"Closing of American Mind"

by Allan Bloom

BUILDING THE INFORMATION-AGE ORGANIZATION:
STRUCTURE, CONTROL, AND INFORMATION TECHNOLOGIES

BUILDING THE INFORMATION-AGE ORGANIZATION:
STRUCTURE, CONTROL, AND INFORMATION TECHNOLOGIES

James I. Cash, Jr.
Robert G. Eccles
Nitin Nohria
Richard L. Nolan

Harvard University Graduate School of Business Administration
July, 1993

IRWIN
Chicago • Bogota • Boston • Buenos Aires • Caracas
London • Madrid • Mexico City • Sydney • Toronto

The Irwin Case Book Series in Information Systems Management
  Building the Information-Age Organization: Structure, Control, and Information Technologies
  Corporate Information Systems Management, Third Edition

© RICHARD D. IRWIN, INC., 1994

Senior sponsoring editor: *Rick Williamson*
Editorial assistant: *Christine Bara*
Project editor: *Mary Conzachi*
Production manager: *Laurie Kersch*
Art manager: *Kim Meriwether*
Compositor: *Carlisle Communications, Inc.*
Typeface: *10/12 Times Roman*
Printer: *R. R. Donnelley & Sons Company*

Library of Congress Cataloging-in-Publication Data

Building the information-age organization : structure, control, and
  information technologies / by James I. Cash, Jr. . . . [et al.].
      p.   cm.
    Includes index.
    ISBN 0-256-12458-2
      1. Information technology—Management—Case studies.
    2. Organization—Case studies.   I. Cash, James I.
    HD30.2.B85   1994
    658.4′038′011—dc20   93–40865

Printed in the United States of America
  2 3 4 5 6 7 8 9 0 DO 0 9 8 7 6 5 4

Preface

There is nothing permanent except change.

—Heraclitus

When information technology substitutes for human effort, it *automates* a task or process.

When information technology augments human effort, it *informates* a task or process.

When information technology restructures, it *transforms* a set of tasks or processes.

This book is for students and managers who understand that sweeping changes are the order of the day. As we approach the twenty-first century, managers are finding that the tools and concepts that drove the twentieth-century, industrial-era organization are insufficient for managing the information-age organization. Concepts that held up well for much of the century—strategy, structure, span of control, organizational boundaries—are shifting on their foundations. Many of these changes are enabled by information technologies, which managers use to fundamentally alter organizational purpose, shape, and practices.

This book blends three previously separate management disciplines—organizational design, management control, and information technology management—in order to offer the student of management an integrated set of concepts and tools for understanding the new roles of the general manager in executing strategy. Our immediate objective is to help students learn how to use organizational structure and management control systems to create flexible, adaptive, and effective organizations. We show how managers can use information technologies to transform their organizations. Our ultimate aim is to help managers build information-age organizations in which the management process itself is a source of sustainable competitive advantage.

The idea for this book was born when a group of Harvard Business School faculty members began to reexamine the MBA program. We had been teaching core courses that largely mapped to traditional functional areas—marketing, finance, control, operations management, and organizational behavior. Yet many of the managers with whom we converse regularly were talking about how difficult it was to improve organizational effectiveness when each employee's vision was limited by the "stovepipe" in which he or she worked. We recognized that managers needed to break out of the "stovepipe" mentality, and so did we.

We also were aware that in some forward-thinking organizations information technology was being used to transform business processes in three fundamental ways:

Shifting from *predicting events* to *managing uncertainty.*

Shifting from *discrete* to *continuous processes.*

Increased emphasis on *horizontal information flows.*

In contrast, many other firms were "automating history" when they should have been "inventing the future." This book, then, represents our attempt to address difficult managerial challenges from an interdisciplinary perspective.

The material in this book was informed by field-based research conducted by Harvard Business School faculty, research associates, and graduate students. We are particularly indebted to the managers and staff members at the case sites, who provided us with time and insights during the course of our research on their organizations. Every example and concept in this book is drawn from observations of actual practice. Without the extensive cooperation of participating organizations, this book would not have come to pass.

Good ideas have many sources. Case development usually involves intensive collaboration between a sponsoring Harvard Business School faculty member and a doctoral student or other research assistant. Our MBA students and Executive Programs participants provide useful feedback when these cases are taught in the classroom. Colleagues from other institutions occasionally participate in case development as well. In addition to the authors' own efforts, we sincerely appreciate the contributions by our Harvard Business School colleagues: Lynda Applegate, Tom Davenport, David Garvin, Janis Gogan, Benn Konsynski, Ken Merchant, Donna Stoddard, and John Sviokla. Finally, the following individuals participated in the development of materials included in this book:

James D. Berkley	Philip Holland	Johathan O'Neil
John Chalykoff	John King	Keri Ostrofsky
Melinda B. Conrad	Robert W. Lightfoot	Jeanne W. Ross
Cynthia Cook	E. Geoffrey Love	Katherine N. Seger
Maryellen C. Costello	C. J. Meadows	Janet L. Simpson
David C. Croson	Boon-Siong Neo	Jeffrey M. Traynor
Julia A. Gladstone	Charles Osborne	

Given such a long list, there is a chance we have forgotten to mention some colleagues who informed our work. We hope they will accept our apologies, but know that we appreciate their contributions.

Rick Williamson and Christine Bara at Richard D. Irwin provided us with motivation and expert guidance. Maureen Donovan, Hillary Gallagher, Nancy Hayes, Rita Perloff, and Judith Tully typed and edited numerous versions of the work. Their patient attention to the many details of our academic lives helped us to concentrate on adding value to this manuscript. Their efforts and loyalty are deeply appreciated.

Without a doubt, the most important nonauthor contributor was Janis Gogan. She helped us weave together the loose threads in our ideas, contributed many of her own, and served as production manager for development of the manuscript. Her patience and persistence were greatly appreciated.

Finally, we thank Dean John H. McArthur for making available the time for this work, and F. Warren McFarlan, head of the Division of Research, for providing financial and other support of these efforts.

Table of Contents

PART I *Foundation Concepts*   *1*

1 Basic Concepts and Tools   **2**
Introduction   3
Part I Overview   6
CASE 1–1: Mrs. Fields' Cookies   *9*

2 Introduction to Organization Structure   **24**
Introduction   25
Central Concepts of Organization Structure   25
Organization Structure: Basic Forms   28
Evolution of Organization Forms   32
CASE 2–1: Appex Corporation   *36*
CASE 2–2: Hill, Holliday, Connors, Cosmopulos, Inc. Advertising (A) *53*
CASE 2–3: Jacobs Suchard: Reorganizing for 1992   *68*
READING 2–1: The Coming of the New Organization   *85*

3 Introduction to Control Systems   **94**
Chapter Overview   95
Management Control: Definition and Concepts   95
What Is a Management Control System?   97
How Are Control Systems Designed?   100
Issues in Management Control Systems   103
CASE 3–1: Controls at the Sands Hotel and Casino   *105*
CASE 3–2: Crompton Greaves Ltd.   *129*
CASE 3–3: Compaq Computer Corporation   *142*

4 Introduction to IT Architecture   **158**
Introduction   159
The Need for an IT Architecture   160
IT Architecture: Basic Building Blocks   161
Technology Generations   166
Developing an IT Architecture   171
CASE 4–1: Air Products and Chemicals, Inc.: Project ICON (A)   *176*
CASE 4–2: Symantec   *191*

PART II   *IT and the Organization*   205

5   IT and the Individual   206
Introduction   207
IT and Changing Work   208
IT and Employee Privacy   209
CASE 5–1: The Internal Revenue Service: Automated Collection System 211
CASE 5–2: The Incident at Waco Manufacturing   225
READING 5–1: Informate the Enterprise: An Agenda for the Twenty-First Century 226
CASE 5–3: Otis Elevator: Managing the Service Force   233
IT and the Individual: Ethical Concerns   247

6   IT in Organizations   252
Introduction   253
IT Eras   253
Stages Theory of IT Adoption and Organizational Learning   259
IT-Driven Changes in Organizational Structure   262
IT in the 1990s   264
READING 6–1: No Excuses Management   268
CASE 6–1: Allen-Bradley's ICCG: Repositioning for the 1990s   286
CASE 6–2: Phillips 66 Company: Executive Information System   303
CASE 6–3: Connor Formed Metal Products   320

7   IT between Organizations: Interorganizational Systems   338
Introduction   338
Motivations for IOS   340
Issues for IOS Hosts and Participants   344
IOS in the Future   349
CASE 7–1: Lithonia Lighting   351
CASE 7–2: Hong Kong TradeLink: News from the Second City   365
CASE 7–3: Singapore Leadership: A Tale of One City   372
CASE 7–4: Singapore TradeNet (A): A Tale of One City   375
CASE 7–5: Singapore TradeNet (B): The Tale Continues   388

PART III   *Toward the 21st Century*   397

8   IT and Business Transformation   398
Introduction   399
The Goal: Organizational Effectiveness   400
Determining the Degree of Required Change   401
The Tools: The Role of IT in Business Transformation   403
Business Process Reengineering: A Path to Business Transformation   406
Sustaining IT Innovation   414

CASE 8–1: Safeway Manufacturing Division: The Manufacturing
Control System (MCS) (A)   420
CASE 8–2: Capital Holding Corporation—Reengineering the Direct
Response Group   433

9 Information Technology and Tomorrow's Manager   454
Introduction   455
Emerging Technologies and the Challenge of Change   456
CASE 9–1: KPMG Peat Marwick: The Shadow Partner   462
READING 9–1: Information Technology and Tomorrow's Manager   472

PART I

Foundation Concepts

Chapter 1   *Basic Concepts and Tools*
Chapter 2   *Introduction to Organization Structure*
Chapter 3   *Introduction to Control Systems*
Chapter 4   *IT Architecture*

To build the information-age organization, start with the foundation. Part I lays out the necessary foundation concepts. Chapter 1 provides an overview of the fundamental concepts and frameworks, which are reviewed in Chapters 2, 3, and 4. Chapter 2 introduces the concepts of organizational design, and explains why organizational structures are changing. Chapter 3 explains the purpose of management control, and the changing design and uses of management control systems. Chapter 4 explains the concept of an information technology architecture, describes its components, and discusses how managers design a flexible and adaptable IT architecture.

Chapter 1

Basic Concepts and Tools

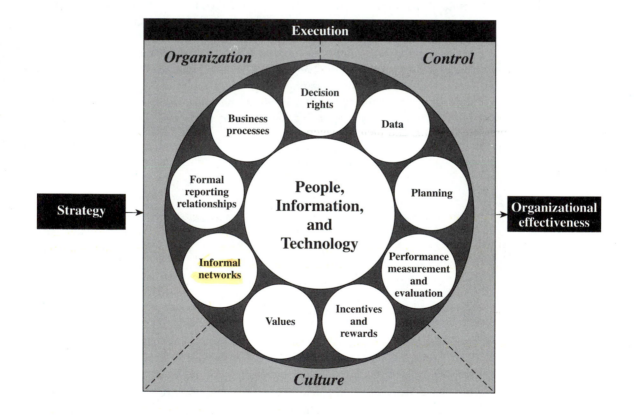

INTRODUCTION

Today's managers need all the help they can get. Their firms are being buffeted on all sides by strong, frequently shifting winds of change. Organizations' *strategic objectives* (chosen markets, product strategy, expected outcomes) and their *business processes* (such as research and development, production, cash-flow management, and order fulfillment) are undergoing significant and volatile changes, placing great pressure on firms and their managers.

Strategic Objectives

Globalized Markets. The world is shrinking. Companies are expanding their reach, targeting new markets throughout the globe. Improvements in transportation and distribution time and costs are helping mass marketers such as PepsiCo and Coca-Cola Co. expand beyond their saturated domestic markets. Niche-marketers such as manufacturers of custom computer chips and electric compressors are also thinking "global," yet giving their customers "local" attention. Even professional-services firms, such as consulting and advertising agencies, have gone global.

Shorter Product Development Cycles. *Fast response* is the name of the game in many industries. Those firms that take the lead in identifying a new customer need and delivering a response to it are capturing impressive market shares. Some of them are using that early lead to lock in patent protection or drive down the learning curve to ensure higher profits over the long haul. Other firms are becoming effective practitioners of "fast followership," especially where patent protection is not a critical element of success. These firms are learning to profit from the leaders' work in defining new markets. No firm can afford the luxury of a leisurely product development cycle.

Higher Performance Hurdles. In addition to getting products out faster, firms are upping the ante for customer satisfaction, thanks to pressure from both more knowledgeable and demanding customers and tougher competitors. Today's customers expect higher and more consistent levels of product quality and safety. They are increasingly impatient with delivery delays and broken promises. They expect every interaction with a firm to be pleasant and productive. When these expectations are not met, the customer usually has another firm to which to turn.

Business Processes

Tighter Cross-Functional Linkages. In order to achieve faster response, produce higher-quality products, and present a unified face to the customer, firms are seeking ways to achieve tighter linkages between functions, for example, research and development (R&D), engineering, marketing, and manufacturing; or between geographically dispersed units. This is in marked contrast to the approach many firms successfully employed a few decades ago, in which each functional area was encouraged to maximize the efficiency of its activities, and senior general managers provided the necessary coordination. Many organizations today are faced with higher complexity and are moving too fast for the old "stovepipe" approach to continue to be feasible.

Work Force Diversity and Changing Career Paths. The Organization Man of 1955 was white, male, and had a western European name. Today, the homogeneous White Male Club has given way to unprecedented work place diversity, a trend that will continue. Today's organizational members speak a variety of languages, draw from a variety of experiences, and represent a far richer mix of talents, skills, and potential. In addition, today's aspiring manager no longer expects to remain in the same organization his/her entire career, and has different expectations about balancing work, family, and leisure than the prototypical post–World War II employee.

Globalized Operations. Even where a firm chooses not to compete in global markets, it may nevertheless engage in global operations, in order to take advantage of a superior national infrastructure, lower labor costs, or a highly skilled labor pool. This adds further complexity to the work force diversity issues mentioned above, as well as to the coordination costs necessary to sustain cross-functional and cross-border linkages. The general manager in this environment juggles a complex set of financial and human resources measures in response to a complex set of global capital markets, government regulations, and societal norms.

Rapid, Unpredictable Technological Innovations. The rate at which knowledge doubles is accelerating, placing increasing burdens on managers trying to keep up with changes in the technologies that affect their business. Furthermore, technological breakthroughs in materials science, information technology, biotechnology, and other arenas can be unpredictable, making it difficult to plan for improved manufacturing and other processes.

Technology changes can be *incremental* or *discontinuous.* Some incremental technical innovations can be readily absorbed into a firm's production and distribution processes; others render these processes obsolete. For example, the computer industry is being completely transformed by the microprocessor. Giants of the industry, such as IBM and Digital, are sustaining heavy losses at the hands of trendsetters like Microsoft and Apple. Developments underway in biotechnology may cause similar upheavals in the pharmaceutical and agribusiness industries.

Many of the above-mentioned pressures on strategic choice and tactical execution are driven by new capabilities for storing, processing, and transmitting information, a phenomenon that ups the ante for management education. Today's general manager needs to understand the increasing importance of information technology as a management tool for engaging in global operations, achieving cross-functional integration and rapid product introductions, developing future managers from a more varied pool of skills, and other managerial tasks. Organizational structures and management control systems, long a part of every general manager's tool kit, are taking new forms, in response to both these pressures and the unique enabling capabilities of networked information technologies.

As illustrated in Figures 1–1 and 1–2, this book addresses how managers translate *strategy* into day-to-day *business processes* (or execution) in an environment that is becoming increasingly complex and interdependent. Managers work with four highly interrelated components:

People, the primary resource, who must be supported and leveraged with appropriate structures, systems, and processes to achieve organizational effectiveness.

Organizational structure and structuring processes, which are contingent upon varying internal capabilities and external conditions.

Management control systems, for planning, monitoring, influencing, and evaluating individual and organizational performance.

Information technologies, for supporting data acquisition and flexible decision making and communication under conditions of change and uncertainty.

Organizational structure, information technologies, control systems, and human resources enable skillful general managers to extend their reach and to affect their organizations' destiny. Effective managers understand these tools and resources, and know which to use for what purposes and under what circumstances. The primary objective of this book is to ensure your familiarity with and understanding of how to effectively manage these components.

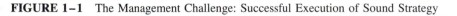

FIGURE 1–1   The Management Challenge: Successful Execution of Sound Strategy

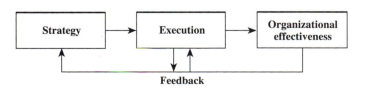

FIGURE 1–2   Managerial Levers: Overview

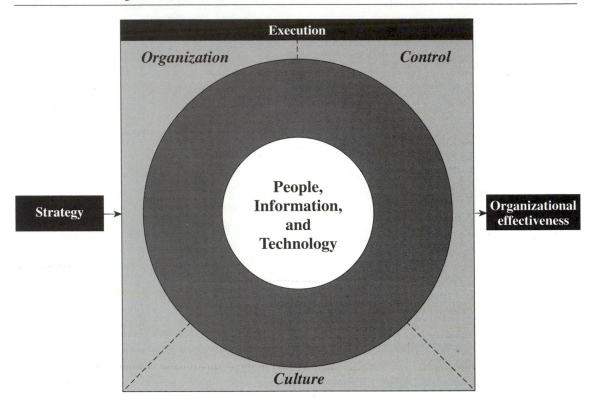

This book comprises three parts, summarized in Figure 1–3. Part I, composed of this chapter as well as Chapters 2, 3, and 4, introduces the basic concepts and tools for designing and effectively using organizational structures, management control systems, and information technologies. Part II examines the impact and evolving roles of IT on individuals, organizations, and relationships between organizations. Part III examines how, by effectively deploying information resources to support organizational structure, management control systems, and people, business transformation can be achieved.

PART I OVERVIEW

Organizations exist to enable groups of people to effectively coordinate their efforts and get things done. The structure of an organization is the pattern of organizational

---

FIGURE 1–3   Book Overview

Part I   IT Foundation Concepts
1. Basic Concepts and Tools
2. Introduction to Organization Structure
3. Introduction to Control Systems
4. IT Architecture

Part II   IT and the Organization
5. IT and the Individual
6. IT in Organizations
7. IT between Organizations: Interorganizational Systems

Part III   IT and Business Transformation
8. IT and Business Transformation
9. Information Technology and Tomorrow's Manager

---

roles, relationships, and procedures that enable such coordinated action by its members. *Organization structure* serves the following functions:

- It enables the members of the organization to undertake a wide variety of activities according to a division of labor that defines the specialization, standardization, and departmentalization of tasks and functions.
- It enables the members of the organization to coordinate their activities through integrating mechanisms such as hierarchical supervision, formal rules and procedures, and training and socialization.
- It defines the boundaries of the organization and its interfaces with the environment or the other organizations and institutions with which it must interact.

Shaping an effective organization structure is a central function of general management. While only those at the highest levels have the ability to change or redesign the overall structure of an organization, all managers have to get things done within this framework. Moreover, most managers must structure those activities that fall within their own sphere of responsibility. Therefore, understanding how organizations are structured is vital to being an effective manager.

Chapter 2 provides an introduction to principles of organizational structure and structuring processes. Three cases are presented—Appex Corporation; Hill, Holliday, Connors, Cosmopulos, Inc., Advertising; and Jacobs Suchard. All are examples of firms coping with change and uncertainty. One is growing rapidly, one is coping with an economic downturn, and one must deal with political and economic changes in Europe. General managers in each case modify organizational structure as a means to improve organizational effectiveness in these changing environments.

After management has adopted a specific strategy and basic implementation plans are developed, the next task is to take steps to ensure that day-to-day execution of business activities leads to desired outcomes. Systems that are established to ensure consistency of effort and achievement of desired outcomes must also be capable of signaling when conditions warrant changes in strategy, tactics, or ongoing business activities. This is the function of *management control systems.*

This book examines how traditional definitions and tactics of control systems have changed to fit the environment of the 1990s and twenty-first century. Management control is defined as creating conditions that will improve the probability that desirable outcomes will be achieved. There are two aspects of this new definition of control that distinguish it from traditional definitions of the term. First, control is defined in *probabilistic* terms. Even though the traditional definition recognizes (largely implicitly) that objectives can never be achieved with certainty, the very purpose of control is to reduce this uncertainty as much as possible. Second, control is defined in terms of *flexible goals* rather than fixed objectives. This is because, as stated in the introduction of this chapter, firms' products, marketing, production, and logistics strategies are rapidly evolving in response to changing customer requirements, underlying technologies, and competitors' moves. In an ambiguous and uncertain world where causal relationships are only partially known and change over time, we need a more probabilistic notion of control.

Chapter 3 discusses the concepts and tools of management control, and illustrates these with a case about the Sands Hotel and Casino. Next, this chapter addresses the issues of individual and organizational performance measurement. Firms are beginning to view financial figures as but one of a broader set of measures for tracking success in meeting strategic objectives. The Crompton Greaves Ltd. case illustrates one approach to performance measurement, and some of the issues involved in identifying appropriate measures and systems. The Compaq Computer Corporation case shows how flexible management control systems replace traditional strategic planning systems in a firm facing a highly volatile competitive environment.

Information resources include information technologies (computer-based hardware and software) and data (numeric, textual, graphical, image, etc.). In a few decades, information technologies (IT) have come to permeate all functional activities of organizations, with impacts on individuals, work groups, the organization itself, and interorganizational relationships. Indications are that this penetration will continue over the foreseeable future, as IT costs continue to drop significantly while processing capabilities and managers' awareness of IT-driven business benefits increase.

In 1975 only a small percentage of clerical and technical employees used computers, whereas today employees at all levels of the company use IT as an important tool for accomplishing their work. The Institute for the Future predicts that by 1995, 90 percent of American white-collar workers will use a personal computer in their jobs.[1] Personal computers are shrinking and becoming increasingly portable. Some are equipped with disk drives containing as much information as an encyclopedia. Users can access enormous volumes of data on databases and communicate with

---

[1] "Information Technology: The Ubiquitous Machine," *The Economist,* 315 (7659): S5-S20 (June 16, 1990).

one another by means of electronic mail over networks. These capabilities enable work to be done in any location, at any time. The pervasiveness, connectivity, and portability of information resources will enable further redefinition of organizations and markets.

In the early 1980s, managers debated whether and how soon to acquire personal computing tools. Now, nearly all employees have ready access to these tools, and managers are assessing whether the organization is getting the greatest possible benefit from them. In many firms, this assessment is long overdue, since the tools were acquired in a somewhat random process that did not explicitly consider the full range of implications that the new technologies brought. Many previously manual tasks have been automated, when greater gain may have resulted from redesigning processes to take full advantage of IT capabilities. Similarly, management control systems in many cases were placed on top of networked personal computing platforms, rather than redesigned for maximum benefits. Many IT initiatives of the past decade have had both intended and unanticipated, positive and negative effects.

IT is also having a significant impact on organizational structure. Where once an organization was defined by bricks and mortar, IT has helped to break down those walls, creating in their place networks of intraorganizational and interorganizational relationships. Through effective exploitation of information technologies, many organizations have redefined their work from primarily creating physical products to primarily offering information-based products. IT has revolutionized both the products some firms offer and the ways some firms do business.

Chapter 4 defines the concept of an IT architecture and a process for defining an appropriate and flexible IT architecture. The chapter also examines how evolving information technologies are assimilated into organizations, and the ramifications of technological discontinuity on the organization and management of information resources. The Air Products and Chemicals, Inc., case presents a multinational firm looking to consolidate its mainframe applications in a single US data center by taking advantage of improved processing and networking capabilities. The Symantec case describes a rapidly growing young firm trying to improve its companywide information flows through more effective IT management. Figure 1–4 expands upon the initial framework to show its primary components (in simplified form) and the linkages among them.

Who should design these components: general managers or their functional staff? The answer is both, and the process is analogous to building your own home. Sure, you need an architect—you don't want that cantilevered balcony to fall down—but the major design decisions are yours. They must be, if the house is to reflect your taste and style, and suit your family's needs. And *you* are going to live in it. Managers live in a network of systems, processes, and relationships—a used house, if you will—frequently inherited from their predecessors. Modifications are not only feasible, they are almost mandatory. Management systems, structures, and human and information resources change and evolve as external pressures dictate change and as successive general managers exercise their design prerogatives.

CASE 1–1: MRS. FIELDS' COOKIES

The Mrs. Fields' Cookies case depicts a young, rapidly growing company that is able to "start from scratch" (pun intended) in designing its organizational structure, management control systems, and information resources architecture. The case provides an introduction to the basic concepts that will be used in this book. As previously noted, subsequent chapters will refine those concepts and illustrate the issues and opportunities facing managers in the future.

Figure 1–4 can be used as a framework for identifying and assessing the choices made by Debbi and Randy Fields.

Preparation Questions

1. Describe and evaluate the organizational structure of Mrs. Fields' Cookies. What alternative structures might Debbi and Randy Fields have pursued?

FIGURE 1–4

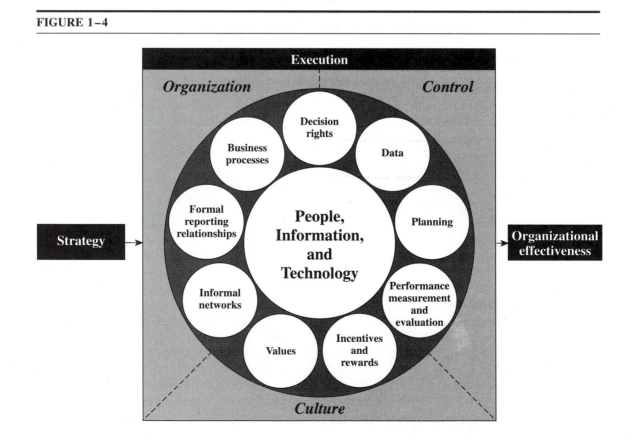

2. Describe and evaluate the approach to management control systems at Mrs. Fields' Cookies, in terms of those systems' ability to help management monitor operations, evaluate performance, and make strategic decisions.
3. Describe and evaluate the role of information technology (IT) at Mrs. Fields' Cookies.
4. Given their goals and the competitive environment in which they compete, have Randy and Debbi Fields made coherent choices about organizational structure, management control systems, information resources, and people?

Case 1–1 Mrs. Fields' Cookies*

Creating something new, given the old and familiar, is an art rather than a science. The late, latter-day da Vinci, Buckminster Fuller, has been credited with this ability. "Part of Fuller's genius," wrote Tom Richman,[1] "was his capacity to transform a technology from the merely new to the truly useful by creating a new form to take advantage of its characteristics." What Fuller's geodesic designs had done for plastic, observed Richman, the administrative management processes Debbi and Randy Fields developed for Mrs. Fields' Cookies did for information technology.

Fuller, who once suggested that a particularly awkward application of a new technology to an old process would be "like putting an outboard motor on a skyscraper," would very likely have approved of the Fields' creation— "*a* shape, if not *the* shape, of business organizations to come," according to Richman.

It gives top management a dimension of personal control over dispersed operations that small companies otherwise find impossible to achieve. It projects a founder's vision into parts of a company that have long ago outgrown his or her ability to reach in person.

*Keri Ostrofsky prepared this case under the supervision of Professor James I. Cash, Jr. Copyright © 1988 by the President and Fellows of Harvard College. Harvard Business School Case 189-056 (revised 1989).

[1]Tom Richman, "Mrs. Fields' Secret Ingredient," *Inc.* (October 1987): 67–72.

In the [Fields'] structure . . . computers don't just speed up old administrative processes. They alter the process. Management . . . becomes less administration and more inspiration. The management hierarchy of the company *feels* almost flat.

Debbi Fields had created the business. Randy had devised a corporate structure fit to be wed to an information system. Theirs was a case of putting an outboard motor, not on a skyscraper, but on a boat.

The Company

In 1988, Debbi Sivyer Fields, as president of Mrs. Fields' Inc. and Mrs. Fields' Cookies, had dominion over 416 Mrs. Fields' Cookie outlets, 122 La Petite Boulangerie Stores, 129 Jessica's Cookies and Famous Chocolate units, 2 Jenessa's retail gift stores, Jenny's Swingset (a children's casual clothing store in Park City), Mrs. Fields' Dessert Store (a Los Angeles store that sold ice cream, cookies, cakes, and pies), Mrs. Fields' Candy Factory (in Park City), Mrs. Fields' Cookie College (for training store managers and assistant managers), and a macadamia nut processing plant in Hawaii. Mrs. Fields' Cookies operated 370 cookie stores in the United States, 10 in Canada, 6 in Hong Kong (through 50 percent ownership of Mrs. Fields' Cookies Far East Ltd., a joint venture with a local company, Dairy Farm Ltd.), 7 in Japan, 6 in the United Kingdom, and 17 in Australia. The company employed 8,000 people, 140 in staff positions at the Park City corporate offices.

Mrs. Fields' Cookies, like many of Buckminster Fuller's designs, achieved elegance of function by marrying what might at first seem to be incongruous elements. Customers knew Mrs. Fields' Cookies as the upscale brown, red, and white retail outlets that dispensed hot, fresh, chewy cookies like grandmother used to bake. Few were aware that by 6:00 AM Utah time, a computer in Park City, high in the Uinta Mountains, would know of their purchase and every other purchase made at the more than 500 Mrs. Fields' Cookie stores in 25 states and five countries on four continents.

The cookies, of course, came first. Debbi Sivyer began baking cookies as a teenager. "Chocolate chip cookies were an easy project . . . just the thing to keep you busy on a rainy afternoon. . . . The Sivyer clan was always delighted to discover a plateful of chocolate chip cookies, and they weren't expensive to make."[2] Debbi perfected her recipe while a teenager, working first for the Oakland A's baseball club (retrieving foul balls on the third base line) and later for a local department store. These experiences fueled her enthusiasm and drive, and were a source of the fundamental philosophies she would later bring to the management of Mrs. Fields' Cookies.

At 19, Debbi married economist and Stanford University graduate Randy Fields, then 29. Finding her expertise in demand by her husband's clients, who often asked that she bake for their visits, Debbi convinced Randy that she should go into the cookie business. The couple borrowed $50,000 and, in August 1977, within a year of being married, Debbi opened her first store, Mrs. Fields' Chocolate Chippery, in Palo Alto, California. Debbi sold $50 worth of cookies on her first day in business, and $75 worth on her second day, thereby winning a friendly bet made between Debbi and Randy regarding the total sales she would make each day.

More than a year passed before Debbi opened a second store in a high-traffic tourist area of San Francisco. "With the first store, I had what I wanted," Debbi recalled. "As Randy had his thing to do every day, I had mine. When the people at Pier 39 shopping mall called and asked me to open a store there, I was immensely flattered . . . thanked the leasing agent profusely, and turned him down. . . . What I saw as a store, he perceived as a business—a business that could grow. The point wasn't to make money, the point was to bake great cookies, and we sacrificed for that principle." Her employees' desire for growth and greater opportunity finally convinced Debbi to open the second store.

Explosive Growth
The San Francisco store was followed by several others in northern California and, in 1980, by an outlet in Honolulu, Hawaii. Mrs. Fields' next expanded east to Salt Lake City, Utah. By 1981, the company had 14 stores. Seeking further opportunities for expansion, the Fields tried to attract shopping mall managers at a 1982 trade show in Las Vegas, but drew a lukewarm response. At the same trade show a year later, Debbi handed out cookie samples to conventioneers from a booth arranged as a working prototype of a store, complete with oven and mixer. This brought her to the attention of the landlords, some of whom not only let Mrs. Fields' into their existing malls, but asked that stores be opened in future locations, as well. The cookie company's East Coast debut also came in 1983—Bloomingdale's invitation to open a Mrs. Fields' store in its New York location was considered a major milestone by Debbi and Randy.

International Expansion
In 1982, Chuck Borash, a vice president at Mrs. Fields', suggested that international expansion be the next project. The challenge was irresistible and, after some preliminary research, the company formed Mrs. Fields' International and targeted Japan, Hong Kong, and Australia.

---

[2]Several quotations in this case are taken from Debbi Fields, *One Smart Cookie* (New York: Simon and Schuster, 1987).

The Fields searched for a Japanese partner, which they were told was a prerequisite to doing business in Japan. Prospective partners warned Debbi and Randy that the cookies would have to be changed to appeal to the Japanese palate, specifically, that the spices and physical scale of the cookies were wrong. When Debbi, Randy, and several other executives visited a potential partner in Japan, Debbi brought along ingredients to make cookies according to her recipe, a company trade secret. "Agreement was universal that these cookies were all wrong for the Japanese taste," Debbi recalled, "and yet in less than a minute, there wasn't a crumb to be seen." Although that was the end of the partnership, the actions of these executives convinced the Fields that they could sell cookies in Japan, and they opened several stores without a partner.

Adjustments were necessary in some countries, however. For example, it was decided that the practice of encouraging sampling when business was slow should be continued in the international stores. The store manager in Hong Kong, however, was unable to interest people in sampling cookies. When Debbi visited the store and tried offering samples herself, she encountered the same reaction. Observing that neighboring store window displays were very neatly organized, in contrast to her piled samples, Debbi rearranged the tray so that people could take one piece without touching the others, and the passersby became willing to sample. Overall, Mrs. Fields' International looked to be a promising avenue for expansion.

Products and Competition

Mrs. Fields' cookies came in 14 varieties. An early move into brownies and muffins was followed, in 1988, by expansion into candies and ice cream. All baked products were made on premises in the individual stores and were to be sold within a specified time. Cookies not sold within two hours, for example, were discarded (usually given to the local Red Cross or other charity).

Mrs. Fields' Cookies was part of the sweet snack industry, which included the packaged snacks segment (e.g., Frito Lay's Grandma's Cookies; Nabisco's Fig Newtons, Vanilla Wafers, Chips Ahoy, and Oreos; and Keebler's Soft Batch). Competitors for impulse snack dollars included New York's David's Cookies, Atlanta's Original Great American Chocolate Chip Cookie Company, and the Nestle's Company's Original Cookie Co.

Speciality stores selling chocolates, ice cream, cinnamon rolls, and croissants constituted another segment of the sweet snack food industry. Shopping malls represented the largest source of spontaneous business for speciality stores, and some 80 percent of Mrs. Fields' outlets were in malls. Competition for the most favorable mall locations, which were typically next to large apparel stores rather than in areas with other foods stores, was fierce. "Customers," noted one industry observer, "are too busy filling up on traditional 'main meal' fare to think seriously about . . . any edible specialty items. Even if they decide afterward to have them as a dessert, they won't have the patience to stand in line once again."[3] As most malls had few such locations, developers were selective about the stores they allowed outside the "food courts." Said one New York leasing director, "We can only accept operations with some sort of proven production record."[4]

Management Philosophy

The second Mrs. Fields' store raised a host of new issues for Debbi, who recognized that she could not be in two places at one time, yet historically had resisted delegating authority.

> Management theory claims that it is wrong not to delegate authority to those who work for you. Okay, I'm wrong, but in my own defense, I have to say that my error came from caring too much. If that's a sin, it's surely a small one. Eventually, I was forced, kicking and screaming, to delegate authority because that was the only way the business could grow.

---

[3] *Chain Store Age Executive* (September 1986): p. 66.
[4] Ibid., p. 62.

Debbi Fields had no formal business school training. She attributed her success to learning by doing, and imparted her standards to her employees through example. Whenever possible, she visited her stores and sold cookies behind the counter. On a visit to one store in early 1988, she and a data processing employee with no retail experience generated an additional $600 in sales.

Debbi believed in having fun. "We combine intense work with spontaneous wackiness that keeps everybody loose and relaxed in the middle of tension," she observed. She also believed in treating employees as though they were customers. "For all the things we say to be effective, the people in the stores have to believe in what they're doing. . . . If we can sell them on quality and caring, they will sell the customers. . . . If we make them understand how important they are—by deeds, not just words—they will make their customers feel important in turn."

Store designs were closely controlled. Each store was made to look as inviting and accessible as possible, with products displayed so customers could see exactly what was available. Most stores had their ovens directly behind the sales counter so the aroma of baking cookies would fill the store. Each of the store elements was designed to impart to customers a "feel-good" feeling.

The Fields had consistently refused to franchise their stores. The notion went against their ideals, as expressed by Debbi.

This business—every business—works in its own quirky ways, and Mrs. Fields' Cookies was not created specifically to make a profit. I can't imagine a franchisee buying into it for any other reason. And once the profit motive worked its way to a dominant position, it would be downhill. It's a feel-good product. It has to be sold in a feel-good way.

Franchises typically controlled standards by specifying actions and quantifying details for the franchisees to follow. Because Debbi regarded each outlet as an extension of her original Palo Alto store, where each sale reflected her own personal philosophy of making the customer happy, she

viewed franchising as a loss of control over the end product and loss of touch with the customer.

Even in partly owned stores, such as those in Hong Kong, Debbi and Randy played a major role. For example, Mrs. Fields' provided product and technical knowledge for the Hong Kong stores, for which Dairy Farms Ltd. provided real estate and on-site management.

Financing Strategy

Although the Fields had always managed to find bank financing when they needed it, each experience had been more unpleasant than the last. Consequently, when expansion pressed them to find additional capital, Debbi and Randy decided to go public, pay off the banks, and use the rest of the money to finance growth. Their initial offering, made on the London Exchange in 1986, was not very successful. English institutional buyers did not know the company (there was only one store in London), and doubted that growth could be sustained without franchising. The stock settled, and then began to rise slowly. In 1987, Randy announced that future growth would be funded by cash flow and debt, not by further public offerings.

Accounting was straightforward. Expenses incurred in a store were charged to the store. Conversely, no corporate expenses were allocated to stores. "When you do that," explained Randy, "you lose track of what corporate is doing." Each store operated as a profit center, with average store revenue of $250,000 per year.

In 1987, Mrs. Fields' Inc. had after-tax profits of $17.6 million on revenue of $113.9 million, a 34 percent increase from 1986 revenue, and a 9.3 percent increase from 1986 net income (see Exhibit 1). In 1988, a write-off of $19.9 million on revenues of $133.1 million for store and plant closings left Mrs. Fields' with an after-tax loss of $18.5 million.

Organization

The Fields believed that "the less hierarchy, the better . . . that with hierarchy, the larger an organization, the more managers turn to managing

EXHIBIT 1 Mrs. Fields' Cookies Financial Information (U.S. $000)

Statement of Operations	1988	1987	1986	1985
Revenues	$133,143	$113,908	$84,751	$72,562
Cost of goods sold	42,049	32,739	19,961	19,165
Selling, G&A costs	74,525	50,643	39,442	38,477
Depreciation and amortization	9,133	5,903	4,505	3,498
Losses from closed stores	19,900	5,397	1,375	577
Income (loss) before interest and taxation	$(12,464)	$ 19,226	$19,468	$10,845
Net interest	6,039	1,540	2,333	4,088
Taxation	0	0	1,000	347
Net income (loss)	$(18,503)	$ 17,686	$16,135	6,410
Dividends paid	0	10,453	4,500	0
Earnings (net loss) retained by company	$(18,503)	$ 7,233	$11,635	$ 6,410

Consolidated Balance Sheet				
ASSETS				
Property and equipment at cost, less depreciation	$ 82,827	$ 82,033	$51,496	$37,838
Leasehold developments at cost, less depreciation	10,672	11,429	5,529	2,809
Other*	1,273	863		
Current assets:				
Inventories	6,640	7,779	4,406	3,198
Accounts receivable	3,816	3,585	3,222	1,522
Prepaid expenses and miscellaneous	8,937	9,363	4,761	2,105
Due from affiliates	5,000	0	740	0
Cash	3,971	6,059	1,543	2,257
	$123,136	$121,111	$71,697	$49,729
LIABILITIES AND SHAREHOLDERS' EQUITY				
Current liabilities:				
Accounts payable, due to affiliates and accrued expenses	$ 18,762	$ 24,963	$11,295	$ 7,006
Income taxes	550	184	514	63
Long-term debt	69,732	42,734	13,187	20,100
Shareholders' equity and retained earnings	34,092	53,230	46,701	22,560
	$123,136	$121,111	$71,697	$49,729

*Other assets include costs of developing computer software for sale or license to third parties.

people and less to managing key business processes." Thus, employees had titles and job responsibilities, but there was no official organization chart. Communication took place between people as needed, regardless of title or position.

Staff. Field sales staff included store clerks, store management, and district and regional managers. At year-end 1987, 105 district sales managers (DSM) reported to 17 regional directors of operations (RDO), who reported to four senior regional directors.

One regional director described her job and the company's management philosophy as follows:

> I manage six district managers, each of whom manages six stores. I also manage a store myself, so I know what my district managers need to know. To do this, I print out about 300 pages of reports a day. My district managers get about 50 pages a day. Daily, I work with my controller in Park City to discuss any accounting differences in my stores.
>
> My store managers are on average 20 to 25 years old and have one to two years of college education. I believe we are split 50/50 between males and females. The turnover of store managers is about 100 percent per year, although many work in that job 12 to 14 months. When they leave, they usually return to college. I think our turnover is above average for this kind of business, however.
>
> My store managers are compensated in two ways. First, they receive a salary which is competitive with other retail food store managers in this area. Second, they are eligible for a monthly bonus if they meet their sales forecasts. They receive 1.25 percent of sales, and if they exceed their quota, they receive 10 percent of all revenue above the goal. The company does not limit the amount of bonus, in fact, one store manager made an additional 90 percent of his salary, I believe.

Quotas, which determined the amount of bonus a store manager could make, were set by the district sales manager. They were based on year-to-year trends. The DSM considered each store separately, looking at past trends, the maturity of the market served by the store, and future projections of how the store could grow. The DSM then forecast how much or how little additional sales could be made at that store and set the quota. They were set on volumes.

Mrs. Fields' "promote from within" policy reflected the high value the company placed on loyalty. Rewarding loyalty extended even to suppliers. In 1987, Mrs. Fields' purchased approximately $6.6 million worth of chocolate from the same supplier it had used on its first day of business, when a company salesman had treated Debbi as if she were his only customer.

The financial side of the stores' business was handled at headquarters. Local marketing decisions were made by the regional and district managers. The average number of stores under the supervision of a DSM decreased from 5.3 to 4.2 in 1987.

Corporate. At corporate headquarters, responsibility for store management fell to store controllers, who reported to Debbi through a vice president of operations. The controllers, each of whom managed between 35 and 75 stores, reviewed daily computer reports summarizing sales overall and by product type for each store; monitored unusual conditions, problems, and trends, as well as cash underages and overages; and contacted field managers for explanations. Within 24 hours of the store controllers' review, Debbi saw the same reports at an aggregate level.

MIS. The objective of being able to run each store essentially as Debbi ran the original Palo Alto store guided the implementation of information technology at Mrs. Fields'. The strategic goal of the MIS area, according to Randy Fields, was "to put as much decision making and intelligence into the store level PC as is necessary to free the manager to do those things that people uniquely do." Randy believed that it was "demeaning for people to do what machines can do." Store managers, he felt, had better things to do than paperwork—such as selling cookies.

Director of MIS Paul Quinn reported directly to Randy Fields and was responsible for implementing his vision. Quinn's 11-person organization was responsible for development, support, and operations for the store personal computers and

EXHIBIT 2   MIS Organization

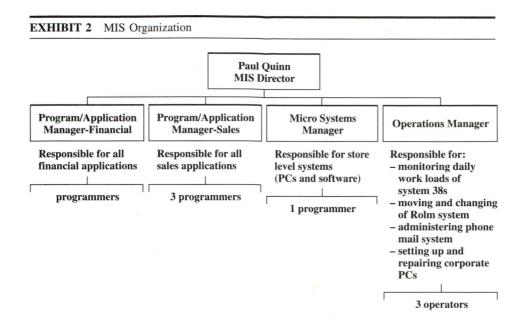

financial and sales systems, and for managing the firm's telecommunications equipment, a Rolm Private Branch Exchange (PBX), and a voice-mail system. The MIS organization chart is shown in Exhibit 2.

With respect to systems development at Mrs. Fields', Quinn explained:

> Anyone can come to me or any of my people and ask for anything. We do an ad hoc cost/benefit analysis and justify a system on one of three criteria:
>
> • Potential payback (will it cut costs and/or save money?)
> • Drive sales (will it generate new sales?)
> • Strategic importance (will it put the company in a position to take advantage of something it could not otherwise do, like the interview system?)
>
> "Strategic" in our industry means promoting sales and controlling labor and food costs. If you can do that you will be successful. I am in an enviable position as the MIS director here, because this company has more information than people can act upon. When someone wants a new report, I have usually already collected the information; it's just a matter of massaging and formatting.

Randy believed that keeping the staff small kept employees solving business problems rather than managing layers of people. He believed this kept jobs interesting and, moreover, that smaller groups of people make decisions faster and better. Randy felt that in order to avoid large groups, a company had to either limit business growth or leverage its people.

Randy saw information systems as a way to accommodate growth without expanding staff. He consistently encouraged the people working with the technology to think up new, creative applications. "Suppose you could not have any people working for you," he would say. "What must the computer do for you then? Don't be limited by what you think the computer can do." An accounts payable clerk, who routinely paid invoices that were regular and consistent, had wondered whether this redundant activity might be automated. This employee's initiative gave rise to the development of an expert system, which was designed to not only automate the routine elements of the activity, but also learn how to respond to exceptions by prompting the manager for input each time an exception was encountered. As the system learned, the exceptions became routine, and the system was able to respond to them automatically without further input from the manager.

Cookie Store Operations

Mrs. Fields' cookie stores were typically divided into two areas (see Exhibit 3). The ovens faced the retail area, fronted by an island of counter space used to fill and unload cookie sheets. Customers were drawn into the store by the openness of the design, and by the aroma of hot cookies fresh from the ovens plainly in view under the lucite-covered display. The back room contained the mixers, a workspace, a small office area with a personal computer, and sufficient storage space for ingredients. This was Mrs. Fields' at the level of the friendly, inviting retail outlets located in high-density shopping areas around the world.

EXHIBIT 3   Typical Mrs. Fields' Store Floorplan*

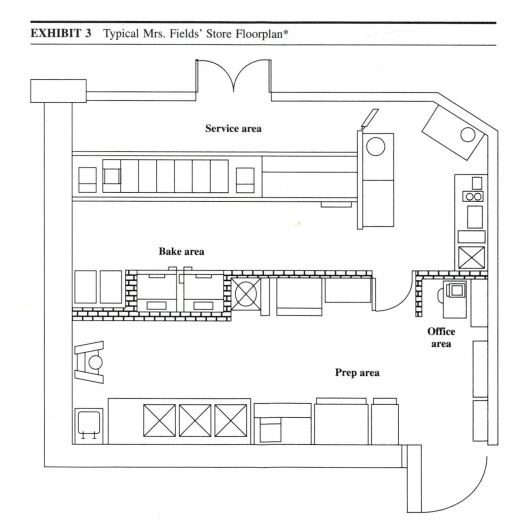

*Note: This floorplan is approximately 600 sq. ft. Stores range from 400 sq. ft. to 1,250 sq. ft.

But there was another level to Mrs. Fields'—the level of the sophisticated management information system that tracked the financial performance of each company-owned outlet and provided comprehensive scheduling of activities within stores, including marketing support, hourly sales projections, and even candidate interviewing for prospective employees.

Each store's personal computer accessed a sophisticated store management system designed by Randy and the MIS organization (see Appendix A). Menu-driven applications included day planning, time clocks, store accounting and inventory, interview scheduling, skill testing, and electronic mail (see Appendix B). One application dialed the headquarters' computer, deposited the day's transactions, and retrieved any mail for store employees.

A store manager's day began in the back room at the personal computer. After entering workday characteristics, such as day of the week, school day or holiday, weather conditions, etc., the manager answered a series of questions that caused the system to access a specific mathematical model for computing the day's schedule. The manager was subsequently advised how many cookies to bake per hour and what the projected sales per hour figure was. The manager would enter the types of cookies to be made that day and the system would respond with the number of batches to mix and when to mix them. For example, the following mixing information

When to Mix	Length of Time	# of Batches to Mix
8 AM	10 AM–3 PM	31
1 PM	3 PM–6 PM	7

would tell the manager: "At 8 AM mix 31 batches of cookies. Use the dough from 10 AM to 3 PM. At that time the dough is no longer up to our standards, so discard any remaining dough. At 1 PM mix 7 batches of dough for use from 3 PM to 6 PM."

As store sales were periodically entered throughout the day, either manually by the manager or by an automated cash register, the system would revise its projections and offer recommendations. For example, if the customer count was down, the system might suggest doing some sampling. If, on the other hand, the customer count was acceptable, but average sales was down, the system might recommend that more suggestive selling be done. Store managers could follow or disregard these suggestions.

From sales and inventory information stored in the computer, the information system computed projections, and prepared and (after being checked by the store manager) generated orders for supplies. A single corporate database tracked sales in each store and produced reports that were reviewed daily. Headquarters thus learned immediately when a store was not meeting its objectives, and was able to respond quickly. Exhibit 4 shows a schematic diagram of the overall information system.

The information system had been explicitly designed to reflect the manager's perspective in order to foster the kind of symbiotic relationship described above, according to Debbi. "Asking store managers making salaries of $20,000 to $25,000 annually to meet an annual quota of a half-million dollars," she explained,

is like asking them to fly to the moon. They cannot really relate to those big numbers. But if you break it down to $50 or $60 an hour, the quotas become easy goals. Even if an hourly quota is missed by $5 or $6, our employees feel they can easily make it up the next hour.

The most efficient way for managers to communicate was via electronic mail, but they also daily called their phone mailbox in Park City for audio messages. Debbi, who had from the outset promised to respond within 48 hours to electronic and voice mail directed to her, sent messages through this network several times a week. Thus, the manager did not simply read memos from the president, but often personally heard her voice.

The information system helped Debbi maintain a degree of personal involvement with each store

EXHIBIT 4   Mrs. Fields' Information Systems Diagram

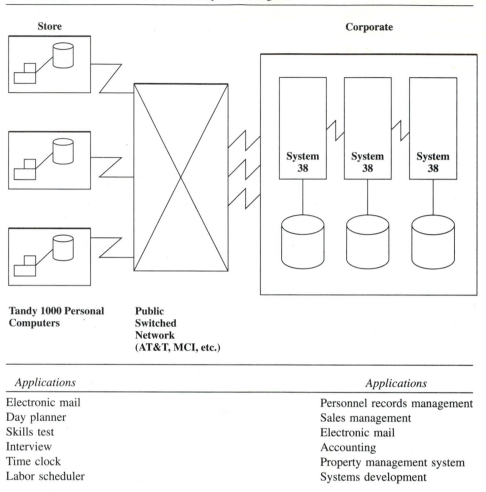

Applications	Applications
Electronic mail	Personnel records management
Day planner	Sales management
Skills test	Electronic mail
Interview	Accounting
Time clock	Property management system
Labor scheduler	Systems development

manager. "Even when she isn't there, she's there," wrote Richman, "in the standards built into the scheduling program, in the hourly goals, in the sampling and suggestive selling, on the phone. The technology has 'leveraged' Debbi's ability to project her influence into more stores than she could ever reach effectively without it."[5]

The information system also helped the manager make hiring decisions. After conducting initial interviews, the manager entered information from the handwritten applications into the computer, which compared it with stored information on previous applicants who had been hired. The system thus helped the manager to narrow the field to applicants who were "Mrs. Fields' kind of people," people who possessed attributes the company valued highly—for example, honesty,

---

[5]Richman, "Mrs. Fields' Secret Ingredient," p. 67.

punctuality, availability, education, experience, salesmanship, knowledge, and attitude—and hence would fit into the corporate culture. Promising applicants were recalled for an interview conducted interactively with the computer. The applicants' answers were compared with those of existing employees and became part of the personnel database. The manager could override the system's final recommendation on hiring by going to the personnel department. The manager could do this, or "go" anywhere else within Mrs. Fields' for that matter, electronically.

Diversification

In April 1987, Mrs. Fields' Holdings Inc. acquired from Pepsico a 119-store French bakery/sandwich chain, La Petite Boulangerie (LPB). In the month following the acquisition, Randy reduced the subsidiary's administrative staff from 53 to three, explaining: "We absorbed many of the overhead functions into our existing organization including accounting, finance, personnel, human resources, training, and development. We left two people in operations and one in R&D."

This was not Mrs. Fields' first acquisition. The company had acquired another retail cookie chain, the Famous Chocolate Chip Company, in 1984. The forerunner of Mrs. Fields' current MIS system had been designed to incorporate that chain's cookie stores into the Mrs. Fields' fold. But the LPB acquisition was different, primarily due to the size of the company, which Randy estimated would add $45 million in revenue in 1987. LPB stores baked (from frozen dough) and served croissants, breads, and other baked goods as well as hot soups and sandwiches. "It was," according to Randy, "a logical extension for the bakery aspect of Mrs. Fields' Cookies."

The focus of the company's "expanded store" strategy was Mrs. Fields' Bakeries. "These," explained Randy, "are destination outlets combining full lines of both cookies and bakery products." La Petite Boulangerie provided the real estate and Mrs. Fields' the "feel-good" element, for these upscale, sit-down cafes. This was not mere expansion; this was a new concept for Mrs. Fields'. Debbi was involved with designing the new combination stores, and planned to have existing senior managers work in them for a month or two in order to become familiar with their operation.

Randy was excited about the combination store approach. It presented an opportunity to carve out a niche in a highly fractionalized market, and the size of the operation constituted an investment barrier to competition. The Mrs. Fields' name was demographically well established, and Randy believed whatever they put it on would sell. Furthermore, a recent market analysis had suggested that enormous, demographically driven growth in the popularity of quality baked goods would not be significantly affected by fluctuations in the economy.

Randy wanted to pay for future expansion with profits, and he was convinced that the greater profits generated by the combination stores would enable them to open more new stores.

As you will see from the financial results, our strategy required a comprehensive rationalization of our real estate portfolio, including consolidating and closing a number of stores that either did not complement the bakery store concept or were performing poorly. This necessitated a real estate write-down of $19.9 million, which we consider R&D expense related to opening our new combination stores. This program is now completed, with the cost fully provided for the 1988 accounts. This has enabled us to establish both a broader and more solid base with greatly enhanced potential for generating future profits.

Corporate direction was clear. "Our bakery strategy," Randy explained,

is long-term, and is based on our operational experience and extensive market and consumer research. But it will take some time for the company to reach its full potential due to the significant expenditures inherent in the bakery store program and the sheer size of the market we intend to dominate.

These changes caught the attention of the financial press, which suggested that Mrs. Fields' faced the characteristic management dilemmas of a growing business. Its expansion, both domestically and abroad, had precipitated changes in organizational and financial structure. The company was in a state of flux. It was attempting to diversify, some claimed belatedly, into combination stores. Earlier it had begun to sell its proprietary information system. Finally, what Randy viewed as record revenues were reported by the press as record losses in 1988 (see Exhibit 1).

Future Growth

What was a cookie company to do? Just a year earlier, explaining what he meant by "having a consistent vision," Randy Fields had said that he could have described as far back as 1978, when he first began to create it, the system that exists today. But he doesn't mean the machines or how they're wired together. MIS in this company, has always had to serve two masters. First, control. Rapid growth without control equals disaster. We needed to keep improving control over our stores. And second, information that leads to control also leads to better decision making. To the extent that the information is then provided to the stores and field management level, the decisions that are made there are better, and they are more easily made.[6]

Had Mrs. Fields' lost control? Just a year earlier, the MIS director had remarked that he had more information available than people could act upon. Was the information system still that cornucopia? The Fields had accommodated past expansion by modifying their information system. Was that what was needed now? Randy Fields wondered as he walked purposefully through corporate headquarters, one floor below the Main Street shopping mall in Park City.

---

[6]Ibid., p. 72.

Appendix A: Mrs. Fields' Information Systems—Hardware

Mrs. Fields' standard personal computer configuration was a Tandy 1000 (a MS-DOS system with 8086 CPU) with one floppy disk drive, a 20 megabyte hard disk, and an internal 1200 bps modem used for communication with the Utah data center. Tandy was chosen because of a favorable service arrangement. Mrs. Fields' maintained a 24-hour service contract with Tandy, but most managers simply contacted the nearest Radio Shack if they had problems.

Software was the responsibility of the Micro Systems manager in Park City. The data center in Park City utilized three IBM Systems 38s, each equipped with six 9335 hard disks. Chosen for their database strengths, the Systems 38s were each dedicated—one to sales systems, one to financial systems, and one to applications development.

With all significant corporate data residing in one database, disaster planning was of critical importance. The company had experienced several system failures, and had a simple disaster plan: if one of the Systems 38s failed, one of the remaining two would back it up for critical functions. Store PCs that had not transmitted their daily work would store the information locally and transmit later. If data had already been transmitted, but nightly backup tapes had not been run, the information would be lost. Such problems had not yet occurred, though there had been recoverable disk failures.

Appendix B: Mrs. Fields' Information Systems—Applications

Randy Fields' notion of having "a vision of what you want to accomplish with the technology" was reflected in the applications he had developed. The most frequently used applications are described below.

Form mail, the menu-driven electronic mail application, was used mainly for brief messages between managers and staff. Managers decided when mail was transmitted to headquarters—whether immediately or when their daily paperwork was sent.

Day planner, the first application a store manager used each morning, produced a schedule for the day based on the minimum sales target (in dollars), the day of the week, and type of day (holiday, school day, etc.). This schedule was updated every time hourly sales information was entered into the system. (Manual entry by the manager was to be eliminated by cash registers custom designed to automatically feed hourly sales into the personal computer.)

Labor scheduler was an expert system that, given requirements for a specific day, scheduled staff to run a store.

Skills tests was a set of computer-based multiple choice tests any employee could take to be considered for raises and promotions. The system indicated how many questions were answered correctly and provided tutorial sessions for questions answered incorrectly. Scores were sent to the personnel database when other information was transmitted to the corporate offices.

Interview helped store managers make hiring decisions. Managers entered information from applications filled out by candidates into the program, which made recommendations based on the historical demographics of people who had previously interviewed and worked for Mrs. Fields'. Prospective employees were called back to the store for an interactive interview with the program, which made a final recommendation for hiring.

Time clock was a planned application that would enable employees to punch in and out via the Tandy computers. The automatic time card maintained by the system would facilitate the payroll process.

Chapter 2

Introduction to Organization Structure

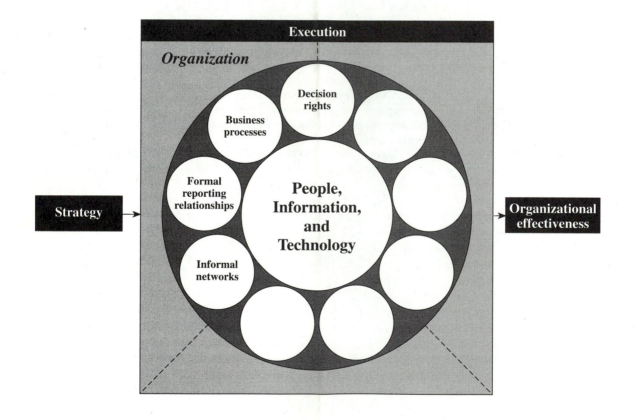

INTRODUCTION

As noted in Chapter 1, organization structure serves the following functions:

- It enables organization members to undertake a wide variety of activities according to a division of labor that defines the specialization, standardization, and departmentalization of tasks and functions.
- It enables organization members to coordinate their activities through integrating mechanisms such as hierarchical supervision, formal rules and procedures, training, and socialization.
- It defines the boundaries of the organization and its interfaces with the environment or other organizations and institutions with which its members must interact.

This chapter begins with an introduction to the key concepts and factors that must be taken into account in designing organization structures. Some archetypal forms of organization structure and their strengths and weaknesses are described, followed by a discussion of emerging trends in organization structure.

CENTRAL CONCEPTS OF ORGANIZATION STRUCTURE

Organization structure is much more than an organization chart of lines and boxes. In thinking about structure, issues that must be addressed include the division of labor and decision rights, coordination mechanisms, organizational boundaries, and informal structures and processes.

Division of Labor. This includes deciding upon the following:

- *Differentiation:* The extent of horizontal and vertical specialization of jobs; for example, job *breadth* in terms of the number of different activities to be performed, and job *depth* in terms of the extent to which the conception, execution, and administration of activities are combined.

- *Departmentalization:* The grouping of activities according to the goods and services the firm markets, to whom it supplies them, or the functions, skills, and knowledge the firm uses to produce them.

Deciding on the division of labor involves trade-offs. For example, highly specialized jobs focus attention, permitting the development of skills and standards. However, extreme specialization increases coordination costs (see below) and leads to monotonous jobs that provide low satisfaction.

Division of Decision Rights.   Who should make which decisions? Decision rights include the authority to initiate, approve, implement, and control various types of strategic or tactical decisions. These rights are distributed along both vertical and horizontal dimensions. The vertical dimension spans the different levels of an organization, leading to the problem of determining an appropriate degree of centralized or decentralized authority. The horizontal dimension concerns activities at the same level of an organization. For example, should the marketing or engineering department have the right to decide on new-product specifications?

Ideally, decision rights are given to those with greatest access to relevant information. For example, a manufacturing manager usually has the best information concerning production capacity, while a field sales manager knows most about customers. However, it may not always be optimal to allow the manufacturing manager to make plant loading decisions or the sales manager to make pricing decisions, because they may not have information about other relevant factors. Even if each had all the necessary information, they might make suboptimal decisions if their interests are at odds with those of the firm as a whole. The manufacturing manager, for instance, may be inclined to increase production if she is compensated for capacity utilization; the sales manager may tend to offer deep discounts in order to meet a unit-sales quota.

Coordination Mechanisms.   Because labor and decision rights are divided among the various members of an organization, differentiation must be balanced with integration. Integration can be achieved through coordination mechanisms that include such formal means as direct supervision, the use of formal rules and procedures, standardized work processes and outputs, standardization of skills, and also through ad hoc or informal mechanisms such as task forces. The choice of coordination mechanism depends in part on the degree to which issues are *routine* versus *exceptional:*

- *Routine* coordination includes such matters as integrating across stations in an assembly line or monthly processing of paychecks. Standard operating procedures and direct supervision typically accomplish this coordination.
- *Exceptional* coordination includes the resolution of infrequent or unusual matters or allocation of limited resources. Plans and budgets, negotiation, committees, and task forces are often used for this form of coordination.

Though important, coordination is costly. For example, coordination meetings, while helpful, can be an expensive use of time.

Organizational Boundaries.   Structuring an organization also involves deciding what to do inside and what to do outside the boundaries of the firm, which in turn leads to make-versus-buy decisions and choices of strategic partners. How much raw materials and components inventory should be held in-house in order to ensure adequate supplies, as compared with managing the relationship with the supplying vendors? How much finished-goods inventory should be held in order to buffer the organization from fluctuating customer demand? To what extent will back-office functions, such as payroll or training, be managed in-house versus contracted with outside suppliers? Should workers in the manufacturing plant be allowed to interact directly with customers, or is this the sole prerogative of the sales force? Overall, such choices define the boundaries of the organization and how it interacts with its environment.

Informal Structure.   Formal roles and relationships are not the sole basis of social interaction in organizations. Although rank and title do count, they do not provide a complete picture of who has authority in an organization. Authority can also arise from social status, expertise, and access to influential others. Just as important as formal roles are informal relationships, which are based on proximity, friendship, shared interests, and other factors. It is also important to recognize that all organizations are political to some extent, since there are always coalitions with competing interests. The political lines may be drawn across departmental, functional, or divisional lines, or they may cut across formal boundaries. Effective managers are cognizant of the informal network and are skilled at assessing the political landscape.

General managers can willfully manipulate and change the division of labor and decision rights, coordination mechanisms, and organizational boundaries. Informal structure is less amenable to managerial influence, but no less important.

Organization structure can vary in terms of the five dimensions listed in Figure 2–1, and the strengths and weaknesses of different structures can be evaluated according to several criteria. These include:

Efficiency: The ability of organizational members to perform their tasks reliably, with minimal errors, and with economy of effort and resources (such as labor and capital).

Timeliness: The speed and timeliness with which tasks are completed.

Responsiveness: The ability to satisfy the demands of the organization's environment.

Adaptability: The ability of the organization to foster innovation and to change dynamically over time.

Accountability: The ability to hold individuals accountable for the performance of defined activities that contribute to organizational performance.

While managers strive for improvements along all of the dimensions listed in Figure 2–2, trade-offs are often necessary. In different organizations, different criteria may take precedence, and structures should be shaped accordingly.

FIGURE 2–1   Organization Structure: Central Concepts

Division of Labor

Degree of differentiation
Grouping of activities

Division of Decision Rights

Vertical authority
Horizontal authority

Coordination Mechanisms

Formal mechanisms
Informal mechanisms
Routine versus exceptional

Organizational Boundaries

Horizontal and vertical integration
Interorganizational relationships

Informal Structure

Social networks and influence processes
Political coalitions

FIGURE 2–2   Criteria for Assessing
Organizational Effectiveness

Efficiency
Timeliness
Responsiveness
Adaptability
Accountability

ORGANIZATION STRUCTURE: BASIC FORMS

In theory, there can be a large number of organization structures. In practice, three basic structural forms—functional, divisional, and matrix—describe most contemporary organizations. These are defined next.

Functional Form.   When an organization grows beyond the affairs that can be handled by a single group of people and one boss, management usually opts to form a

FIGURE 2–3 Functional Structure

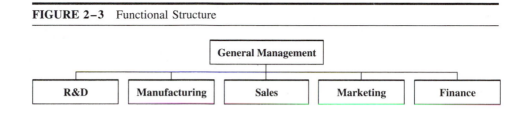

functional structure (Figure 2–3). This creates an initial division of labor in terms of the main functions, such as engineering, production, sales, and finance. As the organization grows, functions may be subdivided and new functions may be added.

In a functional structure, common activities are grouped together. All engineers, for example, are located in an engineering department headed by a vice president of engineering. Their activities are coordinated vertically by means of hierarchical supervision. Planning and budgeting are by function, and reflect the cost of resources in each department. Careers are normally defined on the basis of functional experience, and employees within a function adopt similar values, goals, and orientations. This similarity encourages collaboration, efficiency, and quality within the function, but makes coordination and cooperation with other departments more difficult.

Since an organization's performance is dependent on all functions working together in a coordinated manner, the functional structure requires extensive information exchange among functions. Cross-functional procedures have to be created to process orders, manage inventories and cash, coordinate product development and design changes, and execute other business processes. The cross-functional information processing load falls primarily on the general manager, who also mediates any conflicts that arise among the functions. The general manager may add a central staff and create formal mechanisms for coordination—such as planning and budgeting systems—to manage this integrative load. Using such mechanisms, some organizations have been able to scale up immensely while retaining a basic functional structure.

The functional form works well when the organization's dominant competitive issues stress functional expertise, efficiency, and quality, and when its environment is relatively stable. This is because the functional form promotes economies of scale. Consolidating manufacturing plants may enable an organization to acquire expensive but efficient machinery and reduce duplication and waste. This structure also promotes functional skill development of employees by providing a well-defined career ladder.

The weakness of a functional structure is its inability to respond to a differentiated environment or one in which the firm must respond differently in each product category or customer segment in which it operates. The structure is also weak when the firm must respond rapidly to environmental changes that require coordination between departments. Where change (and hence uncertainty) is high, cross-functional coordination mechanisms can become overloaded. Decisions pile up and top management cannot respond quickly. The functional organization also restricts each employee's view of the overall goals and operations of the organization, leading to local

FIGURE 2–4   Divisional Structure

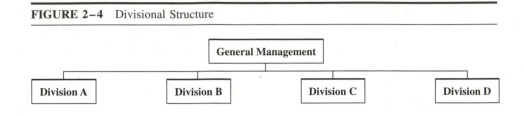

optimization at the expense of firmwide goals. Accountability may also be diffuse, since profit and loss accounts can be calculated for the firm as a whole but not for each separate function.

Divisional Form.   The divisional structure, illustrated in Figure 2–4, groups diverse functions such as manufacturing, research and development, and marketing within each division. While the functional structure is organized according to *inputs,* the divisional structure is organized according to *outputs.* Each division may be responsible for a different set of products, geographical markets or segments, or clients. Thus, one can have product, region, market-segment, or client-based divisional structures.

Within a division, cross-functional coordination is stronger than coordination in a functional form. Employees identify with their division rather than with their functional specialty. Decisions to promote managers are typically based more heavily on integration skills—such as the ability to communicate with and motivate individuals of varying backgrounds, and understanding the interrelationships among functions—than on the basis of functional expertise.

Each division can be held accountable for its performance by defining it as a revenue center, cost center, profit center, or investment center (Chapter 3 includes a discussion of these four approaches to business-unit accountability). A key issue in this structure is the degree of autonomy granted to divisions in making decisions that are strategic and involve significant resource commitments. Coordination across divisions is overseen by a group of managers at corporate headquarters, who are responsible for allocating resources among divisions and setting long-term strategy.

The divisional structure works well when coordinated action is required to develop innovative products, satisfy client expectations, or maintain a market segment. It is most often seen in medium- or large-sized organizations that have adopted a diversified strategy of producing multiple products, operating in different businesses and markets, serving different sets of customers, and/or selling products in different geographical regions. Since each division has the full complement of functional resources, it can respond to the requirements of individual products, markets, customers, or regions, and adapt quickly as these needs change.

One potential disadvantage of this form is a reduction in efficiency due to a loss of scale economies. For example, instead of 50 engineers sharing a common facility in a functional organization, 10 engineers may be assigned to each of five divisions. The necessary mix of skills required for in-depth research may not occur, and physical facilities have to be duplicated for each division. In-depth competence and technical specialization may also be weakened, since employees identify with and invest in the division rather than with a functional specialty. Coordination across divisions can also be difficult. Further, in pursuing their own goals, divisions may work at odds with one another. For example, salespersons from different divisions may compete for the attention of common customers.

Matrix Form.   Some organizations have equally compelling needs for the benefits of both the functional and divisional structures. These organizations need both techno-logical expertise within functions and tight horizontal coordination across functions. For instance, a multinational firm may need to coordinate across functions, products, and geographic locations.

The matrix organization, whose structure is shown in Figure 2–5, addresses this dilemma by simultaneously implementing both structures. Division managers and functional managers have equal authority within the organization, and employees report to both of them. Most employees have dual assignments. An engineer, for example, may be assigned both to a project and to the engineering department. Upon completion of a particular assignment, the engineer returns to the engineering department and is assigned to a new project. The engineer has a home base, but works full time on different projects. She reports to both project and department manager. Since the necessary resources in a matrix organization are distributed between functions and divisions, resource allocation in the form of scheduling and priorities must be negotiated among these groups.

The matrix is appropriate when the following conditions obtain. First, environmen-tal pressures are from two or more critical dimensions, such as function and product or function and region. These pressures mean that a dual authority structure is needed to achieve a balance of power in reaction to environmental pressures. Second, the task environment of the firm is both complex and uncertain. Frequent external changes and high interdependence between units require extremely effective linkages in both vertical and horizontal directions. Third, economies of scale in the use of internal resources (people, equipment, information, cash) are needed.

The matrix enables an organization to meet multiple demands from the environment. Resources can be flexibly allocated and the organization can adapt to changing competi-tive, regulatory, and resource conditions. It also provides an opportunity for employees to acquire either functional or general management skills, depending on their interests.

A basic problem with the matrix structure is determining responsibility and authority relationships between, for instance, functional and project managers. There is commonly a lack of jurisdictional clarity, and each person who reports to two bosses will sometimes face conflicting directions. People in a matrix spend a great deal of time in meetings. Some of the conflict built into a matrix form is healthy, since it forces discussion and coordination to resolve issues that pertain to both functions and projects. It also provides top management with the ability to influence which dimension gets more or less attention in different situations. However, dual reporting relationships and assignments can cause role ambiguity, hamper career development, and weaken employees' ties with professional reference groups.

FIGURE 2–5   Matrix Structure

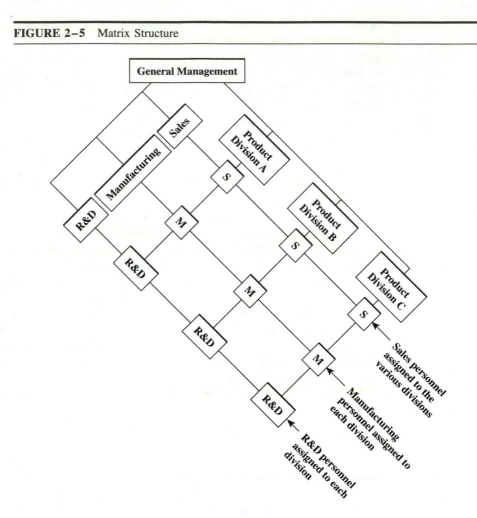

If managers do not adapt to the information- and power-sharing required by the matrix, it will not work. They must collaborate with each other, rather than rely on vertical authority in decision making. This form has been found to be difficult to institute and maintain in many organizations. When it fails, it is usually because one side of the authority structure dominates or because employees have not learned to work in a collaborative fashion.

EVOLUTION OF ORGANIZATION FORMS

Organization structure is organic and evolutionary. The three forms described above represent simplified views of the key features exhibited in organization structure. In practice, however, organization structure is best understood as a pattern of organizational arrangements that evolves over time.

Most organizations begin with a functional structure. As they become larger and more complex in terms of the products and services they offer or markets and clients they serve, they are reorganized into some form of divisional structure, perhaps with a few centralized functional departments. Along the way, firms may modify the pure functional structure or divisional structure. Two types of hybrid structures are found quite frequently. In one hybrid form, project or product groups are overlaid on the functional structure in order to facilitate coordination across functions. In another hybrid form, some key functions that require economies of scale and specialization—such as manufacturing or sales—may be centralized and located at headquarters, thus superimposing a functional structure on a divisional one. By combining characteristics of both functional and divisional structures, hybrid structures can take advantage of both forms of structure and avoid some of their weaknesses. If environmental uncertainty places strong demands along two or more dimensions, such as product and function or product and geography, the firm may adopt a full matrix structure.

The functional, divisional, and matrix structures all share a common, hierarchical heritage of layered reporting relationships. Formal mechanisms—decision rights, work rules, planning and budgeting processes, etc.—are emphasized over informal, ad hoc processes. Lately, however, something is happening to our traditional notions of organizational structure. Some formal mechanisms, such as a formal hierarchy of positions, seem to be decreasing in importance or disappearing altogether. The informal organization seems to be a more significant determinant of organizational effectiveness than ever before, partly because companies are organizing and reorganizing more frequently.

Reorganization often leads to the elimination of entire layers of employees, especially middle managers. Those remaining managers have a broader span of control, which in turn leads to delegation of significant decision making lower in the organization. Information technologies are being used to distribute information for decision making throughout the organization, replacing the middle managers who used to filter and relay this information.

Boundaries between functions and organizational units seem to be blurring, as more work is accomplished as "projects" by "teams" than ever before, and more of the work is accomplished by so-called "contingent" (nonpermanent) employees. The external boundaries of the firm are also becoming harder to identify. Just-in-time production processes link the firm so tightly with its suppliers as to make them seem to be a part of the organization. Other alliances with vendors, customers, and even competitors have a similar blurring effect on organizational boundaries.

Although none of these phenomena, taken separately, makes for a new organizational structure, taken collectively they do. Peter Drucker, whose *Harvard Business Review* article, "The Coming of the New Organization," is included at the end of this chapter, argues that a new form is emerging. We will call this emerging form the network structure (Figure 2–6). As Drucker notes, this form may look "flatter," because there are fewer "command-and-control" layers. It may comprise a larger number of specialists, with fewer general managers—and fewer permanent employees.

FIGURE 2–6   Network Structure

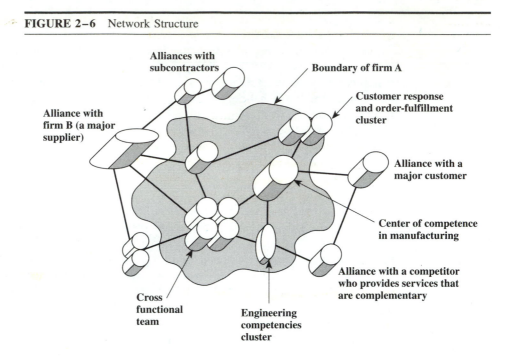

It is characterized by teams that form and disband as required. Most importantly, Drucker says, this new form marks a sea-change move from the traditional "command-and-control" organization to an "information-based" organization. The traditional hierarchical form and its associated planning, control, and human resources systems were geared toward predicting and managing events. In contrast, the new network form is geared toward exploiting uncertainty, rather than reducing it. It emphasizes flexible adaptation in a constantly changing environment.

This adaptability is the main advantage of the emerging network structure. Because people, decision rights, roles, and reporting relationships are contingent upon the particular project or event, they can be altered as required. In turn, this gives the network form an advantage of being fast and responsive to changing events, such as unexpected technology breakthroughs, competitor moves, or other phenomena. On the other hand, a network structure may lead to duplication of resources and ill-defined accountability of action. The network form seems best suited to volatile environments that change rapidly and dramatically, and when innovation is the primary basis of strategic advantage. Many firms in the personal computer hardware and software industries seem to have taken on a network form, and IBM's difficulty in maintaining its lead may have something to do with its reliance on a hierarchical structure. Under more stable conditions, the network structure may not be as effective as the hierarchical forms.

Figures 2–7 and 2–8 compare the chief characteristics and relative advantages and disadvantages of the functional, divisional, matrix, and network structures. Finally, it is

FIGURE 2–7   Comparison of Organization Structures

	Functional	*Divisional*	*Matrix*	*Network*
Division of labor	By inputs	By outputs	By inputs and outputs	By knowledge
Coordination mechanisms	Hierarchical supervision, plans and procedures	Division general manager and corporate staff	Dual reporting relationships	Cross-functional teams
Decision rights	Highly centralized	Separation of strategy and execution	Shared	Highly decentralized
Boundaries	Core/periphery	Internal and external markets	Multiple interfaces	Porous and changing
Importance of informal structure	Low	Modest	Considerable	High
Politics	Interfunctional	Corporate division and Interdivisional	Along matrix dimensions	Shifting coalitions
Basis of authority	Positional and functional expertise	General management responsibility and resources	Negotiating skills and resources	Knowledge and resources

FIGURE 2–8   The Relative Advantages and Disadvantages of Different Structures

	Functional	*Divisional*	*Matrix*	*Network*
Resource efficiency	Excellent	Poor	Moderate	Good
Time efficiency	Poor	Good	Moderate	Excellent
Responsiveness	Poor	Moderate	Good	Excellent
Adaptability	Poor	Good	Moderate	Excellent
Accountability	Good	Excellent	Poor	Moderate
Environment for which best suited	Stable environment	Heterogeneous environments	Complex environment with multiple demands	Volatile environments
Strategy for which best suited	Focused/low-cost strategies	Diversified strategy	Responsiveness strategy	Innovation strategy

important to remember that organizational structure is not an end in itself—it merely sets the context for action. No structure guarantees that desired actions will follow. Structure is but one useful tool that managers can employ to mobilize individual and collective actions with the greatest economy of resources and the best prospects of effective outcomes.

The cases selected for inclusion in this chapter describe senior managers contemplating a change in organizational structure as a result of new pressures. At Appex Corporation, a high-tech firm serving the cellular phone industry, Shikhar Ghosh used structural reorganization as a frequent management lever during a three-year period. At beleaguered Hill, Holliday, Connors, Cosmopulos, Inc., a Boston-based national advertising firm, management of the Boston office contemplated changing to a matrix-like structure after thriving for years with a functional structure. At Jacobs Suchard, managers considered how to reorganize their firm to meet the challenges of the Common European Market in 1992.

CASE 2–1: APPEX CORPORATION

This case describes the challenges faced by the new COO/CEO of Appex Corporation, a young, loosely managed, and faltering firm in the rapidly growing cellular telephone industry. The protagonist of the case, Shikhar Ghosh, leads the company through six changes in organizational structure over a 30-month period. As you analyze this case, consider the comparison of organizational structures in Figure 2–7 of this chapter and the relative advantages and disadvantages of different structures as summarized in Figure 2–8.

Preparation Questions

1. What were the challenges that Shikhar Ghosh faced when he joined Appex in May 1988?
2. Evaluate each of the six structural changes. How important was each change? What problems did each new structure address? What problems, in turn, did it create?
3. Were all the changes necessary? If you were Ghosh, what would you have done in the years before Appex was acquired by EDS?
4. Under what circumstances are structural changes a useful management tool? When might such changes be inappropriate?
5. What should Ghosh do now that Appex is owned by EDS?

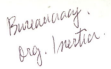
Bureaucracy.
Org. Inertia.

Case 2–1 Appex Corporation*

In May 1988, six months after being made a partner at the Boston Consulting Group, Shikhar Ghosh decided to accept a position as chief operating officer (COO) of Appex Corporation, with the understanding that shortly thereafter he would be made Appex's chief executive officer (CEO). At BCG, Ghosh's specialty was organizational structure, particularly how to create rapid-response organizations. "I left BCG with my head full of ideas of how to structure organizations. I was eager to try out my ideas at a small company where there was little hierarchy," Ghosh stated. Appex, at the time, was a relatively small company, with 25 employees, and $2 million in revenue. The company was entrepreneurial, technology-driven, and loosely structured. But it was losing money rapidly and the venture capitalists who had invested in the firm were hoping that Ghosh would be able to turn it around. Ghosh commented on the nature of Appex when he arrived:

> Everybody just did what they felt like. For instance, customer service people were supposed to start at 8:00 AM. They wouldn't arrive until 10:00 AM, but they would work until 2:00 AM. Everybody did things on their own time, and the attitude toward the customer was—"We'll call you back."
>
> The chief financial officer of one of our customers told me of an incident he experienced at Appex. He arrived at 8:00 AM to find few employees present. He waited for two hours. The Appex group was playing basketball at a court nearby, and showed up at 10:00 AM. Sweaty, and in their athletic clothes, they greeted him. Needless to say, we lost that account.

Reflecting on his initial impression, Ghosh stated: "I knew what had to be done. Appex needed control and structure."

Company Background

Appex Corporation, headquartered in Waltham, Massachusetts, provided management information systems and intercarrier network services to cellular telephone companies. The company was founded in May 1986 from the merger of Appex, Inc., and Lunayach Communications Consultants (LCC). LCC specialized in design and engineering of cellular radio networks for cellular companies. Appex, Inc., founded in 1984 by Brian E. Boyle, focused on management information systems for the cellular industry and credit scoring systems for financial service companies. The consolidated company, named Appex Lunayach Systems Corporation (ALS), integrated LCC's engineering expertise and Appex, Inc.'s business and systems expertise. ALS changed its name to Appex Corporation in May 1989.

In 1990, *Business Week* rated Appex the fastest growing high-technology company in the United States. Revenues grew 1,600 percent between FY1987 and FY1990 (fiscal year September 1– August 31), and were expected to continue to grow rapidly.

Total Revenues (million)			
1987	1988	1989	1990
$1.0	$2.3	$6.8	$16.6

As of April 30, 1990, Appex employed 172 people, of whom 153 were salaried and 19 were compensated on an hourly basis. Due to its growth, the company added about 10 new people every month.

*Julie A. Gladstone prepared this case under the supervision of Professor Nitin Nohria. Copyright © 1991 by the President and Fellows of Harvard College. Harvard Business School case 491-082 (Revised 1992)

The Cellular Telephone Industry

The cellular industry in the United States began in 1982 when the Federal Communications Commission established guidelines for the creation and structure of the industry. Cellular telephone service was capable of providing high-quality mobile telephone service to a large number of simultaneous users via telephones that were either vehicle-installed or hand-held.

Cellular service divided a market into large groups of contiguous "cells." Each cell was generally a few to several miles in radius and was covered by a base station that consisted of a receiver, transmitter, and antenna. When a person placed a call from a cellular telephone, the base station in the cell in which the caller was located would pick up the call. The call was relayed over either landline telephone lines or a microwave relay to what was called the mobile telephone switching office (MTSO). The MTSO then hooked the call into the regular telephone network, and the call reached the receiving party on the regular system. If a caller from a regular telephone called a cellular phone, the process worked in reverse. The MTSO received the call from the local telephone office, sought out the cell in which the receiving cellular phone was located, and instructed the base station to make the connection. If a call was being placed from one cellular telephone to another, the call could bypass the regular telephone system entirely. The signal would go from the caller's cell to the MTSO, and the MTSO would locate the receiving party and relay the call back to the base station in the receiving party's cell. The MTSO controlled the "hand off" of a call from one base station to another as either of the parties moved from one cell to another.

"Roaming" was the ability to use a cellular phone outside the area of the caller's "home" system. When a roamer made a cellular telephone call in a market outside his/her own, the host company would bill the call back to the subscriber's company, and the subscriber's company would pass the charge through to the subscriber. The economics of the transaction were governed by a "roaming agreement" between the two cellular operators. Roaming was usually billed at a substantial mark-up to regular per-minute rates. Because roaming service did not involve any incremental cost to the two operations, roaming was generally more profitable to operators than regular service. As of 1991, roaming represented approximately 10 percent of cellular subscriber revenues.

The cellular telephone industry in the United States had grown from 92,000 subscribers at the end of 1984 to 3.5 million at the end of 1989. Industry analysts expected the rapid growth to continue with subscribers growing to over 5 million by the end of 1990, to approximately 7.5 million by the end of 1991, and to nearly 20 million by the end of 1995. The growth in subscribers was due to the availability of lighter, lower-cost phones, improvement in the quality of equipment and service, increased coverage, increased roaming activity, and enhanced marketing. The government anticipated establishing over 400 rural service area markets, the establishment of which would increase roaming activity. International markets were expected to expand greatly, particularly those in Europe, Latin America, and Asia. Furthermore, analysts predicted that the cellular telephone system might become the primary telephone system in regions of the world where conventional telephone systems were underdeveloped.

Appex's Products and Services

Appex provided service to cellular carriers to allow them to manage their customers in their "home" and "roam" territories. From the very outset, owing to the merger that resulted in its creation, Appex's products and services could be divided into two different categories: intercarrier services (ICS) and cellular management information systems (IS).

The ICS business consisted of a set of on-line services that managed the information required for carriers to provide service to cellular subscribers to and from other markets ("roamers"). The primary services included an on-line national verification system that was used by carriers to authorize roamer calls (Positive Roamer Verification), a national financial clearinghouse for settlement of roamer charges between carriers (Intercarrier Settlement Services), and a national location and call forwarding system for automatically locating roamers and forwarding their cellular calls to them (Roaming America). ICS was a high volume transaction processing service that contributed approximately 60 percent of total company revenues in 1990.

The IS business was very different from the ICS business. It consisted of an integrated software system designed to manage the primary functions of a cellular carrier in its home market. CMIS (Appex Cellular Management Information Systems) was an on-line software system that included customer information, billing information, accounts receivable, credit and collection information, equipment inventory control, and cellular network engineering analysis. ABS (Appex Billing Service) was offered to customers that were either too small for the full CMIS system or preferred to have a professional IS service organization manage their systems. Appex would operate the software for the customer and charged a fixed fee per subscriber of $3.00 to $4.00 per month. IS products contributed approximately 40 percent of total company revenues in 1990.

As of April 1990, Appex had approximately 75 customers, including BellSouth, Cellular Communications, Inc., and Southwestern Bell. Contracts with customers generally were multimarket, multiproduct, multiyear service agreements that ranged in value from $100,000 to over $2 million. Appex served 250 markets in the United States and 34 markets in Canada.

The company marketed its services directly to cellular carriers primarily through trade and industry publications including *Cellular Business* and *Mobile Phone News*. In addition, Appex published a monthly newsletter describing its services and potential product applications, and distributed over 1,000 copies of the newsletter per month to existing and prospective customers.

The Start-Up Stage

The first CEO of Appex was Brian Boyle, who had been CEO of Appex, Inc. before its merger with Lunayach Communications Consultants. As Appex's CEO, Boyle instituted few business procedures; formal procedures seemed unnecessary, given the relatively small size of the company. The key executives made all decisions, and all other employees were involved in developing and selling products. As Boyle stated: "People had particular expertise, but everybody did anything." Ted Baker, presently vice president of operations and service management, described the culture of the company when he joined in October 1988: "If you were interested in something, you just did it. Nobody had any sense of what their job description was."

The structure was very informal and fluid. Employees were focused, committed, and hardworking, and worked in close interaction with each other. As a result, Appex was very responsive and effective at getting things done quickly and relatively cheaply. The company's ability to bring products to the market quickly and Boyle's innovative technical solutions enabled the company to compete against established firms that had an abundance of resources, such as GTE. At one point, some of Appex's competitors, including GTE, Cincinnati Bell, and McDonnell Douglas, put out an RFP (request for proposal) to establish a joint entity called ACT, which would address a particular service need in the cellular industry. ACT had all the resources, expertise, and capital it needed. While ACT was busy planning how to address the need, Boyle created a solution and installed it in the market. As a result, ACT was disbanded.

In the early days, the market was growing quickly and so was Appex. The company was project-based, meaning work was organized around projects. As the number of projects increased, people worked on more and more projects at once. When the workload began to seem overwhelming, the company hired more people. Appex was spending cash quickly and not monitoring its expenses.

Shikhar Ghosh was recruited in May 1988 to head Appex because Appex's investors believed that the company was spending cash too haphazardly. Ghosh had graduated from Harvard Business

School in 1980, and had spent eight years as a consultant at BCG. The investment group that owned Appex Corporation had hired other BCG consultants to run companies, and targeted Ghosh to bring more control to Appex.

Ghosh realized early on that the atmosphere at Appex was changing from "entrepreneurial" to chaotic. People arrived at work and would react to whatever crisis the company happened to face that day. There was only "fire-fighting" and no development of an underlying planning structure. Anything a week away had no priority. Denise Allen, sales manager, described the way in which the organization functioned: "Brian [CEO] came up with ideas. Michael [Engineering Manager] converted them to reality. I sold the service. Mark [Finance Manager] made sure we didn't run out of money." Nobody had time to plan schedules or meetings. Eventually, it became difficult to accomplish basic tasks, such as the preparation of price analyses of new products. People who could not withstand the chaos quit.

Customers began to complain too. One customer claimed to have called 150 times before he received a response. Appex could not address all the technical assistance requests of customers. Those customers who received assistance were pleased with the quality of Appex's support, but other customers requesting assistance did not receive any. The volume of customers and orders had increased, and the company could not handle the increased demand.

Appex started to fall behind schedule, and to miss installation dates. The company experienced failures in product development. For example, one developer would not know what another developer was doing. So, developers, working on the same system, would develop software codes that clashed, causing the system to crash. Information flow, in general, was becoming more difficult.

There was no financial planning, and all planning seemed useless. For example, in a plan written in June 1988, Appex predicted it would go from 36 people by the end of calendar year 1988 to 55 people by the end of calendar year 1989. At the end of 1989, the company had 103 employees. (See Exhibit 1.)

Ghosh recognized that the way in which Appex functioned had become unproductive: "This complete project-orientation and looseness did not work." Ghosh believed that Appex needed to address both long-term planning issues and immediate issues, such as who should attend which meetings, how to pay people, and how to begin employees on a career path. There had to be defined areas of responsibility. As Ghosh explained, "We needed a system of accountability. We needed structure."

Innovative Structures

As the new CEO of a rapidly growing company, Ghosh was eager to try out some of the innovative organizational structures he had been exposed to or had envisioned as a BCG consultant. The first structure he implemented was a circular one similar to what he had seen being used by Japanese companies.

A circular structure meant that there were concurrent circles expanding out from a middle circle. At Appex, the innermost circle contained the senior executives. The next circular layers out included the managers of functions, and the employees in the functions. In the environs around the circle were Appex's customers. The intention of the circular structure was to create a nonhierarchical organization in which information flowed continuously and freely within the organization and between the organization and its environment. (See Exhibit 2.)

Ghosh soon realized that a circular structure did not suit the company for several reasons. One reason was that employees could not relate to the circular structure. They were completely unfamiliar with the structure. The new hires, in particular, who were not accustomed to Appex's culture, could not understand how they were meant to fit into an organization. Ghosh stated: "People who joined Appex expected to see a more traditional

EXHIBIT 1   Forecasted and Actual Growth in Number of Employees

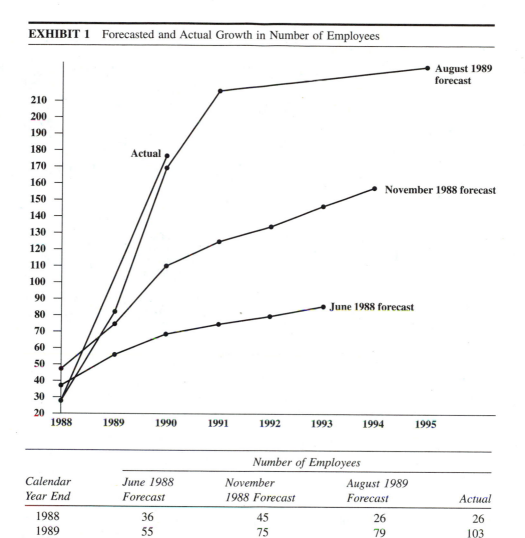

Calendar Year End	June 1988 Forecast	November 1988 Forecast	August 1989 Forecast	Actual
		Number of Employees		
1988	36	45	26	26
1989	55	75	79	103
1990	66	112	176	180
1991	72	130	265	
1992	77	134	369	
1993	83	145	480	
1994		159	586	
1995			675	

organization chart. They did not know with whom to talk to get things done. They did not know the power structure and who had authority to make which decisions. They did not know how their performance was evaluated. The circular structure did not answer any questions or achieve anything." Another reason the circular structure did not work, according to Ghosh, was because "a mentality developed that the customer was the enemy." A third reason was that it was completely

EXHIBIT 2 Circular Structure

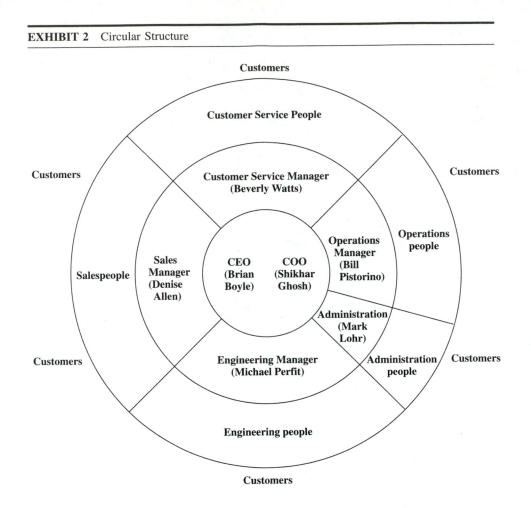

geared toward responsiveness, not toward any form of planning. Those tasks that required planning did not get done.

He next tried a horizontal structure—the traditional, vertical organization chart turned on its side. The employees did not respond enthusiastically. For instance, when Paul Gudonis, senior vice president of sales and marketing, called a meeting of his new direct reports the first day the horizontal structure was implemented, nobody showed up for the meeting.

Within two to three months, it became clear that the innovative structures were inadequate. "My creative notions about network, nonhierarchical,

team-oriented structures blew out the window," Ghosh stated. Following the failures of his innovative structures, Ghosh adopted a new strategy: "I realized that I first needed control, and the way to get it was through a traditional, hierarchical structure. After I achieved a minimal threshold of control, I could begin to break down the structure. Bureaucracy has some purpose."

Hierarchical, Functional Structure

In February 1989, Ghosh established a hierarchical, functional structure. The functions were organized as teams: there was a sales/marketing team, a software development and services team, an engineering and technology team, an operations team, and a finance, human resource, and administrative team. In creating the functional structure, Ghosh was faced with several issues: How many distinct functional teams should he create? For example, should marketing be a separate group or part of sales? Should there be separate finance and accounting and human resources teams? Who should head each of the teams? Could the personnel given certain management responsibilities now handle the responsibilities that would come with the rapid growth of the company? For example, could the person who was vice president of sales at a time when sales were $2 million/year handle the function when sales were $20 million/year?

While firmly believing in the importance of hierarchy, Ghosh wanted to diagram the structure in a way that minimized the sense of hierarchy. He illustrated the functions as reporting to him in a horizontal fashion. This displeased the board of directors that wanted Ghosh to present a traditional diagram of a hierarchical organizational structure. (See Exhibit 3.)

At first, titles were given out rather informally. Soon, it became apparent that people cared a great deal about what titles they were given. For example, someone wanted to be called senior vice president, not vice president. Also, people became concerned with desk locations; that is, who sat where. Ghosh commented, "Even though we were a relatively small company, politics came into existence."

The team structure succeeded in focusing the company on completing tasks. The salespeople now focused on sales. The financial people did financial planning. The structure improved the company's basic capabilities. There was a system of accountability, in which the team heads reported regularly to Ghosh. As Ghosh reflected, "I was involved in everything."

After the functional structure had been in place a few months, various things began to occur. The heads of each team displayed a natural tendency to create subfunctions within their team. For example, the sales team divided into sales and marketing, and then into sales, marketing, and product management. Each of these functions had a manager and then assistant managers. Soon national sales managers and regional sales managers were appointed, and they managed subgroups. All these changes within the sales team occurred within six months of the establishment of the functional structure. (See Exhibit 4.) Every three to four months after the functional structure was originally established, the organization chart grew vertically and horizontally; more layers were added and more subfunctions created.

Over time, the teams became polarized. For example, in the past, Appex had an engineering department run by one person. The distinction between engineering and operations, that is, building a system and operating it, did not exist. After an operations team was established, the operations people proceeded to clearly define their area of responsibility and to restrict engineering's involvement in operations' functions. The structure inhibited a working relationship, and Appex ended up having to spend more money on system development and operation than previously.

The role of "personalities" became more pronounced. Standards were set by individuals rather than company policy. The way in which tasks were handled reflected the influences of particular personalities more than notions about how best to accomplish a task. Ghosh told about a meeting he had with the engineering and operating people that went terribly, until Ghosh devised a plan: "Midway through the meeting I told everyone to take out their egos and put them in an imaginary box— 'the ego box' —which we then tossed out the window. After that, the meeting was more productive."

Another ramification of the functional structure that proved problematic was that the source of authority was functional, not managerial, expertise. The head of engineering was the best engineer. The same held true for the other functions.

EXHIBIT 3   Functional Structure

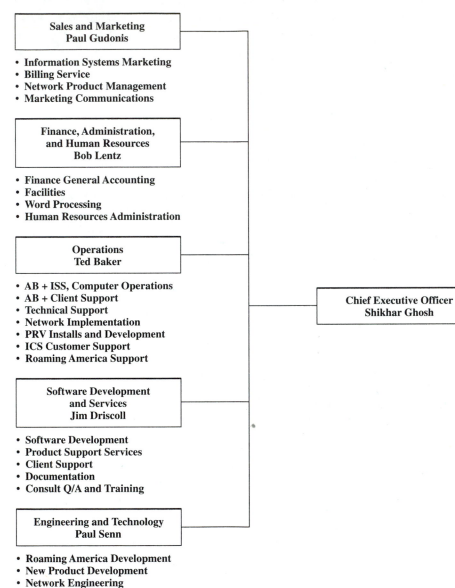

Sales and Marketing
Paul Gudonis

- **Information Systems Marketing**
- **Billing Service**
- **Network Product Management**
- **Marketing Communications**

Finance, Administration,
and Human Resources
Bob Lentz

- **Finance General Accounting**
- **Facilities**
- **Word Processing**
- **Human Resources Administration**

Operations
Ted Baker

- **AB + ISS, Computer Operations**
- **AB + Client Support**
- **Technical Support**
- **Network Implementation**
- **PRV Installs and Development**
- **ICS Customer Support**
- **Roaming America Support**

Software Development
and Services
Jim Driscoll

- **Software Development**
- **Product Support Services**
- **Client Support**
- **Documentation**
- **Consult Q/A and Training**

Engineering and Technology
Paul Senn

- **Roaming America Development**
- **New Product Development**
- **Network Engineering**
- **Software Development**

Chief Executive Officer
Shikhar Ghosh

EXHIBIT 4   Sales and Marketing Team's Organizational Structure (August 1989)

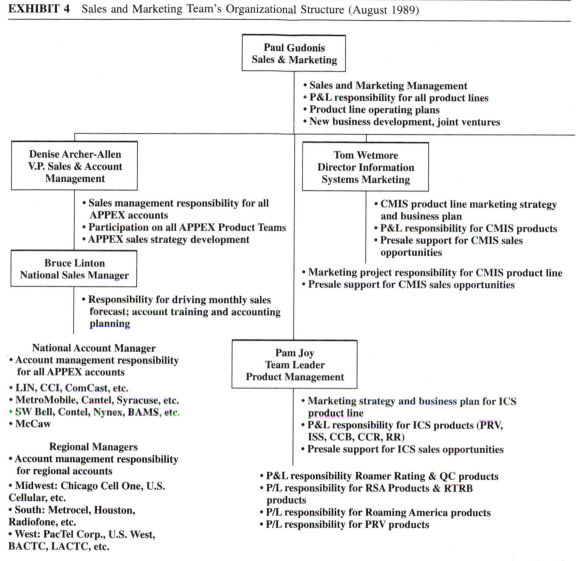

(continued)

EXHIBIT 4   *(concluded)*

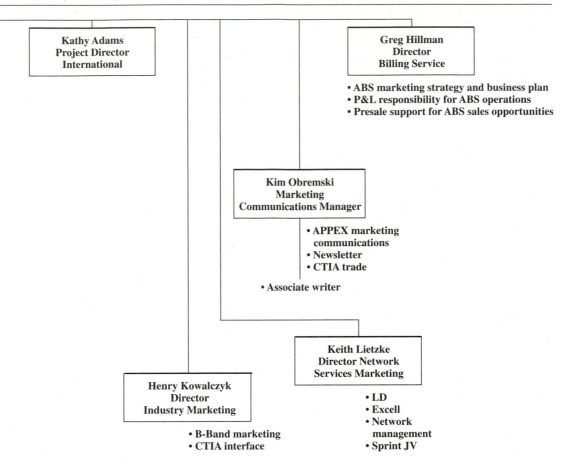

Ghosh hired outside people experienced in management to head teams, but they did not know the product as well as did the people in the team. It was often difficult for new managers to gain the respect of the teams because employees had not valued managerial competence traditionally. Ghosh also found that it was very difficult to measure managerial competence.

In addition to finding people with managerial expertise, Ghosh needed people with broader functional expertise. Employees who had the skills appropriate to a small company or a certain company culture did not necessarily have those skills needed in a larger organization. Ghosh adapted to the expanding demands by reshuffling people, hiring new people, and promoting and demoting people. For example, some of Appex's first engineers were "great band-aid" people, according to Ghosh, but did not have the skills to address the emerging need of the company—quality control. Ghosh hired engineers better skilled in quality issues, and had them assume responsibility for the engineering function. The company, in general, had to learn to value new types of aptitudes and to adjust to the attendant changes in the power structure of the company.

EXHIBIT 5   Paul Gudonis's Organizational Audit (March 1989)

Observations about functional structure:

1. There is no operational plan, just fire-fighting and multitudes of projects. There are no financial forecasts.
2. Nobody, except the president, is acting as "integrator" with responsibility for products and projects across departments.
3. The company's growth has outstripped the management capabilities of certain personnel.
4. There is no "checks and balances" system among departments.
5. No one has responsibility for the system architecture, capacity planning, and the integrity of the network.
6. There is limited senior management teamwork.
7. There is a lack of accountability, unclear job definitions. People do not know who is responsible for what.
8. There is a lack of tactical planning, and scheduling of meetings and trips. Meetings are called at last minute.
9. The culture permits laxity in meeting commitments. People take a "who cares" attitude.
10. There are staffing delays because of recruiting problems. There is no evaluation about why we are not getting the people we need.
11. The technical culture implies "it's good enough" attitude rather than an effort to truly meet customers' needs.

Recommendations

1. A "three-page business plan" should be created for each product line (CMIS, ABS, PRV, ISS, Roaming America). The plan should include financial information, quarterly tasks and milestones, departmental tasks, and staffing requirements.
2. There should be product managers responsible for product teams. The role of product managers should be announced to the company. Product team members should be appointed from the functions. Product managers should be coached about how to do their job.
3. The company should reduce the scope of management responsibilities, and hire product managers from outside.
4. A product team organizational chart should be diagrammed, showing the responsibilities of the product team, and relationships within the product team and between the product teams and senior management.
5. There should be regular meetings to review the progress of the structure.
6. Clear job descriptions should be written, and people should be told what their responsibilities are.
7. Everybody should be required to write four-week advance plans.
8. Senior management should lead the way by setting an example of good managerial practices.

(continued)

In March 1989, four weeks after joining Appex, Paul Gudonis, senior vice president of sales and marketing and general manager at the time, submitted a letter to Ghosh; in it, he expressed his observations of the existing functional structure's deficiencies, and proposed that Ghosh set up product teams. Gudonis believed that there should be separate product teams for each of Appex's main products, and that each product team should be comprised of a product team manager and representatives from the functional areas. The product team managers would write business plans for the products, and integrate the functions represented in the product teams. (See Exhibit 5.) Ghosh liked Gudonis's ideas and gradually began to hire product managers and to establish product teams.

EXHIBIT 5   (*concluded*)   Example of Product Team Structure for RoamAmerica

---

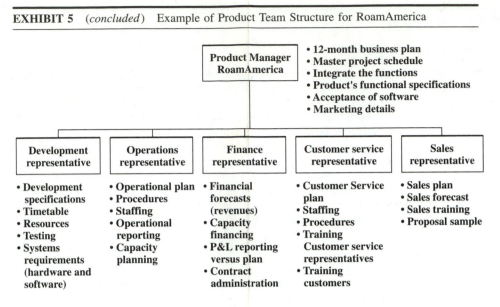

The product teams co-existed with the functional teams. Through this arrangement, the functional teams were informed about product happenings on a daily basis. Although the creation of product teams ameliorated some of the problems of the first functional structure, it generated new problems.

Within the multifunctional product teams, there was no system that specified who had the authority to make which decisions. For example, who had the right to decide a product's features? Should salespeople be allowed to decide discounts? Should the product manager be allowed to tell engineering what its priorities should be? The product teams became larger and larger, and the question of who had authority became more troublesome. The conflict between product managers and operations people became acute. The product managers, who developed marketing strategies, often did not know the products as well as the operations people; thus, the operations people believed that their ideas for the product were what should be implemented. According to Ghosh, "there were constant battles among the functional representatives in the product teams. There would be several people in the product team working on one account, each of whom looked at the same problem a different way and none of whom had the authority to make the final decisions. We couldn't afford this."

The product teams did not know where their authority ended. For example, product managers would try to set a sales price, and would be overruled by senior management. The engineering person on the product team would try to commit to the product team's engineering plans, but had no authority to change the engineering team's schedule. Each product team would want its product to be the highest priority of the engineering department. Every product team wanted the most senior person from the functional team to be on its team, in the hope that that person would have more influence within their respective functional team. A solution to the authority problem was to have senior executives attend all product team meetings and make all decisions; some senior managers did this for a while. For example, the head of operations spent over 40 hours per week in product team meetings. However, this was not a feasible solution because the senior executives needed time for their other responsibilities.

The product teams also generated more resource allocation problems, both within the product teams and among them. The product teams had no system to set priorities about how resources should be divided within the team. In addition, the corporate management team was faced with new allocation decisions. For example, each product team wanted a strong marketing department, which made sense, but it was difficult for corporate to justify spending so much on marketing when other functions lacked some resources.

In response to the authority and resource allocation problems, Ghosh created business teams. The business teams were intermediaries between the product teams and the corporate management team, and had the authority to make decisions, including resource allocation decisions, regarding the products. The business teams included representatives from senior management. Those product teams that operated on the same network and shared the same customer base reported to one business team. Business teams were established in November 1989. (See Exhibit 6.)

Overall, the functional structure overlaid with a product team/business team structure proved to have many shortcomings. One shortcoming, in

---

EXHIBIT 6 Product Team/Business Team Structure

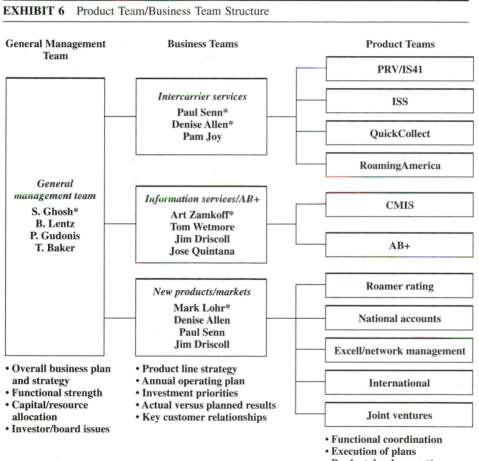

Ghosh's words, was that "there was more tail than tooth." He explained: "In the past we had many revenue-producing people, people who were consultants, dealt with customers, built products. Now we had a lot of people planning, counting, and greasing the wheel." As the company created new products and extensions of existing products, there were more product groups, meetings, and layers of management. The company had approximately 120 employees, many of whom were recent hires. Bob Lentz, senior vice president and general manager for IS division, explained that training costs were high: "We kept stretching the organization, and bringing in new people. The new people generally had no experience in the cellular industry because the industry was only seven years old. They had to be introduced to the industry and the product." The infrastructure costs kept escalating, and this was problematic because the company's pricing policy relied on Appex being a very lean organization.

Moreover, customer focus diminished. People became more concerned with internal processes and issues than with meeting customers' needs. For example, people began having many meetings about how to communicate, and how the product teams/business teams should make decisions.

Finally, people became less concerned with meeting companywide financial goals. One reason for this was that there was no system of profit and loss accountability. Ghosh explained: "There were too many variables for any individual to control in getting a task done, so it was unclear who was responsible when something did not happen. People could get away with a 'who cares' attitude." Profit and loss statements at the end of the month did not meet expectations. Ghosh stated the general outcome of functional/product team/business team structure: "Appex moved from an organization where everybody was doing everything to one with a lot of process and where things were not getting done." It was time for a structural change.

Divisional Structure

In August 1990, Ghosh implemented a divisional structure. He established two broad divisions (businesses): intercarrier services (ICS) and cellular management information systems (IS). Appex's products logically could be divided into one of the two businesses. At the same time, he created a third division, operations, which included utility functions that serviced the two businesses. Each division had one head who was responsible for the entire division and reported to Ghosh. The vice president of finance and administration and the director of human resources also reported to Ghosh. (See Exhibit 7.)

EXHIBIT 7   Divisional Structure

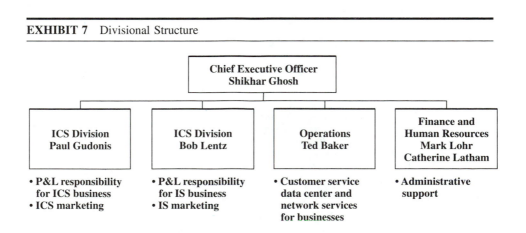

The divisional structure had many advantages. It improved accountability, budgeting, and planning. Employees focused on meeting financial targets. Within divisions, there was a great deal of cooperation. Ghosh was able to spend less time addressing the day-to-day operations of the company and more time planning its strategic direction. Ghosh commented on how his role changed: "One year ago, I was involved in everything. Under the functional structure, all information came to me. In the divisional structure, there was a lot of information I didn't see. We keep moving to the point where the company could run without me."

In time, the divisional structure generated its own problems and challenges. Some problems of the functional structure persisted after the implementation of the divisional structure. One such problem was resource allocation. The senior executives' decisions about resource allocation were not always perceived as equitable. Ghosh explained: "People think senior management is violating some intrinsic equity code, but sometimes it is necessary to allocate resources in a way that to some might seem unjust. The problem of shared resources has led to antagonism between the divisions." Ghosh provided an example about the politics involved in resource allocation: The person made head of IS was previously the company's chief financial officer. He was told about his new position three days before the plan was implemented. After it was implemented, members of the ICS group accused him of securing resources for IS when he was still chief financial officer. As Ghosh stated, "There was a lot of second guessing going on." Ghosh decided to remove all development money from each division, and have the divisions present funding requests on an individual project basis.

Another resource allocation issue was that divisions wanted control over all their resources; they did not want to share resources. For example, each division wanted its own database manager. When the first database manager was hired for the whole company, the person was told to report temporarily to one of the division heads. Right away, that database manager was subsumed into that division, and Ghosh had to hire a database manager for the other division. Ghosh found that he often had to buy things in triple because that was necessary or because it was difficult to coordinate the sharing of resources among the divisions.

A second problem with the divisional structure was that while there was cooperation within them there were high walls between them. There was little communication flow across divisions, and little cross-pollination of ideas. Ghosh noted that once the divisional structure was implemented, he received few new product development ideas. Appex's forte had always been new product development. Ghosh hypothesized that certain products did not get developed because they did not fall neatly into the narrow confines of one division or the other. He received many product extension or improvement ideas, but few brand new ideas.

Ghosh hoped to spur product development and communication across divisions by setting a company theme of quality and creating multidivisional, multifunctional quality teams. He also established other centralized teams, such as a centralized product development team (in addition to the divisional product development teams). He rotated employees across divisions, and made the head of one of the divisions the head of the centralized product development team.

Another phenomenon Ghosh observed was that after a short while the divisions began to act like small companies. They each developed their own business procedures. For example, each division wanted to use a certain technical platform. The company, though, could not support more than one technical platform. As each division grew (in fact, each division was becoming two to three times the size that Appex had been when it was organized functionally), the division faced structural questions similar to those Appex faced as a young company. For example, each division questioned whether it should divide itself into functions or if that would impede cooperation within the division. The divisions began to "play games" with their financial statements (e.g., setting aside an unreported pool of money) to meet financial objectives. As the divisions subdivided into more layered structures, each subdivision "played games" with its numbers, and it became difficult for the senior executives to gain an accurate sense of the financial status of the company.

Ghosh's Structure Philosophy

Ghosh anticipated that the next structural change would be implemented in mid-1991. He believed that Appex's structure should be altered regularly: "Every six months by design I change the organizational structure. I changed it in January 1991, and I'll change it again in June 1991. We're growing at 10 percent a month. I feel when a company has grown 50 percent, it is time to change." Many structural changes reflected employees' suggestions: "Changes come about because people identify a problem and propose a solution to me. I get confidential suggestions about what structural changes to make."

One suggestion, proposed by Ted Baker, was to have the operations division's functions be incorporated into the other two divisions, and operations as a division be disbanded. Data processing would be the exception; it would be a centralized, shared function. In February 1991, Baker stated: "The current structure is untenable for any length of time because the divisional heads want to control all the major components of their respective divisions. I think the divisional structure as it exists now will only last one more month." He expected that a third division—international business—would be established to position Appex abroad.

Ghosh was always surprised by the immediacy of the impact of structural changes: "What's strik-

ing to me is how quickly behavioral changes occur in reaction to structural changes." He asserted that although structural changes created some anxiety among employees, they were necessary: "As we hire new people and the business changes, we need to change the structure to match the people and the business with the structure. People feel a lot of confusion. I tell them, 'whatever you're sure of will change.' " He mitigated the uncertainty caused by structural changes by clearly communicating company financial targets. Targets established stability. Ghosh stated: "I create the semblance of control by setting targets. Targets send a clear message that everyone can understand. Everyone has a point they can focus on."

Ghosh also asserted that changing the structure involved more than cosmetic changes to an organization chart or changes in the reporting structure. The incentive scheme, resource allocation system, and other systems had to reinforce the structure. For example, in 1991 Ghosh established a bonus system, which in his view seemed to be fostering teamwork.

Post-EDS Acquisition

In October 1990, Electronic Data Systems (EDS), a $6 billion information systems management company owned by General Motors, acquired Appex. As a division of EDS, Appex had to follow EDS's requirements, such as its financial planning systems, resource allocation systems, and administrative procedures. Ghosh's role changed after the acquisition: "I spend my time dealing with EDS and planning the strategic direction of Appex within EDS." Following the acquisition, Appex's challenge was to work out its own divisional structure and structural changes in the context of its role as a division of a larger, bureaucratic organization.

CASE 2–2: HILL, HOLLIDAY, CONNORS, COSMOPULOS, INC. ADVERTISING

Hill, Holliday is experiencing declining revenues and rising costs in a tough economic climate. Felice Kincannon, managing director of the Boston office, is contemplating a reorganization from a functional structure to a matrixlike form. Do the new economic pressures warrant this change? If not, why not? If so, is Kincannon's proposal the right change?

Preparation Questions

1. What are the challenges confronting Hill, Holliday in January 1990?
2. What are the strengths and weaknesses of the existing organization structure?
3. What are the strengths and weaknesses of the structure that Kincannon is considering?
4. What structural changes, if any, would you recommend? How would you implement your recommendations?

Case 2–2 Hill, Holliday, Connors, Cosmopulos, Inc. Advertising (A)*

In January 1990, after years of double-digit growth, Boston-based Hill, Holliday, Connors, Cosmopulos, Inc. Advertising found itself confronted by one of the steepest challenges in its history.

The New England economy was in a downturn. The lagging economy affected the entire region's advertising industry, and revenues had been flat for months. As clients tightened their advertising budgets, even strong firms like Hill, Holliday began to feel the repercussions acutely. Compensating for the sagging business climate was proving difficult: since Hill, Holliday already had about 25 percent of the New England advertising market—with clients distributed across many categories—there

were few sizable new accounts it could win in the New England geographical area.

Not everything could be blamed on the economy. Over the past year, Hill, Holliday had met with limited success in its attempts to attract new business. Although the numerous uncertainties and chance events involved in the winning of new business made it hard to assess the reasons for this lack of success, it was perceived internally that the firm had suffered from the loss of "star" creative talent. There was some concern that the firm was no longer able to deliver the "breakthrough" creative advertising that had built the firm's reputation.

The agency's account executives, who were directly responsible for satisfying client needs, saw the necessity for broad change. They communicated their concerns to the agency's top management, who, upon looking at the firm's financial

*Cynthia Cook prepared this case under the supervision of Professor Nitin Nohria. Copyright © 1991 by the President and Fellows of Harvard College. Harvard Business School case 491-016

EXHIBIT 1   Hill, Holliday Growth

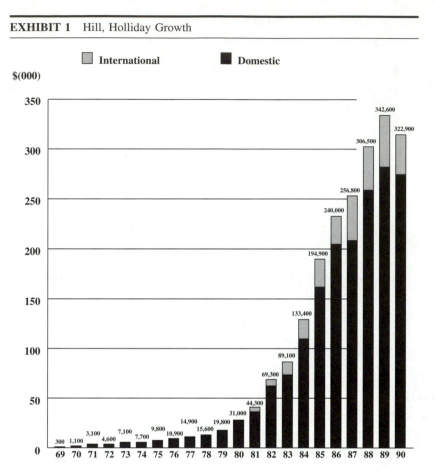

(continued)

projections for the 1991 fiscal year (beginning May 1, 1990), realized that the problem was indeed significant (Exhibit 1). Jack Connors, president/CEO and one of the two principals in the company, believed that flat revenues and increased costs would have a profound impact on the firm's profitability, and that action needed to be taken immediately.

Since the costs in an advertising business were primarily wages, with little capital investment (Exhibit 2), Connors concluded that "either everyone could take a reduction in pay, or Hill, Holliday could reduce manpower." His inclination was to seek ways to do the latter because Hill, Holliday, he felt, "had more layers of people than could possibly be efficient." Convinced that greater efficiency was necessary, Connors communicated his concerns to Felice Kincannon, managing director of the Boston office, and charged her with coming up with a proposal as quickly as possible.

The Advertising Business

History

Advertising, the attempts of a company to promote its products to potential customers, has existed as a formal industry for over a century. A feature article in *The Economist* on June 9, 1990, described the history of the advertising industry:

> The original advertising agents sold space on behalf of newspapers. N.W. Ayer's agency, which was founded in 1863, was the first to start buying space on behalf of clients. Shortly afterwards another

EXHIBIT 1   (*concluded*)   Hill, Holliday Growth

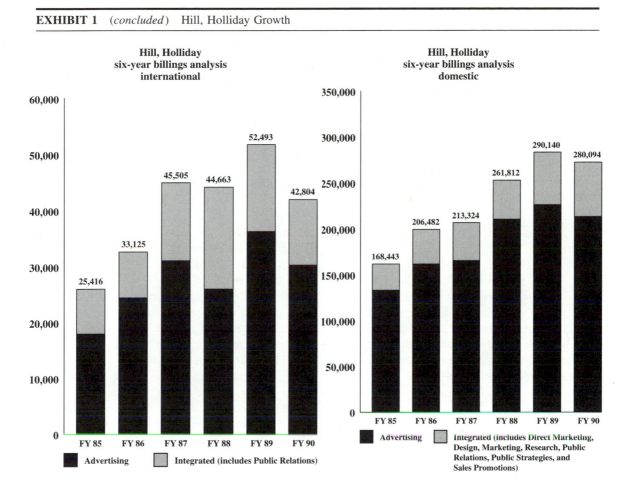

EXHIBIT 2   Hill, Holliday Fiscal Year 1990 Costs Worldwide

Payroll	53.9%
Fringe benefits	11.2
Total payroll and fringe benefits	65.1
Office and related expenses (rent, depreciation, etc.)	15.3
All other*	19.6
	100.0%

*Includes nonbillable client expenses, subscriptions, computer/office equipment, and office supplies.

American, James Walter Thompson, offered to design advertisements for his clients.

Most of the first generation of mass-produced branded goods, such as Coca-Cola and Ivory soap, date from the same period. The new brands relied on cheap mass-manufacturing techniques to undercut local storekeepers' products. And they used advertising to appeal directly to the customer—first through newspapers, magazines, and billboards and then through radio and television.

Last year such media advertising, still known as "above-the-line" marketing, cost companies worldwide $240 billion. Add in other selling gimmicks such as packaging design and sales promotions (which are all referred to as "below-the-line" advertising) and the total marketing budget was $620 billion—or $120 for every person in the world.

In 1990, there were hundreds of advertising agencies in the United States, ranging from tiny two-person "shops" —as firms in the industry were called—to global corporations with thousands of employees. Even the largest firms, though, were smaller businesses than their financial reports indicated. As explained in *The Economist:*

> Firms measure their own size by the media-spending plus production costs ("billings") of their clients. Yet, the agencies get only a commission, traditionally 15 percent, on that expenditure. Last year the commission revenues of the biggest western agency, Saatchi & Saatchi Advertising, were $890 million; Procter & Gamble's advertising budget alone was over $2.4 billion. The stock market value of the world's biggest advertising business, WPP Group, which owns J. Walter Thompson and Ogilvy & Mather, was $450 million.

The conglomerate or "mega" agencies, such as WPP Group, had numerous domestic and international offices and could offer global advertising for multinational clients. Hill, Holliday and its competitors, including Chiat/Day/Mojo, Ammirati & Puris, Weiden and Kennedy, Fallon McElligott, Scali McCabe Sloves, and Hal Riney & Partners, were smaller in size and positioned themselves as national "boutiques" that were able to produce innovative and award-winning advertising. These boutiques claimed that the very success that enabled an advertising firm to establish a global presence tended to subvert its creative edge, since agencies with more and larger clients tended to become increasingly risk averse. As competition among these "full service" agencies grew, the industry was also being shaped by firms that specialized in offering specific advertising services such as media brokerage, direct marketing, sales promotions, design, and public relations.

Agency Performance

The success of advertising agencies depended on their ability to win and retain clients. Client companies choosing an advertising agency usually invited a number of agencies to make a new business presentation. In general, potential clients gave the agencies no more than a few months to come up with a solution to meet needs that often were only vaguely specified. While companies occasionally offered a small retainer to the competing agencies, the sum rarely began to cover the cost of making the new business pitch. The stakes were high: the gain or loss of one sizable account could have a large impact on an advertising agency, and could often serve either to create or to disband an entire organization. For example, Hill, Holliday's Los Angeles office, which employed over 100 people, was set up to handle Nissan's Infiniti account. On the other hand, several international offices were closed when Wang's fortunes in the international marketplace declined.

Clients, once won, could prove at turns loyal and fickle. While only approximately 10 percent of accounts were transferred annually, companies could terminate an account at any time. Since agency performance was not concretely quantifiable, it was difficult for clients to assess the effectiveness of the relationship. Clients could enjoy and measure sales increases, but it was hard to prove that success was due to a particular advertising campaign. In the absence of more quantifiable measures, a firm's reputation was absolutely crucial. There were many highly competitive advertising award shows every year, and recognition for an agency's creative work was vital in the securing of new clients.

Companies also paid careful attention to whether an agency served any competitors, and agencies normally only worked for one company in any particular industry. When Hill, Holliday won Infiniti as a client, it resigned from the smaller Ford Dealers of New England account.

Once a company selected an advertising agency, the agency had to work continuously to develop and maintain the client relationship. Clients usually committed to 18-month affiliations, but could and did fire agencies at any time. An account executive worked to create a good relationship with the client, by understanding its needs, communicating these needs to the creative staff, and helping explain the agency's product—the creative ideas—to the client. Account executives performed a balancing act between the client's desire to have advertising with which it felt comfortable and the creative department's desire to provide innovative work. It was a cliché of the business that an agency's best and most creative work was never seen by the public, as it was perceived by the client as too unusual to release. But as Jack Connors said, "There is no such thing as the right ad. There is only the one that is placed. That is the one that sells the product."

Hill, Holliday

History

Hill, Holliday was founded in 1968 by four people who left BBDO/Boston and struck out on their own (Holliday and Cosmopulos have since left the company). The very survival of the agency was doubtful during its first months, as the partners encountered a number of unexpected and unforeseeable difficulties. For example, a telephone strike that coincided with the opening of the first office forced them to go to the bank every day, purchase rolls of dimes, and cold call potential clients from street corner phones.

The firm grew dramatically in its first 20 years of operation. During its first decade, total billings grew from $250,000 in the first year to $15 million in the tenth. With seven years of 50 percent growth in the 1980s, Hill, Holliday could claim annual billings of $300 million by the end of its second decade.

Hill, Holliday's success was traceable in part to the breakthrough creative work that the firm provided. In the 1980s, the award-winning team of creative director Don Easdon and writer Bill Heater set the tone for the rest of the agency and created advertising that was mimicked by the rest of the industry. An example of this work was the "real life, real answers" campaign produced for John Hancock Life Insurance. Later, the winning of Nissan's Infiniti account underscored the creative success of Hill, Holliday. The controversial advertising for Infiniti received much critical acclaim. The Zen-inspired scenes of nature—unusual in being the first automotive advertising that did not portray a vehicle in any way—built a unique image for the product and created an extremely high level of brand awareness.

Culture

Hill, Holliday employees ascribed a large part of their firm's success to the corporate culture. Kathy Sharpless, director of the design group, summed it up as a "family culture, which starts with Jack Connors, a relatable, caring person." Connors figured prominently in employees' descriptions of the company culture. He was often described as "a charismatic leader," "a street-smart salesman," and "visionary." Felice Kincannon echoed the reactions of many when she said, "He's phenomenal! He has a very strong personality, and is very dynamic. He can talk anybody into almost anything." Employees had a sense of Hill, Holliday as being a place where only people who were "smart and nice" were rewarded. The premium placed on being "nice" was such that there were instances of valuable "smart" employees being let go when they did not meet the "nice" standard. The emphasis Connors placed on maintaining a supportive environment was expressed in his desire to make sure that "Hill, Holliday provided employees with the opportunity to take care of their lives." From 1986 to 1989, *McCall's Working Mother* cited the agency as being one of the best workplaces for women in America.

Hill, Holliday's culture was closely tied to its emphasis on promoting breakthrough creative work. The agency's emphasis on creativity led to a concern about getting bogged down with "too much organization" and "too many rules." As Dr. Jack Sansolo, the firm's president, declared, "We are not in a business that can be run by the numbers. We thrive on intuition. The ultimate rule in advertising is to have flexibility."

There was also an emphasis on being responsive to the needs of clients and being service-oriented. Hill, Holliday prided itself on its very high client retention rate, its ability to maintain relationships longer than was usual in the industry. The agency considered this a result of being able to work with and understand clients, instead of trying to force-feed them undesired and "too-creative" advertising.

The culture of Hill, Holliday was shaped to a great extent by the kind of people it attracted. The creative departments were staffed with creative directors who had often studied art or design, and writers who had an even wider variety of backgrounds. Account executives and the managers of product groups were recruited out of undergraduate and business school. There were few MBAs. It was difficult to attract MBAs unless they had previous advertising experience and wanted to get back into the field, because there was no point in paying them significantly more than others who faced the same learning curve. The people at Hill, Holliday were young, driven, worked long hours, enjoyed public exposure, were conscious of style, and enjoyed the creative aspect of advertising. As Jack Sansolo described, "We attract very competitive people who can cope with the highs and lows which result from the constant need to prove oneself, accompanied with the imminent risk of getting fired from an account." These individuals, as was typical in this industry,

often moved across firms as they tried to build their personal careers and reputations by seeking opportunities for growth.

Growth

Product Expansion

As Hill, Holliday grew from a local to a national firm, it moved from being an agency that provided print and media advertising materials to being a full-service communications company. Billed on a project basis, these services consisted of market research, design, direct marketing, and sales promotion. Market research helped clients with market and competitive analysis, concept testing, strategy development, product positioning, new product development, and tracking advertising success. The design department did work in such areas as corporate identity and logos, information and collateral materials, annual reports, product design and packaging, exhibits for trade shows, and point-of-sale advertising materials. Direct marketing worked with clients to enable them to reach customers by mail or other targeted media using advertising material such as brochures, catalogues, or coupons. The sales promotion department had been recently formed to meet clients' increasing needs for promotions that would build brand loyalty in light of the growing parity of most major brands. Hill, Holliday had also tried at different times to break into the public relations and public strategies areas. Management believed that these "integrated services" (also known as *integrated disciplines*) served as a source of competitive advantage over the other creative boutiques, and that they enabled Hill, Holliday to match many of the services of the largest global agencies. (Exhibit 3).

Despite the firm's expansion and diversification, however, Connors had no desire to let Hill, Holliday become a typical large advertising agency. "Hill, Holliday is a niche player," he said. "We're not and will never be a global or one-market

EXHIBIT 3   Hill, Holliday: Annual Growth Analysis

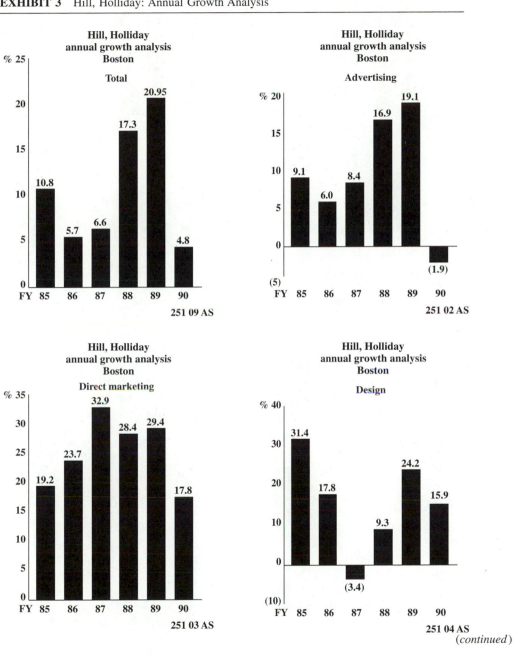

Hill, Holliday
annual growth analysis
Boston
Total

251 09 AS

Hill, Holliday
annual growth analysis
Boston
Advertising

251 02 AS

Hill, Holliday
annual growth analysis
Boston
Direct marketing

251 03 AS

Hill, Holliday
annual growth analysis
Boston
Design

251 04 AS

(continued)

EXHIBIT 3   *(concluded)*

**Hill, Holliday
annual growth analysis
Boston**

Marketing research

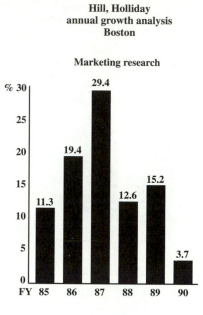

FY 85: 11.3, 86: 19.4, 87: 29.4, 88: 12.6, 89: 15.2, 90: 3.7

**Hill, Holliday
annual growth analysis
Boston**

Sales promotion

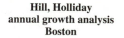

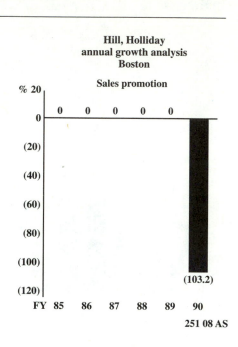

FY 85: 0, 86: 0, 87: 0, 88: 0, 89: 0, 90: (103.2)

251 08 AS

**Hill, Holliday
annual growth analysis
Boston**

Public Strategies

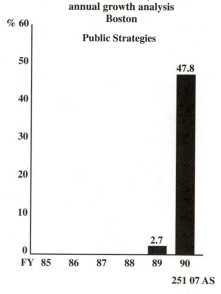

FY 89: 2.7, 90: 47.8

251 07 AS

**Hill, Holliday
annual growth analysis
Boston**

Public relations

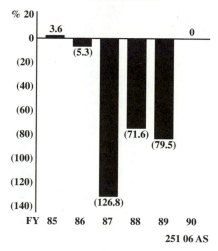

FY 85: 3.6, 86: (5.3), 87: (126.8), 88: (71.6), 89: (79.5), 90: 0

251 06 AS

company . . . In a world of service, this is a family business. The person whose name is on the door will greet them, feed them, and make sure their meal was satisfactory." Although Connors claimed that he did not want Hill, Holliday to become a stereotypical national firm with a "vanilla" creative product, the need for growth remained. He had to consider his and Jay Hill's investment in the company, as well as the needs of his employees. Hill, Holliday personnel had become used to an extraordinarily high level of growth, upward mobility, and a constant expansion in their responsibilities. Without growth, account managers had begun rubbing shoulders, at times uncomfortably.

New Offices

In order to win national accounts, Connors decided it was important to open an office in New York, the center of the advertising industry in the United States. An office was opened there in 1982 and was initially successful, but the managing director, who had previously worked at a much larger agency, soon began to have disagreements with the parent company in Boston. He left, and took a number of accounts with him. Originally, Boston management had wanted to transplant Hill, Holliday's unique culture to New York. Frequent tampering with the New York office to achieve this meant that the office was never given a chance to be independently successful. The New York office struggled for clients, even as its existence became a matter of pride for Connors, who felt that closing it would condemn Hill, Holliday to regional stature.

To service the international Wang account, Hill, Holliday opened overseas offices in Paris, Frankfurt, Sydney, Toronto, London, and Hong Kong. The original plan was to use the Wang account as a "seed" for business in the new markets, but only the Hong Kong office achieved any measure of success. Paris, Frankfurt, Sydney, and Toronto were subsequently closed, and London remained a money-losing venture. Wang's financial troubles were a significant factor in the closing of the offices.

Most recently, Hill, Holliday had opened a Los Angeles office to service Nissan's Infiniti account.

The opening of the Los Angeles office, however, drained the Boston office of some of its best talent, as several key employees from both the creative and client services areas moved to the West Coast. The migration included Don Easdon, member of the Easdon/Heater creative team, who was excited about the opportunities involved in working on Hill, Holliday's largest account. Easdon's partner, however, did not want to uproot his family and leave Boston, so the creative team was broken up. Without Easdon's support and protection from administrative pressures, Heater was not happy, and quit to become an author. He continued to work with Easdon as a part-time consultant.

Hill, Holliday personnel viewed the opening of the Los Angeles office and its concomitant problems as part of the ordinary digestion process of winning a new, large account. The drain of staff and work—as the Los Angeles office grew from needing Boston office support to being able to stand alone—was unavoidable. In the Los Angeles office, there was intense pressure to retain Infiniti as a client, as that account was the mainstay of an office that would close without it. Over time, however, the Los Angeles office was able to serve Nissan successfully and won other accounts, including projects for the Los Angeles Times and Pacific Telephone. Having learned from the agency's experience in New York, and assisted by the distance between the two cities, Boston management avoided the temptation to meddle in the daily operations of the new office.

Creative Department

While the Los Angeles office matured, Hill, Holliday's creative staff in Boston suffered from the loss of the Easdon/Heater team. No new sizable accounts were won by the Boston office after their departure through the end of 1989. Dick Pantano was the creative director of the Boston office, and had the responsibility for checking the quality of the general advertising work presented to clients. Managing the creative department in an advertising agency was complicated; creative talent had tremendous egos and needed to be stroked and carefully nurtured. Pantano had to direct and inspire the creative staff, but also needed to produce his own work to maintain his creative reputation and credibility. In his own view, he had more creative talent than administrative expertise, so to some extent the managing of the creative staff fell to Ann Finucane, who was also in charge of account services for general advertising.

"In every creative field, advertising included," Pantano pointed out, "there are the stars, and then there is everyone else." Easdon and Heater were true advertising stars, and during their tenure in Boston they dominated the rest of the creative staff. After their departure, Pantano looked hard for replacements who would be worth the expense of up to a million dollars a year that the best creative talent could demand. Hill, Holliday management also decided to attempt to grow the firm's own talent into new stars, a lengthy process, but one that had successfully been done before—with Heater and Easdon, for example.

Structure

As Hill, Holliday grew and incorporated different services, the company was organized into different profit centers. General advertising, the mainstay of the firm and its largest profit center, had a client services department staffed by 38 account executives and a creative department that had 26 people. Each integrated service was a separate profit center. The areas of market research, direct marketing, and design (with roughly 12, 40, and 20 full-time professionals, respectively) all had their own account executives, and the latter two their own creative departments. While the public strategies, public relations, and sales promotion departments had been organized as profit centers, they had since been disbanded due to their lack of success.

There were a few centralized services that were not profit centers. One of them was the media department that negotiated and monitored contracts for various media such as television spots or magazine pages to place client advertisements. Most of the media department's services were employed by general advertising clients. The only integrated discipline that used them was direct marketing and the media department charged them on the basis of the personnel who were dedicated to that work. New business development was another centralized group that was responsible for canvassing for new business and coordinating and managing new business presentations.

Each of Hill, Holliday's other offices in the United States and abroad was a self-sufficient entity and an independent profit center. Clients that used the full range of services offered by Hill, Holliday were often served by account executives and creative persons from a number of different disciplines. They formed what was known as a "core team" that provided all the services required by the client. Generally, the account manager responsible for general advertising had the responsibility of putting together and managing the core team.

Management Structure

Jack Connors and Jay Hill ran Hill, Holliday for 20 years, as it grew from a tiny boutique to a national firm. Connors led the account management team and set the course for the agency, while Hill and a series of creative directors managed the creative department. But Connors was an entrepreneur, not a professional manager, and as the firm continued to grow, he decided to hire a manager to make the increasingly large numbers of day-to-day operating decisions. He asked Dr. Jack Sansolo to take on this task. "Dr. Jack" (a Ph.D. in social psychology from Harvard University) had an unusual background for a manager of an advertising agency—he had run a marketing research firm in New York City before coming to Hill, Holliday to run its research department.

Dr. Jack later became president of the firm's entire U.S. operations, including the Los Angeles and New York offices, and had to pull back from making daily decisions in Boston in order to concentrate on national strategy. A management committee was put together to make decisions for the Boston office.

The management committee, which varied between six and eight members, consisted of individuals from different functional areas of the firm. The diverse viewpoints of the various members were all considered during the decision making process. Predictably, the democracy of the system tended to impede the pace at which decisions could be made. Also, since decisions were made by committee, accountability was diffuse. Carolyn Clark, director of marketing services, claimed that "the management committee worked okay, but was blamed for a lack of vision. It became an administrative group, not a leadership group. There was no one leader, and there was constant debate." "The Jacks" (Connors and Sansolo) decided that a reorganization was required in order to eliminate the problems inherent in the management committee structure.

In September of 1989, Connors and Sansolo disbanded the management committee. They promoted Felice Kincannon to the position of managing director of the Boston office. Her duties specifically included the provision of leadership and vision for the office. Carolyn Clark was given responsibility for managing all the integrated marketing services. Ann Finucane was put in charge of client relations for general advertising, overseeing Tom Woodard and Justin Harrington who managed groups of accounts (Exhibit 4).

EXHIBIT 4   Organization Chart (January 1990)

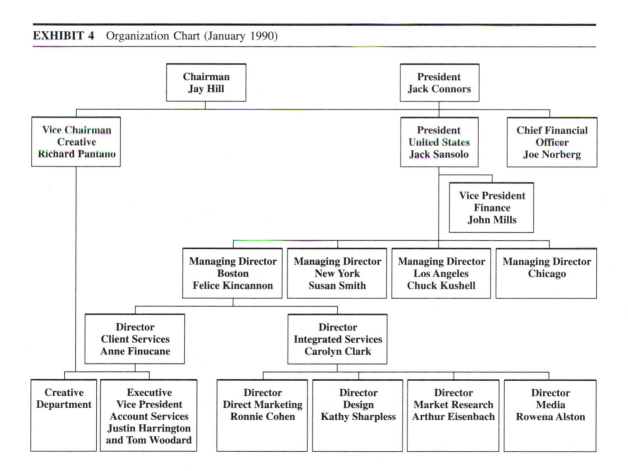

Control Systems

Accounting System

Hill, Holliday had two sources of revenues, general advertising and the integrated services. Revenues consisted of both commissions on total media placements (for general advertising) and time-based fees. Costs consisted mostly of salaries and overhead. The company employed two broad approaches to allocating costs and revenues. For the general advertising part of the business, revenues and costs were measured on a client-by-client basis. Billings were measured by client and could be directly translated into revenues. Costs were allocated on the basis of the time spent by the account managers and creative staff assigned to each of the general advertising accounts. Both account managers and creative staff were required to report their time allocation by client on a weekly basis. Production costs were assigned to clients and an additional general administrative overhead was charged as a fraction of the total staff costs. By this method, general advertising had complete profit and loss statements available on a per-client basis. For the integrated services profit centers, salaries, direct costs, and overhead were not allocated per client. These areas produced only an aggregate profit and loss statement.

Budgeting and Capital Allocation Systems

Though each profit center was required to submit a yearly budget that was reviewed quarterly, the system was not seen by the profit center managers as being very important to the way they ran their business. Dr. Jack's sentiment that the advertising business could not be run by numbers alone was widely accepted among executives. Nevertheless, profit center managers did consider it important to broadly satisfy their budgeted targets for revenues and profits.

There were few capital allocation decisions that had to be made at the level of the profit center manager. The major capital allocation decisions that had to be made for the firm as a whole were decisions regarding new business pitches. These could often cost the firm as much as $300K, and since there was "no reward for second place," questions of allocation were taken seriously. Since allocation decisions regarding new business pitches were infrequent (four to five per year) and did not recur on a regular basis, there was no well-defined process for arriving at them. In general, the top management of the firm would wrestle with the issues, finally arriving at a consensus view of whether they would participate in the pitch and how much they were willing to spend on it.

The Reorganization Dilemma

Barely settled into her role as the managing director of the Boston office, Felice Kincannon now faced the challenge of responding to the charge of Connors and Sansolo to come up with a new plan of organization that would increase efficiency and cut costs. The simplest solution, in her view, "would have been to ask every department for a list of the people who could be let go. Then we would have haggled about the names on the list and finally arrived at a hard decision."

While there were precedents for this sort of response, Kincannon felt that layoffs were not necessarily the solution. Mass layoffs were not unusual in the advertising business, and Hill, Holliday itself had fired 17 employees a few years earlier. Kincannon, however, believed that the current situation was an occasion to develop more than a stopgap solution, and that it was instead an opportunity to reassess the entire organization to see if there were any genuine efficiencies to be gained. After all, one new medium-sized client could increase revenues to the point of profitability and make the layoffs unnecessary. As Jay Hill pointed out, "If we landed a 30 million dollar [in billings] account it would solve a lot of problems." However, Kincannon could not rely on winning a new client any time soon, and costs were an immediate concern.

Her objective, therefore, was to devise a plan that allowed Hill, Holliday to efficiently satisfy three objectives: (1) to be able to provide a fully integrated communications strategy to their clients; (2) to provide improved relationship management to increasingly cost-conscious and savvy clients; and (3) to continue to be a top-quality agency that attracted the best talent in the industry to work there. To develop such a plan, she invited the former members of the management committee to join her in developing a course of action.

While all the members of this group shared the view that there were some inefficiencies in the present organization, they diverged in their assessment of its advantages and disadvantages. Much of the debate centered on the profit center structure.

Advantages of the Current Organization

One of the strongest supporters of the profit center structure was John Mills, executive vice president of finance. "In the beginning," he reminisced, "we established different profit centers when we added different functions with different skill sets. This had a number of justifications. Primarily, the integrated disciplines of market research, direct marketing, and design were distinctly different from general advertising, and people in those departments had dissimilar skills. Designing a corporate logo or a merchandise catalogue to sell products was an art unlike that involved in designing a one-page print or 30-second television advertisement intended to attract attention and create brand awareness. The creative training and expertise varied tremendously. Likewise, the talents of the account management staff were different. Account managers had to have extensive knowledge of their particular discipline." This logic, in his view, had not changed, and hence the profit center structure needed to be maintained.

The current structure allowed the various disciplines of the integrated services to maintain their own relationships with each client, separate from those of general advertising. Integrated services management felt that although this could lead to a redundancy in account management personnel, it was necessary. There was no guarantee that general advertising account managers would effectively cross-sell the value-added integrated services. Moreover, about 25 percent of the revenues

of the integrated services came from clients that were not general advertising clients. It was felt that these clients could receive short shrift if not separately serviced.

A related argument for maintaining the independence of the integrated services was that account managers in general advertising and the integrated services often dealt with different contacts at any particular client firm. The corporate person who approved advertising campaigns was not necessarily the same person who approved logos, or who commissioned marketing research, or who decided on a direct mail campaign. Ed Bernard, creative director of direct marketing, said, "People make direct marketing and advertising decisions differently. Direct marketers speak a different dialect." There were few benefits to be gained by integrating the management of a particular account when individual clients might have numerous purchasing points of contact that were not directly connected. Instead, by maintaining the account executives in each integrated discipline, as Kathy Sharpless, director of design, noted, Hill, Holliday had "a lot of hooks to the client. It's easier to retain them than if there was just one key contact person who could leave."

Each integrated discipline also recruited from separate labor markets. Attaining the required expertise in each integrated discipline meant a high degree of specialization, which reduced the ability to move among departments. Certainly, account managers and creative persons in the integrated disciplines could with proper training perform the tasks of general advertising, and vice versa. In reality, however, there was limited movement among disciplines and between the disciplines and general advertising. Vic Cevoli, creative director of design, said, "Creative skills in general advertising and design are not really translatable. Most creative people make that choice in school." The division of the firm along disciplinary lines allowed each area to tap into its related external labor market with ease.

Finally, the profit centers of the integrated disciplines facilitated both measurement and accountability within each department. Each discipline had to justify its existence financially. Management could easily judge what functions were financially successful, and had the latitude to add new ones with the knowledge that they could be easily measured and removed if not profitable. Management considered this an important part of the growth strategy. Jack Connors said, "We start things all the time. Most of them fail. You only need a couple of winners. And these winners have to be measurable."

Disadvantages of the Current Organization

The organization of Hill, Holliday into a collection of functionally distinct profit centers was not without its shortcomings. Perhaps of most concern was the replication of effort involved in having separate creative departments and account management teams. Each function had its own hierarchy of people who worked on a particular account. Especially during a slow economy, the costs of such redundancy seemed excessive.

This division of functions also meant that Hill, Holliday was unable to present clients with one point of contact and responsibility. Clients had to divide their approach to Hill, Holliday just as the agency divided its approach to the client.

Associated with the lack of a single locus of responsibility was the problem of internal communications. It was important for everyone working with a particular client to have an idea of the full scope of the work being done for that client, to avoid the embarrassment that might result from not being aware of all the elements of the client's program or from suggesting ideas that the client had already rejected or accepted. Yet the need to coordinate all the relevant knowledge, in Dick Pantano's view, "sometimes caused people to step on each others toes." In an organizational structure not geared toward interfunctional communication, it was increasingly difficult to assemble and disseminate the information people needed to do their jobs.

The divided nature of the agency also meant that it was more difficult to present consistent Hill, Holliday quality. Different creative departments meant the work sent to a client ran the risk of not always being thematically unified.

Finally, when a client used only one functional area of Hill, Holliday, there was the risk that there would be insufficient cross-selling of services. Market research could not be expected to have responsibility for convincing an account to use the design department. And the design department in turn could resent the other departments for not doing a sufficiently good job of selling its services.

Proposed Reorganization

After due consideration and much discussion with the former members of the management committee, Kincannon felt she had an initial plan for the reorganization. She decided to alter the structure of the profit centers and make "clients the basis of analysis instead of disciplines." Rather than just having profit centers organized along internal departmental lines, Kincannon planned to put together account groups, perhaps five in total, and make each one a separate profit center. Each account group would have representatives from general advertising and all of the integrated disciplines. They would also be fully staffed with creative directors and writers. Kincannon could then divide the accounts among the newly formed groups, which would be able to unite all the services performed for each client. This would remove some of the double staffing in the account services area, and would thus cut costs, meeting Connors's requirement. The basic idea, according to Ronnie Cohen, director of direct marketing, was "to organize mini-agencies by client and hold each group accountable for the performance of its client accounts."

A key factor of the proposed reorganization was that the groups would have to compete with each other for new business, in a process similar to the internal "beauty contest" creative groups traditionally held before presenting the winning idea to clients at new business pitches. This could be a divisive force at Hill, Holliday, as people fought to find a place in successful groups and as rancor was created between the competitors. Kincannon predicted that group management would have to negotiate for talented employees, arranging trades or loans if necessary. Rather than viewing the process negatively, as divisive, she thought that it would force managers to manage better and smarter, and that Hill, Holliday's friendly culture and small size would encourage people to overcome any short-term problems. "The new proposal will create tension, and good relationships will be key," she said.

The proposed reorganization also meant that the existing decision-making structure would be changed. Questions arose as to who would decide what work should be done and who should do it, how work would be charged, who would control quality, assess performance and determine rewards, and so on. Since decision rights would be rendered unclear, they would have to be shared or negotiated across disciplines and account groups. It was difficult to say who would hold ultimate accountability in the new organization.

Accountability within integrated disciplines had given a clear responsibility to particular individuals for maintaining high product quality and excellent client service. If the disciplines became part of general account groups, accountability within the integrated disciplines would become more problematic and persons without direct experience or control of that discipline would be accountable for its successful integration into the client's overall marketing plan.

New control systems would have to be devised. Formerly, profits and losses could be assigned to each department and conceivably to each client within each department, although the latter only took place for general advertising clients. Under the proposed reorganization, each account management group as a whole and each individual client could be its own profit center. However, there would be no clear way of assessing and assigning costs for the integrated disciplines and general advertising as separate functions, because the same account management and creative per-

sonnel would perform all functions for particular clients.

The proposed reorganization threatened the integrity of the integrated disciplines, which required professionals with specialized knowledge. Ronnie Cohen said, "We could have a big, happy, efficient relationship if we integrated, but we have to guard against losing expertise." If personnel from the integrated disciplines were divided among the account services groups, Kincannon would have to devise a method of keeping them on top of their respective fields. The plan called for retaining small departments for the integrated disciplines, with the department heads, according to Carolyn Clark, "being responsible for nurturing and integration." There were further apprehensions that if the integrated disciplines were completely eliminated, it would be difficult for Hill, Holliday to continue to offer cutting-edge services in these areas.

The plan also raised concerns regarding individual career paths and performance measurement. According to the plan, individuals with integrated discipline experience would be assigned to one of the account groups. Along with maintaining specialization, the functional profit center structure had allowed for career paths within each discipline. As knowledge and skills increased, people could be rewarded with increased tasks and responsibility. It was no longer clear how promotion ladders would be designed in the context of the account group structure.

If persons with integrated discipline skills were assigned to general advertising groups, performance measurement could be problematic. They would no longer be working in a department where their performance could be compared to their peers and evaluated by experts. Instead, their work might be judged by nonexperts who did not fully understand it. There needed to be a clear assignment of responsibility for performance assessment and measurement of individual contributions.

Some worried that the dispersal of Hill, Holliday's specialized services could lead to morale loss, as individuals with integrated discipline expertise lost the camaraderie and nurturing that came from working with people in their own fields. Kincannon understood that "advertising people have tremendous egos, and they need to be fed. Constantly."

There were other concerns regarding the proposal. It did not address the question of whether Hill, Holliday was overstaffed at the upper management level. The young, talented managers of Hill, Holliday already worked for the most prestigious Boston firm, and did not want to leave Boston's quality of life, which they considered unattainable in the city 220 miles to the southwest. Instead of letting some of them go, Kincannon could give upper management more operating duties and eliminate members of middle management. Kincannon also had to consider the effects of a young top management team on recruitment. Potential hires had to be convinced that the career ladders at Hill, Holliday were still open and that they had opportunities for growth.

Hill, Holliday employees had traditionally been rewarded with frequent promotions and salary increases. If the new proposal was adopted, they would have to adjust to a structure that would differ from that of other firms in the industry, which were for the most part organized along disciplinary lines. Titles were used as a reward, as a means of creating and recognizing status within the firm. "Jack Connors hands them out like candy," one employee said. But Hill, Holliday was not alone in having title inflation; it was endemic to the industry. Employees were concerned that if the new reorganization was adopted, it would lead to the creation of titles that were not industry standards, and that other firms would not recognize their position and level of responsibility at Hill, Holliday.

Titles were only part of a reward system that also included a monetary incentive structure. Salaries at Hill, Holliday were high for the Boston advertising market, and were essentially on par with New York. Kincannon wondered if there existed a more effective, and less expensive, way of encouraging high performance. Bonus incentives in the advertising industry were not common, and were usually received only by top managers. Kincannon had to determine if an effective incentive bonus system could be designed for people at all levels. Since there was a large luck factor in the winning of new accounts, bonus systems that were tied to new business would not necessarily reward excellent performance. Moreover, bonuses at Hill, Holliday did not always seem to be explicitly correlated with performance in the first place: employees felt that those working more closely with Connors at bonus time were often more generously rewarded. This may have been unintentional, but Kincannon still had to develop a less subjective method of measuring and rewarding performance.

Kincannon's most important task was to achieve a consensus and convince her fellow Hill, Holliday employees to accept and support the final proposal. No matter what its relative advantages and disadvantages, no plan for reorganization would succeed unless it could win the support of the firm as a whole.

CASE 2–3: JACOBS SUCHARD: REORGANIZING FOR 1992

Jacobs Suchard is a Swiss manufacturer and producer of coffee and confectionery products. In 1989, its managers were looking ahead to the opportunities and challenges that would arise with the advent of the European Economic Community, which was to remove many physical, technical, and fiscal barriers to trade that currently stood between 12 European countries. Jacobs Suchard managers believed these political changes could provide opportunities to achieve enhanced economies of scale, more effective marketing and financing, and other benefits—if the organization was structured so as to respond in new ways.

Preparation Questions

1. How would you react to the changes that have already been announced at Jacobs Suchard if you were:
   a. A country manager?
   b. A manager of an international manufacturing center (IMC)?
   c. A global brand sponsor?

2. What would be your recommendations for the future if you were:
   a. A country manager?
   b. A manager of an international manufacturing center (IMC)?
   c. A global brand sponsor?

3. Looking ahead, what should Klaus Jacobs, the chairman and CEO of Jacobs Suchard, do?

Case 2-3 Jacobs Suchard: Reorganizing for 1992*

Klaus J. Jacobs, chairman and chief executive officer of Jacobs Suchard, had presided over much change in the past year. Now it was May 1989, and more change was still to come.

The main impetus to change had come from the European Economic Community's (EEC) plan to "bring down the frontiers" by 1992, freeing the flow of goods, people, and capital across the borders of the 12 member countries. It meant for Jacobs Suchard, the Swiss-based producer of coffee, chocolate, and sugar confectionery (or confectionery, for short), that no longer would it face an EEC of 12 unique and independent markets, each serviced by autonomous business units, producing and selling for their own local markets; now the EEC would be unified, and the company could take advantage of the larger scale, eliminating some factories and marketing its brands more globally.

*Philip Holland prepared this case under the supervision of Professor Robert G. Eccles. Copyright © 1989 by the President and Fellows of Harvard College. Harvard Business School case 489-106

Since confectionery was already more "global" across Europe in taste than was coffee, Jacobs had been able to move faster in its confectionery operations to change the organization and eliminate factories. People in different countries preferred different coffee blends, so there was less immediate opportunity to produce and sell one brand for all countries. Nevertheless, the coffee business, under Charles Gebhard, was preparing to launch a few global brands, one, for example, called Night & Day.

Gerhard Zinser managed the confectionery business. In preparing for the coming common market, Jacobs and the chief executive office had already appointed "global brand sponsors" within Zinser's organization, to begin struggling with how to market the five basic brands across Europe, rather than independently in each country. Jacobs had also moved the manufacturing functions from Zinser to Hermann Pohl, the new corporate manufacturing and logistics manager, reporting to Jacobs. Thus, much had already been done.

Yet there was still more to do in organizing and setting new measurements and procedures. One proposal, made by a team formed to look again at the organization, called for breaking up the independent business units even further. But the proposal was very controversial and few supported it. So the question remained: What more had to be done?

Jacobs Suchard

Jacobs Suchard was a Swiss-based producer and marketer of coffee and confectionery products. Klaus Jacobs, chairman and CEO, was the major-ity shareholder. He had joined the company at the age of 18, and in the next 16 years took assignments not only in Switzerland, but also in Austria, Germany, and Central America. In 1970, aged 34, he succeeded his uncle and became chairman and CEO.

The company's 1988 revenues of 6.4B SFr were divided between its three businesses: coffee (2.7B SFr), confectionery (2.9B SFr), and trading, industrial and finance (0.8B SFr). (See Exhibit 1). In 1971, Suchard purchased the chocolate manu-facturer Tobler, to form the Interfood company, and in 1982 Jacobs, the coffee manufacturer, purchased Interfood to combine the two popular

EXHIBIT 1   Consolidated Financial Statements of the Group—Important Corporate Data
(Five-Year Summary; Million Francs, Except Per Share Data)

	1988		1987	1986	9185	1984
Sales	6,382		6,104	5,236	5,382	5,111
Operating profit	476		471	338	265	244
Income on ordinary activities	307	*	265	191	150	120
Cash flow (net income and depreciation of buildings and plant)	441	*	394	294	243	205
Income as percentage of average shareholder's equity (%)	19.7*		20.5	13.6	14.1	16.6
Income as percentage of sales (%)	4.8*		4.3	3.6	2.8	2.4
Current assets	3,556		2,206	2,920	2,008	1,390
Fixed assets	1,024		886	832	674	666
Shareholders' equity	1,980		1,143	1,450	1,352	776
Total assets	4,580		3,092	3,753	2,682	2,056
Capital expenditure	211		158	85	100	153
Employees	16,799		16,053	10,063	9,260	10,632
Income per bearer share†	503	*	503	414	353	351
Dividend per bearer share	165‡		165	160	155	150
Dividend as percentage of net income (%)	33‡		31	35	39	34

*Excluding the extraordinary income of 36.4 million Fr.
†Adjusted figures
‡Board of directors' proposal before considering the extraordinary income of 36.4 million Fr. and the proposed bonus of 50 Fr.

products. To further expand its markets, the company in 1986 purchased the Van Houten Group, a German-based confectionery manufacturer, and in 1987 E. J. Brach, the confectionery manufacturer based in Chicago, and Cote d'Or, the Belgian chocolate manufacturer. Jacobs Suchard employed roughly 16,800 worldwide, 76 percent of whom were in the confectionery business.

Its basic confectionery brands featured the famous Milka line, with the recent additions, Lila Pause and Nussini (bars), I Love Milka (filled chocolates), Milka Dream (sponge cake), Lila Stars (small foods, such as nuts, covered with chocolate), and Milka Drink (chocolate powder and liquid). The other main brands were Toblerone, popular worldwide, Cote d'Or, and the Suchard assortments. Jacobs Suchard was first in market share of confectionery products across the EEC, though not in all individual markets, its largest competitors being Nestlé, Mars, and Lindt. The company had offices in Switzerland, Germany, Austria, France, Italy, Denmark, Belgium, the Netherlands, Great Britain, Spain, Greece, North and South America, Japan, and Australia, as well as principal licensees in Portugal, Africa, Asia, and Latin America.

Corporate Principles

In 1982, after acquiring Interfood, the company set down four corporate principles to guide all decisions.

- *Swiss:* Jacobs Suchard is a Swiss public company. The character of the firm is fostered and practiced by the management through its entrepreneurial orientation, its spirit of personal relationship and its value for historical cultures.
- *Leading:* The Jacobs Suchard Group is an international leader in the manufacturing and marketing of confectionery and beverage products. Its leading position is achieved by the high image of the various products as supported by the quality, the low manufacturing cost orientation, and company know-how.
- *Innovative:* The Jacobs Suchard Group is an innovation-oriented corporation. This is true for the products, the technology applied, the people, and the relationships with the client and consumer.
- *Growth-oriented:* The Jacobs Suchard Group is growth-oriented and prefers long-term performance to short-term profit thinking. Growth will be concentrated in markets with products such as confectionery and beverages or in markets where potential business opportunities can be identified.

A Company of Entrepreneurs

"Jacobs Suchard is an enterprise of entrepreneurs." So read the opening statement of the company's 1987 annual report. It had been the company's basic philosophy since its three founders began their respective ventures: Philippe Suchard in 1825, and Johann Jakob Tobler in 1867, with their confectionery shops; and Johann Jacobs, in 1895, with his coffee shop.

Decentralization. The principle of entrepreneurship meant for the modern Jacobs Suchard corporation a great degree of decentralization, both in decision-making authority and Klaus Jacobs's determination to keep a small corporate staff. Based on this principle, Jacobs in 1986 approved a new organization structure. One person would manage each core business (coffee and confectionery) and would supervise general managers, who each had clear profit responsibility for an independent business unit. For confectionery, the manager was Gerhard Zinser, to whom 13 general managers reported. (See Exhibit 2.) This restructuring cut two levels of management between Jacobs and the general managers. In a letter sent to his top executives, Jacobs said of the new structure:

> We want to have as flat an organization as possible; personal relationships are what make this organization work and not hierarchical reporting relationships.
>
> Our type of business succeeds—or fails—at the front line; our money is made or lost at the business

EXHIBIT 2 1988 Organization Chart

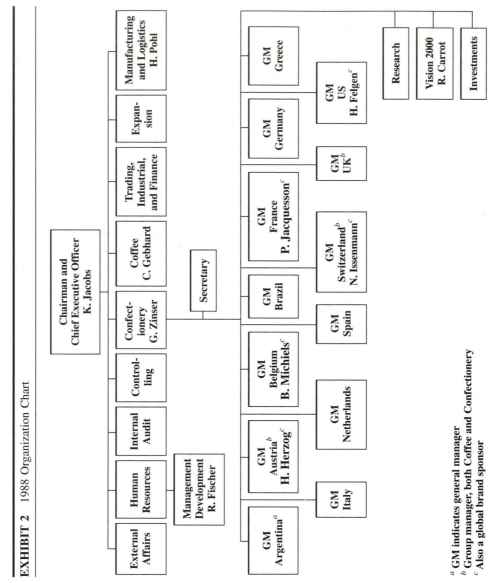

External Affairs

Human Resources

Internal Audit

Control-ling

Chairman and Chief Executive Officer K. Jacobs

Confection-ionery G. Zinser

Coffee C. Gebhard

Trading, Industrial, and Finance

Expan-sion

Manufacturing and Logistics H. Pohl

Management Development R. Fischer

Secretary

GM Argentina[a]

GM Italy

GM Austria[b] H. Herzog[c]

GM Netherlands

GM Belgium B. Michiels[c]

GM Spain

GM Brazil

GM Switzerland[b] N. Issenmann[c]

GM France P. Jacquesson[c]

GM UK[b]

GM Germany

GM US H. Felgen[c]

GM Greece

Research

Vision 2000 R. Carrot

Investments

[a] GM indicates general manager
[b] Group manager, both Coffee and Confectionery
[c] Also a global brand sponsor

72

unit level depending on how effectively we run the business and at the very top-management level where we set global strategies, allocate resources, and plan and execute strategic alliances.

Any organization layers between these two levels must be justified on the basis of their value to the business units; most of our headquarters units are the servants, not the masters of the business units.

No cost centers, but we should be striving for profit centers in all areas, including administrative activities.

"Entrepreneurial," said Zinser, "means that people take their own decisions. It's a 6 billion SFr company with only 60 people in the corporate office." To Jacobs, it was unfortunate that they even had 60: he wanted fewer. Said Rudy Fischer, manager of corporate management development, "Here we have fast decision making. Often major decisions are made in 10 minutes! The worst thing in this company is if you don't do anything." People were expected to learn by doing. They could make mistakes, so long as they didn't try to hide them. Decentralization also meant that management typically used task forces to make the highest level decisions. They appointed managers from across countries and functions to achieve a bottom-up solution to problems.

The role of the CEO and chief executive office. Jacobs saw himself not as a traditional CEO but as the "major coach" or "cheerleader" or "friend." In his memos to others in the company, he often opened with "Friends." To make decisions or review policy, he worked with the chief executive office, which he had formed about four years earlier. Making up the chief executive office were Jacobs, Zinser, Gebhard, Pohl, Gunter Bolte (manager of the trading, industrial, and financial business), and Robert Jaunich (manager of expansion). Jacobs did not want to be, nor have the others in the office be, decision makers, "controllers," or "supervisors." Instead, he wanted the general managers to make most of the decisions. He had chosen the name of the chief executive office with this role in mind; he could not, for example, have

called it the "executive committee," because that name would have implied that it "executes."

Jacobs's own style was informal. Sometimes he would give others complete autonomy; sometimes he would make decisions at the business unit level, particularly around issues of marketing. Other top managers described him as supportive, while still being very much involved with the business. His aggressiveness, many said, his willingness to take risks and commit resources to new opportunities, was uncommon in Europe.

Job rotation. Another key practice related to the aggressive committing of resources, was to rotate people frequently—usually within three years—to avoid letting them fall into routines and "sit too long." Jacobs feared that otherwise managers would associate themselves too strongly with one role and would not build the informal links, beyond the formal structure, that he wanted to rely on. As he put it, "Culture equals relationships." The idea was that people who had a wide exposure to different parts of the business and different problems would work together and cooperate more effectively. Jacobs wanted them to be "round"—that is, to have a broad view of the company and its products—and to have a world view. He wanted them, in the spirit of the corporate principle that the company was Swiss, to have, culturally, an open mind.

As a result of this practice, "There was no clear separation of jobs," as one chief executive office member put it. Managers often recommended actions to others. "If you're strong enough," he said, "if others will listen to you, you can get your way."

The practice of job rotation also fit with Jacobs's view of how to organize. "I don't believe in structure," he said. "I believe in people. The people are the structure." Managers typically were assigned additional responsibilities more because they were capable of them or could handle the workload than because the assignments matched their current position in the organization. "All assignments are temporary, anyway," Jacobs would say.

The Ideal Manager

The company thought a great deal about the type of leader it wanted to encourage and develop. At a seminar, five teams of 20 top managers had worked to define the ideal Jacobs Suchard leader. The following is a consolidation of what they listed:

1. Daring entrepreneur.
2. Motivating leader.
3. Pertinent product know-how.
4. Seasoned professional with international experience.
5. Able to attract good people.

The General Manager

The key position in the decentralized structure of Jacobs Suchard was the general manager of a business unit. Typically, the general manager was responsible for a core business in one country, such as confectionery in France or coffee in Germany. In a few cases, such as with Switzerland, the general manager managed both the coffee and confectionery businesses.

The general managers had total profit responsibility for their businesses. They had trade marketing (sales), consumer marketing (marketing), and manufacturing functions reporting directly to them. They sold to their own local markets, and they produced what those markets demanded. (See Exhibit 3.) They made almost every decision pertaining to their businesses. Zinser described the position as "a man in his own market acting as an entrepreneur, making share and profit in his own business."

A general manager could receive a bonus of up to 100 percent of base salary; the average bonus was 50 percent, and nearly all fell within the range of 20 percent to 80 percent. The bonus was calculated by weighing the general manager's performance in three areas: corporate profit after tax (PAT) and return on total assets (ROTA); business unit PAT and ROTA; and personal MBO objectives. The weight given to corporate performance was 20 percent (10 percent each for PAT and ROTA), business unit performance, 40 percent (20 percent each for PAT and ROTA), and personal objectives (40 percent). Within each area, the general manager was measured on a nine-point scale versus budget, 1 being the lowest score, 5 being "on target," and 9 being "outstanding." The scale was calibrated as follows:

EXHIBIT 3   Typical General Manager Organization Prior to Changes for Globalization

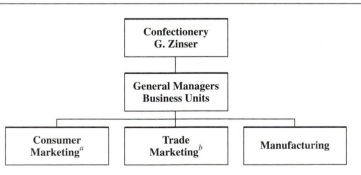

Performance

• **General manager: Profit (profit after tax [PAT], return on total assets [ROTA])**

[a]The equivalent of what might normally be referred to as "marketing"
[b]The equivalent of "sales"

Score	% of Target	Bonus
1	< 90%	0%
3	90 - 100	30
5	100 - 105	50
7	105 - 120	70
9	>120	100

For example, a general manager could earn a 5 in corporate PAT (bonus = 50 percent) and a 7 in corporate ROTA (bonus = 70 percent), a 1 in business unit PAT (bonus = 0 percent) and a 5 in business unit ROTA (bonus = 50 percent), and finally a 5 in personal objectives (bonus = 50 percent). Thus, the general manager's annual bonus would be

(10% weight)(50% bonus) + (10%)(70%) + (20%)(0%) + (20%)(50%) + (40%)(50%) = 42% of salary

Those who reported directly to the general managers and sometimes those one more level down, depending on the size of the business unit, could also receive bonuses, though without the tie to corporate performance. For these managers, half the bonus came from business unit performance (PAT and ROTA) and half from performance against personal objectives.

To be a general manager was the career goal of many within the business units—they would move up the hierarchy of a particular function—and many general managers did not want to move any higher in the organization. To many, it was *the* position. One general manager, Pierre Jacquesson (France, confectionery), when asked why he thought general managers stayed in their positions, said: "They are the position. They think, 'It's my results, my people, my company.' They feel they are the owners."

European Economic Community: 1992

On March 25, 1957, representatives of six European countries—Belgium, France, the Federal Republic of Germany, Italy, Luxembourg, and the Netherlands—signed the famous Treaty of Rome, establishing the European Economic Community. In 1973, three more countries joined: Denmark, Ireland, and the United Kingdom; Greece joined in 1981; and with the addition of Spain and Portugal in 1986, the total in the community became 12.

Then, in February 1986, the 12 governments took their greatest step toward creating a common market: they signed the Single European Act, which aimed "for the citizens of the European community to wake up on the morning of 1 January 1993 in a frontierless Europe." The commission set out more than 300 measures for removing the border obstacles, about a quarter of which had already been implemented by May 1989. Lord Cockfield, the program's architect, in discussing the EEC's lagging economic performance, commented:

> The fragmentation of the European markets into 12 penny packets is not the only reason for this indifferent performance but it is one of the major reasons. It means that we impose on ourselves quite unnecessary costs in complying with frontiers and frontier controls; we deny ourselves the economies of scale that would flow from being able to manufacture and market on the basis of a market of 320 million consumers.

Three types of barriers existed between borders: physical, technical, and fiscal. Physical barriers were the customs, frontier controls, and restrictions on the importation of certain products. Transport vehicles commonly spent days trying to cross certain borders. Technical barriers were the different standards and regulations that producers had to comply with in each country. For example, most countries had differing limits on the amount of vegetable fat permitted in chocolate and ice cream. By 1992, these would all be eliminated. Finally, fiscal barriers were the value-added and excise taxes levied on products crossing borders. In 1989, they varied greatly from country to country. By 1992, though not eliminated, they would be harmonized.

Most likely the slowest to become common would be the differing tastes of each country's consumers. But as people began to travel more freely across Europe and to live and work where they chose, even these were likely to become more uniform.

For countries not in the EEC, such as the EFTA (European Free Trade Association) countries—Switzerland, Sweden, Norway, Iceland, Finland, and Austria—what was happening in the EEC was still a call to action. Some, like Austria, might try to join the EEC; others, like Switzerland, that wished to remain politically independent, might try to negotiate for reduced external barriers to the EEC.

The Globalization of Jacobs Suchard

Because of tariffs, duties, and difficulties with transportation between countries, the original Suchard company, rather than expand by exporting, decided to set up independent offices and factories in the countries it entered outside Switzerland. It placed many of its new factories just across the Swiss border. Tobler had pursued a similar strategy, though on a smaller scale. This strategy, along with Suchard's—and later, Jacobs Suchard's—acquisitions strategy, left the company with 19 different confectionery manufacturing plants across Europe, some of which, because of what was happening in the EEC, were redundant.

No longer were 19 small, low-volume factories needed; now Zinser could take advantage of greater economies of scale by producing in fewer, larger factories, and then shipping the products more easily across Europe. And no longer would he have to produce the same brand with different recipes and packaging for each country, but could reduce the variation in the products. Even advertising and pricing could become more global.

Jacobs and his managers began to move on these opportunities. Now there would be "global brands" and someone would have to coordinate this work. Now, too, instead of having a factory in every country, reporting to a general manager, the company could have fewer factories, servicing many general managers; someone would need to coordinate this work as well. Globalization became the top issue for the company. It was fea-

tured in the 1988 annual report and was the chosen theme for the first year of the Marbach Center of Communication, Jacobs Suchard's brand-new management development center.

The company took a number of steps to make itself more global. The chief executive office had begun a task force, "Vision 2000," that addressed how to reduce the number of factories. It appointed "global brand sponsors." It ran another task force and sent one team to the Harvard Business School to look at how to reorganize for the changing responsibilities. And it appointed a manager of manufacturing and logistics, after eliminating some factories and pulling the responsibility away from the general managers.

Vision 2000: Creating the International Manufacturing Centers

Even before the EEC had voted to create a frontierless Europe, Jacobs had seen the need to eliminate some factories and improve the economies of scale. He hired consultants from McKinsey to study which plants to eliminate. The name of the study became Vision 2000; its goal was to make manufacturing a low-cost producer.

Each factory had become part of an autonomous business unit that reported directly to a general manager and produced everything it needed to serve its local market. Every factory produced all brands and all combinations of forms: fillings (hard, crunchy, and layered); baked (wafers, cookies, and crusts); molded (chocolate poured into a mold); and enrobed (chocolate dripped over a solid filling). Furthermore, each country produced its own cocoa liquor (from roasting and grinding the cocoa beans) and chocolate mass (from adding cocoa butter and sugar to the liquor), as well as handled all packaging, including flowpacks (vacuum sealed), folded (wrapped flat around a chocolate bar), and twisted (sealed in a wrapper by twisting one or two ends). Thus, the countries handled many products, each of limited volume—a loading that hurt productivity.

Not only were there 19 factories all producing a similar set of products, but each also used different processes to produce the same product, in order to satisfy local laws that required different processing temperatures or durations. For example, one factory might roast the cocoa beans, or "conch" the chocolate (the final mixing), differently from another.

Jacobs reviewed the Vision 2000 recommendations in December 1987, then appointed Robert Carrot, manager of the Strasbourg factory, to coordinate the implementation. The main recommendation was to cut the number of primary factories to six (not including two or four smaller factories and third-party manufacturers that would remain for flexibility and new product start-ups). These factories would then be expanded, retooled for automation, and loaded with certain brands or forms to be shipped throughout Europe. Two of the factories would be new. Each would produce from between 80,000 to 100,000 tons of chocolate a year, whereas some of the old plants produced only 5,000 tons a year. The six factories would be:

Berlin, Germany (new)	Countlines and Milka Lila Pause
Bern, Switzerland	Toblerone
Halle, Belgium	Cote d'Or
Herentals, Belgium	Wafer products (e.g., Nussini)
Lorrach, Germany	Milka tablets and bars
Strasbourg, France	Pralines (boxed chocolates)

The six factories would be called international manufacturing centers (IMCs). Given the company's entrepreneurial philosophy and decentralized decision making, the more centralized IMCs presented a challenge. How would they fit into the organization? And how could they be made acceptable to the general managers, who had been responsible for manufacturing?

Global Brand Sponsors

The next major step in making the confectionery business more global came in early 1987, when the chief executive office began appointing "global brand sponsors" for the five major confectionery brands. Each sponsor was also a general manager of a business unit, who now would be responsible for both the local business and for coordinating the strategy and implementation of one global brand. The following were the five sponsors in May 1989, the countries of the business units they already managed and the global brands they were assigned.

Hans Herzog (Austria)	Suchard
Nico Issenmann (Switzerland)	Toblerone
Pierre Jacquesson (France)	Milka
Baudoin Michiels (Belgium)	Cote d'Or
Frank Schiesser (Hong Kong)	Brach/Sugus[1]

Neither the chief executive office nor Zinser specified what the job would involve. Essentially, the managers were told that they were responsible for the global brand. Each manager got a separate budget to cover this new activity, but no additional people.

The Issenmann Task Force

The plant closings begun after Vision 2000 had raised questions about pricing and delivery procedures, so Jacobs kicked off a task force in March 1988, chaired by Nico Issenmann, the business unit manager responsible for both the confectionery and coffee businesses in Switzerland. The goal of the task force was to define the roles of the international manufacturing centers, the general managers, and the global brand sponsors, and the rules by which the three should interact. Six other managers joined Issenmann on the task force: one came from headquarters in Zurich, the others were general managers, factory managers, and finance managers from Switzerland, Germany, and France.

---

[1]Frank Schiesser was the only sponsor who did not work for Zinser (he worked for Robert Jaunich). This appointment exemplifies how assignments were handed out less to be consistent with any structure and more to match capability and workload.

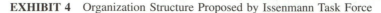

EXHIBIT 4   Organization Structure Proposed by Issenmann Task Force

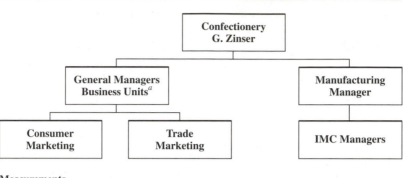

<u>Measurements</u>
- **General manager: Profit (revenue minus cost of goods bought from IMCs)**
  ROTA (current assets)
- **Manufacturing manager: COGS, productivity, ROTA**

[a]**Five of whom are also global brand sponsors**

Source: Company records.

The task force focused on the confectionery business, but suggested that its recommendations could apply to the coffee business as well. The team published its recommendations in August 1988.

Organizationally, the group recommended the appointment of one "manufacturing center sponsor" to manage the six new manufacturing centers. They suggested the following responsibilities for the different managers:

- *General manager business unit:* Brand penetration and business development in countries (i.e., business units).
- *Global brand sponsor:* Brand, product, pricing harmonization, standardization, and inspiring new product and subbrand development in all countries/business units and thus on a global basis.
- *Manufacturing center sponsor:* Optimization of manufacturing economies of scale by concentrating on standardized "global product" production in few large-scale manufacturing centers allowing for competition and entrepreneurial production of new/test products at the same time.

Under this organization, the general managers would keep trade marketing and consumer marketing, but lose manufacturing. Five of the general managers would become global brand sponsors as well. The manufacturing center sponsor would be an independent manager, reporting to Zinser, manager of the confectionery division. (See Exhibit 4.) In addition to its organization recommendations, the task force also proposed how each manager should be measured, and on how the transfer pricing—or, the "intercompany business regulations"—between the IMCs and general managers should take place.

General managers. As before, the general managers would be measured on PAT and ROTA. (Profits were calculated by subtracting total costs from revenues for the business unit, net of taxes.) However, "costs" now would be the cost of goods sold incurred at the IMCs and charged to the general managers, and ROTA now would be based on current assets, such as inventory and accounts receivable, rather than the previous total assets, since the fixed assets now belonged to the IMCs.

Regarding the general managers' role, the task force said that the "focus lies on consumer marketing, trade marketing (sales), and economic affairs (finance), based on agreed strategies with relevant global brand sponsor and core business manager." In other words, the general managers would still be responsible for consumer marketing and trade marketing, though now under the coordination of the global brand sponsors.

Global brand sponsors. Since they were also general managers, the global brand sponsors had a lot to do. As the task force put it, they "have responsibility for a rather vast area of activities they cannot handle all by themselves. The individual sponsor is therefore encouraged to form a team of people from his own and other sister units."

The global brand sponsors would have to "develop and safeguard the financial well-being and share growth of (their brands) on a global basis." They would develop and get agreement from the general managers regarding the following:

- Actions to be taken to increase the importance and share of the global brand in terms of tons or sales units and return on sales.
- International advertising strategies for the global brands, helping the general managers with the implementation.
- Standardized sales units packaging for international usage.
- Activities together with the general managers and corporate R&D to introduce new products for the global brands.
- Activities together with the manufacturing center sponsor to use existing capacities to a maximum and to facilitate and make less complex intercompany relations and logistics.

The task force did not specify how the global brand sponsors should be measured, beyond their measurements as general managers of business units.

Manufacturing center sponsor. The manufacturing center sponsor, who was to report to Zinser and to whom the six IMC managers would report, had the responsibility to ensure that all manufacturing sites were state of the art, and that capacity was shared among the global brands based on the demand

statements from the general managers. The global manufacturing sponsor was to allocate where each brand or form was to be manufactured and for which business units, taking into account capacity, productivity, logistics, and duties (if any).

The task force recommended that the appropriate performance measurements should be productivity (both in terms of sales units per labor hour and tons per labor hour), maximization of raw materials usage, and ROTA for the total corporation.

IMC managers. In the past, the managers of the manufacturing plants had reported directly to the general managers and for the most part served only them. Now, however, the IMC managers would report to the global manufacturing sponsor and "provide the business units only with products prior agreed to by the manufacturing sponsor and the responsible global brand sponsor." Based on the sales plans prepared by the local business units, each IMC would consolidate its orders and in turn provide delivery plans for each business unit.

One of the most difficult steps for manufacturing in terms of the variability of the product line was packaging. In the past, the business units in each country had used different labels, largely because of language difference, and packages of different sizes; for example, three versus six bars to a package. Now the IMCs would get their packaging instructions from the global brand sponsors, who would try to standardize the products. The IMC managers would be measured on productivity and maximization of raw materials usage, and would add to the prices they set a ROTA charge of 4 to 5 percent, to ensure that they were generating enough capital for reinvestment.

Harvard and Managing Change

In August 1988, just after Issenmann task force had published its recommendations, Fischer, Carrot, and Christian Bridoux went to Harvard to attend the managing change program. The team's mission was to take another look at how to organize marketing and manufacturing for Europe 1992. Carrot had been a member of the Issenmann task force.

EXHIBIT 5   Organization Structure Proposed by Harvard Managing Change Team

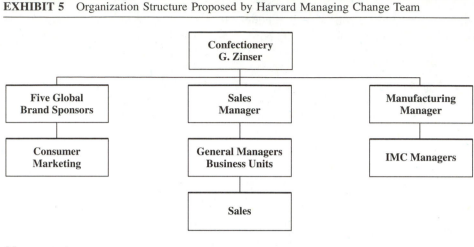

Measurements
- **Global brand sponsors: Profit (based on revenues and costs from all functions)**
- **Sales manager: Total volume and volume/brand**
- **Manufacturing manager: Cost of goods sold**

Note: In actual organization announced February 1989, H. Pohl named manager of IMCs reporting directly to K. Jacobs, not G. Zinser.

Source: Company records.

They recommended the following for the confectionery division, which might later be followed by the coffee division (see Exhibit 5):

1. Establish each global brand as a clear-cut profit center. The five profit centers' executives report directly to the executive vice president (EVP) of the confectionery division.
2. Change the current business units to sales units, reporting directly to one European sales executive who reports to the EVP, confectionery division. The performance of the sales units are measured on total volume and on volume per brand. In this structure the global brand executive and the sales unit general manager will be two different people.
3. Establish independent core factories reporting directly to one manufacturing executive. This manufacturing executive will report to the EVP, confectionery division. There is no organizational link between the core factory managers

and the sales unit. The cost of goods sold of the core factories are to be charged to the global brands.

The team believed that the global brand managers should get profit responsibility; otherwise, "the gap between the authority and responsibility will be too wide." In addition, unlike what the Issenmann task force had proposed, they thought that the global brand managers and the sales unit manager had to be different people: a single person doing both jobs, they felt, could get into conflicts between global strategy and local sales unit profits.

The old business units would be called *sales units,* because consumer marketing would be moved from them to the global brand managers. The business units would also lose manufacturing, which would be independent of both the global brands and the sales units. The team also recommended having regular meetings between the global brand managers, the manufacturing and sales managers, and the confectionery EVP. Summing up their proposal, the members wrote:

> The above sketched model allows us to stay as close as possible to the competitive attitude that characterizes Jacobs Suchard. Many sources of conflict are reduced since there are always direct line responsibilities to only one superior. For example, consumer marketing reports directly and only to the global brand executive and the sales unit, general managers directly to the sales executive, etc. However, the level of potential conflicts will still be substantially higher than in the present organization, for intensive negotiations between the centralized manufacturing, centralized consumer marketing, and the local sales units have to take place.

The Announcement of Hermann Pohl, IMC Manager, and Follow-On Task Forces

In February 1989, Jacobs announced that he was appointing Hermann Pohl head of corporate manufacturing and logistics. Pohl reported directly to Jacobs, and the six IMCs reported to Pohl. Thus, Zinser no longer had responsibility for manufacturing, even though both the Issenmann task force and the Harvard team recommended that the global manufacturing sponsor remain under the core business unit manager. Pohl, who had previously reported to Jacobs as manager of corporate economic affairs, had been working to implement Vision 2000 and clarify issues of structure, pricing, and complexity reduction. Pohl had been the most available of the chief executive office members and the most knowledgeable on these issues. He felt also that it would take someone at his level to get the position established, though perhaps it could be moved into Zinser's organization in a few years.

The Issenmann task force had dealt with the broad issues of roles and responsibilities, so many specifics still had to be worked out before anything could be implemented. In March 1989, therefore, five new task forces began meeting to address the following: transfer pricing, ordering and delivery procedures, reporting procedures between the IMCs and the business units, information services support, and a new cost accounting system. Each task force had from four to eight members, representing different countries and areas of responsibility. Pohl oversaw the task forces.

May 1989: Status of the Changes

By May 1989, many of the 19 old factories had been closed. The organization had been changed as far as it would be for now; what remained was to work out the implementation of the follow-on task force items and to further reduce the product and packaging variability so that the brands became truly global. Whether the organization at the general manager level should be further changed was also still in debate, although most people believed that they should not go as far as Bridoux, Carrot, and Fischer had recommended; that is, to separate the role of global brand sponsor from the role of the general manager and give them consumer marketing, leaving the general managers with only trade marketing. Some thought that such an organization might be possible in the future; others disagreed, believing the general managers had to remain the key position in the company.

Global Brand Sponsors

With no clear direction as to how they should carry out their new assignments, the global brand sponsors began experimenting with how to work with the general managers on global brand strategies. Themselves general managers, the global brand sponsors understood the strong incentives their peers had to maximize profits for the business units, incentives that would make the general managers balk at standardization if it hurt local sales. Since the global brand sponsors had no consumer marketing or trade marketing support of their own—all the consumer marketing and trade marketing managers reported to the local business unit general managers—the challenge for the global brand sponsors was to get the general managers, as Issenmann put it, to "think globally and act locally."

Zinser saw the relationship working this way. The global brand sponsors should make strategy in cooperation with the general managers, who then would try to develop that strategy in the local market. "For example," he said:

> Italy is developing a Milka sponge product and Belgium is developing a marshmallow Milka. Both will be tested in the local markets for global possibilities. Who will pay for this development? The local managers. Why would they? One, because they benefit; and two, it's fun to contribute to the global business. A general manager knows that success with a product will get global attention.

The same idea applied to research and development, which resided both in the business units and at the corporate level. To promote entrepreneurship and decentralization and to keep the bottom-up decision-making process, Zinser expected the business units to come up with new product ideas and develop them locally for ultimate distribution in the global market.

The global brand sponsors and general managers worked together informally, and whether the relationship worked or failed depended on how much both parties respected and trusted each other. According to one top manager, those global sponsors who tried to be "tough" failed, and those who worked "nicely" succeeded. Many of the rules that would govern the relationship were still being worked out in the task forces, and the global brand sponsors were still searching for how to unify the different business units' objectives. Jacquesson, general manager of French confectionery and global brand sponsor for Milka, began by holding formal meetings with the consumer marketing managers from the different business units to discuss global consumer marketing strategy, but stopped the meetings after six months. The business unit consumer marketing managers couldn't make decisions, because the general managers to whom they reported often changed those decisions later. Then he tried holding regular meetings with

15 general managers, but couldn't get agreement on anything. Finally, he set up a steering committee of four of the general managers with the largest markets—Germany, Belgium, England, and France—and asked them to meet every two months. This system, at least, produced some recommendations that the others felt some pressure to accept. Jacquesson characterized his role as "nearly an impossible mission." What did he think were the conditions for success? "The ability to fight, to be fair, to be open—to be young!"

Inevitably, there were conflicts—every day, according to Zinser. What the global brand sponsors wanted often clashed with what the local general managers wanted. There were conflicts over packaging sizes, what language to put on packages, how to advertise, who would pay for international media, which factory to source from (there were still options, and some general managers preferred certain factories), who would pay for investments—and many others. Sometimes a global brand sponsor and the general managers would agree on a European advertising strategy, but when it came time to share the costs, some general managers would refuse. In such cases, the global brand sponsor would be stuck with the cost in his/her own local budget, thereby hurting his/her own profits, and would have to go to Zinser to get the general managers to pay. Sometimes general managers refused to go along with a global advertising strategy because of cultural differences, such as the hair color of the people in the advertisement.

Jacquesson explained how he handled such conflicts. If a general manager refused to implement the global strategy, "I listen to the facts," he said. "If he makes a strong enough case, maybe I'll let him do what he wants. If he just says he doesn't feel the strategy will work, I won't accept that. Much of the conflict has to do with personalities. I try to be fair and take into account what they're concerned about."

When a global brand sponsor and a general manager reached an impasse, then the global brand sponsor could go to Zinser for resolution. This was a last resort, however, because Zinser had such a large span of control and so couldn't get involved in every difference of opinion. Some believed that Zinser would most often support the local business unit management, fearing that otherwise he would hurt profits.

Despite these conflicts, Issenmann and Jacquesson all believed that, contrary to what Bridoux, Carrot, and Fischer had proposed, the global brand sponsors had also to be general managers. They contended that a separate global brand sponsor would have no credibility with the general managers—the general managers would not want to take orders from someone who did not also have to take the same risks with a local business— but also that setting up a separate global brand sponsor might threaten the independence of the general managers, who still had *the* position. Said Issenmann, "A purely global manager would become like a staff member and would just get frustrated, trying to deal with the line managers." Jacquesson gave an example of when he had needed that credibility. He had had to launch a new product globally, Lila Pause, and so had to decide on a package size. He insisted on six-packs, which was different from the traditional three-packs. When he tried the six-packs in his own country, he got 2.4 times the expected sales, which then made it possible for him to convince Germany to use the six-packs. Otherwise, he thought, Germany never would have gone along.

Yet if they agreed that a global brand sponsor also had to be a general manager, they also agreed that the workload was excessive. "We can't do it all," said Issenmann, "but it's the best way to do it." Said Jacquesson, simply: "The workload is too much."

The global brand sponsors were measured for bonuses as general managers, with the personal objectives part of the bonus formula reflecting the additional duties. Typically, the global brand sponsors were expected to complete projects associated with globalization, such as launching advertising campaigns, and were measured according to the number and effectiveness of those projects. Those general managers who were not global sponsors were not measured on how much they contributed to the globalization projects.

The International Manufacturing Centers

By May 1989, the confectionery business had moved about 80 percent toward concentrated production in the six IMCs. By the end of the year, all the extra factories would be closed.

Like the relationship between the general managers and the global brand sponsors, the relationship between the general managers and IMC managers was also fraught with conflict. Where the IMCs sought standardization of a product line to maximize volumes and reduce costs, the general managers sought distinctive packaging and other requirements to serve their local markets.

Having Pohl as their manager, with direct access to the chief executive office and Jacobs, gave the IMC managers a new independence. When they were still reporting to the general managers, the IMC managers had had to follow what the general manager wanted. They could not act against the general manager's profit goals, even if they thought it was best for globalization. Now, however, they reported only indirectly to the general managers.

The general managers had not liked losing manufacturing, but, according to Pohl, most now saw the benefits. The key was how the change was handled. "People realize," he said, "that when the top guys get involved with change, it's serious. Plus, they know they'll be involved. We have to involve them in how we do it." Pohl always sought agreement from the general managers on what he was trying to do. On some issues, getting this agreement took a long time; on the issue of standardized pricing, for example, it took four months.

The general managers still were responsible for profit in their business units, and so when the IMCs wanted to do something that would affect their bottom line, the general managers fought it. For example, the first fully international brand, I Love Milka—which had one recipe and one box— would soon be produced solely in Strasbourg,

France, to be sold across Europe. Currently, it was sold mainly in Germany. Nevertheless, before the Strasbourg line was even completed for I Love Milka, Germany was already developing four new recipes, which would greatly expand the need for space and capacity at the IMC. Whether or not Strasbourg would respond to what Germany wanted, depended on the agreed-upon global strategy. Said Carrot, now IMC manager of Strasbourg, "We are awaiting a decision from the global brand sponsor on this. What's holding them up? Consumer marketing is still independent and local." Consumer marketing managers still reported to the general managers, and did not always have the incentives to follow what the global sponsors wanted.

Pohl described another standard conflict:

> We wanted to have one Milka language wrapper for all of Europe, but people screamed, because we couldn't fit all the languages on the package. So, to compromise, we decided on three different packaging versions: one for the Mediterranean countries, one for the German-speaking countries, and one for the others. I agreed to this for now, because I needed the full commitment of all the general managers. It's the only way to get movement.

Jacquesson thought that many of the problems would not exist if there was a clear financial structure, outlining who had to pay for what. "The IMCs have good ideas, but they don't care where the profit is," he explained.

> The unwritten rule is, "Help yourself." There's no formal decision structure. It's conflict management by design—which is very tough! For example, I wanted Germany to pay for the start-up of a product made in France for Germany, but they originally said no. Sometimes I need to bring in Zurich as an arbitrator. Case by case, issue by issue, we are trying to establish a philosophy for dealing with these cases, to build rules.

For Pohl, the most important issue to be dealt with was product complexity. Before standardiza-

tion had begun, there were about 1,500 stock-keeping units (SKUs) for confectionery, considering all the variations of flavors, sizes, and language. Pohl didn't want to begin centralizing manufacturing with this "chaos." So he began task forces with the consumer marketing managers to try to reduce the SKUs. Others had tried the same thing before Pohl, and twice had gotten nowhere, because no one would compromise and no one could get beyond the issue of package design. The third time, Pohl took package design off the discussion table and simply asked the teams for a big reduction, wanting to let them recommend what was to be done. When they were finished, it looked as though they could cut the number from 1,500 down to 750.

Another open issue was how the IMCs should be measured and compensated, and how the IMCs should charge the general managers. Should the IMCs charge by standard costs, and if so, who would cover the risk of the volatile swings in the commodity prices of cocoa beans and cocoa butter, as well as fluctuations in currencies? A number of these related issues still needed to be worked out in the task forces. Once the task forces were done, they would have to present their recommendations to all the general managers for acceptance, and then to Jacobs.

How Far to Go?

Was the present organization sufficient to create the incentives and priorities for a successful launch of the global brands, or did the company need to separate the role of global brand sponsor from general manager? Jacobs hadn't said no to the idea, but neither did he think the organization was ready. And, could the company maintain its decentralized structure and entrepreneurial spirit, while trying to deal with products and markets that seemed to require more centralization? As Fischer put it, "We are trying to both centralize and keep a small staff." Finally, what was the future of the general manager? Many were already upset at losing functions; most would resign without profit responsibility. In a truly global business, it wasn't clear precisely what the role of the general managers might be. What further complicated the problem was the fact that there would always be local brands. These were some of the questions facing Jacobs as he looked ahead to EEC 1992, which was fast approaching.

Reading 2–1

In the following article, Peter Drucker, a well-known observer of management practice, proposes that business firms are rapidly shifting from "command-and-control" organizations to "information-based" organizations, due largely to the capabilities of information technologies.

Preparation Questions

1. What does Drucker propose about the future roles of specialists versus generalists? What are the implications for management education?
2. Do you agree that the organization of the future will look more like a symphony or an orchestra? Why or why not?

THE COMING OF THE NEW ORGANIZATION

By Peter F. Drucker*

The typical large business 20 years hence will have fewer than half the levels of management of its counterpart today, and no more than a third the managers. In its structure, and in its management problems and concerns, it will bear little resemblance to the typical manufacturing company, circa 1950, which our textbooks still consider the norm. Instead it is far more likely to resemble organizations that neither the practicing manager nor the management scholar pays much attention to today: the hospital, the university, the symphony orchestra. For like them, the typical business will be knowledge-based, an organization composed largely of specialists who direct and discipline their own performance through organized feedback from colleagues, customers, and headquarters. For this reason, it will be what I call an information-based organization.

Businesses, especially large ones, have little choice but to become information-based. Demographics, for one, demands the shift. The center of gravity in employment is moving fast from manual

*Reprinted by permission of *Harvard Business Review.* "The Coming of the New Organization" by Peter F. Drucker (January/February 1988). Copyright © 1987 by the President and Fellows of Harvard College; all rights reserved. Reprint 88105

and clerical workers to knowledge workers who resist the command-and-control model that business took from the military 100 years ago. Economics also dictates change, especially the need for large businesses to innovate and to be entrepreneurs. But above all, information technology demands the shift.

Advanced data-processing technology isn't necessary to create an information-based organization, of course. As we shall see, the British built just such an organization in India when "information technology" meant the quill pen, and barefoot runners were the "telecommunications" systems. But as advanced technology becomes more and more prevalent, we have to engage in analysis and diagnosis—that is, in "information"—even more intensively or risk being swamped by the data we generate.

So far most computer users still use the new technology only to do faster what they have always done before, crunch conventional numbers. But as soon as a company takes the first tentative steps from data to information, its decision processes, management structure, and even the way its work gets done begin to be transformed. In fact, this is already happening, quite fast, in a number of companies throughout the world.

We can readily see the first step in this transformation process when we consider the impact of computer technology on capital-investment decisions. We have known for a long time that there is no one right way to analyze a proposed capital investment. To understand it we need at least six analyses: the expected rate of return; the payout period and the investment's expected productive life; the discounted present value of all returns through the productive lifetime of the investment; the risk in not making the investment or deferring it; the cost and risk in case of failure; and finally, the opportunity cost. Every accounting student is taught these concepts. But before the advent of data-processing capacity, the actual analyses would have taken man-years of clerical toil to complete. Now anyone with a spreadsheet should be able to do them in a few hours.

The availability of this information transforms the capital-investment analysis from opinion into diagnosis, that is, into the rational weighing of alternative assumptions. Then the information transforms the capital-investment decision from an opportunistic, financial decision governed by the numbers into a business decision based on the probability of alternative strategic assumptions. So the decision both presupposes a business strategy and challenges that strategy and its assumptions. What was once a budget exercise becomes an analysis of policy.

The second area that is affected when a company focuses its data-processing capacity on producing information is its organization structure. Almost immediately, it becomes clear that both the number of management levels and the number of managers can be sharply cut. The reason is straightforward: it turns out that whole layers of management neither make decisions nor lead. Instead, their main, if not their only, function is to serve as "relays"—human boosters for the faint, unfocused signals that pass for communication in the traditional pre-information organization.

One of America's largest defense contractors made this discovery when it asked what information its top corporate and operating managers needed to do their jobs. Where did it come from? What form was it in? How did it flow? The search for answers soon revealed that whole layers of management—perhaps as many as 6 out of a total of 14—existed only because these questions had not been asked before. The company had had data galore. But it had always used its copious data for control rather than for information.

Information is data endowed with relevance and purpose. Converting data into information thus requires knowledge. And knowledge, by definition, is specialized. (In fact, truly knowledgeable people tend toward overspecialization, whatever their field, precisely because there is always so much more to know.)

The information-based organization requires far more specialists overall than the command-and-control companies we are accustomed to. Moreover, the specialists are found in operations, not at corporate headquarters. Indeed, the operating organization tends to become an organization of specialists of all kinds.

Information-based organizations need central operating work such as legal counsel, public relations, and labor relations as much as ever. But the need for service staffs—that is, for people without operating responsibilities who only advise, counsel, or coordinate—shrinks drastically. In its *central* management, the information-based organization needs few, if any, specialists.

Because of its flatter structure, the large, information-based organization will more closely resemble the businesses of a century ago than today's big companies. Back then, however, all the knowledge, such as it was, lay with the very top people. The rest were helpers or hands, who mostly did the same work and did as they were told. In the information-based organization, the knowledge will be primarily at the bottom, in the minds of the specialists who do different work and direct themselves. So today's typical organization in which knowledge tends to be concentrated in service staffs, perched rather insecurely between top management and the operating people, will likely be labeled a phase, an attempt to infuse knowledge from the top rather than obtain information from below.

Finally, a good deal of work will be done differently in the information-based organization. Traditional departments will serve as guardians of standards, as centers for training and the assignment of specialists; they won't be where the work gets done. That will happen largely in task-focused teams.

This change is already under way in what used to be the most clearly defined of all departments— research. In pharmaceuticals, in telecommunications, in papermaking, the traditional *sequence* of research, development, manufacturing, and marketing is being replaced by *synchrony*: specialists from all these functions work together as a team, from the inception of research to a product's establishment in the market.

How task forces will develop to tackle other business opportunities and problems remains to be seen. I suspect, however, that the need for a task force, its assignment, its composition, and its leadership will have to be decided on case by case. So the organization that will be developed will go beyond the matrix and may indeed be quite different from it. One thing is clear, though: it will require greater self-discipline and even greater emphasis on individual responsibility for relationships and for communications.

To say that information technology is transforming business enterprises is simple. What this transformation will require of companies and top managements is much harder to decipher. That is why I find it helpful to look for clues in other kinds of information-based organizations, such as the hospital, the symphony orchestra, and the British administration in India.

A fair-sized hospital of about 400 beds will have a staff of several hundred physicians and 1,200 to 1,500 paramedics divided among some 60 medical and paramedical specialities. Each specialty has its own knowledge, its own training, its own language. In each specialty, especially the paramedical ones like the clinical lab and physical therapy, there is a head person who is a working specialist rather than a full-time manager. The head of each specialty reports directly to the top, and there is little middle management. A good deal of the work is done in ad hoc teams as required by an individual patient's diagnosis and condition.

A large symphony orchestra is even more instructive, since for coming works there may be a few hundred musicians on stage playing together. According to organization theory then, there should be several group vice president conductors and perhaps a half-dozen division VP conductors. But that's not how it works. There is only the conductor-CEO—and every one of the musicians plays directly to that person without an intermediary. And each is a high-grade specialist, indeed an artist.

But the best example of a large and successful information-based organization, and one without any middle management at all, is the British civil administration in India.[1]

The British ran the Indian subcontinent for 200 years, from the middle of the eighteenth century through World War II, without making any fundamental changes in organization structure or administrative policy. The Indian civil service never had more than 1,000 members to administer the vast and densely populated subcontinent—a tiny fraction (at most 1 percent) of the legions of Confucian mandarins and palace eunuchs employed next door to administer a not-much-more populous China. Most of the Britishers were quite young; a 30-year-old was a survivor, especially in the early years. Most lived alone in isolated outposts with the nearest countryman a day or two of travel away, and for the first hundred years there was no telegraph or railroad.

The organization structure was totally flat. Each district officer reported directly to the "Coo," the provincial political secretary. And since there were nine provinces, each political secretary had at least 100 people reporting directly to him, many times what the doctrine of the span of control would allow. Nevertheless, the system worked remarkably well, in large part because it was designed to ensure that each of its members had the information he needed to do his job.

Each month the district officer spent a whole day writing a full report to the political secretary in the provincial capital. He discussed each of his principal tasks—there were only four, each clearly delineated. He put down in detail what he had expected would happen with respect to each of them, what actually did happen, and why, if there was discrepancy, the two differed. Then he wrote down what he expected would happen in the ensuing month with respect to each key task and

---

[1]The standard account is Philip Woodruff, *The Men Who Ruled India,* especially the first volume, *The Founders of Modern India* (New York: St. Martin's, 1954). How the system worked day by day is charmingly told in *Sowing* (New York: Harcourt Brace Jovanovich, 1962), volume one of the autobiography of Leonard Woolf (Virginia Woolf's husband).

what he was going to do about it, asked questions about policy, and commented on long-term opportunities, threats, and needs. In turn, the political secretary "minuted" every one of those reports—that is, he wrote back a full comment.

On the basis of these examples, what can we say about the requirements of the information-based organization? And what are its management problems likely to be? Let's look first at the requirements. Several hundred musicians and their CEO, the conductor, can play together because they all have the same score. It tells both flutist and timpanist what to play and when. And it tells the conductor what to expect from each and when. Similarly, all the specialists in the hospital share a common mission: the care and cure of the sick. The diagnosis is their "score"; it dictates specific action for the X-ray lab, the dietitian, the physical therapist, and the rest of the medical team.

Information-based organizations, in other words, require clear, simple, common objectives that translate into particular actions. At the same time, however, as these examples indicate, information-based organizations also need concentration on one objective or, at most, on a few.

Because the "players" in an information-based organization are specialists, they cannot be told how to do their work. There are probably few orchestra conductors who could coax even one note out of a French horn, let alone show the horn player how to do it. But the conductor can focus the horn player's skill and knowledge on the musicians' joint performance. And this focus is what the leaders of an information-based business must be able to achieve.

Yet a business has no "score" to play by except the score it writes as it plays. And whereas neither a first-rate performance of a symphony nor a miserable one will change what the composer wrote, the performance of a business continually creates new and different scores against which its performance is assessed. So an information-based business must be structured around goals that clearly state management's performance expectations for the enterprise and for each part and specialist and around organized feedback that compares results with these performance expectations so that every member can exercise self-control.

The other requirement of an information-based organization is that everyone take information responsibility. The bassoonist in the orchestra does so every time she plays a note. Doctors and paramedics work with an elaborate system of reports and an information center, the nurse's station on the patient's floor. The district officer in India acted on this responsibility every time he filed a report.

The key to such a system is that everyone asks: Who in this organization depends on me for what information? And on whom, in turn, do I depend? Each person's list will always include superiors and subordinates. But the most important names on it will be those of colleagues, people with whom one's primary relationship is coordination. The relationship of the internist, the surgeon, and the anesthesiologist is one example. But the relationship of a biochemist, a pharmacologist, the medical director in charge of clinical testing, and a marketing specialist in a pharmaceutical company is no different. It, too, requires each party to take the fullest information responsibility.

Information responsibility to others is increasingly understood, especially in middle-sized companies. But information responsibility to oneself is still largely neglected. That is, everyone in an organization should constantly be thinking through what information he or she needs to do the job and to make a contribution.

This may well be the most radical break with the way even the most highly computerized businesses are still being run today. There, people either assume the more data, the more information—which was a perfectly valid assumption yesterday when data were scarce, but leads to data overload and information blackout now that they are plentiful. Or they believe that information specialists know what data executives and professionals need in order to have information. But information specialists are tool makers. They can tell us what tool to use to hammer upholstery nails into a chair. We need to decide whether we should be upholstering a chair at all.

Executives and professional specialists need to think through what information is for them, what data they need: first, to know what they are doing; then, to be able to decide what they should be doing; and finally, to appraise how well they are doing. Until this happens MIS departments are likely to remain cost centers rather than become the result centers they could be.

Most large businesses have little in common with the examples we have been looking at. Yet to remain competitive—maybe even to survive—they will have to convert themselves into information-based organizations, and fairly quickly. They will have to change old habits and acquire new ones. And the more successful a company has been, the more difficult and painful this process is apt to be. It will threaten the jobs, status, and opportunities of a good many people in the organization, especially the long-serving, middle-aged people in middle management who tend to be the least mobile and to feel most secure in their work, their positions, their relationships, and their behavior.

The information-based organization will also pose its own special management problems. I see as particularly critical:

1. Developing rewards, recognition, and career opportunities for specialists.
2. Creating unified vision in an organization of specialists.
3. Devising the management structure for an organization of task forces.
4. Ensuring the supply, preparation, and testing of top management people.

Bassoonists presumably neither want nor expect to be anything but bassoonists. Their career opportunities consist of moving from second bassoon to first bassoon and perhaps of moving from a second-rank orchestra to a better, more prestigious one. Similarly, many medical technologists neither expect nor want to be anything but medical technologists. Their career opportunities consist of a fairly good chance of moving up to senior technician, and a very slim chance of becoming lab director. For those who make it to lab director, about 1 out of every 25 or 30 technicians, there is also the opportunity to move to a bigger, richer hospital. The district officer in India had practically no chance for professional growth except possibly to be relocated, after a three-year stint, to a bigger district.

Opportunities for specialists in an information-based business organization should be more plentiful than they are in an orchestra or hospital, let alone in the Indian civil service. But as in these organizations, they will primarily be opportunities for advancement within the specialty, and for limited advancement at that. Advancement into "management" will be the exception, for the simple reason that there will be far fewer middle-management positions to move into. This contrasts sharply with the traditional organization where, except in the research lab, the main line of advancement in rank is out of the specialty and into general management.

More than 30 years ago General Electric tackled this problem by creating "parallel opportunities" for "individual professional contributors." Many companies have followed this example. But professional specialists themselves have largely rejected it as a solution. To them—and to their management colleagues—the only meaningful opportunities are promotions into management. And the prevailing compensation structure in practically all businesses reinforces this attitude because it is heavily biased toward managerial positions and titles.

There are no easy answers to this problem. Some help may come from looking at large law and consulting firms, where even the most senior partners tend to be specialists, and associates who will not make partner are outplaced fairly early on. But whatever scheme is eventually developed will work only if the values and compensation structure of business are drastically changed.

The second challenge that management faces is giving its organization of specialists a common vision, a view of the whole.

In the Indian civil service, the district officer was expected to see the "whole" of his district. But to enable him to concentrate on it, the government services that arose one after the other in the nineteenth century (forestry, irrigation, the archaeological survey, public health and sanitation, roads) were organized outside the administrative structure, and had virtually no contact with the district officer. This meant that the district officer became increasingly isolated from the activities that often had the greatest impact on—and the greatest importance for—his district. In the end, only the provincial government or the central government in Delhi had a view of the "whole," and it was an increasingly abstract one at that.

A business simply cannot function this way. It needs a view of the whole and a focus on the whole to be shared among a great many of its professional specialists, certainly among the senior ones. And yet it will have to accept, indeed will have to foster, the pride and professionalism of its specialists—if only because, in the absence of opportunities to move into middle management, their motivation must come from that pride and professionalism.

One way to foster professionalism, of course, is through assignments to task forces. And the information-based business will use more and more smaller self-governing units, assigning them tasks tidy enough for "a good man to get his arms around," as the old phrase has it. But to what extent should information-based businesses rotate performing specialists out of their specialties and into new ones? And to what extent will top management have to accept as its top priority making and maintaining a common vision across professional specialties?

Heavy reliance on task-force teams assuages one problem. But it aggravates another: the management structure of the information-based organization. Who will the business's managers be? Will they be task-force leaders? Or will there be a two-headed monster—a specialist structure, comparable, perhaps, to the way attending physicians function in a hospital, and an administrative structure of task-force leaders?

The decisions we face on the role and function of the task-force leaders are risky and controversial. Is theirs a permanent assignment, analogous to the job of the supervisory nurse in the hospital? Or is it a function of the task that changes as the task does? Is it an assignment or a position? Does it carry any rank at all? And if it does, will the task-force leaders become in time what the product managers have been at Procter & Gamble: the basic units of management and the company's field officers? Might the task-force leaders eventually replace department heads and vice presidents?

Signs of every one of these developments exist, but there is neither a clear trend nor much understanding as to what each entails. Yet each would give rise to a different organizational structure from any we are familiar with.

Finally, the toughest problem will probably be to ensure the supply, preparation, and testing of top management people. This is, of course, an old and central dilemma as well as a major reason for the general acceptance of decentralization in large businesses in the last 40 years. But the existing business organization has a great many middle-management positions that are supposed to prepare and test a person. As a result, there are usually a good many people to choose from when filling a senior management slot. With the number of middle-management positions sharply cut, where will the information-based organization's top executives come from? What will be their preparation? How will they have been tested?

Decentralization into autonomous units will surely be even more critical than it is now. Perhaps we will even copy the German *Gruppe* in which the decentralized units are set up as separate companies with their own top managements. The Germans use this model precisely because of their tradition of promoting people in their specialties, especially in research and engineering; if they did not have available commands in near-independent subsidiaries to put people in, they would have little opportunity to train and test their most promising professionals. These subsidiaries are thus some-

what like the farm teams of a major-league baseball club.

We may also find that more and more top management jobs in big companies are filled by hiring people away from smaller companies. This is the way that major orchestras get their conductors—a young conductor earns his or her spurs in a small orchestra or opera house, only to be hired away by a larger one. And the heads of a good many large hospitals have had similar careers.

Can business follow the example of the orchestra and hospital where top management has become a separate career? Conductors and hospital administrators come out of courses in conducting or schools of hospital administration respectively. We see something of this sort in France, where large companies are often run by men who have spent their entire previous careers in government service. But in most countries this would be unacceptable to the organization (only France has the *mystique* of the *grandes écoles*). And even in France, businesses, especially large ones, are becoming too demanding to be run by people without firsthand experience and a proven success record.

Thus the entire top management process—preparation, testing, succession—will become even more problematic than it already is. There will be a growing need for experienced businesspeople to go back to school. And business schools will surely need to work out what successful professional specialists must know to prepare themselves for high-level positions as *business* executives and *business* leaders.

Since modern business enterprise first arose, after the Civil War in the United States and the Franco-Prussian War in Europe, there have been two major evolutions in the concept and structure of organizations. The first took place in the 10 years between 1895 and 1905. It distinguished management from ownership and established management as work and task in its own right. This happened first in Germany, when Georg Siemens, the founder and head of Germany's premier bank, *Deutsche Bank,* saved the electrical apparatus company his cousin Werner had founded after Werner's sons and heirs had mismanaged it into near collapse. By threatening to cut off the bank's loans, he forced his cousins to turn the company's management over to professionals. A little later, J. P. Morgan, Andrew Carnegie, and John D. Rockefeller, Sr., followed suit in their massive restructurings of U.S. railroads and industries.

The second evolutionary change took place 20 years later. The development of what we still see as the modern corporation began with Pierre S. du Pont's restructuring of his family company in the early 1920s and continued with Alfred P. Sloan's redesign of General Motors a few years later. This introduced the command-and-control organization of today, with its emphasis on decentralization, central service staffs, personnel management, the whole apparatus of budgets and controls, and the important distinction between policy and operations. This stage culminated in the massive reorganization of General Electric in the early 1950s, an action that perfected the model most big busi-

nesses around the world (including Japanese organizations) still follow.[2]

Now we are entering a third period of change: the shift from the command-and-control organization, the organization of departments and divisions, to the information-based organization, the organization of knowledge specialists. We can perceive, though perhaps only dimly, what this organization will look like. We can identify some of its main characteristics and requirements. We can point to central problems of values, structure, and behavior. But the job of actually building the information-based organization is still ahead of us—it is the managerial challenge of the future.

---

[2]Alfred D. Chandler, Jr., has masterfully chronicled the process in his two books *Strategy and Structure* (Cambridge: MIT Press, 1962) and *The Visible Hand* (Cambridge: Harvard University Press, 1977)—surely the best studies of the administrative history of any major institution. The process itself and its results were presented and analyzed in two of my books: *The Concept of the Corporation* (New York: John Day, 1946) and *The Practice of Management* (New York: Harper Brothers, 1954).

Chapter 3

Introduction to Control Systems

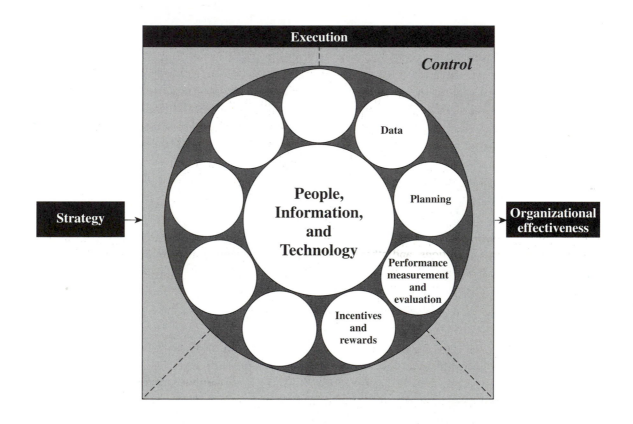

CHAPTER OVERVIEW

This chapter introduces the concepts and tools of management control systems. It starts with a discussion of management control. *Management control systems* are then defined as consisting of *measures* for defined entities, *criteria* for comparing them against standards or expectations, and *processes* for obtaining and evaluating measures. Next, the process of designing control systems is discussed, followed by an exploration of issues in the design and use of control systems.

MANAGEMENT CONTROL: DEFINITION AND CONCEPTS

The purpose of control is to create a set of conditions that improve the likelihood that desirable outcomes will be achieved, despite changing technologies, markets, competitive conditions, and other features of an organization's volatile environment.

Note that this definition of management control explicitly accounts for change and uncertainty, both of which characterize most industries today, in varying degrees. As noted in Chapter 1, managers face a situation of changing strategic objectives and changing business processes. For example, new biotechnologies are transforming how some drugs are produced (processes), and leading to the discoveries of entirely new drugs and treatments with significant market potential (objectives). Similarly, networked information technologies and flexible new database management tools are enabling firms to eliminate layers of management without sacrificing span of control (processes) and also leading to information-based product enhancements as well as entirely new industries, such as purveyors of online news filtering and retrieval services (objectives).

If production technologies and processes, labor and raw material supplies, customer needs, regulations, capital markets, and competitors' moves were stable, control could be defined more simply as the actions management takes to ensure that goals are attained. Instead, in today's ambiguous and uncertain world, management control is based on flexible processes and probabilistic objectives.

Three ways in which managers exert control include: selection and assignment of *people* to tasks, specifying and rewarding appropriate *actions,* and identifying whether appropriate *results* were obtained.[1]

- *People control:* Managers increase the likelihood of achieving desirable outcomes by selecting people with appropriate skills, values, and personality characteristics; training employees to strengthen skills or reinforce values; and assigning employees to positions that develop their breadth or depth of knowledge.
- *Action control:* Managers specify the decisions and behaviors that individuals and organizational subunits should take to achieve desirable outcomes. Job descriptions, policies, procedures, and codes of conduct are among the formal mechanisms of action control. Less formal means are also used to influence employees to act appropriately. These include socialization, persuasive rhetoric, and rewarding effective practices (distinct from rewarding results).
- *Results control:* Managers compare individual and organizational performance with planned or expected performance, and make appropriate adjustments. Some managers rely heavily on a philosophy of management by exception: where results are not in line with expectations, the individual or unit is closely examined to determine the causes. Managers also choose the relevant time period for monitoring performance. While quarterly reviews are widespread, managers in some firms rely on monthly, weekly, even daily performance reviews.[2] Determining an appropriate performance-measurement time interval is largely a function of determining (1) how long it takes for an identifiable trend to show up and (2) at what point can constructive action reasonably be taken.

As discussed in Chapter 2, managers also exert control through organizational structure, by grouping activities, specifying reporting relationships and decision rights, establishing coordination mechanisms, and delimiting organizational boundaries.

Managers choose whether to impose "tight" or "loose" controls. "Tight" control provides clear, narrow specifications of acceptable behaviors and results, and over relatively short time periods. "Loose" control offers considerable latitude within a framework of general guidelines; individuals are expected to use discretion in determining an appropriate course of action and in assessing whether they are achieving appropriate results. In practice, of course, managers choose a variety of control measures representing points along a "loose-tight" spectrum.

The extent to which controls are applied in a tight or loose fashion depends on the predispositions of individual managers, the pace of change within the firm and its industry, the need for innovation versus the need for consistency of effort, and other factors. McDonald's and Mrs. Fields', for example, emphasize consistency (in

[1]Kenneth A. Merchant, *Control in Business Organizations* (Cambridge: Ballinger, 1985).
[2]Robert S. Kaplan, "Texas Eastman Company," Harvard Business School case 9-190-039.

products and in the people working at the counter) over innovation. In contrast, 3M managers, who attribute much of their firm's growth to the successful translation of discoveries into new products, heavily emphasize innovation-oriented action controls geared toward "falling forward" (learning from ideas and innovations that do not succeed).

In general, tight control of actions and results is appropriate in a situation of relatively high stability and certainty. That is, if management is confident of the appropriate actions to be taken, and certain of the goals to which they are directed, then tight control may be appropriate. McDonald's, Mrs. Fields' Cookies, and Disney are three companies that have successfully exemplified this approach. However, the measures that ensure consistency of effort and results tend to stifle creativity and innovation. Hence, in a less stable, less certain situation, looser controls may be more appropriate. *Loose* does not mean that managers abdicate control; rather, the term implies two conditions. First, controls are more flexible; that is, a broader range of acceptable actions or outcomes are accommodated than in a tight control setting. Second, control is shared rather than dispensed by managers, on the assumption that empowered employees, given access to appropriate feedback, will identify both appropriate actions to take and new opportunities that may modify their expected results.

WHAT IS A MANAGEMENT CONTROL SYSTEM?

Management control systems are the primary tools of results control. They provide measures of what has happened (actual performance) and what is likely to happen (estimated performance), which are used by managers to evaluate whether present conditions are likely to lead to desirable outcomes. The term *system* is widely used in management parlance to describe very different processes. In this book, a management control system is defined as being comprised of the following elements:

- *Measures* of performance (financial, nonfinancial) for defined entities (individuals, subunits, products, projects, competitors, etc.).
- *Criteria* for comparing measures against expectations or standards (yardsticks or benchmarks).
- *Processes* for obtaining and evaluating measures.

Measures are quantitative estimates of the value of some variables, which are derived from available data. For example, "first-quarter sales" is a measure calculated by totaling the dollar value of all invoices of the first quarter. "Forecasted second quarter sales" is an estimate derived from applying a growth formula and other constraints to the first-quarter sales figure. While the first estimate, based on past data, is more precise than the second, based partly on future data, both are measures that can be used in a control system. A measure is always an approximation of the "true" value of a variable, and the "true" value itself is partially a matter of social construction.

Measures require data, which can be collected from paper or on-line documents (e.g., purchase orders, invoices), physical inspection (e.g., taking inventory), interviews,

FIGURE 3–1   Performance Measures for Management Control Systems

External

Timeliness of service	**Market share**
Product returns and complaints	**Customer satisfaction**
Number of sales calls/day	**Percent new product sales**
Product servicing calls	**Product returns**
Cost of capital	**Market capitalization**
	Order fulfillment times

Actions/means – – – – – – – – – – – – – – – – –|– – – – – – – – – – – – – – – – – **Ends/results**

New product introduction time	**Revenues/growth**
Number of patents filed	**Return on assets, investment**
Hours of employee training	**Return on equity**
Productivity	**Profitability**
Number of employee suggestions	**Sales growth**
Inventory turns	**Cash flow**

Internal

and other means. Computer-based control systems at many large firms were developed in the 1970s and 1980s as a byproduct of transaction processing and financial accounting systems developed earlier. This partly explains the predominance of financial measures in control systems. The greatly enhanced ability to collect and store information in electronic form today has enabled managers to gather a wider variety of data, including many nonfinancial measures, for use in control systems.

Measures in a control system are taken for defined entities, including individuals, products, projects, organizational units, customers, vendors, market segments, and competitors. Note that this list includes the performance of people and activities within the firm, as individuals and as members of organizational units. Control systems may also measure the performance of people, activities and organizations outside the firm (vendors, customers, competitors). It follows that the data required for performance measures will not all be generated internally; some information must be gathered from entities outside the organization, such as customers, trade groups, suppliers, etc. Figure 3–1 presents a taxonomy of control measures.[3]

Criteria

A measure in and of itself has little meaning until it is compared to a standard or expectation. The purpose of a measure is to inform the manager about the likelihood that present conditions will achieve desirable outcomes. Hence, the manager needs to know if the measure is an accurate indicator of whether things are on track.

One yardstick long used in management control systems is a comparison of current results with those taken in previous periods (e.g., this quarter's earnings versus last

---

[3]See also Robert S. Kaplan and David P. Norton, "The Balanced Scorecard—Measures That Drive Performance," *Harvard Business Review* (January–February 1992), 71–79.

quarter or same quarter last year). A similar yardstick is comparison of actual versus expected results. In this case, expected results may have been estimated according to a model that predicted the impact of a management program such as a product promotion strategy. Other criteria for evaluation are absolute standards and subjective judgment about what the measure should be (such as "zero defects").

Many companies are finding it useful to engage in competitive benchmarking.[4] This involves identifying competitors or companies in other industries that exemplify "best practice" for each of several relevant management processes. Comparison with these benchmarks helps managers identify new actions that they might take to improve performance, and may lead them to set a significantly higher threshold for expected results.

Distinguishing between measures and criteria for evaluating them helps to clarify the meaning of a control "system." A system requires both measures and assessment criteria. For example, a capital budgeting system needs measures such as projected return on investment, as well as criteria for evaluating them, such as a hurdle rate.

Processes for Obtaining and Evaluating Measures and Criteria

Measures are a result of actions taken by people to collect data and, by using calculations and other processes, turn it into meaningful information. Measurement *processes* define what data will be collected, who will collect it (and from whom), how often it will be collected, and how measures will be generated from it. For example, in a capital budgeting system the process for obtaining measures is defined by the responsibilities assigned to the people putting together a capital requisition, the information required in the request, when it is due, and how the value of the expenditure should be calculated.

As business conditions evolve, so should performance measures, the entities at which they are targeted, and the time periods over which they are collected. For example, when an investment is made in new manufacturing equipment it may be appropriate to collect data on production efficiency, quality, scrap, and so on, on a daily basis. Once the equipment is performing in a stable manner it might be appropriate to shift to collecting these measures over longer time periods or in a more aggregated fashion.

Because measures are always approximations involving human judgment, taking measures involves inherent imperfections. Furthermore, trade-offs are made in determining the cost versus the value of increased measurement precision. Hence, measurement processes lend themselves to manipulation, gaming, and even fraud. Processes are thus needed to protect against inappropriate manipulation of performance measures. Some measures are verified by third parties, such as auditors for financial measures. Verification processes for nonfinancial measures—such as quality, customer satisfaction, and innovation—are less well developed.

---

[4]See Robert G. Eccles, "The Performance Measurement Manifesto," *Harvard Business Review* (January–February 1991), 131–37.

Processes must also be developed for identifying, developing, and periodically reassessing appropriate benchmarks or yardsticks (evaluation criteria). These processes can include examination of the relationships between criteria and actual performance. For example, criteria that represent very ambitious goals may be perceived as unattainable, and thus serve to demotivate employees; correspondingly, criteria that represent easily attainable goals may not provide sufficient motivation.

The next section addresses in greater detail the activities and choices involved in designing the performance measures, criteria, and ongoing processes that make up management control systems.

HOW ARE CONTROL SYSTEMS DESIGNED?

Effective control systems help direct managers' attention to activities and results that make a difference in the organization's performance. Unfortunately, there is no one right way to design a control system, since each firm is unique in terms of its competitive opportunities and risks, resource constraints, and capabilities. Appropriate control systems "fit" the environment in which a firm operates, the people it employs, and its organizational structure.

Measures affect behavior. People tend to act in ways that affect measures, especially when rewards are linked to measures. Hence control systems can be powerful tools. In order to ensure that they are used appropriately—to create conditions that will improve the probability of achieving desirable outcomes—careful attention needs to be paid to the design of control systems.

Control systems are inextricably linked to organizational structure, since the measures in a control system are taken for defined entities, including organizational entities (individuals in specific roles, organizational units, etc.). Control systems give further definition to reporting relationships by specifying the measures and criteria by which units or individuals will be evaluated.

Structure and measurement combine to define *responsibility centers,* including revenue centers, cost centers, profit centers, and investment centers. These organizational units are defined below:

- *Revenue center:* Primary performance measure is revenues (example: sales function).
- *Cost center:* Primary performance measure is cost (example: manufacturing function).
- *Profit center:* Primary performance measure is profit—revenues minus costs (example: business unit).
- *Investment center:* Primary performance measure is return on investment (example: division).

Although these definitions are straightforward, they lead to difficult issues about financial performance measurement, which vary for each type of responsibility center. Illustrative examples are given below.

- In a *revenue center,* management must decide how to define a "sale" (when an order is received? when it is shipped? when the invoice is sent? when the customer pays?).

Internal transfer prices—which may or not be the same as the external selling price—must also be set.

- In a *cost center,* measurement decisions hinge on conventions concerning allocation of joint and byproduct costs, as well as allocation of corporate overhead.
- *Profit centers* give rise to both revenue and cost decisions. Some profit center managers are accountable only for "controllable" costs, while others must fully allocate corporate overhead and other costs that are uncontrollable or only partially controllable. Decisions regarding transfer pricing will also affect the extent to which a profit center actually shows a "profit."
- *Investment centers* entail all of the measurement issues identified for profit centers, as well as decisions concerning how the investment base is measured. The choice of assets to be included, depreciation methods for fixed assets, and corporate asset allocations all affect the return on investment measure.

Note that there is nothing intrinsic in the resources of a responsibility center that makes it a revenue, cost, profit, or investment center. Rather, this is determined by the choices managers make about how to value its revenues and/or costs and how to measure its financial performance. The particular definition assigned to a responsibility center will heavily influence the actions of its members. Thus, in a revenue center, employees' actions will be directed toward generating revenues, possibly with low attention to costs.

The process by which control systems are designed is a very important issue. The designers—be they internal staff or external accounting or consulting firms—may not be important users of the system. At issue here is the extent to which the designers involve those who will use it. Failure to do so can result in a control system that lacks credibility or is missing important features. On the other hand, a control system generally cannot be all things to all people. Too much user involvement can lead to excessive resources (people and time) devoted to developing an overly complicated and expensive system.

Some managers design their own control systems, assisted by powerful and increasingly usable information technologies. Here there are two risks: First, the manager may be unnecessarily "reinventing the wheel" if other managers are likewise designing their own, similar control systems. This incurs unnecessary costs. Second, this manager, in addressing his/her particular concerns, may overlook potentially dysfunctional consequences of his/her control system.

Although individual managers need some discretion in designing control systems for their areas of responsibility, a firmwide view is also needed. Senior management can ensure that the following steps are taken:

1. *Identify and define relevant information requirements.* Despite managers' apparent desire to improve customer service, quality, timeliness, and so forth, few companies have developed a clear definition of the data that can be used for developing measures of these activities and outcomes. Hence, identifying these data is crucial. Managers begin by asking the following questions:

Given our strategy, what are the most important measures of performance?

How do these measures relate to one another?

What measures predict long-term financial success in our business?

Establishing a common vocabulary of standard definitions for key information categories is also imperative. At a minimum, a corporate data dictionary defines those terms that have meaning across organizational units (such as *sales, costs, customer identification,* etc.). Those companies that have gone to the effort of establishing a common vocabulary for information feeding into control systems have been able to reorganize quickly without sacrificing control.

In order to achieve coherence in the information going into control systems, it is necessary to assign responsibility for developing both financial and nonfinancial performance measures. Identification of information sources will include the internal data items alluded to above, as well as various external data to be obtained from surveys, trade associations, consumer groups, and so on. Specification of information flows (such as who will have access to which information) is necessary. These tasks are sometimes delegated to the finance department, sometimes to the MIS department, or—to signal that this is an important new initiative—to a new organizational unit. A key challenge here is to ensure that nonfinancial information is placed on an equal footing with long-established financial systems.

2. *Select information technologies that support the information requirements.* Chapter 4 will outline the technical choices (hardware, software, data management, systems development methodologies, etc.) managers make in defining an information resources architecture. Appropriate choices will provide organizations with systems that are responsive, adaptable, cost-effective, and flexible.

3. *Design a process for continuous, ongoing review.* Since business conditions are not static, neither should control systems be static. Periodic reviews will help ensure that the control system is adequately supporting managers' needs to identify whether present conditions are likely to lead to desirable outcomes. Both top-down and bottom-up assessment are useful. Senior managers offer a strategic perspective based on knowledge of the interrelationships among functions and awareness of long-term goals. They view control systems from the top down in order to identify whether appropriate measures are being utilized, the extent of alignment with broad strategic goals, and inconsistent or unexpected responses. Middle managers and their subordinates offer a perspective based on day-to-day familiarity with their business practices. Their bottom-up reviews can help determine perceived equity of measures, disparities or conflicting messages in performance measures, and suggested new measures.

The next section discusses the key issues that need to be periodically addressed in order to ensure that a management control system adequately serves its purposes.

ISSUES IN MANAGEMENT CONTROL SYSTEMS

In ongoing reviews of management control systems, the following questions can be asked:

1. *Are we measuring the right things?* In order to know what variables should be measured, managers need to know both what variables indicate desirable outcomes and what variables contribute to these outcomes. Ideally, an explicit model of the business specifies empirically valid cause/effect relationships. This is not common practice, partly because it is difficult to do and partly because much business modeling has been restricted to financial variables.

Measures of financial results are more highly refined than are measures of nonfinancial results, such as "quality" and "customer satisfaction." Where items can be counted (number of units sold/returned/rejected), defining the underlying data and developing the measures are reasonably straightforward.

Perceptual measures are more difficult to develop, in part because the relationship between specific actions (such as coaching subordinates) and specific outcomes (such as customer service improvements) may not be well understood. Managers may be tempted to measure those actions that are unambiguous (average length of customer service call, number of calls per day, number of meetings held). However, if managers believe that other harder-to-measure actions (such as effective communication, motivation of subordinates, or selection of an advertising campaign) are equally or more important, they are better off measuring them imperfectly than not at all. Managers can borrow measurement concepts from behavioral sciences. A "valid" measure accurately captures the phenomenon it purports to measure. A measure is "reliable" if it consistently yields the same answer under comparable conditions. Statistical techniques help establish the validity and reliability of perceptual measures.

2. *Are measures being taken for the right defined entities?* In order to manage a product on a global basis, it is necessary to have global measures of product quality, profitability, and so forth. Yet many companies that claim to be global still place greater emphasis on geographically defined measures than global ones, and in some cases do not even have these measures on a global basis. Measuring the right variables for the right entity also means knowing what not to emphasize. For example, stressing divisional profitability over product profitability may encourage managers to make decisions that sacrifice product profits in order to maximize division profits.

3. *Are the right people receiving performance measurement information?* Detailed data on product quality that are very important to a first-line supervisor may not be particularly useful to a division general manager. Similarly, whereas the general manager may find it helpful to know the number of prospective new customers contacted in the past month, this information may be of little value to the first-line supervisor. Deciding what information each person should receive requires understanding whether this information will help them improve the probability of achieving desirable outcomes, given their roles and responsibilities.

4. *Are our performance measures compatible with our management philosophy and organization structure?* Earlier we discussed the conditions under which tight versus loose controls are appropriate. Control systems can be designed to reinforce either tight or loose controls, depending on choices of organization structure (roles and responsibilities, decision rights). In the case of a tight control system, the organizational structure greatly restricts the latitude managers have to make decisions. It basically lets the system make the decision for the manager. In the case of a loose control system, the structure permits managers broad latitude in how much weight to place on measures and the criteria for evaluating them.

To illustrate, consider resource allocation. In the most general sense, the fundamental purpose of control systems is to influence resource allocation, in that employees' time is a valuable resource that is constantly being allocated through actions taken and not taken. In the tight control case, the control system completely determines resource allocation. For example, if all projects achieving a specified hurdle rate are funded, while those falling below it are not, then the capital budgeting system is controlling the capital investment decisions (of course, sharp managers might get around this by ensuring that their return on investment figures "come out right"). Loose control systems, in contrast, guide but do not determine resource allocation. In this case, projects that do not pass the corporate hurdle rate but are nevertheless considered strategically important will be funded.

5. *To what extent are rewards aligned with control systems?* It is a truism to state that employees should be rewarded in proportion to their performance on the measures that truly matter. In practice, tying rewards to performance is fraught with difficulty. Linking rewards to results can have a positive impact in providing an explicit signal about desirable actions and results. It can also have negative consequences. People may manipulate measures, ignore important things that are not measured or that are measured but not rewarded, and take actions that they know are not in the best interests of the firm as a whole. Simple formulas tying a few key performance variables to performance may leave important measures out, with dysfunctional consequences. Complex formulas may be confusing, leading to unpredictable results. Furthermore, the relative importance of different activities will change along with changes in the business environment, yet incentive systems need to be reasonably stable or they will be perceived as unfair. Finally, how and to what extent should individual versus group performance be rewarded?

Although there is clearly a link between management control systems and performance appraisal, this link cannot be treated as a simple, one-way mechanical relationship. Regardless of the extent to which specific performance measures count in compensation decisions, it remains the responsibility of the manager to candidly explain promotion and compensation decisions to subordinates.

6. *Is the system being used in ways for which it was not intended?* Controls designed by someone or some unit for one purpose may be used by others for different purposes, and these purposes can evolve over time. For example, a performance measurement system designed by the financial staff for external reporting may eventually be used by senior management to make capital allocation decisions. There is nothing intrinsically right or wrong about this, but managers should be aware of the different uses that are being made of a system. For example, the defined entities in a performance measurement system may not exactly match the defined entities in a reward system that is designed from scratch.

Once designed, control systems rarely stay fixed in time. New structures, new managers, new strategies, and changing circumstances all create pressures to change control systems. Advances in information technology—such as networks, personal workstations, relational databases, and prototyping—mean that it is now easier and quicker to redesign control systems. Control systems can more easily adapt and evolve over time, creating more refined tools for managers coping with a changing world.

CASE 3–1: CONTROLS AT THE SANDS HOTEL AND CASINO

This case illustrates one approach to control in a high cash-transactions setting where theft is a constant threat. Although the casino industry is in some ways unique, the controls observed in the case may be applicable to other settings. As you read through this case, try to determine which of the controls used at Sands Hotel might be applicable elsewhere, and under what circumstances.

Preparation Questions

1. List the controls described in the case. What control problems is each designed to address?
2. Focus on three key roles in the casino: blackjack dealer, blackjack pit boss, and vice president of casino operations. How would you characterize the control strategy used over each of these roles?
3. Is Stephen Hyde justified in being proud of his company's control system? Why or why not? Are any of the controls at the Sands applicable to firms in other industries?

Case 3–1 Controls at the Sands Hotel and Casino*

In July 1983, Stephen F. Hyde, president of the Sands Hotel and Casino in Atlantic City, commented on his company's control system which, he was convinced, was a model of excellence:

> Our controls are probably as good or better than those in use in any other company. Most companies couldn't afford the controls we use, but we really have to have them. In the casino, which is our major attraction and our most lucrative business,

there is a lot of money changing hands, and that provides a lot of temptation for our employees and guests to try to take that money away from us. Our controls help us ensure that we get our fair share of what is wagered.

Many of *our* controls are legally required, as the state of New Jersey has an extensive list of regulations to make sure it gets its share. But we would have those controls whether they were required or not, because it makes good business sense to do so. In support of that contention, I can tell you that we used almost the same set of controls that we have here in our Las Vegas casino, even though the Nevada regulations are not nearly as stringent as those in New Jersey. Also, our

Jeffrey M. Traynor and Professor Kenneth A. Merchant prepared this case. Copyright © 1983 by the President and Fellows of Harvard College. Harvard Business School case 184-048 (Revised 1991)

controls exceed even the New Jersey requirements, in some cases, because we feel that despite the expense an outstanding system of controls is in the best interest of our shareholders.

Gambling in New Jersey

In 1976, New Jersey voters amended their state's constitution to allow casino gambling in Atlantic City. The hopes were that this once glamorous city would be rejuvenated and that taxes on gambling would provide a lucrative source of revenue for the state.

To regulate the new gaming industry, the New Jersey Casino Control Commission (NJCCC) was established. The NJCCC's first action was to develop a comprehensive set of regulations that established minimum guidelines to be followed in all phases of the gaming operations. Every organization that wanted to build gaming establishments in Atlantic City had to prepare a detailed application that included an in-depth discussion of the casino layouts, strategies, and controls that would be used, and these had to be approved by the NJCCC.

The gaming industry moved into Atlantic City very rapidly. The first casino (Resorts International) opened in 1978, and by 1982, nine large hotel/casinos were operating under such well-known gaming names as Harrah's, Caesar's World, Bally, Playboy, Tropicana, and the Sands. In 1982, 20 million people visited Atlantic City, making it the most-visited city in the United States, and combined gambling revenue for the nine casinos was approximately $1.5 billion.

After the casinos began operations, the NJCCC continued to exercise close scrutiny over them. Full-time NJCCC inspectors were required to be present on the floor of each casino and in the count rooms (where the winnings were counted) to ensure that the regulations were being followed and that the casinos were maintaining an orderly house. In addition, NJCCC personnel had to approve all major policy decisions made by casino management, even including how they promoted their businesses.

The Sands

The Sands Hotel and Casino was the operating unit of the Great Bay Casino Corporation (GBCC). In 1982, the Sands's (and GBCC's) gross revenue was $184 million, of which $144 million came from gaming (casino) operations and the rest from hotel operations, which included rooms, entertainment, and food and beverage. (Exhibit 1.)

The casino and hotel were run as separate profit centers. The unique feature of the organization (Exhibit 2), as compared to that in most corporations, was the relatively large size of the finance staff. Of a total of approximately 2,600 people in the organization, over 400 were in the finance organization, reporting in a direct line to the vice president–finance, Ed Sutor (Exhibit 3). Strict separation was maintained between operations and recordkeeping, and the finance organization was large because it had responsibility for cash control and recordkeeping, both important functions in the casino and food and beverage parts of the business, particularly. Thus, the finance organization included cashiers, casino change personnel, pit clerks, and count room personnel, in addition to people who were normally part of a finance organization, such as accounting clerks and financial analysts.

In the casino operations area, the Sands operated 1,077 coin-operated gaming devices (slot machines), 59 blackjack tables, 20 crap tables, 10 roulette wheels, 2 baccarat tables, and 2 big six wheels. The games operated on a two-shift basis—day and swing shifts—covering a total period from 10:00 AM to 4:00 AM weekdays and 10:00 AM to 6:00 AM weekends. A total of 930 people were employed in casino operations (Exhibit 4).

Controls in the Casino

The controls used in the casino were intended to ensure that the Sands and the state of New Jersey each kept their fair share of the money that was wagered. In a short case, it is not possible to

EXHIBIT 1   Income Statement and Balance Sheet for Greate Bay Casino Corporation

Income Statement

	Year Ended December 31,		
	1982	*1981*	*1980*
Revenues			
Gaming	$144,236,000	$ 91,614,000	$ 27,278,000
Rooms	11,775,000	8,700,000	2,833,000
Food and beverage	20,875,000	15,686,000	5,450,000
Other	7,449,000	4,563,000	793,000
Gross revenues	**$184,335,000**	**$120,563,000**	**$ 36,354,000**
Less: promotional allowances	20,899,000	13,031,000	2,802,000
Net revenues	**$163,436,000**	**$107,532,000**	**$ 33,552,000**
Costs and expenses			
Operating	$113,178,000	$ 79,712,000	$ 34,864,000
General and administrative	17,607,000	16,131,000	9,567,000
Depreciation	6,005,000	4,773,000	1,816,000
Interest	11,402,000	12,822,000	2,754,000
	$148,192,000	$113,438,000	$ 49,001,000
Income (loss) before income taxes and extraordinary item	$ 15,244,000	$ (5,906,000)	$(15,449,000)
Provision for income taxes	7,783,000	—	—
Income (loss) before extraordinary item	**$ 7,461,000**	**$ (5,906,000)**	**$(15,449,000)**
Extraordinary item-utilization of tax loss carryforward	6,561,000	—	—
Net income (loss)	**$ 14,022,000**	**$ (5,906,000)**	**$(15,449,000)**
Net income (loss) per share of common stock			
Income (loss) before extraordinary item	$1.42	$(1.12)	$(2.93)
Extraordinary item	1.24	—	—
	$2.66	**$(1.12)**	**$(2.93)**
Average common shares outstanding	**5,279,000**	**5,279,000**	**5,279,000**

Balance Sheet

Assets

Current assets		
Cash and temporary investments	$ 8,243,000	$ 8,198,000
Receivables		
Gaming	$ 15,044,000	$ 8,108,000
Other	990,000	1,227,000
Less: allowance for doubtful accounts	(5,633,000)	(1,965,000)
	$ 10,401,000	$ 7,370,000
Inventories	$ 957,000	$ 656,000
Other current assets:		
Prepaid advertising and promotion expenses	$ 1,678,000	$ 806,000
Other prepaid expenses	2,258,000	1,463,000
	$ 3,936,000	$ 2,269,000
Total current assets	**$ 23,537,000**	**$ 18,493,000**

(*continued*)

EXHIBIT 1 *(concluded)*   Balance Sheet

	December 31,	
	1982	*1981*
Property and equipment		
Land	$ 5,022,000	$ 5,022,000
Buildings	60,311,000	54,036,000
Furniture, fixtures, and equipment	24,957,000	17,678,000
Less: accumulated depreciation	(12,594,000)	(6,589,000)
	$ 77,696,000	**$ 70,147,000**
Other assets	**$ 1,131,000**	**$ 349,000**
Total assets	**$102,364,000**	**$ 88,989,000**
Liabilities and Shareholders' Equity		
Current liabilities		
Current portion of long-term debt	$ 11,088,000	$ 6,245,000
Accounts payable and accrued expenses:		
Trade accounts payable	$ 12,243,000	$ 6,380,000
Salaries and wages	2,303,000	1,955,000
Taxes and licenses	2,026,000	3,892,000
Progressive jackpot accrual	2,017,000	538,000
Interest	332,000	1,889,000
Other	1,200,000	700,000
	$ 20,121,000	**$ 15,354,000**
Other current liabilities	**$ 3,010,000**	**$ 1,241,000**
Total current liabilities	**$ 34,219,000**	**$ 22,840,000**
Long-term debt	**$ 48,108,000**	**$ 60,530,000**
Other long-term liabilities	**$ 310,000**	—
Total liabilities	**$ 82,637,000**	**$ 83,370,000**
Commitments and Contingencies		
Shareholders' equity		
Class A common stock, $.25 par value; authorized 10,000,000 shares; issued and outstanding 5,287,642 shares in 1982 and 1,479,017 in 1981	1,322,000	370,000
Class B common stock, $.25 par value; authorized 5,000,000 shares; issued and outstanding -0- in 1982 and 3,800,000 in 1981	—	950,000
Capital in excess of par value	26,913,000	26,829,000
Retained earnings (deficit)	(8,508,000)	(22,530,000)
Total shareholders' equity	**$ 19,727,000**	**$ 5,619,000**
Total liabilities and shareholders' equity	**$102,364,000**	**$ 88,989,000**

EXHIBIT 2 Organization

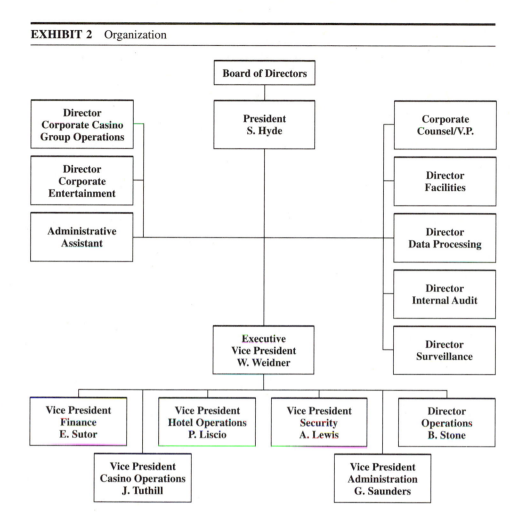

describe all of the many controls that were employed in the casino, but the function of many of them can be described in terms of how they enabled casino management to control: (1) cash and the movement of cash within the casino, and (2) the operation of the casino table games.

To simplify the discussion, all references will be to the table game of blackjack.[1] The following section provides a brief description of blackjack and the personnel involved in running it.

Operation of Blackjack Game at Sands Casino
Blackjack is a very popular card game where up to seven patrons play against the house. The players' object is to draw cards whose total is higher than the dealer's total without exceeding 21.

---

[1]This is done with little loss of generality. Control over all the table games in the Sands was nearly identical. The one major exception was that one extra level of supervision (box-person) was used at crap tables. In the coin-operated gaming devices area, control was simpler because machines eliminated the human element (dealers). Machines did, however, have to be inspected regularly for evidence of tampering.

EXHIBIT 3   Finance Organization

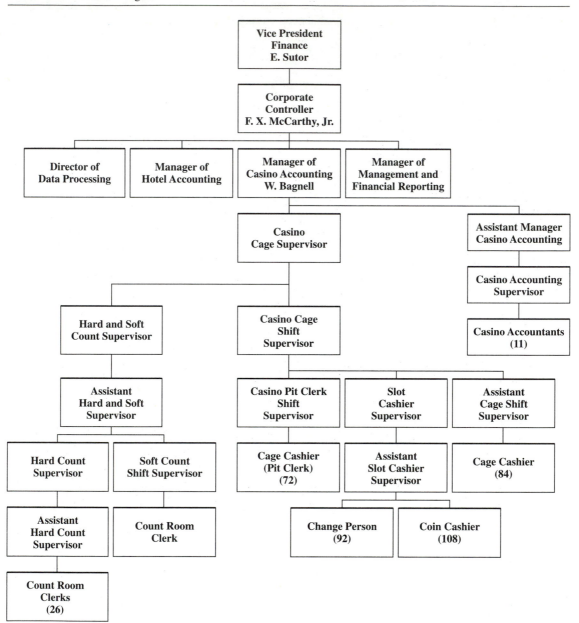

EXHIBIT 4   Casino Operations Organization

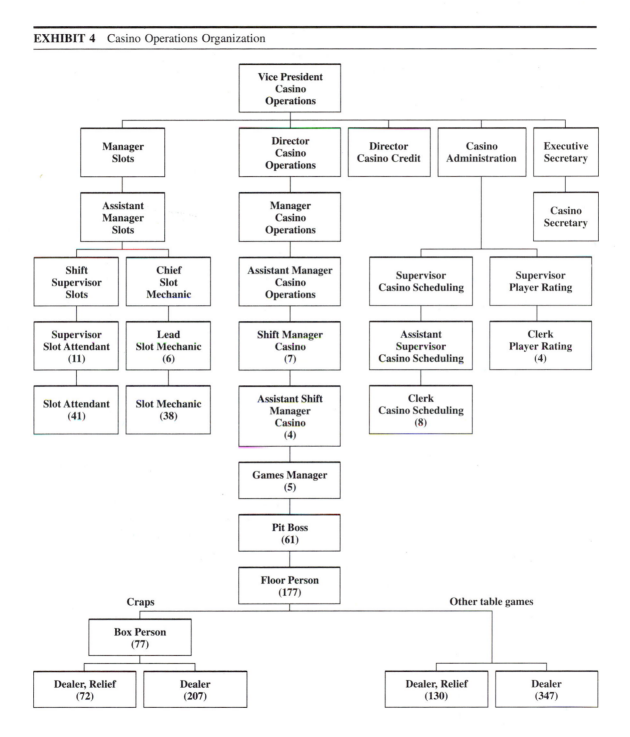

In 1983, the Sands Hotel operated 89 gaming tables, 59 (66 percent) of which were for blackjack. In May 1983, the blackjack drop[2] was $23 million and the win[3] total was $3.2 million. These totals were the highest for any table game or type of coin-operated gambling device in the casino except for the $.25 slot machines.

Each blackjack table was run by a dealer whose job was to sell chips to customers, deal the cards, take losing wagers, and pay winning wagers. Dealing was a skilled profession that required some training and considerable practice. Experience was valuable, as the dealer's value to the casino increased with the number of games that could be dealt within a given time period, and speed usually increased with experience. Experience was also valuable in identifying players who might be cheating.

Dealers received a 20-minute break every hour. Dealers assigned to a table worked for 40 minutes and then were replaced by a "relief dealer" during their break. Relief dealers worked at two different tables for 20 minutes each and then received their break. The frequent breaks were required because the job was mentally and physically taxing—dealers were required to be standing up while they dealt; they had to maintain intense concentration, as errors in paying off bets were not tolerated; and they had to maintain good humor under sometimes difficult conditions (e.g., dealing to players who became irritable because they were losing).

Dealers were paid well. New dealers earned approximately $23,000–$25,000, including tips (which were shared among all dealers).

Two levels of direct supervision were used over the blackjack tables. A "floorperson" was assigned to monitor two blackjack tables. A "pit boss" supervised eight tables.

_____
[2]Drop refers to the total amount of cash and credit exchanged at gaming tables for chips. In slot machine areas, drop refers to the total amount of money removed from the drop bucket.
[3]The term *win* refers to the difference between gaming gains and losses before deducting costs and expenses.

Control of Cash

Because most of the casino business was conducted in terms of cash or cash equivalents (i.e., chips), it was important to have good control over the many stocks of cash and chips that were located within the casino and to be able to move these stocks without loss. The Sands's cash control system can be described in terms of three main elements: (1) individual accountability for cash and (cash equivalent) stocks, (2) formal procedures for transfers, and (3) tight control in the count rooms.

Individual Accountability for Cash Stocks

All cash stocks—with the exception of those kept at a game table or those taken from a game or slot machine for counting—were maintained on an imprest basis. This meant that most personnel who dealt directly with cash, such as change personnel, coin redemption personnel, cashiers, and chip fill bank personnel, were held individually accountable for a specific sum of money that was charged out to them. These personnel were required to turn in the exact amount of money for which they were given responsibility, and any large shortages or persistent patterns of shortages were grounds for dismissal.

Formal Procedures for Transfers

For transfers of cash or chips to or from nonimprest funds (e.g., a game table), very strict procedures had to be followed. All required the creation of formal transactions signifying the transfer of accountability for the money involved. These procedures can be illustrated by describing what was required to move cash or chips to and from a blackjack table.

When a blackjack table was opened for playing, the dealer and floorperson had to count the inventory of chips and complete and sign an *opener* slip that simply provided a listing of the inventory (Exhibit 5). One copy of the opener slip was deposited in the incoming dealer's *drop box,*[4] and

_____
[4]This was a locked container affixed to the gaming table into which the drop was placed.

EXHIBIT 5   Opener (Blackjack Table 40, Swing Shift, 6/23/83)

Sands

HOTEL & CASINO   ATLANTIC CITY

271

DATE _____ 6-23-83

OPENER	GAME BJ	TABLE 40

SHIFT		DAY/SWING	X	SWING/DAY	

CHIP DENOMINATION	AMOUNT	
500	$ —	
100	4 000	.—
25	3 025	.—
20	— —	.
5	1 020	..—
2.50	90	.—
1	66	.—
.50	34	50
.25	— —	
TOTAL	$ 8 235	50

DEALER/ BOXPERSON	*[signature]* 5 3435-11
OUTGOING CASINO SUPERVISOR	*[signature]* 1634-11
DEALER/ BOXPERSON	*[signature]* 9=4 — 11
INCOMING CASINO SUPERVISOR	*[signature]* 1634-11

CCA-7 4-81

EXHIBIT 6   Counter Check

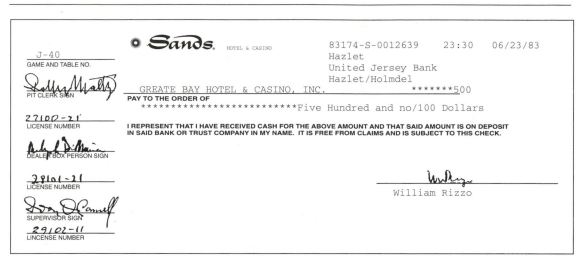

a second copy was delivered to the finance department for input into the computer system.

As the game was played, several different kinds of transactions would take place. One involved players buying chips from the dealer for cash or credit. Cash was deposited immediately in the drop box. Credit had to be approved by checking the customer's credit authorization limit through the use of a computer terminal located in the pit. If the credit was approved, a *counter check*[5] was prepared, signed by the customer, dealer, and pit boss, and then deposited in the drop box. (Exhibit 6)

Players could not make reverse exchanges (chips for cash) at the tables. They had to take their chips to the casino cage[6] where this type of exchange was made.

When the floorperson noticed that additional chips were needed at the table, he or she prepared a "request for fill." This request for a particular mix of chips was input into the computer terminal in the pit and relayed to the fill bank cashier in the

casino cage. The fill bank cashier would fill the order, have the computer print out a *fill slip* (Exhibit 7), sign the fill slip, and have a security guard transport the chips and fill slip to the dealer. Bill Bagnell (manager of casino accounting) explained a unique form of control that came into play at this point:

> The computer keeps track of the time it takes to consummate fill transactions. The security guard may be walking around the casino with $10,000 or more in chips and it should take only a few minutes to get to the table and get the transaction completed. If the whole process takes more than x minutes,[7] a message flashes on the computer screen in the security center, and they start looking for the guard. This is just an extra control we use to make sure the chips get to the table.

When the guard arrived at the table, the dealer and floorperson both counted the chips and signed the fill slip indicating receipt, and the clerk at the computer terminal in the pit entered a code indicating that the fill transaction had been completed.

---

[5]These were also known as *markers.*
[6]This was a secure work area within the casino where the casino bankroll was kept.

---

[7]Actual time programmed into the computer was secret.

EXHIBIT 7 Fill Slips (Blackjack Table 40, Swing Shift, 6/23/83)

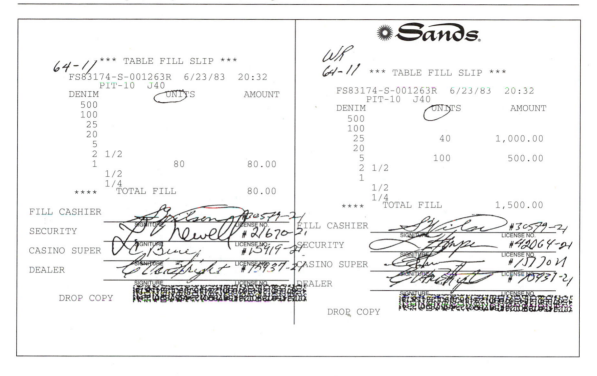

The security guard made sure a copy of the fill slip was placed in the drop box and then returned the original fill slip to the fill bank cashier.[8]

When the dealer's shift was over, the dealer and the floorperson counted the table inventory, and prepared and signed a *closer* slip (Exhibit 8), which was deposited in the outgoing dealer's drop box. In the case of a shift change, a copy of this slip would also serve as an opener for the incoming dealer. The drop box of the outgoing dealer was sealed and security personnel carried it directly to the room where the money was counted.

Exhibit 9 shows a page of a summary report of the transactions that occurred at each table. The transactions illustrated in Exhibits 5–8 occurred on blackjack table #40 on the swing shift of June 23, 1983, and a list of these transactions is shown in the middle of this page of the report.

Tight Security in Count Rooms

Wins (or losses) on a particular game table (or slot machine) could not be determined until the money in the drop box was counted. All counting of money from table games was done in the soft count room,[9] a highly secure room located adjacent to the casino cage. NJCCC regulations required that count rooms be equipped with a metal door, alarm, closed-circuit television cameras, and audio and video taping capabilities. In the middle of the room was a "count table" constructed of clear glass or similar material.

---

[8] A similar procedure was followed when the dealer wished to send an overabundance of chips to the chip bank for credit.

[9] This money was mostly bills and counter checks; hence the name *soft count* room. Coins taken from the slot machines were counted in the hard count room.

EXHIBIT 8   Closer (Blackjack Table 40, Swing Shift, 6/23/83)

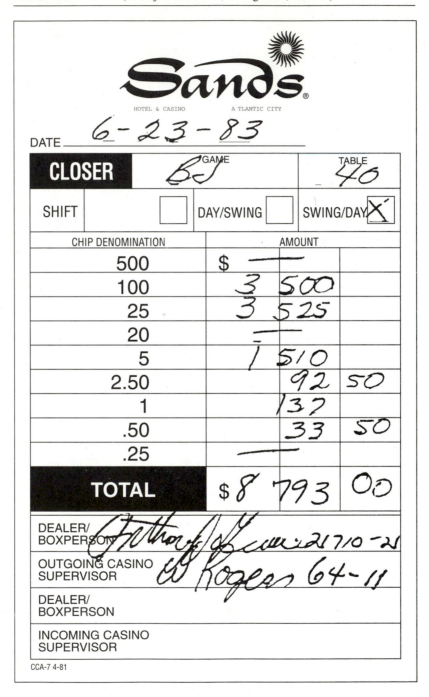

CHIP DENOMINATION	AMOUNT	
500	$ —	
100	3 500	
25	3 525	
20	—	
5	1 510	
2.50	92	50
1	137	
.50	33	50
.25	—	
TOTAL	$ 8 793	00

DATE 6-23-83

CLOSER   GAME *BJ*   TABLE 40

SHIFT   DAY/SWING   SWING/DAY [X]

DEALER/BOXPERSON   *Anthony ... 21710-21*

OUTGOING CASINO SUPERVISOR   *W Rogers 64-11*

DEALER/BOXPERSON

INCOMING CASINO SUPERVISOR

CCA-7 4-81

EXHIBIT 9 Table Games Daily Transaction Report

| Run Date 6/24/83 | Time 8-41-33 | | Table Games Daily Transaction Report | | | | | | | |
| | | | Initiated | | Acknowledge | | Consummated | | Cr. Acct. | |
Serial Number	Transaction	Amount	By	Time	By	Time	By	Time	No.	Remarks
83173-S-0012299	Closer-previous day	7,846.00	22364	02-49						
83174-D-0012300	Opener	7,846.00	45290	12-05						
83174-D-0012301	Fill	2,130.00	45290	12-19	45290	12-54	23960	12-54		
83174-D-0012302	Closer	8,565.00	18354	18-20						
83174-S-0012303	Opener	8,565.00	18354	18-21						
83174-S-0012304	Counter check	500.00	12896	19-03					25758	Yuhl, John
83174-S-0012305	Fill	1,300.00	12896	20-43	12896	20-59	33998	21-23		
83714-S-0012306	Closer	7,328.50	22364	04-01						

Table 39 Table Open for Shifts—Day, Swing, Document Range—12426 to 12625

Game—Blackjack

Serial Number	Transaction	Amount	By	Time	By	Time	By	Time	No.	Remarks
83173-S-0012533	Closer-previous day	6,698.00	22364	02-38						
83174-D-0012534	Opener	6,698.00	45290	12-04						
83174-D-0012535	Fill	4,110.00	45290	12-15	45290	12-35	23960	12-41	4179	Rosenberg, Max
83174-D-0012536	Counter check	500.00	45290	14-23	14757	14-29				
83174-D-0012537	Fill	500.00	18354	16-25	18354	16-47	30579	16-51		
83174-D-0012538	Closer	9,864.00	18354	18-23						
83174-S-0012539	Opener	9,864.00	18354	18-23						
83174-S-0012540	Fill	60.00	12896	20-31	12896	20-48	33998	21-23		
83174-S-0012541	Closer	7,583.50	22364	03-42						

Table 40 Table Open for Shifts—Day, Swing, Document Range—12626 to 12825

Game—Blackjack

Serial Number	Transaction	Amount	By	Time	By	Time	By	Time	No.	Remarks
83173-S-0012632	Closer-previous day	12,656.00	22364	03-23						
83174-D-0012633	Opener	12,656.00	45290	12-09						
83174-D-0012634	Credit	4,500.00	45290	12-13	45290	12-53	23960	12-57		
83174-D-0012635	Fill	600.00	45290	12-14	45290	12-52	23960	12-53		
83174-D-0012636	Closer	8,235.50	18354	18-25						

(continued)

EXHIBIT 9 *(concluded)*   Table Games Daily Transaction Report

Run Date 6/24/83   *Time 8–41–33*   *Table Games Daily Transaction Report*

Serial Number	Transaction	Amount	Initiated		Acknowledge		Consummated		Cr. Acct.	Remarks
			By	Time	By	Time	By	Time	No.	
83174-S-0012637	Opener	8,235.50	18354	18–25						
83174-S-0012638	Fill	80.00	12896	20–32	12896	20–58	33998	21–23		
83174-S-0012639	Counter check	500.00	12896	23–30	29554	23–38			5406	Rizzo, William
83174-S-0012640	Fill	1,500.00	12896	23–57	27823	00–02	33998	00–03		
83174-S-0012641	Closer	8,793.00	22364	03–26						

Game—Blackjack   Table 41 Table Open for Shifts—Day, Swing, Document Range—12826 to 13025

Serial Number	Transaction	Amount	Initiated		Acknowledge		Consummated		Cr. Acct.	Remarks
			By	Time	By	Time	By	Time	No.	
83173-S-0012883	Closer-previous day	30,680.50	22364	03–41						
83174-D-0012884	Opener	30,680.50	45290	12–07						
83174-D-0012885	Credit	20,000.00	45290	12–17	45290	12–37	23960	12–41		
83174-D-0012886	Fill	600.00	45290	12–17	45290	12–36	23960	12–41		
83174-D-0012887	Fill	1,600.00	18354	14–09	18354	14–23	23112	14–25		
83174-D-0012888	Closer	10,073.50	18534	18–33						
83174-S-0012889	Opener	10,073.50	18354	18–33						
83174-S-0012890	Counter check	500.00	12896	20–01	15555	20–07			17217	Weiss, Melvin
83174-S-0012891	Counter check	500.00	27823	21–53	15555	21–59			26864	Famighette, George
83174-S-0012892	Closer	6,636.50	22364	03–39						

Game—Blackjack   Table 45 Table Open for Shifts—Day, Swing, Document Range—13626 to 13825

Serial Number	Transaction	Amount	Initiated		Acknowledge		Consummated		Cr. Acct.	Remarks
			By	Time	By	Time	By	Time	No.	
83173-S-0013735	Closer-previous day	8,066.50	30739	03–46						
83174-D-0013736	Opener	8,066.50	20806	11–03						
83174-D-0013737	Fill	1,610.00	20806	11–13	20806	11–25	23112	11–28		
83174-D-0013738	Fill	2,600.00	14750	14–36	14750	14–43	23112	14–44		

Tight security and supervision was necessary in the count rooms to ensure that the revenues were tallied accurately and that all the money to which the casino was entitled was added to stores in the casino cage. During the actual counting processes, very strict procedures were followed. (Excerpts from the procedures required in the Sands's count-rooms are described in Exhibit 10.) In order to prevent the pocketing of currency, counting personnel were required to wear jumpsuits without pockets while they were in the count room, and personal belongings had to be carried only in clear plastic bags. The counting process took place under the supervision of an NJCCC inspector, and it was filmed by the television cameras located in the room. After the money was counted, it was transferred to the casino cage.

Only after the cash and counter checks in the drop box had been counted was it possible to calculate the winnings for each table. The win for Table 40, swing shift on June 23, 1983, was calculated as shown in Figure A.

The results for all games for each shift were reported on the master game report (MGR), which was produced daily and summarized by type of game. The uses of the MGR as a control report are described in a later section of this case.

FIGURE A   Calculation of Win on Blackjack Table 40, Swing Shift, 6/23/83

Cash in drop box		$1,640.00
Counter checks issued		500.00
Total drop		**2,140.00**
Less: Beginning table		
inventory	$8,235.50	
Fills	1,580.00	
	9,815.50	
Ending table	(8,793.00)	
inventory		
		1,022.50
Win		$1,117.50

Control of Games

The table games and the slot machines provided the only ways by which the casino made money. The table games were particularly difficult to control because of the need to rely on people (dealers) who might be tempted by the extremely large amounts of money that could exchange hands very quickly.

In response to this difficult control problem, multiple forms of control were required by the NJCCC and used in the Sands to help ensure that the casino kept the cash to which it was entitled. These included: (1) licensing of casino personnel, (2) standardization of actions of personnel running the games, (3) careful supervision and surveillance of the action taking place at the table, and (4) monitoring of results. These are discussed in the following sections.

Licensing

All employees working in the casino had to be licensed by the NJCCC, even personnel such as cooks, clerks, and barmaids who were not directly involved in gaming. The intent of licensing was to eliminate from the casino people who had been involved in crimes or violations of casino rules, or those who might be attracted because of a need for some quick cash.

In order to get a dealer's license, prospective dealers had to complete an accredited six-month course in gaming and to demonstrate their knowledge of New Jersey gaming procedures. Separate licenses were granted for each type of game (e.g., blackjack, craps). In addition, dealers had to complete a 23-page license application that requested a detailed personal and family history, the details of which were checked by NJCCC investigators.

Those personnel in supervisory and policymaking, including pit bosses, accounting supervisors, and corporate officers, had to pass an even more comprehensive background check. The application for this highest-level license was 86 pages long and required a very extensive list of information, including five years of personal financial statements and tax returns.

EXHIBIT 10   Excerpts from the Sands's Soft Count Procedures

Immediately prior to commencement of the count, one count team member will notify the person assigned to the closed circuit television monitoring station that the count is about to begin, after which such person will make an audio-video recording, with the time and date inserted thereon, of the entire counting process which will be retained by the surveillance department for at least five (5) days from the date of recordation unless otherwise directed by the commission or the division. The entire count will be performed in full view of the television monitor.

Concurrently, on both sides of a clear plastic count table (both sides of the table used only during peak periods), a count team member will open the drop box, empty its contents onto the table and verbalize *in a tone of voice to be heard by all persons* the game, table number and shift, all in full view of the closed circuit television camera. After the drop box is empty, the count team member will show *the inside of the drop box* to the closed circuit camera, another member of the count team and the commission inspector and then the drop box will be locked in the storage area for empty drop boxes. Currency sorters on both sides of the count table will separate the denominations of currency, coin, and the forms, records, and documents by type. The paperwork will be passed to the count room bookkeeper who will match the opener, closer, fills, and credits to the drop verification report.* Upon completing the currency sort for each drop box, the sorters will attach to the currency a game/table identification card.

The currency and game/table identification card are passed to a first verifier who enters the game and table number into a currency count machine. The currency is passed through the count machine by denomination with a tape produced indicating all detail and the total of drop box currency. The currency is passed to a second verifier *in full view of the closed circuit television camera* while the supporting tape is retained for comparison to the second count.

The currency verification process described above is repeated by the second verifier with the resultant tape compared to the one retained by the first verifier. Any count discrepancies are resolved at this point to the satisfaction of both verifiers, the soft count supervisor or assistant and the commission inspector.

After the second currency verification, count team members located at this area of the count table bundle and consolidate currency as counted. The currency and both count tapes are forwarded to a count team member located at the end of the count table. The currency is verified in total to both count tapes and placed in a holding area near the count table.

Standardization of Actions at the Tables

At the gaming tables, most of the dealers' physical motions were standardized in order to make supervision and surveillance easier. For example:

1. All cash and chip exchanges were to be made in the middle of the gaming table to make them easier to see by supervisory personnel.
2. Tips were to be accepted by tapping the cash or chips on the table and placing them in a clear, locked "toke" box attached to the gaming tables. This was done to distinguish these exchanges from normal wagers.
3. Before dealers left their tables, they were required to place their hands in the middle of the table and to show both the palm and back of

their hands. This was done to prevent them from "palming" money or chips in order to take it from the table as they left. Dealers were also required to wear large, pocketless aprons over their clothes to make it more difficult for them to pocket cash or chips.

Initial knowledge of the required actions was tested as part of the licensing procedure, and the Sands provided regular training sessions to make sure the dealers did not forget them.

Supervision and Surveillance

Front-line gaming personnel (e.g., dealers) were subjected to multiple forms of supervision and surveillance. Direct supervision was provided by

The count tapes are passed on to the count room bookkeeper or assistant who enters the total currency *paid coin* drop by gaming table. The count room bookkeeper or assistant generates printing of the master game report, which indicates win by table game and shift. The master game report is used by the count room bookkeeper to agree the total of openers, closers, fills, and credits to that reported on the drop verification report. *Upon completion of the count for each drop box shift, a main bank cashier will be called into the countroom to verify the cash count. The main bank cashier bulk counts the cash by bundle; all loose straps and clips are individually verified. The main bank cashier then compares the total to the totals listed on the master game report and resolves any differences. The main bank cashier then signs the master game report attesting to the amount of cash received.*

The master game report will be signed by the commission inspector evidencing his or her presence during the count and the fact that both the cashier and count team have agreed on the total amount of currency and coin counted, the soft count supervisor, all count team members, and the cage representative summoned to the count room to assist in the transfer of currency to the main bank for inclusion in the overall cage accountability after it has been recounted, either manually or mechanically.

The master game report, along with all supporting documents removed from the drop boxes, are forwarded to the accounting department for review and posting to the gaming income journal.

The counting and recording of drop box contents will continue over two normal work shifts. Each shift will complete the count of one shift of drop boxes before the other count team shift begins.

The master game report fills, credits, and table inventory slips (opener and closer slips) will on a daily basis be:

- Taped and the totals agreed with the totals indicated on the master gaming report.
- Reviewed on a judgmental basis for the appropriate number and propriety of signatures.
- Tested for proper summarization and recording.
- Subsequently recorded, maintained and controlled by the accounting department as a permanent accounting record.

*A list of transactions affecting drop box contents, similar in format to the transaction report shown in Exhibit 9 of this case.

---

the floorpeople and pit bosses. These people were highly experienced gaming people who were highly paid for their expertise.[10] One of their primary functions was to watch the gaming activity and spot events that were out of the ordinary. They had a keen sense of the activity going on around them and thus were generally good at spotting nonroutine events, such as dealers paying losing bets in blackjack or customers counting cards in blackjack or switching dice in craps.

Extra surveillance of table games was provided through the "eye in the sky" and a system of closed-circuit cameras. The term *eye in the sky* referred to surveillance provided by security personnel who viewed the gaming tables from catwalks located above the gaming floor. They could view the activity of any gaming table from directly overhead without dealer or patron knowledge.[11]

The closed-circuit camera system included over 100 cameras located throughout the casino. They were situated to provide a view of every table on the floor and had lenses powerful enough to zoom in to view objects as small as the date on a dime on the table. The pictures were viewed in a

---

[10]For example, pit bosses were paid an average of $55,000 per year plus overtime.

[11]In some casinos, surveillance was through one-way mirrors.

security room located on the mezzanine level of the casino. The system provided the capability to record the activities shown on videotape for later viewing, or, if necessary, as evidence (e.g., if malfeasance was suspected).

To ensure that the surveillance was done objectively, strict separation was maintained between the personnel working on the casino floor and those working in the surveillance areas.

The levels of casino management above the pit bosses—shift supervisors, casino manager, vice president of casino operations—did very little direct supervision of the gaming activity. They were mainly involved in keeping good customers happy, resolving special problems that arose, and improving the casino operation.

Monitoring of Results

The MGR provided three key indicators of the results of the gaming activity: drop, win, and hold percentage.

1. *Drop* was interpreted as the total amount of money the customers were willing to bet against the casino. The drop number had some limitations as an activity indicator, however, as it was biased upward when table game players exchanged money for chips at the table but did not bet, thereby creating what was called "false drop," and it was biased downward when players gambled with chips bought at another table, perhaps on another shift or day. A better indicator of activity would have been the "handle," the total value of wagers made, but there was no way to determine this number for the table games.
2. *Win* was the casino's gross profit number. It was calculated as shown in Figure A.
3. *Hold percentage* (also called the *hold ratio*) was the primary measure of casino profitability. It was defined as the win divided by the drop.

A comprehensive set of reports was produced that provided these performance measures in various levels of detail, by table and shift and by time period. Exhibit 11 shows a detailed report of the performance of individual blackjack tables on each shift. Exhibit 12 shows a summary by type of game. Special analyses were also prepared using similar formats to see, for example, how much play the casino got from particular customers or junkets.[12]

Sands's management watched the drop and hold numbers carefully. The drop number was the best available measure of the volume of betting activity, and, as such, it was useful as an indicator of the success of the company's marketing strategies and credit policies. It was used, for example, to determine what entertainers attracted the best betting crowd to the casino.

Hold percentage was the best available measure of casino profitability. Ed Sutor (vice president–finance) explained how Sands managers used hold percentage reports for control purposes:

> We look for patterns. We know that each table game should maintain a certain hold ratio; for example, the blackjack hold percentage should average 14–16 percent. The managers in casino operations, particularly, look at the hold generated on each shift in each pit and at each table. The dealers are not always assigned to the same tables, so we have no information to tie them to except that they always work in the same pit. But the floorpeople are always assigned to the same two tables, and the pit boss remains in the same pit. So we can go back to those people and ask them to explain why the hold was down. It may just have been a high-roller who was on a hot streak, but if we suspect something is not right, the casino operations people can call for some extra surveillance.
>
> I also watch the hold percentages. If the hold percentage is low across the casino, on all shifts and all tables, and that pattern persisted for a period of several weeks, I'd take a hard look at our control system to see if there was a leak somewhere.

---

[12]A junket was an arrangement made to induce a group to travel to a casino to gamble. Frequently, the transportation, food, and/or lodging were paid directly or indirectly by the gambling establishment.

EXHIBIT 11 Master Game Report—Detail

Run Date—6/24/83   Time—18-07

Play Date   6/23/83—Thursday

Pit/Game	Table	Game	Shift	Today Drop	Today Win	Today Hold %	Casino Report Month to Date Drop	Win	Hold %	Preliminary Year to Date Drop	Win	Hold %
09	33		Total				47,559	6,721	14.13	504,474	62,698	12.43
	34	Blk Jack	Day				16,897	2,927	17.33	166,774	26,482	15.88
	34		Swing				38,345	13,457	35.09	283,698	44,733	15.77
	34		Total				55,242	16,384	29.66	450,472	71,215	15.81
09	35	Blk Jack	Day				17,633	3,634	20.61	168,301	3,070	1.82
	35		Swing				35,324	3,011	8.53	250,123	45,217	18.08
	35		Total				52,957	6,645	12.55	418,424	48,288	11.54
09	36	Blk Jack	Day				17,386	-1,501	-8.64	189,628	9,107	4.80
	36		Swing				30,207	5,116	16.94	310,561	62,461	20.11
	36		Total				47,593	3,614	7.59	500,189	71,568	14.31
10	37	Blk Jack	Day	2,099	605	28.82	88,998	6,415	7.21	615,023	103,584	16.84
	37		Swing	5,962	91	1.53	116,715	23,316	19.98	814,801	143,076	17.56
	37		Total	8,061	696	8.63	205,713	29,732	14.45	1,429,824	246,660	17.25
10	38	Blk Jack	Day	1,890	479	25.34	66,344	10,030	15.12	493,801	57,558	11.66
	38		Swing	4,319	1,782	41.27	96,090	10,778	11.22	655,642	136,971	20.89
	38		Total	6,209	2,261	36.42	162,434	20,808	12.81	1,149,443	194,529	16.92
10	39	Blk Jack	Day	1,680	236	14.05	64,137	13,308	20.75	493,189	68,554	13.90
	39		Swing	2,447	106	4.35	96,951	19,412	20.02	642,658	119,755	18.63
	39		Total	4,127	342	8.30	161,088	32,720	20.31	1,135,847	188,310	16.58
10	40	Blk Jack	Day	1,478	957	64.78	71,599	7,529	10.52	533,117	59,239	11.11
	40		Swing	2,140	1,117	52.22	90,788	18,345	20.21	696,361	123,855	17.79
	40		Total	3,618	2,075	57.35	162,387	25,875	15.93	1,229,478	183,094	14.89
10	41	Blk Jack	Day	2,904	97	3.34	79,812	11,836	14.83	605,173	84,041	13.89
	41		Swing	3,601	164	4.55	107,602	31,754	29.51	766,816	144,548	18.85
	41		Total	6,505	261	4.01	187,414	43,590	23.26	1,371,989	228,589	16.66
10	42	Blk Jack	Day	1,091	439	40.28	74,250	8,213	11.06	524,339	98,634	18.81
	42		Swing	2,817	1,285	45.63	90,864	24,017	26.43	635,928	151,603	23.84
	42		Total	3,908	1,725	44.14	165,114	32,230	19.52	1,160,267	250,237	21.57

(continued)

EXHIBIT 11 (concluded) Master Game Report—Detail

Run Date—6/24/83   Time—18–07

Play Date   6/23/83—Thursday

Pit/Game		Table	Shift	Today			Casino Report Month to Date			Preliminary Year to Date		
				Drop	Win	Hold %	Drop	Win	Hold %	Drop	Win	Hold %
10	Blk Jack	43	Day	1,782	839	47.11	75,804	10,970	14.47	503,059	100,334	19.94
		43	Swing	4,047	167	4.14	88,382	15,547	17.59	609,689	106,484	17.47
		43	Total	5,829	1,007	17.28	164,186	26,517	16.15	1,112,748	206,818	18.59
10	Blk Jack	44	Day	4,204	803	19.10	79,166	9,924	12.54	585,815	110,009	18.78
		44	Swing	5,224	1,649	31.58	104,119	10,743	10.32	702,022	103,927	14.80
		44	Total	9,428	2,452	26.01	183,285	20,667	11.28	1,287,837	213,937	16.61
11	Blk Jack	45	Day	3,425	997	29.11	93,084	15,524	16.68	669,637	92,277	13.78
		45	Swing	3,394	1,363	40.17	148,392	23,242	15.66	838,985	143,274	17.08
		45	Total	6,819	2,360	34.62	241,476	38,766	16.05	1,508,622	235,551	15.61
11	Blk Jack	46	Day	3,362	-402	-11.96	74,266	2,956	3.98	502,424	63,373	12.61
		46	Swing	7,673	1,267	16.52	108,432	13,599	12.54	696,141	118,120	16.97
		46	Total	11,035	865	7.84	182,698	16,555	9.06	1,198,565	181,493	15.14
11	Blk Jack	47	Day	3,544	-1,515	-42.76	80,907	5,861	7.24	494,976	71,358	14.42
		47	Swing	2,983	606	20.32	98,051	23,637	24.11	647,812	141,205	21.80
		47	Total	6,527	-909	-13.93	178,958	29,498	16.48	1,142,788	212,563	18.60
11	Blk Jack	48	Day	6,285	2,676	42.58	71,304	5,824	8.17	521,703	84,121	16.12
		48	Swing	3,731	1,940	52.00	106,631	24,142	22.64	682,084	157,292	23.06
		48	Total	10,016	4,616	46.09	177,935	29,966	16.84	1,203,787	241,413	20.05
11	Blk Jack	49	Day	1,270	296	23.25	95,993	21,307	22.20	577,840	75,079	12.99
		49	Swing	2,025	-990	-48.89	83,185	13,887	16.69	643,847	139,857	21.72
		49	Total	3,295	-693	-21.05	179,178	35,194	19.64	1,221,687	214,936	17.59
11	Blk Jack	50	Day	4,323	2,477	57.30	73,435	12,798	17.43	506,423	92,065	18.18
		50	Swing	5,265	-1,595	-30.30	78,904	9,662	12.25	555,499	95,321	17.16
		50	Total	9,588	881	9.19	152,339	22,460	14.74	1,061,922	187,386	17.65

EXHIBIT 12 Master Game Report—Summary

Run Date—6/24/83   Time—18—07

Play Date   6/23/83—Thursday

Final Total Page

Pit/Game		Today			Casino Report Month to Date			Preliminary Year to Date		
		Drop	Win	Hold %	Drop	Win	Hold %	Drop	Win	Hold %
Blk Jack	Day	237,569	62,395	26.26	7,060,821	1,055,062	14.94	51,908,803	7,003,734	13.49
	Swing	346,867	158,114	45.58	8,586,885	1,779,110	20.72	62,486,716	10,716,594	17.15
	Total	584,436	220,509	37.73	15,647,706	2,834,172	18.11	114,395,519	17,720,329	15.49
Baccarat	Day	10,971	-8,716	-79.45	797,246	88,467	11.10	6,659,386	876,993	13.17
	Swing	15,014	-2,453	-16.34	1,245,670	97,566	7.83	10,359,402	1,473,800	14.23
	Total	25,985	-11,169	42.98	2,042,916	186,034	9.11	17,018,788	2,350,793	13.81
Craps	Day	254,164	11,925	4.69	7,251,450	783,554	10.81	53,409,701	5,548,571	10.39
	Swing	339,832	16,324	4.80	8,596,480	1,654,711	19.25	56,120,257	9,490,489	16.91
	Total	593,996	28,249	4.76	15,847,930	2,438,265	15.39	109,529,958	15,039,060	13.73
Roulette	Day	26,042	10,351	39.75	772,208	231,272	29.95	5,942,310	1,704,971	28.69
	Swing	39,986	15,265	38.18	988,944	228,291	23.08	6,748,677	1,559,351	23.11
	Total	66,028	25,617	38.80	1,761,152	459,563	26.09	12,690,987	3,264,322	25.72
Big Six	Day	4,553	2,291	50.33	129,600	52,843	40.77	933,157	410,771	44.02
	Swing	4,583	2,329	50.83	135,217	63,312	46.82	902,712	438,282	48.55
	Total	9,136	4,621	50.58	264,817	116,155	43.86	1,835,869	849,053	46.25
All game	Day	533,299	78,247	14.67	16,011,325	2,211,198	13.81	118,853,357	15,545,041	13.08
	Swing	746,282	189,580	25.40	19,553,196	3,822,992	19.55	136,617,764	23,678,517	17.33
	Total	1,279,581	267,827	20.93	35,564,521	6,034,191	16.97	255,471,121	39,223,558	15.35
Credit drop		505,500			13,324,095			92,628,515		
% of total drop		39.51			37.46			36.26		
Daily average—credit drop and table win					579,308	262,356		532,348	225,423	

(*continued*)

EXHIBIT 12 (concluded) Master Game Report—Summary

Daily Marker Activity

Beginning balance	5,374,595
Less markers	
Deposited	82,560
Redemptions	490,045
Consolidations	13,500
Plus markers	
Issued	711,160
Consolidations	13,500
Ending balance	5,513,150
Returned markers outstanding	8,929,121
Total receivable	14,442,271

Safekeeping

Beginning balance	120,535
Deposits made	20,200
Withdrawals	30,400
Ending balance	110,335

Casino Final Total

	Today	M-T-D	Y-T-D
Total win	447,870	10,890,542	68,583,941
Daily average		473,502	394,161

Daily Slot Activity

Denomination		Drop	Win	Daily Average
Nickels	Daily	6,142.35	5,592.35	
	M-T-D	154,311.80	92,907.55	4,039
	Y-T-D	1,240,086.25	1,052,211.15	6,047
Dimes	Daily	4,115.80	3,915.80	
	M-T-D	98,539.90	93,439.90	4,063
	Y-T-D	566,698.00	435,918.00	2,505
Quarters	Daily	147,199.50	130,209.90	
	M-T-D	3,918,959.75	3,520,276.29	153,055
	Y-T-D	25,290,262.00	22,459,384.48	129,077
Halves	Daily	11,637.00	11,337.00	
	M-T-D	377,953.00	315,759.60	13,729
	Y-T-D	2,239,143.00	1,722,115.75	9,897
Dollars	Daily	31,588.00	28,988.00	
	M-T-D	912,368.00	833,968.00	36,259
	Y-T-D	5,480,027.00	3,680,753.80	21,211
Total all denominations	Daily	200,682.65	180,043.05	
	M-T-D	5,462,132.45	4,856,351.34	211,146
	Y-T-D	34,816,216.25	29,360,383.18	168,738

The drop, win, and hold percentage measures were standard throughout the gaming industry, and competitive analyses were facilitated because summaries were prepared and distributed by the Atlantic City Casino Hotel Association. (Exhibit 13.)

Bonuses

The results measures are figured in bonuses paid to management personnel. Managers at the Sands received an annual bonus based on the bottom-line performance of the hotel-casino. This bonus could be doubled if the personal management-by-objectives (MBO) targets that were set during the annual budgeting process were met.

Some of the MBO objectives were based on standard annual performance measures, such as increased volume (drop), good hold percentages, and decreased costs, but as Stephen Hyde explained, these measures had to be supplemented with factors that were more difficult to quantify:

> The standard measures of performance are important indicators of our success, but we try to be careful not to place too much emphasis on them, because we don't want to be encouraging our people to sacrifice everything for bottom-line growth this year. We want them to be building the company and doing everything they can to ensure that we're going to be successful three to five years from now, and even further out. In our MBO program, we supplement the quantitative measures with factors that are usually more difficult to quantify. A good example is customer relations. If a customer has a complaint, we want our managers to make [him or her] happy, even if it costs us something today, so that [he or she] will come back. Other examples might be the successful completion of a project such as installation of a new computer system or maintenance of good employee relations.

Future Controls

In response to a request for a speculation as to what controls in the casino might look like in the future, Ed Sutor responded:

> In the gaming areas, the ultimate form of control for us would be to be able to record every transaction.

Then we'd have a good record of who has done what, and we'd be able to capture a lot of information that would be very valuable for decision-making purposes.

> But I can't visualize how we could record every transaction. Over and above the direct costs that would be involved in such record keeping, there would be some perhaps sizeable indirect costs. We're in the entertainment business, and we can't do anything that would diminish our customers' enjoyment. Furthermore, we don't want to do anything that would slow the games down too much; the number of wagers handled per hour is a standard measure of productivity in this business. So, unless there is some technological innovation that I can't foresee right now, I don't think the controls would be much different from what we have right now.

Control improvements were always being made or contemplated, however. Stephen Hyde explained:

> We're always looking for ways to improve. This is a tough, competitive business. We continually have to make sure that the controls we've got are still working, and we have to be alert for new trends and new ruses. I'll give you a couple of examples.

> Right now, we are going through training programs for all of the various positions. The programs have been reinstituted, and everybody who has gone through them (some as much as two years ago) is going back through them. Theoretically, with the improved training, we will improve the controls in the casino.

> In the blackjack area, we are working on our shuffles. You may find this hard to believe, but we have found that some people seem able to track some cards through the shuffle and they can derive some advantage from it in their plays. So about every six months we have to change our shuffle, and that is one of the things we're looking at right now.

> We're also working on improving our information systems. By the end of the year, we'll have a new computer system that will provide better information for control of credit and complimentaries. If, for example, a pit boss is asked for some complimen-

EXHIBIT 13 Example of Industry Results Report

Report 91500	00.00.00			Sands—Atlantic City Table Game Market Share Analysis Month of May			Run Date 06/14/83		Schedule C-5
	% of Blackjack Tables	% of Blackjack Win	% of Craps Tables	% of Craps Win	% of Roulette Wheels	% of Roulette Win	% of Baccarat Tables	% of Baccarat Win	% of Big Six Wheels	% of Big Six Win
Sands	10.4	9.2	9.3	10.5	10.6	10.0	8.3	11.7	6.7	7.7
Claridge	6.0	7.2	8.1	7.1	8.5	6.9	8.3	6.3	6.7	5.0
Bally	13.3	9.1	12.8	12.7	12.8	11.5	12.5	9.2	13.3	11.6
Caesars	10.5	12.1	16.3	16.2	11.7	12.2	16.7	24.3	10.0	8.9
Playboy	9.3	7.5	8.1	6.4	8.5	8.5	12.5	5.2	6.7	8.3
Resorts	14.7	21.6	11.6	12.5	11.7	13.0	12.5	17.5	20.0	15.8
Harrahs	11.9	8.8	12.8	10.1	12.8	10.6	8.3	6.4	10.0	11.0
Golden Nugget	10.7	13.4	10.5	14.6	10.6	15.2	8.3	24.2	13.3	18.1
Tropicana	13.2	11.2	10.5	10.0	12.8	12.0	12.5	(4.6)	13.3	13.5
Total	**100.0**	**100.0**	**100.0**	**100.0**	**100.0**	**100.0**	**100.0**	**100.0**	**100.0**	**100.0**

tary tickets, he or she could go to a computer terminal and get detailed information about the requestor's betting history (regularity, size of drop) and find out if that same person had just been given other "comps" by another pit boss. Then the pit boss will have the information to make the judgment as to whether the request should be filled. The key is the player's profit potential.

CASE 3–2: CROMPTON GREAVES LTD.

Control systems require making choices about what to measure, how to set targets and review performance against these measures, and how to reward people and make adjustments in light of their performance. At Crompton Greaves, Kewal Krishan Nohria employs a performance-driven control system to motivate employees. Aggressive growth targets and a wide variety of performance measures are used. Will the system continue working as the company continues to grow? What about when Nohria retires—is the control system dependent on his leadership style?

Preparation Questions

1. Evaluate Kewal Krishan Nohria's (KKN) approach to control at Crompton Greaves.
2. What assumptions regarding human motivation and behavior underlie KKN's approach to control?
3. How robust is this approach to control? What are its strengths and weaknesses?

Case 3–2 Crompton Greaves Ltd.*

When Kewal Krishan Nohria (or KKN, as he was often called) became president and managing director of Crompton Greaves, Bombay, India, in 1985, the company's performance was at its lowest level ever. Revenues had flattened and profits had been declining sharply and steadily since 1982 (See Exhibit 1 for Crompton's financial performance in the 1980s). KKN attributed this declining performance to Crompton's inability to respond to changing environmental conditions. Beginning in the early 1980s, he reasoned, the electrical equipment industry in India, from which Crompton derived most of its revenues, shifted from a "seller's market" to a "buyer's market":

> When we were in a seller's market, demand exceeded supply, so firms in our industry were able to get away with adequate quality and high costs. Now that we are in a buyer's market and our supply capacity exceeds demand, we can no longer afford to ignore the demands of the customer. Nor, can we neglect our competition.

Driving this shift was reduced demand from the Indian State Electricity Boards, the largest buyers

*Copyright © 1990 by the President and Fellows of Harvard College. Harvard Business School case 491-074 (Revised 1992).

EXHIBIT 1   Crompton Greaves Ltd.: Performance Record

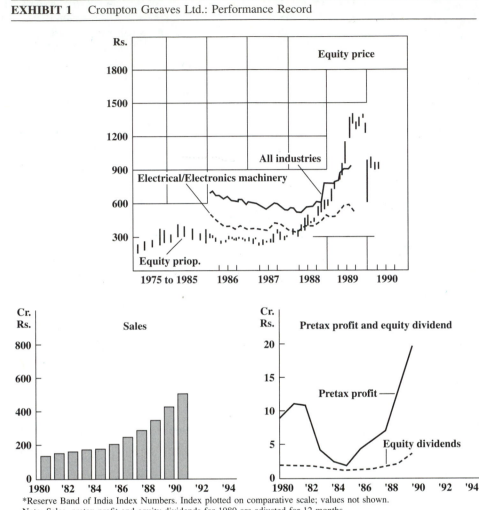

*Reserve Band of India Index Numbers. Index plotted on comparative scale; values not shown.
Note: Sales, pretax profit and equity dividends for 1989 are adjusted for 12 months.

of electrical equipment in India. This led to over-capacity in the industry and to fierce competitive discounting that severely depressed profit margins. Crompton's profitability was particularly hurt because 70 percent of its production was concentrated in Bombay, which had among the highest wage rates and real estate costs in India.

According to KKN, the challenge that Crompton faced when he became president was two-fold. First, Crompton had to adapt to the changed conditions in the electrical equipment industry. In addition to bringing costs under control, Crompton had to respond to the buyer's market through quality and service. Second, to achieve continued profitability, Crompton had to grow aggressively and diversify into new business areas. Including inflation, the Indian economy as a whole was growing at the rate of 10–12 percent. Crompton's costs, on the other hand, because of its base in Bombay, were growing at the rate of 15 percent. In order to improve its profitability, KKN concluded, the firm not only needed to reduce cost, but also had to grow at a rate of about 20 percent per year.

Growth was also a way for the firm to shift the center of gravity of its cost base outside Bombay. Since opportunities for growth in the electrical equipment segment were limited, KKN set his sights on electronics and telecommunication products. In these areas he felt Crompton could hope to leverage some of its existing capabilities. The question was how to achieve this turnaround without borrowing a lot of money or hiring a lot of people, both of which KKN wanted to avoid.

KKN's solution was to leverage what he considered his primary asset—Crompton's employees. He explained:

> When things look bad, one is tempted to find blame with one's people. But these were the same people who had once made Crompton successful. I saw no reason why they couldn't do it again. I believe you have to motivate people first, and make them look to the future with confidence. You must build morale throughout the company and inspire in people the will to succeed. I have no doubt they will rally to the challenge.

By 1987, the success of his strategy was evident. Revenues had grown to Rs. 300 crores, increasing more than 50 percent over revenues in 1985 (1 crore Indian rupees is approximately equal to 0.6 million U.S. dollars). Profits before tax rose from a low point of about Rs. 2 crores in 1985 to over Rs. 7 crores. Since then, the upward trend had continued. In 1990, revenues were over Rs. 500 crores and profits before tax over Rs. 20 crores. When KKN had become president, Crompton was the 54th largest Indian firm (not accounting for government-owned or public-sector enterprises); by 1990 it was ranked 28th.

KKN spoke confidently about Crompton's future, and set ambitious goals for the firm, some of which he hoped would be realized before he retired in 1998, and others that were long term. These goals included Crompton's doubling revenues every four years, and setting up a new plant every three months, as it did in 1989 and 1990. His goal had been translated into a slogan that symbolized the company's strategic intent—"2000 by the year 2000"—meaning that the company should achieve revenues of Rs. 2000 crores by the turn of the century. Profit before tax in 1988 was 2–2.5 percent. KKN wanted that figure to improve to 4 percent in two years, and reach 6–7 percent after five or six years. By the time he retired, KKN's goal was for Crompton to be the number one electronics company of India; it already was the number one electrical company.

Background

Crompton Greaves was incorporated in April 1937 as a private limited company under the name The Crompton Parkinson Works Ltd., England. At the time, the marketing was handled by another firm—Greaves Cotton Crompton Parkinson. In 1966, both manufacturing and marketing were brought together to form Crompton Greaves. As of 1990, Crompton Parkinson, a subsidiary of Hawker Siddley of UK, held 37.5 percent of the shares of the company, and Greaves Cotton, a company of the Thapar Group of India, held another 37.5 percent. Of the balance, 12 percent was owned by financial institutions and 13 percent rested with 6,000 shareholders. As per an understanding among its owners, Crompton Greaves had always been independently and professionally managed.

Crompton produced a broad range of electrical equipment for the public utilities, manufacturing, agricultural, and consumer sectors. In the late 1980s, Crompton launched many new products in the area of computers, telecommunications, industrial electronics, consumer electronics, and home appliances. The company had over 40 technology collaborations with large companies throughout the world including Westinghouse, Hitachi, Mitsubishi, Siemens, and Voest-Alpine.

Structure

Crompton was a diversified multidivisional, multiproduct company. It had 25 product divisions, each of which manufactured a related range of products such as transformers of different ratings, and motors of different sizes. Marketing was a central function and was organized according to customer orientation—stock-and-sell or distributors segment, manufacturing industry segment, services industry segment, and government-orders segment. To cover the geographic spread of the Indian market, the marketing organization was also divided into four regions: north, south, east, and west. Each region was further subdivided into branch offices that served as hubs for local marketing. A central corporate office handled finance, human resources and personnel, MIS, and other administrative functions.

The firm employed approximately 9,000 people, including 1,000 managers or "officers," 2,000 white-collar workers or "staff," and 6,000 blue-collar workers, or simply "workers."

Crompton's board of directors included representatives of Hawker Siddley, the Thapar group, the financial institutions, and some of the earlier managing directors of the firm. KKN, as president and managing director, was the only director with executive responsibilities and he was accountable to Mr. N.M. Wagle, the nonexecutive chairman of the board.

As shown in the organization chart (Exhibit 2), reporting to KKN were several vice presidents. Most of them were responsible for the performance of several divisions that were grouped together according to product or technological similarity. There were also vice presidents for marketing and finance and administration. Each division and region was in turn managed by a general manager. KKN required the vice presidents of the product divisions and marketing regions to also manage at least one division or region directly like a general manager. This, he believed, pressured the vice presidents to "earn their authority over the other divisions by their own performance instead of relying solely on their formal position." It also gave them "less time to meddle with the operations of the other general managers."

Designing and Implementing the Turnaround

To successfully respond to the challenges of a buyer's market and the need for diversified growth, KKN believed that Crompton first and foremost required a new attitude and set of values toward business. The direction in which the company's values had to change was articulated by KKN in terms of five dimensions—a concern for customers, people, products, cost, and innovation (Exhibit 3).

As the new president, KKN travelled to all of Crompton's divisions and regional offices to meet with his employees and discuss his ideas. At each plant, he held open houses to discuss these ideas for 40 employees at a time to cover 1,000 officers during the year. He encouraged his managers to do the same at lower levels so that workers were also engaged in this dialogue. The primary purpose of these visits was to unite the employees of the firm around a shared vision for renewal. KKN wanted Crompton's "9,000 people working *for* the company and not just *in* the company." As Mr. P.H. Rao, general manager, southern region, remembered:

> This was the first time that we were collectively able to focus on what the customer wanted and what we as a firm had to do. Everyone—from the engineer to the general manager who has to deal with the customers and dealers—was able to communicate face-to-face as opposed to through reports. These open houses were not one-sided affairs. Everyone joined in the discussion. This had two effects. First, people realized that top management is approachable; and second, they also realized that the top management had a clear point of view and vision of where we needed to go.

The product of these meetings was a simple statement of the strategy for change: "Excellence through a Concern for QPCE—Quality, Productivity, Cost, and Employees." The strategy was graphically illustrated using a triangle that had Quality, Productivity, and Cost along the edges and Employees in the middle, and was displayed throughout the organization (Exhibit 4).

Having developed a shared strategy of change and a means for communicating it clearly, KKN turned his attention to the task of translating the strategy into action. In his view, the task of management could be divided into three distinct dimensions along which a manager's performance

— create a little anxiety to get output from people.

— pat on shoulder give people credit. for what they have done.

recognition.

EXHIBIT 2 Crompton Greaves Ltd.: Organization Chart, 1990

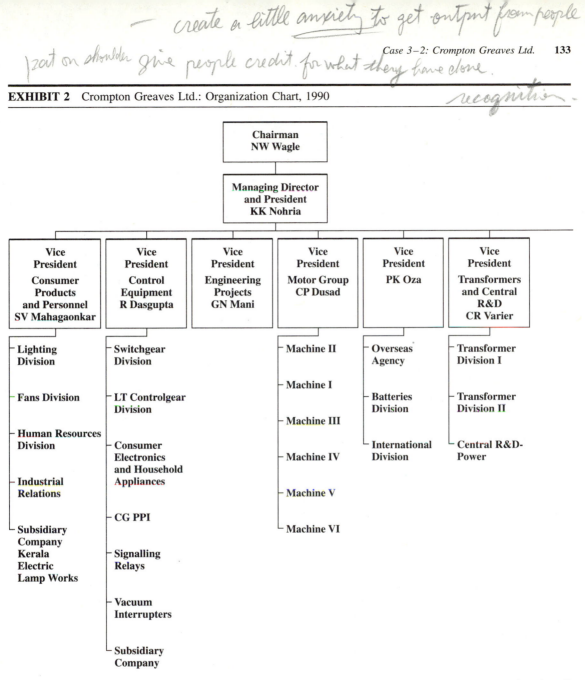

```
                        Chairman
                        NW Wagle
                            |
                   Managing Director
                    and President
                     KK Nohria
```

Vice President	Vice President	Vice President	Vice President	Vice President	Vice President
Consumer Products and Personnel SV Mahagaonkar	Control Equipment R Dasgupta	Engineering Projects GN Mani	Motor Group CP Dusad	PK Oza	Transformers and Central R&D CR Varier

- Consumer Products and Personnel SV Mahagaonkar
  - Lighting Division
  - Fans Division
  - Human Resources Division
  - Industrial Relations
  - Subsidiary Company Kerala Electric Lamp Works

- Control Equipment R Dasgupta
  - Switchgear Division
  - LT Controlgear Division
  - Consumer Electronics and Household Appliances
  - CG PPI
  - Signalling Relays
  - Vacuum Interrupters
  - Subsidiary Company

- Motor Group CP Dusad
  - Machine II
  - Machine I
  - Machine III
  - Machine IV
  - Machine V
  - Machine VI

- PK Oza
  - Overseas Agency
  - Batteries Division
  - International Division

- Transformers and Central R&D CR Varier
  - Transformer Division I
  - Transformer Division II
  - Central R&D-Power

(continued)

could be concretely measured: operations management, improvement management, and strategic management.

Operations Management

Operations management emphasized that the responsibility for the outcomes of their actions fell squarely on the shoulders of management. While paying attention to operational performance was not a new idea in Crompton, KKN felt that his approach differed from the past practice at Crompton in two important ways. First, he had simplified the indicators of performance so that attention was not dissipated by details, but remained focused on

delegate authority

EXHIBIT 2 (concluded)   Crompton Greaves Ltd.: Organization Chart, 1990

span of control 3-7.

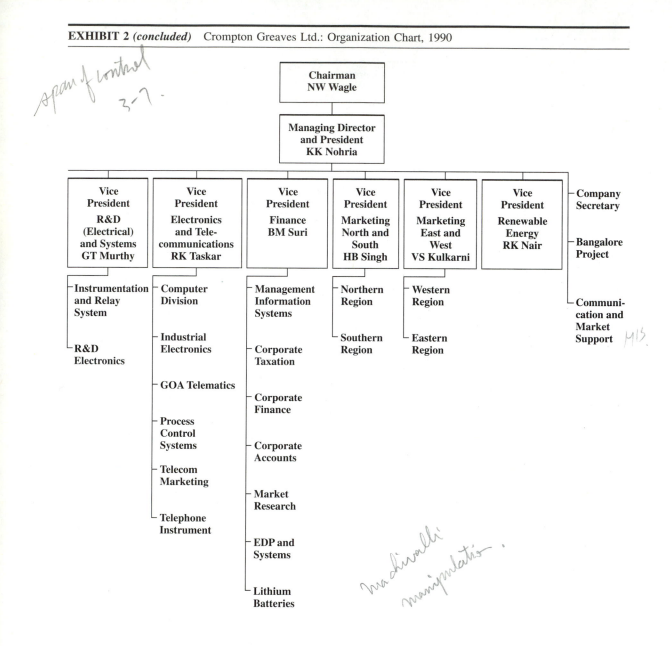

madivalli manipulation.

MIS.

a few key measures. He held all his managers responsible for their commitments on five key measures of their performance: profit before tax, revenues and revenue growth, cash flow, manpower, and capital expenditure. Second, he had pushed his managers to own responsibility and be fully accountable for their actions. KKN believed that "managers must own responsibility, live with the burden of responsibility, and achieve according to their commitment of results."

EXHIBIT 3   Crompton Greaves Ltd.: Statement of Values

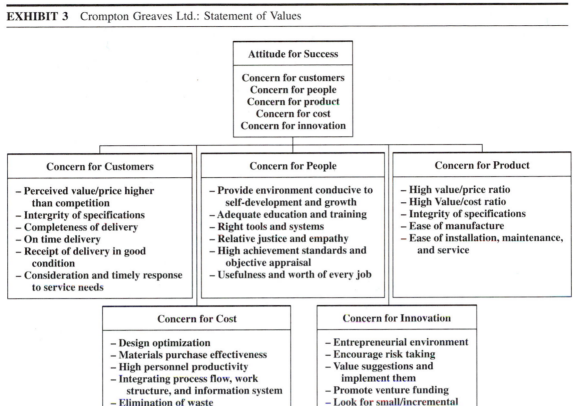

In keeping with these views, he abolished the distinction between cost and profit centers and treated all units of the firm—product divisions, regions, and even the corporate functions—as performance centers:

> Profit and cost centers are accountants' terms, not managers' terms. They take away the burden of responsibility for performance from the manager and lead to useless finger pointing. My general managers will all say that their operation is a performance center.

The response of Mr. P.H. Rao, one of the regional general managers, was testimony:

> Being in marketing, I do not constitute a profit center. But, I view my region as a performance center. I have made commitments for revenues, cash flows, manpower, and expenditures for which I am fully accountable. I believe my contributions have a direct impact on the profitability of the firm.

The importance of bearing the full responsibility for commitments was underscored by Mr. Ranjan Dasgupta, vice president of control systems:

> If I cannot deliver on my own operational commitments, then only I am held responsible. Since I am not told what to do, my inability to meet my commitments reflects a failure in either my judgement or my actions, and neither can be condoned. Even if failures result from environmental contingencies, there may be compassion for me, but I am still not off the hook. I am expected to forecast and hence held to be responsible for the impact of contingencies.

EXHIBIT 4   Crompton Greaves Ltd.: Strategy for Change

Excellence through

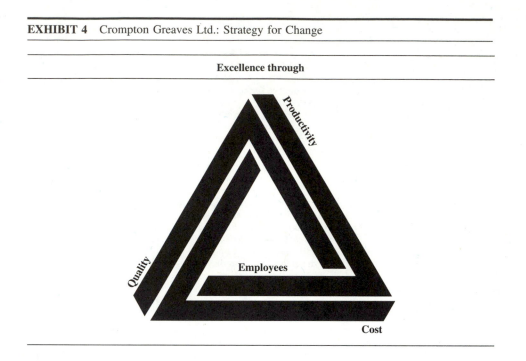

Productivity

Quality

Employees

Cost

Improvement Management

Improvement management was a novel idea that KKN had introduced to Crompton that he acknowledged borrowing from Japanese management. It emphasized that a vital aspect of a manager's task was to strive for constant incremental improvement. While operations management focused on *outcomes,* improvement management focused on the management *processes* that produced different outcomes. In keeping with Crompton's strategy for change, KKN concentrated the attention of his managers on improvements in quality, productivity, cost, and employee involvement. Each area of improvement was defined in quantitatively measurable terms.

Quality was measured by (1) the number of customer returns and complaints, (2) test-bed rejection rate, (3) in-process rejection, and (4) incoming inspection rejection. Quality assessment was being considered at earlier stages in the production process. While the ultimate target was zero defects, KKN had set his managers the

incremental target of halving their quality failures each year. In the marketing organization, quality was being tracked in terms of the speed of response to requests for after-sales service. The target was to increase the speed from its present level of 10–15 days to 2–3 days.

Productivity was defined and measured as sales per employee. KKN felt that while this was not the most sophisticated measure of productivity, it had the benefit of being simple and easy to understand. The drive to constantly increase productivity was treated as a top priority. In 1981–82, when the company had 9,851 employees, revenues were about Rs. 150 crores. In 1987–88, with 1,000 fewer workers, the company's sales revenue was more than twice the 1981 level. But KKN felt that there was considerable room for improvement. In 1988, he estimated, the United States had a productivity level of $100,000/employee in the electrical equipment industry, so KKN believed that even accounting for its more labor intensive technology, a reasonable expectation for Crompton was a productivity level half that of the United States, or $50,000 as opposed to the level of $20,000 it had achieved in 1988.

To encourage all managers to cut costs, KKN devised what was called the profit improvement plan (PIP). This was a list of tangible actions that a manager could take to reduce costs and improve profitability for the firm as a whole. Thus, managers were required to prepare an annual PIP budget based on actions they would take toward cost reductions such as higher price realizations, reduced debtors, reduced stocks, reduced expenses, reduced credit notes, increased advances, uniform production or billing, better interest rates, and so on. The PIP performance of all units in the firm was reviewed every month. The ongoing aspect of PIP was intended to remind managers that cutting cost was not a one-shot deal, but that there was always room for cost reduction.

Employee involvement and training were viewed by KKN to be vital for continuous improvement. Involvement in small group activities was also considered an important device to prevent the creation of a rigid vertical organization with an "empire mentality":

> I tell the people lower down, "The top people are trying to build an empire, and you should try to stop them by building regular interaction at the horizontal level." I say that to them in a joking way, but it's an idea I take quite seriously.

With this in mind, a number of small group activities such as quality circles and value engineering groups had been initiated. Mr. C.P. Dusad, vice president of motors, was one of the major champions of small group activities. In some of the divisions that reported to him, there were as many as 65 different small groups:

> Small groups have been the source of numerous improvements in our manufacturing processes. We have found that people who are actually involved directly in doing things have a much better sense than their managers about opportunities for making small changes that can have a direct impact on the bottom line. My divisions have had so much

success with groups, that we are getting requests from other divisions to help them organize such activities on a broader scale.

To institutionalize this activity, KKN had developed an involvement index that measured the fraction of employees involved in small group activities. The target was, by 1995, for officers to be 100 percent involved, staff 40–50 percent involved, and the rest of the organization 30 percent involved. To further encourage these efforts, annual companywide symposia like a quality circle convention and value engineering convention were organized, so that the participants in small groups across the company could come together to talk about and share their experiences.

Training was also given explicit attention. KKN conceived of a measure of "training exposure rate" for the organization, which was computed as the sum of the number of people in all training courses divided by the total number of employees. KKN set a target for 1990 of three, which meant that on average each employee had been a participant in three training programs. To ensure that training would continue at an expanding rate, KKN had also set a target for the number of people in the company who could act as internal trainers to be 1 percent of the total work force. This target was benchmarked to equal the best practices of Japanese firms.

Through maintaining a high level of worker involvement and constant training, KKN hoped to reduce headcount from 10,000 to 9,000 and stabilize it at 9,000, even as the company continued to double its sales.

Several additional initiatives were also being launched in the spirit of continuous improvement. For instance, the company had been working with a U.S. consulting firm, Productivity Inc., toward developing a value-added management program that was aimed at reducing "business lead time," or the time taken from the receipt of an order to its complete execution including the collection of money. The underlying concept behind this program was that the customer was willing to pay for everything but idle time. So, the program dealt with minimizing idle time at all stages of the business process. Another initiative required every marketing division to submit a sales call plan, which was a plan designed to increase the number of direct sales calls made by each and every person in the sales organization, from the general manager down. The target was to increase the number of sales calls per worker-day by 100 percent. To improve inventory management, twice a year the marketing organizations were being asked to accomplish a zero-stock-to-order day (ZESTO) and divisions a no-overdue-delivery day (NOD).

Strategic Management

The strategic management task focused on performance relative to competitors. As KKN bluntly put it:

> If your operational results such as profitability and sales growth are worse than the industry average, then you must have the modesty to accept that you are less than mediocre.

Mr. N. Rajagopal, the MIS manager, was charged with setting standards for performance based on the relevant competition. His focus was on operational indicators of competitive performance. He tried to find data on the competition in terms of their market shares, relative cost structures, relative working capital management, relative productivity, and revenues and profits. He highlighted the difficulty of getting accurate data on the relevant competition and felt that Crompton still had a long way to go with regard to good competitive intelligence and forecasting.

Most of the firm's top managers, including KKN, felt that this was the area in which the firm had made the least progress to date and would have to devote the most attention in the future. One of the recent initiatives by the marketing region was to try to measure customer preferences in each of Crompton's product groups to see if Crompton was one of the top three preferred suppliers in each category.

Capital expenditure decisions were viewed by KKN as being an important element of strategic management. In making decisions about entering into new businesses, he focused on two questions: (1) was the market segment of interest to Crompton in terms of technology and size; and (2) did Crompton have the ability to be among the top three firms in the industry in the light of existing and potential competition. For existing businesses, capital expenditures that focused on productivity and quality improvements were always given preference over capacity improvement. While KKN required formal business plans for capital investments, he did not take formal analyses like discounted-cash-flow or hurdle rates too seriously. He reasoned:

> Any bright manager can come up with the numbers to justify an investment. Moreover, once an investment is made, its too late even if you do find out that your numbers were wrong. So at end of the day, what really counts is your management ability to be one of the top two or three firms in the business, because in any business, these firms will always make money.

Budgeting and Monitoring

KKN firmly believed that "performance needs to be budgeted, monitored, and managed." The entire top management of the firm, a total of about 60 people including all divisional and regional general managers as well as the vice presidents, were involved in the budget formulation and review process. The new budget cycle began in October when KKN requested everyone to submit their initial budget for the next fiscal year (Crompton's fiscal year ended on March 31). In January, managers presented the broad outlook of their budget, primarily in terms of the key operating parameters. This initiated a discussion that led to a one-on-one discussion between each general manager, the respective vice president, and KKN, held in his office in the first week of February. During this meeting, which lasted four to five hours, general managers had to present in detail their budgets on performance. measurement / what to measure. how to collect? what's the std.?

Case 3–2: Crompton Greaves Ltd. **139**

all three dimensions: operations, improvement, and strategic management. By the end of March, these budgets were refined and reconciled among the product divisions and marketing regions. The final budget was presented by the general managers in May to the board of directors.

Budgeted targets were considered both a personal judgment and commitment. Managers were expected to set targets that were achievable, not wishful. Targets were expected to have a variance of −0 to +5 percent. Over the course of the budget preparation cycle, managers were given three chances to revisit their targets. KKN believed that people tended to overestimate what they could accomplish, so he only adjusted targets downward:

> Most of us overestimate our capacity and ability. Managers always will be optimistic about targets. I will let someone reduce their numbers, but I've never asked someone to increase their target.

On some occasions, KKN had cut targets by 10 percent in order to ensure that his managers would achieve their targets. In his opinion:

> Success teaches success. Failure does not teach success. I'd rather discuss success than failure. The moment people start succeeding, their own self-image is enhanced and that enables them to set higher standards in the future.

To monitor performance against the budget, the entire top management group met every quarter (in January, April, July, and October) for two days. One day was spent in reviewing the previous quarter's performance and to update the year-end outlook. The other day was spent in discussing more qualitative issues.

At the budget review meeting, each manager was required to present his/her results to the whole group. The tone of this review was summed up by KKN in the following way:

> Success need not be explained. Failure cannot be explained.

Managers were expected to assume responsibility for their failure and were never allowed to revise their budget estimates in midstream. However, they were encouraged to provide as accurate a year-end outlook as they could at the end of each quarter. The rationale behind this inflexibility was to ensure that managers felt complete ownership and responsibility for their judgment, particularly since their budgets were never revised upwards. Previously, KKN felt, Crompton managers had been allowed to disavow their responsibility far too easily. Now most managers, as Mr. R. Dasgupta disclosed, took their "hit ratio," or ability to meet targets consistently, very seriously:

> Every three months all of us can see crystal clear how good we each are at meeting our commitments. Though we are not pressurized by KKN, none of us want to admit that we have failed. Right now, I am failing at my budgets, so I am shuddering about the April meeting. I am already working hard to make sure that I meet my commitments in the July meeting. What all of us want is to be able to strut into that meeting as opposed to slinking out of it.

In addition to the quarterly reviews, KKN reviewed the performance of each product division and marketing region by visiting them about three to four times every year. This task consumed about 15 to 18 days of his monthly schedule. KKN's monthly schedule was published and distributed to all managers on the 15th day of the previous month, so that everyone would know when he was going to visit them. The one day meeting with each general manager and his/her direct reports was the way KKN "got a feel for what is happening in the company." Otherwise, he gave the general managers full latitude in making decisions regarding their division: "Twenty-nine days a month the general managers do not hear from me, and I don't hear from them. They would say that I am a hands-on manager but I don't interfere with them too much."

Peer groups across the divisions at lower levels were also encouraged to hold quarterly meetings that KKN attended biannually. There were meetings among works managers, materials managers, marketing managers, design and development managers, personnel managers, administrative managers, engineering managers, and quality managers. These meetings were considered to be ways for managers to learn from each other's experiences as well as to set a shared agenda for improvement.

Performance Assessment and Incentives

> People will work as hard as they can. They are driven toward being the most they can be. Moreover, people like to test themselves in a community of peers. They often don't mind failing in the presence of their boss, but do mind in the presence of their peers.

Crompton's incentive system corresponded with KKN's above-mentioned assumptions about human nature. The incentives to excel were not monetary rewards but rather rewards of self-fulfillment: promotions, job satisfaction gained by setting and accomplishing personal commitments, and peer recognition. There was no bonus system at Crompton, and the pay scales, in line with the norms in Indian industry, were very conservative, even at the CEO level. Promotion, which brought with it a modest increase in salary and considerably more responsibility, was the main formal reward. This meant that the company had to continually grow in order to create promotion opportunities.

KKN strove to make Crompton's performance evaluation system as open, transparent, and fair as possible. Toward this end, he had the marketing regions rank order the product divisions in terms of their ability to satisfy customer needs. The product divisions, in turn, were asked to rate the marketing regions in terms of their efforts at promoting and selling their products. These peer rankings were tabulated and presented at one of the quarterly reviews attended by the entire top management group. While there occasionally were disputes about these rankings, KKN minimized these squabbles by reminding managers that there was no reason why any general manager should single out another as being a poor performer. It was the responsibility of the manager who was perceived as a poor performer to prove to the other managers that this assessment was inaccurate.

In terms of his own evaluation of the managers, KKN focused on their demonstrated performance and not their innate ability. While he admitted that there might be variations among his managers in terms of their intrinsic abilities—some were brighter than others—he paid little attention to these differences. Instead, he concentrated on their demonstrated accomplishments. These accomplishments included the manager's track record on budgeted commitments as well as their relative competitive performance. Thus, a manager who had reduced the losses in a loss-making division was viewed more favorably than one whose profit levels or market share had declined. As KKN pointed out, a manager of a division that was responsible for a large fraction of the total profits of the firm was rated unfavorably because during his tenure the division had lost market share from 20 percent to 16 percent.

By focusing on demonstrated performance which was reviewed in the presence of everyone at the quarterly review meetings, KKN felt he had made the system totally transparent for all to see. In fact, he observed:

> I have made the performance evaluation system so open that I have taken away from myself the prerogative to promote anybody. I have to promote people based on their relative performance which is known to everybody. The track record of the managers and their relative rankings are common knowledge.

One of the great benefits of having such a transparent performance assessment system in KKN's view was that in addition to being perceived as fair in terms of who got rewarded, it also prevented those who were not rewarded from being demotivated. As KKN explained:

> What is often ignored in most incentive systems is the effect the system has on those who are not rewarded. I am much more concerned about that. After all, those who are not rewarded make up the

majority. So if they are left demotivated, we can be in big trouble. I have found that in the system we have established at Crompton, those who are not rewarded can live with the results more easily, because they can understand it fully.

In addition to promotions and salary increases, there were numerous symbolic rewards such as trophies and prizes that were given to the managers of those divisions and regions that had outstanding performance relative to others on measures such as financial results, quality, productivity, cost, and employee involvement. Managers fiercely vied for these awards. As Mr. P.H. Rao stated:

> Each year there are awards for the best marketing branch and region. These are very prestigious. The award is given in the quarterly review meeting in front of all the vice presidents and general managers. Your accomplishments are celebrated in front of all your peers. These are the moments we all live for.

KKN wanted those who set targets and worked to achieve targets to feel a long-term commitment to the division and its goals. As a result, he did not rotate managers frequently: "If managers feel they are there temporarily, they will think in the short term. I want them to think—'All decisions I make I will have to live with.' "

In the case of poor performance, failures were considered the fault not only of the subordinates but also of their managers. KKN believed that when workers failed, managers should not blame the workers but should question themselves. As he stated, poor performers reflected ineffectual managers: "There will not be many incompetent people in an organization unless the CEO or the general managers are incompetent."

KKN's first approach toward incompetent managers was to encourage self-improvement: "When people fail temporarily, I help them seek improvement. It is my job to make sure other people are capable of doing their jobs." KKN believed that improvement came from people helping themselves: "Ultimate improvement comes from self-discipline, self-analysis, self-competition, and

self-reliance." Managers that did not improve, even after being given help, were not fired but rather were deprived of responsibility and status, or in KKN's terms, were kept in the organization as "decorative pieces." These individuals, he said, usually left of their own accord. If, however, they chose to stay, he felt he had no right to fire them, because at some level they were as much a sign of his own failure as theirs.

KKN believed his management practices could be transferred to other multidivisional companies in other industries and countries. When asked if he would change any aspect of his management style if he became CEO of an American organization, KKN stated: "I wouldn't run a company in the United States any differently, except I would take away my personal right to fire anybody."

Conclusion

Crompton Greaves certainly thrived under KKN's management, but some questions were beginning to be raised. One of the issues was the extent to which the present management system was suited to a much larger and more heterogeneous organization. Given the rapid growth of the company, could a management style that relied so heavily on face-to-face interaction function if Crompton had 80 divisions instead of 25? As Susan Varghese, human resource development manager, observed:

> We may be outgrowing our present structure. The firm needs to be more responsive to external market forces. For instance, our new electronics divisions are in very different labor markets than our traditional power equipment divisions. Should we be paying software and telecommunications engineers differently from our other engineers and risk internal inequity or should we preserve equity and risk getting the worst engineers? We have to find a way of being more heterogeneous internally. Systems and procedures that apply to traditional businesses need not apply to our new businesses. Also, it is only going to become harder for KKN to continue to keep on top of an ever larger organization. Will our systems be as good or robust without his intense involvement?

Crompton was also facing very stiff competition in some of the new fields that it was entering. The company was having a hard time making a success of its entry in the television and personal computer segments. In these areas, new entrants had been enjoying much greater success. Some managers were beginning to become nervous about the company's rapid entry into new businesses, wondering what might happen if more of these initiatives failed.

Finally, some of Crompton's executives were troubled about whether the company would continue to sustain this performance after KKN retired. Questions arose concerning the future of Crompton Greaves, the dependence of the organization on KKN, and the transferability of his management style. For example, had KKN's management philosophies become deeply enough embedded in the company so that the attitude he had fostered would persist after his retirement? Would this culture suit another CEO's style?

CASE 3–3: COMPAQ COMPUTER CORPORATION

Compaq is among the new breed of young, rapidly growing firms in the evolving computer industry. This case takes a look at management control systems and issues in the face of rapid product obsolescence, the continual rise and collapse of competitors, and increasingly sophisticated customers. Compaq's approaches to planning, budgeting processes, and financial control are markedly different from those seen in many large, older companies. The relationships among competitive environment, company culture, and financial controls are examined.

Preparation Questions

1. Analyze Compaq's approach to financial planning and control.
2. Would you anticipate that Compaq will have to make any changes in its approach to financial planning and control as it grows and diversifies?
3. How applicable is Compaq's approach to financial planning and control to other companies? Under what circumstances?

Case 3–3 Compaq Computer Corporation*

Background

In early 1982, three former Texas Instruments employees held a meeting at a Houston pie shop. The three used a placemat to sketch the design of what would become Compaq Computer Corporation's (Compaq's) first product, an IBM PC-compatible portable microcomputer. First shipped in January 1983, the Compaq Portable was a tremendous success. It led Compaq to the highest first-year revenues of any corporation in U.S. history.

Compaq later had several more striking successes. It achieved *Fortune* 500 status after only four years, becoming the fastest company ever to do so. Sales reached $1 billion in 1987—again, the fastest ever at the time. Sales reached almost $3 billion in 1989, by which time Compaq had become the leading industry-standard[1] microcomputer manufacturer. In early 1990 Compaq employed over 9,000 people and marketed systems in over 60 countries (Exhibit 1).

Compaq's growth was remarkable given the dynamic, competitive nature of its market. Besides IBM, several other major computer manufacturers had tried to dominate the microcomputer market, among them Xerox, DEC, Hewlett-Packard, AT&T, ITT, Olivetti, and Wang. Apple Computer's well-known Macintosh had also had considerable success in several market segments. Several start-up companies, such as AST Research, Televideo, and Wyse, had entered the market with varying degrees of success.

Compaq had remained focused on the industry standard marketplace, launching several generations of new products. Its philosophy was to wait until technology could provide a "no compromises" solution to users' needs, rather than rushing a product out as soon as technology made it barely feasible. This approach had produced consistently successful products (Exhibit 2).

Compaq had initially marketed through dealers only and had retained this single-channel focus. By 1990 Compaq had a network of over 3,000 dealers. It had concentrated on addressing the dealer channel's traditional weaknesses (e.g., training, service, and support) rather than multiplying distribution channels and thus creating interchannel conflicts. Compaq's pricing strategy was unusual: it had not tried to underprice IBM, as most of its competitors had. Instead, it emphasized superior functionality and quality, symbolized in its advertising theme, "It simply works better."

Compaq went international in 1984, establishing European and international headquarters in Munich and initially marketing in France, Germany, and Great Britain. International sales enjoyed remarkable growth: sales at least doubled every year from 1984 to 1988. In 1989, Compaq became the number two[2] PC manufacturer in Europe with a 9 percent market share, eclipsing Apple's 8 percent. In the first quarter of 1990, Compaq's international sales exceeded North American sales for the first time ever.

Management and Organization

Rod Canion, CEO, was the unquestioned leader of Compaq. A veteran of Texas Instruments' (TI) terminals and peripherals division, he had founded

---

*E. Geoffrey Love prepared this case under the supervision of Professor Robert G. Eccles. Copyright © 1990 by the President and Fellows of Harvard College. Harvard Business School case 491-011 (Revised 1991)

[1] After IBM introduced the PS/2 and Microchannel architecture in 1987, the term *IBM PC-compatible* was replaced by *industry standard* to avoid confusion, since few non-IBM machines were compatible with the Microchannel architecture.

[2] By revenue as measured through the dealer channel.

EXHIBIT 1 Sales Growth*

	1983	1984	1985	1986	1987	1988	1989
Sales (millions)	$111	$329	$504	$625	$1,224	$2,066	$2,876
Total assets (millions)	121	231	312	378	901	1,590	2,090
Percentage of sales international	0%	5%	10%	19%	26%	39%	45%
Sales	100.0%	100.0%	100.0%	100.0%	100.0%	100.0%	100.0%
Cost of sales	72.4	70.6	64.7	57.7	58.6	59.7	59.6
Gross margin	**27.6**	**29.4**	**35.3**	**42.3**	**41.4**	**40.3**	**40.4**
R&D	3.3	3.3	3.2	4.3	3.8	3.6	4.6
Marketing and sales expense	10.3	12.8	13.5	15.3	11.7	11.4	11.6
General and administrative	9.7	7.3	8.4	9.0	6.8	7.8	7.2
Other	−0.2	1.0	1.7	1.5	0.5	−0.3	0.2
Total operating expense	**23.2**	**24.4**	**26.7**	**30.1**	**22.8**	**22.5**	**23.5**
Income before taxes	4.4	5.0	8.7	12.2	18.6	17.8	16.9
Employees (at end of period)	615	1,318	1,860	2,200	4,300	7,000	9,500

*Discrepancies in tallying are caused by rounding.

Compaq with fellow TI veterans Jim Harris, senior VP, engineering, and Bill Murto (no longer with Compaq). Many other senior managers at Compaq were also TI veterans, including the presidents of the North American and the Europe and international business units, the CFO, and several senior VPs.

Canion explained that one reason Compaq had grown so fast was its practice of "hiring for tomorrow." New managers' responsibilities were expected to grow to levels that matched, and then exceeded, their prior experience. For example, Eckhart Pfeiffer, president, Europe and international, had already run a $500-million division at TI when he joined Compaq in September 1983. He joked that he had left Houston with a check for $20,000 and the charge to lead the startup of Compaq's international operations; international sales reached $1.3 billion in 1989.

Canion also emphasized "balance." Compaq managers tried very hard to have all the elements for success (product design, marketing, manufacturing, service, finance, etc.) grow together, rather than emphasizing one to the exclusion of others. Canion described Compaq's philosophy as "doing the basics right." He believed if Compaq could maintain the culture and processes that had made it successful, then success would continue.

Canion's personal abilities were highly regarded. Daryl White, CFO and senior VP, described him as especially strong in working with people: "He's one of the few people I've dealt with who truly doesn't 'type' people's opinions or hold grudges in any way. He takes every issue as a brand new issue to discuss to the fullest. He is fair and he leads by example." Canion apparently had a talent for bringing up sensitive issues in the middle of meetings in a way that avoided bruising egos. Canion's impact was felt throughout Compaq. One production worker said, "What meant the most to me was when he stopped by and talked with us for a few minutes. I was at AT&T for 17 years and I never even saw the president."

Compaq had been organized functionally except for a brief period with a divisional structure in

EXHIBIT 2 Brief Product History

Date	Product	Comments
1/83	Portable	Shipments grow from 200/mo. in January to 10,000/mo. in December.
1/84	Portable Plus	Adds hard disk (expanded storage) capability to portables.
6/84	Deskpro	1st Compaq desktop; helps Compaq triple sales in 1984.
4/85	Portable 286	First portable to use 80286* processor.
4/85	Deskpro 286	Led Compaq to #2 in 286-based systems sales in US.
2/86	Portable II	Compaq's best-selling product within 5 months of introduction.
9/86	Deskpro 386	Compaq was first major manufacturer to introduce a microcomputer based on the 80386 processor.
2/87	Portable III	Best-selling, full-function portable in the world in 1987.
9/87	Deskpro 386/20	Fastest, most powerful PC in the world at introduction.
9/87	Portable 386	Most advanced full-function portable at introduction.
6/88	Deskpro 386/25	Successful follow-on to Deskpro 386/20.
6/88	Deskpro 386s	Used economical 80386SX processor. Compaq's best-selling product in 1989.
10/88	SLT286	Laptop computer. Captured 40% of domestic laptop market within six months.
Late 1988	EISA Standard	Compaq helps form industry alliance to establish the Extended Industry Architecture (EISA) as an alternative to IBM's proprietary Microchannel architecture.
4/89	Deskpro 286e	Continued development of line; better integrated, sleeker.
5/89	Deskpro 386/33	Successful follow-on to Deskpro 386/25.
10/89	LTE/286 & LTE	Notebook computer. Most orders in first three months of any Compaq product to date.
11/89	Systempro	Power comparable to DEC VAX minicomputer; 80386 (later 80486 processor); Compaq's first EISA product.
11/89	Deskpro 486/25	Most powerful desktop PC in world at introduction.

*The processor is the "brain" of a microcomputer. The type of processor (80xxx) determines how powerful the microcomputer is. The 80286 ("286") replaced the slower 8086 and 8088; the 80386 ("386") was yet more powerful; and in 1990 the 80486 processor, the most powerful yet, was just coming into general use. To add to the complexity, each processor had different versions that ran at different speeds or had somewhat different capabilities. On some Compaq products (e.g., the Deskpro 386/20) the processor number is followed by a slash and a second number, which indicates the clock speed in megahertz (faster is better).

EXHIBIT 3   Organization Chart

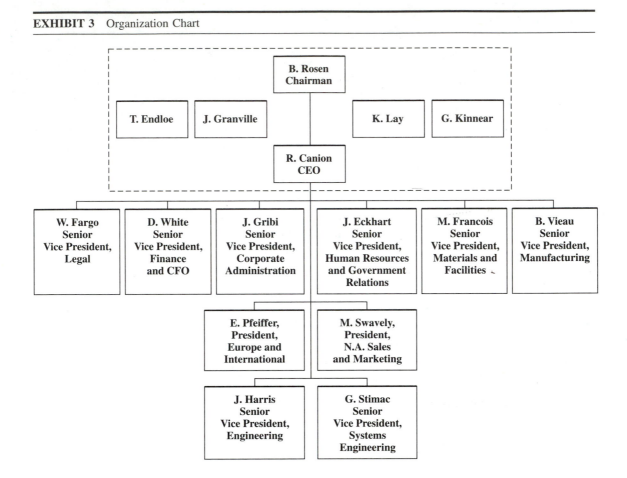

1984. The divisional structure had been intended to stimulate new-product development, but it resulted in overlap and conflict. Management soon concluded that Compaq was not really in separate businesses, so it returned to a functional organization to retain focus.

There were two profit centers in 1990: North America and international. Their two presidents (Michael Swavely and Eckhart Pfeiffer, respectively) reported to Canion, along with several functional senior VPs (Exhibit 3). The functional areas were subdivided into cost centers. Most of Compaq's senior executives had been with the company since 1983 or earlier, so they had seen almost all of its growth.

Internationally, the organizational structure was based on country subsidiaries. Compaq established a separate subsidiary in each major country it sold computers in. The largest were in Great Britain, France, Germany, Australia, and Italy. Country managers reported directly to Pfeiffer and had considerable initiative in marketing and sales planning and operations, although major decisions (involving pricing, advertising programs, or dealer discounting policies, etc.) required approval from international headquarters and/or Houston.

Compaq had three manufacturing locations in 1990. Most manufacturing was done in Houston. In 1987, Compaq opened a manufacturing plant in Erskine, Scotland; by 1990, it employed 800 people and supplied more than half of European market needs. In 1987 a printed circuit board manufacturing plant was opened in Singapore. Compaq's manufacturing facilities were state of the art. They did mainly circuit board and final unit assembly and testing. Mechanization had contributed significantly in reducing the labor content to about 1 percent of overall product cost.

Product Planning

Compaq's marketplace was characterized by short product life cycles, making fast development cycles extremely important. If a product was not right, it was usually too late to change it if problems were noticed after formal introduction. Canion characterized the battle for product success as a "game of inches": a difference of six months to market could make or break a product.

It was very important to match marketplace needs with technological possibilities. Canion said one of Compaq's differences was that "we believe you can determine beforehand if a product will be accepted, through the right kind of market research." For example, Compaq had held back while other companies introduced laptops, and introduced its own only when the technology had progressed so that a true no-compromises laptop was possible. The resulting product, the SLT/286, was an instant success.

Canion said, "Compaq's planning is based on a product strategy team that merges strategic and product planning, focusing on where technology is leading. I spend a third of my time on strategic and product-planning issues. I can justify the time easily; the strongest thing in our market is to have the right product at the right time." Compaq had had a separate strategic planning group, but it was disbanded in favor of the product strategy team.

The product strategy team included Canion, Swavely, Harris, Gary Stimac (senior VP, systems engineering), and a few other top managers. They met Tuesdays and Thursdays for four hours. Each meeting focused on specific, ongoing, potential product development projects, which were consid-

ered in light of the key strategic issues facing Compaq. One or two key people from those projects attended the meeting as full participants while their projects were discussed. The product strategy team maintained a prioritized list of usually about 50 projects; priorities were reassessed periodically. Projects were funded when their priority was high enough for the marketing and development organizations to assign personnel to them.

Once a project was funded, project teams were formed. Marketing and engineering efforts for funded projects worked in parallel, and manufacturing was also involved early through a "design for manufacturing" philosophy, wherein members of a manufacturing liaison team participated in design reviews of new products right from the start. Approval of a development project did not mean the product would reach the market. Stimac said, "If we decide a project is a bad idea, we raise our hand early and make 'kill' decisions." He felt this had been a key to Compaq's enviable product success record.

Culture

Compaq's culture was based on a few ideas about how people act. The most important assumption was that people were inherently honest and would use every tool available to try to do the right thing. Trusting employees was also very important. The main cultural precepts of treating people with respect, trust, open communications, candor, and team spirit were consistent with these ideas. To help maintain the culture, Compaq tried to hire "nice" people, people with integrity, compassion, and a can-do attitude. Considerable resources were invested in finding the right kind of people.

Compaq's main rule for action and decisions was "do what makes sense" for Compaq as a whole, rather than focusing too closely on fixed goals, familiar solutions, or standard procedures. Bob Vieau, senior VP, manufacturing, commented that he guarded against the "it has always been done this way" syndrome and instead was a heavy promoter of "does it make sense today?" The whole idea was that "doing what makes sense prevents the system from getting you hung up in procedures."

The Process

The Process was the method Compaq used to make important decisions and to determine how to do what makes sense. The Process encompassed a whole range of ideas, including (1) the rule of inclusion, (2) teamwork, (3) "working the issue," and (4) consensus building.

First, if the decisions and issues affected several groups, it was important that each group be represented and that everyone who could make a unique contribution to the issues at hand be included.

Second, when a manager committed to do something, he/she committed for his/her team, and to work with the rest of the organization as needed. Team performance was emphasized over individual performance. Even when an individual had screwed up, that was secondary. The important thing was making sure the team succeeded.

Third, the idea of working the issue was to resolve an issue by gathering information, taking full account of the issue's impact on different areas of the company and thoroughly discussing different alternatives. As Canion said, "The more information you have, the more you can work the issue." A key cultural precept was to speak up with any concerns, even if they were uncertain or vague, as long as there were reasons behind them. Senior managers were particularly concerned that all sides of an issue were carefully considered. Canion and Swavely acted as devil's advocates to ensure that competing alternatives were fully represented.

The fourth key aspect of The Process, consensus building, often required repeated cycles of discussion, information gathering, and working the issues. Sometimes everyone agreed on a course of action even though some were not in full agreement with every aspect. The senior person decided for the team only when this level of agreement could not be reached. The Process was meant to ensure that everyone felt their concerns and those of their group had been represented, and that everyone involved understood the decision and its issues, even when a consensus could not be reached. White said the key was that after the decision was made, "everyone marched in the same direction."

Following The Process sometimes meant it took a long time to reach the right decision. Pfeiffer recalled the time the entire international top management group and Swavely spent a whole day discussing only the top item on their agenda: the pricing of one new product. Nevertheless, Compaq executives felt that it was almost always worth taking time to ensure that everyone understood a decision.

Open Communications

Open communications were a key element in all aspects of Compaq's operation. Canion said he could not overemphasize the importance of an open environment in stimulating candid feedback. John Gribi, senior VP, administration, thought communication in many large companies was limited and information was often hidden or camouflaged. Managers generally agreed there was a great deal of freedom to speak out at Compaq.

The open-communications ethic particularly stressed early notification of problems and "don't shoot the messenger." It was acceptable to have made a mistake, as long as you informed the appropriate people as soon as you recognized it. The ethic also stressed integrity of presentation, that is, presenting the facts as they were rather than concealing or distorting them to advance a vested interest. By reducing game-playing with numbers, better decisions could be achieved, and destructive politics were kept to a minimum. Sharing of information was strongly encouraged. Swavely said, "Someone in international can request any piece of data—and ask us to explain it. Allowing others access to information requires a lot of trust, but that trust exists at Compaq."

Compaq's information systems helped provide an open-communications environment. Individuals could send a message directly to nearly anyone in the company via a worldwide network, including top management. The network was extremely active, and the importance of electronic mail (called *B-mail* at Compaq) in tying the company together was widely emphasized. But David Schempf, VP and corporate controller, did have a concern: "B-mail can be a trap, if it eliminates human face-to-face contact."

International Culture

The culture in Compaq's international operations was largely similar to that in the United States. But the culture took more time to assimilate internationally, due to the dispersed nature of Compaq's international operations, differences in each country's indigenous business practices and customs, and the necessity for integrating those practices and customs with Compaq's own culture. Compaq depended heavily on individual country managers to spread the culture as well as to attain business success.

Maintaining the Culture

When asked what was most important for Compaq's continued success, managers always mentioned maintenance of the culture first or second. And maintaining the culture by leading by example was mentioned often. Senior managers felt that setting an example of how The Process worked was particularly important in meetings when problems in process arose. To do this, a manager had to be willing to stop the meeting and discuss the process by which the meeting itself should be conducted.

Opinion varied on how difficult it would be to maintain Compaq's culture. Canion felt the period of greatest risk to the culture had been when Compaq went from hundreds of people to thousands. It had been growing so fast that at one point 79 percent of the people had been with the company for less than a year. But Harris felt it had been relatively easy to maintain the culture during fast growth and that it might become more difficult to maintain as growth slowed. Canion had held

several top-level meetings to find ways to maintain the culture as Compaq grew.

Finance Function

The challenge in a fast-growth environment was to achieve a balance: to have appropriate systems in place, but not to impose too many policies and procedures that made the system inflexible. Compaq's financial policies were designed to avoid overcontrol, but to have information available when needed.

Compaq had had sophisticated financial controls from its inception. Gribi, Compaq's first CFO, had drawn on his experience at Price Waterhouse and TI and set up the financial-control systems to handle a *Fortune* 500–size company. In 1982, he had brought in an integrated financial software system (called *ASK*), which provided material requirements planning, procurement, sales, order entry and processing, and corporate accounting applications. Later versions of ASK were still in use across Compaq in 1990.

Financial staff contrasted their role at Compaq with what they believed were traditional norms. For example, White discussed the financial stereotype of the operating manager. "This manager can't be trusted, so financial procedures and controls are required. Finance becomes responsible for monitoring ever-increasing numbers of controls, many of them overly standardized to make finance's job easier. But any good operations manager can and will get around controls if necessary. After a while, finance is viewed as a spy, and financial policies are seen as hurdles." Several executives believed that unreasonable controls led to "gaming" of systems and could also slow down the company's reaction time and demotivate people.

Compaq's philosophy of the finance function was to help managers maintain control of the business, but not hold it up. For example, Gribi often stressed that all finance staff must view themselves as a service organization. Rather than being judgmental or adversarial, finance could ensure that appropriate and necessary controls—but only those needed—were in place. White even felt that such control could be the opposite of constraint. It could help enable consistent, strong growth. The idea was "to get behind and push in the right direction." Finance could help managers by focusing on business issues, ideas, and concerns instead of just crunching the numbers.

Finance staff were assigned throughout Compaq as full members of cost-center business teams. They attended all key staff meetings, participated broadly in business decisions, and contributed in all areas, even product features. The finance representative raised financial issues for discussion, but in the context of the business issues at hand. This allowed appropriate controls to be in place without managers viewing them as outside interference in "their" business.

The finance staff formed a network of people who "have their fingers on the very pulse of the business. I have the best grapevine in Compaq," White joked. Because of their network, finance staff acted as communication links and coordinators across the various functions. Further, the flow of financial and business information up the hierarchy was ingrained in the very process of Compaq's operations. This helped make it possible to have only a limited number of regular formal reports. White could always use his networked PC if he needed more detailed information.

The key integrating meeting for the finance function itself was the monthly Corporate Forecast Review, attended by 15 to 20 top financial staff. Financial staff at international headquarters "attended" by phone for much of the four-hour meeting. Senior staff presented a corporatewide perspective on current financial and business issues, and issues specific to the finance function were discussed and resolved.

White summarized Compaq's view of financial control by citing the false dilemma of "whom should the controller report to?" He thought the controller needed broad involvement and had to be a full member of two teams: the cost-center business team and the financial team. Whom the controller reported to was less relevant. In fact,

finance was thinking of moving financial staffing costs out to the line organizations.

Cost-Center Management and Finance

The view of finance as a true support organization dovetailed closely with Compaq's philosophy of managerial responsibility. The basic idea was that authority and responsibility should go to the manager making the decisions. The cost-center manager was trusted to make major decisions for the business unit.

With authority to make decisions came responsibility for them. Cost-center managers were responsible for their unit's business performance—particularly the financial measures of its performance. They "owned" the numbers and presented them to their management. Cost-center managers had to be ready to explain the numbers and their impact on current programs and future performance. This made for particularly quick decisions, since managers were able to quickly understand relations between business alternatives and financial implications. (By contrast, in companies where the financial staff was responsible for and presented the numbers, White and Gribi thought managers had little knowledge of the numbers.) Working closely with the cost-center manager, the finance person on a manager's business team helped interpret the consequences of the cost center's business decisions, especially as related to Compaq's broad financial goals.

Top management took a relatively hands-off approach to most individual cost-center financial matters. The major areas they were directly involved in were decisions that were unalterable or that truly changed Compaq's financial position. For example, at Canion's weekly staff meetings, White presented financial updates that focused on the overall financial situation and key trends rather than individual cost-center performance.

Financial Forecasting

For Compaq, financial forecasting extended out only one year. Although longer-term planning was done for broad product strategy and facilities

EXHIBIT 4   Monthly Forecast Revision Process

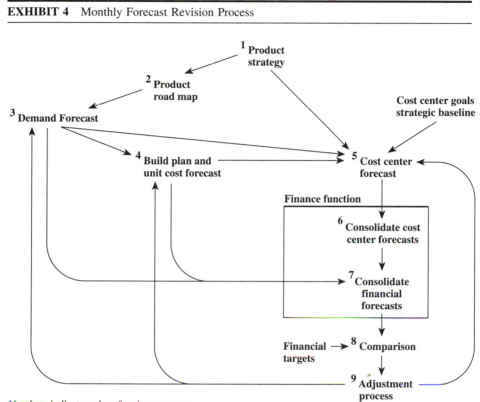

Numbers indicate order of main sequence

expansion, Compaq did not set detailed financial targets beyond one year because experience had taught that the business changed too fast for such planning to be meaningful. Financial forecasts were revised every month. Recent events in technology, markets, manufacturing, and operations were evaluated, and the forecast was brought into line with them. Frequent forecast revisions were forced by fast changes in Compaq's business. As Swavely said, "The only thing I'll guarantee you about the forecast is that it is wrong." Compaq also had an annual planning process, but it was better considered as an adjunct to the monthly planning process rather than entirely separate.

Monthly Forecasting

The major steps in the monthly forecast revision are shown in Exhibit 4. Compaq's "product road

map" detailed new products and introduction dates and was frequently updated, as part of product planning. Product specifications and expected introduction dates were quite firm in the near term (six months or less) and became less so beyond that.

The product road map and the current sales performance were used along with extensive industry competitive and market data to produce the demand forecast, which broke down expected sales by month and model. Demand forecasting was done on a rolling 12-month basis. Each month the 12th month out was added to the demand forecast.

The demand forecast was critical to Compaq's operations. If it was too aggressive, inventory would quickly accumulate. Forecasting conservatively had its own dangers: if sales and marketing based their staffing and spending on conservative demand estimates, they might not have the resources to achieve the maximum possible sales. Or if demand came in above the (conservative) forecast, manufacturing might not have the resources to meet that demand.

The demand forecast was built on a combination of extensive information and the judgment of Compaq managers. Current sales performance was a particularly important input. Field sales personnel entered dealer orders into the ASK system daily. Throughout each month, Swavely, his staff, and the financial staff monitored performance and assessed current and likely future demand conditions. They focused particularly closely on the performance of Compaq's top 25 dealers, who made up 90 percent of sales.

Information from all sources was brought together each month at the "demand forecast issues" meeting, where 15 to 20 people from across Compaq examined that month's issues. These ranged from market research on dealer sales and inventory levels to competitive new-product introductions and pricing changes. Meeting participants often challenged each other about the implications of issues and events. The issues meeting was meant mainly to develop baseline assumptions for the next step, the demand forecast finalization meeting. Teams were formed at the issues meeting to further investigate questions that could not be resolved in the meeting itself.

The finalization meeting was held two days after the issues meeting, with slightly fewer participants. The sales organization would have put together a provisional demand forecast to use as a starting point, based on the results of the issues meeting. At the finalization meeting, product demand estimates were adjusted based on the most up-to-date information and judgments Compaq could gather.

The demand forecast became the main input to manufacturing, which revised the "build plan" every month. The build plan specified production levels by model and month for each manufacturing facility.

Product pricing and product costs were also forecast for the period covered by the demand forecast. A small team of marketing and finance staff drew on Compaq's formal price change approval system, market and competitive analyses, and product introduction plans to develop pricing forecasts by model and month. The unit cost forecast, specifying expected costs for each model in each month, was closely linked with the build plan. Finance coordinated development of this forecast with the help of purchasing, engineering, manufacturing, and marketing. The forecast incorporated expected cost changes, such as component pricing reductions.

The product road map, strategic objectives, build plan, and demand forecast were all used by different cost centers for financial planning. Each of the 400 cost centers estimated its requirements to meet both strategic and its own "baseline" objectives. Strategic objectives were set by top management; for example, Compaq was implementing a companywide total quality commitment program in 1990. Baseline objectives were the daily routine tasks the cost center was charged with. Cost-center resource requirements were broken down by month into detailed categories, including expected capital expenditures. Cost-center planning used Lotus 1-2-3 spreadsheets as what-if tools and Microcontrol networked planning software as the main data collection and transmission tool.

Finance consolidated cost-center forecasts using Microcontrol software, which also had provisions for easy collection and consolidation of Lotus spreadsheet data. The consolidated forecast used less detailed categories than individual cost-center forecasts. Finance combined the consolidated cost-center forecasts with expected revenues from the demand and pricing forecasts and with expected manufacturing costs from the build plan and unit-cost forecast. The result was projections for the income statement and some key balance sheet lines.

Compaq executives shared beliefs about appropriate target levels of expenses in broad categories like G&A, R&D, marketing, and sales, as well as appropriate profitability levels. These beliefs, developed through their extensive experience in the industry and at Compaq, summarized their conception of how the business should be run and were formalized as a "financial model" in which the targets were expressed as a percentage of revenues. The target expense and profit levels had historically changed with the business environment. For example, beliefs about the appropriate level of R&D expenditures had gradually been revised upward as products became ever more complex.

Financial projections were compared against the financial model, with the key targets being the gross margin and the profit-after-tax percentage, and the projected earnings per share. Measures like ROI or ROC were not used at this overall level, for managers were convinced these measures were ineffective in a fast-growth environment like Compaq's.

If financial projections were not within acceptable ranges on key targets, they were adjusted. This process started with members of Canion's team, who worked the issues within their own unit to determine what tradeoffs were required to reduce expenses. Some expense reductions could usually be made without putting Compaq at significant risk. If target percentages could not be met this way, the whole top management team discussed the issue. For example, if Swavely asked his managers to cut $8 million, he would also ask them, "Tell me what you have to do that's stupid." If the cuts required did not pass this "do what makes sense" test, he would not ask his managers to make them. Instead, he would bring the issue back to the full top management team. Another function might be able to make up the shortfall. Alternatively, the financial forecasts could be approved, knowing that the target percentages would not be met. The decision would be made to consider this an "investment" period, during which lower returns would be accepted temporarily.

Annual Planning

This process involved gradually extending the time horizon of the monthly forecasts, so that by January of each year an annual plan for the year was completed. Annual planning started in June. By then, the demand forecast extended through the first half of the next calendar year, for it was done on a true rolling-12-month basis. But the build plan and cost-center forecasts were done on a calendar-year basis, so they would be projected only to the end of the current calendar year. In June the build plan and cost-center forecasts were extended to incorporate the first quarter of the next calendar year, and in July, the second quarter. By September, preliminary forecasts of the entire next calendar year had been made. The discrepancy in time horizons between the demand forecasts and the build plan/cost-center forecasts was at times inconvenient; moving the latter to a 12-month rolling basis was being considered in early 1990.

Early in January of the new year, the annual plan was completed and fixed. After that, the plan was used mainly within the financial function as a stable base to compare against as the year developed. The monthly forecasts, not the plan, were the main management tool.

Forecasting versus Budgeting

Canion said everyone understood the financial forecast was more of a starting direction than a fixed goal. Keeping things balanced as events changed was critically important. As forecasts changed each month, management made changes at whatever level was appropriate: strategy, product programs, marketing and sales programs, staffing, or even capital spending.

White emphasized that to call the financial forecast a budget was misleading, for a budget implied a fixed constraint. For example, cost-center forecasts were forward-looking control mechanisms, simply a manager's statement that "this is what I will do," and were subject to revision. Finance staff were less likely to consider the forecast a budget than were operations staff, who tended to say they had a budget while acknowledging that it changed as needed. There was no formal comparison against last year's performance internally.

Flexibility through Forecast Revisions

Although the monthly revision was time-consuming, it helped Compaq respond to market changes quickly and flexibly and had given top managers a very sophisticated, measured understanding of the business. White, Schempf, and other financial staff monitored overall progress against the forecast almost daily. A sophisticated what-if model enabled quick estimation of current performance's effects on financial forecasts. The model contained a projected income statement, balance sheet, cash-flow statement, and key indices and ratios; it was updated as soon as information was available. Information was gathered from many sources, including weekly status meetings in various functions, pricing actions, and demand-forecast updates from weekly sales-status meetings.

Results from the what-if model were constantly reviewed with an eye to action. Variances against the forecast were analyzed particularly carefully, with the critical question being: was this a one-time anomaly, or was a new trend emerging? White reported findings and concerns to the management team at Canion's weekly staff meetings, allowing them to react intelligently to events almost immediately.

For example, unforeseen circumstances during the fourth quarter of 1989 resulted in sales significantly below forecast levels. The decline was not evident until the start of the quarter's second month. White worked with top management to reduce expenses successfully without harming the business. As a result, Compaq came far closer to meeting its profit goals than would otherwise have been possible.

But Canion emphasized he would not go too far just to reach financial goals. Even if forecasts were not being met, it was important to maintain Compaq's consistency in decisions and to safeguard its image and "tone." Top management would act after considering both these factors and financial goals. For example, they might accept temporarily lower profit margins during development of a new product if they felt it would improve the com-

pany's long-term health, instead of simply reacting with an austerity program aimed at narrow cost-saving goals.

Different Approaches to Financial Control and Measurement

Individual top managers used financial controls and treated financial measures in different ways. Canion himself looked at only a very few financial measures. He relied on White to present important financial information and issues at Canion's weekly staff meeting.

Swavely "managed to the forecast," since performance against the demand forecast was an appropriate measure for his sales teams. Expenses were managed to a percentage of conservatively judged revenues; the level of "judged" revenues was based on a somewhat lower sales level than that in the demand forecast.

Swavely viewed the financial organization as "the glue that holds Compaq together," rather than as a constraint. For him, current financial data were the "backbone," which along with up-to-date market and competitive information was key to making specific decisions. He carried a quick-reference binder filled with information to every meeting (Exhibit 5); other senior managers had similar binders.

Vieau called White and the financial function "the conscience" of the business. White and the financial people in Vieau's group checked if manufacturing was meeting financial expectations; if it was not, they gave "guidance." The manufacturing business team took this information and did its best to adjust its plans. But cost was only the fifth of manufacturing's priorities (Exhibit 6).

Financial controls were least complex in the engineering functions. Stimac in systems engineering used headcount and development project priorities as his main measures, since most of his other expenses were directly related to them. Harris in engineering relied on finance staff to let him know about problems; when there were none, he focused on product development.

EXHIBIT 5   Swavely's Quick-Reference Binder
Sections

- Expense and people forecast.
- Financial data (P&Ls).
- Storeboard (market research).
- International data.
- Market share, size, and growth data.
- Sales, inventory, and channel analysis.
- Demand forecast.
- Price forecast.
- Product road maps.
- Weekly staff reports.
- Financial models (what if?).
- Press releases.
- Canada.
- Service.

EXHIBIT 6   Manufacturing Priorities (in order)

1. Product quality.
2. Short delivery cycle.
3. Short product introduction cycle.
4. Flexibility for mix changes.
5. Product cost.
6. Flexibility for volume change.
7. Asset use.

International Financial Controls

The geographically dispersed nature of Compaq's international operations led the headquarters staff to emphasize financial procedures and controls somewhat more than in the United States. International headquarters was farther away from the countries and could not take corrective action as quickly or easily.

Compaq's international financial forecasting process was similar to that used in the United States, though the target expense percentages were more formally specified. Each country subsidiary's forecasts were compared against the target percentages individually. Larger, more mature subsidiaries were expected to have lower expenses, on a percentage-of-revenue basis. Andreas Barth, managing director, Central Europe, stressed that for him the most important number in the financial model was the total expense percentage he was allowed. As long as he met that target, he felt he was basically meeting expectations.

The forecasts were consolidated in Munich. Before sending them to Houston, Pfeiffer made his own judgment of them, increasing or decreasing the overall demand projections.

Performance Measurement

Canion described Compaq's performance measurement as being "almost the opposite of an MBO [management by objectives] system." He treated numbers and concrete results as a starting point and tried to understand the driving forces at work. Performance measures were intentionally not that objective. Canion believed this helped managers maintain a broad vision and prevented them from "optimizing their personal goals rather than the company's." He believed working closely with people was the key to developing the knowledge necessary to make this approach work.

By not focusing too closely on results as such, Compaq tried to encourage people to be innovative and to do what made sense. Whether Canion was dealing with a failure or a success, he tried to analyze the results the same way. It was almost more important for the proper process to be followed than simply for goals to be met.

Vieau said Compaq asked extraordinary things of its people, so if people failed to meet goals, they were not punished. When a project failed, the question was "Did we do all that we could?" If the answer was yes, a "project should not feel like it was a failure."

Vieau also felt that commitment, not goals, led to achievement: "Goal attainment is deemphasized a little. If we had set more goals, I don't think we would have been so successful. A goal of $20 million in sales in 1983 would have seemed unrealistic; instead we made $111 million through commitment and following our process." Canion felt it was important to keep a feeling of success; he preferred to have realistic goals rather than extremely aggressive ones. White said Compaq limited "sandbagging" (presenting too easily achieved forecasts) by deemphasizing simply "making your numbers" and by revising forecasts monthly. He was adamant about the particularly high importance of this: "If someone was to 'sandbag' and so the company spent less elsewhere, it would be unconscionable." It could also disrupt information sharing and teamwork, which were central to Compaq's operations.

An important part of each manager's performance assessment was his/her own ability to manage according to cultural precepts, and how well he/she was training his/her people about the culture and its processes. The culture's emphasis on team performance was also evident. When asked, "How do you know you are doing a good job?" most managers first talked about how they knew whether their team was doing a good job; several said separation of team and individual performance was very difficult.

Compaq's formal performance appraisals varied in format and importance across different functions. For example, Stimac asked his reports to rate their five weaknesses and five strengths and to rate themselves on performance toward quarterly goals. Stimac rated his reports the same way; then he and the manager compared the ratings.

Internationally, measuring performance had been quite difficult. The country subsidiaries had consistently exceeded their goals. Pfeiffer said it was hard to criticize a country manager—whose main goal was a sales target—when that target had been exceeded by a considerable margin. Like Canion, Pfeiffer tried to get beyond numbers. In particular he focused on ascertaining whether a subsidiary was being managed consistently with Compaq's culture and procedures, in addition to meeting its sales targets.

Compensation

Compaq set salaries using job grades in relatively standard fashion. The goal was for Compaq's pay levels to be in the top quartile of industry pay averages. It also had an annual cash bonus system. Bonuses were drawn from a corporate pool, the size of which was determined by profitability and comparison with other companies' bonus policies. Again, the goal was for Compaq to be in the top quartile in the industry. Compaq's growth and profitability had allowed the bonus pool to grow consistently.

Bonuses were based on individual performance, contribution (the impact of an individual's actions on company performance), and position. They could be a significant portion of the annual salary of some managers and key individual contributors. Half the bonus was based on performance during the past year, and half on future potential. The idea was to reward both current and future talent and key long-term managers. Basing the bonus on position and contribution allowed it to grow as an individual's capabilities grew.

Stock options were also perceived as very important for motivating a long-term growth perspective. The idea was for people to start thinking of Compaq's money as their own. Every employee received a stock option package, with the size and frequency of awards being based on salary, position, contribution, and potential. Gribi said that if you included stock options, "you won't find a better total compensation package than Compaq, anywhere." The return on the stock had been exceptional (Exhibit 7).

The salary, ranking, and bonus systems used internationally were all similar to U.S. ones, although cross-country equity in compensation was an important additional consideration.

Interestingly, Compaq's top management often deemphasized the importance of compensation and incentives. Several said it was important that pay levels and bonuses be perceived as fair, but Stimac summarized the prevailing view: "Once a certain level [of overall pay] is achieved, financial incentives have a diminishing return." Working with good management, having fun, and making personal accomplishments were all mentioned as additional important reasons people enjoyed coming to work each day.

EXHIBIT 7 Compaq Stock Prices, 1984–1989 (Bars Indicate High and Low for Year)

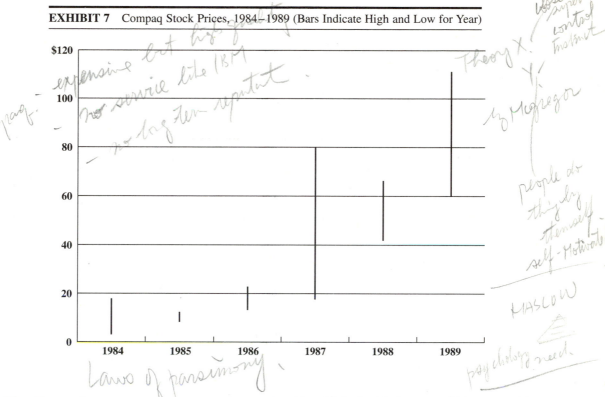

Looking Forward

Compaq faced several challenges in early 1990. The overall U.S. PC market was maturing, with market growth expected to slow to less than 10 percent in 1990, although growth in the international market was expected to continue at a faster pace for some time. Compaq had also attained such size and market share that growth rates would inevitably come down from historical levels. But Compaq's growth was expected to still be faster than overall PC market growth, due to its participation in high-growth segments of that market.

Canion was upbeat. He believed Compaq would still have considerable room to maneuver within its traditional markets, using the dealer channel. He thought the most important challenges would be internal. Several top managers, including Can-

ion himself, had said that one of his most critical roles was as Compaq's "conscience." He was constantly looking for things that might go wrong. His concerns were evident as he assessed Compaq's challenges in early 1990: "The number-one lethal disease is the overconfidence that comes with success. The biggest danger is to stop looking back, to stop understanding the real reasons for our successes." Improper analysis of success could lead to "assumptions that become 'killers' down the road." It was critical that people not stop looking back, that they continue to examine why a particular project was successful and why another failed. For Canion, the key was hard work and maintaining consistency, knowing what was going on at all times. For him, Compaq's business had been, and would remain, a "game of inches."

Chapter 4

Introduction to IT Architecture

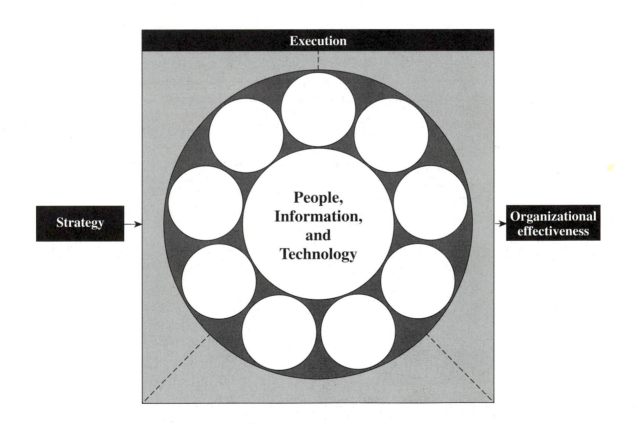

158

INTRODUCTION

Information technologies (IT)—computer-based hardware and software tools—store, transport, and transform data into meaningful information. An *IT architecture* specifies the tools that will be utilized and the structures and processes by which data and applications will be acquired or developed and made available to users. The components of an IT architecture, and the process of developing it, are discussed in the first half of this chapter. Two cases—Air Products and Chemicals, Inc.: Project ICON and Symantec—are then presented to illustrate issues in achieving a coherent IT architecture.

Information technologies are unlike the equipment that drove the Industrial Revolution in two important aspects. The first is *flexibility*: while older industrial equipment was constrained by the laws of physics, newer IT tools are constrained primarily by our ability to identify useful applications, develop them, and put them to effective use. The second difference is the *pace of change*: successive generations of hardware and software tools very rapidly render IT investments obsolete.

Information is a critical resource. Accurate, timely, and relevant operating information improves organizational effectiveness by improving its members' communication and understanding. Information is the "glue" that connects functions, divisions, projects, processes, within the firm and between a firm and its suppliers, customers, and others.

Data, the "raw material" from which information is constructed, is a *nondepletable resource:* unlike capital and physical materials, data may be used repeatedly. IT decreases the costs of acquiring, transforming, and transmitting data and increases its accuracy, timeliness, and availability. However, because data is nondepletable and easily shared, investments in IT can lead to information overload and conflicting data. Organizations that effectively harness IT reap the benefits of improved access to timely information, while minimizing problems of information overload and conflicting data.

159

Choices about IT have fundamentally changed the way some business is conducted. For example, United and American Airlines, which took the lead in developing computer-based reservation systems, reaped impressive gains in market share and profits. Airlines that jumped in too late or chose not to participate in this IT revolution—such as Frontier and People's Express—are now permanently grounded.

In the tough economy of the 1990s, some companies have survived by using IT to redesign business processes and slash payrolls without sacrificing productivity. For example, from 1980 to 1990 the US paper industry increased output by 30 percent while eliminating 245,000 jobs.[1] This IT-enabled downsizing, which is occurring in both the manufacturing and service sectors, is causing managers to take a fresh look at management controls, organizational structure, human resources policies—and their own resumes.

Managers' choices of when and what IT tools and data to acquire or applications to develop are complex. This chapter outlines the range of choices, and the fundamentals of designing an appropriate and flexible IT architecture.

THE NEED FOR AN IT ARCHITECTURE

An IT architecture defines the policies and guidelines that govern the arrangement of IT tools and data. By establishing a logical, coherent plan, an IT architecture ensures that decisions about technology investment and use are in keeping with corporate strategy and capabilities. For example, if corporate strategy aims for fast-cycle custom manufacturing capability, it follows that marketing, sales, engineering, and manufacturing will need mechanisms for tight coordination. An IT architecture can support tight coordination by specifying how issues of systems compatibility, interconnection, and integration will be accomplished.

Consider the IT architecture at Dartmouth College. John Kemeny, the president of Dartmouth from 1970 to 1981, articulated a consistent vision of using information technology to support undergraduate instruction. In contrast, at some other universities, the strategy was to use IT primarily to support administrative or research tasks. When competing requests for technology purchases at Dartmouth were presented, those proposals that would support instruction received higher priority than, for example, highly specialized research computing facilities. A standard hardware platform—offering a consistent graphical user interface and cross-program compatibility—was selected to simplify the delivery of instructional applications. Dartmouth's IT architecture was guided by a clearly articulated vision.

Where an architecture has not been clearly defined, there is often high uncertainty and conflict in determining what tools and data to acquire. Information sharing may be difficult because incompatible software and hardware are selected by separate

---

[1] Anonymous, "Paper and Paperboard" *The Wall Street Journal* (January 28, 1993: p. A1).

organizational units. Proliferation of products can lead to unwieldy service organizations, lost opportunities for volume discounts, and underutilized equipment.

The term *architecture* is a useful metaphor. To build a skyscraper, owners start with a vision of a building that will meet their needs. They work with an architect who translates the vision into a construction plan. Contractors assemble the resources necessary to create the specified structure. The owners did not need expertise in steel girders and structural engineering, but they did need to have a clear idea of the functional characteristics of the building, and enough understanding of design basics to communicate the vision to the architect. Similarly, senior executives do not need highly technical expertise in computer science, but they do need to clearly articulate for the information architect their business strategy, organization structure, management control systems, and related IT requirements.

The skyscraper metaphor falls short, however, in conveying the level of uncertainty in specifying information requirements. Building owners stand on fairly solid ground (pun intended) when they predict how the building will be used. In contrast, executives face a less certain future when designing an IT architecture. New hardware and software may render earlier investments obsolete. Their firm may become the target of a takeover, or may acquire another firm. They may abandon some lines of business and pursue new opportunities. Lawmakers may impose or release regulations. Just as organization structure and management control systems evolve to keep pace with changing conditions, an IT architecture must also be sufficiently flexible and adaptable to accommodate to technical, strategic, and environmental changes over time.

IT ARCHITECTURE: BASIC BUILDING BLOCKS

Figure 4-1 depicts the foundations of an IT architecture—tools and basic operations.

FIGURE 4-1   Foundations of an IT Architecture

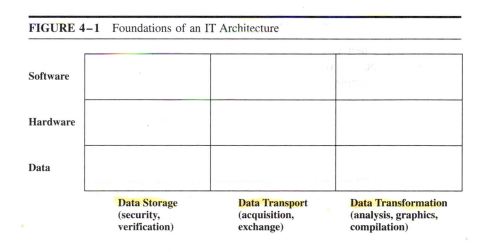

	Data Storage (security, verification)	Data Transport (acquisition, exchange)	Data Transformation (analysis, graphics, compilation)
Software			
Hardware			
Data			

FIGURE 4–2   When Data Become Management Information . . .

Currency pricing information helps a finance manager put corporate cash to best use.

Quality information—numbers, graphs, still photographs, video—help a manufacturing manager identify and fix problems in fabrication and assembly processes.

Scholarly information helps an R&D manager become aware of scientific discoveries that might be incorporated into the firm's products or operations.

Retail sales reports, superimposed on mapping software, help managers identify stores that are underperforming, and identify the problem (e.g., location? employee turnover?).

Focus group videos help a marketing manager determine new product specifications.

Tools: Data, Hardware, Software

Data.   Data include numbers, graphs, text, still and moving images (animation, video), and sound. Data originate in many nondigital media, all of which can be converted to digital form. Data in digital form can be represented by a machine language comprised of combinations of 1s and 0s, each of which in the computer becomes the discrete presence or absence of a signal. ASCII is a coding scheme for representing letters and numbers in machine code. PICT form, another format, represents an image as pixels that are turned on or off.

Paper media—correspondence, invoices, reports—can be converted to digital form. A facsimile machine converts documents into digital form for transmission over a telephone line; the receiving fax machine converts it back to an image on paper. Optical imaging systems—successors to microfilm and microfiche devices—convert extensive paper records into compact digital images. If the text is printed in a standard font, the document can also be converted into ASCII.

Analog media capture conversations, music, other sounds (e.g., wind, water flow, pulse rate) and video on tape. Data in analog form are represented as waves along a continuum, rather than discrete on/off signals. A modem (modulator/demodulator) converts analog data to digital form by identifying peaks and valleys of wave signals. Older televisions and telephones are analog devices, but these and the networks on which their signals are transported are being rapidly converted to digital form. Data become "information" when they are analyzed and interpreted; that is, given meaning (see Figure 4–2).

Hardware.   Computer systems are classified by size and speed into four categories: microcomputers, minicomputers, mainframes, and supercomputers. Few companies have the resources or expertise to acquire and manage supercomputers, which are very fast and costly. Some companies form consortia to acquire and maintain these systems. Mainframe computers are large systems that typically handle very large corporate databases and transaction-processing applications. Minicomputers provide midrange (moderate-sized databases and transaction processing) or specialized computing capabilities. Microcomputers, introduced to most businesses in the 1980s, were first acquired for stand-alone personal productivity applications, such as word processing and electronic spreadsheets. Increasing numbers of powerful microprocessor-based workstations are being acquired and networked so that users can readily share information. Many firms have shifted to client-server computing, a technique in which a "server" microcomputer provides software and/or data to link "client" PCs as needed. Client-server applications are replacing many mainframe applications.

Organizations base their computer purchase decisions on technical performance issues (e.g., processing speed, input/output speed, capacity), price, and organizational issues such as the relative importance of data integration and sharing, centralized versus decentralized control, and other concerns. The distinctions among computer categories are blurring. For example, researchers are linking many microprocessors together to achieve processing speeds that rival supercomputers.

Regardless of its classification, every computer system includes one or more *central processors* and one or more *input, output, and secondary storage devices*. These hardware components may be connected to additional devices by means of a network.

Central Processors. Large-scale integration (LSI) replaced the intricate wire connections of early mainframes with a CPU on a silicon microchip the size of your fingernail. Today, CPUs are embedded in household appliances, automotive antilock braking systems, and numerous other everyday items.

Computers convert data to binary (0 or 1) digits. Machine language is expressed in bytes, each of which consists of eight binary digits. Binary digits are converted to electrical currents called *digital signals*. The *central processing unit (CPU)* consists of electronic circuits that carry out instructions in machine language and control the devices attached to it. The CPU contains three major components:

Main control unit: Supervises programs and operations.

Arithmetic logic unit (ALU): does calculations, logical comparisons.

Read-only memory (ROM): contains hard-wired instructions for starting and keeping the computer running.

The hard-wired instructions and data stored in ROM are not lost when the machine is turned off. In contrast, RAM (random access memory), which is contained within or connected to the CPU, temporarily holds data or application programs currently being processed. RAM size is an important determinant of a microcomputer's speed. The first IBM PC used an Intel 8086 chip, which processed fewer than 500,000 instructions per second. The Intel 80586 chip, the Pentium, introduced in 1993, has 3 million transistors. It processes 100 million instructions per second, enabling enhanced multimedia input and output, increased memory capacity, and multitasking capabilities.

Input, Output, and Secondary Storage Devices. *Input devices,* such as keyboards, mice, joysticks, digital gloves, and light pens, capture and enter data into the computer. Other common input devices include optical scanners, optical character readers

(OCR), sensing devices (to record temperature, fluid flow, resistance, etc.), and speech recognition devices.

Secondary storage devices include floppy, hard, and CD-ROM diskettes—commonly used with microcomputers—and DASD (direct access storage devices), which are used with mainframes and minicomputers. The cost of storing data has dropped dramatically, thanks to techniques for compressing data on magnetic and optical media. A floppy diskette holds about a megabyte (1 million bytes) of data, a hard disk holds 200 or more megabytes, and optical media such as CD-ROM can store 500 megabytes or more.

Output devices include monitors, terminals, printers, plotters, projectors, and sound devices. Multimedia computer systems may include the capability to input, output, and edit full-motion video, stereophonic music, and artificial speech (voice synthesis).

Network devices connect components within and across systems so that digital data can be sent between them. Network devices include computer-based "traffic managers" such as routers, multiplexors, and PBX (private branch exchanges), and the wire or optical media over which the data traffic passes. *Bandwidth,* the carrying capacity of a network link, determines the speed at which data can be transmitted, how many separate communication exchanges can share the link, and, consequently, the practical range of applications it can support. Numbers, text, and sounds are "low-bandwidth" data; they can be sent rapidly over a narrow transmission channel such as twisted-pair wire, which is common to older telephone systems (1,200 to 56,000 bits per second). Images and graphics are "medium-bandwidth" data, and video is "high-bandwidth." Coaxial cable is a medium-bandwidth channel, and fiber-optic, at 2.5 billion bits per second, offers very high bandwidth. Airwave channels, such as microwave, cellular, and radio-frequency transmission, are rapidly growing to accommodate portable computing needs.

Networks are classified into local-area networks (LANs), which are geographically close (within a building or across a small campus), and wide-area networks (WANs), which connect distant locations and may combine cable, microwave, and satellite transmission. WANs are further classified as *public, value-added,* or *private* networks. *Public* networks such as AT&T and MCI, also called *common carriers,* include general-access dial-up lines and leased lines. Dial-up lines have a higher error rate and a slower transmission rate than leased lines. Value-added networks (VANs), such as Tymnet and Telenet, provide enhanced network services, such as gateways between equipment with dissimilar protocols over leased lines from common carriers. VANs give firms the high data-transport capabilities they need without the management overhead. *Private WANs* may use dedicated lines or less expensive, very small-aperture terminal satellites (VSAT).

Software.   Computer devices are directed by software, which consist of sets of instructions that are translated into *machine language* (strings of 1s and 0s triggering on/off states), which the machine executes. First-generation programmers laboriously coded in machine language. Assembler code substitutes simple words like ADD and GET for machine language, but its very limited vocabulary requires programmers to be very specific in instructing the computer to perform operations. *Higher-level languages* (COBOL, C, BASIC) substitute words for sequences of assembler code, so machine code can be generated with fewer commands. *Translators* and *compilers* convert these higher-level instructions to machine code. Very high-level languages are closer to natural English. Object-oriented languages represent sets of operations or data as "objects." For example, in Microsoft Windows (on an IBM-compatible computer) or on an Apple Macintosh, a user clicks on an icon representing a printer to initiate the sequence of instructions that result in data being sent to the printer, translated into instructions, and printed. Generally, lower-level languages are harder to use, but skilled programmers can create efficient code with them.

Applications software—such as a payroll program or a spreadsheet package—instructs the computer to perform user functions. *System software* allocates processing resources between executing programs and handles the flow of data between computing devices. Operating systems, such as MS-DOS or OS/2 for IBM-compatibles and System 7 for Macintoshes, are examples of system software. Operating environments, such as Microsoft Windows, are system software that work in tandem with operating systems. The programs that control data communications are also system software.

Software *standards* make it possible for designers to develop compatible software products. This benefit is traded off against nonstandard design breakthroughs. For example, MS-DOS, long the personal computer standard in business, does not take advantage of the larger RAM size and faster speeds of newer chips. IBM has attempted to move its customers to a newer operating system, OS/2. Microsoft, formerly an IBM partner that developed MS-DOS and now a competitor, has encouraged users to stay on DOS with the addition of its Windows product. Meanwhile, Apple Computer is trying to sway IBM users over to Macintoshes, and other firms are promoting newer operating systems such as PenPoint. The most technically advanced software does not necessarily become a standard.

Software may be purchased commercially ("off the shelf" or "packaged" software) or developed in-house ("custom" software). Software development, despite systematic methodologies and automated development tools (computer-assisted software engineering, or CASE) is rather unpredictable, giving rise to two widespread problems. First, software projects are notoriously difficult to plan and monitor; significant delays and cost overruns are common. Second, new versions of packaged software are often announced by vendors well before they are completed and debugged; this "vaporware" problem makes it hard for managers to plan for upgrades.

The line between hardware and software is not as distinct as the above discussion implies. Machine instructions can be hardwired onto chips, and many devices—such as pocket spell-checkers—use no external software. At the same time, the cost of RAM and secondary storage has decreased so dramatically that highly compact and efficient code is less critical. Since programs are easier to change and update than hardware, many functions that used to be hard-wired are now in the software.

Basic Operations

We have described the foundation components—data, hardware, and software. We next describe the basic operations they support, which fall into three categories: data storage, data transport, and data transformation.

Technology Generations

This section summarizes the evolution of information technologies over five decades. The pace of technological change has not always been linear and predictable. Some IT developments created periods of *technological discontinuity*. Indeed, advancement of information technologies has occurred at nearly blinding speed in comparison with other technologies. What in the 1940s weighed five tons, took up six rooms, processed about 10,000 instructions per second, and cost about $5 million, now may sit on your desk, process at 50 MHz or faster, and cost less than $2,000. And in two more years, it will seem rather slow and stodgy!

1940s and 1950s

The ENIAC, produced in 1945, was the first general-purpose, stored-program digital computer. Programming was in machine language, and 18,000 vacuum tubes performed 333 operations per second. Univac II, the first business computer, was introduced in 1952. FORTRAN, the first high-level language, was introduced in 1956. Also in 1956, the US Justice Department barred AT&T from computer-related activities, a decision that significantly impeded networked computer applications.

1960s

Transistors replaced vacuum tubes, and magnetic-core memory made it possible to efficiently store and retrieve programs and data. The IBM 360 was introduced in 1964, launching the dominant family of upwardly compatible mainframe computers. IBM set the standard for marketing large computers. Punched cards were primarily used for input, but keyboard entry and cathode-ray tubes subsequently replaced card readers. Operating systems were developed to handle input/output, file allocation, and other tasks. COBOL, the most widely used business programming language, was developed in 1960. Time sharing, interactive real-time computing, and multiprogramming (processing several programs simultaneously) were developed to use expensive computing resources more efficiently. Long-distance data transmission was made possible by Telstar, the first communications satellite, which was launched in 1962.

1970s

Integrated circuits, first developed in 1971, quickly led to a new product—the pocket calculator. By the end of the decade, very large-scale integration placed hundreds of thousands of circuits on a chip, including all the circuitry of a CPU. Minicomputers, produced by Digital Equipment Corporation and Wang Labs, were in high demand, and so-called "distributed processing" (in which minicomputers were housed and managed in user departments rather than the corporate data center) was an alternative to centralized, mainframe computing. Many programming languages and applications tools (for querying databases, doing statistical analysis, etc.) were introduced, offering more efficient code generation but new compatibility problems. Database management systems were rapidly developed—hierarchical models at the beginning of the decade, and relational by its end.

Technology Generations (*Continued*)

1980s

This was the decade of the microcomputer. The IBM PC, introduced in August 1981, dominated the business market for several years, until low-cost "clones" were introduced. The first electronic spreadsheet, Visicalc, gave nontechnical business users a reason to acquire desktop computers. A second wave of PC buyers was drawn to word processing software. Intel and Motorola introduced faster, better microprocessors every two to three years, creating a highly turbulent personal computing market. The Apple Macintosh, introduced in 1984, whetted users' appetites for a graphical interface that was consistent across applications. Hard disks and optical media expanded data storage capabilities. Supercomputers offered speeds of 500 million instructions per second and faster, enabling highly complex computations. Deregulation of the telephone industry in 1983 stimulated networked computing initiatives. Progress was made in developing data communication standards, and fiber optics enabled high bandwidth transmission capabilities.

1990s

Smaller, faster, cheaper, easier—the trends continue. The CPU and computer memory have continued to evolve most rapidly, followed by secondary storage devices and software development languages and techniques. Stepping back from the details, we can observe the following overall technology trends:

1. The time between developing a new technology and its practical use is becoming shorter, as is its useful life. This has major implications for both vendor and customer strategies.
2. Information technologies are available to many more individuals. In the 1940s and 1950s, computers were accessible only to a small group of pioneers. In the 1960s and 1970s, they were the domain of computer scientists and MIS professionals. By the 1980s, the PC was a ubiquitous appliance sitting on 50 million desks in the United States alone.
3. Thanks to very large-scale integration, information technologies are now embedded in other devices—elevators, automobiles, and coffee makers, for example. IT pervades an increasing range of activities and goods.
4. The legal and technical lines that used to separate telephones, televisions, copiers, and computers no longer exist. In the all-digital era, new devices will take their place.

Data Storage. Data storage includes verifying the *accuracy,* ensuring the *viability,* determining who will have *access,* and protecting the *security* of data resources. Inaccurate data cannot be transformed into meaningful information. Someone must decide on an accuracy standard (e.g., how many digits of precision for numeric data) and a process for verifying data accuracy (e.g., who is responsible for verification; what software code should be used to prevent or resolve data "collisions" in real-time, multi-user systems), and timeliness (e.g., how often will the database be updated; how will users verify the update version they are viewing). Data *viability* refers to the value of the data. Although data storage costs have declined dramatically, retrieval can be costly when users must navigate through unnecessarily large databases. Hence, data storage processes must include measures for periodically and systematically purging data that are outdated, inaccurate, or no longer useful.

Data management software and techniques have evolved to handle these and other data storage issues. There are two important principles of data management. First, data are *separable* from applications. Early-generation systems did not employ this principle; the applications programs defined the data they would operate upon. A single data item could exist in multiple locations, leading to redundancies and inaccuracies (where data conflict, which is the "right" item?). This greatly inhibited data sharing and caused other problems. For example, in many firms the first-generation payroll systems defined "employee number" as a four-digit field. That worked fine as long as the firm had no more than 9,999 employees. When employee number 10,000 was hired, the four-digit field had to be adjusted in every application in which it was used—a costly and common exercise for many companies.

The second principle is that data definitions are *durable.* That is, the definitions of data used by an organization, if *well specified at the outset,* are stable over time, even though the actual data may be volatile. Hence, once an organization has undergone a rigorous process of specifying data definitions and relationships, and established a data administration function, ongoing modifications are reasonably straightforward. Data managed according to these principles are readily accessible for transformation into meaningful, timely information. Unfortunately, many organizations did not take that first step and now apply Band-Aid solutions to serious data management problems.

Many organizations have data stored in *hierarchical* database management systems, which are analogous to traditional file cabinet systems (first locate the file cabinet, then the drawer, the folder, the document, and finally the data item). Hierarchical databases work well for predefined searches that conform to the file structure (such as, "find all books written by this author"). However, data retrieval is slow or impossible when the query involves complex logic or a search that does not start at the top of the hierarchy (e.g., "find all books written before 1980 and containing the word *computers* in the title and published by Irwin"). A more recent approach, *relational* database management, stores data in a more flexible form. Examples of relational DBMS are DB2, INGRES, and ORACLE for mainframes and RBase and Paradox for microcomputers. Using techniques based in set theory (relational algebra) data in separate files can be easily extracted and combined, as long as they share common fields, or "relational keys." But retrieval can be slower than in a hierarchical database. *Hypertext* systems enable even greater flexibility in managing data, since any hypertext data element can be related to any other data element. However, systematic methodologies for developing and maintaining hypertext databases (which would be the equivalent of relational algebra), have not yet emerged. Lately, *object-oriented* databases have also emerged. This approach adds efficiency and flexibility by treating images, film clips, groups of data or programs, and so on, as objects that can be accessed and manipulated as single units. Software designers are also working on techniques that produce the rapid retrieval possible in hierarchical databases while preserving the flexibility of relational, hypertext, and object-oriented databases.

Data access and security issues are becoming more critical in firms with matrix, hybrid, or network organizational structures, and/or firms confronting high uncertainty and rapid change. In hierarchical organizations, data access could be specified according to reporting relationships and other readily identifiable criteria. In stable environments, disputes over data access could be resolved in an orderly fashion. This is now a time-consuming luxury that many organizations can no longer afford. Access to the right data at the right time by the right people may mean the difference between winning or losing a bid, identifying and fixing a small problem before it becomes a big one, and jumping on a profitable opportunity ahead of the competition.

Data Transport.   Data transport describes the processes involved in *obtaining* and *exchanging* data and information, including sending/receiving digital information, and converting analog or paper to digital or digital to paper or analog. Data transport may occur between similar or dissimilar computers, computers and peripheral devices, and computers and telephones, video machines, tape recorders, and so forth.

The simplest forms of data transport are keyboard input and "sneakernet" (copying data onto a diskette and walking it over to another computer). Sneakernet requires that either the data be stored in a form compatible with the target application, or that the target application contains conversion utilities that can make it so. Online data transport requires other levels of compatibility.

The open system interconnect (OSI) model (Figure 4–3) was proposed by the International Standards Organization with a goal of making network choices vendor-independent, but that ideal has not yet been realized. The model describes seven network "layers," for which standards are being negotiated. For each layer of the OSI model, competing technologies exist. For example, *network protocols* specify how data get compressed for sending over a channel and decompressed by the receiving computer. Two popular LAN protocols are Ethernet and Token Ring. Electronic Data Interchange (EDI) protocols specify the form and process by which two or more organizations will exchange data. WAN protocols include international communication standards such as X.21, X.25 and X.75. The ISDN protocol (Integrated Services Data Network), which has been widely adopted in Japan and France but less so in the United States, specifies standards for transmitting voice, data, graphics, and video over the same transmission channel. New compression/decompression techniques may render ISDN obsolete or lead to competing protocols. GSM (Global Standard for

---

FIGURE 4–3   OSI 7-Layer Model

---

7. Application (the user's application program)
6. Presentation (user interface/screen display)
5. Session (exchange between two nodes on the network)
4. Transport (protocol for encoding messages)
3. Network (mechanisms for separating multiple messages)
2. Link (data encoding schemes)
1. Physical (wires, connectors, voltage)

Mobile Communications), IS-54, and CDMA (Code Division Multiple Access) are competing standards for cellular communications.

Choices of data transport tools and standards can affect the exchange of information within and between organizations. In turn, these capabilities can strengthen management control systems and improve organizational adaptability to changing conditions. Yet, as the discussion of ISDN suggests, "leapfrog" technologies may emerge at the expense of a technology that seemed highly advanced at the time it was acquired. Decision makers must evaluate whether the technical merits of a new data-transfer device or protocol justify the risks of being on the leading edge. The selection process also involves establishing priorities among conflicting objectives. For example, twisted-pair wiring is inexpensive and easy to install, but coax and fiber-optic cable offer higher bandwidths. Or, investments in devices or software that increase network security may come at the cost of a more cumbersome user front end.

Since voice and data (including video) communications are moving to digital form, most organizations now include telecommunications within the IT architecture.

Data Transformation.   Data transformation includes the processes for transforming raw data into meaningful information. The lowest level of transformation is the process by which the machine language is converted into text or images on a page or screen. Other transformations include conversion, computation (adding/subtracting, calculating square root, etc.), sorting (alphabetically or numerically), producing a graphical representation of numbers (regression line, bar chart, etc.), and executing programs that may include all of the above transformation processes.

Traditional programming languages like COBOL and BASIC use *algorithms,* which specify all steps toward a solution. In contrast, expert-systems languages, derived from *artificial intelligence* techniques, use "inference engines" (heuristic and probabilistic logic) to offer conclusions based upon "rules." For example, a "Wine Advisor" expert system contains rules such as "If main dish is beef, wine color is red," and "If main dish is poultry, wine color is white; unless poultry is turkey, then wine color is red or white." Further rules specify whether a wine should have a light or heavy body, fruity or dry flavor, and other characteristics, designed to fit both the meal and the user's general preferences. When the user describes a particular meal, the Wine Advisor matches the rules with the preferences and generates a set of conclusions ranging from "highly" to "reasonably" likely.

Processes of data transformation have themselves been transformed over the last two decades, for several reasons:

- *Database management systems:* Since data characteristics need be defined but once, and data are stored independent of applications, programming is far more efficient.
- *Personal computing:* "Friendlier" programming languages are increasingly accessible to end-users with little or no formal IT training. End-users now develop many applications without assistance from technical staff.
- *Software development methodologies and tools:* What was once an "art" is becoming a "science." Computer-aided software engineering (CASE) combines a systematic development methodology with automated generation of data-flow

diagrams and cross-referencing data calls. In addition, object-oriented programming (OOP) is rapidly becoming incorporated in CASE tools. An object is a self-contained unit consisting of a subroutine and its necessary data. When represented by icons, multiple objects can be "dragged" into an application window to create a program. Advanced CASE tools generate code by calling objects into applications.

These changes in access to data, personal computing tools, and systems development tools have resulted in many benefits (e.g., faster applications development, more satisfied users, and better applications documentation and maintenance), but new issues have also arisen. For example, what happens if an end-user makes an error in developing a critical application? A construction company won a major bid but nearly went bankrupt because a user-developed spreadsheet model contained an error that resulted in an unrealistic estimate of costs. Since end-users are not IS professionals, they may not recognize when they are exposing their organization to an unnecessary application-related risk. Hence, end-user computing has created new pressures to forge a strong and productive alliance between independent users and IS professionals.

DEVELOPING AN IT ARCHITECTURE

An IT architecture specifies the arrangement of *tools* (hardware, software, data), *processes* (data storage, transport, and transmission) and *structures* (support services, reporting relationships, budgeting and cost-recovery mechanisms, etc.). How does management assemble, from among the great variety of tools, processes, and structures, a coherent IT architecture that is responsive to the organization's needs? How does management determine an appropriate set of support services, such as application planning and development, documentation and maintenance of data and systems, and user training and consultation? At a minimum, the architecture should point to answers to these questions:

Do we have the right technologies? Are they structured appropriately?

What levels of information access, sharing, and security should we support?

Which applications will we develop, and which will we buy off the shelf?

Who will maintain and upgrade tools, data, and applications?

Who will assess whether our IT architecture is meeting the firm's needs?

Answers to these questions vary, depending on the firm's core competence, its strategy, management's orientation to risk, and other factors. Just as construction architects are constrained by the site on which the building will be located and by the functional requirements specified by its future occupants, information-resources architects work within frameworks that describe the current and anticipated states of the firm and its environment. The architecture choices should be based on both an understanding of "where we are" and "where we are going," and should complement the firm's organizational structure and management control philosophy and systems.

FIGURE 4–4   Overview: Developing an IT Architecture

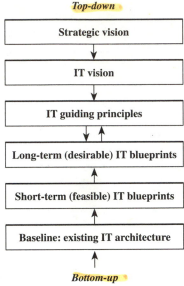

Developing and refining an IT architecture involves both "bottom-up" and "top-down" processes (Figure 4–4). The "bottom-up" process takes stock of the existing (baseline) IT architecture, while the "top-down" process translates management's strategic vision into a set of guiding principles for a new IT architecture. Out of these two processes, both a short-term "feasible blueprint" and a longer-term "desirable blueprint" are developed. These processes are discussed next.

"Bottom-Up": Assessing the Baseline IT Architecture

Only start-up firms have the luxury of building an IT architecture "from scratch." Mrs. Fields' Cookies (see Chapter 1), for instance, was able to develop a coherent architecture using networked microcomputers and relational database management systems, without the burden of "undoing" an earlier architecture of less flexible tools. Most firms, however, must start with a clear picture of "where we are today" in order to identify the steps necessary to move to a more powerful set of tools, processes, and structures.

Baseline assessment is summarized in Figure 4–5. This assessment plays two roles. First, it creates a baseline from which change can be measured, and second, the process of gathering this information reveals relative areas of strengths, weaknesses, and constraints in the current mechanisms for acquiring and utilizing IT tools and data.

FIGURE 4–5   Baseline Assessment: The Existing IT Architecture

IT Structures	*IT Processes*	*IT Tools*
Who pays? Chargeout/allocation policies	**Data storage** How/where stored? How maintained and updated?	**Hardware inventory** What H/W vendors? Standards? Upgrade schedule?
Who manages? Centralized/ decentralized responsibilities	**Data transport** What types of networks? What network services? How maintained?	**Software inventory** What S/W vendors? Languages/packages? How many? Standards? Upgrade schedule?
How much? IT capital investment; IT operating costs	**Data transformation** What applications? What development tools and processes? What maintenance tools and processes?	**Data inventory** What data? From what sources? How much? How often?

"Top-Down": Strategic Vision

Management articulates a vision based on a shared understanding of business objectives, expected challenges, and the organization's core competence. The strategic vision statement is meaningful, inspiring, and captures the essence of what the firm must do well to prosper in the coming decades. In turn, the strategic vision is translated into an IT vision. Three examples are presented below:

• Managers at a regional utility articulated this IT vision statement:

> We operate in a regulated environment with long planning horizons. We have time to make careful information-resources decisions. Since we are under considerable pressure to minimize costs, we seek IT investments that pay back quickly and provide long-term efficiency gains.

• Contrast that vision with the vision statement for a technical consulting firm:

> Our firm does specialized technical consulting in a variety of disciplines, each of which requires its own state-of-the-art tools. Our consultants are highly educated professionals who understand their IT requirements. Information sharing across units is not extensive. Our core competence is maintaining the capability to provide our clients with sophisticated analyses and technically superior solutions.

• A third organization, which produced and sold snack foods, had yet another vision:

> We face limits to future growth in our traditional, mass-marketed product lines. We have to develop new products targeted at specific regional or psychographic segments. Simultaneously, we must bring manufacturing and distribution costs down, even though production planning is becoming more complex. In order to implement this new strategy yet bring down production and distribution costs, tighter integration among these three functions is required. Decisions about tools, applications, and data must support timely sharing of production, marketing, and sales information.

How does the IT vision translate into a workable architecture? Just as a building architect creates blueprints to translate aesthetic and functional requirements into specifications of wiring, plumbing, structural support, windows and doors, so the IT architect creates "blueprints" that show the resources to be acquired, structures to be put in place, and the work to be done. We next describe the essential process of moving from baseline and vision to working blueprints.

The Blueprint

The key to an effective IT architecture is linking the top-down vision with the organization's current staff and capabilities, or bottom-up capacity. IT "blueprints" specify what and how information resources will be acquired or developed, and by whom. They further specify who will have access to various resources, how that access will be controlled, and how and by whom maintenance, upgrades, and user support services will be provided. "By whom" is often organized in three broad categories: central IS organization, business unit, or individual.

Blueprints map directly to the baseline assessment by explicitly noting which IT structures, processes, and foundations will remain, and what new structures, processes, and tools will be put in place (Figure 4–6). Developing workable blueprints is not easy. There is usually a wide gap between the desired IT architecture and the baseline, and that gap cannot be eliminated in one "fell swoop." Blueprints may at first be loosely linked to the IT vision, reflecting resource constraints and the existing infrastructure. Over time, the linkage should become more tightly coupled, even though the IT vision will also shift to reflect changing business conditions. Many firms acknowledge the difficulty of moving from "where we are today" to "where we want to be" by specifying both a near-term, "practically feasible" set of IT blueprints, and a longer-term, "optimally desirable" set of IT blueprints.

"Guiding principles" link the IT vision with the blueprints, taking into account the baseline architecture. By way of illustration, we return below to the three firms whose IT visions were presented above:

- Regional utility vision statement:
  We operate in a regulated environment . . . We are under considerable pressure to minimize costs, so we seek IT investments that pay back quickly and provide long-term efficiency gains.
- Representative guiding principles:
  - *H/W and S/W:* Technology selections should be tested and proved, not leading edge. We will select a standard set of hardware, operating systems, and software packages. Requests for nonstandard tools will be subject to the approval of an IS steering committee.
  - *Data transformation:* A central IS organization will develop and manage those systems costing more than $50,000. Wherever possible, we will buy applications software off the shelf rather than incur the expense of building our own applications. Software must be compatible with standards (above). When applications must be developed in-house, a standard development methodology will be employed.

FIGURE 4–6   Developing an IT Architecture

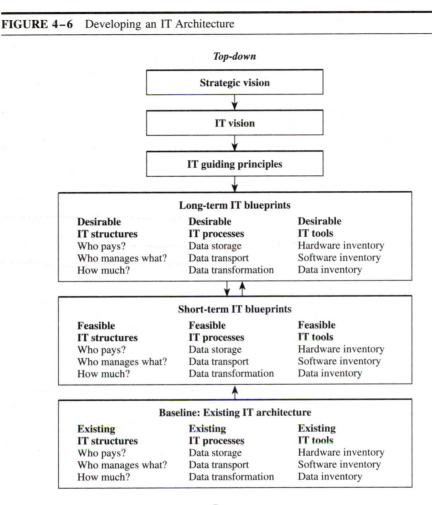

- *Data storage:* Data used by multiple units will be maintained in one location.
- *IT structures:* IT planning and user support will be provided by a central IS group.

- Technical consulting firm IT vision:

    Our consultants are highly educated professionals . . . Our critical success factor is maintaining the capability to provide our clients with sophisticated analyses and technically superior solutions.

- Representative guiding principles:

    - *H/W and S/W:* We will have a multivendor hardware and software operating environment.
    - *IT structures:* Each unit is responsible for its own end-user support services. Where possible, the cost of acquiring tools or developing applications should be allocated to the clients for which they were purchased. Acquisition of tools will be at the discretion of the

unit manager, except for large purchases that cannot be allocated to specific engagements. A central IS unit will provide a limited range of administrative IS services and network administration.

- Snack foods producer IT vision:

  In order to implement this new marketing strategy yet bring down manufacturing and distribution costs, tighter integration among these three functions is required.

- Representative guiding principles:

  - *IT structures:* Decisions about tools, applications and data must support timely sharing of production, marketing, and sales information. A significant multifunctional, information resources planning effort must be undertaken in order to set systems development priorities.
  - *H/W and S/W:* Hardware and software standards are required to ensure compatibility between applications.
  - *Data storage:* A comprehensive, centrally administered dictionary of data definitions is required to ensure that outputs are understood and data can be shared across functions.
  - *Data transformation:* Because cross-functional systems will be critical to our marketing and manufacturing strategy . . . a significant in-house application development effort will be undertaken. CASE tools, modular code, and a standard methodology will be adopted.

For each of the above organizations, only a sampling of guiding principles are presented, and they were articulated at a single point in time. The full process of developing these guidelines, and translating them into specific blueprints, is beyond the scope of this introductory chapter. Suffice it to say that an IT architecture is a "participatory sport," with participation of senior executives fundamental to achieving a strategic IT vision, and participation of front-line managers fundamental to moving from the current baseline state to a responsive and flexible new architecture.

CASE 4–1: AIR PRODUCTS AND CHEMICALS, INC.: PROJECT ICON (A)

This case describes a proposal to use computer and telecommunications equipment to consolidate a multinational company's US and UK data centers. The case illustrates the risks and challenges associated with the IT architecture choices that general managers must make.

Preparation Questions

1. Compare the baseline IT architecture in place at the time of the case with the proposed IT architecture of Project ICON.
2. What do Shepherd and Mather propose to accomplish with Project ICON?
3. How would you characterize the risks associated with Project ICON? From Shepherd's perspective, what issues need to be managed? As Mather, what concerns do you have?

Case 4–1 Air Products and Chemicals, Inc.: Project ICON (A)*

In 1989 and 1990, the economic climate was getting tough, and I foresaw a challenging budget coming from corporate headquarters. I wanted to grow the base of applications we offered, serve more customers, and live within a budget. I faced a choice of reducing application development people or rationalizing other technologically advanced programs. The last thing I wanted to do was cut application development.

—John Shepherd

One early December 1990 afternoon, John Shepherd—motorcycle racer, family man, and spirited MIS director of Air Products–Europe (APE)—and Peter Mather—the no-nonsense vice president of MIS for Air Products and Chemicals, Inc. (APCI) and fellow Englishman by birth—were locked in discussion. Each had read the results of a feasibility study suggesting that the implementation of Project ICON would be possible. Now, they had to decide whether or not to proceed.

In August 1990, Shepherd had identified a unique opportunity to achieve several business and MIS goals. By transferring the processing of IBM mainframe applications from APE's data center in Hersham, United Kingdom, to APCI's corporate data center in Allentown, Pennsylvania, Shepherd thought he could save a great deal of money—particularly important given a deteriorating economic climate—and provide many financial benefits. New technology and declining telecommunications costs made it possible—theoretically—to reap cost savings by running all of Europe's IBM mainframe applications on an IBM mainframe computer operated by APE's parent, APCI. With the money saved, Shepherd could develop more applications and serve more customers without increasing costs.

Potentially, this arrangement would eliminate the need for a new IBM mainframe in the United Kingdom and result in capital savings. However, it would also obviate the need for several of Shepherd's UK employees and perhaps undermine the importance of the European MIS organization. Any plan would require careful thought about implementation, because the project needed support from the employees whose jobs would most likely be affected. Furthermore, both APE's MIS employees and end-users would likely be critical of any "American" solution to a European problem. European employees and users alike could suspect that the larger APCI might force the Europeans to use APCI-written applications not totally consistent with European business requirements. Finally, APE MIS customers might believe that computer performance and customer service would deteriorate following the move.

Shepherd discussed his plan with Peter Mather, and the two men authorized a top-secret feasibility study of the proposal in October 1990. Beyond cost savings for Shepherd's MIS organization, Mather considered the potential benefits of a worldwide system, as he recalled:

The project would make it easier to share applications, where appropriate, between Europe and the United States. For example, top management has encouraged the engineering department within our process systems group to implement global engineering, which would enable teams from

*Robert W. Lightfoot prepared this case under the supervision of Professor Donna B. Stoddard. Copyright © 1992 by the President and Fellows of Harvard College. Harvard Business School case 192-097

EXHIBIT 1   Air Products and Chemicals, Inc. Financial Highlights, 1986–1990, Fiscal Year-End September 30 (in Millions of Dollars, Except per Common Share)

	1990	1989	1988	1987	1986
Sales	$2,894.7	$2,641.8	$2,431.9	$2,132.2	$1,941.5
Operating income	407.7	388.1	376.5	328.4	240.6†
Net income	229.9	222.1	213.7	155.6*	4.7
Adjusted earnings per common share:					
Continuing operations	4.15	4.04	3.90	2.83	1.82
Net income	4.15	4.04	3.90	2.76	.08
Total assets	3,899.5	3,365.7	2,999.5	2,705.1	2,661.0
Shareholders' equity	1,688.4	1,444.9	1,272.2	1,146.6	1,100.1
Return on sales	7.9%	8.4%	8.8%	7.5%	5.5%
Return on average shareholders' equity	14.7	16.4	17.6	14.2	9.2

*Net income for fiscal 1987 includes an extraordinary charge of $4.1 million, or $.07 per share, for early retirement of debt.
†Special items reduced operating income in 1986 by $45.9 million.

different parts of the world to work on different parts of one engineering project. This would be easier to implement if there were one worldwide engineering system and database.

In spite of the potential benefits, both Mather and Shepherd recognized that the execution of an IBM consolidation project (referred to as ICON) would be challenging. For example, whereas "channel extension" technology (see the glossary at the end of this case) had been commercially available for at least a decade, APCI would be among the first to deploy the technology across an ocean. Further, some of the most promising channel extender vendors were small. Joe Schulter, APCI's director of telecommunications services, explained: "No one else had done this before without encountering problems. Only one major rental car agency had tried it but had problems with vendors." Second, if they decided to go forward with the ICON project, any delays would be prohibitively expensive and would damage the credibility of the MIS organization. Third, successful implementation depended on absolute co-operation between Hersham employees, seven of

whose jobs would be eliminated by the project, and their counterparts in Allentown.

Company and Industry Overview
In its half-century of existence, APCI grew to almost $2.9 billion in sales and over $400 million in operating income in 1990; during the 1980s, sales grew at an average rate of 7.6 percent per year and net income about 7.3 percent per year. (Exhibit 1) In more than 150 plants worldwide, the company employed 14,000 people.

APCI produced industrial and specialty gases, chemicals, and environmental and energy products, and it designed custom plants for industrial consumers. Its four business segments were industrial gases, chemicals, environmental and energy, and equipment and technology. (Exhibit 2)

Contributing one-fifth of APCI's sales and operating income, APE's business differed significantly from that of its American counterpart. APE depended on industrial gases for 87 percent of its sales, and had only a fledgling chemicals

EXHIBIT 2 Air Products and Chemicals, Inc., Business Segments, Products, and Markets

Segment	Technologies	Products	Markets
Gases and Equipment Operations in 24 countries around the world. In Far East, most operations are joint ventures with local partners. Equipment manufacturing sites in United States and United Kingdom.	Air separation Cryogenic Adsorption Membranes Natural gas liquefaction Hydrogen recovery and purification Flourine chemistry Helium recovery/purification	Oxygen/nitrogen/argon Hydrogen Helium Specialty gases and equipment Food processing and freezing systems Welding products Organometallics	Cryogenic process Gas handling systems Ultra-high purity Special advanced needs Electronic chemicals	Chemicals Construction Electronics/semiconductors Food and beverage Glass Medical Metals Oil exploration	Petroleum refining Pulp and paper Research Rubber and plastics Aerospace Power Paint Advanced materials
Chemicals Manufacturing operations in US, UK, Italy, and Germany. Exports around the world with emphasis on Europe, Asia, and Latin America.	Polymer chemistry Carbon/nitrogen chemistry Polyurethane chemistry Acetylene chemistry	Emulsion polymers Polyvinyl alcohol Pressure-sensitive adhesives Alkyl amines Specialty amines Specialty surfactants Corrosion inhibitors Cement modifers Epoxy additives	Polyurethane Catalysts Surfactants Release agents Prepolymers and curatives Intermediates Acetic acid Nitrogen fertilizers Methanol	Adhesives Agriculture Transportation Construction Furniture and bedding Health and beauty products Oil production Packaging Plastics	Paint, coatings, and inks Paper Textiles and nonwovens Chemical intermediates Advanced composites Appliance insulation Footwear Electronics
Environment and Energy Businesses that address issues related to cleaning the environment and developing alternative methods of producing low-cost electricity. These businesses utilize skills developed in other parts of the company—project management, plant operations, financing, design/construction. Includes joint ventures with other companies to complement internal skills.	Circulating fluidized bed combustion Solid fuel combustion Flue-gas desulfurization Landfill gas recovery and purification Mass burning of trash Aqueous phase oxidation sludge treatment	Cogeneration facilities Coal-fired utility flue-gas clean-up Landfill gas recovery Waste to energy Sludge treatment		Municipalities Industrial manufacturers Natural gas utilities Electrical utilities	
Equipment and Technology	Plant design, engineering, and manufacturing	Cryogenic and gas processing equipment and plants		Industrial users, utilities, municipalities	

Source: *This Is Air Products*, Air Products and Chemicals, Inc., 1991; annual reports.

business; in the United States, 46 percent of sales came from industrial gases and 42 percent from chemicals.

APCI's various business segments had different clients and customer service processes, manufacturing technologies, and distribution channels. Technology transfer and software or data interchange among segments depended on the different needs of the businesses. Additionally, customer service processes and distribution channels for industrial gases differed in the United States and in Europe.

The gases and chemicals businesses were capital intensive, and competition was formidable. Many of APCI's outputs were commodity products, so small cost advantages translated into healthy profitability gains. APCI was the world's fourth-largest industrial gas company behind L'Air Groupe (France), BOC Group (United Kingdom) and Union Carbide (United States). With about 14 percent of the European industrial gas market, it was tied with BOC for second place in the European market. (L'Air Liquide led with a 25 percent share.) In the chemicals industry, APCI was the world's tenth-largest chemical company and about one-seventh the size of Dow Chemical, the world's largest; it did not have a major presence in the European chemicals market.[1]

MIS Organization

The corporate (APCI) MIS organization (Exhibit 3), headed by Mather, underwent a major reorganization in 1989, the effect of which was to distribute applications development and operations research resources out to the business units.[2] However, because some European business segments were too small to justify their own applications

development resources, applications development in Europe was still centralized (Exhibit 4).

In 1990, the APCI corporate data center included two large IBM mainframes and associated input/output devices (including 165 billion bytes of disk storage and about 4,000 workstation devices). The APE European data center included an IBM 3081 mainframe computer and associated input/output devices including 65 billion bytes of disk storage, 200 terminals/PCs that were channel-attached to the mainframe, and 150 remote terminals/PCs. In addition, APE had 10 Hewlett Packard 3000 and Spectrum minicomputers installed throughout Europe, four of which were located in Hersham and connected to one another on a local area network.

APE ran a mix of large batch and interactive applications on the IBM system. Using the HP network with distributed processing in Europe reduced the need for expensive intra-European telecommunications links.

The IBM system software (e.g., operating system and database/data communication software) APCI and APE used was generally the same, though software sometimes differed at the version or release level. Said Schulter:

> We had cooperated with Europe on major software decisions before, so we had a fairly consistent technological base with products such as CICS, IDMS, and SAS.[3] If we consolidated IBM operations, we would reap good economies of scale. We would have no software licenses to buy and only a very small increase in technical support.

APCI MIS end-users were fairly supportive of the organization but with some reservations. Before the APCI MIS reorganization in 1989, some business segments wanted control over application development. Even after they got it, they were suspicious of large-scale MIS projects, especially

[1]*Chemicalweek* (May 9, 1990), p. 22; and *Chemicalweek* (September 13, 1989), p. 18; and *1991 Business Rankings Annual* (Detroit: Gale Research, 1991), pp. 135–36, 270.

[2]See Harvard Business School Case Studies *Air Products and Chemicals, Inc.: MIS Reorganization (A)* (190–015); and *Air Products and Chemicals, Inc.: MIS Reorganization (B)* (190–016).

[3]These products are explained in the glossary at the end of the case.

EXHIBIT 3   Air Products and Chemicals, Inc., MIS Organization, 1990

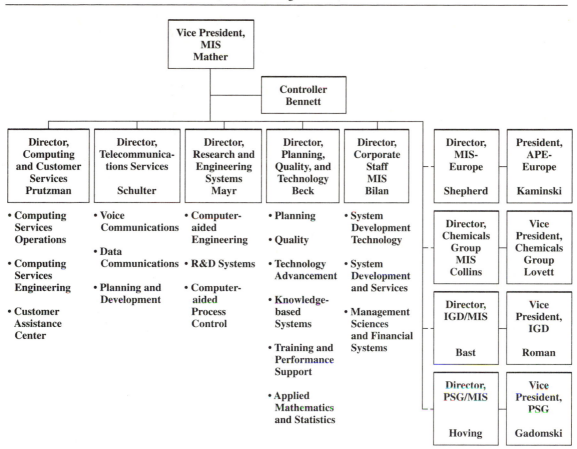

those relying on network solutions. European users were satisfied with the existing computing environment. Because they were extremely risk-averse about any decline in service, they thought change had only a downside potential. From the beginning, Schulter realized, "For users, there was simply no compelling need for ICON."

Both APCI and APE had significant telecommunications expertise and experience. Corporate personnel managed an extensive IBM telecommunications network that connected APCI's various locations around the world to one another and to the corporate headquarters. In a similar vein, APE

had extensive experience with both IBM and HP networking environments. The APCI data center's size gave it bargaining power with IBM; similarly, APE's extensive HP network made it an important customer of HP Europe.

A satellite link between Allentown and Hersham, in place for almost five years, provided data communication between the two data centers. It also carried voice traffic between the United States and Europe, although overflow was handled by the public switched network. APCI leased a 56 kilobyte (kb) circuit to connect its Ethernet local area networks and a dual 56 kb dial-up video confer-

EXHIBIT 4   Air Products–Europe, MIS Organization Chairt, 1990

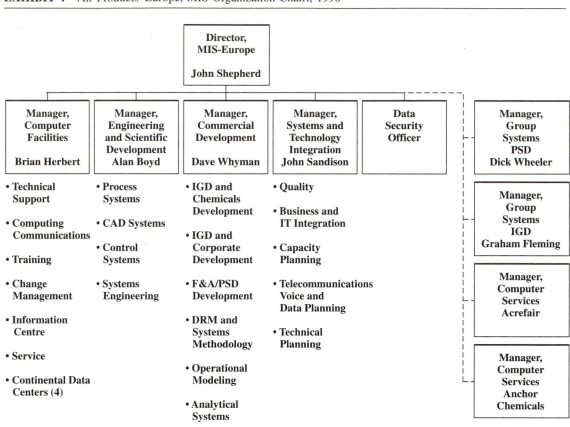

encing circuit to provide additional communication between Europe and the United States.

Project ICON

Mather and Shepherd chose a 10-member team to explore the feasibility of ICON. The two executives wanted the project leader to be a Briton and wanted British and American representation on the team to be equal. Dick Wheeler, APE's manager of group systems–PSD, was chosen to be the overall project leader and to lead the European team, and Joe Schulter led the U.S. side of the project from Allentown. (See Exhibit 5 for the project team roster.)

Opportunities

The 1991 fiscal year presented a serendipitous opportunity for a major reengineering of the computing and telecommunications networks such as Project ICON. First, mainframes in both Allentown and Hersham were running near capacity and were already scheduled for upgrades in 1991. Second, industrial gas division–Europe (IGD) was scheduled to move its employees to a new building in Basingstoke, about 30 miles from the APE data center. When Albert Lee, manager of telecommunications in Europe, became project manager for the Basingstoke move, colleagues assumed the solution would be to build a new data center at

EXHIBIT 5   ICON Initial Project Team*

APE	APCI
Dick Wheeler, manager, group systems–PSD (ICON project leader and European team leader)	Joe Schulter, director, telecommunications services (APCI's US ICON feasibility study team leader)
Brian Herbert, manager, computer facilities	Paul Prutzman, director, computing and customer services
Albert Lee, manager, telecommunications, systems and technology integration	Rich Kroll, manager, computing services engineering
Lawrie Mylet, technical analyst, systems and technology integration	Virgil Palmer, manager, telecommunications planning and development
Gary Pettifer, manager, technical services	Bill Townsend, manager, computer services operations

*Over the fall of 1990, the project team grew from its original 10 members as the involvement of others was needed to carry out the feasibility study.

Basingstoke. Lee looked at a variety of scenarios, and found the potential for a network solution to a computing problem:

> I became confident that we didn't need a data center in Basingstoke. The relative decline of telephone tariffs within the United Kingdom made a network solution appealing. And the costs of opening an additional data center were quite high—*not* hardware costs, but software licensing fees, staffing requirements, and the cost of building the physical environment.

Third, the lease on APCI's Airlink satellite line was due to expire. If the planners built excess capacity into the ICON network, traffic that had been carried via satellite could be carried on ICON's new network. The ICON planners forecast savings of $50,000 in Airlink voice and data

communications in fiscal 1991 and $262,000 annually thereafter.

These opportunities were also constraints, however. If ICON could not be implemented by the target date in June 1991, APE's mainframe would have to be upgraded and some solution for the IGD unit in Basingstoke would have to be found. Summer vacations would make it difficult to implement ICON in July and August, and fiscal year-end reporting activities in September and October would preclude the possibility of implementing ICON then. Planners agreed on a backup date for implementation in November, though that solution was considered quite undesirable. Shepherd noted:

> Although the backup plan, on paper, was to implement ICON in November, I felt strongly that if we could not implement it by July, we would have great difficulty in holding the team together.

Brian Herbert, the manager in charge of APE's MIS facilities department, also pointed out the burden of undertaking the ICON Project:

> The fiscal 1991 project list was already long—the Basingstoke move, a Brussels move, rolling out Windows technology, and the requirement to upgrade several HP machines. And we had acquired a Strasbourg [French] company, which meant consolidating their systems with ours. We needed ICON like a hole in the head.

Quality of Service

At the beginning of the feasibility study, Mather and Shepherd identified the key technical issue as "our ability to cost-effectively and reliably provide consistent subsecond response times to locally attached Hersham and Basingstoke users. This will be especially critical for certain users (engineers, customer service representatives, and accountants). Additionally, service to remote Continental European users must be at least equal to current levels." Longer response times would reduce the productivity of all computer-users. Customer service representatives would not have the same quick, on-line access to information that they were accustomed to, and service would deteriorate.

Perhaps more important, customer dissatisfaction would have been incurred due to the longer time taken to satisfy their information requirements. Additionally, managers would have been required to hire more employees just to finish the same amount of work. This would be especially true in administration, where some computer users were entirely dependent upon on-line transaction services.

Technical specialists on the project team thought ICON would result in a marginal degradation of service response time to local users in Hersham, but would benefit other European users. ICON would improve turnaround for APE batch computer processing jobs, because the corporate data center mainframe would be faster than APE's mainframe. Because the ICON proposal included network upgrades for UK-Continent lines, ICON would actually result in improved response times for remote Continental European users.

European users had also come to expect top quality technical support from APE's MIS organization. Technical support providers in Europe could provide multilingual responses to questions from Continental European users. Also, in the event of failures, Hersham users could go down to the MIS offices and speak with people to get the problem resolved. Dick Wheeler, ICON's project leader, was well aware of the political implications of the project for users:

> I was concerned about how users would see ICON. They would expect excellent performance of the equipment, with the same reliability and responsiveness that they were used to. And it was clear that if we were running jobs on US machines that there would be pressure to take US systems— both to reap economies of scale and to drive commonality. John [Shepherd] and I thought about how to ensure against this, and contemplated drafting a "declaration of independence," in which we would assert our right to veto any application which was inconsistent with European business requirements. We didn't know how the United States [APCI] would respond to this.

In preliminary work on the feasibility study, Rich Kroll, APCI's manager of computing services engineering, suggested service level management procedures. He noted:

> A service level management (SLM) agreement should be developed as part of the feasibility study. We should not be afraid of an SLM agreement. A key item after executing this project will be to ensure that we have satisfied customers, and this is one way to make that happen. I believe the agreement should be driven by APE personnel, preferably both MIS and key customer representatives for major application areas.

Telecommunications Environment in the United States and the United Kingdom

The feasibility of consolidating the two IBM data centers depended on the cost and availability of reliable and responsive telecommunications services. The quickly changing regulatory environment created opportunities for negotiating with various telecommunications companies, whose involvement was essential for Project ICON.

In the United States, the divestiture of AT&T, the American telephone monopoly, had fostered competition in long distance communications among competitors such as AT&T, MCI, and Sprint. The consent decree that ordered the breakup of the system also required the eventual unbundling of network services to promote their reselling and repackaging by third-party service providers. The increased network usage resulting from lower prices made it feasible to update much of the public switched network with fiber optic cable, digital switching, and, in some areas, ISDN.

Cross-subsidies of local access by long distance rates kept those rates artificially high and encouraged many large users of telecommunications services to bypass the public switched network by building their own facilities for local and long distance communication. APCI, for example, had used satellite communication for voice, fax, and limited data between Allentown and Hersham since 1985. In 1986, when APE's mainframe was running near capacity, the company experimented with processing APE's engineering work on AP-CI's IBM via the satellite link. High line error rates and high cost, however, prevented that arrangement from lasting more than three months.

Albert Lee characterized European telecommunications providers as less competitive than their American counterparts, but noted that as a heavy telecommunications user, Air Products had some bargaining power:

> British Telecom (BT) and the other European PTOs [post and telephone operating companies] will do anything to avoid dropping rates.
>
> Companies with high-volume telecommunications business may not be able to get price breaks, but where there are competitive alternatives to the PTOs, they will offer bundled services. When we researched buying fractional T1[4] services, we found the marginal price differences of moving from 512 kbps to 768 kbps to a full T1 quite small. And by buying T1 circuits and managed network services, we could get free tariff circuits between Hersham and Basingstoke which we could use for domestic traffic as well as backup routing for international traffic.

In the United Kingdom, price regulation of BT had given the telephone monopoly incentive to develop new services and markets for them. Price regulation set the rates that BT could charge according to a formula that adjusted them for inflation and expected productivity increases. Although the company could not set its own prices above the calculated ceiling, it could keep as much money as it could earn. As a result, this system, although it fostered competition, provided some incentive to let quality deteriorate. Another characteristic of the U.K. telecommunications environment, independent telephone companies such as Mercury Communications competed with BT in national markets.

In 1990, significant competition in telecommunications network services did not exist in Continental Europe. PTOs provided postal and telephone services, and European governments jealously guarded telephone monopolies as a source of cross-subsidy for postal services. High intra-European tariffs and outdated links in the network (such as analog switches) made it difficult to employ sophisticated, intra-European telecommunications network solutions. Still, APE planned new telecommunications links between the UK and selected Europe locations. Lee predicted, "We will expand networking solutions with France before the rest of Europe, because their telecommunications traditionally has been the cheapest."

In 1990, major telecommunications companies jointly owned two fiber optic cables that spanned the Atlantic Ocean between the United States and the United Kingdom. These two cables afforded an opportunity to build resiliency into the network. Additional fiber links were planned between the United States and the United Kingdom, and between the United Kingdom and Continental Europe.

The Proposed Post-ICON Network

ICON would require a new network. Topologies of the existing and proposed networks are shown in Exhibits 6 and 7. APE's European data center would lose its IBM mainframe, and APCI's data center would upgrade its mainframe computer. APE would run its IBM mainframe jobs on the upgraded equipment.

The IBM mainframe would be partitioned using IBM's PRISM technology, which would preserve APE technical standards and conventions. The APE partition would be connected to its own disk storage system, and APE's tape processing would be implemented on the Allentown data center's cartridge and reel tape drive subsystem. All APE software would be replicated onto the partition in the corporate data center.

To create resiliency in the network, APCI would use two fractional T1 circuits (each with a capacity of 768 kbps) located in two separate fiber optic cables that ran between the United States and a BT facility in England. One circuit would run from that facility to Hersham, United Kingdom, while the other would run to the new Basingstoke facility. The circuits would be run through TIMEPLEX

EXHIBIT 6   Air Products and Chemicals, Inc., Existing Network Configuration

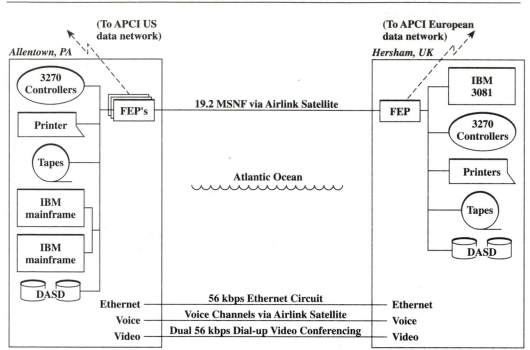

Legend: FEP = front-end processor; DASD = disk storage; Tapes = tape storage. (The glossary explains these terms.)

Link II Time Division Multiplexers (TDMs), which would be programmed to switch from one ½-T1 transatlantic circuit to the other in the event of failure. Excess traffic, voice, fax, video, or data would be automatically switched over to the public network in such a failure. An additional line between Hersham and Basingstoke would provide communication between those facilities and add resiliency to the network.

The US data network would still be connected to the IBM mainframes in Allentown via front-end processors, attached directly to the mainframes through channels.

Alternatives to ICON

Planners in the United Kingdom considered many alternatives to their problem—running out of memory—with the IBM mainframe. First, APE

could have purchased a bigger, cheaper machine, such as an IBM 3084Q. This would have doubled capacity, and cost about half as much as the 3081K. This option would have required about £200,000 up front, and, like any option that involved maintaining a separate mainframe in the United Kingdom, would necessitate maintenance and license fees of about £30,000 per month.

Alternatively, APE considered a solid state device using auxiliary storage to relieve the burden on the mainframe during computations. The SSD paged in frames of memory more quickly than ordinary storage to disk, and could relieve strain on current memory. This option would have cost about £50,000, but would only have worked for about one year.

Finally, APE considered buying an IBM 3090-200E, which had been budgeted at one time.

EXHIBIT 7   Air Products and Chemicals, Inc., Proposed Network Configuration

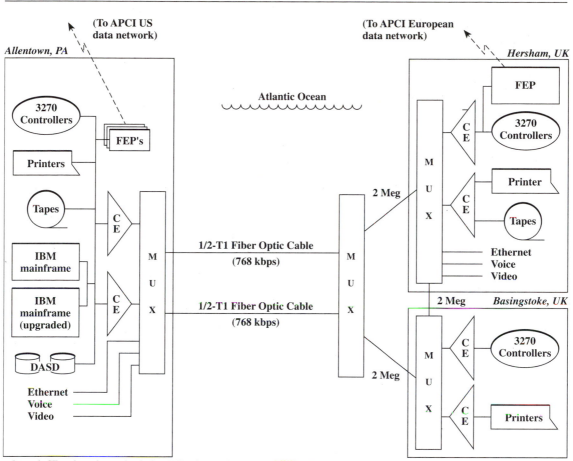

Legend: CE = channel extender device; FEP = front-end processor; MUX = TIMEPLEX multiplexer; DASD = disk storage. (See glossary.)

Though Gary Pettifer, the manager of technical services for APE's IBM group, conceded his IBM specialists "would have just loved it," this option would have cost about £750,000 plus maintenance and license fees.

Project Team Findings

At the end of November 1990, the project team concluded that ICON was technically feasible and presented Mather and Shepherd with projections of potential benefits, quantifiable and otherwise.

ICON Costs and Benefits

The project team concluded that ICON would have quantifiable net savings of more than $1.0 million in fiscal year 1992, $1.4 million in fiscal 1993, and $1.9 million in fiscal 1994. Direct net cost savings and cost avoidance for 1992 would represent approximately 8 percent of Shepherd's budget (Exhibit 8). The gross benefits would result from reduced software expense (33 percent), equipment depreciation (31 percent), staff (18 percent), and equipment maintenance (17 percent). The gross benefits would be offset by

EXHIBIT 8   Air Products and Chemicals, Inc., Project ICON Cost-Benefit Summary

Item (£000/$000)	FY 1991	FY 1992	FY 1993	FY 1994
APE gross savings				
Depreciation	£ 143	310	380	500
Maintenance	40	220	232	270
Software	42	361	415	520
Labor		285	285	285
Other minor		18	19	19
Asset disposal value		40		
	£ 225	£ 1,234	£ 1,331	£ 1,594
	$ 428	$ 2,345	$ 2,529	$ 3,029
Telecommunications and equipment costs				
Dual network circuits	£(170)	(350)	(350)	(350)
Continental upgrades	(12)	(74)	(74)	(74)
Channel extensions	(27)	(107)	(107)	(107)
TIMEPLEX multiplexers	(23)	(70)	(70)	(70)
Miscellaneous	(9)	(27)	(27)	(27)
	£(241)	£ (628)	£ (628)	£ (628)
	$(458)	$(1,193)	$(1,193)	$(1,193)
Telecommunications savings				
Airlink voice/data	£ 26	138	138	138
Intergraph/video/voice overflow	63	179	232	274
	£ 89	£ 317	£ 370	£ 412
	$ 169	$ 602	$ 703	$ 782
APCI incremental costs				
CPU upgrade	£ (33)	(132)	(132)	(132)
Disk and tape storage		(120)	(120)	(120)
Manpower	(10)	(120)	(120)	(120)
	£ (43)	£ (372)	£ (372)	£ (372)
	$ (82)	$ (707)	$ (707)	$ (707)
Travel	£ 27	£ 3		
Total quantifiable net savings	£ 3	£ 548	£ 701	£ 1,006
	$ 6	$ 1,041	$ 1,332	$ 1,912

Note: Exchange rate equals $1.90/£1.00.

EXHIBIT 9   Air Products and Chemicals, Inc., Project ICON Capital Expenditures and (Savings)

	APE £000	APCI £000	Total £000	Total $000
Telecommunications equipment				
Continental TIMEPLEX multiplexers	£ 60	£	£ 160	$ 114
Ocean TIMEPLEX multiplexers	178	41	219	416
Channel extension equipment	350		350	655
APCI incremental cost				
APCI mainframe configuration				
Incremental CPU and disk capacity		630	630	1,200
APE hardware				
Tape drive and controller upgrades	50		50	95
Network management workstation	26		26	49
Total	£ 664	£671	£1,335	$ 2,539
Less: capital savings				
Basingstoke channel extension	(90)		(90)	(171)
Airlink capacity increase	(40)		(40)	(76)
APE mainframe configuration upgrades	(525)		(525)	(998)
Other	(25)		(25)	(47)
	£(680)	£	£(680)	$(1,292)
Net capital addition	£ (16)	£671	£ 655	$ 1,247

Note: Exchange rate equals $1.90/£1.00.

increased incremental costs at the corporate data center from upgrading CPU capacity and disk storage and by increased data network expense. More than half of the costs would be applied to existing and budgeted US-UK communications services, including voice, video, and engineering data.

ICON would also increase US-UK voice/video/fax capacity (70 percent) at no additional cost. If it included upgrades for the network links to Europe, ICON would also improve reliability and response times for end-users on the European continent. ICON could also improve turnaround for APE batch computer processing.

Nearly all quantifiable savings would accrue to APE. Indeed, Mather thought he would have to add the equivalent of two or two-and-a-half employees in operations and technical support. However, Mather and Shepherd agreed to put aside questions of charge-out until after a real summary of ICON's costs and benefits to the company had been completed.

The president of APE stated that the fiscal 1991 MIS budget should not be exceeded. Therefore, capital expenditures on ICON and the project implementation costs had to be defrayed by reduced capital expenditures and savings elsewhere (Exhibit 9).

Organizational Challenges

Because even minor "hiccups" in communication across the Atlantic could cause major disruptions in European operations, if a decision was made to go forward with ICON, there would be no room for error. Implementing ICON by June would place a heavy burden on the employees of APCI's and APE's MIS organizations as well as requiring an unprecedented level of communication between them.

Most project team members saw ICON as a great personal opportunity. For example, Lee was motivated by the technical challenge:

> Working on project ICON was a great chance to find a highly network-oriented solution to a computing problem. It could facilitate reengineering of the network, and because of the technical challenge, it was good for the company and also very satisfying personally.

For IBM specialists, however, ICON would not be quite the same kind of opportunity. Pettifer would face the proposition of motivating the IBM specialists. If the decision was made to go forward with ICON, he strongly favored the June "cutover date" to November because he anticipated it would be difficult to motivate those employees for a long period. Further, he recognized that at the same time that they would be expected to work overtime on ICON, they would be looking for other jobs. He recalled:

> The market for IBM specialists in southeast England was not strong in 1990, and it was unclear whether those whose jobs would be affected could easily find work elsewhere.

The project would be a technical challenge to them and would bring them experience. The world was changing, and they couldn't rely on specialist areas like the IBM.

Managers within APCI were aware of the difficulty of learning the European ways of doing things. Paul Prutzman, APCI's director of computing and customer services, commented:

> There was a lot of knowledge resident in human beings that would have to be transferred to the United States from Europe. APE operators knew a lot about their jobs and procedures that had not been written down. That knowledge would have to be transferred to the United States. Although we identified this issue early on in the planning process, we had to figure out the best way to do so. We could send people over there on short-term assignments, but we don't usually have international assignments for computer operators, and visa and work permit problems were bound to be a nightmare.

The Executive Decision, December 1990

In December 1990, Peter Mather and John Shepherd reviewed the findings of the feasibility study. They needed to assess ICON's risks and potential benefits, and consider whether they should implement it. Further, if they decided to go forward, how would they decide what technology to use? How would they announce the project? What would they tell employees and users? What would they do with displaced employees and how would they motivate them throughout the implementation process?

Glossary of Key Technical Terms

Channel	A physical path (i.e., hardware) that allows independent, simultaneous communication between a computer and a number of simultaneous operating input/output devices.
CICS	Customer information control system. A program that enables transactions entered at remote terminals to be processed concurrently by user-written application programs. It includes facilities for building, using, and maintaining databases.

DASD	A direct-access storage device (DASD) is a data storage medium that gives direct access to individual records; there is no need to read from the beginning of a file to find a desired record.
Ethernet	A local area network standard developed by Xerox, DEC, and Intel and widely used in large organizations. Ethernet allows 1024 devices—including workstations, file servers, print servers, and communications servers—to be connected to each other and allows data transmission at a rate of 10 million bits/second.
Front-end processor	A communication control unit that converts data from the form used by telecommunications equipment to a form acceptable as computer input. A front-end processor also performs functions such as error detection and recovery when signals are lost or distorted during transmission, adding or deleting message headers, or other control information used in routing data.
IDMS	A database management system.
ISDN	Integrated services digital network. An international telecommunications standard for transmitting voice and data, simultaneously, over the same telephone line without a modem. Digital transmission is used, allowing for improved speed for data, multiple line appearances, and increased clarity and reliability for voice. An ordinary line is partitioned into two channels (for voice or data) and a third network control channel that can be used to provide many different services (e.g., automatic call back, caller identification, distinctive ringing for different parties using the same telephone).
LAN	Local area network. A high-bandwidth, bidirectional communications network that operates over a limited geographic area, usually an office building. Connects microcomputers, minicomputers, and communication devices (e.g., Vidoetex, facsimile, and communicating word processors).
Multiplexer	An electronic device that combines data from or to several low-speed communication lines onto a single, higher-speed line. Multiplexers do this by dividing the frequency band into narrower units ("frequency-division multiplexing") or by allotting the channel to several different inputs successively ("time-division multiplexing").
PRISM	Processor resource/systems management (also PR/SM). An IBM software product with hardware assists that allows a mainframe computer to run up to 16 different operating systems simultaneously by creating a logical partition in the computer's processor.
SAS	A statistical analysis application used for regression modeling and other statistical applications.
T1 circuit	A fiber optic cable with a capacity of 1.536 million bits/second.

CASE 4–2: SYMANTEC

Symantec is a rapidly growing software company that has expanded primarily through a strategy of acquisitions. Due to its rapid growth, the firm is beginning to experience some internal communications problems that need to be resolved soon.

Preparation Questions

1. Given the industry in which Symantec competes and the firm's strategy, what are its employees' communication needs?
2. What are the problems facing Symantec?
3. As Gordon Eubanks, what would you do? As Bob Dykes, what would you do?

Case 4–2 Symantec*

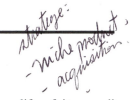

Symantec designed, delivered, and supported a diversified line of software for the information management, productivity, and software development needs of business users. In the eight years since its founding in 1982, the company achieved startling growth (Exhibit 1). The number of employees grew from 30 to 316. It achieved revenues of $50 million and earnings per share of $1.05 for fiscal year 1989. It added nine new products, upgraded and developed different versions of old ones, prided itself on not having missed a scheduled product release date, and established these products as leaders in their respective market segments. It became a major player in the software industry, competing with well-established companies like Lotus and Ashton-Tate. Although employees were pleased with the company's rapid growth, they were concerned about some of its internal processes, particularly those relating to information flow.

Gordon E. Eubanks, CEO, worried about the effect of communication problems on employees: "I think most people view Symantec positively. But the information systems are not working, people are complaining about them, and that

whole problem is taking on a life of its own." People at all levels expressed concern about information flow. As a product manager remarked:

> When you are a company of 30 people, you shout over the side of a cubicle. But as you grow, you need proper communication flow or else you cripple the company. A methodology for getting information to flow among different departments was never set up at Symantec.

Background

Symantec was founded in March 1982 by Gary Hendrix, an expert in artificial intelligence and language processing. Eubanks, founder of another company, C&E Software, merged C&E with Symantec in September 1984 under the name Symantec Corporation. After the merger, Hendrix became vice president in charge of advanced technology, and Eubanks became president/CEO. Corporate headquarters were in Cupertino, California.

In 1987 Symantec acquired three companies: Breakthrough Software of Novato, California; Living Videotext of Mountain View, California; and Think Technologies of Bedford, Massachusetts. Eubanks believed in acquiring the best products possible, no matter where the product companies were located. Once acquired, the companies became Symantec product groups and stayed in their original locations. Eubanks did not believe in relocating workers or imposing a culture on the new product groups. The particular composition

*Julie Gladstone prepared this case under the supervision of Professor Nitin Nohria. Copyright © 1990 by the President and Fellows of Harvard College. Harvard Business School, case 491-010 (Revised 1991).

and dynamics of the original development teams, he asserted, accounted for their innovative products, so they needed to be maintained. Thus, while acknowledging the communication and control problems of a geographically dispersed company, Eubanks was adamant in his decision not to relocate product groups after acquisition. He stated:

> Once you obtain the products, you must keep building and maintaining them. You can't lose the spirit and the people behind the product. People do not want to be relocated. Essentially, what we've done is a trade-off between being in one location and being able to get the products we wanted and keep the people.

After an acquisition, Eubanks sent an executive staff member to the new product group to facilitate the transition and assess the performance of its managers. In all cases, Eubanks chose to replace some top managers but kept the development,

technical support, and marketing infrastructure. He planned to continue to make acquisitions, so Rod Turner, executive vice president (EVP), worked to identify acquisition prospects.

Structure

Symantec was organized into product groups and centralized functions. There were five product groups; each controlled its own product development, marketing, quality assurance, support, and management. Most other functions (finance, human resources, and sales) were handled by centralized departments at corporate headquarters (Exhibit 2). Some functions were centralized but not at headquarters; for example, purchasing and manufacturing were in Santa Clara, California, and training was in Novato, California.

Two of the five product groups, database management and utilities, had been at corporate headquarters from the start. Of the other three, project

EXHIBIT 1 Statement of Operations ($ in thousands, except per-share data)

	Year Ended December 31, 1986	1987	Quarter* Ended March 31, 1988	Year Ended March 31, 1989	Year Ended March 31, 1990
Net revenues	$ 6,126	$ 14,331	$6,092	$39,886	$50,111
Cost of sales	1,952	2,735	1,449	9,413	9,669
Gross margin	4,147	11,596	4,643	30,473	40,342
Operating income (loss)	(2,044)	(966)	69	4,044	8,150
Pretax income (loss)	(2,071)	(1,003)	57	4,107	8,708
Operating expenses:					
R&D	857	2,915	1,131	6,514	7,496
Sales & marketing	3,857	5,655	2,703	15,556	21,049
General & administrative	1,504	3,992	740	4,359	3,647
Total operating expenses	6,218	12,562	4,574	26,429	32,192
Earnings per share	(.76)	(.55)	(.14)	(.08)	1.05
Number of shares used to compute data	2,370	3,650	5,258	5,277	6,375

*When Symantec went public in 1988, it changed its fiscal year from April 1 to March 31.

EXHIBIT 2 Symantec Corporation Organization Chart (March 1990)

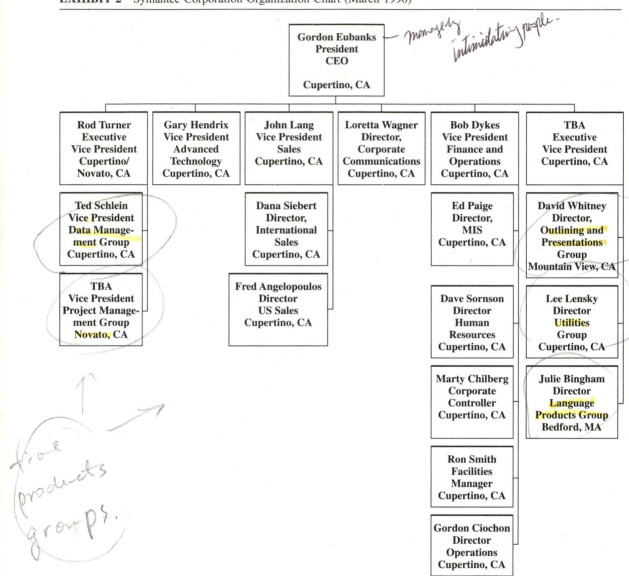

managed intimidating people.

five products groups.

management was in Novato (a one-and-a-half hour drive from Cupertino), outlining and presentation was in Mountain View (a 10-minute drive from Cupertino), and language products was in Bedford, Massachusetts. Symantec's product line included 15 main software packages; some operated on IBM MS-DOS systems, others on Macintosh systems. (Exhibit 3).

A product's life cycle was started by its product development team. Each team conceived its products independently of the other product groups, receiving outside help, if necessary, from Hendrix.

EXHIBIT 3   Symantec's Principal Products

Products	Date of First Shipment	Operating Systems	US 1989 Suggested Retail List Price
Applications Software			
Data management:			
Q&A	November 1985	MS-DOS, OS/2	$349.00
Q&A Network Pack	March 1988	MS-DOS, OS/2	299.00
Q&A Write	July 1987	MS-DOS	199.00
SQZ Plus	May 1986	MS-DOS	99.95
The Budget Express	May 1988	MS-DOS	149.00
Project management:			
Time Line	September 1984	MS-DOS	595.00
Time Line Graphics	September 1986	MS-DOS	195.00
Time Line LAN Pack	November 1988	MS-DOS	195.00
Outlining and presentations:			
GrandView	April 1988	MS-DOS	295.00
MORE II	July 1986	Macintosh	395.00
Systems Software			
Language products:			
THINK C	April 1986	Macintosh	249.00
THINK Pascal	August 1986	Macintosh	149.00
Macintosh Pascal	August 1988	Macintosh	125.00
Utilities:			
Symantec Utilities for Macintosh (SUM)	June 1988	Macintosh	99.95
Symantec AntiVirus for Macintosh (SAM)	May 1989	Macintosh	99.95

After developing a product, the product group educated the sales force, the technical support staff, and the customer service staff.

Product group managers were involved in all stages of the product's life cycle. For example, the product group managers worked with the development team to choose special features for the product; the quality-assurance staff to ensure that the product was effective; and the public relations staff to devise a product launch strategy. The marketing managers in each product group handled the product's advertising, developed collateral material, prepared seminars and demonstra-tions for resellers, and coordinated promotions for distributors. They spoke regularly with the field sales force to inform them about the product and to find out what tools the sales force needed to sell the product.

The field sales representatives reported to sales managers at headquarters. Each of Symantec's seven sales managers managed a field sales force in a certain geographic region and communicated with software distributors. The field sales reps traveled to retailers to encourage them to sell Symantec products. Symantec had a separate distribution sales group that worked with its six major

problem: lack of I.T. infrastructure, to support communication so the corp can exchange expertise.

distributors on managing orders, promotions, inventory levels, and sales to retailers. Its telemarketing group handled major dealer and corporate accounts. Its products were marketed in 23 foreign countries through 41 independent distributors.

Other departments besides the sales force helped promote Symantec software. About the time of shipping, the corporate communications department announced the new product or product upgrade to the press. Corporate communications also planned corporate, regional, and local-market trade shows. Symantec participated in about 300 shows a year, sending to a major show as many as 30 to 35 employees. Corporate communications also prepared two external newsletters (for registered Macintosh owners of Symantec products and for registered DOS owners) to provide product information, a corporate brochure, and a corporate presentation that ran on Symantec software. The EVPs in charge of product groups met with journalists and Wall Street analysts to alert them to new product launches and with corporate customers to learn what features they would like in a product. The training department gave customers workshops and seminars and prepared product information packets.

Orders were placed with the order administration department, which handled order processing and shipping to distributors and corporate customers. Once entered into the database, the order printed out at the manufacturing department. Along with the product, customers received a product registration slip, which they were asked to complete and return to Symantec. The information was entered into a database, which the marketing groups and order administration departments used to inform customers of product upgrades or to send them maintenance shipments.

Symantec had technical support departments within each product group and a centralized customer service department. Technical support representatives answered technical questions over the phone between 6 AM and 5 PM weekdays. Customer service representatives handled all nontechnical questions (e.g., on the status of orders or a prod-

uct's basic features), and also had the authority to authorize returns and enter on-line orders for upgrades.

Information Flow

Given Symantec's structure, information flowed across all of its boundaries. On any given day, the following information flows might occur:

- Rod Turner, EVP and formerly director of international sales, would speak with Dana Siebert, current director of international sales, about establishing Symantec partners and distribution strategies abroad. Siebert would speak with certain Symantec partners, exclusive distributors, or subsidiaries about customizing marketing strategy to their particular market. The international partners would share ideas about marketing strategies. Because the international sales were growing, Siebert would speak with people in finance and personnel about hiring additional employees.

- Ron Kisling, manager of financial analysis, in preparing monthly performance statements for each product group, would speak with product group managers to learn their sales and expense forecasts for the product. Product group managers would talk to sales managers about product launches and changes in launch or shipping schedules. Sales managers would speak with product-group and marketing managers to learn a product's new features, pricing issues, how the new product differed from previous ones, and the scheduled release dates for new products. They would convey marketing information to the resellers and make sure they had appropriate literature and demonstration diskettes to give to customers.

- Product marketing managers would discuss which distributors were more effective in selling Symantec products, and they would speak with field sales representatives about product launches.

- The corporate events division of the corporate communications department would talk to the sales force about getting Symantec equipment to the next trade show and about which Symantec employees should attend the show. The creative services group would discuss with people in manufacturing and operations about manufacturing schedules and how a product should be packaged.

- Fran Stewart, order administration manager, would speak with the production control manager about shipping orders, back orders, changes in a product's shipping schedule or release date, and delivery problems. She would speak with the customer service manager about upgrade order processing. Product managers would speak with her about upgrade policies and strategies and the revenue ramifications of upgrades, such as whether a certain customer should receive a free upgrade. Turner would speak to the operations and finance departments to find out how many units of a certain product were purchased daily.

In addition to these information exchanges, there were scheduled meetings and regularly issued internal publications and reports. Each department and product group held staff meetings. Top executives met weekly; managers at Cupertino met quarterly. Sales managers and customer service representatives attended weekly training sessions to learn about products, upgrades, and new features of a certain product. Customer service representatives attended meetings held by product marketing managers to learn about pricing and selling policies. The human resources department met twice a week to tell new employees about Symantec's benefits and policies.

Symantec printed a quarterly newsletter, *IN-SITE,* which included general company information and was distributed throughout the company. Information was shared also through internal newsletters. The international sales department prepared a biweekly mailing and a monthly newsletter for international partners and Symantec's exclusive distributors, with product and sales information. Corporate communications prepared a monthly internal newsletter describing product launches, advertising campaigns, and reviews of certain products. Bob Dykes, CFO, used to take notes at executive meetings and distribute copies of them to all managers; he planned to resume this practice. The marketing groups of the product groups prepared weekly sales bulletins describing a product's new features and tips on promoting it.

Eubanks planned to have informal lunches, where a small, random selection of employees would meet with two or three executive staff members to discuss issues broached by the employees. Eubanks gathered information also by walking around the Cupertino office and talking to people. This allowed him to hear information that might not reach him otherwise, and symbolized to employees that he was interested in their ideas. Eubanks solicited information from employees and readily shared it. (Because Symantec was publicly owned, certain information could not be shared with the whole company.) But Eubanks sensed that he intimidated some people: "I'm aggressive. I have very little patience and have strong opinions. There are people who are scared of me." Interviews with some employees confirmed this impression. Those wanting to talk to a member of the executive staff tended to approach Hendrix. Hendrix said:

> People who are afraid of going to Gordon come to me with their concerns. I'm glad people see there's a line of communication open. I could foster that, but listening to the company could become a full-time job.

Despite all these communication channels, many employees expressed frustration that some information was not shared and certain groups (especially product groups) did not communicate with each other. The marketing and engineering departments of the product groups had much to gain through sharing information but rarely did so. Turner thought this was because the product groups were geographically dispersed. The product groups (formerly self-contained, entrepreneurial companies) were not used to sharing information or being accountable to a parent organization.

Eubanks speculated that the groups did not communicate because each believed it knew the best way to do something and did not need to solicit information from others. Pam Fleming, product marketing manager for Time Line, expressed the need for more communication among the marketing departments: "All the marketing groups realize we don't communicate enough. Ultimately we're going to save ourselves a lot of time and trouble because, if we share information rather than try to recreate the wheel every time we do a new plan, it would help all of us."

To address these issues, Symantec planned to hold regular product marketing and engineering meetings bringing together all employees in those respective departments. In February 1990, the first companywide marketing meeting was held, and in May 1990, the first companywide engineering meeting. The benefits of communication across certain groups were more evident in some cases than in others. For example, Q&A and Time Line product groups were beginning to meet regularly, which was logical since both were managed by Turner, both made software for MS-DOS systems, and they were in geographic proximity. But the two groups rarely spoke with the Bedford group that developed language products for the Macintosh because they did not see an immediate need to do so.

Some found the information flow from marketplace to company was insufficient. For example, software engineers complained that sales representatives did not give them enough feedback about what customers liked or disliked about current Symantec products. As for communication flow from Symantec to the marketplace, groups serving customers directly complained that at times they did not receive necessary information. For example, the customer service supervisor stated that the product groups did not inform her of problems with the product, which meant the customer service representatives heard about problems first from customers.

One recurring explanation for the lack of some information exchange was that employees did not

have time to communicate. As Turner stated, "This is a high-pressured, fast-paced company. There isn't always time to communicate thoroughly. And if people talk to another product group, they do not necessarily get an immediate benefit from it. So they think it cannot possibly be worth their time." Hendrix, who was responsible for solving problems in software development and designing software, felt that product-development people did not reserve enough time to communicate the development interests of the marketplace: "I want to design software that the product-development people need, but they're too busy to tell me what they need."

Eubanks hoped to have a meeting for the entire company because he believed that having people meet each other would facilitate communication.

Control Systems

to foster ~ Encourage competition among groups. is a good strategy!

All departments—both the functional and product groups—prepared annual budgets every six months. The budgets, completed in June and December, did not correspond to the fiscal year. Since many of the same people both prepared these budgets and reported information for annual fiscal reports, this system was intended to prevent their having too many reports due at the same time.

The product groups budgeted for profits, revenues and costs of product development, quality assurance, marketing, and technical support. They also wrote an annual marketing plan, describing the competition, market, and the group's marketing strategy. This plan was written fully once a year and refined semiannually.

Budgets were submitted to the finance department, which wrote semiannual corporate business plans and forecasts. It also prepared monthly financial statements, describing the product groups' performance, with information gathered from the accounting department, the sales staff, and product group managers. These statements focused on forecasting, for example, what the product groups should expect for the rest of the quarter and how to respond to its market conditions. The statements were sent to the product group managers and presented in a meeting to Marty Chilberg, corporate controller, and Dykes, who presented a summary of them to the executive staff. The financial division forecasted revenues weekly and reported them at the weekly executive staff meeting.

For sales, the key targets were measured in terms of "sell-through," not "sell-in." The sales force sold products to distributors ("sell-in"), who sold them to dealers ("sell-through"), who then sold them to the end-users. Measuring sales-through, Symantec's financial analysts agreed, more accurately measured real sales. Dealers, who carried very low stocks of products, could get supplies from distributors overnight; what the dealers bought reflected customer demand. The sales force was compensated through commissions based on sell-through in their respective geographic areas.

All sales representatives were equipped to sell all Symantec products and were largely free to divide their time among products in any way, although 15 percent of their commission was based on achievement of specific objectives, including specific product goals. As a result, a product groups' performance depended on how effectively it encouraged the sales force to promote its products. The product groups felt they needed to vie for the limited time and resources of the sales force and other centralized functions and for Symantec's financial resources. Eubanks thought a certain amount of competition was productive:

> As in any matrix, people are competing for resources. Part of the system is to keep the tension up. How you get more resources is to keep identifying the need for more.

All corporate functions also had to submit annual plans. For instance, corporate communications wrote an annual PR plan listing anticipated major launches and submitted it to the finance department.

Each quarter, all Symantec employees were supposed to write a list of objectives for the coming quarter and discuss it with their boss and, in some cases, their subordinates. This was known as management by objectives. Besides measuring performance against those objectives quarterly, overall performance was supposed to be evaluated annually, beginning a year after an employee's hiring date. The evaluation form had two parts: overall performance (measures like dedication and punctuality), and success in meeting quarterly objectives. Although objective reports seemed to have been completed regularly, performance evaluations had been done sporadically. In a few departments some people had never had a performance evaluation, or it was done months after deadline. The human resources department believed that having one evaluation form for the whole company was unsatisfactory. As Dave Sornson, director of human resources, explained: "The whole performance system needs to be refined. We're using the same form for all employees, whether you're a receptionist or a senior engineering manager. We need to customize it to particular types of jobs." Human resources was drafting a new form. Some managers had written their own forms before there was an official company one; later they supplemented the official form's questions with their own.

Incentives

As of 1990, Symantec instituted a new bonus plan, a profit-sharing plan that included all employees: managers, nonmanagers, and all software developers. The product groups and functional departments were given a pool of money to divide among their members. Guidelines specifying a bonus of 2 percent to 25 percent of base salary were provided. A third of a product group's bonus payout would be based on its performance and two-thirds on company performance. When assessing performance, product-group managers considered how effective the employees had been in meeting their written objectives.

Decision Making

At the managers meeting for the final quarter of FY1989–90, Eubanks began by stating that employees must recognize the difference between an opinion and a policy. He explained that his opinions should not necessarily be considered policies. At the end of the meeting, someone asked: "Was that an opinion or a policy?" Eubanks replied, "It's an opinion." Reflecting on that question, Eubanks said, "It was a great comment because it pointed out the ambiguity in trying to communicate as the company gets bigger." He wanted his employees to stop passively accepting and implementing all his ideas, but to question them and provide creative input. To do this, he thought, they needed first to believe in the decision-making structure and to feel that executives and managers valued their input:

> What expedites communication is giving people confidence in the decision-making structure and letting them know the CEO believes in it. I must continually communicate and reinforce the importance of the organization to the managers because if they think all decisions are arbitrary and made by a few people, then they will not execute them. Managers should feel confident in their judgments and not feel they are always going to be overridden. You get the best results from people when they feel comfortable providing input and that their input's been heard. Meanwhile, if I want to effect something, I will. I will get the right person to do the job and clearly communicate what I want done. If the person thinks it can't be done or should be done another way, I want to hear a clear explanation why.

Several managers reflected on the meeting, and the nature of communication flow. Some affirmed that there was ambiguity about what was an opinion and what was a policy and when to follow a directive and when to provide input. The result, they asserted, was a lack of direction or instructions when guidance was needed. Eubanks acknowledged that top executives did not stress the importance of sharing information: "We have people who are entrepreneurs who come into the company without much management experience. We have no management training programs. And I don't think I've set as much of a tone as I should about this need for more communication." To address this issue, Eubanks planned to follow communication procedures more rigorously, such as completing his performance evaluations promptly.

Information Technology

Symantec had two basic information technology systems: a Hewlett-Packard (HP) system for accounting, manufacturing schedules, and inventory control; and a network system linking all Symantec employees and allowing them to communicate through electronic mail (e-mail). The company also used a ROLM phone-mail system extensively.

The Hewlett-Packard System

When the Hewlett-Packard 3000 was installed in January 1988, it was running at full capacity, could not be expanded to ingest any more information, and could not accommodate all the order-entry people. When he joined Symantec in October 1988, Dykes had to find a larger system to support the company's growth. He chose the HP 935, a computer with a RISC (reduced instruction set computation) architecture, which meant the system bypassed rarely used instructions, focused on high-volume transactions, and could thus process instructions more rapidly.

After choosing the HP 935, Dykes set out to hire a new MIS director to oversee the transition to the new system. The MIS manager at the time, according to Dykes, was "totally burned out." The network system was constantly crashing, and the HP 3000 was overloaded. Before finding a new MIS director, Symantec temporarily had its software engineers assume MIS responsibilities. This arrangement, according to Hendrix, "was a poor use of our engineering resource." There were also problems with e-mail and phone-mail, but the executive staff decided that accounting problems should be handled first. So Dykes looked for someone experienced with HP systems and with ASK, the commercial software used on the HP. He hired Ed Paige, who proved effective in converting to the HP 935.

The HP system's basic modules, called OMAR (order management and accounts receivable), included accounts receivable, accounts payable, general ledger, and manufacturing modules. OMAR was designed to handle high-value order entries, such as those from distributors. OMAR's front end was POPS (prepaid order processing system), which handled mainly upgrade orders. Not a commercial product, POPS was written in-house. Symantec decided to write its own software because Dykes and the MIS department reasoned that whatever system it bought would have to be customized for the input and type of access that it wanted. Because Symantec orders came in one at a time, it needed a very efficient system, meaning that orders could be entered on average in 30 seconds and did not require many inputters. But producing the software in-house rather than buying it proved more costly, created a lot of work for its programmers, and made Symantec very reliant on its MIS department if POPS had problems.

POPS interfaced with a customer database that included a customer's address and buying history. If a customer wanted an upgrade, the only information the order-entry people needed to process the order was the customer's credit card number. When the upgrade order was entered, it was immediately transferred to the manufacturing department, and then shipped to the customer. POPS could print lists of customers (e.g., all 300,000 end-users of Q&A), which were then used for upgrade mailings. Order entries were completed during the day and then batch-processed and sent to the bank in the evening. Credit card information was captured and returned to the order-processing group. Once the order administration department received the information back from the bank, it used pieces of that order information to update files in the ASK software about revenue, shipping history, and other relevant order information.

Until mid-1989, the HP 935 system and POPS worked well. But as Symantec grew, the system could not process the greater number of orders and began to break down regularly. Dykes had anticipated some problems with HP or POPS, but he had preferred to have some system functioning rather than to wait until the system was deemed perfect to install it:

> I don't like having a department that studies things for a year and says, "This would be exactly the perfect way to do this; now let's proceed." In a company that's growing and changing rapidly, whatever architecture you install will be obsolete and the software uncertain. So I pushed MIS to get something up and running, to just write their first cut, implement it, and then gather people's feedback and refine it. The inevitable problems have cropped up, and they're causing major heartache.

Many employees were frustrated with the system. Those in the order-entry department, who relied on the HP, were forthright in expressing their frustration. Stewart said: "One day I had 11 people with literally nothing to do, and I had the same problem a few days later. Some people's job is data entry, and they are set up to do only that. Now I have to tell them to do something else. When that happens, it affects my department's productivity perhaps more than any other." Chilberg said: "Probably between one-third and one-half of the Saturdays and Sundays that I came in on my own to get things done, I couldn't because the HP was down."

The Network System

Symantec's second major information system was the Novell LAN, which connected all of the 320 IBM-PC and IBM-PC-clones in the company. Through these PCs, most of which were IBM clones, all employees had access to the network on which e-mail ran, and software developers had access to the central file service used for code development and programming. Symantec also had 80 Macintoshes, which could not be linked to this e-mail software. Where the Macintoshes were used (usually sites of the product groups that produced software for Apple computers), there were also IBM PCs or clones for network access.

Symantec's e-mail system, Network Courier, enabled a user to send a message to a person, a group, or the entire company; recipients were able to print out a copy of their messages. Employees also communicated through phone-mail, regular phones, and, in the cases of Novato and Cupertino, through interoffice mail. The international sales department communicated mostly through regular phones and faxes, as many field sales representatives and international partners did not have e-mail or phone-mail. Some partners used an e-mail package called CC Mail, but because only a handful of Symantec employees had CC Mail, its effectiveness as a company communication device was limited. The MIS department allowed employees to choose their own hardware, but it set standards for how e-mail should operate and what types of phones and phone switches employees should use.

Because Symantec was extremely reliant on e-mail and phone-mail, breakdowns frustrated employees. According to Dykes, a problem seemed to arise somewhere in the Novell LAN system at least once a week. Once a month, e-mail corrupted files for no apparent reason. And Symantec's e-mail package was intolerant of noise, making it impossible to communicate from places like New York City whose phone lines were noisy. Cupertino's network wiring was a maze which had caused some systems failures there.

Practically everyone at Cupertino who was interviewed expressed frustration with e-mail's and phone-mail's unreliability. Ted Schlein, product group manager of Q&A, said: "My engineer consultants in Monterey, California, and Fairfield, Iowa, need to send files back and forth to Cupertino for the Q&A developers to create the product. When the network is down, this directly affects engineering schedules." Schlein also expressed frustration with the phone-mail system: "Every so often, all of a sudden you will be cut off. The telephones get overloaded. You can't dial. Last

week we had just started a major upgrade of a product, so lots of phone calls were coming in and tying up all the lines. So we couldn't dial out." Turner stated: "E-mail is unreliable. You can send it to everyone, but only some people will get it some of the time, and you don't know who and which times." Eubanks complained: "Today, for some reason, I can't dial a number with the area code 408. It's funny how a little thing like that can be so annoying." Paige wanted Symantec to install a new e-mail system, but deciding which one to buy became controversial. He wanted to buy CC Mail, but a Symantec board member, who also served on another company's board, wanted to buy its e-mail package. Paige claimed that the e-mail package did not have the same reliability as CC Mail, and that instead of being able to proceed to buy the "best" system, the MIS department had to keep justifying why it did not want to buy the other e-mail package. As for the hardware on which the network ran, Hendrix believed employees should be required to buy name brand PCs instead of PC clones, the wide use of which he thought caused some system failures.

The MIS Department

When there were systems failures or technological problems, the MIS department was notified. It established a code whereby each service request was given a priority number. Certain people such as Eubanks, Dykes, and product group managers had top priority. In assigning other priorities, MIS considered whether the problem was a group or an individual one and its urgency to Symantec's functioning. Individuals requested MIS services and repairs via e-mail, phone-mail, conversations with MIS people in the hallway, and written service-request forms. MIS preferred the forms because they helped MIS keep track of and prioritize requests. The information on the request form was input into a MIS database. Employees complained that the process of prioritizing requests was time-consuming and that MIS took a long time to respond to requests. Stewart commented:

The MIS department's priorities have a huge effect on my ability to meet objectives. I often feel I have to include less significant things in my objective report because I can't control the MIS piece of those objectives. When I need a systems problem solved, I don't fill out a request form. I walk around the building, corner the MIS people, and say, "This is what I need now." I spend half my day chasing people whom I need to continue to function.

Schlein bypassed MIS if he needed technology support:

If you need a cable in a day or two, you do not go through purchasing. You go outside. You buy it, expense it, and install it yourself.

Offices not at headquarters had smaller, more organized LAN systems and seemed to experience fewer technology failures. These off-site locations had no need to use the HP system but relied on e-mail. The director of training at Novato stated: "We've been using e-mail for quite a few years now, and I can't imagine surviving without it. We check it constantly." Some employees commented that there were "too many ways to communicate." Retrieving messages might involve checking e-mail, phone-mail, a telephone answering machine, a fax machine, and a mailbox.

Conclusion

Employees presented a number of explanations and solutions for the communications problems, whether MIS or technology problems or broader communications issues. Interpretations seemed to depend on one's position in the company.

Dykes believed that advances in companywide communications depended foremost on management's willingness to communicate. In his opinion, MIS problems were temporary and due to poor systems decisions made early on:

We've had numerous mechanical problems with our systems. MIS argues that the company is pushing too fast and in too many directions at once. Symantec is doing what it has to do, and we need an MIS department that can respond to company

needs. We can't slow down to accommodate MIS. It has to be the other way around. The MIS problems have become a crutch for managers to not communicate. Human resources training and other methods are required to improve the ability of managers and executives to communicate.

Hendrix ascribed the communications problems to the lack of proper initial planning and believed that establishing the right technologies would eradicate them:

problem

The basic reason for systems failures is that the systems just evolved and weren't planned. As we grew, it was always too inconvenient to make a big change, and the existing antiquated system got more entrenched. Also, we did not put creative personnel in MIS or take time to figure out what ought to be done, and then implement it in a reasonable way. The MIS people spent all their time fighting fires. It was a vicious cycle because the more they patched, the less they created innovative solutions to replace what was there, and the more fires there were. The only way to break that cycle is to have a major influx of money and cure it, which is what we have done recently.

Paige felt that given Symantec's rapid growth and the erratic development of its technology systems, the MIS department did not have the time or resources to devise and implement an effective MIS strategy:

problem 2

This company has a do-it-now, fix-it-later mentality. Most of my time is spent reacting to things as they happen. We've created systems that are very dependent on the MIS department, so when things are not working users do not know how to address the problems. We've had no time to create documents or train users on the software we've built. I feel we need more people in MIS to provide the level of service that this company demands.

problem 3

Eubanks believed that resolving the MIS problems depended on having the right person as the head of MIS:

solution 1

Things in MIS are not working. We're not getting the results people need. This usually means that we don't have the right leadership in place. To solve the MIS problems, Bob has to get the right MIS director, a real leader.

Stewart thought that Symantec, given its structure, needed an ethos stressing information exchange:

> As our jobs become more complex, so do our communication needs. We're structured in such a way that there are inherent limits to communication flow, but more can be done to facilitate it. We need to build communication mechanisms into the structure as much as we build financial plans. This should be done, not necessarily electronically, but through fostering a companywide commitment to communication.

Loretta Wagner, director of corporate communications, stressed the importance of face-to-face communications: "Many interactions do not take place because people are too swamped. I think we need to make the time because face-to-face contact within a company is an imperative, as is such contact with the press and customers."

Sornson, who believed managers were unclear about what to communicate and inexperienced in communicating in a corporate setting, felt that training managers would help:

> Many managers are inexperienced and do not know what they should be communicating. They are uncertain about how to conduct a staff meeting and present information. I think communication and management development are linked, and are the two issues we need to focus on.

Kathy Johnson, director of product marketing for Q&A, felt Symantec needed to institutionalize a unified corporate philosophy that emphasized communications and to establish a policy whereby managers were expected to communicate that philosophy to newly hired employees: *solution 2*

> We need managers with good personal communication skills who, when they hire people, could tell them what our company objectives are and what it means to be an employee of Symantec. We need to tell new hires that we have an open-door policy of really talking to each other and then doing it. The executive staff has begun to recognize the need for a company orientation and identity by setting up a corporate communications department and hiring more senior-level human resources people. But I don't think this philosophy of communication has evolved enough yet at Symantec.

Overall, Eubanks believed that to support its rapid growth, Symantec needed both innovative product development teams and strong managers who were competent in communicating and decision making. He commented: "One of the most important things as we're growing is to make sure we have the right managers. If I'm not willing to share management responsibilities, then we're not going to be as successful as we could be." He thought creating products would continue to be Symantec's foundation, but the greater challenge would be managing the company.

PART II

IT and the Organization

Chapter 5   *IT and the Individual*
Chapter 6   *IT in Organizations*
Chapter 7   *IT between Organizations: Interorganizational Systems*

An effective IT architecture supports the work of individuals, is aligned with organizational objectives, and provides for linkages with other organizations. Information technologies are inherently flexible. Managers and their organizations can be changed by IT and they can use IT to make changes.

Part II examines the processes of accommodation—being changed and making changes—among individuals, organizations, and information technologies.

New IT capabilities are leading to new kinds of work, new working arrangements, and new human resources issues. Chapter 5 examines issues concerning information technology and the individual.

IT is a moving target, evolving at a rapid pace. Over time, the reasons for investing in IT and the management structures for assimilating and supporting IT have also evolved. Chapter 6 examines how changing technologies have been accompanied by changes in strategic objectives, organizational structures, and management control systems.

Information technologies are critical tools supporting new arrangements between organizations. While industrial-age organizations sought to integrate business processes by means of ownership, information-age organizations achieve unprecedented levels of integration using IT. Chapter 7 explores the various forms of interorganizational systems.

Chapter 5

IT and the Individual

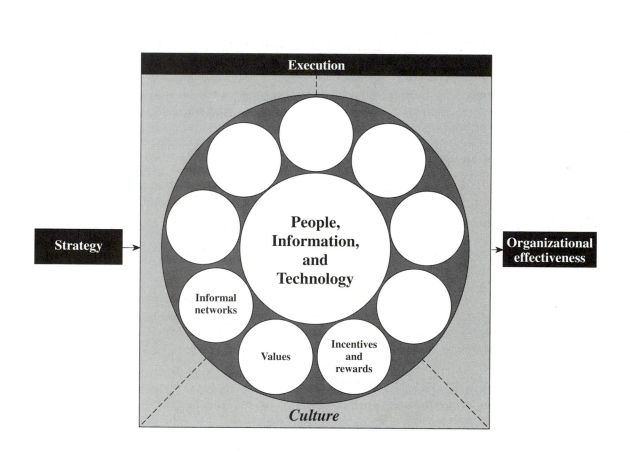

INTRODUCTION

Rapidly evolving information technologies are permeating our lives as employees and as private citizens. This chapter examines some ethical issues associated with expanded capabilities for data storage, transport, and transformation.

The chapter begins by reviewing three broad IT-driven changes in the work of individuals and teams: *new work, new working arrangements,* and *new human resources issues.* Two cases about *employee monitoring systems* are then presented. The Internal Revenue Service case describes an application designed to increase productivity through automating a labor-intensive process. Employees have complained about the new system, and management is contemplating a shift in direction. The Waco Manufacturing case examines the use of a technology that records employees' whereabouts. Has the manager in this case overstepped her bounds? Should firms invest in this technology, and, if so, what guidelines should govern its use?

Next, an important article by Shoshana Zuboff is reprinted. Zuboff contends that organizations need to shift from an IT philosophy of *automating* work to one of "*informating*" work. The implications of using IT as an informating capability are discussed, including changing employees' skills, changing roles and relationships in a "post-hierarchical" structure, and fostering a learning environment.

The last case, Otis Elevator: Managing the Service Force, describes managers assessing the "automating versus informating" potential of IT for improving performance in an important customer-service function.

The final section addresses managers' ethical choices in using IT for automating, monitoring, and informating workers, and issues in gathering and using customer information.

IT AND CHANGING WORK

Rapidly evolving information technologies are altering employee life in three ways: by creating *new work, new working arrangements,* and *new human resources issues.*

New Work

New IT capabilities are leading to enhanced products (such as microprocessor-controlled automobiles and appliances), new products (such as cellular phones), and new industries (such as personal computing software). Literally thousands of small software, hardware, and IT services companies that do business today did not exist a decade ago, and more will form as promising new technologies come along. The Massachusetts Software Council, for example, predicted in 1993 that 33,000 new Massachusetts jobs would be created in this sector over the next five years. Applicants with updated technical skills and adaptable knowledge will find many employment opportunities. Furthermore, jobs are being redefined in traditional industries, as both Drucker (see Reading 2–1 in Chapter 2) and Zuboff (see Reading 5–1 later in this chapter) discuss.

New Working Arrangements

IT is leading to changes in our *relationships* with the organization and its members, in *how we conduct our work,* and in how we are *supervised and evaluated.* The most dramatic changes in the worker's relationship with the organization are the massive downsizings occurring in many firms, and the increasing reliance on a "disposable" or contingent labor pool, comprised of workers hired on a short-term, renewable-contract basis. Contingent employees in 1990 accounted for about a quarter of total US employment, and are expected to comprise half of the labor force by 2000.[1] IT has driven these phenomena in three ways. First, much clerical work has been replaced with automated systems. Second, increased access to timely information about operations enables a broader managerial span of control (more workers report to each manager). And third, the IT-enhanced ability to capture an organization's history and codify its members' expertise enables more efficient transfer of knowledge and skills, which in turn enables more flexible employment arrangements.

Work is being carried out in new ways. There is more team work, and teams are supported by networked technologies such as electronic mail, group decision support systems and authoring systems, video conferencing, and other capabilities. Geography is a far lower constraint, thanks to these technologies. "Telecommuting"—working at

---

[1] Richard S. Belous, *The Contingent Economy: The Growth of the Temporary, Part-Time and Subcontracted Workforce* (Washington, D.C.: National Planning Association), 1989; Lance Morrow, "The Temping of America," *Time* (March 29, 1993); and Clar Ansberry, "Down the Up Escalator: Why Some Workers are Falling Behind," The *Wall Street Journal* (March 11, 1993).

home or in suburban satellite locations while electronically connected to the organization—is a frequently chosen option that helps lower fuel and corporate overhead costs and give workers greater flexibility in where and when they work.

Both new working arrangements and new technologies give rise to new forms of supervision and performance evaluation. As Chapter 3 noted, richer measures for management control are being developed, and many are linked to salary reviews. Electronic employee monitoring is also increasing, especially in insurance companies, banks, airlines, hotels, phone companies, and other service businesses. (See the discussion of electronic monitoring later in this chapter.)

New Human Resources Issues

The new contractual relationships create new personnel issues. A big one is job security and its flip side, employee loyalty to the firm. It is too soon to tell whether the flexibility of a contingent labor pool offers sufficient benefit to offset the threats to employee morale, and unions are likely to use this issue to try to regain the clout they lost in the 1980s. Traditional notions of the "career ladder" may also have to change, as Drucker discusses.

A second issue concerns employee autonomy. Software can be designed to constrain the user or give the user great discretion. This creates a paradox: networked information technologies give individuals greater control over their information processing needs than ever before, yet there is also greater potential for others to exert control over individuals through privacy-reducing on-line performance monitoring and database technologies (more on this topic below).

A third human resources issue arises because of technological discontinuity (see also Chapter 4). Many IT advances are not linear, continuous, or even predictable. It is difficult to predict the effects of a discontinuous technology on employment prospects, quality of work life, and career paths. For individuals and organizations, survival will be less a matter of predicting changes than of adapting to them by participating in new-skills training and other educational programs.

IT AND EMPLOYEE PRIVACY

Networked information technologies make the organization more "transparent," in Zuboff's words, by revealing the data and knowledge going into decisions, and by recording the actions and words of individuals. Project-management groupware, for example, records individuals' deadline commitments. Group authoring systems record each author's comments on a text, yielding a helpful type of audit trail. Sometimes this transparency occurs with the employee's knowledge and consent, but sometimes not. For example, during the US Iran-Contra hearings many details of Oliver North's activities were exposed when backup tapes of his electronic mail conversations were revealed (to his surprise). In another example, an employee was fired after her boss read "inflammatory" electronic mail messages not intended for his eyes. In both cases,

FIGURE 5–1   Typical Examples of Employee Monitoring Systems

Job	What Is Measured
Word processors, data entry clerks	Keystroke speed, errors, time spent working
Telephone operators, customer service workers	Time per customer call, number and type of transactions
Telemarketing/other sales	Time per customer, sales volume
Insurance claims clerk	Number of cases per unit time

the exposed individuals had assumed their messages were private and confidential; and this assumption is widely shared among employees. However, the law currently gives employers the right to monitor messages on their communication media to ensure appropriate use, and it does not require employers to notify employees that messages transmitted over networks may be viewed by others. The law does not view employee information exchanges as "private" matters, except in narrow domains such as employee medical histories.

Under traditional human supervision, employees usually know when they are being observed, and supervision is intermittent. Electronic monitoring, described below, is either constant or perceived as constant, since the employee may not be able to detect when it is or is not in effect. Work habits that the employee may view as private—visits to the washroom, breaks to stretch out a sore back—are not private if the system records where the individual is and/or whether he/she is working on the assigned task.

Formal employee monitoring systems typically do four things:

Set standards for the time it should take to produce certain units of work.

Monitor the actual time it takes to produce each unit of work.

Analyze the variance of actual from standard time.

Provide data for use in planning, cost estimates, productivity improvement, and sometimes wages (when coupled with a pay-for-performance plan).[2]

These systems are in widespread use for routinized office work with large volumes of standardized tasks that are performed repeatedly, such as insurance claims processing and data entry. Figure 5–1 describes some typical electronic monitoring applications.

Electronic monitoring systems can help improve efficiency and reduce errors by providing workers with timely and accurate performance feedback. They also facilitate

---

[2] See also John Chalykoff and Nitin Nohria, "Note on Electronic Monitoring," Harvard Business School case 9-490-044.

telecommuting, since supervision is, in effect, built into the software. However, as discussed above, monitoring systems raise concerns about employee privacy, as well as issues of *deskilling* and potentially *unfair work standards.*

Deskilling

Employee monitoring systems often (though not always) break jobs into small, measurable tasks. This can have the effect of disconnecting the worker from the larger process, which in turn gives workers less opportunity to broaden their skill base and advance in the organization. While a reduction in task complexity facilitates job monitoring, it reduces the challenge and growth potential of the job. Just as manufacturing organizations are addressing the deskilling problem by reexamining work flows and experimenting with job enlargement and self-managed teams, a similar but nascent movement is afoot in the service industry.

Work Standards

Fairness of standards is a major concern, especially when pay-for-performance systems are used. Productivity increases may be gradually ratcheted upward, placing new pressures on employees. Labor advocates point to the increase in repetitive-motion injuries—such as carpal-tunnel syndrome[3]—as evidence that employees may be pushed to produce more than is healthy.

   The Internal Revenue Service case that follows presents one example of employee reactions to a new employee monitoring system. The Waco Manufacturing case that comes after illustrates an even more pervasive form of employee monitoring, and a dilemma posed by its use.

CASE 5–1: THE INTERNAL REVENUE SERVICE: AUTOMATED COLLECTION SYSTEM

To improve collection productivity, the IRS has implemented the automated collection system (ACS). While the system is performing as predicted, the electronic monitoring aspect of ACS has led to greater employee dissatisfaction and turnover. This case highlights the enormous potential of IT to reorganize work flows and improve productivity, but it also reveals some pitfalls.

---

[3]Carpal-tunnel syndrome is an especially common disability among employees who make heavy use of keyboards.

Preparation Questions

1. Evaluate the change from the IRS's COF organizations to the ACS system.
2. As Tim Brown, assistant commissioner for collection, what would you do?

Case 5–1 The Internal Revenue Service: Automated Collection System*

In early 1989, Tim Brown, assistant commissioner for collection of the U.S. Internal Revenue Service (IRS), examined the report on his desk. The first full-scale automation of a major portion of his operation was encountering difficulties. "What has gone wrong?" he thought. "We've completely reorganized the operation, put millions of dollars into new technology, and in some ways it appears worse off than before." Turnover in the newly automated operation had reached a level unprecedented in its history; in some offices it had been reported to be as high as 100%. High turnover was of great concern because of shrinking labor pools and the general difficulty of attracting people to work for the federal government. The report cautioned also that the morale of employees and supervisors was suffering. Even the comments made by his senior managers were equivocal.

- We need an understanding of how to manage an automated environment. I don't think we fully understand the effect of certain things on employees . . . There are unique problems and concerns here. At various times, they have led to some distrust between management and employees.
- It [computer monitoring] has value inasmuch as it keeps employees on their toes. The more they are

monitored, the more they realize there's a cop around the bend.
- Employees like to know how they're doing. The times that I see problems are when employees don't know what they're doing. The thing is how you use the [monitoring] information.

The bright side of the report was that productivity was higher than it had been before automation. Dollars collected had increased about 33 percent annually, inventory levels had declined considerably, and the total number of cases closed had improved 100 percent. And all of these improvements had been made with half the staff employed before automation. However, it was clear to Mr. Brown that productivity was not as high as it could be and would decline if the problems were not addressed. Two issues that required closer examination, in his view, were the way the work was organized and the manner in which computer-aided monitoring of employee performance was handled.

The IRS Organization

Mission
The IRS's primary function was to collect revenue for the US government. Its mission was:

> To collect the proper amount of tax revenues at the least cost to the public, and in a manner that warrants the highest degree of public confidence in our integrity, efficiency, and fairness.

In 1988, for instance, the IRS had received and processed more than 194 million tax returns, col-

*Professors John Chalykoff and Nitin Nohria prepared this case. Copyright © 1990 by the President and Fellows of Harvard College. Harvard Business School case 490-042

lected approximately $935 billion, and dealt with 83 million taxpayer requests for information or assistance. It operated on a budget of $5 billion in fiscal year 1988, with 120,000 employees in more than 700 offices in the United States and abroad.

Technology

Technology had always played a central role in the IRS operations. Mr. Brown commented:

> It is not an understatement to say that every aspect of the IRS's mission has been and will continue to be affected by the technology revolution. For the IRS, it is impossible to look at even our recent past without seeing the enormous impact of information technology (IT). From the way tax returns are processed to the way employees communicate and use office equipment, IT has continually changed the way we do business. And, the IRS of the late 1980s is more dependent on—and benefits by—IT than ever before. There is no question that this trend will continue into the 1990s as the volume of work continues to grow.

IT assumed a central role in the IRS starting in the early 1960s when the agency integrated manual and computerized processing of tax returns into a basic processing system design that remained in place until 1989. Although the IRS had tried to constantly update the system with additions and new equipment, the system was limited by its design, which was based on 1950s technology. This limitation, in Mr. Brown's view, meant that

> No matter how good our intentions were, or how well we trained our people to answer questions and help taxpayers, the system defeated us. We could not give taxpayers the kind of service we wanted and they deserved . . . the kind of one-stop service they expected and usually got from the private financial sector. This failing was unacceptable to those of us charged with managing the Internal Revenue Service. Our only realistic solution was to undertake an unprecedented effort to modernize our entire information processing system—and I mean unprecedented in scope, not just in government, but in private industry as well. But, while we were

committed to automation in order to provide the best service to taxpayers, we wanted to be very careful about the impact it would have on our employees. We were not willing to be like some of the private sector companies that are not very concerned about matters such as turnover, or just believe that one has to live with it. We have always strived to make the IRS a good place in which to work.

The report that Mr. Brown was reviewing dealt with one of the first and most important stages of this general effort at modernization: the automation of one segment of the IRS's collection operations with a system called the *automated collection system (ACS)*.

Collection

The IRS organization consisted of a central office in Washington, D.C., and 63 regional district offices, in which collection was one of six divisions. (See Exhibit 1.) Collection was responsible for handling cases in which the IRS had accounts receivable and that originated in one of 10 national service centers. Service centers were where taxpayer returns were filed and processed and bills for unpaid taxes or notices for unfiled returns were issued. When these situations occurred, the integrated data retrieval system (IDRS), a central information system that maintained data on all taxpayers and the status of their returns, generated a series of notices to the taxpayer. If after the fourth notice the case was not resolved, it was forwarded to collection for further action.

Until 1983–1984, the collection operation, called the *collection office function (COF)*, was organized as 63 district office sites. The IRS then decided to automate and reorganize the COF where a major problem was keeping ahead of the inventory of work. In Mr. Brown's words, "We got swamped with paper, mountains of it, and figured that we were not going to get out from under it without computerizing the operation." Introducing computer technology resulted in a

EXHIBIT 1 Organization Chart of a Typical IRS District

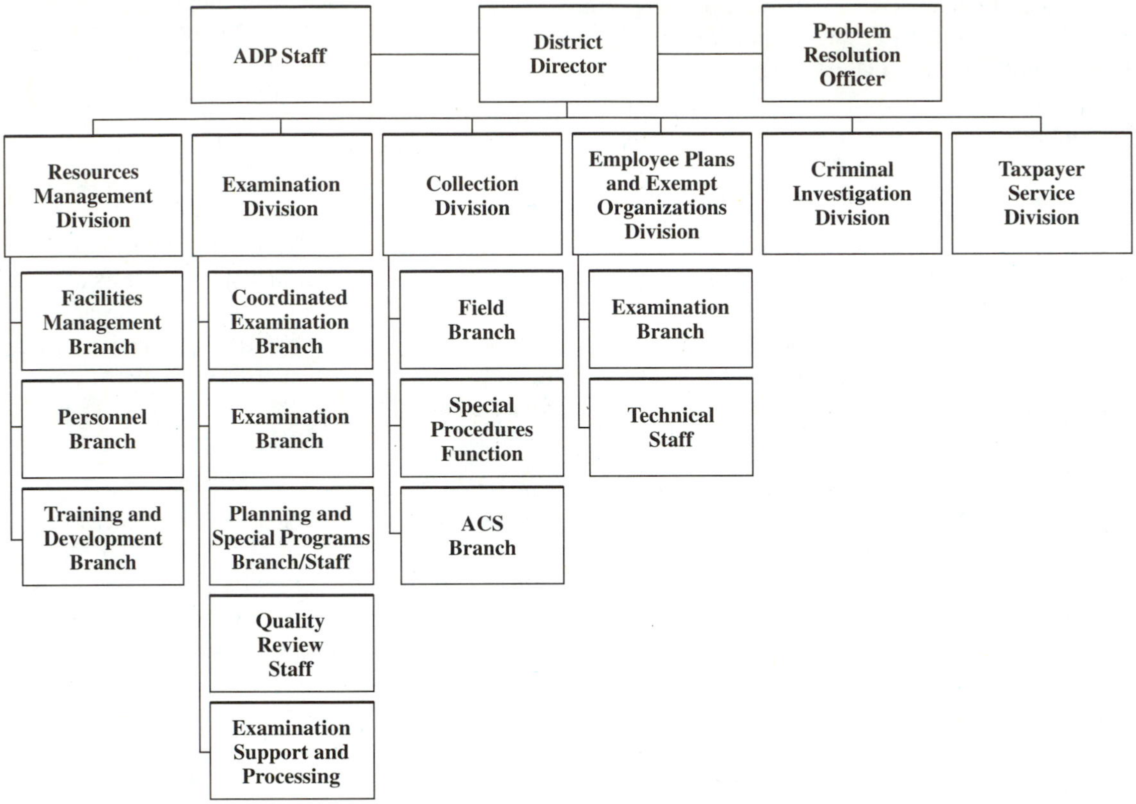

reduction of collection sites from 63 district offices to 20 offices, or "call sites," each of which served multiple districts. It also resulted in a reduction of employees from 5,000 to 2,500. The cases handled by these call sites still originated in the same way as they did for COF. The new operation, intended to create a more efficient and effective collection operation than COF, was called the *automated collection system* (*ACS*). (See Exhibit 2).

Based on further conversations with Mr. Brown and other IRS personnel, brief sketches of the COF and ACS operations follow.

The Collection Office Function (COF)

Structure

COF was organized along six basic functions: (1) process review units, (2) outgoing call units, (3) office field units, (4) incoming call units, (5) a walk-in unit, and (6) a research unit. (Exhibit 3). When cases arrived from the service center they went to the process review unit, where they were categorized by individual and business accounts and batched in large open trays holding up to 500 of these paper documents. If there was no way to contact the taxpayers by phone, a letter was sent or a levy (a judicial order to seize or attach property)

EXHIBIT 2   Listing of ACS Sites by Service Center and District

Service Center	Call Site	District Served
Andover	Boston	Augusta Boston Burlington Harvard Portsmouth Providence
	Buffalo	Albany St. Paul Buffalo
Brookhaven	Manhattan	Brooklyn Manhattan
	Newark	Newark
Philadelphia	Baltimore	Baltimore
	Philadelphia	Philadelphia Pittsburgh Wilmington
	Puerto Rico	Foreign operations (Puerto Rico)
Atlanta	Atlanta	Atlanta Birmingham Columbia Jackson
	Jacksonville	Jacksonville
Memphis	Nashville	Greensboro Nashville Little Rock
	Indianapolis	Indianapolis Richmond
Fresno	San Francisco	Honolulu Los Angeles San Francisco
	Laguna Niguel	Laguna Niguel San Jose Los Angeles
Ogden	Seattle	Anchorage Sacramento Portland Seattle

(continued)

EXHIBIT 2 *(concluded)*   Listing of ACS Sites by Service Center and District

Service Center	Call Site	District Served
	Denver	Aberdeen
		Cheyenne
		Denver
		Fargo
		Omaha
		Phoenix
		Reno
		Salt Lake City
		Boise
		Helena
Cincinnati	Cleveland	Cleveland
		Parkersburg
		Cincinnai
	Detroit	Detroit
		Louisville
Kansas City	Chicago	Chicago
		Des Moines
		Milwaukee
	St. Louis	St. Louis
		Springfield
Austin	Dallas	Albuquerque
		Dallas
		Oklahoma City
		Wichita
	Houston	Austin
		Houston
		New Orleans

placed on any available source. These letters and levies generated the incoming calls and taxpayers, appearing in person at the walk-in unit. Accounts for which a telephone number could be identified were sent to an outgoing call unit.

The outgoing call units primarily made outgoing calls; when incoming call units were overloaded they undertook some of their work. The office collection representatives, as personnel in this function were known, worked at desks with trays of paper accounts, reviewing each one before telephoning the taxpayer. Upon completion of the call, they would note on history sheets what had transpired during the exchange. This information, plus correspondence to and from the taxpayer, added to the amount of paper handled in COF.

The office field unit, consisting of personnel known as *revenue representatives,* handled cases under a certain dollar amount that could not be closed in COF and that did not require more experienced personnel such as revenue officers. Revenue officers, the other major group of employees in the collection field organization, handled high-dollar cases, those requiring visits to the taxpayer, and those that COF revenue representatives couldn't close. Revenue representatives,

EXHIBIT 3   Office Layout of a Typical COF Site

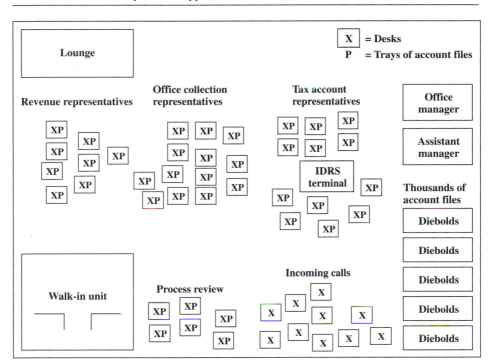

like the office collection representatives, made outgoing calls from the office. In addition, they went to taxpayers' residences to attempt to collect overdue taxes.

The incoming call unit handled calls generated by the letters and levies. When a call came in to a collection representative, he or she would try to get enough information from the taxpayer to become familiar with the case and to take it to the next step, which could be asking the taxpayer to come in or arranging to research the case and return the call later. It was difficult to close incoming call cases. Representatives did not have the cases in front of them and it was extremely difficult to find them among the thousands of paper accounts in the office, many in some stage of transition.

The walk-in unit staff dealt with taxpayers who appeared in person at the office. They could make adjustments to accounts or authorize installment

agreements. They could also release levies pending satisfactory arrangements to pay the account.

The research unit, whose personnel were known as *TARS* (tax account representatives), handled the more difficult cases and special projects such as PRP (problem resolution program) cases. Such cases involving disputes with the IRS over the amount owed, required immediate resolution.

COF was an operation inundated with paper; any action taken on accounts involved paper. Every time an employee worked on an account he or she had to write a summary sheet and attach it to the account. From the time an account was received to the time it was fully processed, anywhere from 10 to 15 separate pieces of paper would be added to it. An individual account could end up being more than an inch thick.

Compounding the paper problem was the rising inventory. According to an IRS report:

In 1976, we had 614,000 accounts receivable in our inventory. By 1982, this inventory had climbed to almost two million accounts. In dollar terms, accounts receivable grew from $1.7 billion in July of 1976 to $7.6 billion in December of 1982.

Consequently, according to this report, COF became "a cumbersome, outmoded, paper-laden system that could no longer handle the work load." Those who had worked in COF underscored that assessment. A former COF branch chief noted: "When a taxpayer wrote to us, we could associate the correspondence with the account only 20 percent of the time." Both managers and employees agreed that COF had come to a point where it was literally out of control and often characterized it as an operation where the better part of one's time was spent trying to locate lost cases. One employee related that her manager used to time, with his stopwatch, how long it took to find a case. It was often more than three hours. Another employee estimated that because at any time about 60 percent of the inventory was in transition, "most of us were always looking for something [we] couldn't find."

The COF system was not very efficient at following up on cases, either. Account representatives would tell taxpayers that they had 10 days to pay; however, that was rarely pursued in a timely fashion. According to one manager:

It got to the point where the taxpayers knew the time frame was slow. So even though you told them that they had 10 days to pay, they knew that there wouldn't be a timely follow up, and that they had at least a couple of months.

There were other problems in the COF organization. Employees in the incoming call units had difficulty handling the calls because they did not have easy access to the taxpayers' accounts. As noted above, accounts were continually in transition. To get the pertinent background information the collection representative would have to ask the taxpayer, adding to the length of the calls, and casting doubt on the information's validity. Lack of easy access compounded the number of errors in the system.

Overall, the climate in the COF was described as very unstructured; the offices consisted of one big open area, with desks almost on top of one another. It was a very hectic environment, referred to as a "boiler room" by some of the employees and a "zoo" by others. Part of the chaos existed because COF employees often worked a case to completion, with a good amount of discussion back and forth among employees over correct procedures. Moreover, employees had considerable freedom to move throughout the office, usually searching for a case or consulting the IDRS terminal for information pertinent to it. In each function—research, contact, and investigation—they were well aware of what others' work consisted of.

Control Systems

At the level of office performance, COF supervisors would track trays of accounts by cycle. Each week was a cycle. They would meet weekly to discuss the status of the work and then shift personnel to whatever area seemed to need help. Supervisors' activities, therefore, consisted primarily of planning, initiating, and following the progress of the work.

Individual performance appraisal was sporadic. To review work, COF supervisors would pull the accounts out of the trays and check that they were handled properly. For the most part the review process consisted of monitoring cases, not individuals, as it was often difficult to trace faulty work to a particular individual. Moreover, going through trays was done about "once every four months," according to one employee. Therefore, employee performance appraisals were only weakly associated with how they actually performed their work.

The Transition to ACS

Mr. Brown, who had begun his career with the IRS in the COF, noted that before the transition to ACS, the majority of the people working in COF had been there a long time. "It was as though they were there forever." These offices were staffed mostly with "older ladies" who knew their jobs well and helped each other in completing cases; they did not receive the proposal to shift to ACS with much enthusiasm.

A lot of the COF staff, particularly those who had the seniority to transfer elsewhere in the system, did not go to ACS. "We lost a lot of the technical knowledge they possessed with the changeover to the new system. We had to hire almost 50 percent of the people from outside the organization and train them from scratch." In Mr. Brown's view, a lot of the senior people did not transfer to ACS because of stories that were circulating about what it would be like—tied to the computer terminal all day.

The Automated Collection System (ACS)

Technology

The automated collection system (ACS) was a computerized inventory control system consisting of three computer components: IDRS (integrated data retrieval system), IBM, and Rockwell ACD (automated call distributor).

IDRS was a master computer located in the service centers and linked to the ACS call sites. Taxpayer information was keyed into this computer at the service center and fed to ACS call sites if, after a fourth notice to the taxpayer, a return had not been filed or taxes were still outstanding. The IDRS also furnished ACS sites with relevant updates regarding account data.

The IBM system consisted of a mainframe that contained the database of ACS accounts and controlled work processing, on a priority basis, to the several terminals staffed by account representatives.

ACD provided for the most cost-effective routing of outgoing telephone calls and allowed incoming calls to be routed to available employees. The Rockwell system automatically connected all incoming and outgoing lines to employee terminals, allowing for a large volume of calls to be handled simultaneously. Outgoing and incoming calls represented the heart of the ACS operation. The overall system also incorporated skip-tracing techniques, third-party contacts, and automated sources for locating taxpayers and their assets.

Cases could be accessed in the ACS by inputting a specific taxpayer identification number or by pressing the <next case> key, which automatically displayed the case with the highest priority in the system. There was a three-tiered priority system in which, in general, workload in the highest tier had to be completed before that in a lower tier. In descending order of priority, the three tiers were: (1) time-constrained cases, (2) assigned-employee cases, (3) scheduled follow-up-date cases.

Time-constrained cases were accessed when a best time to call the taxpayer had been identified. Assigned-employee cases were seldom used since account representatives regularly reassigned their cases for others to follow up. Scheduled follow-up-date cases, which constituted the majority of cases in the ACS system, followed essentially a first-in, first-out method that ensured that all cases were worked on. They were worked on according to oldest follow-up date first and then highest dollar value. Thus, in general, a large-dollar case with today's follow-up date would not be accessed until all of yesterday's low-dollar cases were completed.

Structure

Each ACS call site was organized along three basic functions: (1) contact, (2) investigation, and (3) research. (Exhibit 4). After the respective service center sent out its notices, case information was fed directly into an IDRS terminal located in the call site. It was then stored in the IBM system and could be accessed from employees' terminals.

1. *Contact function:* The contact representative sat at a computer terminal and pressed a key for the next case; then the case with the highest priority in the system flashed onto the screen. After reviewing the salient information, he or she pressed the dial key, and the computer automatically dialed the taxpayer's telephone number. If there was no answer or the line was busy, the computer automatically rescheduled the case for another time. If the contact representative reached the taxpayer, he or she then attempted to resolve the case. Whether successful or not at this point, the employee noted on the screen what action had to be taken as a result of the call. If a form or letter had to be sent out, the employee typed in a code

EXHIBIT 4   Office Layout of a Typical ACS Site

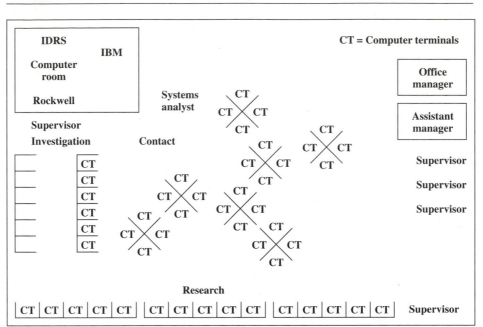

and the document was computer generated overnight at the appropriate service center.

2. *Investigation function:* The investigation function paralleled the work of process review in COF. Investigation staff attempted to find telephone numbers for taxpayers when none were available on the ACS computer file. They scanned available phone directories, or called third parties to locate either taxpayers or their assets.

3. *Research function:* When the ACS sites were first established, the research function handled the more difficult cases, plus incoming calls. Subsequently, in some of the call sites, incoming calls were handled by a contact unit. The research function could access both the IDRS and ACS terminals, with IDRS information used to supplement ACS information when complex adjustments had to be made to resolve a case. The research function also handled correspondence.

Thus, in changing to ACS, the structure became more simplified; of the six functions that existed in

COF, only three were kept in ACS. In part, this new, simplified structure was instituted because of the assumption that ACS would be able to close a lot more cases, as well as higher-dollar cases, than was possible in COF. Those cases that ACS could not close would go directly to revenue officers who were now positioned in the district field office. The walk-in function was also kept separate from ACS. Thus, ACS became a back-room operation, without face-to-face contact with the taxpayer.

This new structure also resulted in an operation isolated from the rest of collection, one not as well integrated. ACS no longer had personnel directly linked with their collection colleagues in the field operation. Concerning the sense of isolation, one senior manager in ACS commented: "The rest of collection thinks we're a dialing-for-dollars operation."

ACS offices were generally bright and roomy. All employees had their own terminals located in private cubicles. On the whole, they were discouraged from discussing case procedures with one another because supervisors felt that it wasted other employees' time. Moreover, because procedures were constantly changing, it was safest to consult with the supervisor.

As cases appeared on the employee's screen randomly (having been assigned to appear on that day), an employee—seeing only pieces of a case—rarely followed them through to completion.

Also, in ACS there was no reason to move from one's station to check the IDRS terminal because it was connected to the employee's terminal. Consequently, employees generally spent their entire working day at their terminal, within their particular function. It was more difficult for them to learn the work of other functions or to get to know other employees.

Thus, in introducing the technology there was a reintegration of three specialized functions, but one that made them—and the employees working in them—more isolated and less likely to follow individual cases through to completion.

From a performance standpoint, ACS addressed many of COF's problems. Because all accounts were on the computer, there was rarely a lost case. Moreover, correspondence could be easily matched to the appropriate case stored in the computer, eliminating time lost looking for cases.

The response time in ACS was much faster than in COF. When a time limit was placed on an account, an account representative entered a code and that case came up on the indicated day for further action.

Because an employee could quickly call up the history sheet of a particular account, follow up on cases was also improved in ACS.

The three factors noted above: the ability to find cases, follow up on cases, and control incoming calls were central to the improvements in work process and productivity of operations that resulted from the changeover to ACS.

Control Systems

Perhaps the biggest difference between COF and ACS was the amount of performance monitoring done in ACS. It was driven in part by the new technology's capabilities, and in part by management's insistence that reviews be done to monitor the benefits of the new automated system and its effect on employee performance.

In terms of office performance, the computer provided timely information that helped managers track the work status. A systems analyst, whose position was created for this purpose, continually monitored the number of incoming and outgoing calls and, depending on the priorities of the site personnel, could "computer gate," or schedule, them accordingly. Consequently, there was less manual scheduling and virtually no tracking of work flow in ACS.

The ACS technology allowed for additional real-time information on a variety of performance indicators. For the entire office, the computer monitored the number of calls received, the number of calls answered, the average speed of answer, the number of calls attempted, the number of calls completed, the average worktime of calls, the number of accounts closed, and the number of dollars collected. However, it was only a portion of the information available. In addition, reports were generated that provided information on resource allocation within the call site, such as inventory levels by type of account (business or individual, not filed, or taxes outstanding); the type of closure on accounts (full payments, installment agreements, or transfers to another part of the IRS); and a breakdown of overaged accounts in inventory.

At the individual level, there were three distinct sources of performance monitoring information: (1) computer monitoring, (2) telephone monitoring, and (3) teach reviews.

1. *Computer monitoring:* Machine monitoring was the most pervasive source of information on work behavior and productivity. The computer provided supervisors and managers with information concerning an employee's average talk time, the number of calls attempted, number of calls completed, time spent away from the computer, and time between calls. This information was sometimes relayed to the employee, especially when one or more of the indicators were judged to be below target. However, the use of machine statistics for formal performance appraisal was not allowed according to the union contract.

2. *Telephone monitoring:* As outlined in the *ACS Management Handbook,* supervisors were required to monitor at least two completed calls to taxpayers, or a minimum of one hour per employee, per week. In this activity, the supervisor listened to the conversation and rated the employee on key criteria such as correct procedure, courtesy, and ability to control the conversation. While monitoring the telephone conversation in process the supervisor simultaneously viewed a screen display of the account the employee was working. According to IRS monitoring guidelines:

> Telephones subject to monitoring must be clearly marked so that telephone users will have full knowledge of the monitoring possibilities.
>
> All employees must be notified, in writing, that their work-related calls are subject to monitoring. This should be accomplished semi-annually. In addition, new employees must be given the same notification prior to assuming monitored telephone duties.

The results of this review were supposed to be given to the employee immediately on completion of the call. Used in the formal performance appraisal process, these reviews had direct implications for promotions and other valued outcomes. Referring to the monitoring reviews, one employee stated: "It's a numbers game; if you don't have the numbers, you're not going to move up."

3. *Teach reviews:* Teach reviews of employees' work, generally done on a weekly basis, consisted of the supervisor using a computer terminal or hard copy to display all cases worked by an employee over a period of time. According to the handbook, the supervisor had to determine whether the employee was:

1. Analyzing ACS data correctly.
2. Making correct decisions and recommendations.
3. Initiating effective follow-up actions.

4. Following procedural guidelines.
5. Encouraging call backs or correspondence unnecessarily.

The results of the review were either communicated to the employee face-to-face or left in his or her drop-box. Regardless of the method of feedback, the results were used in the formal quarterly and annual employee performance appraisal sessions and could have a direct bearing on such outcomes as promotions.

Thus, one of the distinctive features of ACS call sites was the amount of reviews that supervisors and managers were responsible for. Moreover, the technology's capability to monitor both system-wide and individual-level performance made ACS's work operation radically different from COF's. The impact of the transition to ACS on supervisors' and employees' jobs can be summarized as follows. Supervisory work became more singularly focused on the monitoring of employees' work, requiring significant amounts of time. As a consequence, employees were monitored much more heavily than in the past. Moreover, they were much more restricted in their movements; their job consisting primarily of interacting with a computer terminal.

Supervisors' and Employees' Reactions to the Change

Supervisors

The technology in ACS helped to rationalize supervisors' jobs; their work became much less fragmented. However, it had serious implications for how they viewed themselves and the amount of discretion they felt they had.

Most supervisors interviewed stated that on the whole they preferred ACS to COF. However, this view was not without qualification. Some referred to themselves as "glorified watch dogs." One stated:

> I've never been in an environment where employees and supervisors are so scrutinized. Everyone observes everyone else. There's no getting around it.

Supervisory discretion was an issue throughout the call sites. For example, statements similar to "they [senior managers] treat us like babies"; "we have the capability to control but we are not allowed to use it"; or "managers are so concerned with employees' perceptions"; and "we're judged on employees' perceptions of our communications skills," were not uncommon.

There was often a strong feeling of control, of both controlling and being controlled. Some of the supervisors felt that the requirements for telephone monitoring dictated that they give feedback. They saw it being ineffective as it was made routine rather than spontaneous.

However, other supervisors felt differently. They viewed the control potential of the technology as a positive aid to accomplishing their tasks, noting that it was "far easier to identify weak and strong employees." Expressing what she felt was the majority view, one supervisor stated: "Supervisors like it better because they are now able to control the work environment—reward good people, sit on bad people."

Supervisors' activities centered on reviews. When asked to relate their most important activities in a typical week, supervisors nearly unanimously mentioned employees' reviews, particularly telephone monitoring. Representative statements were:

> Telephone monitoring is number one. It probably eats up 60 percent of my time.

> Telephone monitoring! You finish on Friday and you start again on Monday.

In general, a significant amount of supervisors' time was involved in doing one review or another. The following statement by a supervisor may not be typical of the actual time that most supervisors put into reviews, but it is suggestive of the amount of time necessary to meet review requirements:

> Telephone monitoring takes up 15 hours a week minimum. On average, it takes about 20 hours. Counselling employees and presenting feedback on reviews takes another four to five hours. Teach reviews, where I review every fifth case on each employee, takes six to eight hours a week.

Thus, anywhere from 25 to 33 hours of a supervisor's week could be spent on reviews.

Some supervisors noted monitoring's potential for developing employees, viewing it as "a great way to give employees instant feedback on their progress." This attribute was often mentioned. However, the reality was seen as far different in many cases, due to the tension between meeting the monitoring requirement and realizing the feedback potential.

One supervisor stated:

> Supervisors may not use it as the really good tool that it is. It's a positive thing. We resent it because it takes so much time. Supervisors may not want to do it so it turns out to be negative.

Others were clearly disenchanted with what they came to perceive as an exercise lacking value, on the whole more dysfunctional than functional:

> For an employee, the feedback after awhile becomes the same thing. It has little effect.

> I don't see that much difference, whether I monitor or not. Things that I would identify as important don't seem that significant.

> Since I have to do the monitoring, I say something, one way or the other.

> Monitoring just ends up being negative management.

Employees

> We're pretty much tied to the place. All our time is monitored daily. There aren't the friendly hellos or chit-chat, "Did you just get back from your vacation?" and stuff like that. It doesn't bother me. Management is aware of it and has little get-togethers.—ACS employee

The above quote points to the isolation of employees that can accompany computerization in office settings. Whereas in the above statement, the employee was not particularly bothered by the lack of interaction with other employees (indeed, she later stated that she rather appreciated the isolation as it "allows me to do my work"), others were less than enthusiastic. Typical statements were:

> In my supervisor's eyes, if I'm not at the terminal I'm not working.

> It's too confining required to be on the terminal all day.

In the 25 years I've been here [in the IRS] I've never been tied down [as in ACS].

The feeling of confinement resulting from a required constant presence at their terminals was mentioned by employees as the single factor they most disliked in the transition to ACS. Also important was that they no longer worked a case through to completion, which lessened job satisfaction. They noted that their performance was reviewed more, but that had not in itself been a problem. Most employees thought the monitoring was all right if it was conducted properly.

Indeed, the majority of employees interviewed concurred with management's assessment of the general need for monitoring and some of its positive impacts:

We have to do monitoring. I'm sure we don't like to have it done to us all the time, but it's necessary for quality control and as a check on new procedures. It increases performance. I know when I get comments that say you forgot to do something, I try to do it the next time.

Monitoring reminds you not to get careless and to keep up with new procedures . . . I think that when you're first learning, it would be good if all your calls were monitored.

You get good feedback from monitoring. Most of mine was positive.

If we weren't monitored, you'd get all kinds of things going on.

However, another more negative side to monitoring was also raised by some employees:

Some employees think it's like being spied on.

You can get a biased manager who is looking for the bad rather than the good in someone.

I think that monitoring can be good if it's objective. But if they [supervisors] interject with their opinions, then it's not so good. There are different ways of handling calls. Both answers may be right in terms of working a case.

They [supervisors] give the feedback too late. By then you can't remember what happened in the call.

On the whole, employees stressed that how computer-aided monitoring was approached made all the difference. Some even suggested that supervisors "should do more telephone monitoring, but it should be used strictly as a quality control tool." They often felt that instead it was frequently used as a "gotcha!"

Conclusion

Sifting through these reactions, Mr. Brown wondered what to do next. The collection division was committed to making the technology initiative work and to learn from this experience in order to automate other operations. The enhancements in productivity and service that the IRS was able to provide with the introduction of ACS were impressive. Yet, the reactions of the managers and employees who had to make the system work suggested that there was still considerable room for improvement. There were at least three options that Mr. Brown felt worth considering seriously.

The first option was to restructure ACS's work organization into semi-autonomous teams. Such teams would comprise members who, among them, had all the functional expertise necessary to handle cases to completion. They would then be given a batch of cases to work on and their performance would be monitored only as to how they handled the cases. Scheduling work flow and monitoring individual performance would be the team's responsibility. Mr. Brown's technical people had pointed out that this option would require an investment of more than $1 million to redesign the technology so that the teams could handle cases from start to finish. The teams would also have to change to a uniform pay scale instead of the three that then existed for contact, research, and investigation. Such a change was certain to raise the wage bill.

The second option was to retrain ACS employees to become more versatile and able to handle all aspects of the collection function. For example, employees would handle cases as best they could from start to finish. This option, like the one above, would necessitate raising the pay scale to compensate employees for the additional skills required to handle all of the functions in closing a case. In addition, there would be significant retraining costs.

The final option was to work within the present organization but to change the way the system was managed. The report that Mr. Brown was reviewing suggested that seven factors were significant in influencing employees' reaction to ACS. They were: (1) the immediacy of monitoring information feedback, (2) the nature (positive or negative) of the feedback, (3) the clarity of the criteria used to rate performance, (4) the method of monitoring (whether done remotely or with the supervisor sitting next to the employee), (5) the supervisor's knowledge of the job, (6) the supervisor's leadership style, and (7) the employees' prior disposition toward computer monitoring. Taken together, these factors pointed to the importance of effectively managing the way in which the monitoring process was used and the way the information generated from it was communicated to the employees. Experience had shown that the way management approached monitoring did make a difference to its effectiveness and employees' reactions to it.

CASE 5–2: THE INCIDENT AT WACO MANUFACTURING

Preparation Questions

1. What are the benefits of a location-tracking system such as that described in the case?
2. What should Tomaso and Saltz do next?
3. What policies or guidelines would you suggest for governing the storage of and access to location data collected by the system?

Case 5–2 The Incident at Waco Manufacturing*

In 1986, Waco Manufacturing, a leading supplier of custom-machined parts to the automotive industry, installed a security and information system in one of its manufacturing plants. Transceivers (devices that can both transmit and receive radio signals) were embedded in the plant corridors every 25 feet and in badges worn by all employees. This technology supported almost continuous tracking of the location of each employee, a capability that fostered many interesting applications. For example, a telephone call to an employee would ring at the phone nearest that person, which often was not the individual's office phone.

The Incident

During a third-quarter performance review in September 1987, area manager Monique Saltz informed Monk Barber, a plant engineering manager, that she was unhappy that a new set of

*Professor John J. Sviokla prepared this fictitious case. Copyright © 1989 by the President and Fellows of Harvard College. Harvard Business School case 189-142 (Revised 1990)

designs for composite-based products, required in the 1987 plan, was behind schedule. "I have repeatedly met with Sherman McCoy, Telly Frank, and Wanda Gogan, the three engineers assigned to this project," Barber explained, "and I have tried to impress upon them the importance of this set of designs. They simply have not responded. I am at wits' end."

When Saltz subsequently met with McCoy, Frank, and Gogan, Gogan expressed surprise. "I don't know quite how to say this," she told Saltz, "but I had no idea that this project was so important. In fact, I cannot remember meeting with Mr. Barber about the composite design project. We knew it was coming, but we had no idea of its importance." Frank and McCoy concurred. Later that day, Saltz described the situation to plant manager Shelly Tomaso, who suggested that they review the plant record of employee locations as recorded by the transceiver system. Tomaso and Saltz looked first at the record and then at each other—since the beginning of 1987, Barber, McCoy, Frank, and Gogan had never all been in the same room at the same time.

Reading 5–1

Preparation Questions

1. What does Zuboff mean by the term *informate?* How does informating contrast with automating?
2. When an organization commits to informating, what are the implications for employee hiring and retention?
3. How might managers' roles change in an informating organization? What are the implications for management education?

INFORMATE THE ENTERPRISE: AN AGENDA FOR THE TWENTY-FIRST CENTURY*

By Shoshana Zuboff*

Few firms are satisfied with their track records in exploiting the strategic potential inherent in information technology. My own research over the past

*By Shoshana Zuboff. Reprinted with permission from National Forum, Summer 1991.

12 years suggests that the biggest obstacles to achieving significant competitive innovation with information technology lie not in the technology itself, but in the forms of organization and conceptions of management inherited from the nineteenth century that continue to dominate the imaginative

life of today's enterprises. In other words, twenty-first century utilization of information technology requires development of the twenty-first century organization.

The Automate Paradigm

Throughout human history, technology has developed according to one predominant logic. Whether involving a simple tool or a complex machine, that logic has been that technology is designed to substitute for the human body. It is meant to accomplish the same tasks as the human body does, only faster, more reliably, under conditions of greater control, ultimately with less reliance on human skill or intervention, and thus more cheaply.

For these reasons, managers in the modern age have assumed that the more technology they have, the fewer workers they need. A correlative assumption has been that "smarter" technologies require less skill in the work force, because they reduce the scope of human intervention in productive or administrative processes. More smart machines means fewer smart people. The goals associated with deploying new technologies in the workplace have typically been those of cost reduction, efficiency, and productivity.

This generic approach to deployment of technology has come to be known as *automation.* It means applying technology in ways that increase the self-acting and self-regulating capacities of machine systems, thus minimizing human intervention.

There is no doubt that information technology can be applied to automate work according to precisely this logic. What follows are two examples of organizations that applied advanced technologies but remained within the age-old paradigm of "automation."

Piney Wood

The first example is that of Piney Wood, a large American pulp mill built in the 1940s with then state-of-the-art pneumatic-control technology. In that environment, operators typically worked in close proximity to both equipment and product. Over the years, they developed a good deal of tacit knowledge about the production process. This kind of knowledge was felt in their bodies and displayed in their actions, though it was rarely made explicit.

For example, one man judged the chlorine content of bleached pulp by sniffing and squeezing it. Another judged the moisture content in a roll of paper by slapping his hand across it and another by observing the amount of static electricity in his hair. They performed complex sequences of actions that they were unable to describe verbally. Indeed, even the most highly skilled workers had difficulty translating their knowledge into words or breaking it down into logical components. The sentient and physical derivation of their knowledge was the basis for what I call "action-centered skills."

During the early 1980s, a $200 million modernization effort replaced pneumatic-control technology with microprocessor-based integrated information and control systems. Most workers now spent a good deal of their time in control rooms, monitoring digital readout from a vast system of automated equipment and sensors.

Managers at Piney Wood looked to the new technology as a way of increasing control over the production process, and of thus improving reliability, quality, and cost effectiveness, while reducing the dependence on operator skills and judgment. They also believed that the range of information made available by the new control systems would enable improvements to be made in the production process and in product innovations, along with increased flexibility and potential for customization.

Most managers believed that more smart technology would mean both fewer people and dumber people—that is, skill levels could be lowered as more intelligence could be programmed into automatic systems. This was exemplified in the fact that nowhere in the $200 million budget had provision been made for operator (or manager) training. Although this may seem peculiar, my work has led me to conclude that such a practice is common. Few organizations earmark more than a tiny fraction of their technology expenditure for training of any sort. At Piney Wood they said:

> Training doesn't amount to much. No one had training numbers in their budget. We set up menus and teach them to press buttons, but we don't expect them to understand what they are doing.

Although managers believed they were merely automating, they were also creating a very new kind of work environment. Now, remote from product and equipment, workers spent most of their time in control rooms with nicknames like "The Star Trek Suite," engaged with the digital readout from the thousands of microprocessors that both sensed and automated the production process.

In addition to applying programmed instructions, these microprocessors were registering data about the moment-to-moment condition of the product and the process. These data now surrounded operators in the form of glowing blue, green, and red electronic digits, text, and graphics.

It was as if the entire production process had been abstracted and represented in a vast electronic text. In order to monitor the process, operators had to be able to read and understand this new text. Abstract data had become the new medium through which they were required to operate the plant.

If any progress was to be made toward the more complex goals of optimization, innovation, and customization, then operator skills would have to be developed even further. Managers would have had to be able to use the new, more abstract data as the basis for developing new insights into functional relationships, states, conditions, trends, emerging problems, and underlying causes.

Not only did they need to understand what they observed, but they also needed to generate meaningful insights that could translate into value-adding activities, such as learning how to operate better at lower costs, producing high-quality products from less costly raw materials, or tailoring batch runs to customer specifications.

During this period, many Piney Wood managers began, reluctantly, to question some of their assumptions regarding the requirements of the new technology. The plant was experiencing frequent breakdowns, and the new data generated by the computer-based control systems were barely utilized. Gradually, many managers began to believe that they had seriously miscalculated work-force skill requirements in the new technological environment. Instead of their earlier beliefs about opportunities for skill reduction, many now concluded that operating personnel would need to develop new intellectual skills that could provide for a more critical and analytical engagement with the abstract data that now surrounded them. They said:

> We have cut out so many people that there is no one to do the neat things which we could use the information for. It's like having a vast crop and no one to harvest it.

The operators had worked their way around to a similar realization. Many had learned that they now had to develop an entirely different kind of knowledge if they were to remain competent in the new environment. Inarticulate action-centered skills would no longer suffice. They henceforth needed a more analytical and conceptual grasp of their work. As one put it:

> The more I learn theoretically, the more I can see in the information. Raw data turn into information with my knowledge. I find that you have to be able to know more in order to do more. It is your understanding the process that guides you.

Global Bank

Similar dynamics are evident in a wide range of white-collar organizations involving clerks, professionals, and managers in Global Bank.

In the office environment we see connections being made among transaction systems, communication systems, management-information systems, financial systems, customer and supplier systems, epos systems, scanner systems, and imaging systems. Each one may have been developed in order to perform some function faster, more reliably, or at less cost. But as the time frames in which data are collected and presented become accelerated, as more sectors of data are integrated, and as access to the systems becomes more widely distributed, the organization in its myriad functions comes increasingly to be reflected in a dynamic, fluid, electronic text that can be accessed from almost any computer terminal.

Data that were once diffuse, inaccessible, and private—in drawers, on desk tops, in files, or simply stored in people's heads to be summoned up when the occasion demanded—now become codified, rationalized, explicated, and public. This new text is, in theory, accessible to anyone with the appropriate skills to engage it. The business becomes transparent as never before, patterns can be discerned, and opportunities and problems can be anticipated.

For example, in Global Bank, a new business strategy emphasizing targeted marketing of value-added, information-based products and services led to the design of a new database to support the product-development process. Strategists saw database technology as a way to integrate the financial numbers of the bank, which could then be accessed by flexible analytical software. The bank's revenues would depend increasingly upon the ability to use this complex database to perceive new opportunities to serve customers. No longer would it be sufficient to have account officers dedicated to one-on-one dealings with customers while a separate group managed the technology. The new banker would have to be fluent in technology and information analysis as well as relate to customers.

The new technological environment required a change in the nature of a banker's knowledge, similar to that experienced in the pulp mill. Bankers had seen themselves as "artists." An important component of their credit judgment was based on private knowledge, "a feeling in my stomach" or

"a gut feeling" that derived from face-to-face engagements with customers—over drinks, golf, or in the office.

Now an increasing portion of their work depended upon their ability to analyze and conceptualize abstract information, using a broad-reaching database that revealed the dynamics of the bank's business and marketplace more clearly and comprehensively than ever before. This new electronic text would become the "laboratory" from which added value in products and services emerged.

In the old environment, bankers competed for information. Because information was private—stored in memos or reports, spoken out in meetings or luncheon conversation, stored in desk drawers or in correspondence—access to it tended to depend upon either formal status or personal contacts. But as more and more information was made explicit, codified, rationalized, and absorbed into the growing database, access came to depend less on status and contacts and more on the intellectual ability to navigate the database. Competition now depended upon who would create more value from data that were, in principle, widely accessible. Again, interpreting the electronic text was the keystone of a new kind of competence. Bankers described it this way:

> A banker used to be a salesperson—a lot of interaction and personality, flying by the seat of the pants with white scarves and goggles. Now people who are good must manage and use information on a more objective and analytical basis. The new technology provides a sophisticated means of navigating in the business environment. Holding your finger to the wind isn't acceptable anymore.

From Automate to Informate

Even as it is applied to automation, information technology simultaneously accomplishes something very different and much more poorly understood.

What we are learning is that these new conditions defy the old rules of thumb about automation.

Instead of *dumber* people, we are discovering that people need whole new skill-sets as the basis for competence and excellence in this new world.

People who have learned their work relying on physical cues in their environment (interaction with things or people) now require new intellectual skills that will enable them to create meaning and value from the increasingly abstract cues of electronically presented information.

These new "intellective" skills include an emphasis on abstract thinking, problem solving, and inference; an explicit theoretical understanding of the work at hand and its context; modes of reasoning that are analytic, procedural, and systemic; and finally the ability to commit one's attention to systematic mental effort for extended periods.

What we see in these examples are the two faces of intelligent technology. On the one hand, intelligent technology can be used to automate, but even as this occurs the technology has the capacity to translate those automated activities into data and to display those data. Information technology symbolically renders processes, objects, behaviors, and events so that they become visible, knowable, and shareable in a new way.

The word that I have coined to describe this second function is "informate." Information technologies can *informate* as well as *automate*. "To informate" means to translate and make visible; "informating" occurs as processes, objects, behaviors, and events are translated into and made visible as explicit information.

As the informating process unfolds, the organization is increasingly imbued with an electronic text that explicitly represents many forms of data which were once implicit, private, or minimally codified. Thus, the work environment becomes increasingly "textualized."

By "textualization," I mean that an increasing proportion of the information in the work environment is presented through the medium of electronic text.

Under these conditions, to "work" becomes more abstract, since it depends upon an understanding of, responsiveness to, and ability to manage and create value from information. In an informated environment, skills are redefined. The application of an informating technology doesn't simply imply the destruction of older forms of knowledge. Instead, it requires the construction of a new kind of knowledge, one that is more analytical, abstract, and conceptual.

It is in terms of this second informating function that information technology represents a radical discontinuity in the history of work and the evolution of industrial technology. Earlier generations of machines decreased the complexity and substantive content of work tasks, making it possible to employ people with ever-lower levels of skills. In contrast, an informating technology increases the explicit information content of tasks. As a result, it tends to increase the intellectual character of work.

Why is this a fundamental challenge to industrial organization as we have known it? Because over the course of this century, the manager's role has evolved as that of guardian of the organization's explicit information base. A manager's legitimization is derived in large measure from his/her being accredited as someone fit to receive, interpret, and communicate orders based on that information.

An iron curtain was drawn between those whose tasks were simplified and, through automation, stripped of information content, and those who received that information and were expected to preside over it. Indeed, the essential logic of industrial hierarchy rests on the premise that complexity can constantly be removed from the front line and passed up to the management ranks. Automation has been relied upon as a primary means of achieving and maintaining this organizational state of affairs.

But as an informating technology reintroduces substantive content into work tasks at the front line of the organization, this iron curtain is no longer feasible.

An opportunity is created for organizations to deal with complexity at the point where it enters the organization. This may be at the customer interface, at the point of production, or in the process of service delivery. It is an opportunity that should be welcomed by organizations trying to respond to the conditions of hypercompetition, which are increasingly prevalent and which have made such considerations as time to market, customer service, and flexibility of paramount importance.

But it is an opportunity that also requires opening up the information base of the organization to people at every level, in order that complexity may be dealt with at the point where it enters the organization. At each level people must have not only the skills to engage with that information, but also the freedom to express what they know. For the more blurred the distinction among the things which people know, the more fragile and pointless become any relations of domination and subordination among the people themselves.

To summarize these crucial relationships: the informating process makes explicit and visible the internal dynamics of the business as well as its external exchange relationships. This new transparency creates an unprecedented opportunity for learning that can result in added value through improvement and innovation. Information technologies can be a principal force in setting the stage for sustainable competitive advantage, but such advantage does not derive from the technology per se. Instead, it derives from an organization's ability to exploit the learning opportunities made possible by the new transparency, which is in turn a function of the informating process. (See Figure A.)

But how do we create such organizations where the principal axis of human behavior shifts from control and obedience to teaching and learning?

The problem we face is this: industrial history has taught us a great deal about how to design and administer organizations that function successfully within the automate paradigm. But we still know very little about how to design and foster learning organizations that can exploit the opportunities for sustainable advantage created by an informating technology.

FIGURE A

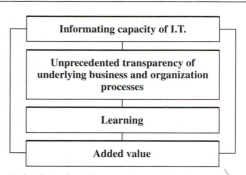

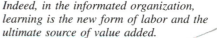

Indeed, in the informated organization, learning is the new form of labor and the ultimate source of value added.

If we are to make headway against this new challenge, we need a paradigm shift—one that transfigures our notions of who people are at work, what they can know, and how they must act together.

The Informated Organization

What is that new paradigm? Rather than search for the one universal template of the informated organization, I believe it is more useful to identify those characteristics that are likely to be a vital part of any organizational response to these emerging conditions.

Intellective-Skill Development

The first level of organizational response involves developing the skills in the work force that can extract value from the electronic text. This requires such skills as abstract thinking and problem solving, conceptualization, analysis, theory-based reasoning, the ability to perceive patterns and relationships, as well as a procedural and functional appreciation of the information systems. In addition, it means a better understanding of the business and its context.

The emphasis is on developing what people have in their heads that they now bring to the information medium. These skills are intellective rather than action centered; they were as important for global bankers in the new database environment as for pulp-mill workers in a highly computerized plant.

Post-Hierarchical Roles and Relationships

Empowering the front lines with information, intellective skills, and the opportunity to act on what they can learn requires, in turn, new forms of roles and relationships, particularly where the role of middle management is concerned. This has been a dominant issue in the organizations that I have studied and worked with.

In an automation paradigm, managers view sharing information and skill as a zero-sum game, in which more knowledge for their subordinates is experienced as a loss of status and power for managers. They fight to retain their role as exclusive guardians of the organization's knowledge base. More automatic processes and fewer skilled people help preserve this hierarchical privilege.

Here's how one worker whose tasks had been informated articulated these new demands on the part of the manager's role:

> The technology lets us know a lot, but we need to know more. As a manager you should teach everybody what you know—keep passing the knowledge on. But they do not give us the knowledge to think for ourselves. I think it's because it would do away with their jobs, or they would look stupid if we had that knowledge.

Too frequently, managers respond to these new conditions defensively as they endeavor to preserve the traditional sources of meaning and prestige in their role. As one manager responded:

> I am not willing to break things down real simply to explain something to operators. I won't give up my terms that I have learned as an engineer. The concepts are hard to understand. I am not here to teach these concepts. I went to college to learn these things and so it proves I have a right to tell people what to do.

But an informating paradigm implies a new conception of roles and relationships. Rather than

FIGURE B   The Concentric Organization

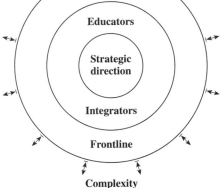

signaling the elimination of middle management, it means that a much wider group of members of the organization take on managerial roles. These roles are likely to differ in terms of the time horizon of the information for which they have responsibility and the degree of integration they must manage.

Those not engaged in front-line activity must be active as educators and integrators. They help develop intellective skills at the front line. They manage the social system in order to create the conditions of collegiality in which the joint problem solving and discursiveness, so vital in an informated organization, can flourish.

Members in these roles are also responsible for managing the heightened interdependencies among a variety of traditional business functions such as development of technology, marketing, human resources, etc. Finally, we can imagine another set of managerial roles that focus on integrating information in order to design and implement business strategy.

The relationships among these roles can be thought of as concentric and interdependent rather than only hierarchical. (See Figure B.) I call this *post-hierarchical management* because it means going beyond the zero-sum games of the traditional pyramid. No longer is there an iron curtain separating the front line from the rest of the organization. Instead, organizational levels are permeable. One can imagine integrated career systems, where one's experience at the front line becomes a multidimensional training ground for promotion to longer time frames of responsibility within the organization.

Structures That Foster a Learning Environment
Managers caught up in such zero-sum games, however, can hardly be blamed. They are actors in a tightly woven logic of reward systems, career policies, and cultural norms. They have been taught not to admit weaknesses or lapses in their own knowledge or understanding. As long as the criteria by which they are evaluated continue to reflect traditional roles, individual behavioral change is very difficult to achieve. This brings us to the third level of innovations—structures and systems must be changed to reinforce and institutionalize new behavioral directions and a redistribution of knowledge.

The real message, then, is that the informating process is unfolding in our organizations. In most cases it is driven by the technology, but in most cases we have failed to develop the people or create the organizations that are capable of exploiting its inherent potential for sustainable competitive advantage.

The point is that informating technologies have put our organizations into play, but these technological processes cannot—will not—ultimately determine what shape the organization takes, what principles it emphasizes, what purposes it embraces, what levels of performance it achieves. This can be done only by *management*. It is a function of the quality of our thinking, understanding, imagination, and leadership. The issues we are facing are systemic. They cannot be treated successfully if we remain trapped within the constraints of today's conception of individual functions, disciplines, and turfs.

These recommendations are neither utopian nor idealistic. In fact, the true idealists express themselves in visions of a perfect clockwork world in which technology can be relied upon to solve all problems.

The real world is a volatile place, where technological solutions fail more often than they succeed and where the demands of flexible adaptation are ruthlessly accelerated. In such a world, human intelligence, combined with smart machines, remains the last best hope for achieving the kind of flexibility, responsiveness, and creativity that have become necessary for organizations to thrive, as well as survive.

These changes have forced us to a new frontier of organizational evolution in which the possibilities of technology and the potentialities of human beings depend on one another as never before. Nowhere is this idea better articulated than in the words of a pulp worker who said:

> If you don't let people grow and develop and make more decisions, it's a waste of human life—a waste of human potential. If you don't use your knowledge and skill it's a waste of life. Using the technology to its full potential means using human beings to their full potential.

CASE 5–3: OTIS ELEVATOR: MANAGING THE SERVICE FORCE

Preparation Questions

1. Describe the information and communication needs of Otis Elevator's maintenance and repair mechanics.

2. Evaluate the approaches taken by field offices to address the organization and communication problems faced by their service field organizations.
3. What difficulties should Bird anticipate with the roll-out of the KDT and OSM software? What actions can Bird take to mitigate some of these difficulties?

Case 5–3 Otis Elevator: Managing the Service Force*

In early October 1990, Rick Whitaker, director of strategic planning for Otis Elevator's North American Operations (NAO), was preparing a new strategic plan for NAO's field-based service operations. Within a week he would present this proposal to the new president of NAO, John Cosentino, and he wanted to review the alternatives carefully before recommending future strategic steps.

Whitaker had no doubt that NAO's service operations needed to be changed to gain significant improvements in productivity and quality. The mechanics needed more information and training as a result of Otis's rapid introduction of new microprocessor-controlled equipment. Intense local competition for Otis's service business added further urgency to the situation. Otis's service market share had declined in many metropolitan areas over the past 10 years, due mainly to the expansion of small, local competitors, who undercut Otis's prices yet stated they offered similar services. Although Otis continued to have a reputation for the best service in the industry, some believed it would have to reduce its costs and its price premium, which was often substantially above the competition's prices.

Whitaker believed the key to regaining Otis's competitive advantage was to "dramatically improve the field service organizational structures,

work methods, and operational tools." He had already seen efforts made throughout Otis toward these ends, and several projects were under way to introduce hand-held portable communications technologies and computer-based scheduled equipment maintenance. In addition, several branch offices with new communications technology were experimenting with using work teams for more efficient and effective equipment service.

Although he was enthusiastic about the potential for implementing some of these changes organizationwide, Whitaker was also wary of disturbing the all-important mechanic/customer relationship, which had been a cornerstone of NAO's market success for more than 100 years. Furthermore, because the service business was NAO's single largest business, there was little margin for error.

The Elevator Industry
In 1990, equipment sales and service in North America represented about $1 billion and $2 billion markets, respectively. The industry was very competitive; Otis, Schindler, Dover, Montgomery, U.S. Elevator, Fujitec, and Mitsubishi were the major manufacturers. But many considered Otis to be the leader in both sales and service. Although elevator sales, being directly correlated to building construction, were cyclical, the market for elevator service was stable. Elevator manufacturers often accepted a low margin on the sale of an elevator to obtain the service contract since service accounted for a significantly higher portion of profits.

The service market attracted many participants because of its steady demand and high profitabil-

*Jonathan O'Neil and Keri Ostrofsky prepared this case under the supervision of Professor James I. Cash, Jr. Copyright © 1991 by the President and Fellows of Harvard College. Harvard Business School case 191-213 (Revised 1992)

EXHIBIT 1   NAO Organization Chart

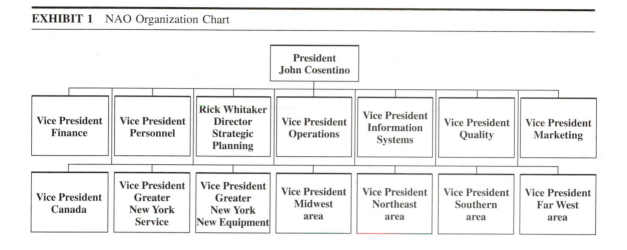

ity. Consequently, many elevator service companies existed, including both manufacturers and small companies devoted only to service. Most of these companies could service elevators from any manufacturer, since all elevators made before the introduction of microprocessor-based control systems used similar, easily understood electromechanical technology.

An elevator service company was usually selected on the basis of responsiveness, quality, and price. An elevator manufacturer was typically awarded 60 percent to 80 percent of the service contracts for its newly installed elevators. As buildings with elevators aged and competition for tenants increased, the cost of service often became the major consideration, and often the lowest bidder received the service contract. Since servicing elevators with microprocessor-based control systems often required the use of proprietary maintenance devices, the manufacturer was more likely to keep these service contracts. While Otis management believed the new technology could be used to help insure the retention of its units on maintenance against nonmanufacturer service companies, most of Otis's installed base of 315,000 units, some of which dated back to the turn of the century, used basic electromechanical

controls. In 1990, Otis had 103,000 Otis units on service contract.

NAO Field Operations

Otis Elevator Company, a subsidiary of United Technologies, was the world's largest manufacturer and service provider in the elevator and escalator market, with 1989 sales of $3.5 billion. In most markets, revenues were split evenly between new-equipment sales and service-contract payments, and gross margins derived mainly from the service business. The North American market, which made up nearly a third of Otis's revenue base, was characterized by similar financial results.

NAO's field operations were organized geographically. The key operating unit was the branch, which had first-line profit and loss responsibility. Branches were managed by region staff offices, which were in turn managed by area staff offices. A total of six areas—Far West, Southern, Northeast, Midwest, Canada, and Greater New York—each reported directly to the NAO president (see Exhibit 1).

The 250 branch offices of NAO were each headed by a branch manager responsible for

EXHIBIT 2   Field Office Structure

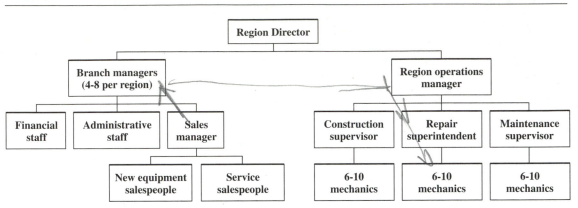

branch finances, administrative staff, and sales-people, who sold new equipment, modernization packages, and service contracts (see Exhibit 2). A typical branch had 2 to 10 salespeople ranging in age from 22 to 65. Branch managers were evaluated on the profitability and revenues of their branches' operations.

The service and new-equipment-construction operations were managed by region operations managers, who reported to the region's director. Region operations managers were responsible for the mechanics in each branch within their regions. Branches were staffed with one to five service and construction supervisors, who managed six to ten mechanics each. The mechanics were highly trained and well paid; including overtime, they could earn as much as $50,000 to $80,000, depending on the location. These mechanics typically had a two-year technical school degree or two to four years of college. They also had extensive on-the-job training and attended company-run courses. Because branch managers had no official authority over the mechanics in their branches, they worked closely with region operations managers to communicate their operations requirements. About half the mechanics and supervisors worked on the service side of the business; the other half worked on new equipment installation. Service mechanics were further subdi-

vided into maintenance mechanics (75 percent) and repair mechanics (25 percent). In 1990, NAO had about 2,500 service mechanics.

Service Mechanic Responsibilities and Organizational Structures

Maintenance Mechanics
The main duty of maintenance mechanics was to perform routine maintenance and respond to call-backs.[1] Most maintenance mechanics were assigned their own route of 40 to 70 units, spread across an area ranging in size from several city blocks to several rural counties. Seven percent of all maintenance mechanics were assigned as "on-site" mechanics for a specific large location, such as the World Trade Center in New York or the Prudential Building in Boston.

Maintenance mechanics were Otis's main representatives to the customer. They typically visited the units on their route between one and four times a month to perform preventive maintenance and/or respond to callbacks. They also discussed the equipment's status with their customers and responded to problems or complaints the customer

---

[1] A callback occurred when a customer called Otis for a mechanic to fix an equipment problem. Callbacks included first-time service calls and return calls, if any.

identified. Before leaving a site, maintenance mechanics received the customer's signature on a work authorization form, providing a record of the mechanic's visit to the site and the only maintenance scheduling tool Otis provided their examiners.

Maintenance supervisors, the maintenance mechanics' bosses, were responsible for checking on units that had extraordinarily high callback levels. Callback reduction efforts, which focused on high callback units, were done by both the supervisor and the maintenance mechanic. Maintenance supervisors also spent much of their time performing annual surveys on each unit under their supervision to ensure that the equipment was properly maintained and working and to train mechanics. Surveys required about two hours per unit, including time going to and from the unit. According to Jerry Robertson, NAO headquarters manager for service operations, "The supervisor is the key to the whole maintenance operation. And the survey is the best way supervisors can ensure the quality of work being done on their routes."

Repair Mechanics

Repair mechanics worked in crews of two, doing repairs that required more than one person or more than one day, such as replacing an elevator's steel ropes or rewinding a motor armature. Repair mechanics were not permanently assigned to specific customers or units; they worked on whatever units needed repair at the time.

Repair superintendents were responsible mainly for coordinating the scheduled and emergency (requiring immediate attention) repairs with available repair teams. The maintenance supervisor ordered materials and provided the repair superintendent with the "benchmark hours" for completion of various tasks. It was the repair superintendent's job to ensure that the repair team stayed within this projection. Although the repair superintendent was responsible for ensuring that the work was performed, it was the maintenance supervisor who originated the request for each repair and inspected and signed off on it. The maintenance supervisor had a budget of "allowed

hours" to allocate to the repair of his or her units, and the repair superintendent "worked for him (or her)."

Scheduling and Work Methods

Both the repair teams and the maintenance mechanics worked independently, with little communication during the working day between mechanics and with their supervisors. Although repair superintendents carefully scheduled their mechanics' time for maximum efficiency, maintenance mechanics typically set their own schedules. The Otis "check chart" (see Exhibit 3) provided guidance on the types of tasks maintenance mechanics did each month. But the timing of activities on the chart bore no relation to elevator usage levels, which was the key determinant of mean-time between failure for most equipment components. Nor did the chart account for all differences between equipment types or the fact that the time needed to perform similar activities varied on different equipment types. Because of this, mechanics often modified their maintenance routines on their own to account for many of the variables associated with the new equipment introduced during the past 15 years. The check chart was updated with just a check mark, when the mechanic completed a procedure, with each mechanic's maintenance visit to a unit; it was kept in the customer's equipment machine room.

The only formal controls ensuring that maintenance mechanics performed proper maintenance were the annual survey, performed by the maintenance supervisor, and the daily update of callbacks on each unit, which was available through OTISLINE ™[2] to the maintenance supervisors.

---

[2]The OTISLINE™ system, implemented in 1983, allowed customers to call a central toll-free number to report a callback and request a mechanic to service a unit. OTISLINE™ was located at NAO headquarters in Farmington, Connecticut, and was staffed by 15–40 operators (depending on the time of day), who answered customer calls and then paged and dispatched mechanics to callbacks. The service was available to all customers 24 hours a day.

EXHIBIT 3 Mechanic Check Chart

BUILDING NAME:
CONTRACT NO.:
TYPE EQUIPMENT: MACHINE NO.:
SUPERVISOR: CONTROLLER: MACHINE:
                   YEAR: EXAMINER:

JANUARY
FEBRUARY
MARCH
APRIL
MAY
JUNE
JULY
AUGUST
SEPTEMBER
OCTOBER
NOVEMBER
DECEMBER

OTIS LUBRICANTS

No. 2   Bearing Oil (Gal.)   VP-418790
        For sleeve type bearings, motors generators, etc.

No. 7   Gear compound (1 lb.)   VP-420040
        For external gears of machines, escalators, etc.

No. 12 Multi-Purpose Grease (14 ½ oz.)   VP-420240
        For ball rollers, friction bearings and general greasing

No. 33 Worm Gear Lubricant (Gal.)   VP-419930
        For gear cases of worm gear machines

No. 35 Dashpot Oil (1 ½ oz. Tube)   VP-419540
        For overload relay dashpots

No. 43 Helical Gear Oil (Gal.)   VP-419820
        For Gear Cases of Helical Gear Machines

CLEANING COMPOUNDS

No. 2   Machinery Cleaning Compound (Gal.)   VP-420540
        For cleaning machinery, guide rails other metals

No. 5   Inhibitor   VP-420465
        to inhibit oxidation and improve appearance of controller switches

No. 6   Controller Solvent Cleaner (Gal.)   VP-420475
        For Controller and selector cleaning

WIPER

        Wiping Cloth (5 lbs.)   VP-743550

UNITED
TECHNOLOGIES
OTIS ELEVATOR

EQUIPMENT	OBSERVE - CLEAN - LUBRICATE - ADJUST
	Run Escalator In Reverse Direction For Short Period
Upper Landing	Handrail Chains - Main Drive Chains - Sprockets - Reversal Device
Machines	Gears - Bearings - Governor
Brakes	Cores, Pins & Bushings - Clearance - Contacts - Switches
Skirt Board	Clearances - Switches - Moldings - Screws
Lower Landing	Step Chains - Wheels - Bushings - Pins - Chain Tension - Switches
	Run Escalator In Reverse Direction For Short Period
Upper Landing	Handrail Chains - Main Drive Chains - Sprockets - Reversal Device
Start/Stop Buttons	Contacts - Springs - Wiring - Key Switches - Covers
Motors	Armature/Rotor Clearances - Connections - Bearings - Clean with Blower
Lower Landing	Step Chains - Wheels - Bushings - Pins - Chain Tension - Switches
	Run Escalator In Reverse Direction For Short Period
Upper Landing	Handrail Chains - Main Drive Chains - Sprockets - Reversal Device
Controller	Clean with Blower - Overload Relays - Airgaps - Contacts Voltage
	Alignment of Switches - Fuses - Condensers
Handrails	Appearance - Brush Guards - Moldings - Clearances
Lower Landing	Step Chains - Wheels - Bushings - Pins - Chain Tension - Switches
	Run Escalator In Reverse Direction For Short Period
Upper Landing	Handrail Chains - Main Drive Chains - Sprockets - Reversal Device
Floor Plates	Wear - Appearance - Screws
Steps	Clearance - Upthrust - Alignment - Switches - Appearance
Lower Landing	Step Chains - Wheels - Bushings - Pins - Chain Tension - Switches
	Run Escalator In Reverse Direction For Short Period
Upper Landing	Handrail Chains - Main Drive Chains - Sprockets - Reversal Device
Truss	Track Wear - Chain Wear - Inspect Stop Welds
	Cleaning of Truss is dependent upon use and building conditions
	and is subject to the discretion of the District Supervisor. When
	steps and complplates are removed for cleaning, a thorough inspection
	should be made and equipment lubricated and adjusted as required.
Lower Landing	Step Chains - Wheels - Bushings - Pins - Chain Tension - Switches
	Run Escalator In Reverse Direction For Short Period
Upper Landing	Handrail Chains - Main Drive Chains - Sprockets - Reversal Device
Handrails	Appearance - Brush Guards - Moldings - Clearances
Steps	Clearance - Upthrust - Alignment - Switches - Appearance
Lower Landing	Step Chains - Wheels - Bushings - Pins - Chain Tension - Switches

EXHIBIT 4   Callback Operations Process

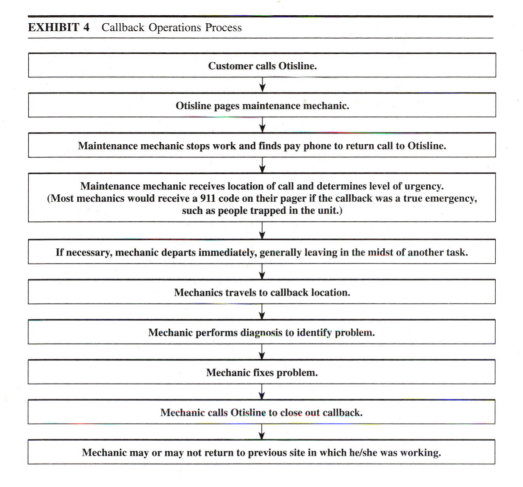

| Customer calls Otisline. |
| Otisline pages maintenance mechanic. |
| Maintenance mechanic stops work and finds pay phone to return call to Otisline. |
| Maintenance mechanic receives location of call and determines level of urgency. (Most mechanics would receive a 911 code on their pager if the callback was a true emergency, such as people trapped in the unit.) |
| If necessary, mechanic departs immediately, generally leaving in the midst of another task. |
| Mechanics travels to callback location. |
| Mechanic performs diagnosis to identify problem. |
| Mechanic fixes problem. |
| Mechanic calls Otisline to close out callback. |
| Mechanic may or may not return to previous site in which he/she was working. |

Maintenance supervisors were held accountable for callbacks on their routes through career evaluation criteria, salary review, and a newly implemented incentive compensation plan that rewarded callback reductions and low callback levels.

OTISLINE™ callback operations involved a multistep process, outlined in Exhibit 4. One maintenance mechanic, responsible for a large rural route, commented on this procedure:

> Performing quality maintenance is the key to reducing callbacks and keeping costs low. But it's not always simple to perform good, efficient maintenance when upwards of 50 percent of your time is taken by callbacks and you have no way to schedule your time. All it takes is two callbacks on opposite ends of my route, and I may as well forget doing maintenance that day.

Field Communications and Information Tools

Communication in the field between individual mechanics and supervisors was complex. Pagers were the traditional and most commonly used method of communicating with field-based personnel. Most pagers were answered from pay phones, which were often unable to receive incoming calls. Consequently, supervisors and mechanics had a difficult time contacting one another. About the only way mechanics and supervisors could communicate efficiently while doing complex equipment maintenance, callback support, and general managerial tasks was to talk face-to-face. One maintenance supervisor remarked, "Although I am in touch with all of my mechanics by phone during the week through my car or office phone, I frequently will see a mechanic only once a week, especially if I'm spending a lot of time at the other end of the city working on a problem unit."

Messages could be sent to and from field personnel through OTISLINE™, which served as a message center and would page field personnel to communicate messages called in by other field personnel. But this mechanism did not allow for two-way interaction. Bob Wesley, a mechanic in the Boston office, elaborated: "It could take me as long as two hours to exchange a message and response with [another] mechanic because of this system."

Communication to and from field personnel was especially important because the number of new products in the field had increased eightfold in the past 15 years. To meet the threat of international competitors who had introduced advanced microprocessor technology in place of the traditional electromechanical technology, Otis had introduced a broad variety of solid-state controlled products. Thus, many mechanics had a broad variety of both electromechanical and solid-state equipment on their routes. Although training programs were in place to teach mechanics how to repair and maintain the full range of equipment, most mechanics had not mastered each equipment type.

Local Solutions and Configurations

Faced with growing product complexities and the geographical distances covered by mechanics, individual offices were taking different approaches to solving the organizational and communications problems faced by their service field organizations. The branch offices in Boston, Dallas, and Glendale provide a cross-section of these solutions.

Boston

The Boston office followed the traditional Otis organizational format. Maintenance mechanics were assigned to individual routes while repair mechanic crews worked on larger jobs involving any equipment in the Boston metropolitan area, which covered about 2,000 square miles.

Bob Wesley commented on how he covered his route for callbacks and maintenance:

> My route requires a lot of driving around because the units cover a big three-town territory. If I could just travel along the most efficient route between units, my travel time would be minimal, but on a bad callback day I can spend as much as 25 percent of my time on the road just running back and forth across my route. It's also difficult to really dig into a big maintenance job when you know you might receive a callback at any time. Many of my units are in buildings without pay phones, which means I have to pack up and drive to the nearest phone just to find out what type of callback OTISLINE™ is calling me about. Many times I find out that I could have waited if I had known what the problem was before picking up my tools and leaving the original maintenance site.

As with all offices in NAO, the increase in equipment diversity had meant that (1) it was more difficult for Boston's mechanics to maintain equipment and (2) that callbacks were often more varied and took longer to complete with the new equipment. Work methods and task scheduling varied among the mechanics and were based on the check chart, past experience, and consultation between individual mechanics and their supervisors. Supervisors and mechanics used the check chart as the first step in determining appropriate preventive maintenance activities for the full range of equipment. Supervisors also worked with maintenance mechanics to tailor maintenance procedures to the microprocessor equipment. Mechanics often developed their own sets of procedures for preventive maintenance on their equipment. The main controls for ensuring that mechanics were doing appropriate maintenance were the callback reports that OTISLINE™ gave the supervisors, and the annual equipment surveys performed by the supervisors.

Communication among field personnel was available only through OTISLINE™, using pagers and pay phones as described above. This system also made it more difficult for maintenance mechanics in faraway areas to work together and share information on equipment problems. Mechanics with such routes would often work for a week at a time without speaking with another mechanic. But in the city of Boston, mechanics could work together more easily due to the closeness of their routes (generally two to five blocks apart). In some cases, mechanics often spoke with other mechanics three to five times a week. For example, Dennis Tooher, a downtown Boston-based maintenance mechanic, commented:

> Because several of [the other] mechanics work within a short walk of my route, we are able to work together to solve technical problems, learn about different equipment types from one another, find out who in the area has a specific part, and on occasion, perform smaller repairs with one another. This teamwork is a big timesaver and also saves the repair mechanics from having to travel downtown to work on a small repair.

Howard Beressi, manager of field operations for the New England region, remarked on the overall Boston branch's organization structure:

> There is a need for improved communications and organizational forms for my field workers, but until I have access to some new type of portable communications technology, it would be difficult to make any significant changes in the current system of one mechanic, one route. We've considered implementing a team-based approach in the more concentrated urban areas, but it would be much easier to do with more efficient communications.

Glendale

The Glendale office, in southern California, used a different approach for its field organization and communications. It called its new service operations organization "pod" maintenance. This structure included one repair mechanic assigned to a group of four to five separately routed maintenance mechanics. While the mechanics worked as a team within the pod, the maintenance mechanics continued to report to their supervisors and the repair mechanics to their superintendents (see Exhibit 5). Glendale had two such pods, each serving approximately 325 units. The regional maintenance supervisor of the Glendale office, Bob Smith, remarked on the pod arrangement:

> The benefit of this approach is a stronger relationship among customers, repair mechanics, and maintenance mechanics. Repair mechanics perform not only the more substantial repairs but now also work on smaller repairs and maintenance (when they are not working on regular repairs). Similarly, the maintenance mechanics act as the second member of the repair crew for major repairs on their route.

Discussing the disadvantages of pod maintenance, Smith suggested that the approach worked best in high-unit-density areas, like downtown Los Angeles:

> With routes spread across a large rural area, you lose efficiency with repair mechanics helping in small repairs and maintenance spread over a several-hundred-square-mile area. In these cases it's better for the route maintenance mechanic to take care of smaller tasks and repair mechanics to work only on the large repairs required in the entire branch area.

Glendale was one of two pilot test sites for the new Motorola keyed-data terminal (KDT) (see Exhibit 6) which allowed all field personnel to communicate via radio frequency to one another's terminal. Brief messages typed into a KDT would then be sent over the network to the recipient's KDT screen. Messages could easily be sent from person to person or broadcast to a group, and

EXHIBIT 5   Pod Structure

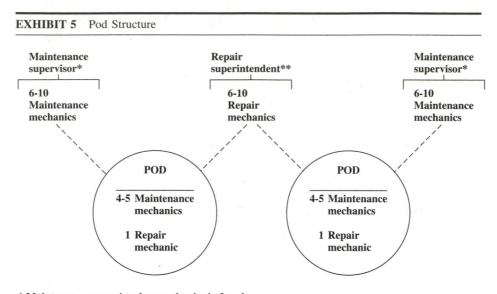

* Maintenance supervisor has mechanics in 2 pods.
** Repair superintendent has mechanics in 3-5 pods involving maintenance mechanics from several maintenance supervisors.

OTISLINE™ was able to page directly into the KDT and send a detailed message about a customer's problem. When a callback was completed, the mechanic could close it out with OTISLINE™ by typing a message into the KDT rather than by finding a pay phone and calling OTISLINE™.

In preparing cost justifications for the KDT's capital allocation proposal, headquarters staff had tried to determine the savings that would accrue as a result of reduced nonproductive mechanic time resulting from leaving an elevator's machine room and going to the nearest pay phone. Using an average of $35 per hour per mechanic with an average of 90 hours a year spent paging and responding to OTISLINE™ through a pay phone, the total cost of nonproductive time per mechanic amounted to $3,150 a year. Most managers agreed that many other less quantifiable savings would occur with the use of better communications systems.

The KDT allowed mechanics to communicate more easily, and it also helped the supervisors. For the first time they could give technical assistance directly without requiring the mechanic to leave the equipment to call from a pay phone.

Dallas

Recognizing the importance of mobile communications, the Dallas branch decided to purchase hand-held, two-way radios (see Exhibit 7). These allowed mechanics and supervisors to communicate either in a group or in one-to-one conversations. One of the radios' shortcomings was that they did not communicate with OTISLINE™. But Dallas field personnel were convinced of the radios' effectiveness because they allowed voice communications. Most were not opposed to a future KDT rollout as long as it was not intended to replace their radios. Some mechanics who had grown used to accessing fellow mechanics and supervisors by simply talking into their radios were leery of trading voice communications for a keyed terminal approach.

In Dallas, the repair and maintenance functions remained separated. Repair used standard procedures similar to those in Boston and other traditional organizations, but the maintenance organization was experimenting with a team approach, which they called *super routes*. In this arrangement, each supervisor had two teams of

EXHIBIT 6   Motorola Keyed-Data Terminal (KDT)

Features

True portability
The extremely rugged KDT 840 terminal is about the size of a video cassette and weighs only 30 ounces — perfect to slip into a briefcase, toolchest or carry on a belt.

The most advanced technology and design
The advanced LCD display has four lines of 40 characters each. Backlighting and contrast adjustment make the display easy to read, even in dim light.

The KDT 840 terminal is easy to use because of the familiar typewriter-style keyboard. User-programmable function keys reduce keyboard entries and increase operator efficiency.

A truly outstanding design feature is the multi-function capability which allows the user to simultaneously send or receive a message while executing an application program.

Exceptional memory
Standard features include 128K bytes of erasable, programmable read-only memory (EPROM) and 32K bytes of random access memory (RAM). All this memory means information such as memos or partially filled out forms can be stored and recalled quickly and easily. User application programs can reside in the terminal thereby reducing network traffic.

Self-diagnostics
Each time the terminal is turned on it automatically goes through a diagnostic procedure to alert the user to any functional problems.

Additional features
A real-time clock provides time and date stamping of transactions to help you maintain accurate records.

The KDT 840 terminal supports a large number of accessories. With the accessory port and optional peripheral cables you can use a range of bar code readers, printers, and telephone modems. A complete line of cases and battery chargers provides the utmost flexibility in carrying and charging options.

A commitment to reliability
Like other Mobile Data products, the KDT 840 terminal was designed with reliability in mind. That's the Mobile Data tradition: superior mobile data communication sytems for the most demanding users. A tradition that pays off in increased efficiency and flexibility for your operation.

Specifications

Physical
Size: W7.88 in. x H4.08 in. x D1.43 in. (W20.0 cm. x H10.36 cm. x D3.62 cm)
Weight: 30 oz (840 g)
Display Type: Liquid Crystal — Supertwist
Format: 4 lines of 40 characters per line
Indicators: 11 operational, 8 application
Character Set: Upper and lower case alpha (A-Z), numeric (0-9), 22 punctuation
Lighting: Electroluminescent backlighting
Keyboard: 49 keys, 38 alphanumeric, 11 terminal function

Environmental
Operating Temperature: -13°F to 140°F (-25°C to +60°C) (EIA standard display 0°C to 40°C RS-316A)
Storage Temperature: -13°F to 176°F (-25°C to +80°C)
Humidity : Up to 95% non-condensing humidity at 10°F(+50°C) for up to 8 hours

Rain: Meets MIL STD 810C Method 506.1 Procedure II
Vibration: Meets EIA standard RS-316B

RF Communications
Data Rate: 4800 bps
Transmitter Frequency Range: 806 MHz - 821 MHz
Receiver Frequency Range: 851 MHz - 866 MHz
RF Power: 4 Watts
Frequency Stability: ±2.5 ppm
FCC I.D. Number: AZ49FT5680

I/O Port
Serial I/F: RS232 (TTL levels available)
Connector: 9 pin subminiature D type

Internal Memory
Read Only: Basic Model — 128K Bytes (64K required by operating system)
Random Access: 32K Bytes
Battery: 7.5 V (nominal) rechargeable

nickel-cadmium provides 8 hrs. average use
Memory Backup: Internal rechargeable lithium battery provides one-hour backup support for volatile memory during main battery replacement

Accessories
Battery Charger   Interface Cables
Bar Code Readers   Desktop Charger

Contact us for more information about what a Mobile Data system can do for you:
MOBILE DATA INTERNATIONAL
Corporate Headquarters:
11411 Number Five Road, Richmond, B.C.
Canada, V7A 4Z3   Telephone: 604-277-1511
Toll Free: 800-678-7MDI (7634)

MOBILE DATA INTERNATIONAL

® IBM is a registered trademark of International Business Machines Inc.
Litho'd in Canada

A Ⓜ **MOTOROLA** COMPANY

EXHIBIT 7   Two-Way Radios

Imagine putting Motorola quality in the palm of your hand

Radius Portable Radios give you clean, dependable communications day in and day out

Imagine how efficient and profitable your operation will be when you can direct field personnel without running back and forth... without looking for a pay phone.

Imagine how satisfied your customers will be — and how many new customers you'll win — when you can respond to needs and opportunities at a moment's notice.

Finally, imagine reaching for a Motorola-built radio so solid, so reliable, you just know it's going to perform for you... without compromise... no matter how rough your treatment. A radio so well designed, it was tested for easy operation with gloves on.

Then you'll see why choosing anything other than Motorola Radius is... simply *unimaginable.*

Features geared for total performance.

Multi-Channel Operation
Choose up to 6-channel flexibility to communicate with different groups.

Coded Squelch
Digital Private-Line (DPL) or Private-Line (PL) Reduces unwanted transmissions by receiving only calls meant for your radio system. Also provides access to additional transmitters for expanded coverage area. Up to two codes available per radio for increased flexibility.

Programmable
Allows your local Radius Dealer to quickly change frequency and operating characteristics of your radio, maximizing up time. For added convenience, a cloning cable allows you to transfer one radio's personality to another. This makes changing radios from one work group to another quick, easy and inexpensive.

Choice of Power Levels
Available in 1 or 5-Watt VHF models or 1 or 4-Watt UHF models. Plenty of power to get your message through — loud and clear.

Time-Out Timer
Limits each transmission to 60 seconds, preventing channel tie-up due to inadvertent keying of the radio.

Quik-Call II Decoding
Quik-Call II, also known as Two-Tone Sequential, allows each portable to be called individually. When the P100 is placed in the Quik-Call II operating mode, only messages preceded by the individual radio's coded signal will be received. When used with a two-tone paging encoder system, Quik-Call II decoding lets your radio double as a pager. This provides you with system flexibility and keeps your personnel out of the communication flow until they are needed.

Motorola-Built
Rugged and reliable — tough enough to withstand on-the-job punishment, with a housing constructed of the same hi-impact material used for football and motorcycle helmets.

Optional Touch Code Encoding Keypad for enhanced performance.

Dual Tone Multiple Frequency (DTMF) tones are encoded through the 3 x 4 keypad for access to the land-line phone network and for remote control. DTMF tones are sent for as long as the radio is transmitting and the touch-code key button is depressed.

Reliable operation at your fingertips.

The Radius P100 is designed to fit comfortably in your hand, even with gloves on, and provide ease-of-operation. All operating controls except the Push-to-Talk button are conveniently located on the top of the unit:

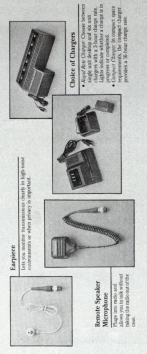

- *Audio Accessories Connector* allows for the addition of audio accessories.
- *Channel Selector* lets the operator choose the frequency.
- *Squelch Control Knob* lets the operator adjust the carrier squelch and switch into DPL, PL or Quik-Call II mode.
- *LED* indicates to the operator that the radio is transmitting. A blinking light when the radio is transmitting indicates a low battery.

The P100 is also equipped with *Radio Self-Check,* which gives the user an audible indication that all radio functions are operational.

Radius Portable Radios
Completing the communications circle.

Motorola-Backed

All Radius Portable Radios are backed by Motorola's commitment to quality and reliability.
- Each and every model must pass Accelerated Life Testing — simulating five years of field stress — before it meets Motorola standards.
- Each and every unit is backed by Motorola's limited 3-year warranty to assure your complete satisfaction.

Optional accessories and flexibility for enhanced use.

Choice of Carrying Cases
The P100 comes standard with a belt clip carry holder. For additional protection, a variety of carrying cases are available for both radio and battery. Choose between standard belt loop or swivel-back covers with restraining nylon strap.

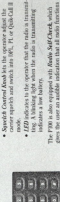

Earpiece
Lets you monitor transmissions clearly in high-noise environments or when privacy is important.

Remote Speaker Microphone
Plugs into radio and allows you to talk without taking the radio out of the case.

Choice of Chargers
- *Rapid Rate Charger.* Choose between single unit desktop and six unit chargers with a 3-hour charge rate. Lights indicate whether a charge is in progress or completed.
- *Compact Charger.* In compact space requirements, the compact charger provides a 16-hour charge rate.

EXHIBIT 8   Dallas Service Organization

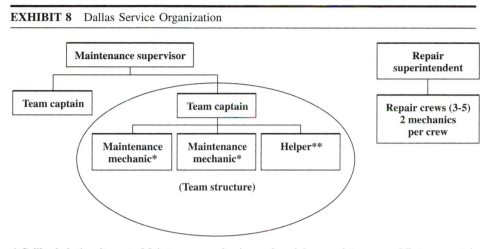

* **Callback duties alternate. Maintenance mechanics work mainly on maintenance, while team captain performs callbacks.**
** **A junior trainee who works entirely on routine maintenance.**

three or four mechanics. Each team was directed by a "team captain," who was typically the most technically proficient mechanic in the team and had displayed some leadership ability (see Exhibit 8).

Team captains used radios to keep in touch with their teams throughout the day and acted as the main callback mechanics. This allowed the other mechanics to work on their routes and perform preventive maintenance in an uninterrupted fashion. In return, the team captain was not responsible for a specific route; instead, each team member was responsible for performing preventive maintenance on about 30 percent to 40 percent more units, bringing their total units to 90 to 100. The team captain helped in preventive maintenance and spent time training the other mechanics on newer equipment when not working on callbacks. These teams were self-directed, since the team captain was more a facilitator than a foreman. Most decisions were made by consensus rather than by mandate from the team captain or the supervisor. Supervisors continued to guide the teams and were fully responsible for the financial and operating results of their mechanics.

To help the maintenance mechanics and supervisors in their maintenance, the Southern Area (SOA), of which Dallas was a part, was rolling out a new maintenance planning system called the Otis maintenance management system (OMMS). Prompted by local management desire to expand the check chart's effectiveness, this system had been developed and tested in the field by a small group of supervisors and maintenance experts in the Texas operations.

OMMS was a paper-based system that planned, scheduled, and tracked the maintenance procedures of all mechanics on every unit of equipment on their routes. At the end of each week, maintenance mechanics and their supervisors would develop a plan for the coming week's maintenance. The mechanic would do this work during the following week and record the completion of these procedures on the weekly planner. At the end of the week, before preparing the coming week's planner, the mechanic would turn in the planner and the supervisor would record the completed work on maintenance history forms for each unit serviced. In this system, the check chart would be replaced by a maintenance history form giving detailed information on the precise work performed, the time and date it was completed, and the counter reading at that time. OMMS would be rolled out to accommodate the Dallas branch's teams, allowing team members to work together to plan weekly schedules.

Under OMMS, the mechanics would receive detailed instructions outlining the frequency of each procedure and the steps it involved. As a result, even a new mechanic would be able to perform optimal maintenance by following OMMS's guidelines and procedures. SOA management also planned to move from their calendar-based maintenance scheduling system to a usage-based program. This change was based on the premise that usage level rather than time was the key determinant of equipment failure. To determine usage levels, simple electronic counters were installed in each unit to count and record motor starts.

Future Activities

NAO headquarters staff was working on a new software package, Otis scheduled maintenance (OSM) that would optimize maintenance scheduling utilizing distributed processing to link the OTISLINE™ mainframe with branch-office PCs and the field personnel's KDTs. OSM would allow supervisors and examiners to jointly develop appropriate maintenance schedules and routines for all maintenance activities. The OSM software would use this input to schedule the daily work of each maintenance mechanic, and mechanics would type in their actual times, dates worked, and counter reading for each activity when the work was performed. Supervisors, with their mechanics, would then evaluate performance and adjust maintenance schedules based on actual experience. Norman Bird, the scheduled-maintenance project manager at headquarters, commented on this innovation:

The OSM software could radically change the mechanics' work habits. Mechanics now follow their

own maintenance schedules, which may or may not rely solely on the check chart to schedule procedures. With OSM, very specific expectations will be set out, and mechanics will be held accountable for performing their maintenance on a scheduled basis. Because the software is interactive, supervisors and, to a lesser degree, mechanics will be able to adjust standards as necessary to accommodate local mechanics' capabilities, equipment conditions, and many other variables.

Although no firm implementation steps had yet been planned, Bird anticipated that the potential technical difficulties associated with the KDT and the OSM software would be small compared to the challenge of gaining acceptance of these initiatives from the 3,000 mechanics, managers, and staff in the field.

Said Bird:

We have spent most of our time working out the details of the software and its application to maintenance procedures and are just starting to formulate a final strategy to respond to possible opposition to the systems by the mechanics. We do plan to prototype scheduled maintenance extensively before full-scale rollout, and we are also planning to introduce the KDT first as just a communications device, with the objective of achieving buy-in by the mechanics before attaching scheduled maintenance to the KDT. It is then hoped that most field personnel will more readily accept the addition of the scheduled-maintenance software to their KDT. But even with these precautions, I am worried about a potential negative mechanic response. A lot of people out there could have their daily work routine seriously changed with OSM, and there is bound to be some reaction to that. However, the competition is around the corner, and we must change our habits, but not the culture that has made, and will keep, Otis number one.

Bird anticipated that the new scheduled-maintenance software would be ready to roll out within 18 to 24 months. Based on the initial success of the KDT in its pilot tests, NAO President John Cosentino had decided to expand the pilot to all the mechanics in North America with the full intention of adding the scheduled-maintenance software as soon as it was available.

Whitaker had visited a number of branch offices that were just beginning to think about using new work methods, communication tools, and organizational structures to address issues related to service productivity and product diversity. He had observed several highly successful variations in Glendale and Dallas and wondered to what extent the use of teams, scheduled maintenance, and new communications technology could be applied in other locations. If they could, what role should headquarters management play in implementing them?

But improvements in organization, tools, and methods were only one part of the picture. The whole picture required matching technology with structure. Whitaker recognized the importance of using mobile field-based communications, for the status quo (pagers and pay telephones) was highly inefficient. The KDT provided a homogeneous portable system to link field personnel and OTIS-LINE™, but it would not be fully implemented nationwide for two years and did not provide for voice communication. In the meantime, would it make sense to invest in cellular phones or radios? Would a voice-based communications system be better for Otis than the KDT? And what were the risks of confusing the field force if headquarters first rolled out portable radios or telephones and then replaced them two years later with KDTs?

The check chart maintenance-scheduling system could clearly be improved upon, but management estimated that the new scheduled-maintenance system being developed at headquarters would not be fully implemented for more than two years. Would it make sense, as an intermediate step, to use a paper-based system that could be rolled out within three months? Many felt such a system would even work to prepare field personnel for the future use of the more sophisticated scheduled-maintenance software. But if such a paper-based system were highly successful in its own right, organizational momentum to continue spending resources on developing the software might be diminished.

In reviewing the rollout of new team-based organizations, communications technologies, and work methods, Whitaker also recognized the importance of determining the proper sequence and approach to implementing new approaches in each area. Would it make sense to introduce new communications technologies first, followed by teams and then work methods? Was there a better sequence? Or should they all be introduced as a cohesive package at the same time? He knew he needed to consider the extent to which headquarters should allow each office to tailor the new approaches to their needs. Otis had always given the local branches a tremendous amount of autonomy, and yet the strategic plan needed to address an organizationwide solution.

IT AND THE INDIVIDUAL: ETHICAL CONCERNS

New IT capabilities raise new ethical concerns, which, if not addressed effectively, may result in disgruntled employees, dissatisfied customers, and lawsuits. As discussed in Chapter 3, the costs of electronically capturing, storing, and exchanging data have dropped dramatically, while the ability to digitally store a richer set of data (including still and video images and sounds) has greatly increased. Information is a renewable, nondepletable resource. Some data have only transient value, such as the room number to which a hotel guest is assigned. Other data, however, have lasting, renewable value—for example, customer purchase data may retain value for a period of years before they are no longer useful for predicting future purchase behavior. Database marketing has created heightened demand for customer information; currently more

---

FIGURE 5–2   Ethical Concerns in Data Management

	Data Storage	*Data Transfer*	*Data Transformation*
Access rights	What customer and employee data should we collect? How long should we store it? Who owns it?	Who can see it? Who can profit from its use? Should permission be obtained to use it?	What data recombinations are permitted? Who profits from employee-developed applications?
Stewardship responsibility	How is accuracy verified?	How do we prevent unauthorized access?	How is alteration or recombination controlled?

---

than 1,000 companies sell lists of names in various categories. Because individual data—about employees or customers, for instance—have value, conflicts may arise in determining who should have access to such data (access rights) and how data should be protected (stewardship responsibilities).

The widespread use of relational database management systems, and the increased incorporation of object-oriented and hypertext technologies, permit dramatically enhanced abilities to combine and recombine data.[4] When preserved separately, data may not carry the same meaning as when they are combined. For example, when income-tax return data are combined with "deadbeat dads" data, authorities can track down those child-support avoiders who are best able to pay up. Birth records, combined with zipcode-tagged socioeconomic data, can help marketers identify customer segments for different infant products. Height and weight information from driver's licenses, combined with credit card purchase data, can yield lists of tall, upscale shoppers.

Capabilities for electronically exchanging information over private and public networks are also pervasive; and even where networks are not well developed, information is easily intercepted or transferred via floppy disks. Hence, data become available to a broader range of recipients than ever before, raising additional questions about legitimate ownership and access.

The three basic IT operations—data storage, data transfer, and data transformation—all give rise to ethical concerns. Figure 5–2 summarizes these issues.

Data Access

The fundamental issue at stake is, who owns data created by or about individuals? Unfortunately, the law provides ambiguous guidance, and different individuals may

---

[4]Richard O. Mason, "Four Ethical Issues of the Information Age," *MIS Quarterly* (March 1986).

have very different opinions on the matter. Personal information is generally not considered legal "property" under common law, although copyright laws protect "intellectual property" such as books and software. Corporate (proprietary) information is given legal protection; for example, when hackers electronically break into a corporate database, the firm can prosecute them. Firms can also use nondisclosure and noncompete agreements to ensure that employees who leave the company are not legally able to immediately put the information and knowledge gained on the job to use elsewhere.

The law is less clear in distinguishing between corporate information and data that are generated by or concerning its employees. The Electronic Communications Privacy Act of 1986 (ECPA) specifies that a service provider can examine messages exchanged on its own system, in order to properly maintain the system. This implies that employee e-mail messages are not private communications. Similarly, employee monitoring is generally not considered an illegal invasion of privacy. However, employee medical histories are considered personal, and their confidentiality must be guaranteed by the employer. In the absence of clear laws, explicit company policies can at least reveal to employees the current "rules of play."

Similarly, the law is ambiguous about customer information. When a customer makes a credit-card transaction, who owns the information about the transaction? Under current legal interpretation, the credit card company does. Furthermore, the company developed or acquired the information systems that transform data into valuable information. Yet many customers feel their privacy has been invaded when such information is sold to a third party, resulting in unwanted mail and phone solicitations. They want to choose who will have access to personal information and for how long such information can be retained. Other customers are pleased to receive database-driven mailings targeted to their special interests (e.g., a person who orders fly-fishing gear from L. L. Bean may be happy to receive a brochure about another company's fly-fishing seminar). Some specific categories of transactions are protected under current legislation. For example, it is illegal to sell lists of customers categorized by their video rental patterns (since having one's name appear on the list of pornographic video renters is considered an invasion of privacy). Blanket protection of customer data would impose severe constraints on database marketers that might not be justified by customers' views of the confidentiality of different types of data.

In an ideal situation, the information-disclosure expectations of managers, employees, and customers are aligned. In practice, they often are not. Database marketing can be a useful tool for matching customers with products or the improper selling of personal information. Workplace monitoring may be a legitimate form of management control or an invasive Big Brother practice. At issue are conflicting views of information access and disclosure, which create a "privacy gap."[5]

---

[5]Janis L. Gogan and Jeanne W. Ross, "Managers and the Privacy Gap," Boston University working paper 91-71 (1991).

Stewardship Responsibility

The above discussion presupposes that information, whether confidential or not, is true. But as the volume of stored data increases, so does the potential for errors. The most common error is "stale" data; for instance, a customer may continue to show up on lists of parents of infants long after the child has moved on to adolescence. An employee may have received a negative evaluation from one supervisor, which remains a blot on the personnel record even though subsequent supervisors have given positive evaluations. Input or transformation errors also occur. For example, practically all the property-tax paying citizens of Norwich, Vermont, received negative credit ratings when their status was mistakenly recorded as "unpaid" instead of "paid." This came to light when a couple were denied a mortgage application and a prominent physician had to cut short an Alaskan vacation because his credit line was withdrawn. In other examples, people have been arrested because police computers incorrectly listed them as out on warrant (perhaps the real criminal had a similar name, or used the innocent victim's name). Another data accuracy concern arises from the increased use of employee psychological evaluations and drug testing methods, which are not fully reliable—"false positives" are common and have grave consequences if treated as true.

Data accuracy, then, must be explicitly protected. Some protection can be built into database and applications software, in the form of various error-checking and backup routines. Administrative procedures, including audits, are also necessary forms of accuracy protection. Since the measures necessary for 100 percent accuracy are expensive, it is also necessary to identify the ramifications of inaccurate personal data

---

FIGURE 5–3   How Managers Address Ethical Issues

Stakeholder analysis:	Identify all parties with a stake in the issue. Who will be affected by this data access decision? What are the consequences to each party of data access and disclosure?
Goal-based analysis:	Select the option that promises the greatest good for the greatest number. Assess costs and benefits, including noneconomic factors (happiness, general welfare).
Rights-based analysis:	Identify and/or articulate specific legal, institutional, and human rights to privacy, free speech, and other information-related values. Identify specific data storage, transfer, and transformation decisions that could violate these rights.
Duty-based analysis:	Identify basic ethical duties, such as honesty, fairness, and doing no harm. Does this action violate any fundamental ethical duties? Are there alternative actions that do not do so?

Source: Mary Gentile and John Sviokla, "New Guidlines for Dealing with Data," *Information Technology Quarterly* (Summer 1990).

in various categories. Ideally, these categories would take into account individuals' disclosure preferences.

A second stewardship issue is security. Once restricted-access data are identified, how will they be protected from unwanted access and disclosure? Data security measures are well developed in financial services firms, but less so in other industries. Breaking into corporate systems is a favorite "hacker" sport, and 100 percent network security is unattainable. However, access passwords and encryption techniques provide some measure of protection. Extremely sensitive personnel data (such as medical histories) may be best stored on diskettes in locked drawers.

Figure 5–3 summarizes a four-pronged approach to addressing IT-related ethical issues. No single analytical approach will resolve all ethical issues, but taken together the four approaches—stakeholder analysis, goal-based analysis, rights-based analysis, and duty-based analysis—can help the manager identify acceptable alternatives. Perhaps the single most important observation is that since information technologies are inherently flexible, managers can shape them in a way that works with the organizational culture and values, and managers need not passively allow IT to compromise those values.

Chapter 6

IT in Organizations

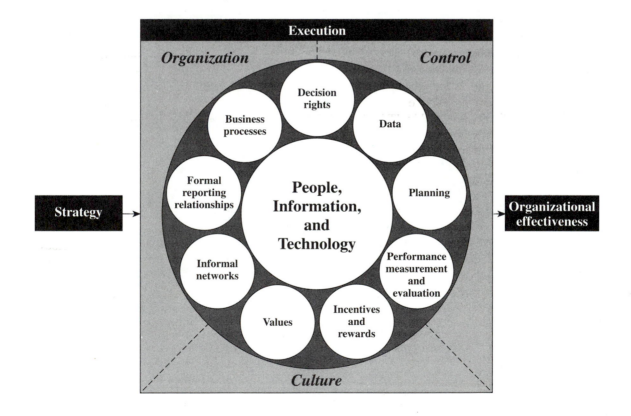

INTRODUCTION

Over the past several decades IT has become intricately woven into organizational "fabric." Where once an organization was defined by "bricks and mortar," IT is now helping to break down the walls separating functions, geographic locations, and management levels, permitting new networks of relationships among the organization's membership. IT is also redefining the primary work of many firms, from creating physical products to managing information.

This chapter explores the evolution in how IT has been managed in organizations, and its impact on organization structure, management control systems, and ability to compete. The chapter is organized as follows:

- *IT eras:* This section describes how, as information technologies evolved over the last several decades, associated IT management structures also evolved.
- *The stages theory of IT adoption and organizational learning:* This section describes the typical life cycle of investment in IT as it is assimilated into an organization, and issues of tight and loose management control during its evolution.
- *IT-driven changes in organizational structure:* This section discusses how the changing roles of IT—for automating, informating, embedding, and communicating—were associated with changes in organizational structure over time.
- *IT in the 1990s:* This section describes the key challenges managers now face in effectively deploying IT.

IT ERAS

Chapter 4 described how information technologies have evolved. This chapter shows how successive IT generations were associated with different IT applications, impacts, and management processes. We characterize these evolving organizational arrangements for IT into three broad eras: *DP era, micro era,* and *network era*.

DP Era *(data processing)*.

(1950s ~ 1970s)

* centralized

DBMS (hierarchical / relational)

During the 1950s and 1960s, mainframe computers replaced legions of clerical workers processing insurance claims, bank checks, accounting records, and other high-volume, transaction-intensive applications. In order to capture economies of scale in terms of machine cycles, storage, and programming staffs, applications development and data-processing operations and planning were typically centralized.

During the 1970s, database management systems (DBMS) were widely adopted. In the early 1970s, *hierarchical DBMS* were used; more flexible *relational DMBS* were introduced in the late 1970s. In addition to the transaction-processing applications developed in the 1960s, management information systems (MIS) and decision support systems (DSS) were developed. MIS compiled data used in the large transaction-processing applications into reports that helped managers monitor business-unit performance. Since MIS were byproducts of DP, they did not necessarily produce all the information that managers wanted, or in the desired form. DSS, thanks to database management systems, query tools, and analytical programming languages, gave managers more flexible access to information for management control. Many data-query and analytical applications could be performed with little or no assistance from the IS professionals. DSS use marked the dawn of "end-user computing."

A third key trend in the 1970s was that minicomputer sales were soaring, and many were not purchased by the central DP department. Instead, managers of a functional area like marketing, frustrated with long applications-development delays, purchased their own equipment and hired their own programmers. Now central data processing and MIS coincided with distributed processing and DSS.

Micro Era *(1980s)*

* technological discontinuity

* decentralized

The decade of the 1980s was driven by the microprocessor. The first PC sales, beginning in the late 1970s, were to users who were frustrated with waiting in the DP/MIS queues, and willing to "get their hands dirty" in exchange for their own relatively speedy application development. Once a critical mass of PCs and spreadsheet software (first Visicalc, later Lotus 1-2-3) were sold, early users began turning to each other for help and advice, and away from the DP/MIS organization. The IS professionals were caught off guard. Many initially viewed the PC as a mildly interesting toy. At first, many central MIS organizations made no attempt to either count or control microcomputers in their firms.

This was a period of *technological discontinuity*. In many firms, the IS group subsequently tried to impose the same controls over PC acquisition, application development, and use as they used for DP and MIS applications. But the issues in purchasing a $3,000 PC are not the same as those in purchasing a $3 million

FIGURE 6–1   Comparison of Traditional DP versus Personal Computing (Technological Discontinuity at Work)

	Traditional DP	*Personal Computing*
Applications	Large, shared applications; used regularly; highly structured (e.g., payroll)	Small, individual applications; often ad hoc; often unstructured (e.g., "quick and dirty" spreadsheet)
Application development	Slow, methodical system development by trained IS professionals, using project management tools and systems life-cycle methods	User customizes off-the-shelf packages to suit own needs; evolutionary, prototyping approach; little need for formal tools and methodologies
Implementation issues	Ensuring user cooperation and correct use; adding requested enhancements	Responding to requests for training and troubleshooting help

Source: Janis L. Gogan, *The Personal Computer in Organizations,* unpublished doctoral dissertation, Harvard Business School (1988).

mainframe, nor is the development and maintenance of a spreadsheet application for use by an individual the same as development of an airline reservation system or a multinational payroll application. Conflict between early PC users and IS professionals was intense in some organizations. The frameworks and techniques that worked well for managing data processing were not very helpful for achieving the benefits and minimizing the problems of personal computing. Figure 6–1 identifies some of the reasons for conflict between PC users and IS professionals by comparing traditional DP with personal computing.

In developing traditional data-processing applications, systematic techniques had been devised to elicit a clear set of user specifications, so that system designers could "get inside the user's head." But when designer and user are one and the same, a separate, formal requirements-definition phase is not necessary. Instead, the user may take a rather idiosyncratic, experimental approach to building his/her application, by developing one or several simple prototypes until the application meets his/her needs. Since prototypes are easy to develop using spreadsheet applications, it would be inefficient to engage in separate steps of requirements definition, designing, and coding.

Traditional data-processing systems were often large, sometimes complex applications designed for long, stable use and managed by DP professionals. The processes they supported were usually predictable, structured, and repetitive. For some applications—such as airline reservation systems or banking funds-transfer systems—highly reliable performance is essential, since a system failure may be devastating to the firm. Hence, substantial measures are designed into these systems to prevent crashes or recover from them. In contrast, early personal computing largely consisted of ad hoc, relatively unstructured, and varied activities. For example, a user might build a spreadsheet forecasting model for use in planning a new-product campaign. That user did not need to incorporate the same level of protective measures in her small application, and indeed such measures would be like hospitalizing a child for a scraped knee. Over time, some users did develop quite sophisticated applications, but these were not characteristic of most personal computing during the transition years.

As Figure 6–1 suggests, other differences between traditional DP and personal computing existed, which placed a strain on the DP/MIS organization. Its managers had spent the previous decade fine-tuning an organization geared toward large, complex, reliable systems. But this organization, its people, and its management control systems could not adequately support personal computing. They possessed formal and experiential DP knowledge, but lacked both formal and experiential personal computing knowledge. This is not to suggest that the need for DP skills disappeared overnight; far from it. Big, shared systems continued to be built, but new structures, people, and control systems were needed to support the new activities introduced because of the microprocessor and other emerging technologies.

Later waves of PC users tended to have other issues. PC training and consultation were in high demand by novice users, and issues of software compatibility became acute as the volume of independently acquired PCs and users increased. Demand for access to data residing on corporate mainframes and minicomputers also intensified. Many firms adopted end-user computing services and policies that balanced control with support. For example, "controls" typically included hardware and software standards; "support" included technology assessment, user training, and user assistance.

Another impact of the personal computing phenomenon was an increase in demand for IT applications of all kinds. Some DP sages had predicted that end-user computing would reduce the strain on the DP/MIS organization. Instead, more users got a glimpse of what could be done with IT, and often their vision exceeded their reach. IS organizations felt even greater pressure to produce more while spending less.

Meanwhile, the microprocessor was making itself felt in other areas of the organization that were not necessarily controlled by the central IS group. Banks were investing in ATM machines. Air conditioning, automobile, aircraft, home-appliance, and elevator companies (to name a few industries) were embedding microprocessors in their products in order to add features and lock in maintenance contracts. Sometimes the IS organization was asked for advice on these matters. At the same time, IS organizations were also trying to exploit other promising new tools, such as CAD/CAM, robotics, and expert systems. Each new technology offered new potential and new pitfalls.

Network Era (early 1990s.

During the micro era, responsibility for many aspects of IT was decentralized to user departments. Further accelerating the decentralization trend was the widespread practice of "outsourcing" many routine IT services, in order to focus the efforts of a central IS group on key priorities. The proliferation of microcomputers led to a lack of integration between centralized mainframe computing and decentralized personal computing.

For many organizations, the early 1990s marked a shift from the microcomputer as a "personal" (i.e., independent, stand-alone) computer to an "interpersonal" (interdependent, connected) workstation. User demand for access to corporate data and to capabilities for electronic communication is growing, leading to data pathways between mainframes, minicomputers, and microcomputers.

Meanwhile, many firms are "downsizing" their mainframe applications to stand-alone or networked microcomputers. For some, this means experimenting with a new approach called *client-server* computing. In addition, faced with severe resource constraints and increasing competitive pressures, many firms are embarking on ambitious programs to minimize organizational layers and reorganize operations for greater efficiency and improved responsiveness. Since many "reengineering" initiatives reduce or eliminate middle management layers, new means of cross-functional and interorganizational integration are required.

These trends point to dramatic increases in networked infrastructures in the coming decade. LANs connect user computers to each other for electronic mail, to high-end printers and other expensive peripherals, to corporate databases, and to outside databases and information services. Today, about 65 percent of corporate PCs are already connected to LANs, and further connectivity will occur rapidly, for two reasons. First, the necessary hardware, software, and minimal data-communication standards are already available for this transition, although higher-level standards are still somewhat unstable. Second, many networked IT applications are "critical-mass" phenomena, comparable to the use of the telephone. For example, electronic mail is of little use unless most of one's correspondents also participate in e-mail. Once organizations begin, they have a strong incentive to quickly achieve critical-mass levels of networking.

Just as the technological discontinuities of the micro era challenged the existing MIS organization, the network era will also bring new IT architecture and management *New Issues:* issues. For example, networked information flows are far more difficult to protect than when users store their data on stand-alone PC databases. Firms are looking closely at data security issues in the new environment. Second, client-server computing takes many forms. Some firms use it to give users access to shared databases, while other firms use it to replace large individually controlled hard disks with server space, and still others use it to distribute software on an as-needed basis. Each approach raises new issues. For example, will users accustomed to the freedom of independent personal computing resist network-based data storage or software distribution? Can the IS organization provide a sufficiently high level of client-server reliability such that this change will be transparent to users? Another issue concerns electronic communication. When is e-mail the appropriate communication medium, versus videoconferencing, the telephone, or face-to-face conversations? Should e-mail users expect their communications to be treated as private or public matters? Numerous lawsuits on the latter concern suggest that this matter is by no means settled (see also Chapter 5).

Long-distance networking, supported by satellite and fiber optic transmission media, minimizes geography as a constraint in doing business. This gives firms the opportunity to hire labor from a broader, not necessarily local, pool, which raises new concerns. For example, telecommuting is becoming a popular work arrangement, but

---

FIGURE 6–2   Assessing Emerging Information Technologies

Questions concerning the emerging IT as a foundation technology
(see Chapter 4, Figure 4–1)

Is this technology radically or incrementally different from others with which our organization is familiar?

What changes in software, hardware, and data does this technology incorporate?

How does this technology affect data storage, transport, and transformation?

Questions concerning the potential impact of the emerging IT on the current IT
Architecture (see Chapter 4, Figure 4–5)

What are the likely roles of this technology in supporting the work of individuals, business units, and the organization as a whole?

Given the characteristics of this technology, and the level of risk that it poses, who should have control over its acquisition and use: individuals, business units, or central IS?

What support services will be required in order to gain expected benefits from this technology? Who will provide these services?

What are the ramifications of investing either too early or too late in this technology? What issues might arise with its acquisition and use?

---

organizational structures and management control systems are not yet in place to fully support this option. Networking also opens up the opportunity to establish new relationships with suppliers, distributors, and other business partners, a topic explored in Chapter 7.

In addition, networking may not be the only significant technology in the coming decade. Other emerging technologies—speech recognition systems, multimedia, and "virtual reality," to name a few—will also make their mark and challenge existing structures and systems. Change will continue to be the order of the day, both in the evolving information technologies and in their applications in the organization. In order to assess how new technologies can contribute to operational processes, and what changes in organizational structure, management control systems, and people are required in order to effectively assimilate them, some firms have established a new structure, the emerging technologies group. This unit is charged with identifying and assessing technologies of relevance to the organization. Managers can use the concepts discussed in Chapter 4 as a frame of reference in conducting an emerging technology assessment. For example, an assessment might include the questions listed in Figure 6–2.

Based on the experiences of companies making the transition from the DP era to the micro era, and based on the observation that information technologies are highly flexible and malleable, it is unlikely that even a sophisticated emerging technologies group will fully answer all the questions listed in Figure 6–2. At least as important as planning for technology assimilation is putting in place mechanisms for ongoing assessment of its expected and unexpected benefits and issues. The next section offers a set of concepts for assessing the assimilation of new technologies in an organization.

STAGES THEORY OF IT ADOPTION AND ORGANIZATIONAL LEARNING

The stages theory, a set of concepts for understanding the assimilation of IT in business organizations, was first proposed in the early 1970s.[1] It is based on the observation that most organizations' computer expenditures formed an S-shaped curve over time, following the familiar pattern of learning curves and experience curves. The theory proposed that the S-shaped curve reflects organizational learning as computers are applied to business processes. In the early 1970s, most firms used computers for data processing, as discussed above. As the next few decades unfolded, new IT and applications—MIS, minicomputers, DSS, personal computers, expert systems, CAD/CAM, videoconferencing, and others—were introduced to organizations. It became apparent that the stages theory predicts not one S-curve, but many.

Since organizational learning is partly formal transfer of recorded knowledge and partly informal accumulation of experiential knowledge, the theory proposes that every organization traverses four stages of learning in sequence. As organizations "learn" how to utilize IT, they spend more and more money to develop this capability. Expenditures accelerate into a growth period, then decelerate and mature into slow-paced steady growth. If organizational learning is explicitly managed through each stage in turn, optimal integration can be achieved. The DP stages are reviewed next.

Stage I—Initiation

In this stage, data-processing technologies are first introduced into an organization's administrative operations for automation of systems such as payroll or accounts receivable.

Stage II—Contagion

In this stage the learning curve moves sharply upward as increasing numbers of individuals or units adopt the technology, and as organizational members experiment with new uses for it. Management concentrates on introducing the innovation at all available opportunities. Experimentation is more heavily emphasized than is efficiency. Management creates some organizational slack, committing more resources than are strictly necessary to get the job done. For example, the costs for training new users may be absorbed into overhead rather than charged directly to them. This extra

---

[1]Richard L. Nolan, "Stages Hypothesis of Computer Growth," *Communications of the ACM* (July 1973).

spending nurtures reinvention, which helps expand the uses of the new tools. With low control and high slack, adoption and usage grows rapidly, but at the loss of some efficiency.

Stage III—Control

By the end of Stage II, the IT budget may be outpacing revenue growth, alarming senior management. Now managers "squeeze out" slack by enforcing tighter control through measures such as budget reviews and full chargeout systems. The rapid growth characteristic of contagion slows as tighter controls are imposed on IT acquisition and usage. High control and low slack promote efficiency but inhibit learning, which may also discourage diffusion of the technology to other organizational functions. *Striking the proper balance between control and slack is a critical management task.*

Stage IV—Integration

Here management succeeds in striking a balance between slack and control as the new technology becomes firmly integrated into the company's operational business processes.

A second key concept of the stages theory is "growth processes." Four growth processes (so-called because they evolve, or "grow," with use of IT over time) describe IT activity and organizational learning in an organization:

Applications portfolio: The use of IT in the business organization. The applications portfolio grows and evolves as new technology and new capabilities emerge.

Resources: The means (money, technology, and people) needed to apply computers in the business.

Management: The techniques and procedures (such as planning, project management, and chargeout) that ensure resources are applied efficiently. The objective of management is to strike an appropriate balance between tight and loose controls for each stage of technology adoption.

User awareness: The ability of users to effectively apply IT to their work. In stage I, users tend to be "hands off," but by stage IV, they are taking an active role in the design and development of IT applications for their needs.

Figure 6–3 shows the characteristics of each growth process by stage in the DP era. Each process changes (grows) as an organization progresses through the stages. Effective management of IT occurs by maintaining balance among the four growth processes, and by ensuring that no one process gets significantly ahead of the others, nor significantly falls behind.

FIGURE 6–3 Stages Theory and Growth Processes

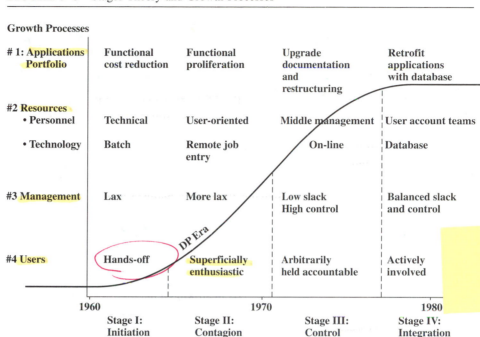

A common imbalance situation occurs when the technology is too far ahead of the organization's ability to apply it. For example, some DP managers acquired advanced technologies—database systems, CAD/CAM, and expert systems tools—before their programmers had the appropriate technical skills or before users were sufficiently aware of the potential benefits to effectively apply the advanced technology. As a result, systems using the advanced technology were expensive to develop and maintain. To achieve a better balance of growth processes, managers can slow down the acquisition of technology or speed up the development of necessary skills.

Earlier in this chapter we observed three principle IT eras, based on the prevailing technology generations. The *DP era* spanned the decades of the 1960s and 1970s and was chiefly characterized by central management of mainframe information resources. The *micro era,* which began slowly in the late 1970s, continued through the early 1990s. The chief characteristic of this era was widespread disperson of information resources, due primarily to the rapid influx, first of minicomputers and later of microcomputers, into virtually every functional area, activity, and organizational level of the firm. The *network era* began for most organizations in the early 1990s. Figure 6–4 depicts the typical S-shaped learning curves of business organizations for each of these three IT eras. The overlapping curves show how the end of one era coincided with the beginning of another, as firms continued to invest in older technologies while beginning to experiment with the newer technologies.

FIGURE 6–4   Three IT Eras, Three Organizational Learning Curves

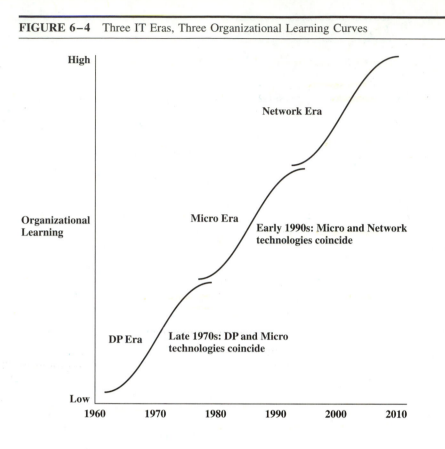

IT-DRIVEN CHANGES IN ORGANIZATIONAL STRUCTURE

IT has been used in four fundamental ways: *automating, informating, embedding,* and *communicating.* In turn, business processes and organizational structure have been significantly changed.

    Automating: Substituting technology for labor. The automation of routine, clerical, information-processing jobs by data-processing technologies is analogous to the automation of factory workers by machinery.

    Informating: Complementing human information-processing capabilities with enhanced capabilities for compilation, analysis, and presentation of data (see also Chapter 5). Technologies such as DSS, query languages, and personal computing software such as spreadsheets help users interpret and evaluate data.

    Embedding: Integrated-circuit chips have dramatically increased in functionality and decreased in price, making it desirable to replace mechanical and electro mechanical controls with microprocessor controls in many products. In turn, this creates new avenues for data acquisition, dissemination, and functionality.

Communicating: Enhancing information-sharing capabilities. Networked technologies such as electronic mail and voice mail remove time and distance barriers to communication, facilitating the formation of new kinds of project teams, organizational arrangements, and product/service features.

Over time, the relative importance of each application approach has changed, thanks both to evolving IT capabilities and to management choices. Automating was a hallmark of the DP era. From 1960 to 1980, over 12 million information-handling jobs were automated by data-processing technologies. Automation of clerical and routine factory work at lower levels of the organizational hierarchy led to substantial reductions in numbers of clerical employees, but did not lead directly to significant changes in organizational structure (except for the centralization of the DP function). Automation did lead to an increase in the amount of data available in electronic form, and from the mid-1970s through the 1980s many organizations developed MIS and DSS to transform transaction-based data into information for managerial decision making. This marked a shift from an emphasis on automating to an emphasis on informating, which is a hallmark of the micro era. Personal computing tools further enhanced these capabilities, both directly by offering the user sophisticated analytical tools, and indirectly by freeing users' time to concentrate on the interpretation and evaluation of data rather than its compilation. Since informating complements workers rather than substituting for them, many mid-level staff members were able to expand their jobs and even carve out new, information-intensive positions for themselves. The hierarchical structure was weakened as middle managers' work was redefined.

Another hallmark of the micro era has been the increased embedding of microprocessors into products that previously were not information-intensive. Often the intent is to simply substitute a microprocessor control for a mechanical one. For example, many automobiles have 10 to 13 embedded microprocessors, which monitor and/or regulate various functions (such as cruise control, fuel consumption, and anti-lock braking systems). Once embedded in a device, these chips can also be used to gather information about the use of the device. In the automobile example, some chips essentially record the car's driving history and may prove useful in diagnosing subsequent maintenance problems. "Smart cards" are being developed by financial institutions to record each customer's banking activities, and by countries to record their citizens' visa status, tax payments, and health histories (Thailand is well along in such a project). Another intriguing example is a running shoe with a microprocessor in its heel. At the end of a run, the athlete plugs the shoe into a device connected to a personal computer and receives an analysis of his/her speed, stride, and other factors. The possibilities for embedded microprocessors are virtually limitless, and organizations are exploring how this technology can help them better serve their customers and better manage their operations.

When enough users have personal computers or terminals on their desks, many firms invest in communications technologies like e-mail and voice mail. These technologies, by dramatically reducing time and distance barriers to communication, support the formation of new organizational arrangements, such as temporary project teams and interorganizational systems. In turn, network linkages drive demand for improved access to information in electronic form, including traditional corporate databases, data generated and stored by individuals (usually on personal computers), customer and supplier data, and other external databases. The network era promises to bring together the long-sundered tasks of data processing and information interpretation. As organizations establish standards for file interchange and tool compatibility, they move toward a goal of equal access to information from all connected computers. *The greater the connectivity and free access to information, the more profound are the implications for organizational structure.* Some firms have dramatically reduced the numbers in their middle-management ranks, even eliminating entire organizational levels while increasing managers' span of control, as the Phillips 66 case in this chapter illustrates. Other firms have used networking capabilities to support a highly flexible organizational structure with permeable and shifting boundaries. The next section further examines the organizational implications of networked IT.

IT IN THE 1990s

Early information technologies, though revolutionary in their impact on process efficiency, nevertheless were accompanied by significant constraints. Mainframe computers were very large investments that had to be carefully justified by the large firms that could afford them. Data storage was expensive, so information was carefully filtered. Application development was time consuming and the sole province of trained IT professionals working from a centralized organizational base. Data communications were constrained by narrow-bandwidth, sometimes unreliable transmission media. In the 1990s, few of these constraints remain, and information technologies have become far more flexible and powerful. Microcomputers are available to the smallest organizations. Storing information electronically is far less expensive than the equivalent paper storage in filing cabinets, when the cost of office space is factored in. CASE tools are yielding big improvements in large-scale applications development, and personal computer users are quickly building many of their own applications. Management of many IT activities is highly decentralized. Finally, bandwidth is no longer a significant constraint, thanks to the replacement of older media with fiber optics and VSATs, and to tools for compressing and decompressing data sent over twisted-pair and coax. As we approach the millennium, the question to ask is not "What can IT do?" but rather "What do we want it to do next?"

"Time-based competition" is a watchword for the 1990s. Many companies are using IT to squeeze excess time out of key business operations, including reducing product development times, production cycles, and order fulfillment. However, as companies tighten up their operations, they sometimes run into new problems. Time is an important buffer that helps organizations cope with environmental uncertainty and internal complexity. Drastic shortening of product development, production, and other business operations, without simultaneously improving the timeliness of management control systems and coordination processes, can lead to dysfunction. Timely and flexible access to information is a critical element of time-based competition (see Figure 6–5).

FIGURE 6–5 Fast Cycle Capabilities

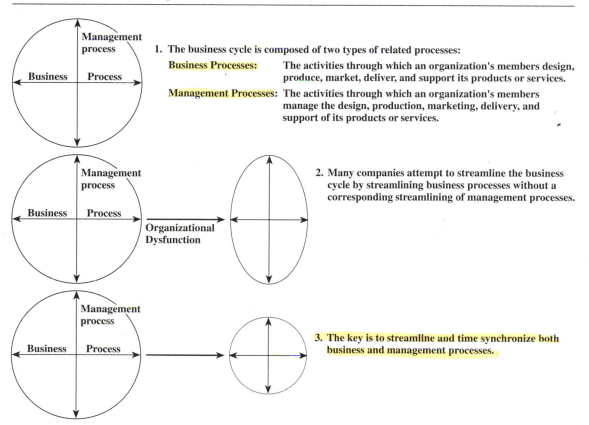

1. **The business cycle is composed of two types of related processes:**

   Business Processes: The activities through which an organization's members design, produce, market, deliver, and support its products or services.

   Management Processes: The activities through which an organization's members manage the design, production, marketing, delivery, and support of its products or services.

2. Many companies attempt to streamline the business cycle by streamlining business processes without a corresponding streamlining of management processes.

3. The key is to streamline and time synchronize both business and management processes.

Source: Lynda M. Applegate, "Information Technology and Organizations," Harvard Business School Note 9-191-136 (February 1991).

The traditional, hierarchical organizations and management control systems of the industrial era allowed managers and their staffs to carefully locate and sift through information before making a decision. Today, fast-paced managers are recognizing that traditional organizational structures, management control systems, and decision-making methods simply won't work. Figure 6–6 depicts the traditional approach to information access in organizations. In hierarchical structures, detailed information about competitors, customers, and internal organizational capabilities resides largely at the bottom of the organization, "where the action is." First-level managers and employees, being knowledgeable about the dynamics of their specific part of the business, tend to make decisions that are locally optimal. Conversely, access to information on corporatewide strategic direction and perspectives, and the dynamics of the business as a whole, usually resides at the top of the organization. Consequently, decisions made at the top often consider corporatewide initiatives and strategic direction but may be based on an inadequate in-depth understanding of business operations.

FIGURE 6–6   The Information Challenge

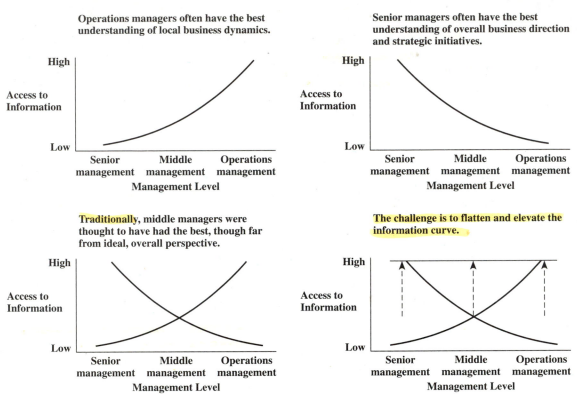

Source: Lynda M. Applegate, "Information Technology and Organizations," Harvard Business School Note 9-191-136 (February 1991).

To minimize the problem of inadequate access to information, most large firms delegate decision making and management responsibilities to middle managers, who are positioned where access to both business-specific and corporatewide policy information intersect. However, critical information from both the top and bottom of the organization may be lost or distorted. In addition, the time it takes to exchange information through middle management layers seriously hampers the speed with which the organization can operate.

As the pace of business increases and the environment becomes more dynamic, many companies are "cutting out the middle," forcing the top and bottom of the organization closer together. To avoid organizational dysfunction, this action must be accompanied by flattening and elevating the information access curve. This does not mean that everyone in the organization receives all information; that would result in dysfunctional information overload. Rather, it implies that all decision makers, regardless of their level in the organization, can gain access to the information they need to make well-informed and timely decisions.

By solving the problem of poor information access, accountability for decision making and control can be based on business imperatives rather than on who has access to relevant information. In dynamic and uncertain environments, where both speed and in-depth understanding of the marketplace are critical, decision making and authority can be pushed down to front-line managers along with the necessary corporate perspective and policy information. By the same token, top management can develop a better understanding of the dynamics of the business and external environment and thereby improve the quality of decisions concerned with strategic direction and management of corporatewide initiatives. This leads to a controversial issue: if systems provide timely, flexible access to relevant information, is a middle-management layer needed? That question is being hotly debated. Regardless of its resolution, it is likely that any new roles that do emerge will require flexible and timely access to information.

In large, complex organizations, solving the information access problem requires the redesign of organization structure, management control systems, human resources policies and procedures, and especially the IT architecture.

Chapter 4 introduced the fundamentals of designing an IT architecture. This can be a massive undertaking, since, as many who have struggled with this process can attest, technology can be a powerful inhibitor of change. In most large organizations, systems implemented many years ago may now seem set in stone, even though many aging applications are dangerously fragile because of years of modification. Because older systems tend to be fragmented and inflexible, and because changing them is a formidable task, they often lock the organization into established structures and processes.

There are two major approaches to IT architecture: revolution and evolution. A revolutionary approach involves a wholesale replacement of the existing infrastructure with integrated and flexible systems. This option is more often chosen in small, rapidly growing companies that have not already made a substantial investment in technology. In an evolutionary approach, an integrated and flexible IT architecture is layered on top of the inflexible, static infrastructure. Data for decision making are pulled from old systems into the new systems, where they become available in a more flexible, integrated, and timely manner. Old systems are gradually replaced over time.

Information technologies are flexible tools, constrained primarily by managers' will to use them, expectations about their roles, and applications choices. The readings and cases in this book show several approaches to harnessing information technologies. The first reading, "No Excuses Management," describes the "no surprises" philosophy at Cypress Semiconductor Corporation, and a controversial system of tight, detailed, computer-based controls. The Allen-Bradley case describes an international firm at a critical juncture, as managers set a new strategic direction. Instead of being a national supplier of industrial control "boxes," Allen-Bradley was becoming a global supplier of integrated "solutions," working in partnership with other firms. Organizational structure, management control systems, and IT architecture all had to be repositioned to support the shift in strategy. The final case describes a small company, Connor Formed Metal Products, in which employees have extensive access to corporate data, and are expected to act upon the information.

Reading 6–1

This article describes a radical approach to management—a "no surprises, no excuses management" philosophy in a young organization. Rodgers, the founder, president, and CEO of Cypress Semiconductor Corporation, describes its information architecture, organizational structure, and management control systems.

Preparation Questions

1. Evaluate T. J. Rodgers's approach to management. What elements of the Cypress IOC do you feel are innovative and effective? What elements would you characterize as ineffective?
2. As a general manager, under what circumstances would you implement a management philosophy such as the one proposed by Rodgers?

NO EXCUSES MANAGEMENT

By T. J. Rodgers*

If everyone in our company made ordinary business decisions in a commonsense way, we would be unstoppable. It turns out that very few people, at our company or anywhere else, make ordinary business decisions in a commonsense way. Most companies don't fail for lack of talent or strategic vision. They fail for lack of execution—the mundane blocking and tackling that the great companies consistently do well and strive to do better.

At Cypress, our management systems track corporate, departmental, and individual performance so regularly and in such detail that no manager, including me, can plausibly claim to be in the dark about critical problems. Our systems give managers the capacity to monitor what's happening at all levels of the organization, to anticipate problems or conflicts, to intervene when appropriate, and to identify best practices—without creating layers of bureaucracy that bog down decisions and sap morale.

Lots of companies espouse a "no surprises" philosophy. At Cypress, "no surprises" is a way of life. We operate in a treacherous and unforgiving business. An integrated circuit is the end result of a thousand multidisciplinary tasks; doing 999 of them right guarantees failure, not success. Last year, we shipped 159 different chips (56 of which were new in 1989) in 7 distinct product categories using 26 different process-technology variations. This year, we plan to add another 50 products to our portfolio. Our watchwords are discipline, ac-

*Reprinted by permission of *Harvard Business Review*. "No Excuses Management" by T. J. Rodgers, July–August 1990. Copyright © 1990 by the President and Fellows of Harvard College; all rights reserved.

countability, and relentless attention to detail—at every level of the organization.

How do we measure success at Cypress? By doing what we say we are going to do. We meet sales projections within a percentage point or two every quarter. We don't go over budget—ever. Our silicon wafer manufacturing plant in Round Rock, Texas, which now accounts for 70 percent of our sales, shipped its first revenue wafer eight months after ground breaking. That performance tied the industry record, which had been set in 1984 by our manufacturing facility in San Jose.

Some who learn about our systems raise the specter of Big Brother or use terms like "electronic treadmill." This is nonsense. Our management systems are not designed to punish or pressure; people put enough pressure on themselves without any help from me. The systems are designed to encourage collective thinking and to force each of us to face reality every day.

At Cypress, we collect information in such detail and share it so widely that the company is virtually transparent. This works against the political infighting and bureaucratic obfuscation that cripple so many organizations. People at Cypress disagree vigorously on many things; in our management meetings, people of any rank are free (and eager) to challenge senior executives. But we disagree over substance and the best ways to make the hardheaded trade-offs that are the essence of management. Nobody gets ahead by using information selectively to win internal battles.

Technological change drives the semiconductor industry, and several of our management systems help us make decisions about technology assessment and product development that are quite specific to our business. But most of our management systems (and certainly the most important ones) address the universal challenges of business—motivating people to perform effectively and allocating resources productively. To succeed over the long term, we have to do at least four things better than our competitors:

1. Hire outstanding people and hold on to them.
2. Encourage everyone in the organization to set challenging goals and meet them.
3. Allocate key resources (people, capital, operating expenses) so as to maximize productivity.
4. Reward people in ways that encourage superior performance rather than demotivate superior performers.

Before I describe several of our most important systems, let me make three points. First, I don't use the word *systems* loosely. Each one involves holding specific meetings, maintaining databases, submitting specific reports, and securing approvals. For example, managers grant raises by using a software package that takes them step by step through the required performance-evaluation procedure, recommends salary increases that they can modify within limits, and alerts them if their final decisions violate company policy. A few of our systems virtually run themselves. We've developed a set of computer applications that automatically shuts down a manufacturing operation if it detects that performance has violated a critical procedure. Dubbed "killer software" by our MIS group, these applications have inspired dramatic performance improvements in our factories, and we are transferring the concept to administrative functions such as order entry and accounts receivable.

Second, we don't confuse systems with bureaucratic planning. In our business (and, I suspect, most businesses), five-year plans, even one-year plans, are obsolete 60 seconds after they are written. So we have plans, but we don't become enslaved by them at an unrealistic level of precision. Our annual marketing forecasts are probably 95 percent accurate, with respect to total revenues for each of our product lines. For groups of products within each line, the plans may be 70 percent accurate. For individual products within groups, it's not that unusual to be off by 100 percent.

At the same time, we are absolute sticklers about meeting quarterly revenue and profit targets. Precisely because we understand that detailed long-term forecasts are so unreliable, we track product shipments and revenues on a *daily* basis, evaluate how they measure up against the plan, and identify what adjustments we have to make to meet the plan in the aggregate. We worry less about meeting product-by-product forecasts than about reacting instantaneously to unforeseen competitive developments.

Finally, top management cannot manage without a thorough mastery of the details of its business. To my mind, no CEO can claim to be in charge of the organization unless within 15 minutes—and I mean this literally—he or she can answer the following questions. What are the company's revenues per employee? How do the figures compare with the competition's? What are the revenue-per-employee figures for each of the company's leading product lines? What explains recent trends in each line? What is the average outgoing quality level in each product line? How many orders are delinquent? Which of the company's top 20 executives are standouts, which are low performers, and why? Which departments could recover from a major competitive shock, and which are vulnerable to change? What are the yields, costs, and cycle times at every manufacturing operation? What explains the company's stock market valuation relative to its competitors'?

By now, I suspect, readers are ready to protest: Isn't this a formula for "micromanagement" by the CEO? Won't top executives get lost in the thicket of details and lose sight of broader strategic imperatives? Being in command of detail *doesn't* mean interfering where you don't belong. Collecting information, reviewing it regularly, and sharing it widely allows me to practice management by exception in the truest sense. So long as we stick to our systems, this organization virtually runs itself. I intervene only to solve problems and champion urgent projects.

How to Hire Outstanding People

Great people alone don't guarantee corporate success—but no company can succeed without

them. Sounds like a truism, right? Yet how many companies are as scientific about hiring as they are about designing new products or perfecting the latest market-research techniques? Hiring is one of the most bureaucratic, passive, and arbitrary parts of corporate life. The day we founded Cypress we understood that our greatest proprietary advantage would be to do a better job of hiring than the big companies against which we would compete. We think we've sustained that advantage.

Cypress now employs more than 1,400 people. Our philosophy of hiring (and the system that puts the philosophy into practice) hasn't changed much since we founded the company in 1982. I know the entire organization is implementing the system because no one can bring in a new employee, no matter the rank, without submitting a "hiring book" that documents the entire process and gives comprehensive results of interviews and reference checks. Until we reached 400 employees, I read every one of those books before we made a job offer. I now share that task with six other senior managers. In no more than 15 minutes, with no verbal communication whatsoever, one of us can determine whether or not a hiring manager has followed our procedures. When the system has been followed, we make the hire. When it hasn't, we don't.

Recently, for example, one of our vice presidents submitted a hiring book that violated a cardinal rule not to offer big raises to job candidates. His explanation was familiar: "At my old company, we had to give big raises to convince people to sign on." My response was unequivocal: "We've hired 1,400 people with this system. Is there any reason we can't hire number 1,401 the same way?" The vice president resubmitted the hiring book two weeks later, and it still contained an out-of-policy raise. To emphasize my point, I tracked down a big pair of scissors, cut the book in half, and mailed it back to him. He now does it right the first time.

The hiring book serves another purpose. When people don't work out, it helps us go back and evaluate what went wrong. Hiring the wrong people is a very expensive mistake. We give no raises to about 3 percent of our employees every year, a sign that they are low performers. This company would die if 3 percent of the products we shipped were defective. We strive for 100 percent quality in manufacturing; we have the same goal for hiring. In many cases, when an employee leaves because of poor performance, we send his or her manager the hiring book, ask how we might have spotted the problem earlier, and use the departure as an opportunity to improve our hiring procedures.

Three strongly held beliefs drive our hiring system. First, the only way to hire outstanding people is for managers themselves to find the people they need. Hiring, like most everything else in business, is an acquired skill. The more people you interview, evaluate, and select, the better you get at interviewing, evaluating, and selecting. Thus if 1 of my 12 direct reports (8 vice presidents and 4 subsidiary presidents) is authorized to hire a new manager, or 1 of our 72 managers is authorized to hire an individual contributor, it is up to *that manager,* not the human resource staff, to locate desirable candidates, prescreen them before they enter the formal evaluation process, and monitor the process as it unfolds. We make almost no use of executive recruiters. The human resource department plays a modest role in suggesting candidates but no role in evaluating them. Indeed, prospective employees don't see anyone in human resources until they report to work and fill out their insurance applications.

Most companies—and certainly most big companies—do just the opposite. Managers sit behind their desks and wait for personnel to parade candidates through their office. Of course, personnel is never as motivated as the hiring manager is to fill an open slot. As the hiring schedule falls behind, the manager grows increasingly desperate and makes an offer to the first warm body that meets rudimentary requirements. This approach guarantees that the quality of the company's work force will nicely (and disastrously) mirror the quality of the available labor pool. The organization drifts toward average.

In our system, managers have only themselves to blame if they can't fill open slots. After eight years, we have a good feel for the employment "hit rate." It takes 10 prescreen telephone interviews to find one person good enough to qualify for the formal evaluation process. We make offers to about 25 percent of the people who go through our evaluation, and about 85 percent of the people to whom we make offers accept. If our managers do their math, they quickly understand that quality hiring takes a lot of work. They'll need to make about 100 telephone calls to find two great people. By the way, if they don't fill their open slots by the end of the quarter, they lose the hiring requisition and have to justify the new position again.

Another weakness with most companies' passive approach to hiring is that executives lose touch with the job market. Regular interaction with the job market provides insights on marketplace dynamics. A few years ago, in a memo explaining our hiring system to a new top manager, I wrote down what I had learned as a result of my own job-related calls and interviews. For example, people didn't like Intel's 8 AM sign-in policy, which the company has since eliminated. Intel and National Semiconductor were paying 15 percent premiums to layout designers on the night shift while Cypress paid none. But most layout designers cared less about shift differentials than about the kinds of chips they were designing. The market value of plasma engineers ranged from $20,000 a year to $50,000 a year, with little variation of price with quality. The list could have gone on for several pages.

We have a second inviolate principle of hiring: We don't buy employees. This is uncommon in Silicon Valley, but it serves as an excellent screen. Someone who will join Cypress for a few percentage points more in salary or a better dental plan is not the kind of career-oriented person we want. Good people want to be paid fairly, in a way that reflects the organization's success over the long term. They are rarely concerned with earning an excessive amount of money relative to their peers. What drives them is the desire to win.

Until 1986, therefore, we had a very simple policy: A candidate who had received a raise from a previous employer within the last four months came to Cypress without a raise. We now offer an 8 percent prorated increase, but the basic premise holds. We do not bid for great talent; people with great talent come to Cypress because they want to win. Members of our team are rewarded with stock options and the highest percentage raises in the industry. Everyone at the company, from the receptionists to the CEO, participates in an aggressive stock-option program. (We recently repurchased two million shares to fund that option program.) As for raises, our formal policy is to survey the competition, calculate the average of the three companies that grant the highest raises, and add one-half a percentage point or more to determine the Cypress raise budget.

We have a third principle: The interview and evaluation process should be tough, fair, and expeditious. Quality interviewing is the most important part of the hiring process—and something most managers are terrible at. We've developed several interview techniques to keep these sessions productive. (See the accompanying box, "The Science of Interviewing.") Although the interview and evaluation process is demanding, it need not take forever. There's no reason a manager can't prescreen a candidate by telephone, bring him or her in for two rounds of interviews, and make an offer within one week. We're not there yet; we meet the one-week target about 75 percent of the time. We also expect the hiring manager to be in *daily* contact with the candidate as the process unfolds.

Set Goals—Then Measure and Meet Them

All of Cypress's 1,400 employees have goals, which, in theory, makes them no different from employees at most other companies. What does make our people different is that every week they set their own goals, commit to achieving them by a specific date, enter them into a database, and report whether or not they completed prior goals.

Cypress's computerized goal system is an important part of our managerial infrastructure. It is a detailed guide to the future and an objective record of the past. In any given week, some 6,000 goals in the database come due. Our ability to meet those goals ultimately determines our success or failure.

Most of the work in our company is organized by project rather than along strict functional lines. Members of a project team may be (and usually are) from different parts of the organization. Project managers need not be (and often aren't) the highest ranking member of the group. Likewise, the goal system is organized by project and function. In Monday project meetings, employees set short-term goals and rank them in priority order. Short-term goals take from one to six weeks to complete, and different employees have different numbers of goals. At the beginning of a typical week, for example, a member of our production-control staff initiated seven new goals in connection with three different projects. He said he would, among other things, report on progress with certain minicomputer problems (two weeks), monitor and report on quality rejection rates for certain products (three weeks), update killer software for the assembly department (two weeks), and assist a marketing executive with a forecasting software enhancement (four weeks).

On Monday night, the project goals are fed back into a central computer. On Tuesday mornings, functional managers receive a printout of their direct reports' new and pending project goals. These printouts are the basis of Tuesday afternoon meetings in which managers work with their people to anticipate overload and conflicting goals, sort out priorities, organize work, and make mutual commitments about what's going to get done. This is a critical step. The failure mode in our company (and I suspect in most growing companies) is that people overcommit themselves rather than establish unchallenging goals. By 5 PM Tuesday, the revised schedule is fed back into the central database.

This "two pass" system generates the work program that coordinates the mostly self-imposed

The Science of Interviewing

You can't hire quality people without a systematic approach to interviewing. Four basic rules guide our interview and evaluation process.

1. *Use the big guns.* If you want job prospects to know that you are serious, high-ranking executives should take the time to get involved in the interview process. At Cypress, all candidates for exempt positions, whether or not they are senior enough to report to vice presidents, interview with two vice presidents. I interview all candidates who would report to vice presidents as well as many important individual contributors who report to managers. This is the technique Jerry Sanders used on me when I was considering joining Advanced Micro Devices. The first day I walked in the door, the receptionist in a building of 2,000 people smiled and said, "Oh yes, Dr. Rodgers, Jerry is waiting for you." She took me right upstairs—no waiting in the lobby—and our session began. That's the way to communicate to job prospects how valuable they are.

2. *Make interviews tough and technically demanding—even for people you know you want.* We are a hard-charging company in a tough business and have a no-nonsense way of communicating. People should know that before they sign on. At the beginning of the evaluation process, candidates receive a form that lists the technical skills the position requires, with whom they'll be interviewing, and the questions they will be asked. This focuses the interviews and alerts the candidates to how rigorous the sessions will be.

After several "technical" interviews and the interviews with two vice presidents, candidates go through what we call the "pack of wolves" session. The applicant sits in a conference room where senior technical people pose difficult questions that the candidate does not know in advance. Some of the questions are virtually impossible to answer, and they come in rapid succession. When the candidate makes a mistake, the interviewers point it out and give the correct answer. The tone of this session is aggressive but not abusive. It is an excellent way to weed out qualified managers and engineers who can't take the pressures of our business.

3. *Interviews should lead to detailed assessments of strengths and weaknesses, not vague impressions.* Our interview evaluation forms include numerical scores (on a scale of zero to five) that mirror the technical qualifications on the requisition. Our people are tough graders. I also insist that the hiring vice president write an interview strategy before my session with a managerial candidate. That strategy highlights the specific strengths and weaknesses of the candidate, particular concerns he or she has expressed about the job or the company, and other critical issues. I'm not reluctant to share the numerical evaluations with a candidate, especially one who has been assessed as weak in a particular area. This candid feedback is usually a positive experience. Good people know their weaknesses and are eager to improve them.

4. *Check for cultural fit.* Most companies claim to do this, but few are very systematic. We probe work attitudes and career goals through a questionnaire that requires brief but direct answers to open-ended questions. The questionnaire forces candidates to be as specific as possible about hard-to-quantify issues that are addressed only obliquely, if at all, in most evaluation processes. Among the questions are: How is the morale in your company or department? Why? What do you expect Cypress has to offer you in the way of a work environment that your employer doesn't offer? What would your boss say is your best attribute? What would the "needs improvement" section of your performance review address? Can you describe your personal experience with a difficult boss, peer, or subordinate?

activities of every Cypress employee. It allows the organization to be project driven, which helps us emphasize speed and agility, as well as functionally accurate, which works against burnout and failure to execute. On Wednesday morning, our eight vice presidents receive goal printouts for their people and the people below them—another conflict-resolution mechanism.

In the early days of the company, until we hit about 100 employees, I read every employee's goals every week. I knew what every person in the company was doing on a week-to-week basis. That's not the role of the CEO in a company with more than 1,400 people, so my approach to the goal system has changed. Today my job is to anticipate problems, largely by sorting through the goal system looking for patterns. I use the system as a kind of organizational speedometer that not only tells me how fast we're traveling but also helps explain what's holding us back.

On Wednesday afternoons at my weekly staff meeting, I review various database reports with my vice presidents. We talk about what's going wrong and how to help managers who are running into problems. The following reports typically serve as the basis for discussion: progress with goals on critical projects; percentage of delinquent goals sorted by managers (their goals plus those of their subordinates); percentage of delinquent goals sorted by vice president (the percentage of pending goals that are delinquent for all people reporting up the chain of command to each vice president); all employees without goals (something I do not tolerate); all goals five or more weeks delinquent; and all employees with two or more delinquent goals, sorted by manager.

As we've refined the goal system and used it more extensively, I've developed some general principles. First, people are going to have goals they don't achieve on time; the key is to sense when a vice president or a manager is losing control of the operation. My rule of thumb is that vice presidents should not have delinquency rates above 20 percent, and managers should not let more than 30 percent of their goals become delin-

quent. When managers do have a delinquency problem, I usually intervene with a short note: "Your delinquency rate is running at 35 percent, what can I do to help?" I often get back requests for specific assistance. Part of my role is to hold people accountable. But it is also to identify problems before they become crises and to provide help in getting them fixed.

Second, people need positive feedback. Every month we issue a completed goal report for every person in the company. The report lists all goals completed over the past four weeks as well as those that have yet to come due. "Individual Monthly Goal Report," an excerpt from a monthly report for a production-control staffer, lists all goals completed in workweek 45 of 1989. The entire report consists of 49 goals, 28 of which were completed on time, 4 of which were completed late, and 17 of which were pending—an outstanding record.

The completed goal report is also a valuable tool for performance evaluation. Like most companies, we use annual reviews to set salary increases. The trouble with annual reviews is that managers succumb to the "proximity effect." An employee who performs outstandingly for the first 10 months of the year but has a subpar 2 months just before the review is more likely to get a poor evaluation than is a colleague who had a lousy 10 months but did a great job in the two months just before the evaluation. At Cypress, the completed goal report triggers a performance minireview; every month managers read through their people's printouts and prepare brief, factual evaluations. At year end, managers have a dozen such objective reviews to refresh their memories and fight the proximity effect.

It's important to note that the goal system does not require big investments in computer hardware and software. Indeed, we have no equipment dedicated exclusively to the goal system. We use personal computers and a DEC minicomputer that also handles the company's administrative tasks. The software is Lotus 1-2-3 and Paradox—two of the most common microcomputer applications.

Much of the system still runs on "sneakernet"— people pass disks back and forth rather than use networking systems, although we are in the process of networking the entire company more effectively.

Indeed, I developed the goal system long before personal computers existed. It has its roots in management-by-objectives techniques I learned in the mid-1970s at American Microsystems (AMI), where I ran the random access memory (RAM) group.[1] Back then my hardware was a blackboard, and my software was chalk. In a typical year, we would develop as many as 10 new chips, and tracking each project became a nightmare. So I got a blackboard, wrote down everything that had to be done before each product could ship, and attached names and due dates to each task. My update routine was an eraser.

After I left for Advanced Micro Devices (AMD), where I was responsible for RAM manufacturing as well as design, it became a bit harder to keep score. So I covered my walls with blackboards, used masking tape to divide them into project panels, and transported the system from AMI. Once a week, my assistant would wheel in an electric typewriter, record the schedule, and send it out to the troops. If people in my organization wanted to know where things stood, all they had to do was come into my office and look at the blackboards.

The Cypress system is just an enhanced, electronic version of what I've been doing for 15 years. The computer record on each goal includes a description of the task, when the goal was set, when it is due, what priority it is, who has agreed to complete it, to what manager that person reports, and to what vice president the manager reports. We are now enhancing the system by recording long-term goals (which we call "strategic" goals) and all quality-oriented goals. Of course, recording that information means I can sort by each of those fields and create special-exception reports. With a few keystrokes, I can check on the performance of any one of my vice presidents, see how a manager is relating to subordinates, or check on the progress of a particular project.

No one can accuse me of not "knowing the details" of my business. Yet I don't have to intervene where I don't belong or try to be in a hundred places at once. The goal system provides warnings when something goes wrong and offers instant access to data in any area that I am concerned about. I'm a big advocate of management by walking around, and I regularly block out time on my calendar to visit our facilities. The goal system lets me practice MBWA all the more effectively. By sorting through the database and following up with telephone calls, I can get up to speed on an operation before I arrive.

I don't want to give the impression that the goal system is strictly a support mechanism. It does give me the ammunition I need to cut through bureaucratic obfuscation. My access to the details means vice presidents and managers know they can't snow me. For example, we recently shafted a valued customer by delivering an emergency shipment of parts one day late. (I learned about the problem because every officer at Cypress is "godfather" to one strategic customer and I happened to be godfather to this customer.) I spent 15 minutes at my computer screen reviewing relevant goal reports and data from a few other systems. With a follow-up telephone call or two, I discovered what went wrong. Shipping was overloaded on the day the parts were scheduled to go out; the parts were not marked as a "JIT order," so they weren't shipped immediately. By the time the department shipped the parts, they were a day late. With another call, I learned that certain people in marketing did not understand the shipping department's priority system. I called the relevant people into my office and asked them to change our

---

[1]Several of Cypress's systems are enhancements of best practices among our competitors or companies with which our executives have been affiliated. For example, the goal system traces its origins to management-by-objectives techniques I learned from former AMI chief executive Glenn Penisten, who brought them over from Texas Instruments. Our expense-control system draws on techniques practiced at Mostek.

procedures so that the problem would never happen again.

Now think what might have happened without the goal system. After I learned about the problem, I would have called in the marketing manager, who would have made plausible excuses, produced nice-looking graphs showing a 99 percent on-time delivery performance—and blamed the jerks in shipping. Then I'd have called shipping, a manager there would have complained about having been overloaded, about how marketing always expects miracles, and the political infighting would have been hot and heavy. I would have been virtually powerless to cut through to the truth.

People at Cypress know I don't tolerate bureaucratic politics—it's one of the items on a very short list of what can get you fired. They also know I have the ability to peer down into the bowels of the organization, drag up relevant data, make a few telephone calls, and find out what really happened in any situation. The knowledge that I can call on so much detail so easily *means I seldom have to.* No vice president or manager wants to be in the awkward position where the CEO knows more about a situation than he or she does.

Allocate Resources for Maximum Productivity

Middle managers can be an organization's most enduring strength. They are more aware of the company's day-to-day business realities than any other group, and they are earnest, committed, and creative. Middle managers can also cause companies to grow fat and uncompetitive, not because they don't do their jobs, but because they think their jobs are the most important in the world and thus lose sight of the broader corporate imperative. I call this phenomenon middle management myopia. In organizations that suffer from this disease (and it afflicts the majority of large companies), middle managers clamor for resources while top managers are chartered to hold the line. Usually, top managers are forced to cave in because middle managers can call on so much

more information and functional expertise. How can a senior executive turn down a request for resources (people, equipment, expenses) when a well-respected middle manager makes a plausible argument that the department will unravel without them—probably taking the company with it?

These "gun-to-the-head" stories are a staple of corporate life. If you don't think any good middle manager can come up with several of them, you are fooling yourself. Consider just two:

- *From a financial manager:* "We have $40 million of excess receivables on which we pay $140,000 of interest every year. I could get the receivables down to $20 million, but I need another clerk to do it. The basic problem is paperwork; sometimes our invoices don't match our customers' records, and we have to work the phones to get them to agree to pay. I know I told you seven clerks was enough. But if we hire one more at $30,000 a year, we can cut the uncollected receivables in half, saving us $70,000. It's foolish not to make the hire."
- *From the engineering manager:* "We generate annual revenues of $20 million with this particular chip. Our final-test yield is 90 percent, which means we're throwing away $2 million a year. If you let me hire two more engineers (they will cost us less than $100,000 a year combined), we can get yields up to 94 percent, saving $400,000—a four-month payback. It's foolish not to make the hires."

The moment senior executives buy into the tunnel vision of their middle managers, they've lost control of the company. If that happens, it's *not* the middle managers' fault; they're simply doing their jobs as they understand them. Our resource-allocation systems are designed to prevent middle management myopia by forcing collective thinking at all levels. Every quarter, based on our revenue projections, we establish total corporate allowances for new hires, capital investment, and operating expenses. We then allocate this overall target by departments and force critical trade-off decisions down to the middle manage-

Individual Monthly Goal Report*

Workweek	Date	Manager	Department	Project	Begin	End	Delinquent	Status	Who	Goal
8945	11/08/89	RF	310	OPLN	35	45		C	GB	Define die kit request queue time; request screen [dev/pkg/grade]
8945	11/08/89	RF	310	OPLN	38	45		C	GB	Killer for purchasing: shutdown purchasing if receipts later than commit
8945	11/08/89	RF	310	OPLN	40	44	45	C	GB	Turn on killer software for "IQA"
8945	11/08/89	RF	310	OPLN	41	45		C	GB	Action request #3561: schedule for remote order entry
8945	11/08/89	RF	310	OPLN	44	45		C	GB	Ignore 7C34x devices in the killer for sort
8945	11/08/89	RF	310	OPLN	44	45		C	GB	Printout of 3Q89 ships for RF
8945	11/08/89	RF	310	OPLN	44	45		C	GB	Publish weekly MIS summary
8945	11/08/89	RF	310	OPLN	44	45		C	GB	Verify that FAB 2 shipreview data is updated (not since WW33)
8945	11/08/89	RF	310	OREN	44	45		C	GB	Train marketing on ED1 forms and getting customers into system

*This excerpt lists all the goals one production-control staffer completed in workweek 45. The entire report consisted of 49 completed and pending goals.

ment level. We get these people into the same room at the same time, with a computer model that allows us to conduct resource negotiations on-line, and cut the deals that would otherwise lead to memo wars and special pleading.

Our resource-allocation systems also address a second source of waste and inefficiency: the false confidence created by prosperity. The seeds of business failure are sewn in good times, not bad. Economic reversals have a wonderful way of concentrating minds and encouraging groups to overcome long-standing differences. During times of prosperity, however, danger lurks everywhere. Growth masks waste, extravagance, and inefficiency. The moment growth slows, the accumulated sins of the past are revealed all the way to the bottom line.

At Cypress, our annual revenues have grown 40 percent or more per year since we founded the company in 1982. We're proud of that record, but we're even more proud of our consistent quarter-to-quarter profitability. Even in 1986, when the semiconductor industry was in the midst of a crippling downturn, we maintained industry-leading operating margins of 20 percent. And we did it on revenues of only $50 million.

This was no accident. The performance measures that drive the company adjust our thinking to control the prosperity illusion. Sure we want aggressive revenue growth. But we *demand* ever-increasing revenue per employee, ever-higher capital productivity (revenue dollars per dollar of undepreciated fixed assets), and ever-lower expense ratios. And we constantly check our performance against the best of our competition. The graphs in "Tracking Performance at Cypress" review our record on these measures.

Our system for controlling head count is one of the three most important systems we have at Cypress. Here's how it works. At the beginning of every quarter, we hold a head-count meeting for the entire company. Our eight vice presidents attend the meeting along with middle managers. Together we review the last quarter's total revenue, total head count, and revenue per employee.

We then use forecast revenues to determine the allowable head count at the end of the quarter and thus the total number of requisitions we can *afford* to open in the new quarter. There are two things to keep in mind. First, we are almost always within 1 percent or 2 percent of forecast revenue—this is not a hypothetical exercise. Second, our target head count is based on continual improvement in revenue per employee. We expect this critical productivity measure to improve every quarter or, in difficult economic times, to hold the line.[2]

Thus, quickly and directly, everyone in the room (which means virtually everyone in the company with hiring authority) understands how many new employees will join Cypress over the next three months. This is not a negotiable figure. The negotiations start once we total up the vice presidents' head-count requests and start adjusting them to meet the new total.

The power of our system is that it presents the real trade-offs to everyone at the same time. Everyone in the room understands that we are playing a zero-sum game. A vice president who insists on all his or her requisitions understands (as does everyone else) that these slots come at the expense of other requests. Such stark trade-offs create incentives for everyone else to think creatively about solving that vice president's problems without hiring more people. In other words, I enlist many allies in my effort to hold the line on resources. Moreover, vice presidents who can't make the number of hires they want don't feel arbitrarily denied. Even if they're unhappy, they understand the logic behind the final decisions.

The negotiations are conducted in great detail—they're not for the faint of heart. Every department has a microperformance index that divides some useful measure of output by head count. These indexes, which we flash on the screen for everyone

---

[2]It's not always possible to improve corporate revenue per employee. When our Round Rock fab went on line, corporate productivity "dropped" until the plant began volume shipments. But we still insisted on continual improvement from the rest of the company, and we adjusted our quarterly figures to measure it.

Tracking Performance at Cypress

Revenues (*in millions*)

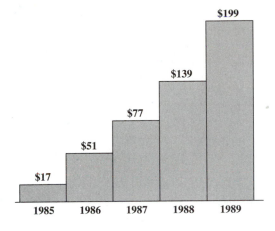

Revenue per Employee (*in thousands*)

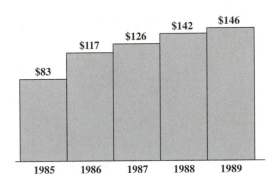

Revenue per Dollar Gross Fixed Assets

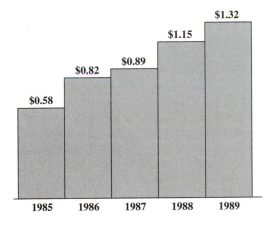

Marketing G&A Expenses (*as a percentage of revenues*)

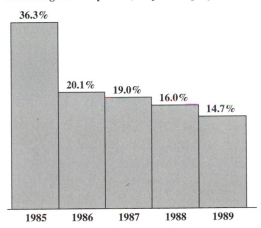

to see, become the basis of the trade-offs between departments. Let's say shipping and receiving has requested an additional clerk. We flash a graph that tracks the department's productivity index—line items shipped per week per clerk—and ask the manager and vice president to justify the request. Or say the vice president of manufacturing needs ten more operators in our San Jose fab. The group reviews weekly wafer output per employee per week, builds in further progress on this perfor-

mance index, and weighs the vice president's request accordingly. In each negotiation, the group knows the number of requisitions we must eliminate to meet the corporate target, the productivity trends for each department making requests, and which departments won't be able to hire new people if other departments make all the hires they've requested.

Our system for allocating capital works much the same way. We track total revenues as a function of undepreciated capital, insist on continual improvement in the macroindex, approve overall corporate targets on this basis, and use the targets to drive capital spending down through the departments. In our capital-intensive business, having just enough capital just in time is even more important than controlling head count.

Our expense-control system goes one step farther. The CEO of any startup company signs every purchase order for the first few years. This is a deadly efficient way to control spending. But there comes a time (at about $40 million of annual revenues for a semiconductor company) when the CEO faces a moment of truth: he or she can spend every waking minute signing purchase orders or develop a new approach. This is where the extravagance usually begins or where a new purchasing bureaucracy chokes off necessary expenditures and creates frustration throughout the company.

We've developed a system that gives senior management ironclad control of spending and that requires no more than five working days for a purchase order to be approved or sent back to the requester for cause. As with head count and capital, allowable expenses in a given quarter start from the top line. We project revenues, insist on improvement in the corporate expense-to-revenue ratio, and then allocate allowable purchases by function and department through real-time negotiation and adjustment.

Then comes a second critical step. We divide each manager's quarterly expenses by 13 and create a weekly budget that governs spending for the quarter. Of course, some spending comes in clumps; a manager may need to make one purchase that exceeds the weekly budget. That's allowed—so long as the manager has accrued enough "credit" in previous weeks so that the big purchase does not bump overall spending for the quarter off track.

This system is rigorous. It also works. If senior management controls the quarterly spending meter, and the meter determines how fast money flows into the corporate pipeline each week, we can't be surprised by what comes out at the end of 13 weeks.

Controlling the meter does not mean I abdicate my role in monitoring expenses. With few "emergency P.O." exceptions, the spending window at Cypress is open for two hours a week. Every Thursday from 8 AM to 10 AM, we hold a purchase-order commit meeting with the vice presidents. They summarize the purchase orders that need my approval that week; I look for questionable expenditures and probe for extravagance. Even more important, the weekly meetings become a way of transferring best practices on spending throughout the organization. I invariably come out of them full of ideas about cost reduction that I immediately share with people who can benefit from them.

A visitor unfamiliar with our system could sit in on a purchase-order commit meeting and conclude that the CEO of this $200 million company still signs every purchase order above the petty cash limit. That visitor would be correct in the literal sense but dead wrong about how the system really works. Indeed, our approach to expense control has cascaded down through all four levels of the company, to a point where I don't worry about missing a purchase-order commit meeting. (I miss one out of three.) Vice presidents routinely take their weekly expense budgets and divide them appropriately among their managers to guide weekly budgets. In turn, managers take their weekly expenses and divide them appropriately among their subordinates, who take their weekly budgets and divide them among their contributors.

Today our expense-control system virtually runs itself. It drives us every week of every month of every quarter. It's no accident we have never exceeded a quarterly budget by more than 1 percent.

Take the Mystery out of Performance Appraisal

Managers shouldn't expect outstanding performance unless they're prepared to reward outstanding performers. Yet evaluation and reward systems remain an organizational black hole for three reasons.

First, managers aren't very scientific about rating their people. They may be able to identify the real stars and the worst laggards, but the vast majority of people (who must still be ranked) get lost somewhere in the middle. Second, even if they evaluate people correctly, managers like to spread raises around evenly to keep the troops happy. This is a deadly policy that saps the morale of standouts who deserve more and sends the wrong signal to weak performers. Third, managers are totally incapable of distinguishing between "merit" and "equity" when awarding increases. *Merit* refers to that portion of a raise awarded for the quality of past performance. *Equity* refers to adjustments in that raise to more closely align salaries of equally ranked peers. Merit and equity both have a place in the incentive mix, but confusing the two makes for mushy logic, counterproductive results, and dissatisfied people.

Cypress is not immune to these problems; I'd say a third of our vice presidents still don't have a good feel for how to review performance and award raises. But I'm not too concerned about that. Our focal-review system, one of the most efficient systems we've ever developed, controls the three big problems I just identified. Our managers follow the system because the only way to grant raises in the company is to use the series of computer templates that walks managers through a series of review-process steps and alerts them to violations against company policy.

As with all our resource-allocation systems, the focal-review system starts with policies at the top and forces middle management decisions to be consistent with that thinking. Senior management and the board of directors review our annual revenue forecasts, survey compensation trends among our competitors, and settle on a total corporate allowance for raises. The "raise budget" is not negotiable, and it drives raises throughout the company. If the corporate budget is 8 percent, then every department must meet a weighted-average salary increase of 8 percent. It's up to managers to distribute the 8 percent pool, which is where the focal-review system comes in.

There are four stages to the process. Everyone at Cypress is part of a "focal group" (there are 132 groups in the company) composed of peers with comparable responsibilities. For example, all vice presidents are in one focal group, all weekend night-shift assembly operators are in another, all RAM circuit designers are in a third. The ranking committee for each focal group includes the members' supervisors as well as managers from other parts of the company in a position to judge each member's performance and service. The ranking committee for our shipping clerks might include representatives from sales or manufacturing. The ranking committee for a group of circuit designers might include representatives from marketing or manufacturing. Before evaluations take place, we post rosters of focal groups and ranking committees to allow people to question their assignments.

Much of the discussion in the ranking committee centers on the monthly reviews stemming from the goal system. This controls the proximity effect I've already discussed and provides an objective record of performance based on goals employees have set for themselves.

The ranking procedure helps control a second problem that undermines so many performance reviews; I call it the mayonnaise effect. Suppose you're running a food company that wants to enter the mayonnaise market. You can make your mayonnaise with olive oil, sunflower oil, or corn oil. You can use vinegar, lemon, both, or neither. You can emulsify with egg yolks, dry eggs, or whole eggs. You can use lots of salt or not much salt. If you put 10 different mayonnaise formulas on a table and ask people to rate each one, chances are pretty good they'll make some big errors. They'll probably recall their absolute favorites and the recipes that made them sick. But what about all the recipes in the middle? Are you confident your tasters will correctly rank formulas three through seven—none of which made a dramatic impression, but each of which has its unique qualities?

This same problem afflicts performance appraisal. It's not too hard to identify the two outstanding performers and the two laggards in a group of ten employees. But to the people in the middle, there's a big difference between being ranked fourth and seventh—and managers can badly muff these rankings. That's why our system forces comparisons between pairs that leave little room for error. Consider a 10-person focal group with members A through J. The ranking committee's job is to review every possible two-employee comparison and determine who was the superior performer for the year: Has A performed better than B? Has A performed better than C? Has B performed better than C? And so on. The software records the outcome of each comparison and develops relative rankings as the basis for merit increases. No confusion, no mistakes, no mayonnaise effect.

These rankings become the basis of merit increases decided by the focal-group leader, the senior member of the ranking committee. (The focal-group leader alone is chartered to divide up the raise budget once the rankings are completed.) And merit means merit. The software reviews the ranking committee's individual judgments and recommends appropriate merit increases. At this point in the process, no salaries have been disclosed—everything is expressed in percentages. The computer uses a pure and uncomplicated process to assign a certain percentage raise for a certain ranking. The leader can make adjustments to these recommendations, but the software checks to make sure the final numbers comply with several principles. There are 20 quality checks in all, including these:

- *Monotonic distribution:* Any group member ranked higher than another must receive a higher merit raise. This check prevents managers from taking money away from a top performer who happens to be highly paid and giving it to a weak performer.
- *Forced differentiation:* There must be a minimum spread (last year it was 8 percent) between the largest and smallest raises in the group. This check prevents the most common managerial cop-out, spreading raises evenly throughout the group.

- *Reasonable adjustments:* Although leaders are free to adjust the computer-generated recommendations, there are limits. This check works against clustering the majority of increases around one figure.
- *Budgets:* The average raise for the group cannot exceed the corporate target. This check emphasizes the point that giving big raises to people who deserve low raises hurts the entire group.

Only after they have awarded percentage increases based strictly on merit can managers make adjustments for salary inequities created by personal circumstances and historical accidents. Again, the software plays a central role. For each and every focal group, it generates a simple graph that compares the *salaries* of each group member (on the vertical axis) with merit rankings (on the horizontal axis). The graph also displays a trend line that describes the desired salary distribution for the department. We operate according to the general principle that the best performer in a department should earn at least 50 percent more than the worst performer in that department. Managers adjust raises up or down to move salaries closer to the trend line. Here too the system checks for mistakes and makes sure the overall increase stays within budget. (See the chart "How Cypress Awards Raises.")

The power of our focal-review system is its simplicity. An easy-to-use software application (it runs on Lotus 1-2-3) rigorously applies a set of principles without usurping managerial discretion. It guides managers on a step-by-step journey through the evaluation and reward process, alerts them instantaneously when their decisions violate company policy, and guarantees that they stay within budget. The system also creates a paper trail that managers can use to explain to employees how raises were determined. We can tell each of our people how the ranking committee evaluated his or her performance ("You rated above average but not in the top 10 percent"), the percentage merit increase awarded by the focal-group leader, and how the manager adjusted the merit increase

How Cypress Awards Raises*

Employee	Rank	Merit Increase		Current Salary	Equity Increase			Final Raise	New Salary
		cREC%	iREC%		cEQ$	cAEQ%	iAEQ%		
BB	1	10.6%	12.0%	$53,400	$ 3,700	0.7%	0.7%	12.7%	$60,200
DD	2	9.7	10.4	59,800	(5,500)	−0.9	−0.9	9.5	62,859
FF	3	8.8	9.3	49,300	3,600	0.7	0.7	10.0	54,245
EE	4	7.9	8.1	50,300	100	0.0	0.0	8.1	54,383
CC	5	7.1	7.1	42,800	5,600	1.3	1.3	8.4	46,398
AA	6	6.2	6.9	53,400	(8,700)	−1.6	−1.6	5.3	56,217
GG	7	5.3	5.0	42,100	1,200	0.3	0.3	5.3	44,323
HH	8	4.4	3.0	41,100	0.00	0.0	0.0	3.0	42,335
Quality checks		**Wt'd avg:** 8.0%		$49,025				8.0%	$52,620

Key: **cREC%** = Computer   recommends   **iREC%** = Leader   awards   **cEQ$** = Equity   differential   **cAEQ%** = Computer recommends   **iAEQ%** = Leader recommends

*This condensed report shows how a focal-group leader awards raises among eight SRAM product engineers. The ranking committee rated engineer DD higher than FF, so the group leader awarded DD a larger merit increase. However, the computer's equity analysis showed that DD was overpaid by $5,500 relative to his peers, while FF was underpaid by $3,600. As a result of equity adjustments, DD received a lower raise than FF.

for equity. Most people will accept an outcome they are unhappy with so long as they understand the logic behind it.

As for senior management, the system becomes yet another tool for management by exception. In a single, effective two-hour meeting, I review the raise of every employee at Cypress by reviewing the printouts the system generates. I can compare an individual's raise with those granted to his or her peers, look at raise distributions in one group versus those in another, or compare this year's raises for an individual or group with raises from the last two years. Of course, I can also check to make sure the system has been followed. Any manager who submits a printout that violates our policy gets it back with a note to do it right—which means very few managers ever submit faulty printouts. The system is simple, effective, and consistent.

How Big Is Too Big?

It's natural to ask whether the systems I've described can work in companies much bigger than Cypress. I don't know. But I do know that if they can't, then these companies are probably unmanageable. We respect the limitations of size. I am absolutely convinced that any small group of smart, dedicated, hard-working professionals can beat any large group of average professionals with superior resources. There comes a point in any organization's evolution when adding more people, more buildings, and more equipment reduces overall productivity.

I believe that point is somewhere in the neighborhood of $100 million in annual revenues for a semiconductor company. Which is why Cypress today is not one company with total revenues of $200 million but *five* distinct companies linked by a common strategy, vision, and management systems. We have chosen to fund our growth with a venture-capital model, seeding new ventures under the Cypress umbrella.

Our first startup, Cypress Semiconductor (Texas), was the Round Rock wafer fab. Aspen Semiconductor was founded in 1987 to design and develop new categories of logic chips. Multichip

---

What to Do when a Valued Employee Quits

February 24, 1988

TO: Vice Presidents and Managers
FROM: T. J. Rodgers

I have not been called on to save a valued employee for some time. Last week, I became involved in two such situations—both were successful—but my job was made more difficult because we did not follow some basic rules.

I realized I have never formally stated our policy on resignations. Here it is:

1. *React immediately.* That means within five minutes. Nothing takes priority over working with a valued employee who has resigned. Delays such as "I'll talk to you after our staff meeting" are unacceptable. Cancel the next activity you have scheduled.

This demonstrates to the employee that he or she takes precedence over daily activities. It also gives you the best chance of changing the employee's mind before he or she makes an irreversible decision.

2. *Keep the resignation quiet.* This is important for both parties. If other employees don't know about the resignation, the employee does not face the embarrassment of publicly changing his or her mind. The company also gets more latitude. In one recent case, the resignation was disclosed. After I convinced the employee to stay, there were multiple rumors (all untrue) that we had "bought back" the employee. Cypress does not negotiate the salaries of employees who have resigned. We may communicate information about upcoming raises and evergreen stock options if that information is available at the time.

3. *Tell your boss immediately and me within an hour.* There is no excuse for not informing me (and everyone in the chain of command between the individual and me) as soon as a resignation occurs. I expect instantaneous communication and can be interrupted in meetings, called out of meetings in outside locations, or called at home. (I am listed in the telephone directory.)

4. *Listen carefully to the employee.* Once a resignation has occurred and the proper people know, the employee's manager and vice president should sit down with the employee and listen carefully to the reasons behind the resignation. Any attempt to retain the employee will be severely impaired unless management listens to *exactly* what the employee says and accepts it. That message should then be transmitted up through the chain of command without any changes, even if it is unflattering to the manager involved.

You should also make an exact determination of the employee's options at the other company. Is he or she looking at a better job, more money, slower pace, faster pace, or fundamental career change? These issues will obviously be imperative in constructing an argument to change the employee's mind.

5. *Construct your arguments.* Once you've gathered accurate data, sit down with your vice president and put together a plan to convince the employee to stay. The only possibly effective argument is one that validly claims the employee's best interests are served by staying at Cypress. Once you and the vice president have formulated your employee-retention arguments, you may want me to become involved to help set the overall strategy. This strategy should be defined and refined on the very same day the employee resigns.

Typically, an employee will have quit because of a "push" of some sort involving long-standing frustration at Cypress and a "pull" from another company where the grass looks greener. In some cases, realism will dictate that we can't keep the employee. Ninety percent of the time, however, we can make a good argument that it is in the employee's best interest to stay at Cypress.

6. *Use all the horsepower at your disposal to win.* With a carefully constructed strategy, we can proceed to win back the employee. Think of what we've already done on day one. The employee got the message that quitting was a big deal because of our rapid reaction to the resignation. We reminded the employee that the company was truly interested in him or her because we took as long as needed to *listen* to what was wrong.

On the second day, the employee should get the message that quitting was a mistake, that the company knows it was a mistake, and that we will single-mindedly try to rectify that mistake. Cypress will accept only two answers to our proposal to stay: yes, or we'll talk about it some more.

What to Do when a Valued Employee Quits—Continued

On the second or third day, as we present our position, the employee should continue to understand that this is not business as usual. We will interrupt our schedules. If appropriate, we may meet over meals during off hours. If the employee's spouse is a major factor in the resignation, the spouse should be involved in the discussions. Bring in any level of management required to get the job done. If it takes the president (and it does in half the cases), then I have nothing more important to do than to sit down with the employee. Many middle managers mistakenly assume that I am too busy to interrupt my schedule to keep a good person in the company. Nothing is further from the truth.

7. *Solve the employee's problems.* If we correct the problems that caused the employee to start looking around, we will succeed more than 80 percent of the time in changing the employee's mind. Most often, resigning employees like Cypress, its benefits, and the people with whom they work. They usually, however, do not like some of the particulars of their jobs or their direct supervisors. Their resolve to leave is further strengthened because they have found jobs (typically) at companies that are poor seconds to Cypress but that appear to offer some relative benefits. By alleviating the root problem at Cypress, and by stressing the fundamental differences between us and the other company, we can usually persuade the employee to stay.

8. *Wipe out the competitor.* Two objectives are important here: to shut down the competitor so firmly that it will conduct no further negotiations with our employee, and to shut down the competitor in such a manner that it believes it has wasted its time trying to hire away from Cypress. The employee should call the competition and turn down the offer and, in doing so, make it clear that he or she does not want counter offers and continuing negotiations.

A model response goes something like this: "There was no counter offer, I just want to stay at Cypress. I think my long-term interests are served by being here. The same hour that I told my boss I was thinking about leaving, I had meetings with my boss, the vice president, and T. J. Rodgers. When they made the comparisons between my career at Cypress and at your company, it was clear that I made a mistake in thinking about leaving. I really do not want to take any time to come over to talk to you; my mind is made up. It would not be helpful to change your offer monetarily; I am fairly paid and have a good stock-option package. Money is not the issue."

9. *Prevent the next problem.* The last step in the process is really the first step: sit down, think about your people, try to anticipate where you might have a problem in the future, and fix it before it starts.

Technology was founded in 1988 to combine multiple chips into memory subsystems. Ross Technology, our fourth new company, has delivered the industry's highest performance RISC microprocessor since it was formed in 1988.

These subsidiaries have true autonomy. But I do expect two major commitments. A subsidiary must use the management systems that have served Cypress so well. It must also send high-level managers (almost always the president) to a few key corporate meetings in which we track and coordinate activities across the subsidiaries.

We intend Cypress to be a billion-dollar enterprise before too long—without the waste, bureaucracy, and complacency that afflict so many large organizations. We'll achieve that goal by seeding new startups, dividing down successful businesses as they get too big to manage tightly, continuing to refine our management systems, and driving them down through our organization and its subsidiaries.*

---

*Author's note: I wish to acknowledge the role of MIS director Rick Foreman and his team in the design and implementation of our management systems.

CASE 6–1: ALLEN-BRADLEY'S ICCG: REPOSITIONING FOR THE 1990s

This case describes a broad set of organizational changes undertaken by a division of Allen-Bradley, driven by an increasing emphasis on computer integrated solutions in the market for industrial automation. The changes being undertaken at Allen-Bradley offer a good example of what Drucker calls "the coming of the new organization" (see Chapter 2).

Preparation Questions

1. What are the major changes at ICCG? Do they make ICCG a more effective organization?
2. How important were these changes for Allen-Bradley's competitive success in the 1980s?
3. What are the challenges that ICCG faces for the future? What should Rody Salas do?

Case 6–1 Allen-Bradley's ICCG: Repositioning for the 1990s*

O'Rourke always said that the second repositioning of Allen-Bradley would make the first one look like child's play. But I don't think any of us knew how difficult it would be.

—Rodolfo Salas, senior vice president, ICCG

Introduction

Although situated a few miles from downtown Cleveland, the tinted glass doors at the Highland Heights, Ohio offices of Allen-Bradley's Industrial Computer and Communication Group (ICCG) bid the visitor welcome in eight languages and several different alphabets. After passing through them,

*Research Associate James Berkley prepared this case under the supervision of Assistant Professor Nitin Nohria. Copyright © 1990 by the President and Fellows of Harvard College. Harvard Business School Case 491-066 (revised December 20, 1990).

one was met by a row of clocks mounted above the reception desk: one showed the time in Amsterdam, another the time in Tokyo, the third the local time in Cleveland. In all, the entrance lobby projected the image of a streamlined enclave of internationalism: the clocks, multilingual framed posters, even a display of the flags of nations using Allen-Bradley products.

Traditionally a supplier of industrial control devices to the manufacturing industry, Allen-Bradley, a Milwaukee-based company acquired by Rockwell International in 1985 for $1.65 billion, had moved swiftly to embrace a dizzying array of new techniques in both manufacturing and in management. In the past decade this had meant pioneering the use of computer-integrated-manufacturing (CIM), and later the introduction of a product—the Pyramid Integrator—that gave customers the ability to bring factory floor data into their information systems. Now under the slogan "Reaching Higher in the 90s," ICCG was instituting a series of management and organizational innovations whose full implementation would prove as difficult as the technical innovations that preceded them.

Rodolfo (Rody) Salas—ICCG's new senior vice president and the primary architect of the recent changes—had articulated five "organizational guideposts" for ICCG:

- Focus on the customer.
- Clarify the direction of the business.
- Simplify the business.
- Measure the critical aspects of the business that determine success.
- Involve and develop our people.

Salas was confident that within the framework of these guideposts, the radical restructuring and repositioning of ICCG's business would indeed help Allen-Bradley to reach higher in the 1990s than ever before. At the same time, however, the sweeping changes would present ICCG with a new set of challenges.

Company Background

The history of Allen-Bradley offered little foreshadowing of the massive changes that were to sweep through the company—and ICCG in particular—in the 1980s and 1990s. The company traced its origin to 1893 when 15-year-old Lynde Bradley developed a homemade motor controller in his family's cellar workshop in Milwaukee. In 1903, with the financial backing of his friend Stanton Allen, Bradley began the Compression Rheostat Company, renamed Allen-Bradley in 1909. Lynde's brother joined the company soon thereafter, and the two brothers ran the business together for the remainder of their lives.

Although the company grew steadily and came to occupy a central position in the city of Milwaukee, Allen-Bradley remained until the 1970s a conservative, privately held manufacturer of electromechanical equipment that, despite a number of foreign ventures, supplied its products to a primarily domestic market.

The typical Allen-Bradley product of the 1970s was, in concept if not in appearance, not far removed from the products on which the company had originally been founded: the business continued to be organized around an array of electromechanical products, or "boxes," that were used to control primary machinery on other companies' factory floors. The company, whose culture had for many years been steeped in the tradition of European artisanship, was renowned for being cautious and paternalistic. The organization of the company was bureaucratic and hierarchical, and a job at Allen-Bradley held the implicit promise of lifetime security. With sales topping a billion dollars and over 13,000 employees, the Allen-Bradley of the 1970s had developed a reputation as the "Cadillac" of the industrial controller business.

The First Repositioning

In the late 1970s, as American manufacturing edged toward a crisis that most did not foresee, J. Tracy O'Rourke—who would later serve as president and CEO—went before the board and proposed what would come to be known as the first repositioning of Allen-Bradley. Although the company had become a leading provider of the control hardware used to mechanize plants and factories and was enjoying the strongest profits in its history, O'Rourke argued that the company needed to expand into international markets and turn its focus toward solid-state products that could be used in an increasingly automated factory environment. The result was a rapid move to become a provider of electronic programmable logic controllers (PLCs), a product that used microprocessor technology in order to control the functioning of machinery on the factory floor.

The shift toward PLCs proved a boon to the young Industrial Computer and Communication Group. PLCs had been developed in the late 1960s by an Ann Arbor, Michigan based company that had been acquired by Allen-Bradley in 1969. In 1970, Allen-Bradley bought a Highland Heights facility called the Numerical Control Systems Division from the Bunker-Ramo Corporation, renamed it the Systems Division, and integrated it with the recently acquired Ann Arbor company. While PLCs had been a marginal part of Allen-Bradley's business during the 1970s, the timely decision to focus on programmable controllers made the Systems Division an increasingly important part of the Allen-Bradley organization. The Systems Division became the Systems Group and finally the Industrial Computer and Communication Group. As this occurred, the Ohio-based facility went through a series of major hiring phases. While marked by the same hierarchical structure evidenced elsewhere in the company, the resulting organization was significantly younger and more freewheeling in style than the rest of Allen-Bradley. By 1990, ICCG had approximately 2,000 employees. Nearly half of these worked in Highland Heights, while the rest worked either in Ann Arbor or in the manufacturing facilities in Twinsburg, Ohio, and Dublin, Georgia.

Structure of ICCG

Until the spring of 1990, ICCG's formal organizational structure was highly conventional. The group, overseen by a senior vice president, had three main product divisions and a fourth product unit. (Exhibit 1 shows the organization of both Allen-Bradley and ICCG at this time.) The most significant part of the business was the programmable controller division, often called simply PC, which had served as the breeding ground for other elements—industrial computer, communication, and the smaller engineered systems unit—that had been "spun off" into relative autonomy within the group. While PC contributed 80 percent of ICCG's revenues and nearly all of its profits, the financial contribution of the other divisions often appeared marginal.

Although manufacturing was centralized at the group level and all sales were by a single companywide sales force, the various divisions of ICCG maintained independent market strategies. Each division was run essentially as a separate business that offered a particular range of products and did so with its own engineering and marketing departments. The same sort of decentralization and diversity also occurred within divisions: functions such as engineering and marketing, for example, tended to have quite different procedures and vocabularies.

Computer Integration and the Second Repositioning

During the 1980s, the concept of computer integrated manufacturing (CIM) became an overall vision both for the products Allen-Bradley would create and for how the company would manufacture these products. When asked to define the notion of CIM, O'Rourke—whom *The Wall Street Journal* was later to call the 'guru' of CIM—was fond of describing his vision of a "single closed loop." According to O'Rourke:

> Computer integrated manufacturing integrates the factors of production to organize every event that occurs in a manufacturing business from receipt of a customer's order to delivery of the product. The ultimate goal is to integrate the production processes, the material, sales, marketing, purchasing, administration, and engineering information flows into a closed-loop, controlled, system . . . CIM is a whole new philosophy of business.

While pitched as a new philosophy, the impetus for CIM as a manufacturing strategy was, even by O'Rourke's own accounts, almost wholly economic. Global competition was increasing in the industrial control industry, and it was no longer safe to assume that domestic customers would buy expensive American products when the same products could be bought from foreign suppliers at a fraction of the price. While foreign firms could compete on the basis of cheap labor, O'Rourke saw the CIM innovation as Allen-Bradley's key to

EXHIBIT 1   Allen-Bradley Organization Chart (abridged)

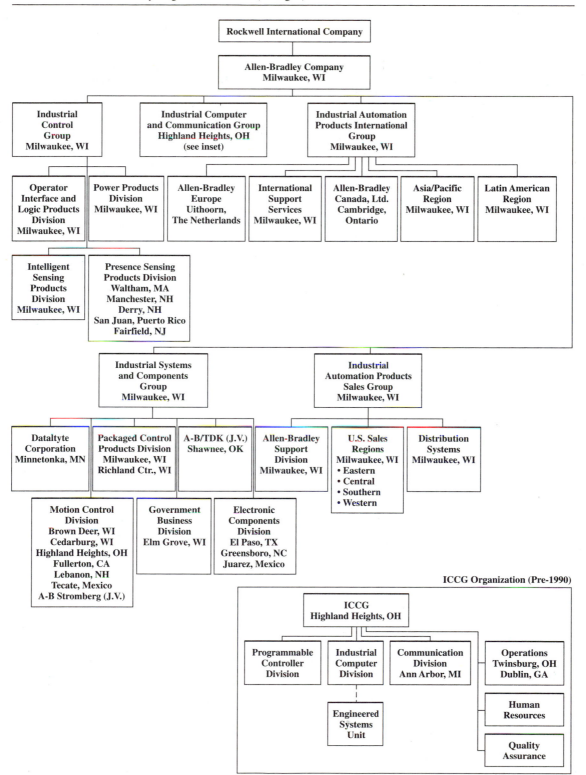

long-term competitive advantage in an increasingly global industry.

As Allen-Bradley migrated toward a CIM environment, so did many of its customers. By the mid-1980s, CIM was seen as a cornerstone in a second, perhaps more radical, repositioning at Allen-Bradley: in an environment that increasingly required the integration of heterogeneous systems, Allen-Bradley would both become a leading user of CIM technology and would move from being a supplier of "boxes" to being a global supplier of computer-integrated "solutions." Such a repositioning, it was reckoned, would require not only a new way of thinking about Allen-Bradley's products, but a new way of thinking about the functioning of the organization in general.

The Twinsburg Facility

Allen-Bradley's decision to adopt CIM as a "business philosophy" led to the establishment of a CIM facility at ICCG's Twinsburg, Ohio, plant. The Twinsburg plant, which assembled printed circuit boards for the different engineering divisions of ICCG, was a low-volume, high-mix facility: average lot size was small (17) and engineering changes were frequent due to the rapidly evolving technology. By 1986, when ICCG decided to adopt the advanced production technique of surface mount technology—a technique that effectively doubled the "real estate" on a given circuit board by allowing components to be placed on both sides of the board—an improvement in the flow of information in the manufacturing function was becoming crucial. Existing information flows could just barely accommodate the processes of the old technology; with denser board designs and shrinking time horizons for the introduction of new products, there would be even less room for the delays and imprecisions inherent in the traditional manufacturing environment.

With the trend to smaller lot sizes and the introduction of surface mount technology, CIM was seen as crucial to the continued success of the Twinsburg facility. According to Vice President of Operations Al Hails, the smooth functioning of the new manufacturing environment was largely a matter of information:

> The idea is to get the right information to the right place at the right time, using common data. The flip side of this is to collect the information at all the distributed points of activity and put it back together in a database that can be accessed by anyone on the other side.

Getting the "right information to the right place at the right time" could mean many different things, as there were lots of "other sides" that could make use of the information generated in a flexible CIM environment. Information needed to be exchanged between the engineering and manufacturing functions, but information also needed to be better controlled and distributed within the manufacturing area itself. Finally, there needed to be a way to bring the information generated on the factory floor into the information systems of the business at large.

Integrating Engineering and Manufacturing

The lack of a streamlined information flow between engineering and manufacturing was a constant headache at ICCG. The manufacturing area was accustomed to exchanging huge quantities of paper with the engineering departments of each product division, a process that generated both errors and large wastes of time. It was doubted whether the transition to surface mount technology could be supported by such a system.

Each of the four different design/engineering areas had its own protocols for how it would generate the designs that it would "throw over the wall" to the manufacturing area. Vital exchanges of information between engineering and manufacturing were done manually, and because each design area had been able to choose its own species of computer aided design (CAD), it was left to manufacturing to make sense of whatever landed in its territory. According to Greg Mesko, a manager on the manufacturing side at Twinsburg, this state of affairs was not that unusual in a company like Allen-Bradley. "I think what we had was typical of every company that had implemented CAD," said Mesko. "What happened was that every engineering group had a different personality for how it generated drawings, and there were no standards internally." Redundant information was being kept on both sides of the wall, and the laborious and inaccurate process of re-entering data by hand was accepted simply as the way things were done. The problem was exacerbated by the close collaboration that was required between engineering and manufacturing even after the initial design phase: engineering change notices (ECNs) occurred as frequently as every two hours, and information continued to pass back and forth between the two areas throughout the product's life.

The initiative to integrate the processes on either side of the fence came from people within the two areas rather than from above. Rody Salas would later stress that this sort of approach was part of the new way ICCG was to work: the CIM vision was articulated at the top yet implemented from the bottom, with empowered employees given the opportunity to architect specific tasks of integration. Mesko was friends with Jeff Kent, a manager in engineering, and the two regularly convened in the mid-1980s to complain about the poor interface between their organizations. Approvingly described by one ICCG employee as "buddies who drink beer and play golf together," Kent and Mesko decided to do something about the communications bottleneck between their respective areas by setting out to design an end-to-end information flow that would bring the various functions together while providing the needed levels of flexibility and security.

It was not easy to sell the merits of a streamlined and integrated design process to many of the engineers at ICCG. While the existing system cried out for change, an entire design culture at ICCG had grown up around it. Kent noted:

Changing the mind-set of the people was the biggest challenge . . . The whole culture [of the design engineers] was built upon drafting and doing drawings, not upon databases and information. They had this whole draftsman mentality and liked to see things on paper.

To create a paperless and standardized environment, ICCG instituted a system whereby a single relational database held universally available CIM files for both design and manufacturing. No longer would a design engineer create a drawing and simply send it over to the manufacturing arena for "translation." Instead, designers became responsible for maintaining a database file that held all the data manufacturing would need; as design revisions occurred, it was necessary to update the database file to ensure the integrity of this data. The files provided full electrical and mechanical descriptions of all component parts using a common part numbering system and supplied all the data necessary to assemble and test the designs.

At first, design engineers resisted the changes, as they found ways of re-inventing the old system and circumventing the database. Eventually, however, they were able to see the benefits of "closing the loop" with manufacturing and developed an allegiance to the new system. ICCG figured that, in the quality test area alone, the new process saved 50 hours in data entry and 40 in debugging per board design, and found that it dramatically reduced the number of undetected errors that propagated through the system.

The implementation of computer aided process planning—which was to the manufacturing side what the single design database was to engineering—allowed people in manufacturing to access the relational database in order to generate the programs needed to direct actual factory processes. In turn, data generated on the plant floor could be gathered and used wherever in the business it was needed. For example, data collected in the manufacturing environment could be used by people in quality or for the purpose of tracking inventories and resources. To help with the various integration tasks, two people from MIS were transferred to Twinsburg to help manufacturing with the process of computer integration.

Due to the relative youth of ICCG's main information systems, the task of integration was not as traumatic as it could have been. Mike Krueger, a manager in MIS who worked along with Kent and Mesko, noted that ICCG had the luxury of living in an environment where the current large-scale information systems were no more than 10 or 15 years old. While Kent and Mesko agreed that the youth of these systems had certainly helped, they felt that the success of ICCG's integration project was due primarily to a spirit of cooperation and teamwork. People in different areas were able to agree on a common goal, and thought it better for their career development to cooperate with one another than to compete. A prime motivation, said Mesko, was "simply seeing things work." There had been no one from above dictating what a "true" CIM implementation would finally look like, a state of affairs that confused people looking in on the process from the outside. Mesko and Kent joked that people always would ask who their CIM czar was. Their reply was that ICCG didn't really have one or need one.

Pyramid Integrator

As ICCG was integrating its internal functions, other people in the group were beginning to explore the development of CIM tools for ICCG's customers. Allen-Bradley had realized that its customers wanted to unite the plant floor with the rest of their companies, and that they were turning to systems integrators, software companies and consultants in order to tackle many of the same integration difficulties that ICCG had faced in Twinsburg. Allen-Bradley perceived a critical opportunity to enter an emerging market for CIM "solutions," although it was evident that no single company would be able to provide all the capabilities required for such a large integration task.

For Allen-Bradley to provide what its customers were beginning to demand, it was necessary for ICCG to join forces with a company whose expertise complemented its own. In 1987, ICCG entered a joint venture with Digital Equipment Corpora-

tion (DEC) to bring out a product that—through the combined resources of DEC and Allen-Bradley—could provide the first step in a customer's CIM solution. Named the Pyramid Integrator, the product would not only serve to capture and integrate the wealth of data generated on the plant floor, but would also serve as an intelligent gateway into the other areas of the business.

In October 1987, a cross-functional control and information integration (CII) team was put together to begin working on the project. Don Davis—then ICCG's senior vice president and later the president of Allen-Bradley—wanted a product announcement by October 1988, but there were absolutely no hard and fast rules as to how the partnership with DEC would work or what it would produce. Pat Babington, a manager on this team, marveled at how freewheeling the project often seemed to those involved. She recalled:

> There was no master plan—just a good concept and strong support. There were no preconceived notions on how to market it, what it would be called, or even on what it would be . . . It was all operating on a handshake and good faith.

A joint venture of such a scope—Allen-Bradley had almost 100 people formally involved in the partnership, with many more on the periphery—opened the company to a sizeable amount of risk and legal sensitivity, but top management was supportive and kept a very "hands-off" attitude. For many months, team members from Allen-Bradley and DEC lived, as Babington said, "in each other's back pockets." People from the two companies would shuttle back and forth between Cleveland and Boston several times a month, working more like members of the same firm than like representatives of two different firms.

On October 4, 1988, Allen-Bradley announced its alliance with DEC and introduced the Pyramid Integrator. Within the Pyramid Integrator chassis was a Digital MicroVAX computer, which was manufactured and sold by Allen-Bradley exclusively. The product was introduced as a platform that would support future Allen-Bradley products from all its divisions and would serve as the first major element in what became known as the company's Pyramid Systems Architecture, the blueprint for the standards and interfaces required to manage the flow of data through information and control systems.

While the creation of the Pyramid Integrator was a landmark technical development, Babington knew that the project ultimately meant much more to upper management:

> We knew we were a pilot in more than just a technical sense, but in an organizational sense too. We needed to learn how to team both internally and with outside organizations. People like Don Davis made this clear and also made it clear that there would be great benefits for the team if we could make it work.

Clearly, the technical capabilities of the Pyramid Integrator were innovative and impressive. Just as impressive, however, was the impact it would have, and had already had, upon the way people worked together. At a media event a few weeks after its announcement, Don Davis expressed his opinion that the Pyramid Integrator was more than just a streamlining of existing technical processes; it was also a "people integrator." He said:

> In addition [to facilitating the flow of information both within manufacturing and the company at large], the Pyramid Integrator is also a people integrator. It can integrate the people within an individual business so that they can work better together using shared information. And, as we have seen, it has been the means of integrating separate businesses into cooperative partnerships. We've learned to cooperate with people in different businesses, across company lines, and that has been a valuable experience for us.

Adapting the Organization

For ICCG, Pyramid Integrator was a whole new way to think about the industrial controller business, and Davis's words plainly stated that the future of ICCG was to lie in the direction that the

Pyramid Integrator project had pointed. Davis's tenure as ICCG's senior vice president had served to reintroduce the customer as the group's focus, and the ethic of customer focus demanded the breakdown of both internal and external boundaries in order to allow people to work together in new ways. In 1987, Davis hired Rody Salas away from IBM to serve as vice president of ICCG's Industrial Computer Division (ICD). In July 1989, when Davis became president of Allen-Bradley, Salas was chosen to replace him as senior vice president.

Consistent with Davis's initiatives and with his own organizational guideposts, Salas initiated four broad management programs at ICCG: priorities, teaming, metrics, and people development. By the end of 1989, the guideposts and programs were evident in changes in both ICD and the organization as a whole.

Priorities and Teaming

Throughout the 1980s, informal "teaming" had become increasingly common at ICCG. CIM required a team mentality, and the Pyramid Integrator project had introduced many ICCG employees to the idea of teaming as a way to conduct business. Furthermore, the entrepreneurial environment at Highland Heights tended to encourage the development of a network of informal relationships that cut across functional boundaries. One person commented that these ad hoc cross-functional relationships would often leave new employees wondering where they fit into the organization. Although there was in theory a clear formal structure, seasoned employees knew how to bypass this structure when it became an obstacle to getting work done.

As teamwork became an increasingly important part of ICCG, it became important to give some structure to a process that—aside from Pyramid Integrator—had typically occurred on an ad hoc basis. In Ann Arbor, the communications division, under the direction of Vice President Bill Little, began in 1989 to experiment with more formalized team structures. It was in Salas's industrial computer division, however, that the need for change was becoming most evident. Functions such as engineering and marketing were interacting both poorly and inefficiently, and Salas responded by hiring Assad Ansari—who had previously worked with Little—as ICD's director of information engineering.

Assessing ICD in 1989, Salas and Ansari faced a situation where the need for focus was becoming critical. Nearly 70 engineering projects were occurring concurrently, and as many as 18 people would regularly convene in a conference room to put in their "two cents" on a given project. While the area was a hub of activity, it was in fact neither particularly productive nor efficient. According to Ansari, "If you were an engineer, you didn't know what project you would work on next. It was hard just to keep track of what was going on."

The first response was to draw up a list of all 70 engineering projects in order of their importance to the company. Those at the top of the list survived; the rest—with few exceptions—were unceremoniously shelved. This "prioritization" brought schedules under control and increased both the productivity and the contentment of the engineers.

After a set of thorough skip-level reviews with ICD employees, Salas and Ansari decided to develop a formal process for guiding the development of individual projects. Under their plan, a cross-functional project team would assume most of the responsibility for overseeing the development of new products. These teams—consisting of representatives from marketing, engineering, manufacturing, scheduling, and quality assurance—would essentially own product development from "womb to tomb." Formed and dissolved as the project warranted, the teams would handle all the aspects of day-to-day project management and would be responsible for their performance in terms of costs, profitability, time to market, and quality.

Related project teams would be supervised by business teams charged with the responsibility for allocating resources and for making decisions concerning strategies and priorities. While business teams would play an important role in approving the goals and activities of project teams, they would do so while keeping interference with these teams to a minimum.

When the team system was introduced as a pilot in ICD, many employees were skeptical. Ansari recalled:

> Some people took it as a management edict. Then, after three or four meetings, they liked it better since no one was second guessing them. We consciously stayed out of their way.

Ansari stressed that the move to a team structure provided structure rather than took it away: "Whether people admit it or not, people really do like structure in their life," he claimed, "and this is a situation where there was a certain amount of structure." While team members were responsible for making their own schedules, they had a new sense of focus and purpose that steered them without intervention from above. People put in reasonable hours, working overtime when their project demanded. In general, there was little of the burnout that came from working on several critical projects at once.

The T60 Industrial Workstation, the fruit of ICD's pilot in formal teaming, was the first product to be developed using the new business team/project team approach. In all aspects, the development of the T60—a personal computer workstation for factory floor applications—met or exceeded expectations: time to market was less than 12 months, final cost was within 2 percent of estimated cost, and both the team and the product were featured prominently in an article in *Control Engineering*.

Quality and Customer Satisfaction

The idea of quality was nothing new at Allen-Bradley, and was now being rethought through the lens of customer focus. The tradition of artisanship upon which the company was founded made quality a significant part of the original Allen-Bradley culture, and the company proudly displayed the word "quality" beneath its name in its corporate logo.

Roger Hartel, vice president of quality assurance, believed that ICCG had remained abreast of the leading-edge techniques in total quality management advanced in the 1980s. Nevertheless, he saw two important new directions for quality assurance in the group. First, Hartel wanted the "white collar" regions of ICCG to examine processes much in the way processes were examined in the manufacturing area. Toward these ends, a business process management program was initiated in February 1990 to examine and improve the quality of management processes at ICCG.

Second, Hartel also believed that quality considerations needed to be made more explicit in ICCG's relationships with suppliers and customers. Under the theory, "you are what you eat," ICCG needed to work with its suppliers to achieve tighter quality controls. Likewise, Hartel fervently believed in the importance of measures of customer satisfaction. Because its goods were sold primarily through distributors, ICCG had tended to be somewhat isolated from many of its customers. Yet with an increasing emphasis on meeting the specific needs of end-users, Allen-Bradley had a growing need to break down this isolation with customer surveys and direct interaction.

On the suggestion of quality assurance manager Jim Weber, ICCG put together a cross-functional team called the total customer satisfaction task-force, popularly known as "Ghostbusters." Ghostbusters consisted of approximately 10 core people from across the entire organization who were empowered to "bust" the almost imperceptible practices that negatively impacted customer satisfaction, and to resolve such problems without elevating them to senior management. In its first few months of existence, Ghostbusters put together an impressive list of accomplishments, including a more readable label font, minimization of loose parts in packaging, and coordination of price changes across divisions.

Metrics

Measurement systems of all kinds had undergone fundamental changes at ICCG. Under Salas's direction, ICCG instituted a new metrics program that emphasized nonfinancial measures in addition to traditional accounting measures. According to Ted Crandall, vice president of finance and business planning, it had been the quality movement of the 1980s—both at Allen-Bradley and elsewhere—that had implicitly driven the evolution toward nonfinancial measures. There was a new sense that financial performance was only the end result of a wide array of operational factors, and that attempts to control only financial measures would tend to overlook important determinants of the group's performance.

The prevailing practice was for upper management to review financial performance on a monthly basis. Under the new metrics program, implemented in the fall of 1989, upper management would also gather separately to examine a wide array of nonfinancial measurements. It was easy for executives to arrive at a general agreement upon four broad categories for these measurements: manufacturing, quality, human resources, and customer service. Determining the measurements to be included within each category, however, was slightly more difficult. Clearly, any given measure had to be relevant to the goals of the category, but it was equally important that it be easily measurable and controllable: it was difficult to measure customer service or satisfaction, for example, unless one could find a way of turning a qualitative measure into a quantitative one. Eventually, executives agreed upon a core list of approximately 20 measures. (See Exhibit 2.)

Once per month, Salas met with all his direct reports and some of their key staff to review the status of all of the measures included in the new program. Actual measurements were compared with a targeted value, and the person responsible for the measurement would generally give a "top five" list of the five factors that inhibited the measurement from a better showing. For example, the measurement for warranty failures might be

EXHIBIT 2   Metrics Adopted Fall 1989

Quality

- Warranty returns (parts per million)
- Finished good audit results (ppm)
- Percentage of lots rejected at incoming
- Scrap and rework cost percentage of total material cost
- Repair: percentage of audit test yield

Customer Service and Support

- Compliance to want date
- Compliance to schedule date
- Shipping/pricing errors
- Training: number of student weeks
- Response to customer calls
- Repair: average turnaround time

Manufacturing

- Percentage of attainment of MPS
- Direct labor productivity
- Utilization loss due to change notices
- Cumulative lead time
- Number of vendors
- Repair productivity

Human Resources

- Percentage of requisitions beyond target date
- Percentage of turnover
- Number of special awards

accompanied by a "top five" list of the five particular products that were causing the most problems. For each component of the top five list, the person had to specify an action plan, a date by which the action would be achieved, and the person who would be responsible for overseeing the remedy. To the outsider, goals for metrics seemed impressively high: under ICCG's policy of continuous improvement, quality measures were charged with the goal of a 20:1 improvement every five years.

Crandall saw the new metrics system as fulfilling an important function at ICCG. He commented:

Establishing these metrics and raising their visibility to the senior management level communicates to the entire organization what is important to senior management. And by the simple act of measuring, you affect people's behavior. These metrics will be the dimensions along which people will optimize, so we have to be especially sure that these are the right dimensions.

To ensure that people would optimize along the right dimensions, ICCG's metrics were allowed to evolve along with the organization and its knowledge about itself. According to Crandall, 1990 was seeing a major reevaluation of all the performance measures for manufacturing, and there was a constant effort to make sure the right variable was being tracked.

Like Crandall, Rody Salas too felt that the metrics program was more than just a way of keeping track of ICCG's business; it was a fundamental means of focusing and understanding its activities. "If you can't measure it," he said, "you probably can't understand it. In areas where we haven't succeeded, we're probably not measuring the right thing." Salas believed the new metrics program fostered a sense of openness and honesty, and while he believed the motivation for cheating or gaming on the measures was low, he wryly commented that the wise manager lived by the motto, "Don't expect, inspect."

Rethinking the Organization

By the end of 1989, ICCG had done much to bring the second repositioning of the firm from concept to reality. Teaming was spreading throughout the organization, the group was forging creative alliances on a global scale, and Pyramid Integrator and the Pyramid System Architecture were making it easier for customers to customize their own CIM needs. Despite the healthy appearance, however, Rody Salas—now settled into his role as senior vice president—saw the group heading for a crisis much like the one that had earlier beset ICD. "Decisions," recalled Salas, "were getting harder and harder to make." For every business or product decision facing ICCG, there were too many people, too much bureaucracy, and too many issues; Salas saw a desperate need to energize and empower the organization.

Consolidation and Reorganization

Salas was impressed with the changes that had occurred in the previous five years at ICCG. But as the 1980s drew to a close it became apparent that something fundamental had yet to change: "With all the changes, one thing that hadn't changed was the organization itself," he noted. "And the organization was suddenly under tremendous stress." Developments at ICCG had led to a situation where overlapping functions, interdepartmental politics, and drawn-out decision making threatened to become the rule rather than the exception, a situation Salas attributed to the fact that recent changes had taken place against an organizational background in which nothing had really changed at all. ICCG was—despite the increasing importance of horizontal, cross-functional, and interorganizational relationships—still essentially a collection of autonomous divisions whose relationships both with customers and with one another had never really been examined or changed.

Phil Bessler, the new vice president of ICD, felt that the divisional structure of the company left him besieged by contradictions. His job was to optimize financial return for ICD, but often the right thing for ICD was hardly in the interests of ICCG as a whole. For example, ICD could optimize its own profits by investing in its line of human-machine interface products, but such a use of resources was foolish if ICCG's interests could be served best by concentrating on customer integration solutions instead. On the other hand, if ICD chose to do what seemed best for ICCG, they would be undermining their own financial performance as a division.

Bessler's dilemma was not unique. Salas believed that the problems being encountered at ICCG could be traced back to the fact that all the components of the organization had been "created

around technologies" rather than created around the needs of the business. Each division had a small technological fiefdom and thought it was out to be a world leader in a particular line of products. But technology, Salas felt, was no longer the differentiator in the factory automation business; technology now disseminated instantly through the industry, and the new differentiator would prove to be how well a company could respond to the special needs of its customers. As the industry changed, the costs of having a divisional structure organized around an aging principle of technology-orientation were becoming evident. Often the products and missions of different divisions overlapped or blatantly contradicted one another, a situation that bred confusion in the sales force. Money was wasted as three separate profit centers introduced conflicting products with no clear strategy across divisions.

Salas's plan was radical: all boundaries between divisions would be effectively struck down, and the group would be restructured according to the needs of the customer and the business. Bessler explained the process as being akin to "throwing all the components of ICCG into a single pot and thinking about how the elements could best be recombined." By analyzing the performance of the group's various product lines, it was determined that ICCG's "core businesses" lay in two basic product lines in the PC division, while everything else played an essentially supporting role that added value to these core products for the customer.

Having identified these two core businesses, Salas oversaw the design of a new concentric model for the organization of the group. At the center would be control systems, the group's core business. A second ring, entitled communication and information systems, would focus on tying these core products together through the use of information technology and would differentiate Allen-Bradley products to the customer. A third layer, application systems, would add value by packaging and integrating systems into end-user solutions. Functions such as operations, human

EXHIBIT 3   ICCG Organization after May 1990

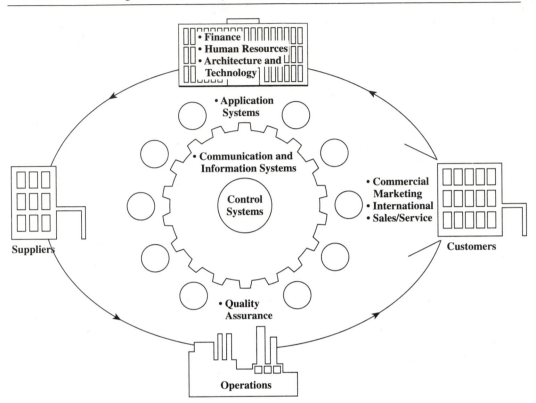

resources, finance planning, and marketing were in an "orbit" around these three rings, along with the suppliers and customers with whom ICCG did business. Profit and loss responsibilities for the old divisions would be eliminated. Although each would maintain a set of financial objectives, the boundaries that had formerly existed between divisions—and between the firm and the outside world—were henceforth to be thought of as provisionary and permeable. (See Exhibit 3.)

In some ways, the new organization of ICCG formalized the ethic of customer focus that had begun with the announcement of the second repositioning several years earlier. The core PC business was at the center of the new organizational chart, and the customer was at the chart's periphery, outside the third ring. As one moved toward the center, one moved closer to the "heart" of the firm; as one moved away from the center one reached the increasingly permeable boundary between the firm and the outside world. At the public announcement of ICCG's consolidation into a single business on May 23, 1990, Salas said:

> This consolidation will improve our customer focus and enhance our ability to develop and deliver superior integrated control and information systems. We will be able to work together better, make decisions faster, and bring higher quality products to market earlier because we are now organized to reflect how our customers are applying our technology.

The world beyond ICCG's third ring contained not only customers, but also other firms, including

EXHIBIT 4   External Teaming for Customer Solutions

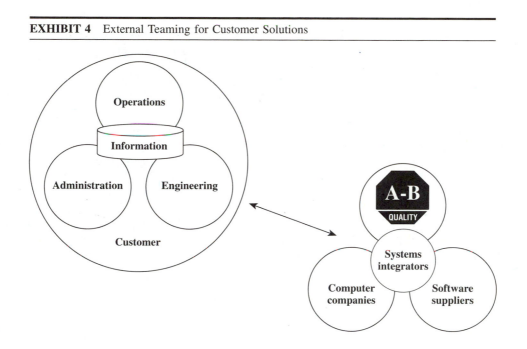

Allen-Bradley's competitors. The new organization was designed to allow ICCG to interact more freely and more successfully with these firms: the new model, for example, permitted Salas to see at a glance which kinds of partnerships made sense for ICCG and which did not. Companies for whom Salas could envision a concentric model similar to that of ICCG could be ruled out immediately; companies with different models—ranging from third-party software vendors to large computer companies such as DEC—could be seen as opportunities for strategic alliances on the firm's periphery. In consolidating the three divisions, ICCG also consolidated the divisions' three distinct marketing departments into a single commercial marketing area. Now a single organization (with the exception of a number of employees who remained behind to do primary marketing for products), the marketing function could better pursue innovative alliances with other businesses, such as software companies or computer companies, all in the interest of providing customers with equally innovative automation solutions. (See Exhibit 4.)

While all of its products belonged to the category of high technology, A-B's new orientation had little to do explicitly with technology. Salas summarized A-B's new mission as "managing processes and systems that deliver value to the customer."

Groupwide Prioritization and Councils

During late 1989, Salas also led ICCG through a groupwide prioritization akin to what he and Ansari had implemented in ICD. The group had been trying to satisfy so many different interests that it often ended up satisfying no one: sales and marketing would say yes to everything, and projects piled up on top of one another until postponements and frustration became inevitable. Salas compiled a list of all the concurrent projects in ICCG and, within nine months, the group reached consensus on a new list one-third the size. The result, he predicted, would be a three-fold increase in the number of products brought to market over the next 18 months.

In Salas's view, less was more. After focusing on the customer and clarifying the nature of the business, the next most important thing was to make things as simple as possible:

> What we're saying is focus, focus, focus . . . It's all the idea of doing the fewest number of things and doing them all exceptionally well.

One example of this ethic of focus and simplicity was evident in ICCG's relations with its suppliers. While ICCG had traditionally been served by a wide range of suppliers, the group now aimed to develop intense partnershiplike relationships with only a select number of these firms. Along these lines, ICCG had reduced its number of suppliers by 45 percent, and had set the goal of trimming 30 percent of the remainder.

To enable the proper focus at the executive level, ICCG also initiated a set of four executive councils, also known as executive teams. Each of these teams—priorities, customer value-added, Pyramid Systems Architecture, and quality, cost, and time-to-market—was headed by a vice president and was charged with the examination of a crucial aspect of ICCG's business.

Groupwide Teaming

By the middle of 1990, the functioning of business teams and project teams had been formalized and instituted groupwide. With a teaming system in place across the entire organization, authority and accountability would be driven down to the lowest levels possible within the group.

The structure and functioning of the new teams closely followed the model that had been used in ICD. Initiatives could be generated anywhere in the organization, but a team could be formed only with the explicit charter of an executive sponsor, normally one of Salas's direct reports. Once formed, business teams were overseen directly by the team's executive sponsor. Project teams, however, were managed by supervisory business teams that only rarely elevated project-related issues to the executive level. While business teams were responsible for defining success parameters and

identifying strategic business issues, most of the responsibility for the management of ICCG's projects now rested entirely within the project teams. (See Exhibit 5.)

Although responsibility had been pushed far down in the organization, ICCG employed a formal review process—known as general manager (GM) milestone reviews—in order to oversee the various stages of product development. At five such reviews during the life cycle of a project, teams met with Rody Salas and his direct reports to give a presentation concerning their status. A successful GM milestone review served as a seal of approval that allowed the team to advance to the next stage of their project. Likewise, if the project was encountering obstacles or was failing to meet certain objectives of cost or scheduling, the milestone review process could serve as a forum for the negotiation of new terms.

In general, leadership of project teams rotated according to where the project was in the milestone process. Marketing assumed the lead role for the business proposal and project definition segment, up through the first GM milestone review. Engineering then guided the team through the design and development phases, followed by manufacturing's lead during pilot activity and full production. Marketing took over again for field performance reviews and the final GM evaluation, which occurred six months after the first shipment.

Looking Ahead

While the comprehensive reorganization of ICCG's divisional structure appeared to put the crowning touches on the second repositioning that had been announced four years earlier, it also raised a new set of issues. The consolidation of the business and the introduction of the concentric ring model were—after many years of piecemeal change—signs that there was no going back for the newly reorganized group. As ICCG settled in for the long term, Salas identified three major challenges that ICCG would have to face in order to capitalize most fully on the bold measures that

EXHIBIT 5   ICCG Teaming Structure

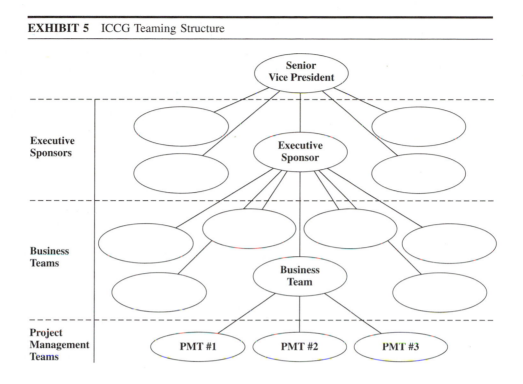

had been taken. First, ICCG needed to learn how best to manage the intersection of its management structure with a team structure that had absorbed many of management's old responsibilities. Second, ICCG faced the challenge of developing a human resources system that would be compatible with the rest of the organization. Third, the group needed to find ways to extend the principles of teamwork and cooperation beyond the "four walls" of ICCG, both to the rest of Allen-Bradley and to the group's suppliers and customers as well.

Salas believed it was very important to arrive at the right set of interfaces between management and teams. While much of the day-to-day running of the company could now be handled at the team level, Salas and his direct reports maintained four crucial "windows" into the organization through financial reviews, metrics, milestone reviews, and executive councils. Ninety-five percent of ICCG's employees, however, did not participate in such meetings, and Salas felt that the prime challenge

was to ensure that teams were properly tied in to the management of the organization. Salas posed the question:

> If I'm a third level manager or director with a team under me, then where do my powers begin and end? What responsibility and accountability should management retain and what should be delegated to teams?

While Salas believed that the proper control systems existed, he noticed that in practice the responses of managers tended to vary. Some managers were not comfortable with letting go of their traditional means of control, while others adapted quickly to embrace the new system.

The reactions of lower-level employees varied as well. While at first there had been a rush to get on as many teams as possible—Jeff Kent joked that the principle seemed to be "Whoever dies with the most teams wins"—some team members were unsure of how to behave in the new environment, while others were flourishing and emerging as future candidates for positions in upper management.

Keith Hamilton, director of human resources, anticipated the need for some considerable changes. In the past years, human resources had realized the need to match Allen-Bradley's new approaches to technology with new approaches to people. Hamilton recalled:

> At Twinsburg, we woke up one day with a terrible feeling that our manufacturing processes were so far ahead of our people processes. People would ask what the link between our new manufacturing processes and our people processes was and we didn't really have an answer.

For some time, human resources had been working to answer this question. Hamilton's area was training people to "understand the transition from functional to project-oriented management," and to give lower-level employees a new sense of empowerment and contribution through awards and recognition programs. For supervisors, Hamilton believed that focus needed to be moved away from strict control to issues of teaming, training, coaching, and boundary management. At all levels, cross-training was becoming prevalent as employees began to require an increasingly wide view of the business.

The working environment at ICCG was now so dynamic that it no longer made any sense to distribute comprehensive employee handbooks. Instead, ICCG now provided only broad policy manuals and relied upon a set of basic principles to guide employee behavior. These four "behavior principles"—customer focus, sense of urgency, ownership, and teamwork—were now displayed everywhere in ICCG: on plaques, posters, even on T-shirts. In November 1989, the group had instituted an informal recognition program by which employees exhibiting behavior relating to one of the principles could be nominated for a T-shirt award. By the end of 1990, over 650 employees had received blue and white Allen-Bradley T-shirts which on one side proclaimed "I did it just right!"

and on the other listed the four guiding principles that would allow Allen-Bradley to "reach higher in the nineties." Salas felt that programs such as the T-shirt award served the dual role of both communication and motivation at practically no cost to the company: "There are ways you can create a motivational environment without having to spend a nickel," he claimed. "People work for pride. When you give them the opportunity to take initiative and you listen to them, they can be as high as a kite."

As informal award programs proliferated, however, questions of formal recognition could be seen waiting in the wings. The sticky issues of compensation and performance appraisal were getting increasingly hard to ignore, both in human resources and elsewhere. Salas and Hamilton both felt that their current performance appraisal systems were not oriented to the new way the organization was working. It was clear that ICCG's appraisal system needed to be made consistent with policies of customer-orientation, continuous improvement, and teamwork, but there were lingering questions about how precisely this might be achieved. A first step toward this goal had been taken when human resources put together a cross-functional team charged with the design of a new performance evaluation system. An engineer who sat on the team would have direct input into the design of a new system, something Hamilton felt would never have been possible even a few years before.

Both Salas and Hamilton felt that traditional compensation programs were "just not going to cut it," but they were as yet unsure of what a new system would require. How was one to go about measuring contribution to a team? What sort of new compensation practices would be required in an increasingly flat organization? Salas was eager for ICCG to confront these issues, but felt there might be a long way to go until they were resolved.

The final challenge for ICCG, according to Salas, would be cooperation and teamwork outside the group's walls. Since customers were looking for solutions that involved multiple products—both from Allen-Bradley and from other firms—ICCG needed to develop close working relationships with other organizations, some of which had traditionally been considered competitors. According to Salas, accomplishing this would not necessarily be easy: "Egos," he said, "must learn to get out of the way." Salas reckoned that it would take some time for this new collaborative spirit to become the norm, just as it would take time for ICCG itself to master its own transition.

CASE 6–2: PHILLIPS 66 COMPANY: EXECUTIVE INFORMATION SYSTEM

The president of Phillips 66, the "downstream" portion of Phillips Petroleum, used information technology to support his restructuring of the organization and to manage the business after two takeover attempts.

Preparation Questions

1. What was the situation faced by Bob Wallace in early 1985? Evaluate the actions he took to manage the company through its crises.
2. Describe Phillips's EIS. What role did the EIS play in the organization's transformation? How has the system influenced organizational structure, management controls, and decision making in the company? What other impacts has the system had on Phillips 66 and its employees?

Case 6–2 Phillips 66 Company: Executive Information System*

At 6:30 PM on December 12, 1988, Gene Batchelder was in his office at Phillips 66 Company headquarters in Bartlesville, Oklahoma. As the controllers division manager in charge of management information systems (MIS) and operations

*Professor Lynda M. Applegate and Research Associate Charles S. Osborn prepared this case. Copyright © 1988 by the President and Fellows of Harvard College. Harvard Business School case 189-006 (revised June 16, 1993).

analysis and control (OA&C), Batchelder was reviewing the status of Phillips 66 Company's executive information system (EIS) in preparation for a meeting with President Robert (Bob) Wallace, who as the main sponsor of the EIS since its inception in August 1985, wanted to discuss the system's future. Batchelder made notes for the meeting, referring to EIS information displays on his desktop workstation to confirm facts and figures.

*Industry and Company Background**

In 1988, the petroleum industry included four distinct vertical levels: production, refining, marketing, and transportation. Production involved the location and extraction of oil and natural gas from underground reservoirs. While the U.S. crude production market was relatively unconcentrated by conventional measures, the common use of joint ventures in exploration and transportation and the merger and acquisition activities of the 1980s combined to produce market dynamics of a concentrated industry. Refining manufactured finished products ranging from petrochemicals to motor fuel to jet fuel. In the 1980s, there was a significant excess in refining capacity worldwide. Wholesale and retail marketers distributed refined oil products to consumers. Most jet fuel was sold by refining companies directly to customers (primarily the Department of Defense and the major commercial airlines), while residential fuel and motor fuel were primarily sold through independent marketers. In the United States, there was substantial consolidation within the retail gasoline segment of the industry during the 1970s and 1980s, with the number of service stations decreasing from 216,000 in 1973 to 112,000 in 1988. The majority of the decline was due to the disappearance of small, independent stations which were replaced by large "superstations." Finally, a specialized transportation industry, which included pipelines, tankers, barges, and trucks, moved crude oil from the fields to refineries and finished product from refineries to marketers. In the United

States, pipelines, which were primarily owned and operated by major U.S. oil firms, were the most important mode of transportation since they permitted the movement of large volumes of oil overland.

In 1988, Phillips Petroleum Company was one of the largest oil companies in the United States. Fortune magazine ranked it 9th in sales and 10th in profits within the petroleum refining industry and 31st in sales among all U.S. industrial firms. In addition to its core businesses, which included producing crude oil and natural gas, oil refining, and marketing of gasoline products, Phillips was also a leading producer of petrochemicals. Phillips 66 Company, a wholly owned subsidiary of Phillips Petroleum Company, provided "downstream" (i.e., nonexploration and production) operations for its parent. Phillips 66 engaged in six major lines of business: supply and transportation, crude oil refining, natural gas liquids, chemicals manufacturing, plastics production, and gasoline marketing. (See Exhibit 1)

The company, which was named after its founders, Frank and L. E. Phillips, was organized in 1917 to acquire their original oil venture, Anchor Oil and Gas Company. During the first three decades of its existence, the company was highly profitable and earned a reputation as a leader in research and development. By the beginning of the 1950s, its natural gas and chemicals businesses were very strong, but it had begun to fall behind in oil exploration and production because of Frank Phillips's opposition to overseas ventures. Determined to keep the company a U.S. enterprise, Phillips turned down the opportunity to join other U.S. majors in joint ventures in the Middle East.

After Frank Phillips' death in 1950, the company embarked on an aggressive program of capital investment to fuel a strategy for growth and expansion both domestically and overseas. But by the 1970s, the company began to show signs of overexpansion as projects failed and profits dwindled due to high capital costs. The late 1970s were a time of retrenchment, and the company

*Material for this section of the case was drawn from: Martin, S., "The Petroleum Industry," The Structure of American Industry, 8th edition. NY: Macmillan, 1990. pp. 41–71; Yergin, D., The Prize: The Epic Quest for Oil, Money, and Power. NY: Simon & Schuster, 1991. p.773; and Sun, D., "Phillips Petroleum Company," International Directory of Company Histories, vol IV. Chicago: St. James Press, 1991. pp 521-523.

"The Fortune 500 Industrial Rankings," Fortune, April 24, 1989.

Sun, D., "Petroleum: Phillips Petroleum Company" pg. 523"Phillips Climbs up from the Bottom of the Barrel," Business Week, January 16, 1989.

EXHIBIT 1   Selected Financial Results ($ in millions)

	1988	1987	1986
Income before taxes			
Petroleum Products*	$ 471	$ 201	$ 458
Chemicals†	911	482	299
Total	$1,382	$ 683	$ 757
Capital expenditures			
Petroleum products	$ 177	$ 131	$ 75
Chemicals	130	78	46
Total	$ 307	$ 209	$ 121
Total assets			
Petroleum products	$2,707	$2,643	$2,500
Chemicals	1,349	1,165	1,053
Total	$4,056	$3,808	$3,553
Key petroleum products sold (millions of barrels per day)			
Auto gasoline	245	256	243
Aviation fuels	36	32	31
Distillates	100	98	93
Chemical sales (millions of pounds)			
Ethylene	720	903	803
Polyethylene	1,585	1,606	1,410

*Petroleum products includes refining, marketing, supply and transportation and natural gas liquids divisions.
†Chemicals includes chemicals and plastics divisions.

instituted extensive planning and control systems to avoid the mistakes of the previous decade.

In the early 1980s, the company began an aggressive series of acquisitions to ensure access to sufficient crude oil to supply its refining capacity and make it a "less attractive takeover candidate." In one acquisition, the company stepped in as a "white knight" to thwart Mesa's takeover attempt of General American Oil. This would not be the company's last encounter with Mesa and its chairman, T. Boone Pickens, who in late November 1984 announced his intention to try for a majority stake in Phillips Petroleum. The company, having anticipated such an action, fought back successfully at a cost of approximately $4.5 billion. Pickens retreated one month later $100 million richer. But no sooner had Pickens left than Irwin Jacobs, Ivan Boesky, Carl Icahn, and other financiers began buying blocks of stock. On February 12, 1985, Icahn, who already owned 5 percent of Phillips stock, offered to buy 45 percent of the company for $4.2 billion, which would give him a controlling interest. Icahn was paid off in March, this time at $62 per share, compared with the $53 per share that Pickens had received. (See Exhibit 2.) By May 1985, the company had sold off $2 billion worth of assets. Debt levels peaked at $8.8 billion, an increase from 20 percent to 80 percent of equity. The task of rebuilding the battered company was left to C. J. (Pete) Silas who

EXHIBIT 2   Phillips Stock Prices versus Standard and Poors 500 (1980–1990)

Value of $1.00 Invested in Phillips Stock on January 1, 1980 versus S&P 500

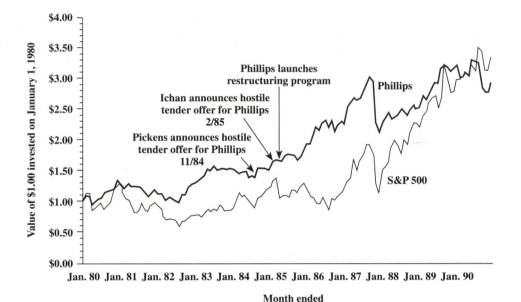

succeeded William Douce as chairman of Phillips Petroleum Corporation in May 1985, while Bob Wallace, president of Phillips 66 Company, took on the task for the downstream portion of the business.

Managing the Crisis

As Wallace contemplated the challenges he faced in managing downstream operations following the 1985 crisis, he defined the major areas of the business that needed to be addressed immediately:

> As I analyzed the situation right after the takeover attempts, it became clear that there were several things that we needed to do immediately. First, we needed to streamline the business to enable us to dramatically increase our cash flow to fund day-to-day operations while servicing the huge debt. Second, senior management needed to become much more involved in the business. We needed to provide operating managers with a clear set of guidelines that would help them focus their efforts

on the key leveraged parts of the business—those parts of the business where we had an opportunity to make, or lose, money quickly. We had to monitor operations much more closely to ensure that we were operating at peak levels of efficiency and effectiveness. Before the takeover, senior management operated on a 45-day reporting cycle. But after the takeovers, if we waited 45 days we could be out of business. Third, we had to break through the internal politics that had caused different divisions to fight with each other more than with the competition. In 1985, our culture did not support collaboration and teamwork across the divisions despite the high levels of mutual interdependence. To survive we would need to pull together and forget the constant bickering that wasted valuable time and energy. Finally, we didn't have time to slowly evolve a new organization and new way of doing business. We needed to turn on a dime.

At the time of the takeover, Phillips 66 was organized into fourteen divisions under two senior vice

EXHIBIT 3   Phillips 66 Organization Chart before June 1985 Reorganization

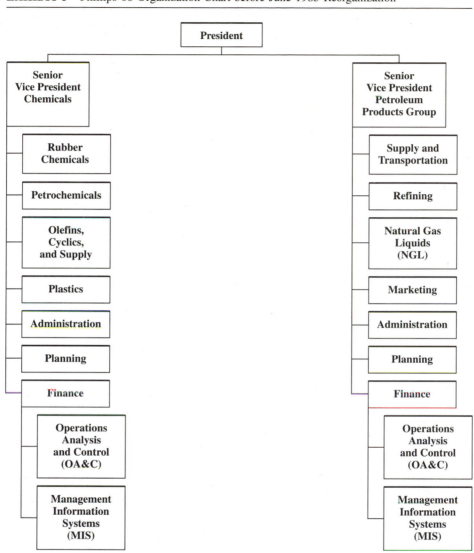

presidents who were in charge of the Petroleum Products (PPG) and Chemicals areas of the business. (See Exhibit 3.) The 14 divisions were managed as independent profit centers and a complex system of transfer pricing was used to coordinate business processes that crossed organizational-boundaries. In June 1985, Wallace reorganized

downstream operations into nine divisions that reported directly to him. (See Exhibit 4.) The two senior vice presidents retired, and six of the nine vice presidents were new to their positions. Below the vice president level, management and support staff were thinned by 40 percent and operating staff decreased by 25 percent. The latter cuts primarily

---

EXHIBIT 4   EIS Main Menu

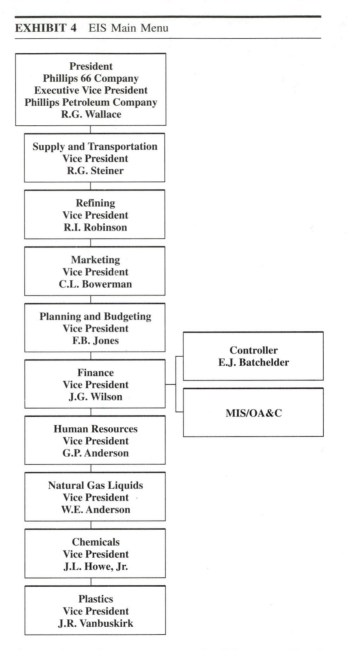

came from discontinued operations. On average, span of control doubled from five to nine or more. Wallace explained:

During the 1960s, Phillips was a very centralized organization. But as we grew, senior management

realized that we could no longer get our hands around the complexity of our operations. In 1973, we brought in consultants who recommended that we decentralize decision making and reorganize around products rather than functions. We changed the structure and pushed decision making down but realized afterwards that we didn't have the information we needed to run the business. Before the restructuring, all information came from one source, the centralized corporate controller. After the restructuring, the operating managers all requested their own controllers. At the same time, senior managers, who were uncomfortable with not understanding the business, added additional staff. Between 1974 and 1978, we went from one controller to over thirty, and the number of staff tripled. We really hadn't decentralized decision making authority now we had checkers checking the checkers. The goal of the restructuring after the takeover attempts was to truly decentralize decision making by pushing down decision rights along with the information, authority, and accountability needed to make and implement the decisions. Our downsizing efforts were targeted to reduce the bureaucracy of control that had developed over the 1970s and early 1980s.

A New Management Information and Control System

Wallace described his philosophy as he transferred decision rights and redesigned management information and control systems in the leaner Phillips 66:

The problem facing senior management was how to transfer decision rights and accountability without losing control of the overall business. Drawing on the lessons we had learned in the 1970s, we wanted to provide operating managers with the information they needed to make decisions before we transferred decision making authority and accountability. At the same time, we wanted to provide senior management with the information they needed to understand the business so they could continue to make informed policy decisions. We did not want senior management looking over the shoulder of operating managers making operating decisions.

Our first task was to analyze our current operating decisions. Because of the debt pressure, we began with those decisions that had significant time value. In the oil industry, those decisions centered on areas of pricing, inventory, and supply. For example, in 1985 Phillips faced market conditions that called for daily pricing decisions but it usually took three to four days to change prices.

If prices for motor fuel were off by a penny, it could mean a difference of as much as $40 million in annual profits. A similar mispricing of polyethelene could reduce annual profits by as much as $15 million. A penny in the oil industry is worth millions of dollars. We wanted to put pricing and inventory information and control in the hands of managers who were in the best position to make those decisions on a daily basis. We developed a business information system to deliver that information to enable us to decentralize decision making.

We then looked at our organization and identified the points of action and reaction. For example, for pricing decisions, that point was at the front line manager, the lowest level in the organization. For every point of action-reaction, there is also a point of control. Our next task was to identify that control point and change the role from active controller to monitor and teacher. In the pricing example, corporate staff used to set and control prices. As we passed decision rights down, these experts (fewer in number) would now serve, first and foremost, as teachers but also as monitors. At first, the front line managers made poor pricing decisions, despite access to improved information. Our approach was to work with them and give them a chance. If they were not able (or willing) to assume the increased responsibilities we would pull them out. We were pleased that most of them quickly became better pricers than our centralized group.

Our last task was to redesign our internal performance measurement and compensation systems to match the expanded set of responsibilities at all levels of the company. Prior to the restructuring, all 14 divisions operated as profit centers and we spent significant management time and energy resolving transfer pricing debates. But, as we pushed decision rights down, it became clear that profitability was not the only criterion that we needed to consider. We needed to measure performance along a broad set of internal and external measures that corresponded to the diverse set of responsibilities that we were setting in place at all levels of the organization. As part of the reorganization, I asked all of the division managers to suggest criteria with which to measure the operating performance of their units. I then added my own criteria, and the combination became the

---

EXHIBIT 5   Phillips Motor Fuel Sales: Upper Midwest Area

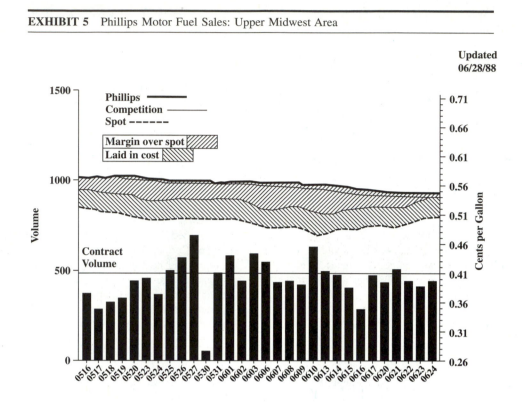

Updated
06/28/88

---

basis for a new reporting system. Each division manager was instructed to cascade this approach to measuring performance down through the organization. We also recognized that quarterly reports would not be sufficient for controlling the more fast-paced, streamlined organization. To solve this problem, I instituted monthly responsibility statements in which all managers reported progress against performance criteria and revised performance measures as indicated. This system improved our yearly planning and budgeting system by giving us a better focus on the critical variables in the business.

Exhibit 5 provides a sample of the pricing information provided by the business information system developed by Wallace to enable decentralization of pricing decisions without losing control. Exhibit 6 summarizes the post-takeover restructuring.

Early on, Wallace recognized the importance of improved access to information and improved communication as critical tools for enabling transformation of Phillips 66. Gene Batchelder, who assumed the position of Phillips 66 controller, recalled the effect that the Phillips 66 reorganization had on Wallace. "Everything that the senior vice presidents had previously condensed, analyzed, and interpreted now reached Bob in raw form. He was learning of problems faster but was swamped with details." Many Phillips managers knew the story he told to illustrate his approach to management:

During WWII, I was an antiaircraft gunner in the Navy. I used binoculars to sight enemy planes sweeping all areas of the horizon, watching for evidence of incoming enemy fighters. At first I was overwhelmed by the vastness of the sky and the

EXHIBIT 6   Summary of Phillips 66 Restructuring

Organization Structure 1984	Sample Decision Rights 1984			Organization Structure 1984	Sample Decision Rights 1984		
	Profit & Loss	Capital Spending	Pricing		Profit & Loss	Capital Spending	Pricing
President (1)	8 Business Divisions in PPG & Chemicals	$3M	Staff Group	President (1)	PPG	$5M	
Senior VPs					Rubber Olefins Petro-Chemical Plastics		
Division VPs (16)				Division VPs (9)			
Regional VPs (15)				Regional VPs (5)		Up to $1M	
Managers (Operating decision level)		$25,000		Managers (Operating decision level)			
Supervisors				Supervisors			
Operations				Operations			Front-line Managers

speed of the aircraft. My superiors taught me to take mental snapshots glancing at different parts of the sky, looking for the specific characteristics that distinguished enemy planes from friendly ones.

Managing Phillips 66 is very similar. There's simply too much information out there on the business horizon. We have to take snapshots of our operations and of world events. To do that we need rapid access to large quantities of information, condensed and reported in a manner that allows managers to quickly identify problems and opportunities. Since the business is changing quickly, the system needs to be flexible and to adapt to the changes. In the Navy, access to that kind of information saved our lives. At Phillips, it saved our business.

In August 1985, Wallace met with Batchelder to discuss the use of a computer-based information system for Phillips 66 managers. He asked that the new system be implemented by the end of 1986.

Information Management at Phillips 66

Improved access to management information had been a major goal of Phillips Petroleum Corporation since the restructuring of the 1970s. In the late 1970s, an IT consulting firm was hired to benchmark the IT infrastructure and to make recommendations on improvements. Like many companies, Phillips had automated in the 1960s by creating specific applications to handle high volume transactions. Over the years, as the company changed the way it did business, each specific application needed to be revised. Redundancy of information across systems resulted in inconsistency of data as revisions affected each application differently. High costs and long time frames were required to keep the inflexible systems up to date. As management information needs intensified in the 1970s, maintenance problems skyrocketed. The IT consultants recommended that Phillips adopt a database approach to information management, and a centralized database was created within Phillips Corporation headquarters that drew information from the inflexible applications and made it available to managers and staff through the use of a software package that enabled sophisticated end-users to customize their own reports.

Decentralized management information systems (MIS) units were set up within Phillips 66's Chemical and PPG business units to work with the decentralized controllers units, which were called operations analysis and control units (OA&C). These two groups worked together to create customized and routine management information reports. Prior to the 1985 restructuring, Phillips 66's Chemicals and PPG SBUs had separate MIS and OA&C units, each reporting to separate managers. These four managers reported to the vice president of finance for each business unit, who in turn reported to the SBU head. With the reorganization, however, Wallace combined all four units (i.e., Chemical MIS, Chemicals OA&C, PPG MIS, and PPG OA&C) into a single organization reporting to Gene Batchelder, who assumed the position of corporate controller and MIS head for all of Phillips 66. (The four previous managers retired.) There were about 25 employees in the newly combined department, about half as many as in its four predecessors. Batchelder had initially been tapped by Wallace to lead the combined MIS/OA&C function because of his broad background as a division controller within Chemicals and over 10 years of experience monitoring Phillips operations within both staff and line functions. He did not have formal MIS training, but he had built a successful management reporting system within Chemicals using a personal computer spreadsheet package.

After the reorganization, the combined MIS/OA&C department initially assumed the same responsibilities as had existed before. Recognizing the need for more timely and flexible access to information as a result of the reorganization, responsibilities soon shifted to the development of an improved business information system, which was initially targeted toward meeting the needs of senior management and, as such, was referred to as the Executive Information System (EIS). The system was developed with the recognition that, as decision rights and control were transferred down, the system would need to be expanded to meet the information needs of those managers lower in the corporation.

Batchelder chose two managers to support him on the EIS project. B. J. (Bobby) Culpepper was hired from Corporate IS to provide information systems expertise. Culpepper had a BS in accounting and an MBA. He had worked for the local office of an accounting firm before coming to Phillips. At Phillips, he had six years of experience with Corporate IS in the corporation's Information Center and User Services Department. Batchelder selected Glenn Jones to provide operations analysis and control expertise. Jones had a master's degree in accounting and had worked at Phillips for eight years. In addition to having international experience, he had broad experience with providing management information to division executives.

In 1985, Batchelder, Culpepper, and Keith Bright, an IBM systems engineer, examined the available PC and mainframe hardware that could be used to run the EIS. Early in the process, they realized that they would need the strengths of the mainframe and PC systems working together. As Culpepper and Bright described it:

> All the data we needed came from mainframe-based production systems and external databases. The mainframe could manage large volumes of data but was too cumbersome and slow for on-line data analysis and presentation to executives. We needed PCs for their ease of use, response time, flexibility, and capacity for executive-quality graphics.

FOCUS, which was already available on the mainframes, was used to access, integrate, and analyze the information for the EIS. But the system still needed software that would create graphic displays of the information and store those displays for fast access by the senior managers. Batchelder and Culpepper worked closely with Keith Bright to locate software that met their

---

EXHIBIT 7   EIS Main Menu

P66/EIS   *Main Selection Menu*   *07/07/88 9:08 a.m.*

Type number and press ENTER→

1. News, Quotes, and Highlights   6. R. G. Wallace
2. Weekly Operating Data   7. Forecasts and Trends
3. Monthly Letters   8. Administration
4. Responsibility Statements   9. File Control
5. Monthly Financial   10. Conference Room Meetings

Function Key Assistance

F1 - Print Profs Note   F5 - Other Printing   F2 - Esc to Introduction

---

specifications. After a long search, Bright found a demonstration software package, developed at IBM's laboratories in Hursley, England, that enabled the creation of sophisticated graphics. The graphics were created on the mainframe but stored and displayed on the PC. Bright and Culpepper then took on the task of rewriting the software program to meet the specifications of the EIS.

Glenn Jones and OA&C analysts were responsible for providing the information for the system. Jones discussed their work:

> The OA&C analysts knew what information the managers were already seeing or wanted to see, and they knew where to find it. Wallace believed that the business divisions should be accountable for their data and maintain control of it. Therefore, we always went to the owner of the data that we wished to obtain. We reviewed how the data would be analyzed and displayed and requested permission to access it directly for the EIS. Although this could have been a sensitive issue, we found that Wallace's sponsorship of the project helped assure that we had the information we needed. If the sponsor of the EIS had been a vice president instead of the president, it would have been much more difficult.

By June 1986, the first fully operational version of the EIS was installed on Wallace's desk. By

November 1986, workstations were on the desks of each of the division vice presidents and their executive secretaries. Shortly thereafter, the system was made available to managers who would be assuming responsibility for pricing and inventory decisions. Batchelder reflected:

> We developed and implemented the system in the time frame Bob Wallace established and within the cost and staffing restraints imposed by our financial condition at the time. We added no new mainframe software and built no new internal transaction systems. In other words, we leveraged off of the existing strengths and data we already possessed.

Managers used a keyboard to gain access to a series of information displays. These displays could include graphics, tables, and text. (Sample displays are presented in the Appendix.) Menus were used to organize the information in the system. The main menu, which could be customized for each manager, organized the information into 10 categories (see Exhibit 7). For example, "News, Quotes, and Highlights" provided a series of text-based screens containing daily news stories affecting the petroleum and chemicals industries, competitors, the parent company, and Phillips 66. The text was prepared by Glenda Fost, an information analyst who had worked with Phillips for many years and had

---

EXHIBIT 8   News Summary

Highlights Edited by P66/MIS from Dow, Reuters, Platts & Other Sources.
05/16/88 - CHEMICALS/PLASTICS

7:30 AM HIGHLIGHTS

Reuters   Rome
ENI says Enichem unit signed Letter of Intent w/China Hainon Petrochem General that could
lead to construction of major petrochem complex on island of Hainan . . . project cost
undisclosed/sources close to ENI say it could involve $800 mln investment . . . ENI says ac-
cord covered possibility of creating joint venture w/China group to construct complex, which
would include 250,000 tonne naphtha cracker plus PE/PP/butadiene prods plants . . .
Snamprogetti unit/Technipetrol to carry out feasibility studies to evaluate project economic
& industrial viability.

Reuters   Rome
ENI says Super Octanos, joint venture w/Pequiven, signed $150 mln finance accord for Jose
petrochem complex to be built by Super Octanos near Puerto La Cruz . . due to be completed
in 3 yrs, will produce 500,000 tonnes/yr MTBE high octane prod which allows lead
compounds to be eliminated fm gasoline, financing, organized by Manufacturers Hanover/
involving 22-bank intl consortium, comprised $70 mln export credit & $90 mln medium-term
loan . . . total project cost expected to be $266 mln . . . ENI participates in Super Octanos thru
Ecofuel sub/Pequivan is PDVSA unit.

*PRINT - Print	PF8 - Page Forward
PF7 - Page Backward	PF12 - Quit

---

broad experience in the operating divisions. Fost
reviewed and summarized news stories from Dow
Jones, Reuters, Platt's, and other oil industry data
services. The text was updated three times a day: at
7:30 AM, when most managers first arrived at work;
at 11:00 AM, before they went to lunch; and at 3:00
PM, before they left the office for the day (see Exhibit 8). Fost described how she prepared the news
summaries.

I come in at 6:30 AM, pull additional information,
and publish the first news summary. Because of
time-zone differences, that issue is mostly Far East
and Middle East news. By 10:00 AM, I have material
on East Coast developments and by 2:00 PM. I have
the West Coast news.

In general, the EIS allows our division managers
to see the news highlights a day before they appear
in the papers. A number of them now get all of their

news information through the system, which can
save them 30 to 45 minutes of reading time a day.

The "Weekly Operating Data" section of the
EIS provided each manager with division-level
operating information that was updated weekly.
The "Monthly Letters" and "Responsibility Statements" sections were used by managers to inform
the management team of the performance criteria
and progress in meeting those criteria. The
"Monthly Financial" section provided budget and
financial information that was updated every month.
Other selections provided key daily operating results. In addition to the information that the managers shared, each manager could specify a personal set
of screen displays that other managers could not
access. Selected personnel information and detailed
operations information fell into this category.

Wallace and the senior managers were active in defining areas where they needed better or more timely information. Glenn Jones described how the process worked:

In the beginning, the managers would tell us exactly what information they wanted and how they wanted to see it. Some would even go so far as to draw a sample of what the chart or graph should look like. As we became more experienced with identifying their information needs, and they gained confidence in our ability to provide the information in the most effective manner, they stopped telling us how to create the information displays and instead focused on explaining the problem area. Gene and I would discuss the problem and design a series of information displays that we thought would provide the information in the most effective and efficient manner. We would show the sample displays to Wallace or the manager who had requested them and then revise them until we had captured what was needed. Sometimes a manager would say, "I think that's right. Go ahead and build that for me and I will let you know how it works." I would then go to the OA&C analysts and have them track down the information and build the display. It usually took us about one to two days to build a new display from the time that the manager made the request to the time that he or she had the display on his or her machine. Often we would not create the electronic links to the data until the manager had used the display and was satisfied that it presented the proper information in the proper format. Instead we would manually update the information until we were sure we had a workable set of displays.

The EIS was linked directly to PROFS, IBM's Professional Office System. Managers used the electronic mail function of PROFS to communicate with other Phillips employees worldwide. PROFS also provided electronic calendars for individual managers, conference room scheduling services, and other managerial productivity tools. The EIS provided meeting agendas, meeting minutes, and copies of meeting presentations for all formal meetings.

At Wallace's suggestion, Batchelder and Culpepper set up a conference room to enable use of EIS displays at meetings. The room had a wall-sized projection screen, a concealed workstation that ran the EIS from a keyboard at the head of the conference table, and other video and audio capabilities. Batchelder described the room:

We designed the room for large-screen presentations. Over time, however, it's become the "EIS meeting center." Wallace started holding his monthly coordination meetings there, using EIS displays rather than sending out for 35mm slides. Now he uses it for most of his periodic meetings, including all of his staff meetings. Other division managers also use it for their staff meetings. Presentation materials and meeting minutes can be circulated on the EIS before and after each meeting.

Introducing EIS to the Division Managers

Wallace played a pivotal role in managing the adoption and growth of the system. By his example and encouragement, he kept the EIS project responsive, visible, and on schedule. Batchelder recalled events from June to December 1986:

In June 1986, Bob was using his EIS workstation several times each day. He insisted that each vice president have an EIS workstation in his or her office, but he did not demand it be used. He allowed each manager to design a customized cabinet to house the workstation that fit with his or her office decor. He wanted each one of them to feel comfortable with it. Above all, he wanted each of the vice presidents to assume ownership of the system. When I suggested that we strongly encourage managers and analysts to support the system, Bob said to go slowly: "Now that they have the workstation, let's not bother them for awhile. They'll adjust to it, and soon they'll come to us." Bob did, however, inform the vice presidents that his meeting schedules and calendar would now be on PROFS and that he would be communicating with them using electronic mail. Bob was right. When the vice presidents saw how well he was prepared for meetings, they also began to ask us for customized information displays. We noticed that the sharing of information through the EIS drastically decreased the amount of discussion during meetings over whose numbers were correct.

After a few weeks, Bob met with the vice presidents to discuss information that they wished to view in common.

Batchelder discovered that three vice presidents were eager to have the system, three were generally indifferent, and three cautious. One of the last three was actively opposed to the system. Ben Jones, vice president of Planning and Budgeting, already had a sophisticated manual information system in place. He initially saw no need for the system. Soon after the EIS was introduced, however, Jones underwent back surgery and was forced to recuperate at home for almost eight weeks. At his request, Culpepper and Bright delivered an EIS workstation to his home and showed him how to use it to stay in touch with the office. When Jones returned, he became one of the EIS's strongest supporters.

By December 1986, the EIS provided 50 reports and graphs. The EIS was running on the Corporate IS IBM 3081 mainframe along with many other IS applications. By January 1987, the increasing load of FOCUS and PROFS use throughout the company overloaded the 3081. EIS performance decreased an occurrence that was immediately noticed by Phillips 66 managers. They asked Corporate IS for a mainframe system with more power, and IS recommended an IBM 3090. Batchelder noted how the relationship between IS and the line operations had changed:

> EIS usage subtly changed the relationship between Corporate IS and our managers. This was the first instance where the managers had requested better computer performance. Before that, the executives usually demanded that IS cost justify and explain in detail the need for computer upgrades. But in this case, Wallace himself documented the need for the new machine to the Corporate Executive Committee. The result was that we purchased new IS hardware during a time of extreme Corporate financial pressure.

The commitment of senior management to expanding the use of technology was also apparent in other areas of the company. During a second wave of cost reductions that followed a drop in oil prices in late 1986 and 1987, the company's spending for IS actually increased. This went against industry trends. Art Wilson, Phillips' IBM account manager who worked with a number of the major oil companies at the time, explained:

> In the oil industry, most companies spend money on IS when times are good and cut back drastically when they're bad. Phillips 66 made a strategic decision to do just the opposite. It is using computer systems to drive a cost-reduction strategy. For example in late 1987, Phillips 66 decided to cut costs by closing several marketing districts. Even so, it did not want to cut its overall marketing effectiveness. In fact, it wanted to improve it. So, while Phillips 66 reduced marketing and sales staff, it added a sales and marketing information system to enable fewer people to cover wider areas more effectively.

By January 1988, the EIS contained over 1,000 information displays for 45 managers and 35 secretaries and staff. Wallace continued to personally approve each new EIS installation to help monitor and manage the growth of the system. Many managers had EIS workstations at the office and at home. More than 1,200 staff analysts and IS professional were using FOCUS on the IBM 3090, and PROFS users exceeded 5,000.

Use of EIS by Phillips 66 Managers

Wallace and his management team used the EIS to institute a new management control system and to build new information channels. One EIS screen, for example, had resulted in tighter control of Phillips 66 inventories. Batchelder recalled this improvement:

> Inventory control was a constant theme in management meetings, but individual managers found it very difficult to estimate their current inventory positions. Understanding 12-month trends in motor fuel inventory levels required the compilation of some 24 spreadsheet reports, which were seldom available at the same time or in the same place. A manager would learn of May inventory levels at the beginning of July. Even with

motor fuel inventories set at 9.5 million barrels, we often had outages.

This situation changed after we distributed an EIS display, updated weekly, that described current inventory levels. The display synthesized the information from the 24 spreadsheet reports and allowed an immediate comparison of current and past-year levels with a target-inventory range. This information is now available to the operating managers responsible for inventory control. Since they began using this display, we have been able to decrease motor fuel inventories to 8.5 million barrels. At about $18 a barrel, that represents a sizable amount of money.

Charlie Bowerman, vice president of the Marketing Division, used the EIS one to two hours each day to better monitor market condition and more efficiently measure the impact of pricing changes:

Marketing negotiates three-year sales contracts with motor fuel distributors, but actual sales fluctuate daily in response to customer needs and changing market conditions. The EIS has made us much more responsive to both these critical factors, with the results being significantly improved inventory, supply, and pricing management. Conservatively, the system has generated increased profits of $20 million.

Dick Robinson, vice president of the Refining Division, used the system for more than one hour per day during short sessions spread throughout the day. He estimated that EIS access reduced the amount of mail passing through his office by 50 percent. He also noted how the system contributed to monitoring his business:

In December 1986, I uncovered a potential scheduling problem at the Borger refinery during my daily check of division news on the EIS. Division engineers were planning to shut down one of the crude oil processing units, called a Heavy Oil Cracker, for 10 days. This cracking unit converted raw crude oil into products such as motor fuel. The engineers wanted to overhaul the cracker to bring efficiency back up. They were unaware, however, that motor fuel demand was exceeding Phillips'

production capacity. Bringing the cracker down would force the company to purchase motor fuel for resale at a lower margin on the spot market. I contacted Borger directly and asked for a catalyst retest. The results were in a range that convinced the engineers it would be safe to postpone catalyst replacement until a general plant overhaul scheduled for the spring of 1988. Operating the cracker for the 10 days that it would have been idled allowed us to produce 337,000 more barrels of motor fuel than had been budgeted, resulting in higher profits and an overall cost saving estimated at $650,000. Soon after, we provided the refinery managers with the information needed to help them recognize these difficulties as they made scheduling decisions. We have found other areas like this where we were unaware that operating managers did not have sufficient information to manage the business.

A few months after the initial implementation, Batchelder surveyed the division vice presidents and found that most used the EIS daily when they were in town. During their frequent travels, many used laptop computers or received EIS reports from their secretaries. Chemicals' Vice President Jack Howe used the EIS to scan news and quotes for 10 minutes two to three times per day. Howe and six of his seven managers were new to their jobs in 1986 and felt that the EIS was a valuable tool for quickly gaining experience with the Chemicals Division's business. Ray Steiner, vice president of Supply and Transportation, had a Reuters terminal in his office before the EIS was installed. Now he used the EIS as well; it was the first thing he turned to every morning.

Wayne Anderson, newly promoted vice president of Natural Gas Liquids, used his previous experience in the Marketing Division to significantly expand the computerization of the NGL Division:

The EIS is changing the way we run the business. For example, LP gas is now priced at each of our 82 individual pipeline terminals. This allows our front-line managers to assume control of the pricing activity and allows us to respond much more quickly to changes in specific markets. Before, we had a much more centralized approach to pricing and only set prices for the three large pipeline

systems that we operate. Customers feel that
Phillips 66 is more responsive, and our competitors
seem to be confused by the new pricing structure.
They are having trouble reacting.

Batchelder described the system's use by Gail
Anderson, vice president of Human Resources:

Gail has used the EIS as a driver to implement
sweeping changes in the availability and use of
individual employee and organizational information.
His leadership has moved personnel data out of the
confines of the large, corporately administered
database and into the hands of our executives and
line managers.

The Plastics Division represented a unique use
of the EIS. Plastics' Vice President John Vanbuskirk had developed an on-line reporting system for
his area before the EIS was introduced. Because of
the specialty nature of his business, the original
data in the EIS were not of great use to him.
Vanbuskirk ran a collection of distinct businesses,
ranging from fibers to plastic pipe and high-
technology composites. These dissimilar businesses were alike only in that they often served the
same customer. Vanbuskirk needed information
displays that treated his businesses by market and
customer rather than on the temporal basis used by
the EIS. Batchelder, Jones, and Culpepper worked
with Vanbuskirk and his managers until they had
completed a full-scale EIS tailored to Plastics.
Vanbuskirk could still gain access to displays
shared by the other division vice presidents, but
his workstation was so fully customized that it
appeared to be a different system.

Managing System Growth

Batchelder believed that the system was entering a
period of rapid growth. The EIS could potentially
have more than 100 users by the end of 1988.
Across the entire Phillips corporation there were
more than 500 managers who could potentially use
the system. He and Wallace were concerned that
growth be managed effectively. So far, the EIS had
been highly individualized. Wallace had personally approved the assignment of each workstation.

All the managers now on the system had been well
known to Batchelder, Culpepper, and Jones. As
more people used the EIS, Batchelder knew these
characteristics would change.

Batchelder anticipated that EIS growth would
make system maintenance more difficult. The EIS
also proved a catalyst for other new systems. The
MIS/OA&C group, which had started in 1985 with
25 people, had grown to 50 by 1988 and was
responsible for more than 25 commercial systems
development projects that involved computer support for managers, the management of information, and the support of their businesses. These
projects were in addition to the EIS project. Batchelder believed that his group served as an excellent
training ground for a new breed of employee who
understood both the business and the role of
technology in supporting the business. As a result,
he encouraged high turnover in his employees to
enable them to "seed" both the business and IS
areas with this special blend of skills.

Batchelder had also shifted EIS management responsibilities as the system became better defined:

At first Culpepper and I worked closely with Bob
Wallace on a small number of prototypes in
management offices. At that time, the system was a
technical challenge. As we became more familiar
with the technology and the number of users began
to increase, we entered a second phase in which the
technical challenge was overshadowed by the
information challenge, and responsibility shifted
increasingly to Glenn Jones and OA&C. Now we
are nearing 100 systems, and installations have
shifted from the vice president level to the operating
managers. They have different needs for information
and system support.

Options for the Future

By late 1988, Phillips Petroleum Corporation appeared to be bouncing back despite sagging oil
prices. A Business Week[1] article reported that

---

[1]Anonymous, "Phillips Climbs up from The Bottom of the
Board," Business Week, January 16, 1989.

Phillips 66 Company NGL Fractionation Summary
Month-to-Date through 5/19/88

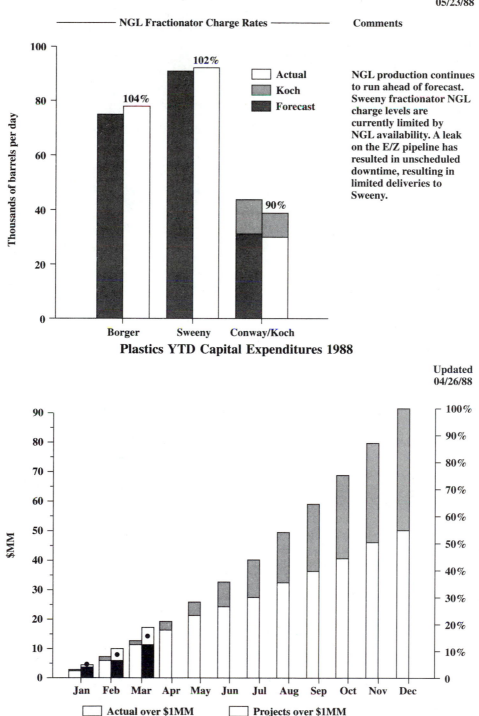

Updated
05/23/88

——————— NGL Fractionator Charge Rates ———————   Comments

NGL production continues to run ahead of forecast. Sweeny fractionator NGL charge levels are currently limited by NGL availability. A leak on the E/Z pipeline has resulted in unscheduled downtime, resulting in limited deliveries to Sweeny.

Plastics YTD Capital Expenditures 1988

Updated
04/26/88

"[Phillips] salvation came from a stunning 1988 performance from downstream operations. . . . They generated $1.3 billion in cash and enabled Phillips to make a $900 million debt payment. As a result, the company's average yearly payments dropped to a manageable $332 million, although it still faced a $939 million payment in 1995."

Batchelder finished his review of the EIS, prepared some screens for his discussion with Wallace, and made a list of further issues he wanted to cover. He wanted to examine some key points:

First, have we successfully assimilated the EIS into Phillips 66 management culture and business? We think the system has reached the stage where it is self-sustaining within Phillips 66. We need to change our approach to managing the system. We must be careful, however, not to move too fast and destroy our ability to support the system.

Second, how can we help the rest of Phillips Petroleum recognize the value of the EIS for their business? For example, our upstream operations—the Exploration and Production group—have a different business process and organization structure from that of Phillips 66 Company.

Third, Bob Wallace is retiring at the end of 1988. What happens when he is no longer an active EIS sponsor? Will we need a new system sponsor? If so, who should that be?

Fourth, we are receiving large numbers of inquiries from other companies about the EIS. We may have an opportunity to license the system as a commercial product in a joint venture with IBM or another partner. What changes would we have to make in the system to make it a commercial package? What parts of it are generalizable to other companies and other industries? How big is the market for such a system? Do we really want to be in that business?

Batchelder had learned earlier that day that Glenn Cox, president of Phillips Petroleum Company, had asked for an EIS workstation. He knew that Wallace had reviewed the system with Cox and was certain that Wallace would want to discuss the impact that Cox's acceptance of the EIS might have on the rest of the corporation.

CASE 6–3: CONNOR FORMED METAL PRODUCTS

Bob Sloss assumed control of Connor Formed Metal Products, a small ($12 million in sales) manufacturing company, in 1984. To help the company survive in harsh economic conditions and fierce global competition, he made dramatic changes. IT was a key tool in this organization's transformation.

Preparation Questions

1. Evaluate the actions taken by Bob Sloss after he assumed control of Connor Formed Metal Products.
2. What role did IT play in the changes Sloss made?
3. The technology developed at the Los Angeles division will be transferred to the San Jose, Portland, and Dallas divisions. What advice would you give Sloss on the implementation?
4. What advice would you give Sloss on future directions for the use of IT at Connor?

Case 6–3 Connor Formed Metal Products*

At the close of 1990, Bob Sloss, president of Connor Formed Metal Products, reflected on his accomplishments since taking the helm of his family company in 1984. The company, a small custom metal spring and stampings manufacturer, had followed a steady but slow course since its founding. When Sloss became president, however, he was determined to shake things up. Now, after six years of hard work and significant investment, Sloss had come a long way, but believed additional changes still needed to be implemented.

One recent change made by Sloss was to hire Michael Quarrey as Connor's human resource and information systems manager. Quarrey, who had a bachelor of science degree in computer science and an MBA and had worked at the National

Center for Employee Ownership was given the mandate for developing an order tracking system that would support Sloss' goal of empowering workers with information (see Exhibit 1). The system significantly changed access to and availability of information regarding the process for designing, manufacturing, selling, and servicing products. At the close of 1990, the system had been up and running successfully in the Los Angeles division for six months. Sloss now hoped to push the technology out to the other divisions in an attempt to improve the firm's profitability.

Company and Industry Overview

Connor manufactured metal springs and stampings for large U.S. original equipment manufacturers. Approximately 20 percent of Connor's business was producing coiled springs, which were "commodity-like" in their composition and manufacturing; the remaining 80 percent was metal stampings, complex wire forms, and assemblies, all of which varied widely in design and therefore

*Research Associate Melinda B. Conrad prepared this case under the supervision of Professor Lynda M. Applegate and Donna B. Stoddard. Copyright © 1993 by the President and Fellows of Harvard College. Harvard Business School case 193-003 (revised September 8, 1993).

EXHIBIT 1   Connor Organization Chart, 1990

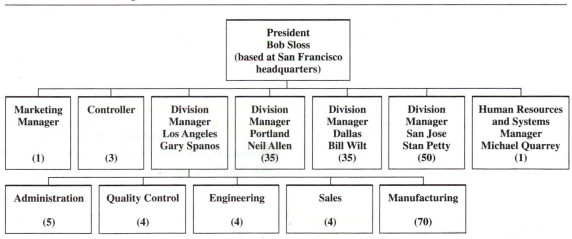

Note: Numbers in parenthesis represent headcount.

required significant engineering expertise to produce. Connor's competition, fragmented around product lines, comprised 600 to 700 primarily owner-operated job shops, most of which had an average of 20 to 30 employees. Customers typically chose their suppliers based on price, particularly since quality and service were notoriously poor within the industry.

In 1947, Joe and Henry Sloss, owners of a family hardware business, purchased Connor as an investment. The Slosses managed the company from afar until the early 1960s, when they sold off their hardware business. The family continued to expand Connor and, by the 1960s, it had opened divisions in San Jose, Phoenix, Los Angeles, and Portland, Oregon. During this time and through the 1970s, the company was run by Vice President of Operations George Halkides, who maintained tight control over the company through traditional accounting and control systems split between Connor's San Francisco corporate headquarters and Los Angeles plant. When Halkides retired in the early 1980s, Joe Sloss's son, Bob Sloss, was in line to fill the position. At age 34, Sloss had worked at the company since 1972. Short on experience but long on enthusiasm, Sloss enrolled in Stanford's summer executive education program. Describing himself as the "wild-eyed dissident," Sloss recalled his experience:

> Halkides had taken a conservative, bottom-line approach to running the company. Connor had no debt, and it was a typical slow-growth, low-investment spring company. The Stanford program served as a catalyst for me because I learned how progressive businesses were changing due to new technology and foreign competition. I realized that Connor could either keep plugging along and eventually get lost, or we could really turn it around and set it apart from the competition.

When Sloss took over, he recognized that the company could not survive by maintaining its traditional way of doing business. Offshore competitors, many with lower cost structures and superior product quality, had entered the US market and were stealing market share from the more traditional small job shops that had supplied the industry in the past. Many of these offshore firms were also attempting to buy the larger more successful U.S. competitors as a way of entering the market. To respond to these threats, Sloss drove the company through significant change. In 1984, Connor opened a new facility in Dallas, Texas. That same year, Sloss decentralized the company, turning day-to-day authority over to the plant managers. Sloss repositioned Connor as a service-oriented business which would focus on providing custom-developed metal stampings and wire forms and would be "100 percent reliable." To reach this goal, he bought new machinery and established a statistical process control system. To increase Connor's technical expertise, he hired engineers for the first time in Connor's history.

Sloss was aware that properly motivating employees was equally important. As a result, he raised wages, established a quarterly cash bonus system, and set up an employee stock ownership program (ESOP). To convey the company's new identity to the outside world, Sloss changed the company's name to Connor Formed Metal Products from its previous name, Connor Springs. He printed new marketing materials, updated sales presentations, and produced a professional videotape on the company.

Word of Connor's new image quickly spread throughout the industry and the company became a vendor to large companies such as Honeywell, Motorola, and Hewlett-Packard. Shipments rose from under $8 million in 1982 to over $17 million in 1988. Despite these telltale signals, however, Connor was not able to see the results in the bottom line (see Exhibit 2). And while the closing of the Phoenix plant and the transfer of its employees to Dallas had accounted for much of the company's 1989 losses, the Dallas plant had not been profitable in its five years of existence and the Los Angeles division was seeing tough times as well. Connor's other divisions in Portland and San Jose were making a significant profit, but the overall results still had not reached Sloss's goals.

EXHIBIT 2   Financial Summary

	Shipments (#)	Pre-Tax Profit ($)	Net Profit ($)
1967	4,242,801	$ 228,282	$140,782
1968	4,828,467	85,237	37,579
1969	4,884,528	76,721	44,021
1970	4,192,626	(173,647)	(91,418)
1971	2,752,046	94,829	48,574
1972	3,253,937	252,343	135,343
1973	4,032,621	414,175	209,175
1974	4,886,381	473,548	245,248
1975	3,835,915	84,288	56,588
1976	5,178,388	491,745	253,728
1977	7,211,058	994,114	503,144
1978	7,900,755	689,759	455,569
1979	10,171,281	1,427,610	741,001
1980	8,457,836	950,442	525,348
1981	8,890,372	947,640	510,483
1982	7,970,621	474,986	269,132
1983	9,742,496	1,059,133	615,323
1984	11,287,189	797,699	519,559
1985	12,367,778	725,406	459,912
1986	12,880,456	897,688	403,688
1987	12,127,989	384,007	240,007
1988	17,031,282	1,122,116	655,116
1989	16,423,298	(143,509)	(79,509)
1990	19,159,542	1,328,754	792,754

Transforming Connor

Structure

Prior to Bob Sloss's presidency, Connor had been divided into two regions, North and South; the Phoenix plant had reported to Los Angeles, while the Portland plant had reported to San Jose. Not only had this perpetuated a structural hierarchy that Sloss disliked, but customers were being traded between plants based on the self-interest of the larger plants in California rather than the needs of the customer.

Upon his arrival in 1984, Sloss's first move was to decentralize the company into four autonomous divisions, giving each full profit and loss as well as capital expenditure responsibility (see Exhibit 3). In his move away from a hierarchical organizational structure, Sloss established a "hands-off" approach to overseeing the business. At the division level, each plant maintained administrative, quality control, engineering, sales, and manufacturing functions. Product pricing was jointly determined by engineering, sales, and division management. Production scheduling was run by the division's production manager. Sloss placed a particular emphasis on the engineering aspect of the business process. Engineers, production supervisors, and salespeople were teamed together and were expected to communicate closely as each order moved through the business process.

The Los Angeles division was the largest Connor plant, with 100 employees and sales totaling $10 million. The plant specialized in high-volume

EXHIBIT 3   Decision Rights (1985)

Organization Structure	Sample Decision Rights						
President	Capital expenses	Pricing	P&L	Business development			
Division Manager		Pricing			Product development	Production scheduling	Shop hold
Product Team (Engineering, Sales, Manufacturing, and Quality Control)							
Production Floor							

Decision Rights (1990)

Organization Structure	Sample Decision Rights						
President							
Division Manager	Capital expenses	Pricing	P&L	Business development			
Product Team (Engineering, Sales, Manufacturing, and Quality Control)		Pricing			Product development	Production scheduling	Shop hold (all divisions but L.A.)
Production Floor							Shop hold* (L.A. division)

*Shop Hold authority was moved down to the production floor in L.A. after implementation of the "L.A. Experiment" in 1990.
Note: This structure did not change with the introduction of the new IT system.

products for the diverse industrial businesses of southern California. The division manager, Gary Spanos, had been with Connor for close to 20 years. Originally hired by Halkides, Spanos had managed both the Portland and San Jose plants. In 1986, seven years after Halkides' departure, Spanos returned to Los Angeles with the mission of restoring the plant to its former role as profit leader for the company.

The San Jose division, with 60 employees was run by a MBA graduate, Stan Petty. Petty had succeeded Spanos as manager of the Portland division, and then succeeded Spanos again when he became manager of the San Jose division. In the 1980s, the San Jose plant had diversified from

its traditional product lines of springs and stampings to specialize in the manufacturing of short-run prototypes for high-technology Silicon Valley companies. Petty was known for his "bottom-line" approach to management, and the San Jose division had achieved record profit margins during Petty's tenure as manager.

The Portland division comprised approximately 30 employees and served primarily Northwest-based trucking companies and related parts manufacturers. The division was run by Neil Allen, who had been in the industry for 20 years and whose father had also worked for Connor. While in the past the Portland division had been perceived as being less sophisticated than the other Connor divisions, it had made efforts to increase the level of technical support available to customers within the past few years and aggressively pursued new "world-class" customers.

The company purchased the Dallas plant soon after Sloss assumed control in 1984. By 1989, when the plant had failed to make a profit, Sloss decided to merge the Dallas and Phoenix plants and relocate both to a new site in Dallas. Sloss brought in Bill Wilt from the Phoenix plant to run the new Dallas division. Wilt had had a long career with Associated Spring, the world's largest spring-maker, and was known for turning around losing operations.

When considering what aspects of the company to change as he moved forward, Sloss was confident that the autonomous division structure needed to remain intact because the company's regional business structure provided a competitive advantage:

> There is no question that we could move everything under one roof, but we would lose our local customers. We would also probably ruin the culture of our company, which is based around working in small groups. Our future plans are to continue to develop our regional markets. There is particular potential in Mexico for both our Los Angeles and Dallas plants. We would even consider opening up new divisions if there was enough demand.

Control

Upon assuming control of the company, Sloss recognized that Connor's control systems needed to be realigned. Halkides had maintained a detached, top-down management approach and shared minimal information with employees. In contrast, Sloss believed in actively involving employees in the business process through the exchange of information. Sloss recalled Halkides' approach:

> Halkides had created an environment of traditional loyalty, but he rarely got the employees on the floor involved with what the business was doing. He managed by "the need to know." And, to him, when it came to the shop employees, they didn't need to know much. There were never any employee meetings with or without management. They just did their jobs out in the shop.
>
> I don't believe in a stringent managerial hierarchy. I want to involve as many employees as possible in the decision-making process because I really believe that the more the employees know, the better off the company will be. I want them to have access to all kinds of information which they wouldn't have if they were working at a company of the "old school." Especially as an ESOP company, we are obligated to operate this way.

To promote the sharing of information within each division, Sloss encouraged the division managers to hold weekly staff meetings with 12 to 15 employees from engineering, sales, customer service, quality control, production management, and personnel. Leadership of these meetings was determined on an informal rotation basis. In addition, weekly production meetings were scheduled and run by the production manager of the plant. In these meetings, the heads of each department reviewed the production schedule for the upcoming week. Product teams met on an ad hoc schedule, often once a week. In all meetings, the designated leader was responsible for filling out a meeting report (see Exhibit 4). These reports were stored in a binder located in the meeting room and were available for reference to anyone in the company. Each division also held monthly departmental meetings with the division manager. Division managers' meetings were held quarterly and Sloss visited each plant regularly.

Halkides had closely monitored all aspects of the company's information flow; for example, he signed his initials on each invoice. Sloss, in contrast, chose to review only a handful of key indicators, such as, sales-in, backlog, and payroll. He believed that if he and the division managers delegated much of this responsibility, details could be handled with more speed and accuracy.

Through an extensive statistical process control program begun in Portland and carried to all the plants, employees were trained to monitor and take responsibility for the quality of their own work. In Dallas, Wilt carried this concept further by initiat-

EXHIBIT 4   Sample Team Meeting Report

Team Meeting Report   Date: ___1-13___

Team Name: ___×_____

Meeting: Regular ☒ Special ☐

Objective: To Discuss the clutch spring testing & process _____

Persons Attending:

Ron W.	Steve B.	
Javiar C.	Bob D.	
Renee C.	Armando L.	
Jim N.	Steve J.	

Production Goals	Backlog	New D.M.R.S.
For the next_____ , _____ PCS. For the next_____ , _____ PCS.	PCS. _____ $ Value _____	Yes ☒ No ☐ If yes, attach

Critical areas:

I Desluger Mach – 3 more will be made when results of looking at 4 Boxes for slugs

II New Cutters – 110,000 cuts without sharpening at all, with old one only 5,000 – 42,000

　　　　　　5 more sets have been ordered

III New -01 Mach – Mach. has all tooling in place ready to make parts

　　　　　Need Electrical for oven

　　　　　Oven & tubing on order

　　　　　Hoping to be up & running by Thursday 1-23-92

IV Position – We are currently having problems holding the 20° ± 20° Free pos.

　　　　　It seems it was easier to maintain before the I.D. was a critical issue with Porter.

　　　　　Itaya feels with a larger I.D. & less of a loaded pos. we may be able to

　　　　　　hold the free pos. better; at this point we are about out of ideas.

V PI Porter testing – Porter is going to send us a list of what they have studied & the

　　　　　　results of the tests

　　　　　The smaller I.D. Parts were tested & 8/10 failed Hemp. 10/10 passed

　　　　　We are going to tumble some of the smaller I.D. parts & retest

　　　　　Porter feels that a smaller I.D. & wire size may be the answer

Action items:

		Assigned responsibility	Target date	Comp
1.	Empty 4 Boxes & look for slugs	Renee C.	1-20-92	
2.	Send out tumbled parts for testing	Armando L.	1-20-92	
3.	Check tang length on tumbled parts	Jim N.	1-20-92	
4.	Order 2 new carts	Javiar C.	1-20-92	
5.	15 pc study on Free Position for parts at 180° & 177° Loaded position	"	1-20-92	
6.	Get some small I.D. Parts back	Steve J.		
7.				

Next meeting will be ___1-20___ **at** _3_ : _30_ PM **Written by** *S J Belling* _____

EXHIBIT 5 Average Stock Holdings per Connor

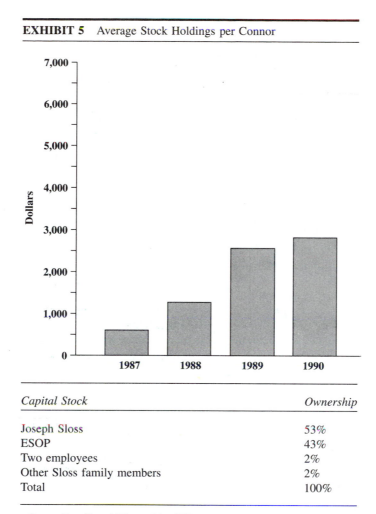

Capital Stock	Ownership
Joseph Sloss	53%
ESOP	43%
Two employees	2%
Other Sloss family members	2%
Total	100%

Source: Duns Financial Report, May 1993.

ing plantwide incentives based on "managing the numbers." In addition to monitoring quality, Dallas employees, recording their progress on bulletin boards, tracked their own efficiency, on-time delivery, and safety. Employees received monthly bonuses based on their improvements.

Sloss also looked outside Connor for information and feedback on the company's progress and overall strategy. Encouraged by Motorola, the company participated annually in the National Baldrige Award competition. Sloss made it a point to learn as much as possible from customers, other ESOP companies, and trade associations through which he and other Connor employees networked frequently.

Culture

The ESOP Sloss established in 1986 had grown steadily (see Exhibit 5). Obsessed with chipping away at Connor's old-fashioned, secretive style of management, Sloss insisted that once employees were actual owners of the company, they should act like owners as well. Sloss and the division managers explained the company's financial statistics to employees, walked around the plant answering questions, and made themselves available for such things as "lunch with the boss" meetings. He also established a monthly company newsletter and began holding periodic on-site and off-site team-building sessions (see Exhibit 6.)

Incentives and Rewards

In keeping with his desire to empower all levels of the organization, Sloss instituted a number of incentives and rewards for lower levels of the company. Prior to Sloss's arrival, Connor maintained standard wages with added incentives only for top executives. Sloss immediately increased the company's base salaries to be the most competitive in the industry and implemented a quarterly cash bonus system. Division managers began to occasionally award bonus checks of up to a few hundred dollars to employees who had shown "exemplary performance."

Employee response to such changes was extremely positive. Mary Kunkel, San Jose's office manager, explained:

> I am pretty pro-Connor. I really enjoy the company. I like being an ESOP company because I think you tend to take more pride in your company and your work. If it's the end of the month, we will seriously go out to the shop and say, "What do you have to get out today?" Give us tacky board, give us the parts, we will put them in the little box and get them out. Because we want that money on the shipping log, we want more bonuses, we want more profit. I started here when I was young enough, so that I can have a lot of money by the time I retire. Either that or I will have an awfully nice boat on a lake!

Sloss also worked to attract the "best and the brightest" to Connor. He recruited at top engineering schools to find younger, high-potential employees. He believed that Connor promised those who were interested in a challenge a valuable experience with a competitive salary.

Information Systems

When Sloss took over in 1984, the extent of the company's information technology was an IBM System 34 mini-computer located at the corporate office, which produced the company's payroll, accounts receivable, and accounts payable. Within the operating divisions, engineers produced estimates by hand, shop orders were typed out on a slip ten carbons deep, sales information was kept in large, loose-leaf notebooks, and order slips were returned following production covered with grease and finger smudges. In an effort to reduce some of this paperwork, Sloss in 1985 brought IBM System 36s into the Los Angeles, San Jose, and Portland plants. Employees used the system for basic office tasks but found the "canned" software too generic for the more complicated procedures, such as, estimating and shop ordering.

Each division responded to the IBM System 36 differently; success with the system could be traced to the level of computer proficiency within each division at that time. In the Portland division, where a number of employees were experienced computer users, the System 36 was used for a variety of tasks. But the San Jose division system had not been used since its installment, primarily because there were no employees who felt comfortable using mini-computers. The Los Angeles division used the System 36 for basic office automation and had even upgraded to the System 38 for more capacity. Yet, they still found the system too unwieldy for anything other than basic administrative procedures.

The Los Angeles Experiment

When considering how to move forward with information management and computers, Sloss noted what Petty had done with personal computers after transferring from Portland to San Jose in 1986. Petty, a strong advocate of increased efficiency through the use of computers, had created a system using personal computers and manufacturing software called "Job Boss." This system, well

EXHIBIT 6   Sample Company Newsletter

CONNOR NEWS

A Publication for the Employee Owners of Connor Formed Metal Products

December	San Francisco

Balancing Multiple Agenda's

One of the reasons our company is so successful is that we continually examine everything we do and try to improve it. Many companies are great at one thing: quality, employee ownership, technology, training, marketing - we strive to be the best in all.

This approach, what we call advancing "multiple agendas," can be overwhelming at times. As we continually re-evaluate our priorities, new ideas are introduced while others are put on hold, or even dropped. Our track record suggests that this works well, keeping us open to rapidly changing business conditions.

But, for employees it can be disorienting, especially if they aren't informed or don't have a chance to have input. Consider, for example, the ESOP committee. Many employees are wondering whatever became of this group. While we have addressed many ESOP issues with employees this year, we haven't yet found a role for the ESOP committee.

It is because of our on-going updating of plans that we spend so much time communicating with this newsletter, in reports, and in meetings. It's also why we're seeking more employee involvement. The more employees participate in setting and carrying out our various agendas, the faster we can move forward.

The Importance of Cash Flow

To understand Connor's finances you have to follow two things: profit and cash. So far the newsletter has focused on profits, reporting the "Income Statement" or "Profit & Loss" (P&L) statement each month.

Now we are going to start reporting on cash also. It is common to think of cash and profits as the same, but they are not. In fact, it is possible for a company to be profitable and go bankrupt, which means it doesn't have enough cash to pay its bills. It's also possible for a company to be unprofitable and yet have cash, although this is less likely.

For now, accept it as true that cash and profits are different. This will become clear as we explain the items in the cash flow statement over the next several issues.

This month we'll focus on **Beginning and Ending Cash**. These include both cash in our checking account and the amount we owe on our line of credit. The line of credit allows us to borrow from the bank on a short time basis. Whenever our borrowing on the line of credit is more than our cash in the bank, we record the difference as a negative amount of cash.

	6 Months 1992	Year 1991
Beginning Cash	166,823	(288,816)
Sources of Cash:		
Pre-tax Profit	1,038,296	1,832,483
Depreciation	488,400	879,257
Total Sources	1,526,696	2,711,740
Uses of Cash:		
Equipment/Bldg	1,030,043	1,228,824
Income Taxes	509,021	693,860
Loan Payments	195,296	250,000
Other	(69,423)	83,417
Stock Repurchase	260,391	0
Total Uses	1,925,328	2,256,101
Cash Surplus/(Deficit)	(398,632)	455,639
Ending Cash	(231,804)	166,823

From the cash flow statement above, you can see that we began 1991 with $288,816 "negative cash," meaning we had short term debt. By the end of 1991, we had generated $455,639 in cash. This allowed us to pay off the debt and put $166,823 in the bank. So far this year we have used $398,632 more cash than we have generated, using up our cash in the bank and resulting in new short term debt.

regarded by employees who used it, automated almost all of the division's office tasks (e.g., estimating, order entry, accounts receivable, and purchasing). At the same time, the Portland division was also experimenting with personal computers. As a result, Sloss began to consider using personal computers combined with custom software to help make the business more profitable. Sloss recalled:

> I wanted to begin doing things on purpose. I wanted to know which department's machinery produced the best margins. I wanted to have answers to questions like, "Are we more profitable manufacturing parts for the irrigation industry or the aerospace industry?" I also wanted to know whether there was a similarity among the kind of customers that bought from us. Could we go out and find more of them? All of this was information that the division managers would know about. However, I wanted to know it empirically instead of by gut feel, and I believed we could do it using PCs and custom software.

During this same period, Sloss was interviewing candidates to fill the newly created position of human resource manager when he met Michael Quarrey, who had just left a small manufacturing company in Worcester, Massachusetts, in hopes of finding a job where he could fulfill his long-term career goal. After having worked at the National Center for Employee Ownership and done extensive research on ESOP companies,[1] Quarrey wanted to test ways of empowering employee owners with information. When his previous employer was unable to set up an ESOP, Quarrey decided to find a company that already had one. He contacted Sloss and explained that with his college-level computer programming expertise and his ESOP background, he could serve as Connor's human resource manager and help Sloss find a solution to Connor's information problem. Quarrey remembered:

[1]Corey Rosen and Michael Quarrey, "How Well is Employee Ownership Working?," *Harvard Business Review* (September/October 1987): 126–129.

Sloss was going through a very typical thing for an ESOP company executive. He or she gets to a point and says, "We now have given our employees 33 percent ownership, yet the employees are responding to us the same as they always have." While Sloss had expected employee ownership to improve Connor's performance, overall margins weren't getting better, and in Los Angeles they were getting substantially worse. Here was someone calling him on the phone out of the blue, saying, "I have a theory about how to do things. I don't know anything about the company, but I have a very strong conviction that information and ESOPs should be married together and I have some tools that can help." For me, the reward would be experimenting in Connor's "lab" to test employee ownership and ways of empowering people with information.

After listening to Quarrey's pitch, Sloss decided to go forward. Since Los Angeles was doing poorly and it was the largest plant, the possibility of computerizing its information flow seemed like a logical step. Sloss had spoken with Spanos about the idea before, but Spanos had taken an "anti-technology" view, claiming that information systems were too inflexible for the custom work in which Connor specialized. Sloss believed, however, that if he could position Quarrey's role as supporting employee ownership, his added responsibility of writing custom software would be better received by Spanos as well as the other employees. Sloss explained:

> The idea of a little company like ours hiring a computer programmer was mind boggling. But, I was convinced it was the way to go and we could justify Michael's payroll expense by having him work on two things, software and the ESOP.

Beginning work in August 1989, Quarrey was instructed to work on increasing the Los Angeles division's employee involvement in the ESOP while also developing an order-tracking and costing system for the plant. The system was developed using a relational database PC package called "Clipper," which was specifically designed to support distributed database management over a network. The cost of the database software was approximately $500. Quarrey's strategy was to begin development of the system by creating the module that would support the estimating portion of the product service delivery process. Once this was in place, he could build in shop order and invoice capabilities and, ultimately, add in all of the administrative procedures included in the manufacturing process. Before long, Quarrey was designing features that set the system apart from a typical "automated" process. Each electronic shop order contained "notes" areas, where departments could make comments about a particular job as it moved through the manufacturing process. "But it was Roy Gallucci, a blunt-spoken machinist in Connor's coiling department, who may have had the biggest impact on the new system," stated John Case in a recent article on the company:[2]

> The machinist's message to the boss was simple. At least one computer should be out in the shop. Blue-collar employees should have the ability not only to enter comments about a job but to somehow force the office to pay attention. He didn't know exactly how it might work, however, if the company was going to put in a whole new system, it had better do it right. Bingo, Sloss thought: Gallucci was touching on a perennial complaint that the office never listened to the shop. Here was a chance to deal with it.
>
> Thanks to Roy Gallucci, every employee has full and instant access to data about the jobs he or she is working on not just the customer's name and the specs but a full history of the job to date, special notes or instructions from engineering or customer service, and management information once thought of as sensitive, such as, the price and the margin. An employee who spots (or develops) a problem with a job can go to the computer and put a "shop hold" on it. Until the engineering department investigates and makes a formal written disposition of the problem the software won't allow Connor to take any new orders for the same part.
>
> In one recent six-week period, Quarrey counted 117 holds emanating from machine operators and

their supervisors. "This grinding can only be done by A-1 Surface Grinding," read one, adding the address, a contact name, and the price per part that the preferred outside vendor would charge. "OK, will change the master," responded engineering. "Change run speed from 850 pcs/hr to 650 pcs/hr," recommended another. "Changed speed from 850 pcs/hr to 700 pcs/hr," answered the not-totally-compliant engineer. Gallucci himself admits to using the feature regularly, for example, to propose sending a three-part order out for heat treating all together rather than one batch at a time. And Quarrey points out that similar holds can be put on a shop order by quality control, by engineering ("Don't allow this estimate to become an order until we have a clean blueprint"), or by customer service (Don't ship without clearance from us").

As a result, employees, using the bare minimum of the "page up/down" keys, would know not only the full history of a job to date, but also have the power to help control the production process. (See Exhibit 7 and Exhibit 8 for samples of an estimate and shop order.) Quarrey explained:

> The system will not allow anyone to create a report on an individual employee's productivity. All the information we collect is sorted by job number, not by employee. This was important so that the system be used not to manage people but rather the other way around—people manage the process. In keeping with his "details are delegated" approach, Sloss wasn't even networked to the system.
>
> Each computer program was designed participatively. I spoke to people in different areas of the plant and got a general overview of how the process worked and what information they needed. Then, after going through a programming phase, I would go back and show it to people to find out what they thought. After a lot of iterations of programming, implementing, and revising we came up with the most effective approaches. Functions were based around simple keystrokes (Page/Up, Page/Down, Escape, etc.) and separate screens were made for "viewing" and "updating" data so that any employee in the shop could "view" any information without accidentally changing it.

By May 1990, Quarrey had the new system up and running in the Los Angeles division (see

[2]John Case, "The Knowledge Factory," *INC,* October 1991.

EXHIBIT 7 Sample Estimate

CONNOR ESTIMATE #14058

Date: 03/16	Part: 07570-00035-1 Rev.: D	Who: DD Copy: 12237 Q-Type: R
Cust:	Desc: CLIP PLATEN	Type: CLIP PLATEN S-Terr: 02

Material Specification

		Quantity:	10,000	0	0	0	0

Material: 301-STAINLESS STEEL   Spec: MIL-s-5059, FULL HARD
   Size: .018±.0009 × 1.220±.005
Supplier: GIBBS   Edge: SLIT
   Contact: BOB V.   Temper: FULL HARD

Ship Wt/M: 0.000 Feed/ea: 3.770   Delivery: 7-10 DAYS Min $: 0
Weight/M: 0+ [24,000 + 5.1% scrap] = 25.224

Weight:	(.253)	(0)	(0)	(0)	(0)
$/lb.:	(2.550)	(0.000)	(0.000)	(0.000)	(0.000)
Freight:	0.00	0.00	0.00	0.00	0.00
Other:	0	0	0	0	0
Mat Cost:	645	0	0	0	0

Operations & Outside Processing

Notes	Seq.	Oper.	Dept	S/U	ReSetPc	Pcs/Hr	S/US	Run$	Mch% Yld Min $				
	01	Four-Slide	F	20	0	2500	50	45		1180	0	0	0	0
	02	Stress Rel		0	0	0	0	0		0	0	0	0	0
	03	Passivate	K	0	0	3000	30	25		83	0	0	0	0
	04	SIZE	S	2	0	600	35	25		487	0	0	0	0
100% SORT	05	100% Insp.	S	1	0	500	35	25		535	0	0	0	0
AND REWORK														
PACK 100 PCS	06	Package	S	2	0	1000	35	25		320	0	0	0	0
PER POLY BAG														

PURCH:

Conv Cost:	2605	0	0	0	0
Out/Proc:	0	0	0	0	0
Cost of Mfg:	3250	0	0	0	0

O & N:

Mat MrkUp: 35	226	0	0	0	0
O/P MrkUp: 35	0	0	0	0	0
Conv Mrkup <L>	(1,412)	(0.000)	(0.000)	(0.000)	(0.000)
Conv MrkUp $:	3678	0	0	0	0
Tot MrkUp:	3904	0	0	0	0
NREC (Amort.):	0	0	0	0	0
TL & TM:	55	0	0	0	0
Other:	0	0	0	0	0
Sub-Asmbly:	0	0	0	0	0

MFG: 1) PACKAGE 100 PCS PER BAG, TAG BAG WITH LABEL WITH
THE PART NUMBER, COUNTRY OF ORIGIN AND PACKAGING
QUANTITY PRINTED ON IT ADHERED TO THE BAG. (100 PIECES)
BOXES MUST BE STAMPED ALSO WITH SPECIAL STAMP MADE UP
2.)2,000 PCS IN STOCK AT LOC. WHR8MR, NOT VERIFIED.

Tot Calc $:	7209	0	0	0	0
Calc. $/ea:	0.7209	0.0000	0.0000	0.0000	0.0000
Final $/ea:	0.7210	0.0000	0.0000	0.0000	0.0000
WREC Charge:					

EST:

Delivery:	7-9 WEEKS A.R.O.
	1 RUN 1 DELIVERY.

No Tooling or NREC

Vendor:
Desc:
   0 (D) + 0 (M) × $50 = 0 (lab) + 0 (mat) = 0
Tool Life (pcs): 2000000 Tool Maintenance (hrs/100,000 pcs): 11

Conversion Hrs:	79	0	0	0	0
% Out of Pkt:	9	0	0	0	0
Avg $/hr:	82	0	0	0	0

EXHIBIT 8   Sample Shop Order

P/N: 39D05098L07
Type: TAP.COMP
Qty: 3,000,000

S/O # 12384

10/17
Pg 1 of 2

BILL TO	SHIP TO
P/N: 39D05098L07 Rev: J CONTACT BATTERY POS. Qty: 3,000,000 $0.4240/E Ship Tol: ±0 Exp$: 0	Cst#: 301961 Ter: 98 Tax: N Trms: 1/2% 10 Days, Net 30	

P/O #: CK.31190PP00
Takn By: JAN
Entd By: JD
Reorder: Yes   Prev #: 11068
Buyer: DOUG OBER
Phone:
Fax:

Mfg Codes

Avg: 121   TV#: 1272000.00
O/P: 46   CV#: 686880.00
Code: 153K1
Est#: 12492

Quality Notes

Material Specification

Type: 302-Stainless Steel
Size: .027+.0005
Spec: ASTM A 313,NICKEL COATED,
     COND B, CLASS1
Edge:
Temper:

Set-up: 0
Lbs./M: 1.000   Tot Lbs: 3000
Ship Wt: 0.000   Feed/ea: 5.750

Supplier: _____
On Hand: _____
P/O #: _____
Est $/lb: 3.100 Min $ 50
Est Frt: 0.00

Contact: _____
Due: _____
Qty Ord: _____
Price/Lb: _____

Issue Date				
Vendor				
P/O #				
Heat #				

Operations & Outside Processing

Notes/Specs	Seq	Oper.	Dept	S/U	ReSet	Pcs/Hr	RunHrs	Mach%	Yield	P/O#	QCP	Process Approval
SET UP 2 MACHINES	01	Itaya	I	50	429	600	5000	35	0			
ON LINE	02	Stress Rel	I	0	0	0	0	0	0			
	03	Passivate	K	1	0	12000	250	0	0			
.000040 MIN PER PRINT	04	GOLD PLATE	O/P	$ 185.00/M					0			
INCLUDING PACKAGING												
	89	Final Insp	0	0	0	0	0	0	0			
$ 1.19 PER TRAY,$.2 TRAYS	99	TRAYS		PUR $ 5.00/M					0			
PER M				Vendor: CAPAC Contact:								

Mfg Notes

1) INSPECTION \ GOLD PLATING \ SPC \ PACKAGING | LOT
CONTROL -- MUST BE PERFORMED IN ACCORDANCE WITH WRITTEN
QUALITY PLANS.
2) PLATING PRICE QUOTED BY $190.00/M
PACKAGED. GOLD SURCHARGE OF .30/M BASED ON $400 GOLD.
USE THESE NUMBERS ON PLATING P.O.

Qualifications & Notes

1) GOLD SURCHARGE OF $0.0003/EA BASED ON #380 GOLD
APPLIES. (SURCHARGE BASED ON PER DOLLAR MOVEMENT
IN THE PRICE OF GOLD. BASED ON ENGELHARDT FAB
PRICE.)

Special Instructions

* ALL SHIPMENTS SHIPPING DIRECT TO   ARE TO
SHIP FED EXPRESS-PRIORITY 1/NEXT DAY SERVICE. FREIGHT
COLLECT.

* 12/31/99 SCHEDULE SHARING - OK TO SHIP ONE WEEK EARLY.
NO OVERSHIPMENTS UNLESS AUTHORIZED.

Shipments Record

Date	Qty.	Bal.	Via	# Cont

Final Shipment Info.

Counted By: Pcs:

Weight: Boxes:

Sched. Releases

Date	Qty
10/25/91	112000
10/30/91	71000
11/18/91	73000
11/25/91	60000
12/02/91	60000
12/09/91	60000
12/16/91	60000
12/23/91	60000
12/30/91	50000
01/06/92	50000
01/13/92	50000
01/20/92	50000
02/10/92	44800
02/17/92	50400
02/24/92	44800
03/02/92	50400
03/09/92	44800
03/16/92	50400
03/23/92	44800
03/30/92	50400

More Page 2

12384

EXHIBIT 9 Los Angeles Division Floor Plan

Note: The number of personal computers in each area of the plant is in parentheses. All of the computers were IBM PC compatible and most were 286s and 386-SXs, costing approximately $1,200-2,000 each. All computers were networked using a Novell local area network that could support up to 100 computers or other input/output devices (printers, fax machines, etc.). The total cost of purchasing and installing the local area network was $75,000.

Exhibit 9). Quarrey held a number of training sessions for the office employees as well as the shop and soon the system was being used throughout the division. Quarrey recalled:

> We quickly showed the system to them and they immediately began using it. Since that day, we have never gone back to the old handwritten way of doing estimates and shop orders. Every day, someone logs in and pulls up the shop order screen. Then, all the employee has to do is type in the shop order number and hit the "page down" or other function keys until it reaches the desired screen, which can be left on all day and then the network shuts it down at night. Since I was working in Los Angeles full time, I was always around if they had questions, but generally, they just asked each other instead of asking me.

One machine operator explained:

> I had never used a computer before. At first, it was really scary. But, the way it is set up, it is easy—anyone can do it. Most of the people here have just asked each other how to use it and that way we don't have to worry about feeling stupid. If there's ever a problem, you can look above the computer where there's a key to the commands.

As a result of this technology, the way the Los Angeles division did business dramatically changed (see Exhibit 10). Customer service representatives eliminated the use of carbon copies and began doing all of their work on the computer. When they received phone calls from customers about a particular job, they immediately pulled the information up on the computer screen instead of weeding through outdated files. The engineers' estimating program reduced the calculation time for trial quotes from hours to minutes. With access to historical information, the customer service representatives did most of their own estimating without the assistance of the engineering department. And salespeople, who had previously relied

EXHIBIT 10 Connor Product Service Delivery Information Flow

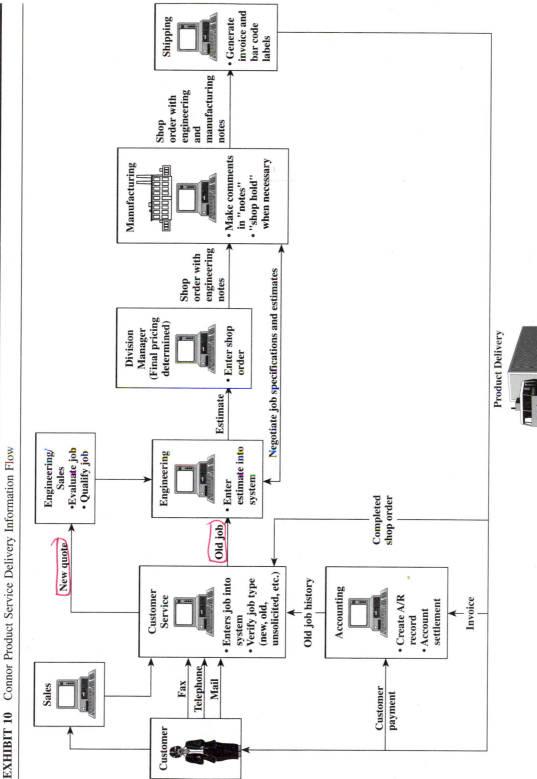

Note: Arrows denote product/service delivery process information flow.

on phone calls and handwritten reports to keep the shop up to date about each customer's needs, began using PCs exclusively.

The Next Step

By the close of 1990, the Los Angeles division had already begun to see dramatic improvements. Just within the first few months of using the system, run speeds on a number of jobs had increased by as much as 20 percent. Repeat defective jobs had reduced from 14 percent in 1989 to 4 percent, and credits issued to customers fell from 4 percent of sales to .5 percent during the same period. Over the past two years, late jobs had declined from 10 percent of backlog to less than 1 percent. The plant's head count had dropped through attrition by 15, while its sales had risen 28 percent to an annual level of $10 million.

Customers began to take note of Connor's service and quality record. Annual quality ratings had soared to near perfection and customers were hiring Connor despite its higher prices. Sloss was even seeing results in his bottom line when Los Angeles's pre-tax profit rose 5 percent in 1990. Employee ownership had reached 42 percent and Connor's stock value had increased 35 percent in the past year.

With such positive results, Quarrey and Sloss were tempted to quickly roll out the system to the other divisions. Quarrey thought back to the meeting during which he had introduced the system to the other managers:

> At that meeting, we brought in a few monitors, hooked them all up to one computer, and went through how the software worked. The meeting went for four hours that afternoon and the discussion continued through dinner. While the managers generally seemed excited, they had a lot of questions. The main one was whether the system would really work in the smaller divisions. In the Los Angeles shop where you have 100 people, things like the "shop hold" really cut through the layers. You may not need to do that in San Jose or Portland, where internal communication is already excellent.

In San Jose, a plant manager noted:

> I have some concerns about switching from Job Boss to the new software. We have already invested a lot in training everyone in the office to use our current system. What if we don't like some of the new ways of doing things? Even if we do like it, we're already making record profits in San Jose—why throw our information systems up in the air?

Others were very enthusiastic. The quality control manager from Portland, Carl Brandstetter, insisted that it would be a wise move for their facility:

> We absolutely want to go to Connor Software. We don't need most of that packaged software, so custom is perfect for us. We have long recognized the limitations of the System 36. We rail against it every day. Data entry is counter-intuitive, and to correct an error is unacceptably complex. Plus, we don't even have word processors or spreadsheets. What we have now is a dog. We'll all probably go out to lunch if we get the new system!

Another manager added:

> Currently, there's a lag between when something is pulled and when it is documented. Since it is done manually, it is also very error prone. In this world, we have to respond to our customer immediately, and if we can pull information up on a screen and answer a customer's question right there on the phone, our relationships with customers will improve.

Another division manager explained:

> This is all about the information chain. People should be able to review any information they want. The system should essentially say, "We're not keeping any secrets from you." Hopefully, it would be a tool in the shop for when people are running a job and they need additional information. They can walk over to the terminal, call up the job, and do something about it. I don't know how much they will actually use it, but I think just the fact that we are willing to share the information will make them feel good.

Quarrey and Sloss considered their options carefully. On one hand, Los Angeles had been a great success—why not push the system out further? However, Los Angeles was large enough and communicating information was difficult enough so that the division easily benefited from such technology. And maybe the smaller divisions, in which communicating information was inherently easier, would find it too structured and bureau- cratic. In addition, Sloss wondered whether the success of the Los Angeles experiment had been largely due to the unique combination of Quarrey's involvement and the circumstances of the particular plant. Quarrey and Sloss wondered how to proceed.

Chapter 7

IT between Organizations:
Interorganizational Systems

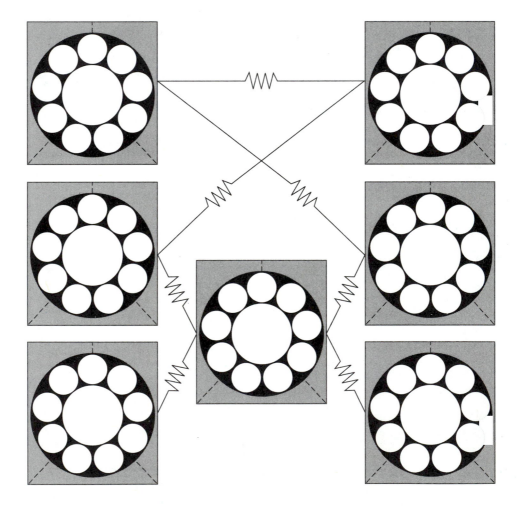

INTRODUCTION

"The right information at the right time is nine-tenths of any battle."

—Napoleon Bonaparte

Chapter 6 described how IT is increasingly being deployed to bring down the "brick walls" that previously impeded information flows between functional areas within organizations. IT is also being used to penetrate organizational boundaries, as firms link with their suppliers, distributors, customers, regulators, and even competitors.

Increasing numbers of firms are using IT to exchange information electronically with other organizations. This chapter discusses firms' motivations for participating in *interorganizational systems (IOS),* and issues surrounding their development and use.

Definitions

An *IOS* is a networked information system used by two or more separate organizations to perform a joint business function. An IOS can be highly automated, with very little human intervention. For example, an IOS connecting multiple components suppliers with a manufacturer may automatically scan suppliers' prices and inventory stock levels and place orders based on the manufacturer's need for certain components. Other IOS are less automated. For example, when travel agents log onto airline reservations systems, they retain control over the flight selection. In contrast, there are automated scanning systems that run overnight, selecting those flights that most closely match the customer's price or departure/arrival preferences.

Electronic data interchange (EDI) describes the standards necessary for exchanging data over an IOS. The universal product code (UPC), combined with network transmission protocols and other standards, constitutes an EDI standard.

An *IOS participant* is a direct party to the exchange of data over an IOS. Participants can include organizations in the buyer-supplier chain, competitors, regulators, or some combination of these. An *IOS host* may serve at one or both of two levels:

Content host: The organization or consortium of organizations that develop and maintain the IOS application software (such as an airline travel-agency reservation system).

Conduit host: The organization that provides the network hardware and software. The conduit host may be a value-added network provider (such as GE Information Services or Tymnet) or a content host using lines leased from a common carrier (such as AT&T or MCI) or private network capabilities (lines, microwave towers, satellites).

Often, hosts are also participants in the IOS. For example, American Airlines and United Airlines each developed travel-agency reservations systems that list their flights in addition to those of others. In exchange for their considerable investments in developing and maintaining these complex systems (approximately $500 million each over about two decades), the hosts gained access to the other participants' flight schedules, prices, and other information.

A content or conduit host that is not a participant and profits from provision of the application or conduit (as opposed to the data exchanged on it) is an *IOS facilitator,* or *nonparticipating host.* For example, CIRRUS, which is not a bank, provides a nationwide network of automated teller machines, giving customers of subscribing banks 24-hour access to their ATM systems. Another facilitator, General Electric Information Services, provides value-added network services such as EDI*EXPRESS, which General Motors uses to exchange invoices, product specifications, and other data with 2,000 automotive parts suppliers in six European countries.

MOTIVATIONS FOR IOS

Reasons for creating or participating in an IOS include the following:

Reduce paperwork and improve transaction efficiency.

Improve control of inventories/suppliers.

Strengthen channel control.

Improve customer relationships.

Share resources/risks.

These are described next.

Reduce Paperwork and Improve Transaction Efficiency

One motivation for an IOS is comparable to the motivation for automating clerical processes: reduce the mountains of paper records, the corps of clerical employees handling them, and the errors inherent in such manual processes. These efficiency gains alone may be sufficient to justify the expense of developing and maintaining an IOS; however, participants may have one or more additional motives.

Improve Control of Inventories/Suppliers

Here the motivation may be to negotiate better prices with suppliers, monitor and resolve components-quality problems more closely, or reduce inventory holding costs (which are driven by the costs of warehouse space and interest expense) by implementing just-in-time or flexible manufacturing. The General Electric appliance division automatically places orders with vendors worldwide, based on predetermined order points. Similarly, automotive-parts suppliers wanting General Motors's business are required to adhere to EDI standards established by an automotive industry association. The supply ordering system, which is integrated with GM's inventory management systems, gives GM the capability to automatically identify which stocks are in low supply, which suppliers have sufficient stock to meet GM's needs, and at what price. In turn, this raises GM's bargaining power and lowers the suppliers' prices. Some plants' CAD/CAM systems (computer-aided design and manufacturing) are also integrated with the IOS so that suppliers' computers can communicate directly with GM's robot-based assembly lines. Clearly, GM's role as host in this example gives them substantial benefits.

Many other manufacturing firms are developing such systems in support of just-in-time manufacturing, a strategy that reduces inventory holding costs by placing orders only when they are needed and having them filled quickly. A supply-side IOS may also be used to strengthen quality control by giving suppliers rapid feedback about goods that do not pass the recipient's quality standards.

Strengthen Channel Control

Channel-oriented IOS may be used to improve distributor product awareness, to raise distributor switching costs (make giving business to a competitor less appealing), or to raise entry barriers (make it harder for new competitors to enter the industry). The airline reservation systems are an excellent example of these motivations. After airline deregulation in 1978, and the resulting proliferation of fares, routes, and carriers, the travel agent's importance as a sales channel increased. Recognizing that, both American Airlines and United Airlines raced to convert their in-house reservation systems to multicarrier systems that travel agents could use. Today, travel-agency airline reservation systems account for 90 percent of all airline ticket sales. Some nonparticipating airlines accused the hosts of unfairly excluding airlines whose routes competed against them. Participating airlines accused the hosts of biasing their screen displays to favor their own flights. Whether or not the specific allegations are true, it remains true that both American and United have direct communication linkages with the travel agencies, giving them increased control over this important selling channel.

Their competitors, who either could not afford to develop their own systems or found that agents were not interested in adding yet another terminal to their crowded desks, do not. In addition, the host airlines have found that the sale of their reservation services to participating airlines is more lucrative than are the profits generated from the actual passenger fares.

In another example, a firm that sells livestock feeds collaborated with a major computer manufacturer to put personal-computer-based systems on the desks of their key selling channel, the local feed and grain distributors. The system included office-management software and network-based order-entry and information applications that tied the distributor closer to the host. Once that system was developed, the host firm then began promoting a new line of personal computer-based systems for sale by the distributor to farmers. This project offered two potential benefits: in the short term, income from sales of the PC systems; in the longer term, the host planned to eventually sell feed and grain directly to larger farmers, bypassing the distributor and increasing its own margins. Virtually any IOS that works to *strengthen* a channel can also be designed to eventually *bypass* that channel, an observation that distributors will do well to keep in mind.

Improve Customer Relationships

Examples in this area are growing as industrial customers have come to expect more and companies are recognizing the opportunities for cultivating long-term relationships with them. The ultimate objective of relationship marketing is to increase the chance that a given customer will buy perishable products repeatedly, and buy upgrades, enhancements, and new products.

Some firms use IOS to make the process of learning about and acquiring their products faster, easier, and cheaper. This was a motivation of American Hospital Supply (AHS) when they developed ASAP, an IOS that took much of the time and paperwork out of ordering their goods. Instead of flipping through pages of a catalog and placing a telephone order, hospital purchasing agents selected and ordered items on their terminal screens. Product and price updates were automatic, and the purchasing manager could store standard orders, minimizing keystrokes. AHS was able to fill the orders more rapidly, since they were fed electronically into the AHS warehouse inventory system.

IOS may also deliver value-added services on top of existing products. The AHS system gave hospital purchasing agents inventory-management software that helped them reduce their inventory costs even though they were paying a little more for each item purchased from AHS. In other examples, Trane and Carrier, both suppliers of air conditioners, provide architectural firms with personal computer software that helps the architect select and design appropriate heating, ventilation, and air conditioning equipment (duct work, compressors, etc.) and incorporate the specifications in the construction blueprints. Each firm's design software, of course, highlights its own product line and is linked to a networked application for ordering those products.

When combined with database marketing techniques, IOS can deliver customized promotions targeted to more and more narrowly defined customer segments. These techniques, commonly used for selling consumer products via direct mail, are increasingly used in industrial marketing as well.

Share Resources/Risks

IOS among nonprofit organizations—government and social services agencies, libraries, universities, etc.—are common. Interlibrary loan systems, for example, make it possible for libraries to focus their acquisitions while still giving patrons broad access to materials. Universities share supercomputing and information-intensive R&D resources over IOS, and firms in some high-tech industries are also doing so. Joining forces can make it possible for organizations to reduce their investment in IOS hardware and software development and their exposure to technical and business risks. For example, in Europe during the late 1980s, two coalitions of airlines were formed—Amadeus and Galileo—to participate in reservations systems as alternatives to SABRE and Apollo. By cooperating, competitors may regain channel-control parity. Another coalition of competitors is IVANS, the Insurance Value-Added Network Services, which gives independent insurance agents access to property and casualty companies' prices and terms, and reduces the channel control of large insurance companies' IOS. In this example, an industry trade association initiated the project. Similarly, another trade association sponsored MEMA/Transnet, an IOS that connects manufacturers and retailers in the auto parts industry.

Integration and Synergy without Ownership

When firms collaborate to share resources through IOS, they challenge traditional management theory. For example, according to conventional theory, *vertical integration* refers to the extent to which a company owns resources from raw materials (through backward integration, by acquiring suppliers) through to the end customer (through forward integration, by acquiring distribution/marketing channels). Scale economies may also be obtained if, for example, the merging firms have similar production requirements or sales forces. When a firm owns its sources of raw materials and its distribution channels, it gains control over these resources but loses flexibility in responding to changes in its environment, because of the fixed expenses of employees, factories, warehouses, and other investments. Firms also acquire other firms in order to capture "synergy" by combining the strongest capabilities of each organization. For example, one firm in the medical-equipment business may have a lock on the distribution channels, yet another that the first firm wishes to acquire has a recent track record of innovative and profitable new products. In acquiring a firm for synergy, the organization also takes on all the weaknesses of the acquired firm. Furthermore, sometimes—a clash of cultures or systems, perhaps—the sum of the combined parts does not add to a viable new whole.

Partnerships based on IOS can sometimes give firms many of the integration and synergy benefits associated with ownership, without its drawbacks. Consider, for example, the travel industry. Management of United Airlines, in acquiring Hertz Rent-A-Car and Westin Hotels, envisioned a single, integrated travel-services firm, under one corporate umbrella—Allegis Corporation. Taking advantage of the sophisticated expertise of United's information systems division, the customer databases of the three would be merged, and new customers identified. Full-service travel packages and a merged frequent-travel plan would increase customer loyalty and the firm's profits. It sounded great—but Allegis did not succeed in achieving these synergies. In contrast, other players in the travel industry are forming coalitions instead of mergers. For example, AMRIS, a subsidiary of American Airlines, is collaborating with Hilton, Marriott, and Budget Rent-a-Car to develop an integrated travel reservation system that can offer most of the vision of Allegis—but without the burden of becoming a merged behemoth.

Access to information and shared IT resources can largely replace control by ownership. As the discussion regarding supplier-manufacturer-distributor relations suggested, an IOS host can achieve ownership-style integration benefits through networked IT, at the expense of other participants in the IOS. For example, GM was able to reduce the bargaining power of its suppliers when they were required to link up. Today, however, potential IOS participants are more sophisticated in understanding the balance-of-power implications of an IOS, so there are fewer opportunities to exert such one-way control. Besides, managers in many industries, like the travel example above, are exploring the long-term advantages of cooperative win-win strategies over "I win, you lose" approaches.[1] Consider the IOS example below:

> Several US retail, apparel, and textile companies . . . have linked their business processes to speed up reordering of apparel. When Dillard's (department store) inventory of a particular pants style falls below a specified level, Haggar (apparel manufacturer) is notified electronically. If Haggar does not have the cloth to manufacture the pants, Burlington Industries (textile manufacturer) is notified electronically . . . Information technology is the major vehicle by which this interorganizational linkage is executed.[2]

ISSUES FOR IOS HOSTS AND PARTICIPANTS

IOS "risks" fall into four main categories: technical, competitive, legal/regulatory, and organizational.

---

[1] See Russell Johnston and Paul R. Lawrence, "Beyond Vertical Integration—the Rise of the Value-Adding Partnership," *Harvard Business Review* (July–August 1988). See also Benn R. Konsynski and F. Warren McFarlan, "Information Partnerships—Shared Data, Shared Scale," *Harvard Business Review* (September–October, 1990).

[2] Thomas H. Davenport and James E. Short, "The New Industrial Engineering: Information Technology and Business Process Redesign," *Sloan Management Review* (Summer 1990).

IOS Classified by Motivation and Structure

Benn Konsynski* assessed IOS according to the hosts' intent (motivation) and the structure of the linkage. He identified four types of IOS:

Marketing and logistics IOS link buyers and suppliers. Marketing linkages offer significant product or service differentiation. Industrial examples: Baxter Healthcare ASAP Express, Levi Strauss LEVILINK, and Haggar HOTS. Logistics IOS influence inventory and ordering procedures (Kmart and Gillette, Caterpillar Tractor SPEED and General Motors EPIC).

Industry platforms represent the initiative of one or more players to bring economies of scale and reduce costs for all participants. Examples: TRANSNET (auto parts), IVANS (insurance).

Virtual systems arise when standards (such as VICS codes, X.12, and EDIFACT) emerge among a community of market participants. Each participant selects and implements their systems. Industry examples: WINS (warehousing) and TALC (textiles). Public examples: Singapore TradeNet, Hong Kong TradeLink, Norway TVINN, and Australia TradeGate.

In *electronic market access forums*, a third-party facilitator performs many essential market functions, such as seller/buyer identification, matching, negotiation, settlement, etc. The facilitator enforces trading rules. Examples: American Gem Market System (gemstones), TELCOT (cotton), Inventory Locator Services (airplane parts), Autoinfo (auto dismantlers), and Reuters INSTINET.

Figure 7–1 illustrates these four types.

FIGURE 7–1

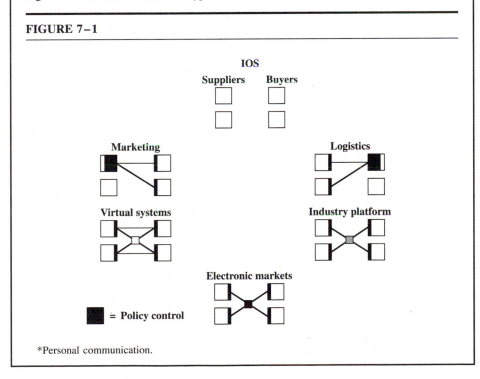

*Personal communication.

Technical Risks

Wide-area networking is a technology that only a small number of firms managed on their own until quite recently. A firm that is already experienced in wide-area networking applications is exposed to less risk as a conduit host than a firm that does not have this in-house expertise. For content hosts, the technical risk of developing the IOS application software can be extensive. A firm that has already developed complex applications software is less exposed to this risk than one that has worked primarily with off-the-shelf software or small-scale systems. Technical risks also increase with increased numbers of participants and increased geographic scope. For example, multinational IOS must accommodate to varied national telecommunications infrastructures, which translate to varied network reliability.

Competitive Risks

Many organizations that joined IOS as participants in the 1980s did so on the authority of rather junior administrators, who justified participation primarily on efficiency grounds. By allowing such decisions to be made without senior-level review, these firms were exposed to the risks of greatly reduced bargaining power, as noted below:

> Under the guise of faster information flow and greater data integrity, the new system suddenly shifts inventory holding costs and business risks to a supplier. Such an imbalance would clearly far outweigh any advantages that the more efficient information system brings to the supplier.[3]

For potential participants, a competitive risk is inherent in the question of whether or not to join an IOS. Many of the airlines that ignored the importance of computerized reservations systems—including Frontier, Eastern, Braniff, and People Express—are no longer going concerns. People Express, founded in 1981, grew to become the world's fifth-largest airline, with $2 billion in revenues, in less than five years. However, in 1985 its fortunes were dramatically reversed, and in 1986: "Losses piled up, and Burr finally sold the business to rival Texas Air Corp. for only $4 a share—about one-sixth the value of People stock at its high in mid-1983."[4]

What happened? Donald Burr, the founder of People Express, points to his own misunderstanding of the changing role of IT in the airline industry. He had decided at the outset that his no-frills strategy had no room for an expensive reservation system like American Airline's SABRE or United's Apollo, which linked those airlines with travel agents and with competing airlines. Burr now maintains that he misjudged the value of the data residing in those systems.[5] United and American were able to use their systems for pinpointed yield management. These competitors could match

---

[3]James I. Cash, Jr., and Benn R. Konsynski, "IS Redraws Competitive Boundaries," *Harvard Business Review* (March–April 1985).

[4]John A. Byrne, "Donald Burr May Be Ready to Take to the Skies Again," *Business Week* (January 16, 1989): 74–75.

[5]See, for example, David H. Freedman, "Canceled Flights," *CIO* 2(7) (April 1989): 48–54.

People's low prices selectively, by selling only as many loss-leader, bargain-priced seats as were necessary to capture People's customers. On the other hand, some airlines—Midway, Southwest, and others—invented new ways to compete that relied less heavily on the travel agent channel, and hence were not dependent on their reservation systems.

Another competitive risk is timing. In many arenas, first-mover advantages can be compelling. For example, had United and American not introduced their reservation systems to travel agents in roughly the same time frame, one of them might have locked the other out of the market, causing a huge loss on the development costs. As it was, they succeeded in locking others out of the reservation-systems business for a number of years, since travel agents were not interested in having many terminals on their desks (now that these applications run on microcomputers, that switching cost has been reduced). Similarly, American Hospital Supply reaped huge rewards from introducing ASAP to its customers long before its competitors could respond in kind. On the other hand, technological advances can help companies "leapfrog" over each other, greatly reducing first-mover advantages. Sometimes being a fast follower can be even more profitable than being the leader. For example, Trane introduced the first mainframe-based IOS with its architects, and converted quite a lot of Carrier customers to its product line. A few years later, Carrier recaptured much of what it had lost by introducing the first microcomputer-based version. Trane rebounded with a system that combined the best of the PC and mainframe worlds, and the "leapfrog wars" continued.

Legal and Regulatory Risks

IOS challenge existing laws and regulations, which were not written with networked IT in mind. For example, when does the electronic message passing over an IOS actually become an order or a contract? What happens when data passing over the IOS are lost or distorted? Both content and conduit hosts face legal risks relating to the integrity and security of the data being exchanged over the IOS. Banks' electronic funds-transfer systems incorporate multiple stringent measures in applications and network software for protecting the security and integrity of customer data. Geographic scope is again an issue, since different countries have varied laws concerning data privacy safeguards, and different penalties for infractions.

In the 1960s, Bunker Ramo tried to develop an IOS for the brokerage business. They were unable to do so because AT&T, at the time a regulated monopoly, had control of the telephone lines over which the data were to be transferred. Deregulation of the telecommunications industry in the United States removed that obstacle, although it remains a hurdle in some nations. Countries also vary in their commerce and labor regulations. When an IOS involves competitors, what constitutes unfair business practice? The case of Frontier Airlines versus United offers an example of competitive success exposing an IOS host to legal and regulatory risks. United made a very large investment to develop the Apollo reservations system. United managers felt that since they built the system they had the right to control access to it, determine prices for its use, and glean from it data useful for rapid decision making. In 1983,

Frontier filed a case against United, which accused them of unfairly restricting access to Apollo, charging excessive and inconsistent fees, and giving itself access to information about participating carriers without offering them comparable access. Frontier went out of business before these concerns were resolved, but lawsuits continue, as regulators consider whether airline reservation systems are anticompetitive. These deliberations will affect the value consumers receive and the innovation-related risks that firms are willing to take.

Organizational Risks

Throughout this book we have demonstrated how a change in one organizational element—structure, control systems, people, and information resources—can lead to changes in the other organizational elements. Not surprisingly, then, IOS can impact structure, systems, and people. For example, McKesson Corporation, a large distributor of health and beauty products, created an IOS for selling its products to independent drugstores. The IOS caused McKesson to eliminate 500 clerical jobs (formerly assigned to taking telephone orders), reduce its buying staff from 140 to 12, and eliminate 80 of its 134 warehouses—all while growing sales from $900 million to over $5 billion.[6] Such changes do not happen automatically; they must be managed well.

As noted above, often the decision to participate in an IOS is made at a low organizational level. When this occurs, the risk of unanticipated impacts increases. For example, if an IOS is effectively used as a marketing and sales tool, what happens to the sales force? Will their commissions decline, and, if so, what measures should be taken to keep them motivated and productive? If an IOS is integrated into a manufacturing operation, what will be the impact on engineering, quality control, and related functions? What about the risk of sabotage by disgruntled employees (such as those that may be displaced by the new system)? There are many instances of an employee being fired and subsequently stealing proprietary information, planting a destructive software virus, or otherwise damaging or compromising corporate information resources. The threat of such damage to an IOS exposes the organization to a far broader range of risks.

Participants and hosts are exposed to different varieties and levels of these risks. For participants, the most compelling issue is, what control do we give up if we join, and what do we lose if we do not join?

As noted above, an IOS host can be involved as a content host, conduit host, or both. In addition, a host may or may not be a participant in the IOS. Variations in these arrangements result in varied levels of exposure to risks, and corresponding variations in the potential financial returns from IOS. Figure 7–2 summarizes the relative risks faced by hosts of varying categories.

The conduit-only host, or facilitator, is exposed to the lowest risk (and correspondingly, low to moderate financial returns) for several reasons. First, technical risks will

---

[6]Johnston and Lawrence, 1988, op cit.

FIGURE 7–2 Varied Risks of Host Arrangements

	Not a Participant	*Participant*
Conduit and content	Moderate risk moderate-high returns	Very high risk very high complexity very high potential returns
Content only	Information utility moderate risk/return	Very high risk high potential returns
Conduit only	Lowest risk commodity business	(Not common)

---

be low to moderate if this firm has already served as a facilitator for other systems. Second, most of the expenses associated with the conduit are not sunk costs. This is because if the IOS application fails, the conduit capacity can be redirected to any number of other networked applications. Third, as a nonparticipant, this host is not being exposed to the same level of competitive, regulatory, and organizational risks faced by the participants. Potential returns (in terms of network fees) may be only moderate, however, especially as networks shift toward a commodity business.

Content hosts that are also participants represent high levels of risk, but also high potential returns. The investment in networking capability and/or IOS applications can be in the hundreds of millions of dollars, a risk that is compounded by the risks of late entry, leapfrogging, and regulatory changes. The returns, however, can be substantial. The investments made by American, United, American Hospital Supply, McKesson Corporation, and others in the "IOS Hall of Fame" were returned many times over in increased market shares. However, as the next section discusses, it is not clear whether similar returns can be achieved in those IOS that are developed in the future.

IOS IN THE FUTURE

In 1966, Felix Kaufman wrote in *Harvard Business Review* of the potential of IOS:

> Information handling could become neutral ground. Information processes could be conducted at a uniformly high level of efficiency, with all users having equal access to the lowest-cost service. Perhaps users could purchase such services from data processing utilities.[7]

In Kaufman's view of information handling as a "utility," information and data-processing activities would be common goods, accessible to all on an equal basis. In one sense his predictions were realized, in that time-sharing companies provided

---

[7]Felix Kaufman, "Data Systems That Cross Company Boundaries," *Harvard Business Review* (January–February 1966): 141.

data-processing services on a consistent basis to all comers in the 1960s and 1970s (until inexpensive mini-computers and subsequently microcomputers replaced most time-shared services). Also, open access to numerous online databases (at a price) provides individual and corporate users with up-to-date information on stock prices, news stories, and scholarly research. On the other hand, many firms have identified ways to develop and use IOS that provide selective, not universal, access. This selectivity gave some IOS hosts and some participants a long-lasting competitive advantage. However, firms are now far less likely to gain a sustainable advantage based on one-way supplier or channel control, because more knowledgeable consumers, regulators, and potential participants are discouraging such IOS.

Although information handling is not likely to become the "neutral ground" predicted by Kaufman, it is less likely to lead directly to competitive advantages in the coming decades. Max Hopper, who directed American Airlines's SABRE system for many years, believes that IOS have shifted from being a strategic advantage to being a competitive necessity in many industries: "Think of it as a technology treadmill: companies will have to run harder and harder just to stay in place."[8] Indeed, the recent turmoil in the airline industry suggests that reservation systems, and the yield-management techniques they spawned, may have contributed to a nearly self-destructing industry, as one company after another fails.

Some observers believe that the real IOS winners in the future will be a new crop of small, flexible organizations that take advantage of IT-driven integration and synergy. The scale economies that helped big companies get bigger in the 1960s, 1970s, and 1980s may no longer be sufficient to offset the disadvantages of size and complexity, especially in terms of flexibility.

> Most historians agree that the development of cheap, centralized power and efficient but costly production machinery tipped the competitive advantage toward large companies that could achieve economies of scale. Today, low-cost computing and communication seem to be tipping the competitive advantage back toward partnerships of smaller companies . . .[9]

The primary driver of this small-business renaissance appears to be interorganizational systems. But instead of using IOS as shackles that bind suppliers to them or raise new technological barriers to entry, many of these firms are concentrating on IOS applications that optimize operations across an industry's value-added chain, thereby delivering greater value to the end-customer. They are based more on models of cooperation than on models of competition.

IOS—whether competitive or cooperative—are likely to continue to emerge and be refined in the coming decades, thanks to several key trends. First, the information infrastructure is rapidly improving. International "electronic highways" are rapidly developing, as optical fiber replaces lower-bandwidth cables. Technologies such as VSATs and cellular and radio-frequency communications augment these conduits. Second, standards are coalescing, although there are still significant issues to resolve.

---

[8]Max Hopper, "Rattling SABRE—New Ways to Compete on Information," *Harvard Business Review* (May–June 1990): 121.

[9]Johnston and Lawrence, 1988, op cit.

Third, where previously IOS hosts faced the hurdle of getting dedicated terminals onto participants' desks, now they face the simpler issue of providing software in a few common "flavors" (e.g., Macintosh, Windows, DOS without Windows) and convincing participants to use their own personal computers as gateways to the IOS.

Whatever shape they take, and whichever participants they bring together, interorganizational systems will continue to permeate and transform organizational boundaries.

CASE 7–1: LITHONIA LIGHTING

This case describes an IOS, Light*Link, that Lithonia has pioneered to facilitate the sale of the lighting fixtures they manufacture. Jim McClung, the CEO of Lithonia, must decide whether he should continue with aggressive further development of Light*Link in the face of declining revenues brought about by a slump in the construction business. Lithonia's information services department has budgeted approximately 2 percent of sales for this project. Are the benefits of Light*Link worth spending that amount of money?

Preparation Questions

1. Evaluate the design and architecture of the Light*Link system. What impact has the system had on the process by which Lithonia sells lighting fixtures?
2. How would you value the strategic benefits of Light*Link? Does it give Lithonia a sustainable competitive advantage?
3. If you were Jim McClung, what would you do? If you were Charles Darnell, what would you do?

Case 7–1 Lithonia Lighting*

Atlanta, GA, March 20—National Service Industries reported today that its net income in the second fiscal quarter ended February 28, 1991, declined 33.9 percent to $14.8 million. As a result, earnings per share decreased 34.3 percent from 46 cents a year earlier to 30 cents in the current quarter.

Sidney Kirschner, president and chief executive officer, noted that the quarter was the first in more than a decade in which operating earnings had declined. "We had expected a difficult quarter, given the slowdown in business activity generally and the severe downturn in the nonresidential construction industry, on which our lighting equipment division is dependent . . . We cannot predict when business conditions will improve, and at this time I do not believe it will happen in time for us to extend our record of annual earnings increases . . ."

—National Service Industries News Release, 3/20/91

Jim McClung—president and CEO of Lithonia Lighting, the largest division of National Service Industries (NSI) and the largest American manufacturer of lighting fixtures—surveyed the immaculate surfaces of his wood-paneled office with a calmness that belied a gnawing concern. Outside his first floor window, it was a bright warm winter day in Conyers, Georgia, a small rural-industrial town at the edge of metropolitan Atlanta. Yet weather could sometimes be deceiving, and McClung was far from certain that Lithonia would be in for sunny times ahead. With a war in the Persian Gulf and a serious slump—some would say depression—in the construction business, McClung was facing the prospect of Lithonia's first drop in sales in over 15 years.

As the future of the lighting business became increasingly uncertain, the traditional zeal of the company's investments in information technology (IT) became more difficult to support. Throughout the 1980s, Lithonia's IMS (information and management systems) function, under the direction of Senior Vice President Charles Darnell, had pioneered the use of sophisticated information tools that tied together the myriad players in the company's distribution chain through a system known as LIGHT*LINK℠. The company's growth had been prodigious and had generated impressive profits for its parent company, NSI. Now, with a potentially severe market downturn, it was time for some sober reevaluation of the company's IT policies. Was the company being prescient, or merely reckless? What really *was* the value-added of Lithonia's aggressive IT practices, and what was the best tactic to take in such an uncertain environment? While Darnell was convinced of the merits of IMS's strategic direction over the long term, McClung was less certain of the near-term benefits. "Have we been overly ambitious?" he asked. "Have we been investing a huge amount of money in things that are not entirely warranted by our customers' needs?"

Industry and Company Background

The Early Years

The emergence of large, nationwide lighting fixture companies such as Lithonia had been a relatively recent phenomenon. Lithonia could trace its origin back to 1946, when founder Sam Freeman began to produce fluorescent fixtures in what had been a garage in Lithonia, Georgia. Many other companies in the industry could also trace their origin back to the years after 1945, when the end of World War II led to the creation of a large number of "mom and pop" operations that served regional markets.

Nearly all of Lithonia's senior management team (including Darnell and McClung, a 1964 Harvard Business School graduate) arrived at Lithonia in the early 1960s to find a strong regional company in the midst of a highly fragmented industry. There were few truly national firms; strong regional manufacturers like Lithonia were still the rule. Lithonia had grown into an $18 million business that was strongest in the southeast, with small footholds in several metropolitan markets. Like most companies in the industry, Lithonia was rather unsophisticated in its business practices. Darnell reminisced: "We had no bills of material, no process sheets, and the only automation we had was in payroll. Our prices were inconsistent, our product lines were limited, and our volumes were low."

The goal of the incoming management team was to transform Lithonia into the "number one force in lighting." True to their intentions, Lithonia did indeed grow steadily and rapidly. The company diversified into nonfluorescent products, established more rational prices, focused on customer service and availability, and—in particular—gave special attention to the care and development of its independent sales agencies. In 1969, after several years of outstanding growth, Lithonia was acquired by National Service Industries, Inc.,

---

*Research Associate James D. Berkley prepared this case under the supervision of Professor Nitin Nohria. Copyright © 1991 by the President and Fellows of Harvard College. Harvard Business School case 492-003 (Revised 1992).

a publicly held company with several diversified lines of business. During the 1970s and 1980s, Lithonia's relationship with NSI would provide the company with the capital for further expansion, including money for the development of the ambitious information systems known together as Light*Link.

Consolidation and Complexity

While Lithonia's growth was—with the exception of a few minor acquisitions—largely internal, the company's recent history was hardly typical of the lighting industry as a whole. Since the late 1960s, the industry had witnessed a frenzy of buyouts and consolidations, which by 1990 had resulted in the reduction of a field of over 1,300 companies into nine major ones that accounted for more than three-quarters of industry sales.[1] As large companies with nationwide sales agencies began to dominate the industry, smaller companies found it increasingly difficult to remain viable.

As the structure of the industry had changed, so too had its complexity. Up until the early 1970s, lighting had been considered a fairly simple business. Because energy was relatively cheap and plentiful, accepted guidelines for light levels were high and most buildings were overlighted with a few basic products. When the oil crunch hit in 1973, however, this simplicity began to fade. Since lighting could consume up to 50 percent of the electricity used in a commercial building, complicated new strategies were devised for minimizing the consumption of wattage. Government standards were proposed, and companies raced to market with sophisticated new products they claimed, often disingenuously, to be more efficient. Suddenly, the once simple question of "the right amount of light at the right place at the right time" became extremely complex, and sales agents found themselves called upon to think more like lighting engineers.

Lithonia fared well in the midst of the industry's new complexity. By the early 1980s, Lithonia had

---

[1] "Why Lithonia MIS Won't Lighten Up," *Information Week* (January 14, 1991): 30.

clearly become the nation's largest manufacturer of commercial lighting products, and was particularly strong in supplying fixtures to the commercial and industrial (as opposed to residential) market. Besides its fluorescent division, the company had two other main product divisions that manufactured downlighting, track lighting, industrial and high-intensity lighting, emergency lighting, wiring systems, and wiring controls. Sales and marketing for these divisions were undertaken by functions centralized in Conyers. (see Exhibit 1). Sales in fiscal 1990 were $717 million, with operating profits of $63.9 million. The company employed over 5,300 people, had 12 manufacturing plants in six states and Canada, and stocked 50 field warehouses across North America. Analysts estimated Lithonia to hold an approximately 15 percent share in the U.S. market for lighting fixtures (see Exhibit 2). Lithonia's mission statement, framed in the early 1950s, still provided the company's two mottos: "To Provide the Best Value in Lighting" and "To Be Easy to Do Business With."

How Lithonia Sold Lighting Fixtures

Agencies and the Distribution Chain

Being "easy to do business with" was no easy feat in the commercial lighting industry. Since Lithonia's products were aimed largely at commercial and industrial builders rather than end-user customers, the company was intimately connected to the construction business. Architects, contractors, electrical engineers, distributors, agents: all played a role in Lithonia's success in the sale of its products. "What it all boils down to," noted McClung, "is an extremely complex matrix of players that all relate to one another, all with somewhat different interests to be served."

Because local relationships were so important in selling Lithonia products, Lithonia—like most other lighting companies—found it impractical to sell through its own company salespeople. Instead, the company worked with approximately 85 independent lighting agencies in the U.S. which

EXHIBIT 1   Organization Chart

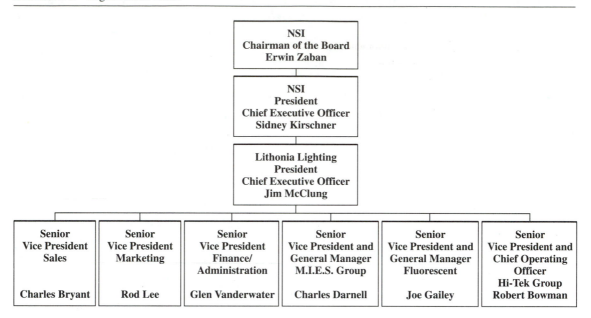

maintained close, often highly personal, relationships with the different players in their geographic area. Despite Lithonia's own internal sales and marketing functions, the day-to-day selling of Lithonia products was handled through these independent agencies, most of which were considered the premier lighting agencies in their market areas. While agents generally sold to electrical distributors which would in turn sell a significant portion of Lithonia products "off the shelf," the major activity of Lithonia agencies was attempting to influence the buying decisions related to specific projects, such as the construction or retrofitting of large buildings.

While agents stocked no products and carried no inventory, they were nonetheless the crucial link between Lithonia and the main buying influences in the construction industry. In a typical scenario, the architect or developer responsible for a building project would hire a consulting engineer (also known as a *specifier*) who, often responding to the wishes of an interior designer, was charged with specifying the type of electrical products the project would require. In turn, general contractors would make bids to meet the specifier's requirements, and would typically subcontract the lighting portion out to an electrical contractor. The electrical contractor who was awarded the lighting job would be responsible for actually purchasing and installing the lighting equipment for the project. This equipment would be purchased through an electrical distributor and often shipped directly to the job site. Since each of these players could play a role in the decision to use Lithonia products, agents did what they could to favorably influence all of them at every stage in the process.

A typical large project involved a large number of people and a considerable amount of politicking. When IBM built an office tower in Atlanta, for example, the building's electrical contractor was based in Dallas. Lithonia's Dallas agency swung into action to persuade the contractor to use Lithonia products, but it was also necessary to persuade a lighting design firm in Philadelphia and IBM's

EXHIBIT 2a Revenues of NSI Divisions, 1990

	Revenues ($ millions)
Lighting equipment (Lithonia)	$ 717
Textile rental	397
Chemicals	233
Insulation service	117
Envelopes	93
Marketing services	49
Men's apparel	42
Total	$1,648

Source: NSI.

EXHIBIT 2b Lithonia Lighting: Selected Financial Data, 1980–1990 ($ thousands)

Year	Sales Revenues	Operating Profit	Assets	Capital Expenses
1990	$717,237	$63,893	$295,059	$30,015
1989	658,657	55,247	263,538	20,299
1988	602,771	50,640	241,741	13,971
1987	559,384	46,977	225,378	16,141
1986	522,056	53,108	214,862	22,877
1985	469,426	47,103	182,432	13,781
1984	383,392	27,651	165,599	8,561
1983	299,794	19,843	138,796	5,990
1982	278,468	23,126	127,114	6,609
1981	263,433	26,580	122,754	6,484
1980	236,730	24,474	103,661	8,216

Source: NSI.

corporate facilities personnel in White Plains, New York. In many cases, the negotiating could begin even before a project was announced, as agencies representing different lighting companies would learn of projects through the grapevine and become factors in the bidding process by which contractors were awarded jobs. Rod Lee, senior vice president of marketing, described the process:

> The whole thing is like an octopus with lots of arms and legs. Right off the bat, all the different people involved immediately say that they're in charge. In

the main, it's very cut-throat and probably one of the purest examples of free enterprise that I know.

While none of Lithonia's partner agencies represented other large companies that could be considered Lithonia competitors, many also sold products of so-called "complementary" companies, mostly small companies whose specialty offerings rounded out the lighting packages sold by Lithonia.

Lithonia versus Its Competitors
Lithonia prided itself on its agency force, and depended upon it perhaps more than other companies

in the industry. Most other large companies in the industry—such as Cooper Lighting, Lithonia's main competitor—had grown through acquisitions. These companies were sometimes represented by more than one agency in a particular area, and some were experiencing difficulties in attempting to consolidate their representation. In addition, companies less successful in securing business often were more dependent upon other members of the distribution chain, such as distributors. Cooper, for example, was strongest in "flow" (off-the-shelf) business of downlighting products, and had forged its strongest alliances with distributors as opposed to agents. Lithonia's strengths, however, were more balanced: while the company was very interested in working well with distributors, its prominence in the "job" segment (which accounted for approximately 70 percent of Lithonia's revenues) served to make Lithonia somewhat less dependent on distributors than other fixture companies (see exhibits 3a, 3b, and 3c). In regions like the Los Angeles Basin, Lithonia had even begun to experiment with the development of "satellite warehouses," large secondary warehouses whose electronic links to distributors made products quickly available to customers. Lithonia's stated objective was to use these capabilities to supplement the capabilities of its distributors. Some distributors had reservations, however, since they felt that these warehouses might eventually serve to undermine the traditional function of the electrical distributor.

The Story of Light*Link

Decentering Lithonia

As Lithonia had grown, the scope and size of its business had become an increasing burden upon agents. Different divisions of the company had to be dealt with separately, requiring order takers to parse out orders to the various divisions. As agencies' business grew, so did support staffs and overhead; for every salesperson actually selling fixtures, there may have been two or three people managing the influx of telephone calls. Agencies often seemed on the brink of chaos: "You'd walk in there and see babies crying, women fainting, snakes hissing . . ." recalled Darnell. "We were this big pervasive company but we were forcing our agents to deal with us as if we were six or seven different ones." In a business in which deals were constantly being made and unmade, the standard practice of relying on the telephone began to look woefully inadequate.

Throughout the company's existence, agencies and customer service had always been viewed as primary to Lithonia's success. Yet it was increasingly obvious that the traditional means of managing information in Lithonia's agencies had become a constraint to future growth. Therefore, in 1979, McClung asked his staff to find ways to improve the flow of information through agencies. The agency throughput project, or ATP, was thus officially established.

Darnell—an irrepressible fan of cutting-edge technology—began to think about how Lithonia might build a computer system that would tie together all the players in the lighting business's matrix together and make it easier for the company to do what it existed to do: sell fixtures. After many weeks of dialogue with agents and company personnel, Darnell and his IMS people went into a design effort that resulted in a new chart of how business information would flow. When the new chart was finally drawn up, it had an interesting quality: Lithonia wasn't at the center; the agent was. As Darnell saw it, there was simply no way to conceive of the business unless the agencies, rather than Lithonia itself, were placed at the hub of the information system. "You think you're at the center of the universe," he explained. "But every time we tried to put Lithonia at the center, we ended up with all these crossed lines. It just didn't work."

In the architecture Darnell foresaw, Lithonia's sales people, divisions, and field warehouses—along with industry contractors, distributors, and specifiers—formed a ring around the agency, which was, despite its essential independence, to

---

EXHIBIT 3a Approximate Breakdown of US Lighting Equipment Sales by Major Categories, 1990

	Project or "Job"	Stock or "Flow"	Approximate Total Sales
Fluorescent	60%	40%	$1.5 billion
Downlighting	40%	60%	$500 million

Note: Total US 1990 market for lighting fixtures was approximately $4.6 billion, excluding vehicular and roadway lighting.

EXHIBIT 3b Approximate Average Markup Realized in Distribution Chain (as % of final selling price)

Project Business		Stock Business	
Agent	6%	Agent	6%
Distributor	3%–10%	Distributor	20%–30%
Electrical Contractor	10%–15%	Contractor	20%–30%
General Contractor	10%		
Specifier	(Fee)		

EXHIBIT 3c Market Shares in US Lighting Fixture Industry, 1989

	% share
Lithonia	14.8%
Cooper	12.0
USI	11.1
Genlyte	11.1
Thomas	6.7
Others	44.1

Source: NSI.

---

be understood as the true center of Lithonia's business. Once Lithonia had been refigured in this way, the kinds of applications that the company needed to develop began to be more clear. It was still only 1979, however, and the era of cheap, powerful personal computers was still years away. Nevertheless, Darnell and the IMS function quickly put together some first rudimentary applications that would form a computer link between the agencies and the Lithonia divisions.

The Structure of Light*Link
Throughout the 1980s, IMS continued to develop new applications and update older ones, eventually

EXHIBIT 4 LIGHT*LINK™ Structure and Primary Applications

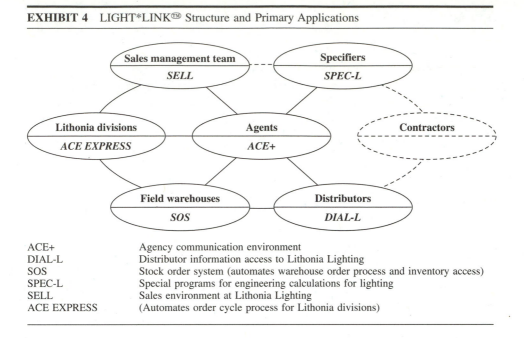

ACE+	Agency communication environment
DIAL-L	Distributor information access to Lithonia Lighting
SOS	Stock order system (automates warehouse order process and inventory access)
SPEC-L	Special programs for engineering calculations for lighting
SELL	Sales environment at Lithonia Lighting
ACE EXPRESS	(Automates order cycle process for Lithonia divisions)

using IBM PCs. By the end of the decade, almost all of the important connections in Darnell's ring structure were made by computerized communication links that circulated business information either in nightly batch jobs or on an on-line basis (see exhibit 4). At the hub of the network was the system known as ACE+, which stood for agency communication environment. Using ACE+, an agency could manage almost the entire range of its dealings with Lithonia. It allowed agency employees to dial into the systems of factories, warehouses, and distributors to communicate about the status of items or projects. Projects could be managed through computerized "job files" that contained all the relevant information about customer orders, and all orders were automated transactions that broke each job down into components to be handled by Lithonia's different manufacturing divisions.

Agents were not the sole beneficiaries of Lithonia's communications network. During the course of the 1980s, Darnell oversaw the development of a host of other applications, and showed a proclivity for coining three- and four-letter anagrams.

Lithonia developed SPEC-L, a set of engineering applications for specifiers (also usable by agencies) that could assist in determining the number and type of Lithonia fixtures required for such varied lighting environments as offices, parking lots, and stadiums. A system called SOS (stock order system) allowed field warehouses to manage inventory and their own ordering processes. DIAL-L (distributor information access to Lithonia Lighting) allowed distributors to dial into agents and warehouses in order to obtain quotes, orders, memos, and status reports. SELL (sales environment at Lithonia Lighting) provided a range of capabilities for Lithonia's internal sales management team. Few four-letter words could resist being commandeered by Darnell:[2] COPS (corporate order processing), MILL (manufacturing information at Lithonia Lighting), ROLL (routing orders at Lithonia Lighting), and BILL (billing information at Lithonia Lighting) were all

---

[2] "Why Lithonia MIS Won't Lighten Up," p. 26.

in the process of being added to the firm's systems roster under the rubric of a program known as One Lithonia Architecture, or OLA, which sought to create an integrated flow of internal and external information about the status of Lithonia's business. By 1992, the company planned to add PACE (pricing and commissioning environment), a sophisticated system that would reduce the agent's need to constantly negotiate prices and commissions with Lithonia's various divisional marketing departments.

Many of these projects were ones that Lithonia had been promising for many years. While they typically appeared late and sometimes delivered less than had been promised, users could be convinced of continuous upgrades and improvements once they had been introduced. Darnell had few qualms about envisioning and describing projects several years in advance: by 1994, he hoped to be able to introduce an idea called "dynamic synchronization," a system by which factory and distribution automation systems could fully be integrated with Light*Link systems for ordering and customer service.

The steady introduction of Light*Link systems caused a definitive change in how the lighting business worked, at least insofar as the game was played by Lithonia. Lithonia's business grew steadily through the 1980s; many agents doubled or tripled their business. Executives and agents were careful to point out that the new systems had been responsible for enabling Lithonia's growth, rather than simply causing it. But it was indisputable that what had once been a game of selling light fixtures by relationships had been enhanced by the introduction of business systems and PC networks. The goal of providing "the right amount of light in the right place at the right time" had been greatly impacted by the new strategy of having the right information in the right place at the right time.

Rod Lee explained:

What we've found over the years is that there's a tremendous demand for information in our business.

All these players want information, and they always want it *now.* What evolved a few years ago with the advent of the information age was the sense that what we needed wasn't simply more people, but the ability to get more information out into the field, out with the agent. Then we began to take a step beyond that, and said, "If we can empower the agent, why not empower the person he or she works with?"

Light*Link from the Agent's Perspective

Larry Davis, the head of Lighting Associates, a leading lighting agency in the Atlanta area, described how Light*Link had changed his firm. In 1980, he recalled, Lighting Associates did $6 to $7 million in Lithonia business. At the time, the agency was staffed with three order-entry people and three quotations people. By 1990, the agency had grown to $20 million in Lithonia business. But it still had only three order-entry and quotations people, even though it had significantly added to its sales force in order to generate the additional business. According to Davis, this growth was to a large extent due to the benefits of the Light*Link system.

Before Light*Link, when distributors or contractors called the agency to get a quote for an order—say for the lighting requirement of a baseball field—it could take the agency as long as three weeks to respond with a quotation. This was because it took a long time to perform the calculations to come up with a specification of the necessary lighting fixtures and to procure price and delivery quotes from Lithonia. The information necessary to quote an order and then fulfill it resided in so many different places that agencies spent most of their time fielding incoming telephone calls and making outgoing calls in order to manage the necessary information flows. In peak times, the agency had to handle as many as 1,000 calls per day. The result was a system that had a high administrative overhead (the ratio of administrative staff people in the agency was 1:1), a slow response time, limited flexibility (since agents were unable to respond easily to the numerous changes in an order as it evolved from an initial to a final specification), and a susceptibility to errors (as agency staff had to keep on top of an increasing volume of paperwork and a large number of changing products and prices).

Davis felt that with Light*Link, the agency had become far more effective. For instance, by asking a few simple questions such as the size of the baseball field and its shape, the agency could use the SPEC-L package to come up with lighting specifications in real time. Through the ACE+ system, they could also generate price quotes and check on delivery schedules for most standard configurations in real time. This allowed the agency to make bids on orders more quickly and to be more responsive to changes in the specifications. The Light*Link system also helped the agencies to fulfill orders more effectively since the system allowed them to track the status of any order within Lithonia. The capabilities afforded by Light*Link had allowed the agency to reduce the ratio of administrative staff to salespeople to 0.3:1. In fact, Davis's order-entry staff now performed other functions; they had been given the authority to quote for small orders and had thus become income producers instead of being merely overhead.

While Davis believed that Light*Link had really helped him differentiate his agency and offer superior service relative to his competitors, he felt that there were some additional features that were vital for Light*Link to be truly effective. Most important, in his view, was the ability of the system to deal with the products of the complementary manufacturers the agency represented, which accounted for between 30 and 40 percent of their revenues. Davis also felt that it was important to see improvements in Light*Link's quotation system so that a greater number of products could be directly priced by the agents instead of requiring interaction with Lithonia's marketing and sales organization.

An Uncertain Future

The Lighting Business in Early 1991
While Light*Link had helped to bring Lithonia sales to new heights, the lighting industry faced

one of its worst quarters in the company's history during the first part of 1991. Statistics on new construction headed for lows not seen in decades and the market for job-related lighting sales looked extremely grim. Lighting followed the fate of the construction business, which in turn followed the fate of the economy in general (see exhibits 5a and 5b on pages 361 and 362). Vacancy rates were high, confidence among builders was low, and financial institutions were increasingly fearful of lending money for real estate development. Suddenly Lithonia's fate seemed jeopardized by forces beyond the company's control.

Lithonia and NSI
With the economy in a slump of unforeseeable length, the costs of maintaining such large investments in IT began to call the workings of the entire IMS function into question. Darnell badly wanted the company to get the benefits he foresaw with new and improved Light*Link applications, which he knew would require considerable IMS resources to obtain. He also knew that all expenses, including those of IMS, must be tempered by economic necessities.

McClung was increasingly concerned about Lithonia's ability to continue to absorb added overhead associated with Light*Link projects. As the market got tougher, margins would continue to be squeezed across the board. The overhead that Lithonia had so easily carried during the booming eighties would become increasingly difficult to justify (see exhibit 6). NSI had always depended upon Lithonia for a healthy portion of its profits; especially in light of their generous support over the years, McClung felt it would be wrong to knowingly act against the interests of the parent company. He commented:

What's the cost premium of Light*Link? It's difficult to say: we have a lot more people involved in MIS technology relative to our competitors and spend a lot more money there. The disadvantage is that when the market goes down, then we have

EXHIBIT 5a   Dodge Construction Index, 1989–1991 (Value of Construction Contract Awards 1982 = 100)

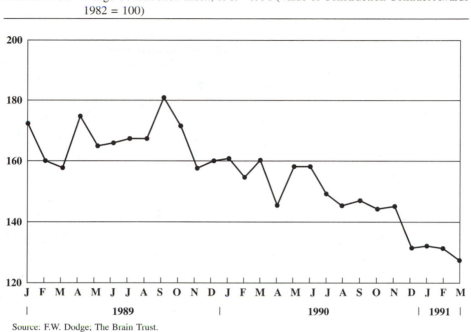

Source: F.W. Dodge; The Brain Trust.

overhead costs that need to be carried that the competition does not. If margins really get squeezed, we have a set of costs to carry that are not very easily dismantled.

If lighting customers were to react to a recession by becoming solely "bargain shoppers," Lithonia could be in for some trouble. According to Jerry Veydt, vice president of sales, Lithonia's whole strategy had been built around the idea that superior service would be important enough to the customer to prevent Lithonia from having to sell at rock bottom prices:

> We are rarely the lowest price or equal to the lowest price in any order opportunity. And that's directly related to the service investments we've made in our business, particularly with Light*Link. Competitors without this overhead find it easier to compete with lower prices, and that's why we try to make sure that it doesn't come down to a pure price game.

The Future of the Industry

Behind the difference of opinion on Light*Link were two very different theories of what was occurring in the lighting industry, and what impact Light*Link had, and would be able to have, upon it.

By one theory, Light*Link had initiated a set of changes that would, over a period of time, completely redefine the way the lighting industry worked. Darnell was quite obviously of this camp. In his eyes, Light*Link was allowing the lighting industry to realize its potential to be reconfigured as the split-second, information-dependent endeavor that the new technology and applications allowed. With evident excitement, he mused:

> The future is going to be electronic. I really believe that. So what we're doing this all for is the future. You're adding value for the present and preparing for the future.

EXHIBIT 5b   Authorized Nonresidential Construction during January 1988–1991 (Excludes Public Sector)

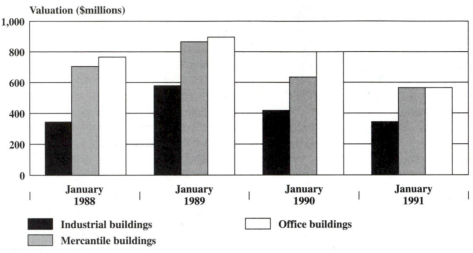

Source: *Construction Review.*

EXHIBIT 6   Budgets and Headcounts in Lithonia Information Services Department, 1982–1991 (All $ in thousands)

Year	Sales $	Annual Budget $	% Sales	Staff
1982	$278,468	$ 3,827	1.37%	62
1983	299,794	4,083	1.36	63
1984	383,392	4,654	1.21	76
1985	469,426	5,989	1.28	93
1986	522,056	7,748	1.48	132*
1987	559,384	9,117	1.63	117
1988	602,771	9,055	1.50	112
1989	658,657	10,039	1.52	115
1990	717,237	11,739	1.64	121
1991 (est.)	652,500	13,086	2.01	130

1986 headcount includes temporary build-up of personnel utilized in installation of ACE field systems.

McClung had doubts that all of the lighting industry would go through the kind of total transformation that people like Darnell envisioned. For example, Cooper Industries—a company with much less investment in information technology along its distribution chain—was clearly a close rival to Lithonia for industry dominance. He explained his view of the scenario:

You could make a case to say that two companies have outperformed everybody else and that Lithonia is the larger of the two, but it would be difficult to say that our information systems investments have made a clear preference in the view of many customers. When it comes down to it, this industry just isn't like American Hospital Supply or American Airlines. Here, IT probably isn't going to make that kind of difference. Information processing in the lighting market is never going to be that sophisticated. A lot of business will always be done by small electrical contractors who go to distributors with very simple demands: product, price, and availability. All that matters is that these demands be met—not the means employed to meet them. We may push the market in certain directions, but there's still an awful lot of lighting business that's strictly bread and butter.

Light*Link: The Immediate Future

Time to Say No?

Few people at Lithonia disputed the importance of the information systems introduced over the past 10 years. There was no doubt that Light*Link and other IMS investments had clearly allowed the company and its agencies to profitably handle rapid growth in sales volumes and in product diversity. Now, however, many questioned whether the means by which systems development had typically been pursued was still appropriate in such an uncertain economic climate.

Alan Suttle, head of the extremely successful Los Angeles agency and another Harvard Business School graduate, said that agents had learned to be wary of Darnell's promises, even as they eagerly awaited the things he promised:

Charles has a tendency to overcommit. He'll get in front of a group of agents and start describing the merits of this system or that system that could be developed. His role is important: he's clearly the dreamer of the company and one of its real driving forces. But because his dreams can be far-reaching and perhaps never implemented, we agents have learned to be very careful about what we expect to get and when we expect to get it.

Charlie Bryant, senior vice president of sales, essentially corroborated Suttle's view, and felt that now was perhaps the time to refocus the use of resources in the IT area:

From an economic standpoint, we'll be hard pressed to do some of these more ambitious projects and justify them in terms of the overhead that will be incurred.

Even Bob Bowman—head of the Hi-Tek division and normally one of Darnell's best supporters—expressed his own reservations about Light*Link's present and future course:

From a purely short-term operating profit perspective, one could say that the investments in Light*Link are not reflected in the results. Yet from a strategic position, you could also say that Light*Link is a terribly, terribly crucial element in maintaining our position in the marketplace. If we were in a strong growth economy with lots of new projects out there, I'd be fully supportive of Lithonia's strategy. But in the short term, there are some questions in my mind over how we should best use our resources.

Many felt that, at least until the economy showed a marked improvement, Lithonia should be more selective in its plans for new applications and enhancements. If nothing else, continued expansion in the IMS area would only serve to fuel interfunctional disputes in the company: while the manufacturing divisions were significantly downsizing their employee rosters, McClung had continued to authorize high levels of IMS staffing and budgets. Although IMS's total overhead was still within 2 percent of sales, Bowman felt that for IMS to pursue a policy of "business as usual" could lead to a sort of mutiny elsewhere in the company.

The Costs of Pioneering

There were other concerns less directly tied to the state of the economy, but which had nevertheless been thrown into sharper focus by the downturn. As sophisticated information systems became more commonplace in American industry, Lithonia had to deal with the inevitable introduction of similar systems capabilities among its competitors. Yet when these companies chose to introduce systems of their own, they would find the technology and the know-how much more readily available than Lithonia had a few years earlier. Charlie Bryant noted:

We've had to invent the wheel, so we really don't have any path that's been blazed for us. Although we originally prospered in the lighting business by being an intelligent follower, now we're paying for all the pioneering work in information systems.

It had been reported from several sources that Cooper would be introducing new and improved field information systems in the fall of 1991. In addition, a former employee from Darnell's group had formed a company that had already begun to market a nonproprietary third-party system that could feasibly handle any manufacturer's products. Agents such as Atlanta's Larry Davis felt that such a system could be very useful, since Lithonia's software was not designed to handle business with the smaller complementary companies. Were such a system to be successful, other companies would have "instant" access to some of the information tools it had taken Lithonia 10 years and 20 million dollars to develop. Thus, even people like Jerry Veydt who felt that the industry was indeed in transition could sometimes feel more than a bit of unease:

> The time will get here—probably during the 1990s- when other companies will have to get more involved with information technology. The time will come when other companies will no longer be able to consider these kinds of information systems a luxury but a necessity. What I'm afraid of is that our competitors will be able to start these things up much quicker and cheaper than we did.

Full Speed Ahead?

As far as some people were concerned, straying from the past formula could only spell trouble for the company. The company's image as the most progressive, forward-thinking company in the business—a reputation underscored by McClung and Darnell's 1988 receipt of a prestigious Society for Information Management award—could be put in jeopardy if Lithonia was to put many of its IT developments on hold. As Alan Suttle remarked:

> Part of Lithonia's strength in the marketplace is a respect for what they've accomplished in the systems area. And as agents, part of our strength is

that the general marketplace believes that Lithonia is always on the forefront, pushing the bubble outward.

He continued:

> Sitting where I sit, Jim McClung seems pretty pessimistic on the long-term market outlook. But at least in our part of the world, we can't get people to believe that the recession will last any longer than 8 to 12 months. Even if business drops off, what doesn't go away are corporate offices, owner-occupied buildings, and such. The kinds of projects we do may change somewhat and we may have less than a stellar year, but I don't think that's reason for Lithonia to totally change its approach.

Marc Conway, vice president of marketing in the fluorescent division, took a similar position:

> Now that they've whet our whistle, Lord, don't stop the investments! Our operational results have been significantly improved by our systems. What I'd like to see now are some resources directed toward our internal systems. Perhaps instead of starting new external ventures, we should look to do some housekeeping, perhaps find new ways of cutting down the interpretation time it takes to figure out the complicated bill of materials and prices we have to generate when orders come in. This can be especially difficult for custom orders that require novel lighting configurations.

Tom Naramore, fluorescent's vice president of operations, largely concurred:

> The Light*Link projects that have been put out there have made it somewhat easier for us to manage our production schedule. And we hope that now the IMS group can really work with us on tying everything together to help accomplish our objective of becoming a world-class manufacturer that can simultaneously provide the highest quality at the lowest cost.

McClung's Dilemma

McClung, on the other hand, was not convinced of the need for new and continued investments; he feared that the market downturn would be severe and unknown in duration. From where he sat, it seemed like it might be time to put on the brakes.

It was difficult to justify the continued deployment of new applications with their associated overhead when Lithonia was facing a decline in sales that would surely cause a steep decline in profits. NSI was becoming increasingly vocal about keeping expenditures down, and McClung felt the pressure from Lithonia's parent becoming "greater all the time, greater all the time." It was time to think long and hard about where his company, and where his industry, were really headed.

CASE 7–2: HONG KONG TRADELINK: NEWS FROM THE SECOND CITY

This description of Hong Kong, the Hotline project and the subsequent Tradelink project, is drawn from various public record sources. The excerpts from newspaper articles cover the period between November 1988 and May 1990. They hint at issues of government versus private-industry control and competitive timing.

Preparation Questions

1. What are the arguments in favor of the Hong Kong government sponsoring an EDI initiative like the Hotline project? What are the arguments in favor of private industry sponsoring an EDI initiative like TradeLink?
2. What do you think of the Hong Kong government's commitment to the $9 million joint venture with TradeLink?
3. What challenges do the TradeLink sponsors face in planning this system?

Case 7–2 Hong Kong TradeLink: News from the Second City*

Background on Hong Kong

Hong Kong was established by the United Kingdom in the early 19th century as a trading colony, part of the British Empire. The colony was built upon Hong Kong Island, which was ceded to the United Kingdom in perpetuity by the Chinese government. As the colony grew, it expanded beyond the island, and eventually came to occupy a significant part of the mainland (the New Territories) leased by the Chinese government to the United Kingdom for the period 1898 to 1997. After extensive negotiations between the United Kingdom and the People's Republic of China during the mid to late 1980s, a joint agreement was reached whereby Hong Kong would become part of the People's Republic of China in 1997. The memorandum of understanding, however, stipulates that Hong Kong will retain its special political and economic character for 50 years past the 1997 hand-over.

Hong Kong is administered by a governor appointed by the Queen of England, though as a

*Marvin Bower Fellow John King and Professor Benn Konsynski prepared this case. Copyright © 1990 by the President and Fellows of Harvard College. Harvard Business School case 191-026 (Revised 4/7/1993).

practical matter the governor reports to UK Foreign Office. The governor is assisted by two councils: a Legislative Council that enacts local legislation and sets budgetary authority, and an advisory executive council. Administration of the Hong Kong government is managed by the chief secretary (formerly called the *colonial secretary*), to whom most of the secretaries running major Government agencies report. The attorney general and the finance secretary also report to the chief secretary, though they have more of a peer status with the chief secretary than do the other secretaries. The attorney general is responsible for all crown prosecutions, while the finance secretary is responsible for the treasury, trade, and industry; government data processing; and other key administrative functions. Numerous advisory committees involving government officials and citizens help with particular policy issues.

Background on Trade-Related Electronic Data Interchange in Hong Kong

In 1983, the Hong Kong Trade Facilitation Council, a nonprofit organization of traders, facility authorities (e.g., the port authority), and trade-related agencies of the Hong Kong government, began looking into the possibility of improving trade activities in Hong Kong through use of electronic data interchange (EDI). A study was organized within the Council to outline a possible EDI project, and in 1984 the Council made public plans for the construction of a system called *Hotline*. Hotline was proposed as a centralized database system of consignment data on all goods exchanged through external trade mechanisms.

The Government, which had been instrumental in creation of the Council and was its initial underwriter, was approached to fund the Hotline project. The Government had problems with the proposal on substantive and procedural grounds. None of the Government officials who would have to approve the Hotline project and provide funding understood what was being proposed in detail, so it was not easy to sell the concept. No other

trade-related EDI was operating in the world, and only limited discussion and planning had taken place in those places contemplating it. Also, the Council had been started with initial support by the Government, but it was the intent from the beginning for the Council to become a self-supporting entity very soon after creation. Government support of Hotline would have significantly increased the government's obligations to the Council, and in the view of Government officials, there were not sound grounds for making the investment in the first place.

The Government response to the Hotline project was that the private sector stood to benefit most from Hotline, and therefore it should undertake the project if it felt the benefits worthwhile. While rational from a market perspective, this suggestion met severe institutional resistance among the members of the trading company. A survey of interested companies revealed the widespread sentiment that the information contained in such a system would be proprietary and competitively sensitive. The Government, in the minds of the various companies, was the only entity that could undertake the project and guarantee fair and equal treatment of all users. Thus, the key blocs within the Council—the Government and the private companies involved in trade—were at a deadlock on Hotline.

From 1984 to 1987, the EDI issue was dormant. None of the Council parties could devise a means of breaking out of the deadlock, and, for a while, interest in the issue waned. In 1987, however, several key events occurred that restarted discussions. One was the establishment of the United Nations EDIFACT standard for EDI. This greatly increased the probability that a single EDI format would be adopted for trading use. Another, more local stimulus was the announcement by the Singapore government of a crash program to develop a trade-related EDI system called TradeNet. TradeNet was to use the EDIFACT standard, and it was targeted to be working within two years. This announcement was significant because Singapore, as Hong Kong's nearest and largest trading competitor, was clearly viewing EDI as a major source of competitive advantage in trade. Also at about this time other, less ambitious trade-related EDI projects were being announced in Norway, the United Kingdom, and other countries. It seemed to some members of the Council that EDI had moved from "desirable" status to "necessary" status in Hong Kong's trade future. And there was official support for moving forward provided by the Hong Kong Government's advisory board on science and technology, which recommended that the government help make some kind of EDI project happen.

In late 1987, several companies that were members of the Council decided to pull out of the Council and form their own EDI consortium for the purpose of commissioning and funding a major study of the viability of a trade-related EDI system for Hong Kong. They formed a special company called TradeLink, and commissioned a major consultancy study with the firm Coopers and Lybrand. The Government, desiring to keep a hand in the ongoing discussion, contributed 10 percent to the cost of the consultancy.

Excerpts from Articles on Trade-Related EDI from Hong Kong Newspapers

Eight Hong Kong Companies Have Started Work on TradeLink Computer Network

Eight Hong Kong companies have begun work on an international computer network linking Hong Kong's freight carriers, banks, and trading companies. These are China Resources, Hong Kong Air and Cargo Terminals, Hong Kong International Terminals, Maersk Line (HK), Modern Terminals, Swire Pacific, Standard Chartered Bank and the Hongkong and Shanghai Bank. The government is not a shareholder of the new company, TradeLink Electronic Document Services. The formation of TradeLink is in response to the increasing use of electronic data interchange (EDI) systems to reduce paperwork. TradeLink is expected to begin operation in 1990, almost a year after Singapore is scheduled to launch its EDI, TradeNet. [*Shipping Times* (November 1, 1988):1]

TradeLink Computerised Paperwork System Given Go Ahead

A final report from Coopers and Lybrand on the practicalities of setting up a computerised network to handle trade paperwork in the territory will recommend that the project goes ahead despite concerns over its economic viability. The Trade-Link consortium proposing the project is expected to decide whether to provide a paperless trading service in Hong Kong before October 4, when the group will participate in a conference on electronic document interchange (EDI). [*South China Morning Post* (Business News) (August 27, 1989):3]

TradeLink Denies Dropping Plans for Electronic Data Interchange Service

TradeLink, the consortium of 11 companies set up to establish a comprehensive EDI service in Hongkong, has said no decision on the project has been made. An EDI feasibility study by Coopers and Lybrand is believed to have run over its HK$6 million government provided funding and is already two months overdue. TradeLink did not say whether Coopers' draft report had recommended the project be abandoned. TradeLink project manager Juletta Broomfield said a statement would probably be made in October. [*South China Morning Post* (Business News) (August 22, 1989):11]

Cable and Wireless to Launch EDI System

Cable and Wireless has decided not to wait for the findings of a feasibility study commissioned by the TradeLink consortium about an electronic data interchange (EDI) system in Hong Kong. The company will launch its own EDI system in Hong Kong on June 5, about a month before the results of the Coopers and Lybrand study are handed to TradeLink. According to Cable and Wireless, the move is nothing unusual. Plans for the system, to be called Intertrade, have been underway since early last year, well before TradeLink was formed. [*South China Morning Post* (Business News) (May 8, 1989):11]

TradeLink Announcement on EDI Expected Next Month

TradeLink Electronic Document Services is next month expected to make a preliminary announcement on its role in setting up a territorywide electronic data interchange (EDI). The group—composed of 11 Hongkong organisations—is investigating the feasibility of EDI in Hongkong. Anthony Charter, managing director of Hongkong Air Cargo Terminals and newly appointed chairman of TradeLink, said: "EDI has already proved its worth in the highly competitive air transport industry and I am not in any doubt that it will become an essential way of doing business for much of Hongkong's trading community in the future. The only question that has to be resolved is to what extent Hongkong would benefit from a coordinated approach." [*South China Morning Post* (Business News) (September 4, 1989):3]

Agenda: Electronic Data Conference

With so many people (still) waiting to hear the recommendations of the Coopers and Lybrand report commissioned by TradeLink on the feasibility of electronic data interchange in Hongkong, the two-day EDI Asia '89 conference which starts at the Exhibition Centre today should generate a lot of interest . . . TradeLink's new chairman, Anthony Charter, will reveal all tomorrow when he delivers a talk on the Coopers and Lybrand consultancy study and the future role of TradeLink in the application of EDI in Hongkong. For most observers, the question of whether or not EDI is the wave of the future for Hongkong has already been answered. It will be. The questions that remain are when substantial services will be adopted by Hongkong, who will provide the services (and the hardware involved), and what kind of system will be implemented. The principal sponsor of the conference program is everyone's favourite computer monolith, Big Blue. Then, sponsoring everything from speeches to lunches to cocktail receptions, are Hewlett Packard, American Telephone and Telegraph, Digital Equipment, ICL, Hongkong Telephone, Cable and Wireless, Intertrade, NYNEX, McDonnell Douglas Information Systems, International Network

Services, Singapore, Computer Systems, and even relational database specialists Oracle. Not to be seen left out of the event, the Government is also involved in the sponsorship program through both the Hongkong Productivity Council and the Hongkong Trade Facilitation Council. [*South China Morning Post* (Business News) (March 10, 1993):12]

TradeLink Electronic Scheme to Process Trade Documents Under Study, by James Riley

The Government is considering a proposal that would allow a private company to provide an exclusive franchise service to process government-related trade documents electronically, according to Secretary for the Treasury Hamish McCleod. The proposal was submitted last week by TradeLink . . . TradeLink's initiative to form a public and private sector "partnership" to process government trade documents was also under consideration, he said. "We do not rule out, at this stage, any possible options in developing trade related EDI in Hongkong," Mr McCleod said. TradeLink chairman Anthony Charter said the report had found that the potential market for EDI services could be as high as $10 billion by the turn of the century, but that due to constraints unique to Hongkong, the realisable market had been estimated between $1 billion and $1.5 billion. He said the market size was restricted by the resistance of smaller companies to computerisation; a lack of standards for the development of Chinese language EDI; a low awareness of the real cost of handling paper documents; and the legal constraints that electronic documents presented. The granting of an exclusive franchise would help overcome these constraints, and speed the overall adoption of paperless trading in Hongkong, he added. The franchise should be granted in return for an obligation to explore low cost access to EDI for Hongkong's numerous small traders and to help develop and establish Chinese-language EDI standards . . . Mr Charter said the setting up of an EDI service could require an investment of up to $500 million over the next 10 years. Mr Charter said that while the EDI gateway to the government should be franchised, the open market should dictate the development of electronic document gateways between domestic trading partners, and between Hongkong and overseas trading partners. [*South China Morning Post* (Business News) (October 5, 1989):1]

Data Interchange Seminars Offered

The latest in a series of seminars organised by TradeLink to prepare Hongkong business for the advent of EDI . . . "Although EDI is correctly described as a business function rather than a technological one, its implementation demands specialist software and telecommunications links," seminar leader John Sanders said. "Therefore the business[person] needs to have a broad understanding of the technical issues involved, so that he [/she] knows the right questions to ask suppliers, and can be sure of acquiring the right software and communications services," he added.

Mr Sanders said that because TradeLink was independent of any vendor, the seminar would not make specific recommendations for any particular EDI product or service . . . [*South China Morning Post* (Business News) (October 16, 1989):4]

World Not Ready for EDI Implementation, by Keith Cameron

It seems that we are subjected to "experts" talking on Electronic Data Interchange (EDI) on a daily basis. The questions which loom up in my mind are: Are the "experts" talking to the right audience? And, even if they are, does the audience understand what they are talking about? It hardly needed a multimillion dollar consultancy study to tell us that there was a myriad of small companies here that would need training in the fundamentals of information technology before any standardised electronic document exchange could be introduced. Taxpayers' funds paid for part of the TradeLink study, for which we are now told that the consultants were given the wrong terms of reference. The TradeLink organisation is claiming that all is not lost because of that and has turned to Government for a commitment of exclusivity for electronic document handling. This, it said, would enable EDI to be introduced on a commercial basis, provided it was linked to a Government-backed no-loss guarantee for the trading organisation. Commercial Utopia supreme, it would appear. While

I have no argument with preparing for the day when all documents will be transferred electronically, I believe that the hype about EDI today is misplaced and premature. There is much to be done worldwide before a total EDI environment can exist, and most of the responsibility lies at the user end, not with the technologists, although some important technological implementations must occur. International standards for documentation must be agreed and implemented by all parties for EDI to be successful. Anyone who has been remotely connected with the freight and shipping industry will be aware that this is no mean task. It not only involves a collaboration between private industry, but it also demands conformity by relevant government bodies all over the world . . . I do not mean to discourage the activity which surrounds EDI in Hongkong today, but I do think that it could be a little more pragmatic and less theoretical. [*South China Morning Post* (Business News) (October 31, 1989):13]

Firms Urged to Seize Lead in EDI Growth

Banks in Hongkong and other major banking and finance centres could lose their traditional data interchange business unless they take the lead in developing a standard global electronic data interchange (EDI) network, according to a banking and finance computer consultant . . . While stressing that "what Hongkong and Singapore are doing is a step in the right direction," Mr Griggs said that, like other major trading centres, "they are responding to market pressures in the fight to remain competitive." Many of the systems now in use worldwide, he said, were solving documentation and information problems and leading to systems that would easily extend to taking over much of the traditional banking aspects of trade finance. "Unfortunately, banks generally are not part of the movement and are in danger of being left out," Mr Griggs said. [*South China Morning Post* (Business News) (November 11, 1989):14]

Group Steps Up Campaign on Data Exchange, by James Riley

The TradeLink consortium has intensified its lobbying of the government for an exclusive franchise to computerise the processing of all government trade-related documents. The proposal has drawn heavy criticism from some sectors of the high technology industry which claim that electronic document processing would be better serviced in a free-market environment . . . The controversial proposal would include a safety net of government subsidies to ensure its profitability during its introduction. TradeLink chairman Anthony Charter said the project would require a total investment of "considerably more" than $500 million over 10 years. Mr Charter said an exclusive franchise should be granted for EDI processing of government documents to ensure that a system of standards was established, and that the territory's vast number of small trading companies were encouraged to adopt the system. He warned that unless the government said it intended to adopt EDI before the end of the year, it was likely that the TradeLink members would withdraw the proposal and dissolve the company. The group said it had spent $14 million investigating EDI in Hongkong . . . Mr Charter said unless Hongkong traders adopted EDI practices they could become less competitive in international markets. "I believe (EDI) should be ranked at least equal in priority to major physical infrastructure projects like the new airport," Mr Charter said. "In this situation where you have a slow take (of EDI) in the early years, there is an implied subsidy that would be required from government," he said. "They subsidise roads and they subsidise airports—this is part of the infrastructure and if necessary they should subsidise it in the early years until it can stand on its own feet." The Hongkong Information Technology Federation (HKITF), a 120-member high technology industry group, has responded coolly to the TradeLink proposal. . . . [*South China Morning Post* (Business News) (November 16, 1989):4]

Council to Promote Joint Research Urged, by James Riley

Legislative Councillor Professor Poon Chung-kwong last week urged the Government to establish an autonomous council to coordinate joint research efforts between the public and private sectors. Professor Poon, who is also the chairman of the Government's Committee on Science and

Technology and the head of Hongkong University's science faculty, said Hongkong lacked a centralised body to formulate and implement long-term technology projects . . . The recent proposal by the TradeLink consortium that it be granted a franchise to establish an electronic data interchange gateway to Government was a good example of where an established and powerful committee could be of use in making technology decisions, he said . . . [*South China Morning Post* (Business News) (November 21, 1989):13]

TradeLink Makes Its Case for EDI to IT Federation, by James Riley

In an attempt to bolster support for its electronic data interchange (EDI) initiative, TradeLink last week met with Hongkong Information Technology Federation (HKITF) representatives in the hope of winning support from the powerful trade group . . . there were some committee members that felt that if a franchise were granted, it be for an EDI gateway alone, and should not include any preprocessing . . . [*South China Morning Post* (Business News) (November 28, 1989):12]

Government to Decide on Trade Uses of EDI, by James Riley

The trading community in Hongkong should know by the end of the month whether or not the Government is serious about plans to introduce electronic data interchange (EDI) to Hongkong. Whatever the Government decides about its EDI plans, any announcement on the subject is likely to raise plenty of eyebrows among the local trading community . . . The Government has given TradeLink a commitment that it will indicate by the end of the month whether the group should proceed with further investigation and pilot projects—or that it deems the idea unfeasible. The Government's thinking on the proposal is not known, so it is impossible to guess whether or not the investment in TradeLink by its shareholders will eventually pay its own way. But even if TradeLink should disband, the company has already been an outstanding success as the principal impetus behind all the current talk about the EDI concept. [*South China Morning Post* (Business News) (March 4, 1990):12]

Seminar on Paperless Trade, by Ian Lewis

The Hongkong Shippers' Council is organising a one-day seminar to increase awareness of existing paperless communication systems while businesses wait for the TradeLink Electronic Data Interchange (EDI) network to start up. The seminar is organised in conjunction with Intertrade, an EDI service run by Cable and Wireless (HK), and will be presented in Cantonese at the Hongkong Convention and Exhibition Centre on April 12 . . . [*South China Morning Post* (Business News) (March 13, 1990):4]

HK "Will Lose Out without More IT," by James Riley

The Hongkong business community must become more aware of the opportunities that information technology (IT) offers and the problems that must be overcome in implementing that technology if the territory is to remain competitive in the region Legislative Councillor Mr Stephen Cheong Kam-cheun said yesterday. Officially announcing the local industry's biggest-ever technology event, Information Technology Week (ITWeek)—which is scheduled for September—Mr Cheong said Hongkong had fallen behind some Asian competitors in the adoption of technology. There were key technology issues facing Hongkong that had to be addressed as soon as possible if the territory were to maintain its position in Asia as a financial and industrial centre . . . "Hongkong has had the misfortune of falling behind other territories like Taiwan, Korea and Singapore," Mr Cheong said. "It is now our duty and our hope that we will catch up—and given the Hongkong people's tremendous appetite for learning and tremendous energy I am sure that we can get on with it," he said . . . [*South China Morning Post* (Business News) (March 20, 1990):12]

Government in EDI Venture with TradeLink, by James Riley

The Government plans to set up a joint-venture project with TradeLink Electronic Document Services to develop a system of "paperless trading," the acting Secretary for Trade and Industry, Mr Joseph Wong Wing-ping announced yesterday.

Funding for the $9 million venture will be shared equally by the government and TradeLink. The project will develop a business plan and technical specifications for a long awaited communitywide system of electronic data interchange (EDI) for Hongkong. Called SPEDI—Shared Project for EDI—the study will be completed by the end of the year . . . [*South China Morning Post* (Business News) (March 21, 1990):3]

EDI Venture "Half-Hearted Step," by James Riley

Local industry groups have responded coolly to the Government's announcement last week that it had entered a $9 million joint venture, Shared Project for EDI (SPEDI), with TradeLink to develop a business plan for the introduction of electronic data interchange (EDI) in Hongkong. Spokes[persons] for the Hongkong Telecommunication Users Group and the Hongkong Information Technology Federation's EDI committee said the joint venture was a half-hearted step forward, and complained that the Government was still dragging its feet in making a solid commitment to adopting paperless trading practices. The spokespeople questioned the likely benefits that would be derived from the study, given its limited $9 million budget, and expressed concern that it would simply retrace the steps of the consultancy study carried out by Coopers and Lybrand on behalf of TradeLink last year. "I am extremely disappointed," said HKITF EDI committee chairman Mr Roy Grubb. "We believe that the Government should be taking the bull by the horns and doing (EDI) for themselves—at the very least for their own paperwork . . ." [*South China Morning Post* (Business News) (March 27, 1990):12]

Talks on Chinese EDI

Talks between Hongkong and mainland electronic data interchange (EDI) experts to develop Chinese-language messaging standards have been scheduled for later this year following an exploratory meeting of representatives in Beijing recently. The discussions will aim to establish common character sets and internal codes for Chinese language data processing, Chinese versions of UN-EDIFACT (the international message standard for EDI), and trading terms and definitions. With the involvement of Taiwan, also represented at the Beijing meeting, it should be possible to develop Chinese-language applications of EDI that can be used throughout China, Hongkong and Taiwan, and internationally. [*South China Morning Post* (Business News): May 22, 1990 12]

CASE SERIES: 7–3 SINGAPORE LEADERSHIP: A TALE OF ONE CITY
7–4 SINGAPORE TRADENET (A): A TALE OF ONE CITY
7–5 SINGAPORE TRADENET (B): THE TALE CONTINUES

These three cases about Singapore and its IT strategy illustrate the use of IOS in support of a government's (in this case, a city-state) trade policy and processes. The cases present the story behind development of an industrywide EDI platform, TradeNet, for trade documentation processing. TradeNet involves a partnership of government agencies, bureaus, statutory boards, private agencies, and private corporations involved in all aspects of the shipment of goods.

Preparation Questions

1. What was Lee Kuan Yew's vision for Singapore? What challenges did he face in reaching his goals?
2. Describe the trade documentation process before and after the implementation of TradeNet. Who were the major stakeholders involved in the process redesign?
3. Evaluate the process used to implement TradeNet. Was it successful? If so, what factors contributed to its success? If not, why not?
4. Compare Hong Kong's TradeLink initiative to Singapore's TradeNet.
5. What impact will TradeNet have on countries outside the Pacific Rim?

Case 7–3 Singapore Leadership: A Tale of One City*

Lee Kuan Yew, the prime minister of the Republic of Singapore, is usually credited with the "Singapore Miracle." Cambridge-educated and widely regarded as a brilliant strategist, Lee has been the central figure in Singapore politics since before the founding of the Republic in 1959. Admirers say he embodies all that is good about Asia. Singapore's rapid economic progress (see Exhibit 1) is accompanied by litter-free streets, a low crime rate, and a high level of public amenities and services. Lee's critics, however, point at Singapore's strict laws governing everyday behavior (e.g., rigorously enforced rules against spitting and other minor infractions) and the suppression of criticism of the government as a high cost the citizens of Singapore pay for their progress.

*Marvin Bower Fellow John King and Professor Benn Konsynski prepared this case. Copyright © 1990 by the President and Fellows of Harvard College. Harvard Business School case 191–025 (Revised April 6, 1993).

Lee has used his People's Action Party (PAP) to create a functioning multiracial, multilingual, multireligious society. The Republic is a parliamentary democracy, with an elected Parliament that elects a president every four years. The president appoints the prime minister and cabinet. Ethnic Chinese make up a significant percent of the population, followed by Malays, Indians, and "Europeans." To help balance the different interests in the society, representation by non-Chinese in Parliament is based on group representation constituencies (GRCs). Opposition parties are allowed to hold up to three of the 81 seats in Parliament as nonconstituency members of parliament (MPs), if fewer than three opposition MPs are returned in the elections. Over the years, PAP has remained strong, holding 80 of the 81 seats as of 1990.

The central question in Singapore politics has for some years concerned Lee's successor. Recent events had set the stage for the immediate succession when Lee was scheduled to retire to the position of a regular cabinet member at the end of 1990. Goh Chok Tong, currently first deputy prime minister and first minister of defense, was named to become prime minister at that time. Lately Goh had become quite visible, for example making policy statements in the sensitive area of relations between Singapore and neighboring Malaysia. Recently, Goh was asked if his assumption of the prime minister's job signaled a long-term direction for the country, or whether he was taking the job as an "interim measure" in anticipation of another prime minister down the line. Goh said a "substantial" victory in the September 1993 election would make him secure in his position, but he also said he would not remain in the office for "long."

The most widely rumored successor to Goh is the oldest son of Lee Kuan Yew, Lee Hsien Loong, known popularly as B.G. (Brigadier General) Lee for his status in Singapore's armed forces. Educated at Cambridge University, Harvard University, and the United States Army General Staff College, he has held important government positions, including second minister of defense and minister of trade and industry. He also has been involved in many key policy debates regarding the future of Singapore. Political commentators have compared him with his illustrious father. Regarding competitiveness of nations, B.G. Lee said:

> What's important is not just the cost of labor. The key is total productivity. There's the labor cost, infrastructure, inventiveness of the leading edge of technology, and the quality of the production process. Not just individual workers but the way

EXHIBIT 1   Comparative Statistics for Singapore, 1965 and 1988

Item	1965	1988
Population at mid-year	1.89 million	2.65 million
GDP (1985 market prices)	6.62 billion	47.9 billion
Indigenous GDP per capita	1,692	15,999
External trade (import and export)	6.8 billion	167.28 billion
Students enrolled in school	15,000	77,000
Labor force	723,000	1,282,000
Sea cargo handled (tonnes)	15.1 million	142 million
Air cargo handled (tonnes)	21,100	512,500
Official foreign reserves	14.2 million	33.28 billion
Balance of payment (current acct)	−150,000	3.34 billion

Source: Singapore Economic Development Board, 1990.

whole plants are organized and structured and efficiency is squeezed out of fallible human digits . . .

In Singapore we have an appreciation for how fragile we are. Why are we here? There is nothing special about this island. It is just one of 18,000 islands in the region. But here you can do business. You have banks, telephones, airports that work, factories that are up and running in six to nine months. What makes it special? The only thing which makes it special is that the place is revved to 99 percent of what it is capable of. And unless you can always run at that efficiency, you'll just sink. There's no reason to be here. Do we have hydroelectric power? Timber, tin, gold, gas? We have none. But if we want to continue to be here, we have to be special.[1]

Being "special" in the Singaporean sense has translated into active government programs fostering economic links with other countries, the encouragement of overseas investment, the establishment of an assertive diplomacy, and the development of "international networking." The fiscal system of Singapore has been characterized as 75 percent private and 25 percent government, with high levels of public investment in infrastructure and the maintenance of sound monetary policy. In recent years, the country has built a state-of-the-art transportation infrastructure, including world-class container ports, airport facilities, highways, and a subway system. It also has an advanced telephone and data communications network. Much effort is focused on building the capabilities of the country's small- and medium-sized enterprises through tax credits and other incentives to encourage investment in computing technology and the hiring of consultants to improve know-how at the firm level.

[1]Brian Kelly and Mark London, *The Four Little Dragons* (New York: Simon and Schuster, 1989), pp. 385, 387.

Case 7–4 Singapore TradeNet (A): A Tale of One City*

As the sun rose over the island of Borneo, the container ship *Kobayashi Maru,* bound for the Port of Singapore near the heart of the city, rounded the southern tip of Singapore Island from the South China Sea. The captain knew the crew would be disappointed by the short stay that would prevent many from taking shore leave. In spite of the extensive off-loading and on-loading planned at the container terminal, the *Kobayashi Maru* would put to sea by nightfall. Singapore's state-of-the-art shipping facilities could turn around an average sized container ship in under 10 hours, as opposed to 20 hours or more for most ports. A major factor in this was the new TradeNet system. Early this

*Marvin Bower Fellow John King and Professor Benn Konsynski prepared this case. Copyright © 1990 by the President and Fellows of Harvard College. Harvard Business School case 191-009 (Revised April 5, 1993).

morning he had sent his ship's cargo manifests, in electronic form, to the freight forwarders in Singapore. Within two hours, using TradeNet, the freight forwarders had already obtained import permits, cleared customs and paid duties for all cargo going ashore, and received export permits for the ship's outbound cargo. Because of TradeNet, together with the other systems in the Singapore port, the days of the long layover in Singapore City were over. Now, shipping there was strictly business.

A city state of 2.6 million people occupying a 625-square-kilometer island at the southern tip of the Malaysian Peninsula, Singapore was prosperous and had sustained remarkable economic growth during the past 20 years. GNP in 1989 was US$ 23.84 billion, and per capital GNP was US$ 9,000. With a literacy rate of over 87 percent and a life expectancy of 74 years, Singapore was on the

EXHIBIT 1   Southeast Asia

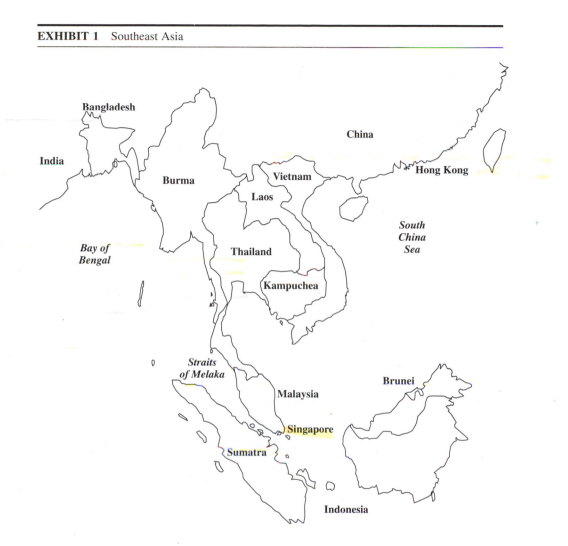

verge of moving into the club of developed nations. The government had adopted a public position that the country would be recognized as a developed nation by the year 2000.

Its position at the tip of the Malaysian peninsula, at the bend in the long sea trade route between the Indian Ocean and South China Sea, had made Singapore a key strategic port for those interested in trade in and around Asia (see Exhibit 1). Its location had been the crucial factor in Singapore's development since its founding in 1819 and was a major source of the country's remarkable economic growth since becoming an independent republic in 1966.

As of 1989, Singapore had the largest port in the world in gross tonnage and in bunkering activity (transshipment of oil and oil products). The second-largest port in container handling, behind only Hong Kong, Singapore was significantly ahead of Rotterdam, the third-largest port. Singapore had also built the region's busiest airport and in 1989 began expanding the airport with new passenger and cargo facilities to be ready in 1991. Trade had grown to be a highly significant component of Singapore's economy. In 1990, external trade alone equaled 3.5 times the country's GDP. Though Singapore was the size of Philadelphia in land and population, in 1989 it was among the top 20 trading nations of the world.

Trade Documentation

Modern trade revolved around transactions involving information on facts, parties at interest, and exchanges. *Facts* included the cargoes that were being shipped, the values of the cargoes, the vessels that carried them, their points of origin and destination, and the dates of departure and arrival. *Parties at interest* included the owners who shipped the cargoes and the recipients, as well as all the intermediaries—agents, freight forwarders, shipping companies, banks, insurance companies, port authorities, and government customs and controlagencies. *Exchange transactions*, the actual interchange of goods and information at the intersections of facts and parties at interest, included transfers of cargo custody, payments of various fees and duties, and payments among the partiesbuying and selling the cargoes.

Trade documentation linked these crucial information components through manifests, bills of lading, letters of credit, customs declarations, and all manner of receipts and reports. Trade documentation in a busy port like Singapore was a complex and expensive activity. Yeo Seng Teck, chief executive officer of the Trade Development Board (TDB), a statutory board[1] responsible for manag-

ing all incoming and outgoing trade activities, explained the situation his agency faced in 1987:

> Our agency (TDB) was loaded with paperwork. In 1987 we were handling about 10,000 declarations each day, and the number was rising. And TDB was only part of the system. The trade process involves agencies such as the port authorities, customs, and so on, each with its own rules. At least four documents had to be completed for each incoming or outgoing shipment. In complicated cases as many as 20 forms might be required. Shipping agents and freight forwarders prepared these reports and physically carried them to service centers where they would be handled manually by government officials and clerks. Two day turnaround was common. The cost of these transactions was high for all concerned. Swedish and U.S. studies of the costs of trade documentation in those countries estimated the cost at 4 percent to 7 percent of the value of goods shipped. And such transactions are error prone. A British study estimated that half of all letter of credit applications were turned down on first application due to errors in completion. This seemed like a lot of work with little payoff. It also provided an opportunity for us. Singapore is a small country. We have no natural resources. Our population has stabilized. We know we cannot compete by just bringing in new labor. If we are to be successful, we must improve our competitiveness in every way and especially in external trade, which is our largest business sector. This means cutting costs. That 4 percent to 7 percent was the best place to start.

The TradeNet System

TradeNet, an electronic data interchange (EDI) system that allowed computer-to-computer exchange of intercompany business documents in a format conforming to established public standards, connected members of the Singapore trading community (see Exhibit 2). Eventually, it would link with the EDI systems of the international community. The TradeNet system (see Exhibit 3) utilized software running on a large IBM mainframe computer owned and operated by Singapore Network Services Pte. Ltd. This system was linked via telephone dial-up or leased lines to all the mem-

---

[1]Statutory boards are an important feature of Singapore's economic structure, responsible for operating vital utilities (e.g., telephone and subway systems), major installations (e.g., the airport and the port), major construction enterprises (e.g., the Urban Redevelopment Authority), and analytical functions (e.g., the Economic Development Board). Each entity with the term *board* or *authority* in its title mentioned in this case is a statutory board. These boards are created by the government through enabling legislation, but they are *not* government departments. Although they are typically tied through their enabling legislation to particular ministries of government, they are not-for-profit corporations whose directorships consist of a mix of leaders from government, the private sector, and labor organizations. They generally must operate without government subsidy and can retain surplus earnings to expand their programs.

EXHIBIT 2   The TradeNet Community

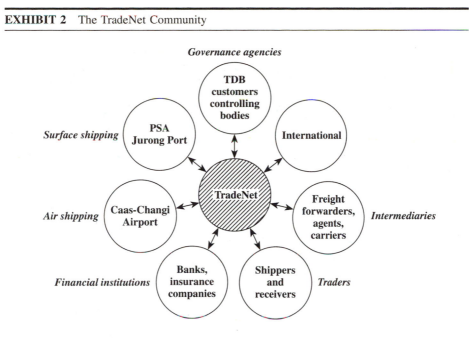

---

bers of the trading community, each of whom used terminals or their own computer systems to interact with the system.

A user, such as a freight forwarder, utilized the application interface (see Exhibit 4) on his or her local computer system to complete the required TradeNet application forms. The local system translated the data from the form into EDIFACT (an international electronic document standard). A communications program then transmitted the EDIFACT document to the TradeNet mainframe. At the mainframe, the Information Exchange Interface received the information and determined the nature of the transaction, who had sent it, and what was being requested. A typical request might be for an approval from TDB and customs and excise to release an incoming shipment for delivery to a destination within Singapore, or to release a shipment that was being exported from Singapore. Relevant data were forwarded to appropriate destinations, such as the TDB, customs, and any other agency with jurisdiction over particular trade–associated requests. The applications man-ager module and the session manager module kept track of the transaction, stored data for future use, and forwarded system use information to the user and system monitor module, which would eventually bill the user's organization for utilizing TradeNet.

TDB and the customs and excise agency were the principal governmental agencies with whom traders interacted via TradeNet, but the system could also provide data on the status of a shipment to other interested parties, such as the port or airport authorities. TradeNet had the ability to support certain financial transactions. A freight forwarder, for example, might send a message to its bank ordering a payment to be made to another freight forwarder for services rendered on a given shipment. TradeNet also supported direct GIRO interbank funds transfer.

Planning TradeNet

TradeNet resulted from discussions on environmental factors and government policies and programs in the 1980s. As part of its program of

EXHIBIT 3   TradeNet Structure

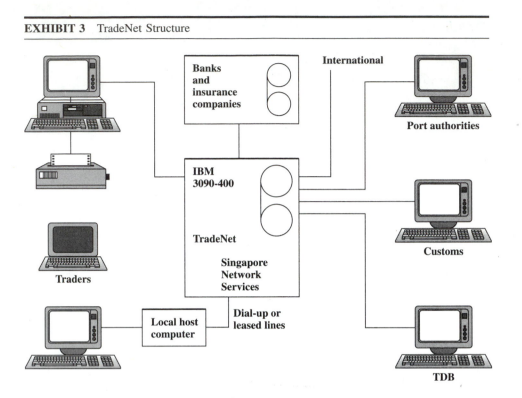

general economic development during the 1970s, a number of opportunities for Singapore's economic growth were explored. These explorations suggested that the broad field of information technology (IT) provided special opportunities for the country. Accordingly, a blue-ribbon Committee on National Computerization (CNC) was established by the government to develop specific recommendations on ways Singapore could pursue a future in the growing information technology field. In 1980, the CNC issued a report stating that Singapore could become one of the world's leaders in the creation and use of information technologies. To do so, however, the country would have to mobilize its efforts and create a coherent plan of development. In particular, it was necessary to build Singapore's IT human infrastructure. Only 850 IT professionals were available in the country in 1980. The CNC estimated that 10,000 would be needed by 1990 to accomplish its goals. Computer educa-

tion at all levels of school became a priority. Also, the country needed to gain practical experience with the technology. A special statutory board, the National Computer Board (NCB), was created under the ministry of finance and charged with creating development programs that would build Singapore into an IT Society. NCB's first major effort, the Government Computerization Project, focused on bringing computerization to government agencies and greatly expanded the skill base. The education programs worked well and by 1986 there were nearly 4,000 IT professionals available in the country. These initiatives provided the base for more ambitious undertakings.

In 1985, a recession hit Singapore, causing concern about the country's economic future and, in particular, the immediate goals of national economic development. A high level committee, convened to consider options, named improvement in external trade as a major goal. This report

EXHIBIT 4　TradeNet Schematic

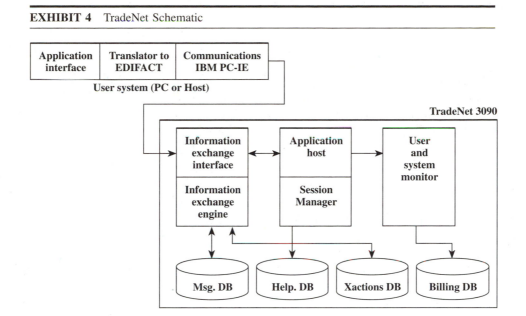

resulted in a concentrated effort to implement IT in both the port and the airport and was an important mobilizing factor leading to TradeNet. Also in 1986, Singapore's main shipping competitor, Hong Kong, revealed that it was working toward creation of a trade-oriented EDI system to be called Hotline (later renamed TradeLink).

Trade is clearly a multilateral phenomenon, involving many groups with differing interests. No single organization could create a workable computer system for trade. Whatever was done, it would have to be built on agreements among a large number of interest groups. Philip Yeo, chairman of the Economic Development Board (EDB) and National Computer Board (NCB), and a graduate of a well-known US East Coast MBA program, met with Yeo Seng Teck, chairman of the TDB, to discuss ways to proceed. Yeo Seng Teck recalled:

> Philip and I knew each other well. The small size of our country makes it possible for key people to get to know one another. In fact, people often hold a

number of key positions in different agencies through their careers. Philip was chairman of EDB, and I had been CEO of EDB before I moved over to TDB. We both understood the problems. We also knew nothing would happen unless we agreed to push it. So the two Yeos got together and agreed to make it happen.

They brought together a disparate group of influential interests and obtained agreement on "streamlining trade." This meant building technological support but, perhaps more important, it meant streamlining the procedures and protocols of many different agencies and organizations into a set of coherent and simplified procedures that could be automated. This challenge was often more political than technical. TDB was given the task of mobilizing the trade community and became the coordinating entity among the government agencies and statutory boards involved with trade, such as customs and excise, the Port of Singapore Authority, and Civil Aviation Authority of Singapore. Yeo Seng Teck called a meeting of

EXHIBIT 5   Interested Parties in the Process

TDB-MTI-EDB-NCB
Port of Singapore Authority
Jurong Town Corporation
Civil Aviation Authority of Singapore
  (Caas-Changi Airport)
Customs and excise
Singapore Telecoms
Other controlling agencies
Singapore National Shipping Association
Singapore Freight Forwarders Association
Singapore Air Cargo Agents Association
Board of Airline Representatives
Federation of Chambers of Commerce and Industry

EXHIBIT 6   TradeNet Committee Structure

the relevant interest groups that would have to come together in agreement if TradeNet were to succeed (see Exhibit 5). Participants included a large, heterogeneous mix of government agencies, companies, hierarchical organizations, and voluntary associations. Through several meetings and much discussion all the participants came to agree that significant savings would accrue from reducing the burdens of trade documentation handling and that streamlining trade would make the entire Singapore trading community more competitive internationally. Eventually, an "agreement to agree" was reached, and the process of streamlining began.

The most important first step in the process was to develop a detailed understanding of exactly what trade procedures were already being followed (see Exhibit 6). The TradeNet steering committee, which was created to oversee the process, was subdivided into three working subcommittees, one each for the maritime community (sea shipping), the air community (air shipping), and the government agencies and statutory boards. Individual NCB staffers were appointed to support each subcommittee. The subcommittees met regularly over several months, investigating trade procedures and developing a profile of essential trade documentation activities that must be incorporated

in any new set of procedures. Each subcommittee produced a report, and these reports were integrated by NCB staffers and members of the whole committee into an "integrated procedures report" that served as the focal point of procedural reform discussions.

Automating the existing procedures would produce nothing more than an automated mess. It would be necessary to reduce the 20+ forms involved in trade to a few or, ideally, one. There was much negotiation, during which organizations with long-standing procedures based on particular forms had to compromise. The result was a single form—actually, a large, formatted computer screen—to serve nearly all trade documentation needs in Singapore. This form would be the substantive core of the new computerized system. Once this agreement was made, the committee prepared a proposal for the creation of TradeNet. At about the same time, TDB began experimenting with a prototype on-line system called Trade-Dial-Up, which allowed traders to dial into the TDB computer system and complete trade forms from their local PCs or systems in terminal emulation mode. Completion of the single form made Trade-Dial-Up effective, and the system was used successfully to prove the concept that trade documentation could be completed on-line.

The TradeNet project was reviewed at the highest levels of government and received the go-ahead. In December 1986, B. G. Lee, son of the prime minister and head of the ministry of trade and industry, publicly announced the TradeNet project. In his announcement he said the new system would be operational within two years. This gave the development team little time, but by its decision the government gave the team the full authority and resources to proceed.

Building TradeNet

By February 1987, the TradeNet team had refined the reports produced in the analysis phase into a set of broad specifications for an EDI system for trade documentation, which they issued to a long list of possible vendors, and it developed a prequalification solicitation, essentially a request for information (RFI) that would provide background on which companies could undertake such a project. They also commissioned Price Waterhouse to do a separate study of TradeNet's likely market. The report suggested a potential customer base of about 2,200 firms engaged in trade-related activities in Singapore, plus the various government agencies and statutory boards that would be users of the system. Price Waterhouse was also asked to conduct a study of the basic information processing requirements of firms within the trading community. The objective of this study was to evaluate the potential applications of computers to these firms. This information would help firms develop applications to make them more productive. But the real objective was to enhance TradeNet's effects. TradeNet would be most useful if it tied directly into the automated systems of the trading firms, and the Price Waterhouse study provided examples of the applications that were needed to enhance TradeNet's value throughout the trading community.

The RFI produced 23 responses, mainly from US and Japanese firms. Most were judged too small or inexperienced to take on the project and were eliminated. To assess the remaining vendors, members of the TradeNet team made visits to EDI installations in the United States and Europe to see the various systems in action. By the summer of 1987, three finalists were chosen: IBM Corporation, McDonnell Douglas Information Systems Company, and General Electric Information Services Company (GEISCO). Each received a formal request for proposal (RFP) in June 1987. The proposals, received in September, were reviewed with special emphasis on each company's "staying power" in completing a project of TradeNet's complexity. In December 1987, a year after TradeNet was announced, IBM was notified that it was the winning bidder.

The specialists in IBM's Singapore office knew that TradeNet was not a trivial system. It would link together a number of existing and new procedural and computerized systems. The project was more of a systems integration effort than a system building effort. To head up the TradeNet technical effort, IBM sent Joe Huber, who had extensive experience in large-scale systems integration through IBM's Federal Systems Division, which builds special systems for the U.S. government. Huber's first decision was to put the contract negotiations on hold while IBM conducted a "detailed design study" of the proposed system. Basically, he wanted to know what IBM was really getting into. The TradeNet team agreed to IBM's study, even though it would take time, because the study would provide useful information for the actual construction of the system.

Since the TradeNet project was proceeding toward a formal contract with significant commitments, it was time to create an official organization to house the enterprise. The decision was made by the four key statutory boards involved in the project—TDB, the Port of Singapore Authority (PSA), which runs the port facilities, the Civil Aviation Authority of Singapore (CAAS), which runs Changi International Airport, and Singapore Telecoms, which runs the telephone system—to create a for-profit company to own and operate the system. On March 18, 1988, Singapore Network Services Pte. Ltd. (SNI) was created. TDB owned 55 percent of the SNS shares, and PSA, CAAS, and Telecoms each owned 15 percent. Pearleen Chan, who had been deputy general manager and head of the government computerization project at NCB, was named CEO of SNS. The core staff consisted of only four people, all of them from the original TradeNet committee. Of the original TradeNet team, only Ko Kheng Hwa did not move. He remained at NCB as head of industry computerization.

The detailed design review took three months and was submitted in April 1988. The results showed that the system could indeed be built as proposed, and minor modifications were made in the proposed contract to accommodate issues discovered during the review. The final contract between SNS and IBM was signed on May 25, 1988. IBM was the systems integration contractor with responsibility for all aspects of the system, except the software that would run at the user site (the application interface, EDIFACT translator, and communications module). IBM's partner in the project was a Singapore-based software company, CSA (Computer Systems Advisers, Pte. Ltd.), which would serve as subcontractor.

The general structure of TradeNet is shown in Exhibits 3 and 4. The actual construction of the system depended on adaptation of existing code and writing of new programs. The core of the system, which is shown in Exhibit 4 as the Information Exchange Engine, was a large, proprietary EDI system built for internal IBM use. Nicknamed the "Tampa Engine" for the IBM Information Networks division in Tampa, Florida, where it was created, it consisted of approximately 1.25 million lines of assembly code and had taken many person-years to build.[2] The Tampa Engine required only minor modifications to serve TradeNet purposes: a total of about 3,000 lines of code were altered in the process.

It was expected that the transfer of the Tampa Engine to the TradeNet application would be a modest undertaking. The basic system was in

---

[2] The "Tampa Engine" refers to the global IBM Information Network service.

place and proven, and the systems engineers (SEs) from Tampa would provide whatever help was needed to transport the system to its new use. IBM's Tampa operation, however, was not positioned to provide the requisite support, and IBM Singapore had to handle the installation on its own. The Singapore office added two SEs to its original complement and dispatched them to Tampa, and later to London, to study the Tampa Engine in detail and learn how it worked. This proved to be an essential factor in bringing the engine on-line for TradeNet.

In the meantime, IBM and CSA began work on the other components of the TradeNet system. CSA had responsibility, under IBM's direction, for writing the information exchange interface, the application host, the session manager, and the modules associated with system monitoring and user billing. All told, these modules constituted about 250,000 lines of COBOL code. CSA's professional staff had little difficulty developing this code as they made use of the well-developed procedural and design documents produced by the TradeNet team and by IBM in the detailed design review. Also, they were writing for the "target" of the Tampa Engine and knew the parameters they had to meet. Although they had only six months to develop and test the modules, they were able to make good progress.

During this period, two procedural steps were taken to help keep the program on track. The first was precipitated by an inevitable problem in complex system integration projects: the emergence of engineering change requests. Any new system poses a dilemma for designers. As the system is built, everyone learns more about what is desirable and undesirable, possible and impossible. Thus, there is a strong temptation to change the design to conform to this new understanding. Huber recognized this problem from his long experience in SI work and knew that the most serious consequence of implementing engineering changes was delay. With B.G. Lee's deadline of January 1989 looming, there was no slack in the schedule. To handle this problem, Huber instituted an "engineering change procedure" (ECP) to deal with all changes proposed by SNS. The procedure was straightforward, albeit demanding. Any proposed change was given a thorough assessment in terms of what it would actually require in time and money. The assessment, and the rationale behind it, was documented in an ECP report. This became the basis of negotiation between IBM and SNS.

The first encounter over a proposed change was stressful for the IBM/SNS relationship. Joe Huber explained:

> The results of the first ECP were startling, especially the projected cost and delay it would cause. Our relations with the customer were probably more tense at this time than at any other time in the project. But our numbers were right, and we stood by them. Eventually it became clear to everyone that changes cause cost and delay. Some delays can be accommodated; some cannot. Once everyone accepted the ECP as standard and took the results seriously, it was possible to make quick evaluations of proposed changes and decide whether to implement them or not. Some of the proposed changes were implemented, but many were not.

The ECP was a major breakthrough in the SNS/IBM relationship because it established a sense of shared purpose in the TradeNet enterprise. Both SNS and IBM were now focused on getting the system up on time; useful changes could wait for later.

The other procedural change was a decision of the top management of the enterprise to engage the SNS systems professionals early in the "customization" phase of the design and development process. This had two effects. Most important, it gave the SNS systems people early access to the major components of the system and allowed them time to learn in detail how the system was to work. This knowledge was instrumental in developing the customized features of the system for various user communities. Also important, however, the early involvement of the SNS systems people cemented the social bonds between IBM and SNS at the crucial level of technical reality. Thus, SNS systems people became effective boundary spanners be-

tween IBM and SNS leadership over important questions about design and implementation that might, under different circumstances, have been a source of serious disputes. This was especially crucial given the deadline. Chan Kah Khuen, a member of the early study team and later head of SNS's technical group, expressed it this way:

> There was real management commitment to this project and clear agreement on project objectives, so decisions were made fast. This helped build *esprit de corps*. The teams were also very skilled, with real expertise coming from IBM, CSA, and SNS. At times there were 100 to 200 people working together very closely, and everyone got on well. There were occasionally disagreements over the "gray areas," but these were resolved quickly because management paid attention to the effort and we were a real team.

In the meantime, SNS had let contracts to four local firms to develop the user interface software essential for the trading community that would use TradeNet. The initial implementations were kept relatively simple by standardizing on MS-DOS machines (e.g., the IBM PC) as the target user computer. This was sensible because the availability of low-priced, powerful MS-DOS systems made them the most common system among Singapore's business community. Also, to help keep implementation simple, SNS mandated use of the IBM PC-IE communications software that would link the user host to the TradeNet mainframe over leased or dial-up lines. In spite of the relative simplicity of the task, there were delays and problems in getting the user software ready for January. SNS spent considerable energy making the software work correctly. In the end, however, usable packages were created.

Delay-producing changes proposed for TradeNet were usually deferred through use of the ECP, but some essential changes were adopted and implemented. Some delays were unavoidable. SNS and IBM decided to concentrate on the basic information exchange and transaction processing components of the system for the January 1989 introduction of TradeNet. They delayed implementation of some database capabilities as well as the user billing modules until after the system was introduced. This allowed the team to concentrate on finishing, testing, and debugging the crucial components of the information exchange interface, the application host, the session manager, and the information exchange engine.

In addition, the progress on TradeNet was rapid because so much of the essential infrastructure was already in place. Pearleen Chan commented:

> TradeNet is the largest single project undertaken to date in the national effort to build IT capability, but it would have been impossible without the government computerization project that preceded it. Also, without the sophisticated computer systems installed in the various boards and agencies, TradeNet would have had nothing to hook up to. It wouldn't have mattered if we could deliver documents quickly to TDB or customs, for example, if they simply went into big stacks to be processed manually. The fact that documents flow through TradeNet into the automated systems at TDB and customs is essential to the main objective of speeding up trade document transactions.

The first transaction on TradeNet was a shipping application sent over a dial-up line by Merchants Air Cargo, a company owned by Mr. Joseph Low, who had served as the representative of the Singapore Air Cargo Agents Association on the TradeNet committee. The application was submitted on January 1, 1989. Ten minutes later, approval of the shipment was returned to the Merchants Air Cargo offices. TradeNet was operational.

In the next six months, the remaining modules were completed, tested, and installed. By June 1989, all of the original design components of TradeNet were in place, and planning had begun on significant enhancements. The direct capital cost of TradeNet's development (i.e., the contract cost to IBM and the other contractors) was more than S$20 million. This did not include the investment made by the various ministries and statutory boards in conceiving the project, developing the requirements and specifications, managing the contracting, or establishing SNS.

Results

The original expectations for TradeNet were ambitious. SNS hoped to capture about 25 percent of the total trade document transactions in the first year of operation, with a subscriber base of about 500. In retrospect, these ambitious expectations looked conservative. By December 1989, TradeNet had 850 out of about 2,200 possible subscribers, and about 45 percent of all trade documentation for sea and air shipments was being handled by the network. The success was so striking that TDB changed the date when use of TradeNet for all trade transactions would be made mandatory from early 1993 to early 1991. Most of the larger firms had already joined the system by the end of 1989. The balance of the 2,200 potential subscribers was comprised of medium and small firms. In anticipation of eventually making use of TradeNet mandatory, SNS began exploring means for facilitating the movement of the medium and smaller sized firms onto the system. As SNS had grown significantly, Pearleen Chan, who had still been working on projects at NCB, moved over to SNS full time in October 1989. By March 1990, SNS had grown to a full-time staff of five managers, 40 programmers and salespeople, and 10 support staff, and was expanding. It had outgrown its offices and was looking forward to moving into larger quarters in a new building under construction nearby. Soon, SNS was meeting its operational costs through revenues from TradeNet subscriptions and user fees.

Joining TradeNet cost a company S$750 for a one-time connect charge, with monthly costs of S$30 for a dial-up port and transaction costs of S$.5 per 1 kilobyte of transmitted information (the average declaration requires .7 kilobytes). In addition, the company needed to have the hardware necessary for local processing of the application and transmission of the coded EDIFACT data. The minimum required PC configuration cost about S$4,000, and the software between S$1,000 and S$4,000. This posed no problem for large companies, most of whom had significant in-house computer capability. Smaller companies were generally willing to buy the hardware since Singapore offered enticing tax write-offs for computer hardware purchased by small enterprises. Nevertheless, SNS and TDB recognized that not all small companies would wish to spend the capital necessary to join TradeNet right away. Therefore, three plans were developed to provide use of the system to those who didn't join. Small companies might, if they did not wish to make the necessary investments, use the facilities of service centers. Also, they might go to the TDB offices where data would be captured by TDB. Finally, TDB was considering opening convenient offices where public terminals and assistance could be obtained for a modest fee. It was anticipated that no more than 5 percent of total TradeNet volume would be conducted in these ways.

The cost of a company's overall changes in procedures and protocols required for moving to TradeNet were less clear than the direct costs. For some companies, the conversion was trivial because their own systems were already in place and ready to accommodate the new ways of doing business. For companies not yet used to doing business with computers, the change would be more difficult. Nevertheless, many small companies with no prior computing experience had purchased computers and begun to use them, due strictly to the availability of TradeNet.

TradeNet's performance effects were beginning to be noticed. Turnaround time for processing of typical trade documents had been reduced from a minimum of one day and as many as four days to as little as 15 minutes. Most transactions were actually completed in 10 minutes. This had had a remarkable effect on the subscribers to the system. An example of this was the experience of MSAS Cargo International, a worldwide multimodal freight forwarder with a major office in Singapore. Ms. Georgiana Yuen, regional systems manager at MSAS, Pte. Ltd. Singapore, explained:

> The productivity improvements from TradeNet have been significant. The turnaround is much faster, and we can speed up the movements of shipments to our customers. There are also major logistics

improvements. For example, we used to have to send clerks as couriers with documents to various offices here, at Caas-Changi International Airport, or downtown. Now there is no need to. The clerks do not have to wait in line and are always here in the office. This saves a lot of time and means better deployment of our staff. Also, we've been able to make better use of our trucks. Fast turnaround makes it possible for us to organize shipments onto outgoing trucks. Mainly, we benefit from improved service to our customers, more effective control of trucks and equipment, and of manpower resources. As a result, we experience higher productivity in our operations. TradeNet has become a key part of our operations.

Great Expectations

While formal analysis of the cost impacts of TradeNet for subscribers had yet to be performed, several freight forwarders reported savings of 25 percent to 35 percent in handling trade documentation. Expectations of benefits by TradeNet subscribers were significant and were indicated by the experiences of Merchants Air Cargo, Pte. Ltd., a freight forwarder based at Changi International Airport. MAC had been an innovator in use of computers for its operations for several years. By 1984, it had computerized most of its back office functions (accounting, statistics, etc.) using a NEC ASTRA minicomputer. Although its software was custom-built by an outside contractor, over time it took all system support activities in-house. In 1985, the company embarked on computerizing significant aspects of its operations, but since most transactions involving shipments were tied to outside entities that were not computerized, the full potential of computerized operations was difficult to realize. MAC was a participant in TDB's Trade Dial-Up experiments in 1986-87, which confirmed the potential of computerization of trade documentation functions. And MAC served as one of the exemplary sites for development of the requirements described in the air community subcommitee report. MAC continued to develop its in-house computer capabilities during the period when TradeNet was being constructed. It expanded its minicomputer system and installed new terminals that gave the company a terminal-to-employee ratio of one to two. When TradeNet went on-line, MAC sent the first transaction over the system.

Mr. Joseph Low, president of MAC, characterized the potential of TradeNet for his company and for his industry:

> TradeNet really makes our business work more efficiently. It is a 24-hour-per-day system, which is a big improvement over having to work through offices that are open only eight hours a day. We can integrate our operations now. For example, we can get information on an incoming shipment prior to the arrival of the aircraft it is on, submit the documents, get the shipment cleared, and meet the plane with all the finished documents in hand. We can get shipments to customers very quickly this way. Also, we can clear whole collections of shipments in a single transaction, which speeds things up. And we can consolidate shipments on our trucks, which saves time and money. We also save money by not having to send people out to stand in line in queues, waiting to have documents cleared. Since we are computerized in our own operations, we save money and time by automatically completing most of the TradeNet documentation using information already entered in our own system. Between 60 percent to 70 percent of the information required for each TradeNet submission is automatically transferred from our own system each time we prepare documentation forms. When the additional capabilities for banking and insurance interactions are installed, the benefits will be greater. Even now, we are completely dependent on our systems. A couple of months ago we had a major power failure here, and the systems were all down. Everyone sat around, unable to work. But I don't mind that. The payoffs are worth it.

The expectation of benefits for the subscribers was matched by the benefits to the various government agencies and statutory boards that used the system. For example, customs and excise had found TradeNet to be a major adjunct to its operations. Customs and excise director General Lee Yew Kim summarized:

TradeNet is part of our larger scheme to improve performance through use of computers. Our earlier computerization efforts made our important procedural reforms work to our advantage. We were able to turn customs and excise into an agency that helps speed up trade, not slow it down. For example, we went from a procedure of postapproval of applications to preapproval. Duties are now prepaid and post approval checks on an audit basis are then made. Violators are subject to penalties, such as fines, and their subsequent shipments are inspected. This makes them uncompetitive, so the responsible companies never even try to avoid customs checks. This procedure change improved throughput dramatically, but most important, it made it possible for our computers to interface directly with TradeNet. We are also using TradeNet as the vehicle for payment of customs duties, which means we get paid much faster. Only a fraction of the traders are paying via TradeNet now, but this will grow rapidly.

Benefits to the TDB, the "clearinghouse" for trade documentation in Singapore, had been substantial in both direct and indirect ways. TDB CEO Yeo Seng Teck summarized the short-run and long-run benefits this way:

> We haven't done a detailed study of the benefits yet, but the system is clearly a success. We have about 50 percent of the transactions going through the system now, and we expect to have 90 percent by the end of 1990. We'll cut over to use of TradeNet for almost all transactions around that time. The local benefits of TradeNet are very nice, but the big payoffs for us are international. TDB is not a trade control agency; it is a trade facilitator. We are trade promoters. TradeNet facilitates trade. It makes it easier to do business in Singapore. That draws foreign investment to our economy and makes us competitive internationally. We are very happy to say that Hong Kong is now looking to us for inspiration.

TradeNet, in conjunction with information systems innovations in the port and airport, permitted faster total turnaround for ships and aircraft. For example, the Port of Singapore Authority installed sophisticated computer-based systems that facilitated registration of incoming vessels, deployment of vessels to port facilities (e.g., container cranes), optimization of off-loading and on-loading sequences, and discharging of vessels that were ready to leave. Similarly, systems had been installed to facilitate movement of cargoes within the free-trade zone, into and out of the free-trade zone, into and out of customs warehouses, and between the port and the airport. The total package of aids to trade was making Singapore into one of the world's most efficient trading centers.

Beyond TradeNet

TradeNet launched Singapore's full entry into the development and deployment of EDI services. SNS was created not only as the owner and custodian of TradeNet, but as a company that would develop and deploy value-added networks throughout the Singapore economy. Already, TradeNet offered interbank GIRO service for electronic payments. This facility was used by customs and excise and would be expanded substantially for all users. In addition, TradeNet would offer interorganizational interchange of many kinds of business documents among subscribers, including invoice, purchase orders, delivery orders, debit and credit notes, and so on. These were intended to facilitate such business practices as just-in-time inventory control and direct store delivery. TradeNet also would be linked to the international trade community.

Beyond the trade sector, SNS was working on EDI networks for the health care, legal, retailing, and manufacturing sectors. A health care network called MediNet was being planned to link hospitals, laboratories, pharmacies, drug distributors, private clinics, and medical supply companies. Among the information to be exchanged in this system were hospital payments via the third-party payments system; public health data that must be reported to government authorities; purchase orders, invoices, and delivery orders for drugs and medical supplies; and patient medical records. The system would also provide access to international medical databases. Preliminary designs were also under way for a supplier-manufacturer network that would permit international multinationals in the electronics industry to order and pay for components from local suppliers. In time, exchange of computer-aided design (CAD) files would be provided via this system, and the system would contain the ability to translate such files from one protocol to another (e.g., between AutoCAD and other formats). Similar network utilities were designed to link major chain stores with suppliers, incorporating data collected from point-of-sale terminals. Pearleen Chan noted:

> Our vision is to extend the use of EDI through every sector of the Singapore economy, to create a more conducive environment for doing business and to give our companies a truly competitive edge. I believe we will see tremendous growth in the EDI industry over the next decade. We at SNS will do our best to be among the leaders in this business.

Case 7–5 Singapore TradeNet (B): The Tale Continues*

"We are quite pleased with our success so far," observed Pearleen Chan, CEO of Singapore Network Services (SNS).

"We've been profitable since our second year of operation. Our revenues grew from about S$4 million in 1989 to more than S$20 million, with S$3.2 million profit, in 1992. We have no debt. Our paid-up share capital of S$24 million was financed from funds provided by our owning boards. We never borrowed a cent from the banks. Our owners told us to concentrate on the business and they would provide the funds we need. We moved into a new building some months ago. We are now up to 150 full-time staff. We installed our own mainframe computer, an IBM ES/9121 Model 440 with a capacity of 30 MIPS, in mid-1991. Most important, we have implemented a large number of the value-added network services we envisioned four years ago."

Singapore Network Services Pte. Ltd. was created in March 1988 to initiate and manage the creation of value-added networks for trade and other aspects of commerce in the island nation of Singapore. Company stock was owned by four "statutory boards," quasi-government agencies with focused missions in the Singapore economy. The Trade Development Board guided development and management of external trade in Singapore (55 percent); the Civil Aviation Authority of Singapore owned and operated Caas-Changi Airport (15 percent); the Port of Singapore Authority managed Singapore's huge container port (15 percent); and Singapore Telecoms was the country's local and long-distance telephone utility (15 percent).

*Professor Boon-Siong Neo of Nanyang Technological University, Professor John L. King of the University of California–Irvine, and Professor Lynda Applegate prepared this case. Copyright © 1993 by the President and Fellows of Harvard College. Harvard Business School case 193-136 (Revised March 25, 1993).

The TradeNet System

Singapore is the 17th-largest trading nation in the world, with total trade exceeding S$220 billion in 1992. Documentation is an expensive aspect of trade; delay in processing documentation not only increases expenses, but also lowers utilization of warehouse and port facilities. TradeNet, an electronic data interchange (EDI) system that links multiple parties to external trade transactions creating a single point-of-transaction for most trade documentation tasks, was SNS's first product. Studies suggested that TradeNet reduced the time required to process most trade applications (requests for approval to export or import) from between two to four days to as little as 15 minutes and reduced the trade documentation processing costs by 20 percent or more. Changes in trade processing secondary to implementation of TradeNet are detailed in Exhibit 1.

In December 1989, after one year of operation, TradeNet was serving 800 of an estimated 2,400 trade-related organizations in Singapore and was being used for approximately 45 percent of trade document transactions. By the end of 1990, 1,500 trade-related organizations were using TradeNet to process about 90 percent of trade documentation requirements. The numbers reached 1,800 and 95 percent by mid-1991. (The remaining 5 percent of trade documents pertained to disparate elements such as personal effects of ship and airline crews and diplomatic staff and commodities such as rice that were subject to sensitive regulations.)

Trade-related services subsequently added to TradeNet included, in March 1990, a module to enable exporters to apply electronically for certificates of origin (COs) which certified sources of manufactured products for purposes of qualifying imports for preferential tax treatment in importing countries. Automation of CO applications reduced

EXHIBIT 1 Trade Processing before and after TradeNet

Characteristics	Before TradeNet	After TradeNet
Submission of documents	By dispatch clerks	By electronic transmission
Trips per document	At least two trips	No trips needed
Interpersonal interactions	Dispatch clerk and TDB counter clerk; TDB supervisor and data-processing clerks	No interpersonal interactions needed
Knowledge of trade codes	Resident in TDB processing clerks	Resident in TradeNet system
Checking and approval process	Manual	Automatic
Turnaround time for document processing	4 hours (urgent) to 2 days (normal)	15 minutes
Fees charged users	S$6–S$10	S$6
Accuracy of data on declaration vis-à-vis documents	100% manually checked prior to approval	Automatic system edit checks; no manual checks; sample audit source checks of supporting documents
Dutiable goods handling	Separate document for customs processing	Same electronic document automatically routed to customs based on harmonized system codes
Controlled goods handling	Separate documents to different controlling agencies for processing	Same electronic document to controlling agencies automatically
Number of staff in TDB documentation department	134	88 (as of July 1992)
Floor space used by TDB documentation department	1,390 square meters	985 square meters

the approval process from two days to half a day and eliminated for exporters one of the two trips needed to collect approved COs. (Printed COs persisted only because many countries of destination, including the United States, continued to require paper COs on arrival.)

SNS expanded its network activity considerably following the launch of TradeNet, which was designed from the beginning to be the first step in the broader strategic objective of learning to build value-added networks. The skills developed in designing and implementing TradeNet were to be applied to the creation of other value-added networks for Singapore and, eventually, other customers. SNS's primary contribution to the Singapore economy was not, observed Yeo Seng Teck, CEO of the Trade Development Board and chairman of SNS, the improvement of trade, per se, but a larger vision. "What SNS is really doing," he explained,

is building information infrastructure. We leveraged the trade documentation application to give us a beachhead. But we knew right from the start that we were investing in an information infrastructure to achieve higher efficiency and productivity. We decided to go ahead with TradeNet even though initial calculations indicated that the payback would take many years. Singapore as a country has never been stingy on infrastructural developments—look at how aggressively we have invested in building our highways, container port facilities, airport, and telecommunications network. We know we have a small population and limited land, and therefore we have to leverage what we have to the fullest. We knew that EDI was the way to go, but we were unsure how it would be perceived by the business community. When the response to TradeNet surpassed our expectations, we became more confident and decided to hasten the pace of EDI usage in trade and other business sectors after the first year of TradeNet operation.

Other Networks

SNS built on its TradeNet experience to develop and implement networks for other sectors of the Singapore economy, mostly in profit-sharing partnership arrangements with government departments and industry associations. Government was particularly keen for such arrangements as SNS could speed implementation of needed systems. Moreover, having a private company bear development costs and business risks made it unnecessary for the cooperating government agency to petition the finance ministry to underwrite the projects, a process that takes considerable time. "Each deal is structured differently," explained Chan about arrangements with partners.

> If we invest in the development of the systems, we take equity interests in the products and ensure that they have sufficient payback to justify the investments. We try to make sure that new projects pay back within three years, although there have been projects that we intentionally invested in for the long term. If we just provide the network service, we do not take equity interests but charge for usage. If the service involves access to information provided by third parties, they get a cut from the service. We try to work out arrangements that are equitable to all parties.

Concepts for systems originated from a variety of sources—government departments, private firms, and SNS—but the expertise required for design resided with SNS, which offered its network as a delivery mechanism for services provided by new systems. Industry associations were enlisted to offer new services to their members and proved effective in persuading their members to use the new services. SNS thus provided the technical infrastructure for new services and gained by having those new services in its portfolio. SNS also reached new groups of customers through its government and industry partners, which marketed new services, recruited customers to make the new services viable, and utilized SNS network capacity more fully and economically.

With TradeNet running, the National Computer Board began to look for opportunities to apply similar network concepts in other industries. Major initiatives were subsequently begun in the medical and legal sectors.

MediNet was a national computer network that linked hospitals, clinics, drug and surgical equipment stores, the ministry of health (MOH), and the central provident fund (CPF), which administered the use of individual retirement funds, a portion of which (termed *Medisave*) could be used to pay hospitalization charges prior to retirement. Developed jointly with MOH and the National Computer Board (NCB), MediNet provided for electronic submission of hospital claims to the CPF Board and medical information to the ministry of health, reducing the need for paper-based forms and speeding the processing of claims. The system was implemented in July 1990.

Like many successful innovations, MediNet was a product that was developed from ideas generated by many sources. NCB proposed the idea for MediNet in 1988, at the same time experiments were under way in such countries as New Zealand, Sweden, and the United States. Of particular interest were experiments in Taiwan, where national patient master indexes and other medical databases were being developed, and the United Kingdom, where EDI was being used for procurement of medicines and medical supplies. Impetus for MediNet in Singapore grew when a new medical insurance scheme, Medishield, was approved. Medishield, to be administered by the CPF Board, was to deduct premiums from CPF individual retirement accounts. Discussions on the implementation of Medishield raised considerations that it and Medisave might use a similar form. Lau Chee Chong, head of the accounts department at the Ministry of Health, recalled how the electronic processing of claims became the core function of MediNet.

> In discussing the use of a form for the submission of Medishield claims, there were concerns that the administrative costs of computing Medisave and Medishield claimable expenses separately could be very high in view of 1.7 million Medisave account holders and with Medishield expected to cover more than one million people. When the issue of using the same form to submit claims for both Medisave and Medishield was resolved, we began to ask whether the claims should be submitted electronically. Although claim processing was listed in the original proposal for MediNet, it was not a feature that was considered to be central to the system. To reduce cost and time for claims, we decided to launch the electronic claims processing module of MediNet at the same time as the launch of Medishield. That was at the end of 1989, giving us only about six months to build and implement MediNet. With cooperation from NCB, SNS, and CPF, we met the target launch date.

SNS was able to implement MediNet quickly, observed Chan Kah Khuen, deputy CEO of SNS, by leveraging the available TradeNet infrastructure. "When we implemented TradeNet," he explained,

> we were fortunate to be able to rely on Singapore's public telecommunication lines for transmission of EDI messages. We bought the EDI message manager ("engine") from IBM to perform the role of a giant electronic mailbox for TradeNet messages. Once that was in place, applications like MediNet could be built on top of the EDI engine very quickly. The logic was the same. Just as TradeNet enabled electronic messages to be

exchanged between traders and government trade bodies, MediNet enabled electronic exchange between hospitals and MOH and CPF. Every electronic message has a six-byte alpha code that identifies message type. When the message is sent to the SNS computer, the message code identifies the application, in this case, TradeNet or MediNet, to be used to process the message. For MediNet, we defined the information required for claims processing, created a new message code to identify and route it, programmed the application to perform the necessary processing and front-end edit checks, and added new electronic mailboxes for hospitals, MOH, and CPF. We used the same TradeNet mainframe computer, operating systems, network control software, and message manager to implement MediNet. This approach has since been used to develop and implement other SNS products and services.

MediNet had functionality beyond its original conception. It enabled hospitals to submit medical statistics to MOH and provided access to a number of medical information services, including a database for cancer treatment procedures and care. Among new services being developed for MediNet were a poison and drug information database, a health care professional register, information on medical service providers, and a utility to allow hospitals to order pharmaceutical and medical supplies directly from suppliers. Development of a national database of patient biographic and other medical information, access to which was to be subject to patient permission, was also undertaken.

Almost immediately upon MediNet's launch, 13 major hospitals began using it to submit claims to CPF. Within a month, more than 90 percent of the 1,200 daily Medisave and Medishield claims were being processed through MediNet, and within a year, smaller hospitals and clinics were using MediNet to submit Medisave/Medishield claims. By 1991, the number of hospitals had risen to 24 and the proportion of claims processed via MediNet came close to 100 percent. Claims approval was also accelerated, with about 80 percent of claims approved within two hours, compared to a minimum of one week under the paper-based system. Payment by check, which was executed within one week of approval, was expected to be done more quickly when the direct bank crediting module of MediNet was implemented.

LawNet, which provided electronic access to legal statutes, was launched in July 1990. "We had begun computerizing the attorney general (AG)'s chambers in 1988," explained Lee Seiu Kin, deputy state counsel in the AG's chambers.

> We had started to work on putting legal statutes on-line so that lawyers could access them electronically. When we began to look into the resources needed to offer statutes on-line, we realized that it would not be feasible for the AG's chambers to do it. We approached SNS in 1989 and coined the name LawNet to sell this service. SNS knew that usage for electronic access to legal statutes would not be high, but was willing to do it in the interest of introducing network services for sectors beyond trade. We said that other services might be added later, but there were no concrete plans. We appreciated their commitment to introduce LawNet. In late 1990, Robin Hu, NCB's information systems manager for the legal sector, proposed that many of the applications and information services that had been planned or developed by individual government departments in the legal sector be integrated and offered to the public as part of LawNet. This included services in the AG's chambers, judiciary, registry of trademarks and patents, and registry of land titles and deeds. In our study visit to the United States in late 1990, we had seen many applications of IT in law firms and county courts, including the Lexis system that contains legal judgments of the United States, United Kingdom, and Australia. But we did not see any integrated system that catered to the needs of the legal community. The concept of LawNet was to allow users to access a host of applications and services through the same screen. When we presented the integrated LawNet system to the chief justice, the law minister, and AG, they were all for it. The "second phase" of LawNet was launched in November 1992.

LawNet subsequently provided modules to facilitate legal research and provide bankruptcy and litigation information and access to corporate law information (profiles of company directors, and so forth). Of special importance is LawNet's recent support of electronic submission of documents to courts and electronic conveyancing, whereby documents required by 11 different government departments in many property-related transactions are automated and can be submitted by entering the data on one screen, an especially useful system for law firms. When LawNet was first implemented in July 1990, only about 200 lawyers in about 30 firms, out of a pool of 2,400 lawyers in 600 firms, used it to access statutes electronically. With the new services added to LawNet since November 1992, the number of subscribers increased to 1,300 lawyers in about 180 law firms.

The success of TradeNet, MediNet, and LawNet gave rise to network projects in manufacturing and engineering, business, real estate, and cargo transport. Among these were GraphNet, BizNet, EPC-Net, RealNet, and StarNet.

GraphNet supported electronic exchange of computer-aided design (CAD) drawings and other graphics and facilitated translation among different types of computer-aided design/computer-aided manufacturing (CAD/CAM) software. Developed by SNS in partnership with Nanyang Technological University's CIM Research Institute and the Construction Industry Development Board, GraphNet enabled companies to access graphical libraries containing drawings of components, symbols, and designs and to exchange product designs among dispersed divisions or business partners. This reduced the need for redrawing, shortened drafting and design time, and speeded up the product development cycle. GraphNet also accommodated the exchange of engineering specifications between manufacturers and contractors and architectural drawings between architects, contractors, and government agencies. The use of GraphNet after about two years was relatively low. SNS was attributed to the high cost of transmission (graphics files are very large) and lack of local technical infrastructure among users.

BizNet provided users access to business information lodged with the registry of companies and businesses (RCB). New business enterprises were required by law to register with RCB and provide information about the nature and profile of the business, its officers, and so forth. Changes were submitted periodically. All businesses were required to file statistical and financial information (turnover, profits, and so forth) annually. Developed jointly with RCB, BizNet enabled users to electronically submit information RCB required and access information about other business enterprises for planning and transaction purposes. This eliminated the need to make physical trips to RCB. Within the first three months of operation, more than 200 firms used BizNet to access RCB information. BizNet was upgraded in mid-1991 to allow firms to file their returns to RCB electronically. A new service, DunsLink, was added in 1991 to enable firms considering overseas business ventures to obtain Dun & Bradstreet reports on international companies and markets.

EPCNet was developed in partnership with seven chambers of commerce and industry associations that jointly established the enterprise promotion center (EPC) to promote development of local Singapore enterprises, particularly smaller-sized firms. The network enabled firm members of the seven associations to communicate and transact with one another electronically and access trade and business opportunities and information about potential trading partners. EPCNet was to be extended to the other five countries in the ASEAN regional economic grouping (Malaysia, Indonesia, Philippines, Brunei, and Thailand) at the end of 1991.

RealNet enabled the real estate community to list properties for sale and search for properties that matched client specifications. Developed in collaboration with the real estate industry, RealNet institutionalized co-brokerage practices among real estate agents, whereby the commission is split between buying and selling agents. The co-brokerage agreement provided the financial incentive for agents to use RealNet for both buying and selling client properties. RealNet-listed properties tended to sell faster because it became *the* database for search by prospective buyers. Buying agents could serve clients faster and better by reducing the time and cost of their searches. By matching client specifications (budget, type of property, size, age, location, and so forth) to the characteristics of properties listed, they could select for viewing only the most appropriate properties and thereby reduce time, cost, and inconvenience to the client. In 1992, RealNet was enhanced to provide price comparisons to past sales records of agents and to past sale prices and present asking prices of similar properties in a particular location.

StarNet supported communication and exchange of information and documents among air cargo agents. Developed in partnership with the Singapore Aircargo Agents Association, StarNet facilitated planning and operations by enabling air cargo agents to buy and sell cargo space electronically, report on lost and found cargo to expedite tracking, communicate changes in clientele, and post notification of cargo arrival. Moreover, it provided E-mail facilities for communication among cargo agents, airlines, consignees, and ground handling agents. Because it was not essential to air cargo agents' operations, StarNet did not meet expectations for usage, leading SNS to explore with customers how StarNet might be enhanced to better serve the operational needs of air cargo agents.

Subsequent projects suggested that SNS was making headway in its expansion program. In 1992, SNS launched jointly with the ministry of defense (MINDEF) a new procurement network, ProfNet, to link MINDEF to its suppliers, vendors, and contractors. ProfNet enabled MINDEF and its suppliers to electronically exchange invitations, awards, purchase and work orders, proposals, invoices, and other documents.

ApparelNet, developed jointly with the Textile and Garment Manufacturers Association, supported communication between manufacturers and suppliers, and provided a database of available products and services needed by the apparel industry. It also facilitated quota management, an important function for a textile producer such as Singapore. ApparelNet allowed manufacturers to offer excess quota to others who may need it in a given period.

ColnNet, the first phase of a system developed for the construction industry in collaboration with the Singapore Contractors Association, was implemented in July 1992. Material prices were updated weekly to enable contractors to more accurately estimate costs in bidding for tenders. More information services were to be added in subsequent phases, including tender results, contractor profiles, and market analyses.

Generic EDI/Network Services

SNS moved beyond its targeted approach to specific communities by building a range of generic network and information services. OrderLink, for example, enabled business firms to electronically exchange business documents related to the procurement and delivery of goods. Buyers could use the network to call for quotations or tenders, issue purchase orders to suppliers, and pay suppliers upon receipt of goods. Suppliers could respond to requests for quotations or tenders, confirm orders, and issue invoices to buyers. OrderLink was begun early, shortly after TradeNet went on-line. One of its first users, Changi International Airport Services (CIAS), employed the system to send purchase orders to suppliers of food, material, and other services to the international airlines that it served. A first step toward an integrated procurement system, OrderLink grew from five users in 1990 to more than 130 in 1992.

MaiLink provided users such routine E-mail services as sending and receipt of messages, maintenance of distribution lists, fax interface, calendaring, and bulletin boards. It, too, was begun shortly after TradeNet. Among the services added since early 1990 were $Link and InfoLink. $Link enabled businesses to instruct their banks to collect or pay commercial bills on their behalf, thereby minimizing checkwriting and issuance and simplifying check receiving and banking procedures. Businesses can use $Link to have their

banks perform much of the mundane payroll function and manage their funds electronically. Begun initially with DBS, one of the four local banks, $Link subsequently was made available by Citibank and the Hong Kong Bank. Many government departments and statutory boards used $Link to pay bills with an eye toward a totally checkless environment. InfoLink provided access to a range of external databases, including stock prices, currency rates, vessel and flight schedules, world news, and trade statistics.

SNS pioneered Singapore's international networking as well. The country's first international linkage became available in March 1990 through an electronic connection to the local node of General Electric information services (GEIS), which provided access to more than 5,000 users in 750 cities. The uses made of this system were impressive. Apple Computer's manufacturing division in Singapore, for example, used the GEIS connection to send orders directly to a Motorola subsidiary in Hong Kong, eliminating the need to go through Motorola's Singapore division and reducing the order confirmation turnaround from three weeks to three days. Three additional international links were established in early 1991. A link to Fujitsu's EDI network enabled users to communicate with 18,000 business users in Japan's retail and manufacturing sectors; a link to the INTIS network in the Rotterdam port in the Netherlands supported electronic transmission of all trade-related documents for shipments between Singapore and Rotterdam and provided the needed gateway for communication with businesses in Europe; a link to the Ministry of Information in Indonesia enabled businesses in both countries to exchange documents needed in trade activities. In late 1991, SNS linked to the Intertrade network in Hong Kong, allowing traders in both countries to exchange all documents necessary for trade transactions.

SNS moved beyond community-oriented network services for business users with the August 1992 launch of Comet, a community network that provided individuals and households with low cost, 24-hour access to electronic services. Marketed as a "community service" and operated on equipment donated by DEC and Racal Electronics, a local vendor, Comet services included self-learning tutorials, bulletin board services, E-mail, on-line chatting, on-line shopping, access to PC shareware, current events, and access to other information and network services. SNS hoped through Comet to familiarize a new generation of computer users with network services; within three months, more than 2,500 individuals had signed on and used Comet.

Services under Development

SNS planned to expand value-added network services for specific sectors of the Singapore economy and targeted, among other sectors, manufacturing. SNS undertook with the Economic Development Board and Institute of Manufacturing Technology the development of ManuNet, which was to link manufacturing firms together in a network.

SNS was also exploring new services that catered to the tourist and leisure sectors. In response to a request from the Singapore Tourist Promotion Board, SNS invested in a prototype tourist information terminal and "smart card" application that was demonstrated at a major tourism and travel conference in Singapore in December 1992. SNS collected feedback from conference participants to help develop a full-scale application for the tourist and travel industry.

In a joint study with the Information Management Research Center of the Nanyang Technological University, SNS investigated the feasibility of moving beyond TradeNet and StarNet by electronically linking all parties in the trading sector. The proposed network would link traders, transportation companies, freight forwarders, warehouse operators, banks, insurance companies, and government agencies, allowing for total integrated cargo, logistics, and information management.

In late 1992, SNS concluded an agreement to provide "managed network services" to NTUC Supermarkets, the largest retail chain in Singapore, with more than 40 outlets and annual revenues in excess of S$40 million. James Kang, SNS's director for business development, explained how SNS won the NTUC deal.

In contrast to services like LawNet, for example, where SNS was approached to provide the delivery mechanism after it was conceived and deliberated in the AG chambers, SNS targeted and pursued NTUC supermarkets for nine months before it was awarded the job. We have wanted to go into the retail sector for a long time and NTUC was a logical target because it was the largest chain in Singapore. In the first phase, we will be linking all 40 branches to headquarters for electronic communication. We will then link the headquarters and branches to their suppliers. NTUC sends more than 4,000 orders to suppliers daily. The new network will have significant benefits to NTUC, and we are pleased to be able to do it for them.

A link to SITA, the airline telecommunications and information services organization, expected to be launched in early 1993, would enable users to electronically communicate with more than 25,000 airlines, freight forwarders, customs administrators, and travel-related businesses in 184 countries and provide access to international cargo booking services and databases and freight tracking applications. By mid-1993, SNS expected to be linked to Spectrum, a cargo community system that would enable SNS customers to book cargo space with airlines and track the status of cargo shipments worldwide.

Business Plans

SNS was developing its own mainframe EDI engine. Its existing engine, licensed from IBM in 1988, had satisfied SNS's needs in its first few years. As TradeNet's reputation grew, and as SNS's success became more visible, many countries in the region sought its advice about implementing EDI networks within their borders. In trying to provide EDI consulting in the region, SNS found that it could not provide a total service package to clients because the licensing agreement with IBM prohibited it from licensing or selling the EDI engine to a third party. By 1990, SNS had begun to see the lack of its own EDI engine as a potential hurdle to future growth, and decided to devote resources to develop one. More than 40 IT professionals worked on the project for two years. A PC-version of the EDI engine was released in late 1992. When its mainframe EDI engine is available in 1993, it will be a major milestone toward SNS's objective of being a total provider of EDI and value-added network services.

With more Singapore businesses expanding into the Southeast Asian region, SNS foresees growing demand for electronic network services and access to information databases, and wants to be a recognized player in the local market of the regional countries. It hopes to expand revenue from its international business from less than 5 percent of its total business to 20 percent over five years. Toward the end of 1992, Chan and her directors began traveling to neighboring countries to make contacts, close some deals, and negotiate others. SNS, she explained, hopes to enter more regional markets while maintaining its dominant position in Singapore.

> We want to be the EDI provider for Singapore. We are in overdrive. We are ahead and we keep moving. We want to make interorganizational networking a way of doing business for every business sector in Singapore. We are now very strong in the trade and distribution sectors, and we are penetrating the manufacturing sector. But we have made few inroads into the financial services sector because it is a mature market. We still have the consumer market that is largely untapped. We also aim to be a major regional player in the local markets of the Asian countries. We are discussing deals with local partners in Korea, Taiwan, the Philippines, Indonesia, and other Asian countries. The region recognizes SNS's headstart in EDI and network technology and is keen to learn from our experience in setting up network services within their countries. SNS tries to respond to all requests for information and services. We expand the business through new projects, but without adding people. I have frozen new hires since last year. We roll our people over from project to project. We have just reorganized and now have three business development groups. I give the groups complete freedom to decide on how to grow the business in SNS. As long as the new projects are commercially viable and we can do them without adding people and without overtaxing the management structure, we will go for it.

PART III

Toward the 21st Century

Chapter 8   *IT and Business Transformation*

Chapter 9   *Information Technology and Tomorrow's Manager*

Business transformation occurs when managers align new technologies, strategies, structures, human resources, and management control systems. To build a successful information-age organization, it is necessary to dismantle much of the existing industrial-age organization. Part III examines how networked information technologies can enable a fundamental transformation of strategic objectives, organizational structures, and management control systems.

Chapter 8 describes how business process reengineering and continuous IT innovation can lead to business transformation.

Chapter 9 looks to the future by examining emerging information technologies and their implications for the information-age organization.

Chapter 8

IT and Business Transformation

INTRODUCTION

When IT *substitutes* for human effort, it *automates* a task or process.

When IT *augments* human effort, it *informates* a task or process.

When IT *restructures,* it *transforms* a set of tasks or processes.

Automating, informating, and transforming are all important IT-enabled activities that can help improve a firm's financial performance, relationship with customers, employee satisfaction, and organizational adaptiveness. In this chapter we focus on ambitious efforts to *transform business processes.*

Information technologies affect how individuals carry out their work, how organizations are structured and managed, and how relations between organizations are structured and managed. As organizations capitalize on networked IT capabilities, the possibilities for transforming work, people, structures, and systems dramatically increase. This chapter and the final chapter address issues associated with IT-enabled business transformation. This chapter is organized as follows:

The goal: organizational effectiveness: What are the characteristics of an "effective" organization? What are the goals of business transformation?

The tools: role of IT in business transformation: How can IT help transform business processes? What are the constraints in using IT for business transformation?

The process: how to achieve business transformation: What can we learn from firms that have already undertaken business transformation efforts? What pitfalls can be avoided, and how?

Sustaining IT innovation: How can organizations foster continuous IT-based innovation in support of continuous adaptation to changing conditions?

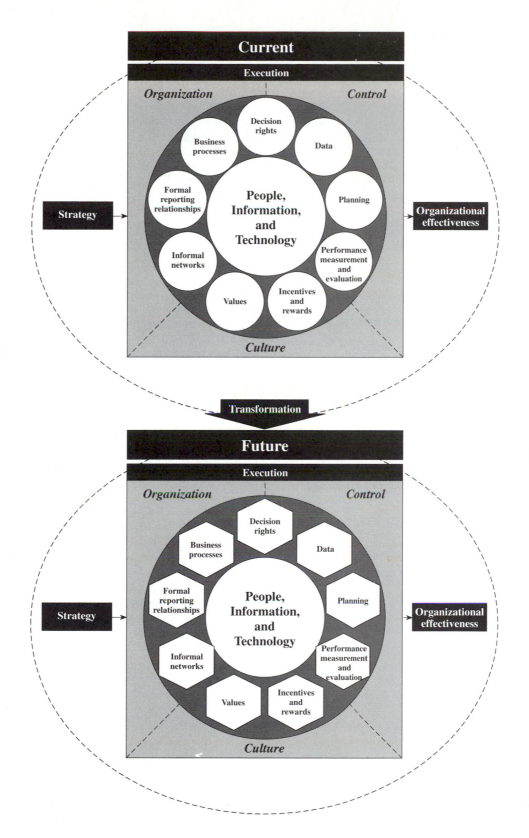

THE GOAL: ORGANIZATIONAL EFFECTIVENESS

The purpose of new strategy, structure, and systems is to improve organizational effectiveness. The starting point for business transformation, then, is an assessment of the organization's current level of effectiveness. Indicators of effectiveness include *financial performance, customer satisfaction, employee satisfaction,* and *adaptability.*

Financial performance: Internal financial measures such as profitability and return on assets, and external financial measures such as stock price and market valuation, are indicators of organizational effectiveness. However, as discussed in Chapter 3, financial results may not reveal developing problems. Managers who rely solely on financial indicators are at a severe disadvantage, since by the time poor performance works its way into financial reports, the problems have existed too long.

Customer satisfaction: This is an important indicator of effectiveness, since erosion of customer satisfaction is usually accompanied in short order by loss of market share. A company is performing well if its customers believe they are paying a fair price, given the perceived value and quality of a product, and if they view customer service as responsive and helpful. Successful firms are finding ways to continuously improve the value they offer their customers.

Employee satisfaction and effectiveness: It is virtually impossible to find an organization that can keep its customers satisfied over the long term without also keeping its employees satisfied and productive over the long term. Satisfied employees feel they can marshal the resources and know-how to make a contribution, and that they are fairly rewarded for their efforts. In this age of "downsizing" and "disposable workers," maintaining employee morale is more challenging than ever.

Adaptability: This is what separates the great information-age firm from the great industrial-age firm. Given that uncertainty is now a constant fact of life, the effective organization is one that develops its members' *capacity to learn and adapt.* Specifically, firms engage in five kinds of learning:[1]

- Systematic problem solving.
- Experimentation with new approaches.
- Learning from past experiences.
- Examination of the best practices of others.
- Transferring knowledge throughout the organization.

The organization's ability to adapt to changing conditions is key to long-term organizational effectiveness. In the past, managers reduced uncertainty by participating in long-range planning exercises that steered the organization toward a clear goal, with a clear set of operational tactics. Today's business environment is too volatile and too uncertain—in the speed of change (shorter product life cycles) and the rules of

---

[1]Personal communication with Harvard Business School Professor David B. Garvin.

play (new players, new forms of competition, new product categories)—for detailed long-term planning to be as useful as it was in the industrial age. In many respects, *we don't known what we don't know,* because scientific, political, and environmental events tomorrow could yield discontinuous changes that alter the rules of play again. Today, much uncertainty cannot be reduced, but it can be managed.

How is uncertainty managed? Companies are making a transition from episodic and discrete assessment and planning processes to continuous processes. Continuous strategic monitoring takes frequent "snapshots" of exernal and internal business conditions. A difficult first step is to identify the activities and outcomes that should be monitored. Chapter 3 outlined performance measures that can be included in management control systems. That discussion also referred to benchmarking, a process by which performance measures are compared with those of competitors by asking questions such as: Are our costs out of line? What is our lead time for new product introduction? Is it longer than for other organizations? What is our lead time for customer-initiated service requests? Do we respond as quickly as our competitors? Competitive benchmarking helps to surface problems early.

Effective organizations use these measures to engage in continuous reassessment of business objectives and tactics, in contrast with traditional strategic planning processes. Traditional planning and budgeting takes place at fixed intervals (quarterly, yearly, five-year plans); costs and performance are measured against the plan and budget over the next quarter or year. Today, strategy formulation and assessment is no longer a discrete, isolated activity; instead, it is a continuous process. By developing and effectively using *strategic monitoring capabilities,* the learning organization responds quickly and appropriately to changing conditions. Budgets and plans are continuously revised to reflect new products, changes in pricing, and other strategic shifts, which occur frequently and incrementally. Adaptability is a function of how quickly and effectively the organization detects and responds to changes in the marketplace.

The Compaq Computer case (Chapter 3) described one tightly integrated approach to strategic monitoring. In an intensely competitive industry, budgets and operational tactics need to be continuously revised based on assessment of organizational effectiveness indicators.

DETERMINING THE DEGREE OF REQUIRED CHANGE

An assessment of organizational effectiveness should yield an understanding of *whether* and *why* transformation is needed (the *stimulus for change*) and *how much* transformation is needed (the *scope of change*). Figure 8–1 illustrates the interplay of these elements.

Stimulus for Change

The best time to transform an organization is when it is in good shape: its financials are solid, customers are happy, and employees are productive and committed to the

FIGURE 8-1   Is the Organization Ready for Transformation?

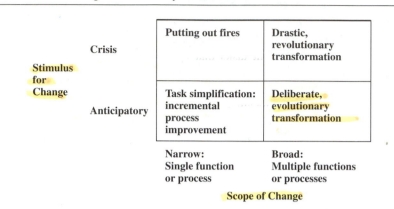

		Putting out fires	Drastic, revolutionary transformation
Stimulus for Change	**Crisis**		
	Anticipatory	Task simplification: incremental process improvement	Deliberate, evolutionary transformation
		Narrow: Single function or process	Broad: Multiple functions or processes

Scope of Change

organization. This is the "anticipatory" mode. Visionary managers may foresee the long-range impact of a new technology, competitor, regulatory change, or other phenomenon on the firm's core businesses. They understand that change is coming, and they successfully interpret the potential impacts on the organization. While this is the "best" time to transform an organization, historically it has proved to be the most difficult context in which to implement significant change. When managers in the anticipatory mode propose changes, critics may say, "If it ain't broke, why fix it?" The answer, in many cases, is "It's not broken yet, so we might have time to act before it is." The challenge is to help organizational members understand why change is necessary, and to motivate them to give up comfortable relationships and patterns of work while there is still time.

A classic example of ineffective anticipatory change occurred in the American automobile industry. During the oil crisis of the 1970s, managers at GM, Ford, and Chrysler had access to information suggesting a growing demand for small, fuel-efficient cars, but they interpreted that information as comprising a short-term trend—and gave that market to the Japanese. Similarly, managers at Wang Laboratories, the dominant leader in word processing until the mid-1980s, misinterpreted the potential impact of the personal computer, and the organization virtually disintegrated in the last half of that decade.

When an organization is in crisis—sales or market share have declined, costs have escalated out of control, employee morale has hit bottom—members of the organization may readily recognize the need for change, and be willing to make personal sacrifices for the sake of organizational survival. A highly visible crisis can be the occasion for completely rethinking structures and procedures. However, managers may be so busy "putting out fires" that they do not take the time necessary to change the status quo. In a crisis, strong, visionary leadership is an essential—and unfortunately rare—commodity.

Scope of Change

Defining the scope of required change is difficult, since it is not easy to draw clear bounds around processes that feed each other. A "business process" is a set of interdependent tasks that together produce a defined outcome. A process can be as broad as "product development" or "insurance claims processing," or as narrow as "approve a bank loan" or "provide a new-employee orientation." Processes can be difficult to locate on an organization chart, since they usually cut across functional, geographic, and organizational boundaries. In addition, many of the information systems that support business processes were designed for functional applications, and cannot simply be merged with other functional systems.

If the scope of change is defined too narrowly, task simplification (*tuning*), rather than transformation, will be achieved. To achieve breakthrough service levels or dramatic cost or time reductions, long-linked complex processes must be significantly altered. However, if the process is defined too broadly, the managers working on its redesign may have trouble determining what can be accomplished in a finite time frame. For example, at a large computer company an extensive effort—involving 16 cross-functional teams—to redesign order fulfillment processes became bogged down when participants could not agree on its scope. Was quoting a price to a customer an "order fulfillment" activity? Was materials management part of order fulfillment? Clearly both activities affect order fulfillment, but eventually the task force concluded that they would have to exclude these activities in the scope of their work in order to make tangible progress. Big change can bring big organizational rewards—but only if it succeeds.

Knowing an organization's starting point in Figure 8–1 is important for the design of an effective change process. In the anticipatory mode, it is critical to initiate the process by unfreezing the organization—shaking loose assumptions about "how we do things around here"—and building a critical mass of support for a change effort. In the crisis mode, it is critical to achieve quick closure on a clear goal. This helps channel organizational members' energy and anxiety into a productive change process.

THE TOOLS: THE ROLE OF IT IN BUSINESS TRANSFORMATION

Several observations can be made about the role of IT in business transformation:

1. *IT, per se, causes nothing.* Information technologies can be powerful enablers of change under the direction of skillful managers. Because information technologies are flexible and malleable, they can be used in many different ways, to accomplish many different business objectives. Poorly managed, IT applications can lead to negative consequences as easily as to positive outcomes.
2. *IT touches everything.* Although there was a time when computing technologies supported a narrow range of computation- or transaction-intensive activities, that

time is long gone. IT is *pervasive* (nearly every worker today uses IT), and it is *extensive,* connecting individuals within and beyond organizational, geographic, and temporal boundaries. Today, it is no longer possible to separate IT decisions from decisions about business strategy, organizational structure, human resources, and management control systems.

3. *IT innovation is not necessarily about being first*

- with a new technology

    or

- with a new application.

In the 1950s, 1960s, and 1970s, computers were accessible primarily to very large corporations. In contrast, today virtually any organization can purchase nearly any IT capability. An IT application is innovative if it significantly changes organizational effectiveness. For example, an application is innovative if it enables the organization to develop new revenue sources, strengthen customer relationships, dramatically reduce costs, or improve the organization's ability to adapt to changing conditions. Acquiring IT puts the organization in the starting gate; using it effectively, in combination with continuous reformulation of business strategy, organizational structures, and management control systems, wins the race.

For about a decade, it was possible for an organization to reap significant competitive advantages from a single brilliant IT application. These early IT leaders formed a small club—United and American Airlines, McKesson Drugs, Otis Elevator, American Hospital Supply, Merrill Lynch, and a handful of others. The applications they pioneered are now strategic necessities rather than sources of strategic advantage. Today, the payback from IT investments comes, not from the one-shot ideas, but from outstanding execution of business processes. These processes are based on IT-facilitated, continuous-improvement design principles that use the technology to transform business processes in three fundamental ways:

Shifting from *predicting events* to *managing uncertainty*.

Shifting from *discrete* to *continuous processes*.

Increased emphasis on *horizontal information flows*.

Shift from Predicting Events to Managing Uncertainty

Although much uncertainty cannot be reduced, it can be managed by comparing organizational performance and activities with competitors and with customer and investor expectations. By dramatically reducing the cost of acquiring and storing data, and by improving managers' ability to understand what the data mean, IT helps manage uncertainty. Specifically, IT can improve managers' *awareness* of relevant events by bringing more information to the manager's attention, improve management *decision making* by providing tools for transforming data into meaningful information, and support timely and extensive *communication* among organizational members, thus helping to marshal the necessary commitment and resources for change.

Shift from Discrete to Continuous Processes

Earlier we described how traditional discrete planning and budgeting processes are being replaced by continuous planning and budgeting. IT is an important component, since it changes the economics of these processes. Previously, the costs of continuously gathering relevant data were too high to warrant continuous planning and budgeting, given the incremental value of doing so in a business environment characterized by only a moderate pace of change. Now the cost of *not* engaging in continuous strategic monitoring is frequently higher than the costs of data gathering and analysis.

Total quality management (TQM) is another continuous process, which makes the assumption that products and processes can always be improved. This, too, is supported by IT, since a key aspect of TQM is gathering statistical and other quality-control data.

Human resources management is also becoming more fluid. Employee career development is now less a matter of climbing discrete "steps" on the career ladder than it is of strengthening one's skill set by participating in a range of activities throughout the firm. IT can support these shifting roles in several ways: new human resources databases contain richer information about employees' skills and experiences than ever before, supporting managers' search for the right mix of people to work on project teams; and communication technologies make it possible for team members to coordinate their efforts even when geographically distant. Project teams are continuously formed, disbanded, and reconfigured. In addition, organizational knowledge bases that capture members' experience and expertise enable more transient relationships and more flexible deployment of personnel within and across organizations. When an employee is transferred to another division or project, the previous division does not lose all of his/her expertise. Similarly, the employee can be more rapidly assimilated into the new division because of the greater availability of information.

Chapter 6 discussed the importance of time-based competition in many industries. There is little advantage to capturing data fast if you cannot absorb it into faster management cycles—for planning, human resources management, quality control, and other business processes. Time-based competition requires this shift from discrete to continuous processes.

Increased Emphasis on Horizontal Information Flows

As was discussed in Chapter 2, organizational structure traditionally reinforced vertical communication, coordination, and control. Networked IT can preserve these capabilities, but also enables extensive horizontal communication, coordination, and control. The result is that traditional concepts of *centralization* and *decentralization* have little or no meaning in new organizational structures. In their place are concepts of *information access* and *decision rights,* which are distributed around the organization to the appropriate people, regardless of job level and location. Previously the decision to centralize or decentralize always involved trade-offs between innovation and control; now control and innovation can co-exist. Most successful business process redesign efforts capitalize on the ability of IT to support horizontal coordination.

In turn, these capabilities support the formation of both ongoing and temporary cross-functional teams, who coordinate the efforts of disparate groups without the costly overhead of a hierarchical centralized structure. These teams are formed on the basis of their members' skill sets, not on the basis of titles or locations. Often cross-functional teams are able to accomplish work *concurrently* that previously was done *serially.* Under the traditional system of specialized functions, each individual developed expertise in specific areas, then these functions were "strung together" in a serial process to produce a product or service, solve a problem, or search for new business opportunities. Now, thanks to the coordinating power of networked IT, team members can work in parallel, dramatically speeding up the process in a kind of "just-in-time" project management. When needed expertise is not available among team members, electronic mail can be used to quickly identify another organizational member (or, for that matter, individuals outside the formal organizational boundaries but connected electronically) who can help out, and that individual may "meet" with team members either over e-mail, video conferencing, or another IT-enabled medium. Expertise is also available to project teams in other electronic forms, such as bibliographic databases, expert systems, multimedia databases, and other IT tools.

The cross-functional team is not a new phenomenon; organizations have used them when the need for coordinated effort was high. What is new, however, is the increased scope of teams' roles, their ability to complete complex tasks far more quickly than before (thanks to IT-supported coordination and information-sharing capabilities), and their freedom from geographic and time constraints. Where previously the project team was an organizational arrangement added to an existing structure, now in many firms the team is at the core of a highly fluid new structure.

BUSINESS PROCESS REENGINEERING: A PATH TO BUSINESS TRANSFORMATION

Business process reengineering identifies new ways of carrying out work, enabled by new IT capabilities. *Business transformation* occurs when managers align new strategies, structures, human resources, and management control systems to take full advantage of redesigned processes.

Business process reengineering consists of a set of techniques for examining and redesigning business processes. A reengineering effort has a clear goal, and its success can be measured. *Business transformation* occurs when, either as a result of deliberate reengineering or of evolutionary change over time, work is carried out in substantially new ways—such as networked project teams and interorganizational partnerships—and often toward new ends—such as time-based competition, mass customization, and new information-based products. IT contributes to organizational transformation by helping its members manage uncertainty, continuous processes, and horizontal information flows.

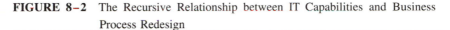

FIGURE 8–2   The Recursive Relationship between IT Capabilities and Business Process Redesign

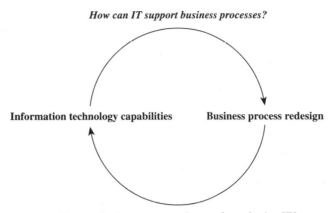

Source: Thomas H. Davenport and James E. Short, "The New Industrial Engineering: Information Technology and Business Process Redesign," *Sloan Management Review* (Summer 1990). See also Thomas H. Davenport, *Process Innovation: Reengineering Work through Information Technology* (Cambridge: Harvard Business School Press, 1993).

In reengineering, all assumptions about "how we do business" are questioned in the light of changes in the competitive environment and changes in available IT capabilities. One consultant describes "the essence of reengineering":

> At the heart of reengineering is the notion of discontinuous thinking—of recognizing and breaking away from the outdated rules and fundamental assumptions that underlie operations. Unless we change these rules, we are merely rearranging the deck chairs on the *Titanic*. We cannot achieve breakthroughs in performance by cutting fat or automating existing processes. Rather, we must challenge old assumptions and shed the old rules that made the business underperform in the first place.[2]

As depicted in Figure 8–2, reengineering is recursive; two questions are repeatedly asked:

How can IT support business processes?

How can business processes be reconfigured using IT?

Reengineering requires "process thinking," which is characterized as follows.

Process Thinking Is Skeptical.   It assumes that existing processes are suboptimal and overly complicated. This skeptical view recognizes that many business processes were organized before IT capabilities enabled rapid, time-and-place independent knowledge encapsulation and information sharing. The phrase "We've always done it

---

[2]Michael Hammer, "Reengineering Work: Don't Automate, Obliterate," *Harvard Business Review* (July–August 1990).

this way" should automatically trigger a red flag, since it signifies that this process could not have been designed with today's IT capabilities in mind.

Process Thinking Focuses on Outcomes.   This is another way of saying that process thinking focuses on *why* a process exists. It should be possible to describe any organizational activity in terms of its position on a logical chain leading directly to a key business goal such as those articulated at the beginning of this chapter. In reengineering we ask, how does this process contribute to customer satisfaction? Or employee morale? When it is difficult to answer simple questions like these, it is probably time to rethink why a process exists.

Process Thinking Is Focused, but Not Myopic.   For most organizations, the time spent cataloging and documenting every possible process is time that would be better spent getting started on reengineering a critical process. Competitive benchmarking or a financial or market-share crisis can reveal the general location of key process problems. Operations that have grown gradually more costly over time may also point toward opportunities for improvement.

Process Thinking Is Flexible.   It acknowledges that there are many paths to a goal. Consider the personal process of vacation planning. There are plenty of inappropriate choices, and quite a few good choices, with no one "best possible" vacation. Similarly, there is no one right design for a given business process, although there are useful design criteria, which we discuss briefly next.[3]

Reengineering Starts with an Understanding of Existing Processes

This is for two reasons. First, as noted in both the performance measurement and IT architecture discussions (Chapters 3 and 4), baseline measures of "where we are" enable managers to measure the impact of subsequent changes. Second, a deep understanding of existing processes reveals both the formal roles and relationships, and informal means of social persuasion and coordination. Managers at the computer manufacturer described above thought they understood what took place between the first customer sales proposal and the final set of specifications. They redesigned the organization to achieve a more rational, simplified approach, only to discover, too late, that they did not understand the informal structure. Sales reps no longer had access to technical specialists they had been routinely consulting with "off line." The new regime led to delays, inaccuracies, and the firm's first operating loss in its history.

Although a little laborious, the best description of a process is a logic diagram depicting specific formal and informal tasks and interdependencies, leading step by step from an identifiable starting point to a clear outcome and its contribution to a clear

---

[3]Thomas H. Davenport, *Process Innovation: Reengineering Work through Information Technology* (Cambridge, Mass.: Harvard Business School Press, 1993).

goal. Drawing a logic diagram is not for the faint of heart; at the computer manufacturer this task yielded a chart covering the entire wall of a conference room, and looking like "very complex, very abstract art," in the words of one participant.

There are two drawbacks in assessing an existing process. First, it can be time consuming, just when the need for change is pressing. Second, participants may focus on ways to simplify the process within its broad structure, rather than thinking more creatively about a wholly new process. This is why some consultants advocate starting with a "clean slate." However, deep understanding of an existing process can point toward a superior new design, if participants in the process are trained to challenge each assumption and identify key roles and working arrangements in the existing process.

An advantage of looking closely at the existing process is that it can help participants identify "low lying fruit," easy opportunities to improve the efficiency of existing processes and reduce costs. Savings from these initial projects should go into a "transformation bucket," which will provide some or all of the funding for the more ambitious subsequent redesign efforts.

Who Participates in Reengineering?

The stimulus for and scope of change are important determinants of who will participate, and at what levels and phases. In general, if the stimulus for a project is anticipatory and it is narrow in scope, smaller numbers of participants at lower levels can be used. Big changes require a big effort. When the scope of change is broad, many participants are involved. Typical roles in large-scale business transformation efforts are summarized in Figure 8–3.

Role of the Sponsor. Reengineering efforts geared toward large-scale business transformation require a strong, clear vision. The sponsor sets the tone for the project, often by articulating an "outrageous" goal—cut head-count in half; cut the time of this process from 30 days to 1 day; move from 40 regional warehouses to 5. The sponsor understands that IT can enable these kinds of "outrageous" improvements because of the unprecedented capabilities for capturing data at its source, coordinating geographically dispersed activities, and informating operational workers without sacrificing management control. Practically speaking, a senior-level sponsor is required to direct resources to the effort, often at a time when the organization is under severe pressure to reduce costs. Consider, for example, the Phillips 66 case (Chapter 6). Even while the organization was cutting costs to the bone, the CEO was approving investments in information technology, which he believed would allow the company to dramatically alter its structure and improve its effectiveness.

Role of the Steering Committee. Early in the process this group, comprised of senior-level managers representing the major functional areas to be affected by change, plays an active role in helping to determine the scope of the project. Subsequently, the group meets periodically to review how the project is going and

---

FIGURE 8–3 Who Participates in Business Process Reengineering?

Sponsor	Senior manager; sees the big picture. Has significant business stake in project success. Can provide necessary resources (people, money). Diplomat: manages criticism, "greases the skids." Sees the project as a top priority.
Steering committee	Peers of the sponsor, representing affected units. Provide guidance, insight. Meet once or twice a month, for a half-day: • review project status, next steps • to identify issues, concerns.
Change partners	From the organization's network of relationships: customers, distributors, suppliers, consultants. Have a stake in the outcome or relevant know-how.
Design teams	Operating managers, professionals with process expertise. The "best and brightest"; high knowledge, good ideas. Have credibility with first-line managers. Cross-functional representation; all at same level. 50 to 100 percent on project; need buy-in from their managers. Collaborative, creative, motivated, see big picture. Meet one day a week.
Champion	Middle manager with strong leadership skills. 100 percent commitment to project; direct line to sponsor. Performance appraisal based on transformation success. Coordinates multiple design teams.
Implementation teams	Often different composition from design teams, but may retain design team leadership. Excellent communicators, well connected, respected. Open to change, want visibility. Focused on the details.

---

resolve conflicts. Conflict is inevitable, since existing processes and systems tend to reward local optimization. For example, when operating representatives from marketing and manufacturing come together on a process redesign team, they tend to point to each other as the source of the problem (marketing may believe that manufacturing is inflexible and doesn't deliver the goods fast enough, while manufacturing may believe that marketing will sell anything, regardless of whether it fits the firm's production capabilities). Senior managers, whose next career goal is top management, are motivated to see beyond their functional area and prove their ability to make decisions that benefit the larger organization. Ongoing senior management review also helps lower-level participants understand the contribution they are making to the larger good, and senior managers may identify connections to other processes that are not apparent to the more narrowly focused participants.

Role of Change Partners. Many business processes—such as purchasing, order fulfillment, or after-sales service—directly involve participants outside the organization. Other processes benefit from contributions by external partners who have not been socialized into the company's "way of thinking." For example, many firms now involve their key customers or suppliers in product or process design. "Change partners" contribute to reengineering by revealing constraints or opportunities at both the input and the outcome sides of the process. Since interorganizational systems promise many advantages for shortening process times, improving product quality, and reducing costs, partnerships are a key element of business transformation.

Role of Design Teams. These are the people who translate the sponsor's "outrageous goals" into workable new process designs. Members of design teams need to be bright, analytical, and motivated to change. Each member should have high credibility in his/her home organization, and solicits ideas from co-workers. To strike a balance between "deep understanding" and "fresh ideas," it is useful to include both outside consultants and experienced insiders on the design team. It is also useful to expose the design team to "best practices" elsewhere. Competitive benchmarking should identify exemplary organizations to visit, not necessarily within the same industry. For example, a hospital team working on processes related to patient comfort might visit Disney World or Marriott Hotels to learn how they keep customers comfortable. The steering committee should also go on some of these "field trips." The output of these visits might be a case write-up and videotape depicting the key features of interest. Such products can be useful down the line in broad-based education programs to help the rest of the organization understand the changes that will be made (since it is easier to look dispassionately at someone else's process than the processes to which one's career ambitions are tied).

The design team is charged with: (1) identifying specific processes to be redesigned (working with the steering committee); (2) understanding and measuring existing processes; (3) identifying IT levers; and (4) designing and building a prototype of the new process. These activities require that team members be free to make a substantial commitment to the effort. The steering committee members negotiate with the design team members' managers to ensure that the team will be able to commit the necessary time to the effort.

A key challenge is to avoid converging too quickly on a solution, since the first *acceptable* design may have a much lower impact than subsequent designs. Just as participants in a redesign effort must be skeptical of existing processes, they also benefit from a healthy skepticism of proposed new processes. A good team will be comprised of both "divergent" and "convergent" thinkers. Divergent thinkers recognize that there is no one right process; they help the team brainstorm alternative approaches to a new design. Since brainstorming could theoretically go on forever, convergent thinkers help the team make a commitment to a reasonable design. The ideal team leader is skilled at avoiding either premature convergence on a solution or excessive "blue-sky" thinking.

To communicate the proposed changes, a practical and effective medium is videotape. This should be a low-budget, quickly produced short video comprised of three segments. The first segment illustrates how a business process or interrelated processes currently work, with an emphasis on current problems. The next segment illustrates the proposed redesigned process(es) and expected new functions to be provided. The final segment reprises the second segment, but pauses at appropriate points to discuss the required changes or investments in technical, organizational, personnel, or other resources necessary to execute each improvement. For example, at the point of depicting a service representative evaluating a customer's creditworthiness, the voice-over might comment upon the need to develop an expert system to support the representative, or a requirement that representatives will now have to be bilingual. Each segment is no more than about seven minutes long.

Use of video, rather than the traditional "white paper," as a medium has several benefits. First, it gives senior executives a tangible view of the changes, and these can be simultaneously and efficiently communicated from the point of view of both the organization and its customers. Secondly, the entire message is communicated. Often managers making traditional presentations are interrupted by a question, which can lead to an off-track discussion and a derailed presentation. Finally, the videotape captures executives' attention, and they may be more receptive to reading about the details in supplementary written materials. The videotape and supplements provide the basis for senior management's decision to endorse the project or to require additional work on the redesign.

Role of the Champion.   Sometimes multiple design teams are established to produce competing designs. More often, each team tackles different parts of a larger process. For example, a new product development process effort might include multiple teams addressing customer needs assessment, product design, and engineering. The "champion" is a middle manager who coordinates one or several design teams. This task is the champion's only job during the life of the project. The champion keeps the steering committee and sponsor informed, identifies resource requirements, and ensures that the teams make progress. The champion has strong leadership skills to keep team members motivated. He/she has strong communication skills, to promote the projects to others in the organization.

Role of the Implementation Teams.   The creative, analytical skills necessary at the design stage are not necessarily what is needed for implementing a new design. Often the teams charged with implementing changes are different in composition from the design team. These individuals need to be skilled at motivating others to change, and attentive to details, since they will be closely monitoring the process to identify and fix unanticipated problems. A risk of establishing new membership for the change process is that these participants will also have their own thoughts about process design. Many redesign efforts have bogged down when the new implementation teams began to dismantle the work of the design teams. This transition must be carefully managed by the champion, who may retain one or two members of the design team on the new team.

Implementation team members need to thrive on ambiguity and challenge, because the early phase of a new process can be rocky going. The implementation team

FIGURE 8–4   An Organizational Prototype Addresses Every Component of Change

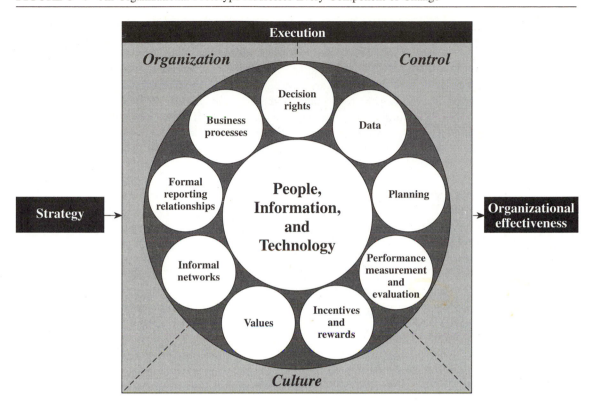

participates in a *pilot test* or *organizational prototype*. A *pilot* is used in a situation where the changes will be narrow, focused, and must be implemented full scale and as quickly as possible. Most companies already have experience in conducting pilot tests. For example, marketing organizations routinely test out a new product by conducting a pilot test in a single region. An *organizational prototype* is developed when broad, sweeping changes will involve numerous interdependent players, systems, and organizational units. An effective organizational prototype specifies both the redesigned process and a changed organizational structure and control systems. Every element of our basic framework is addressed in the organizational prototype (Figure 8–4). For example, before Wal-Mart and Procter & Gamble established an interorganizational system they first tested it out with one product line in three stores. A case write-up or a videotape of the new process (depicting actual practice rather than the earlier design video, which was staged) can be helpful at this point, in order to reveal issues that arise from the point of view of participants in the new process. This is best produced by an informed outsider who is skilled at identifying issues that arise in the new process.

A successful pilot or prototype does not necessarily ensure successful roll-out. Here the change team members, their champion, the steering committee, and sponsors all need to work together on a coordinated effort to communicate the features of the new process and the steps to be taken. A significant internal marketing effort and extensive educational efforts should be undertaken throughout those areas of the organization that will be affected by the change. Since there is a natural tendency to persist in the behaviors that have been successful in the past, organizational members need to understand the reasons for changes and the specific new ways in which they will have to change in order to make the new process work. Case-based training sessions, combining nonthreatening examples from external organizations with the close-to-home pilot test example, can help members move forward in the same direction.

SUSTAINING IT INNOVATION

Earlier in this chapter three observations were made about IT and business transformation:

IT touches everything.

IT, per se, causes nothing.

IT innovation is not necessarily about being first

- with a new technology
    or
- with a new application.

While successful business-process redesign and IT architecture efforts can yield radical transformation, managers should not overlook the value of incremental innovations. There are two reasons for this. First, sometimes small steps do ultimately lead to transformation. For example, American Hospital Supply's legendary ASAP interorganizational system that combined materials-management consultation with an easy on-line product-ordering system started in 1969 as a small-scale effort by a single manager and evolved incrementally for nearly two decades. It was not the result of systematic, exhaustive planning or a redesign process. A second reason for encouraging incremental innovation is that organizations, like the people who populate them, can accommodate just so much radical change. Small improvements are necessary to maintain customer relationships and keep costs under control, and these small steps have an invigorating, motivating effect on employees. *Effective managers create an organizational climate for continuous innovation.*

To effectively plan for continuous innovation, one needs a model of how innovation occurs, and the key managerial levers for influencing the process. Below we describe such a model, followed by a discussion of typical inhibitors of change. The IT innovation process is depicted in Figure 8–5, which shows four key processes—idea generation, idea refinement and development, value analysis, and transformation and organization change—and three key sets of players—executives, middle managers, and first-line (operating) managers. The processes and roles are briefly described next.

FIGURE 8–5   Continuous IT-Based Innovation

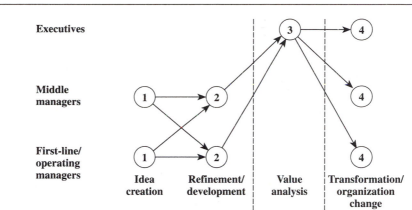

Step 1. In an ideal case, *idea generation* comes primarily from the first-line and middle managers most familiar with operations and with the firms' customers and suppliers. These managers are constantly faced with business problems, some of which IT can help to solve. If these employees are aware of IT capabilities they will generate ideas for technology-enabled solutions.

Step 2. *Idea refinement and development:* Once an idea is generated, it will be tested with peers, superiors, and others. Assuming the requisite IT literacy, innovators may explore their ideas by building inexpensive PC-based prototypes of the proposed applications.

Step 3. *Value analysis:* If the idea is considered robust enough to formally request significant resources, it is submitted to senior management. Executives will assess the business value of a proposed application and decide whether to sponsor the idea or to discourage further work on it.

Step 4. If a decision is made to proceed with the innovation, an implementation project is required to fully exploit the idea. *Execution* may involve all levels of management, since the innovation may require a rethinking of both the broad features and fine details of organization structure, management control systems, and human resources.

Although we necessarily describe these processes in a linear sequence, IT innovation is anything but linear. In fact, it is more likely to be rather disorderly and even chaotic. There are many potential paths to innovation. We believe the best approach to facilitating IT-based innovation is to first identify the major inhibitors or "roadblocks." Figure 8–6 illustrates their locations.

First Roadblack.   Many companies suffer from a nearly total lack of creative ideas for new uses of IT. Frequently this is a result of *self-screening.* This first roadblock has several components. First is the IT literacy level of employees. If first-line or middle managers have little experience with IT, they may have difficulty envisioning how to

---

FIGURE 8–6   Continuous IT-Based Innovation: Roadblocks

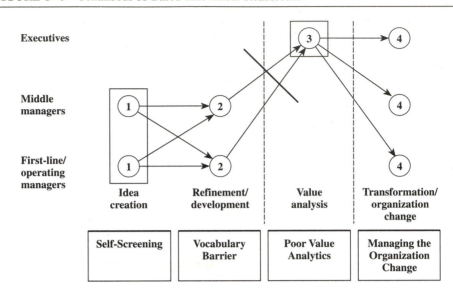

use technology to address their business problems. A second common problem occurs when the company has a culture that discourages use of technology. We have observed organizations that clearly convey that "real executives don't touch keyboards," which discourages aspiring managers to identify themselves as computer users. Firms can head off this roadblock by offering three-pronged IT training, directed toward *awareness* of potential IT applications, *motivation* to use IT, and hands-on *usage skills.* Rotation of employees through multiple functions, or "mixing up" project team memberships can help expose managers to multiple perspectives that can stimulate idea generation and encourage them to communicate the ideas to their managers.

Yet a third contributor to self-screening is when administrative systems discourage use. For example, inappropriately designed IT chargeout systems or inadequate IT support structures can discourage employee experimentation. A tight management control system can also contribute to this roadblock. For example, if strict return-on-investment (ROI) criteria are typically applied, an innovator uncertain of how to value the potential return may never air his/her idea because of the personal risks he/she fears facing. Heavy prescreening of ideas, another form of tight control, may have a similar impact, if ideas are criticized before they are fully explored. If senior managers want to foster innovation, they will want to reward *both* high-impact results *and* innovative behavior.

Second Roadblock.   Assuming successful passage through the first two steps, many innovations incur a roadblock we label the *vocabulary barrier.* This is the tendency of IT innovators to describe their idea in terms of its technical features (such as language or software package used, network capacity, and protocols) to senior managers who

FIGURE 8–7   Assessing the Value of a Proposed IT Application: Using Porter's "Five Forces" Model

Force	Implication	Potential Uses of IT to Combat Force
Threat of new entrants	New capacity Substantial resources Reduced prices or inflation of incumbents' costs	Provide entry barriers: Economies of scale Switching costs Product differentiation Access to distribution channels
Buyers' bargaining power	Prices forced down High quality More services Competition encouraged	Buyer selection Switching costs Differentiation Entry barriers
Suppliers' bargaining power	Prices raised Reduced quality and services (labor)	Selection Threat of backward integration
Threat of substitute products or services	Potential returns limited Ceiling on prices	Improve price/performance Redefine products and services
Traditional intra-industry rivals	Competition: Price Product Distribution and service	Cost-effectiveness Market access Differentiation: Product Services Firm

Source: James I. Cash, F. Warren McFarlen, James L. McKenney, and Lynda Applegate, *Corporate Information Systems Management: Text and Cases* (Homewood, Ill.: Irwin, 1993) p. 93.

don't share the same vocabulary. For effective communication of an application idea to occur, it must be described in terms of its potential business value (strengthen customer relationships, improve manufacturing quality, improve productivity, etc.). Figure 8–7 illustrates one approach to describing the potential value of an IT application, using Porter's Five Forces of Competition.[4]

To illustrate the use of this framework, assume you are in an industry where buyers have significant bargaining power. The implications of this (column 2) are that buyers are able to force prices to decrease or remain constant, while requiring increases in product quality and associated services. They do this by creating competition among multiple suppliers. Creative uses of IT in this context should be communicated in terms of the potential impact on this force (column 3). For example, the airline reservation systems' screen bias mentioned in Chapter 7 influenced buyer selection (where travel agents are considered the buyers). Providing a unique on-line information

[4]Michael E. Porter, *Competitive Advantage* (New York: The Free Press, 1985).

FIGURE 8–8   Benefit/Beneficiary Matrix

	Efficiency	Effectiveness	Transformation
Individual			
Functional unit			
Organization			

The Benefit/Beneficiary Matrix describes the value to be gained from an IT application and the organizational unit employing the application. The Matrix can help executives assess the value of an idea, proposal, or prototype by isolating its potential impacts.

Source: Cyrus F. Gibson and Barbara Bund Jackson. *The Information Imperative: Managing the Impact of Information Technology on Businesses and People* (Lexington, Mass.: Lexington Books, 1988).

service that differentiates a product (and facilitates a higher price) is another example of IT helping a seller regain parity with buyers. Instead of describing an IT investment in terms of its components (e.g., "buying terminals and communications lines to connect with our customers"), it is far more effective to describe the investment in terms of its business impact.

Consider a situation in which the key force is the threat of new entrants. Many firms have deployed information technologies in a manner that raised entry barriers. For example, a company that successfully invests in computer-integrated manufacturing capabilities (which may enable flexible manufacturing, rapid turnaround, and reduced costs) raises the stakes for participation in that industry, reducing the likelihood of new entrants. In another example, a public accounting firm developed computer-based systems for auditing specialized financial instruments (such as mortgage-backed securities) at a dramatically lower cost than their competitors. They captured a large share of this lucrative niche and were able to sustain that lead for several years before competitors developed similar systems.

The Five Forces is one of many useful frameworks for describing the business value of a potential application. Another useful framework is the Benefit/Beneficiary Matrix,[5] depicted in Figure 8–8. This framework helps managers assess the implication of a proposed IT application in terms of a range of benefits and a range of beneficiaries. *Efficiency* means accomplishing a task faster or with fewer resources. *Effectiveness* means producing a higher quality outcome. A *transformation* benefit results in a redesigned process, a new product line, or a new basis of competition. Many traditional IT applications reside on the efficiency slice of the matrix. Proposals to build yet another efficiency-oriented application serving a single functional unit might be deferred in favor of applications geared to the organizational transformation cell, which represents new ways of organizing work or dealing with customers and suppliers. To move past the "vocabulary barrier," an idea initiator must clearly articulate its business value in terms that are meaningful to potential sponsors.

---

[5]Cyrus F. Gibson and Barbara Bund Jackson, *The Information Imperative* (Lexington, Mass.: Lexington Books, 1988).

Third Roadblock: Poor Value Analytics. Sometimes good ideas surface, then recede for lack of a senior-management sponsor. Executives who are uncomfortable with IT may shy away from IT-related projects, especially if they are intimidated by esoteric technical details. Inappropriate criteria can also be a problem here. For example, a strict efficiency focus can impede senior managers' ability to assess an idea's true business value. When IT supports a new product or service, a new way of reaching the customer, or a dramatic reduction in the product development cycle, then an emphasis on "hours saved," "head-count reduction," or ROI can be short-sighted. Again, it is useful to assess the application's impact on the financial measures that drive organizational effectiveness. Frameworks such as the Five Forces and the Benefit/Beneficiary Matrix can help potential sponsors see beyond today's balance sheet. Consider again the "traditional intraindustry rivalry" force. Otis Elevator developed clear differentiation in the elevator maintenance business, their most profitable but also their most fragmented industry segment. By embedding micropro- cessors in elevator control panels, which required proprietary, computer-based tools and techniques, Otis ensured that small "mom and pop" shops could not service these newer models. This application also provided substantial efficiency and effectiveness benefits, since elevators could be remotely monitored for symptoms of component failure. However, quantifying those benefits was less important to Otis management than the recognition that this application would transform the elevator maintenance business.

Fourth Roadblock: Poor Execution. Executives may push an application forward, only to encounter obstacles during full-scale implementation. Sometimes managers fail to consider how the application will impact the existing organization structure, roles and responsibilities, decision rights, or other systems. For example, a new selling channel is likely to affect sales force compensation. In order to understand the potential impact of a new application, managers at all levels need a deep understanding of existing organizational processes and structures. Extensive internal marketing is in order, as members of each functional area that will be involved must "buy in" to the idea. Too often, ideas are believed to generate their own momentum. In practice, inadequate attention to execution sinks many projects.

Figure 8–9 conveys a perspective that can help ensure a company's commitment to continuous, IT-facilitated improvements. To overcome the roadblocks, managers must focus on the key participants' roles in the innovation model. For example, the problems associated with self-screening are addressed with such measures as:

IT training courses for middle and first-line managers.

Relaxing management control systems for IT proposals.

Establishing IT R&D or "internal venture capital" funds.

Implementing reward and recognition systems for idea generation.

The vocabulary barrier and value analysis problems are addressed by IT education courses that involve middle and senior managers and IT professionals. Development of a common vocabulary focused on business impact, and a taxonomy of application

FIGURE 8–9   Preparing the Organization

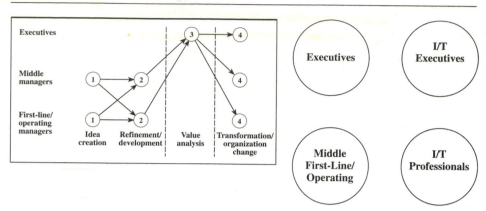

categories and evaluation criteria, are the desired outputs of these sessions. Key to the success of continuous innovation is the active involvement of senior executives, middle managers, and first-line operating managers, in partnership with IT professionals. The challenge for managers is to strike an optimal balance between the sparks generated by an incremental, creative process and the safety net provided by systematic technical and business reviews.

CASE 8–1: SAFEWAY MANUFACTURING DIVISION: THE MANUFACTURING CONTROL SYSTEM (MCS)(A)

This case describes a business considering how best to take advantage of a new IT capability—MRPII (the MCS project)—to improve its manufacturing control. For many organizations, the decision to invest in MRPII is also the occasion to reexamine business processes, since MRPII cuts across many functions within and beyond manufacturing.

What is MRPII? Manufacturing resources planning (MRP) is a technique for determining what materials should be ordered and when. MRPII, the second generation of such systems, links an MRP operating system with a firm's financial system, allowing all departments to work from one integrated set of numbers. A fully integrated MRPII system brings together business planning (goals, expected margins, and profits), sales planning (product projections based on anticipated market demand), production planning (production scheduling, materials planning, capacity planning, purchasing, and shop floor control), and management control systems (with performance measures such as accuracy of product forecasts and production planning, bills of material, inventory, etc.).

As you read the Safeway case, consider whether the MCS project should involve a major initiative to redesign business processes. If so, how would you define the process or processes to be redesigned?

Preparation Questions

1. Assume you are Len Chapman. What do you feel should be your priorities as you move forward with MCS? Where do you think problems will arise?
2. How would you assess the risk of this project? What actions, if any, can be taken to mitigate the project risk?
3. Assume you are Tim Leschinsky. Prepare a detailed implementation plan for presentation to Len Chapman and Walt Schoendorf to outline how the MCS implementation should unfold. Address both human and technical issues.

Case 8–1 Safeway Manufacturing Division: The Manufacturing Control System (MCS) (A)*

In June of 1991, Walter Schoendorf, Sr., senior vice president of Safeway Manufacturing Division (SMD), considered the challenges facing Len Chapman, newly hired manufacturing control system sponsor/coordinator. Chapman had come on board to replace Steve Armstrong, who had been promoted to milk department manager. Chapman's challenge was to manage the implementation of MCS, the largest project ever undertaken within SMD.

The foundation for MCS was an MRPII-based software package, the Pansophic Resource Management System (PRMS), that Safeway had purchased from Pansophic, a software vendor. PRMS would be customized and implemented in SMD's 38 diverse food and consumer product manufacturing plants. MCS would provide an integrated system for inventory control, plant scheduling, purchasing, accounts payable, and other functions across SMD's 38 plants. It was expected to involve major changes into the way work was performed in the division. Schoendorf recognized that the success of MCS would be predicated on

the management of these technical and cultural changes.

MCS was estimated to take five and a half years to accomplish and to cost $37 million. Total project savings were estimated at $147 million over a 10-year period, with annualized savings upon full implementation estimated at $18.7 million (Exhibit 1).

MCS reflected a philosophy of manufacturing control, which Schoendorf implemented in the bakery group during his early years with SMD. Upon his planned retirement in 1992, Schoendorf would have spent 40 years with Safeway in various manufacturing management positions. He believed that MCS was the most important legacy he would leave SMD. Schoendorf described his philosophy of manufacturing control:

My background is really in chemistry and quality assurance. During the late 1950s and early 1960s, I held a number of management positions in the bakery division. At the time, each plant developed its own formulations [recipes]. While baking time and temperature guidelines were a part of those formulations, individual bakers had a lot of autonomy. I quickly noted that the quality of our bread was uneven. Furthermore, there was very little coordination between the person preparing the bread

*Professor Donna Stoddard and Research Associate Maryellen C. Costello prepared this case. Copyright © 1993 by the President and Fellows of Harvard College. Harvard Business School case 193-134 (Revised April 1, 1993).

EXHIBIT 1 MCS Cost/Benefits (in Millions)

	Year 1	Year 2	Year 3	Year 4	Year 5	Year 6	Year 7	Year 8	Year 9	Year 10	Total
Capital spending											
Equipment cost	$(1,900)	$(1,600)	$(1,000)	$(1,000)	$(850)	$(350)					$ (6,700)
Pansophic package	(890)										(890)
Modification/development	(790)	(790)	(270)	(100)							(1,950)
Training/implementation*	(1,630)	(590)	(500)	(275)	(125)	(100)					(3,220)
Contingency		(603)	(422)	(363)	(303)	(224)					(1,914)
Total expense	(5,210)	(3,583)	(2,192)	(1,738)	(1,278)	(674)					(14,674)
Operating cash outflow											
User labor costs	(1,100)	(1,242)	(1,285)	(1,330)	(1,262)	(653)					(6,872)
User training/travel†	(385)	(217)	(311)	(449)	(539)	(18)					(1,919)
Computer charges	(230)	(631)	(1,103)	(1,353)	(1,538)	(1,010)	(369)	(382)	(395)	(409)	(7,420)
Pansophic maintenance	(40)		(129)	(133)	(138)	(143)	(148)	(153)	(158)	(164)	(1,206)
MIS staffing support	(1,025)	(1,113)	(953)	(926)	(820)	(594)	(307)	(127)	(132)	(136)	(6,133)
Supply system interface	(300)	(518)	(107)	(55)	(57)						(1,037)
Total cash outflows	(3,080)	(3,721)	(3,888)	(4,246)	(4,354)	(2,418)	(824)	(662)	(685)	(709)	(24,587)
Total cost	(8,290)	(7,304)	(6,080)	(5,984)	(5,632)	(3,092)	(824)	(662)	(685)	(709)	(39,261)[a]
Operating cash inflows											
Labor productivity[b]				987	1,021	1,057	1,094	1,132	1,172	1,213	7,676
Material cost reductions[c]			2,370	8,086	13,573	18,293	18,933	19,596	20,281	20,991	122,123
Additional sales profit[d]						1,710	1,770	1,832	1,896	1,963	9,171
Inventory control—plant[e]			972	1,533	1,559	2,546					6,610
Operating savings—finance						344	356	369	382	395	1,846
Total cash inflows			3,342	10,606	16,153	23,950	22,153	22,929	23,731	24,562	147,426
Net cash flows	(8,290)	(7,304)	(2,738)	4,622	10,521	20,858	21,329	22,267	23,046	23,853	108,165

IRR—41.9%

*This represents the cost budgeted for training from the software vendor and project consulting/administration. Of the total, $500,000 was budgeted for user trainers who would work with manufacturing plant personnel.

†The bulk (approximately 70%) of the training operating cash outflows was for travel to support the 38 implementations.

aThe MCS implementation team calculated that MCS would cost $37 million in 1991 dollars.

bSMD management estimated they could achieve a 1% improvement in direct labor productivity due to MCS.

cReductions would result from centralized management of contracts with vendors and reduced losses of materials in the plant due to tighter controls.

dSales personnel estimated that with better information on costs, bids would be more accurate and increase sales, yielding higher profits.

eSMD management estimated that each plant could reduce its inventory as a result of MCS.

EXHIBIT 2A Top Three Supermarket Industry Competitors, 1990

	American Stores	Kroger Company	Safeway, Inc.
Sales	$22 billion	$19 billion	$14.9 billion
Number of retail outlets	1,255	2,231	1,117
Number of manufacturing plants	18	37	38
Number of employees	163,900	170,000	110,000

for the oven (the mixer) and the person wrapping the bread.

We implemented a [manual] time line control system, which included a baking schedule that factored in our bottleneck—the oven. With the new system, we improved the flow of goods in the factory and could see where down times occurred.

For a number of years I have envisioned implementing a standard computer-based system in all of our facilities, that would not only enhance our ability to manage individual plants but would provide the information we need to leverage our size when we deal with our suppliers and customers. The challenge that we face as we try to accomplish this is that there are vast differences in the characteristics and life cycles of the products produced in our 38 plants. Yet, if we are successful at implementing a standard system, the opportunity is enormous.

Chapman had an extensive manufacturing background that included design, technology, and engineering. Prior to joining SMD, he had worked as director of operations for another major food manufacturer where the same PRMS software had been implemented.

The SMD senior management team hired Chapman because of his strong operations, management, interpersonal skills, and prior experience with PRMS. Yet, as Schoendorf looked ahead, he acknowledged that implementing MCS would be a quite a challenge. How should he advise Chapman and the MCS project team as they developed an implementation approach? What additional resources would Chapman need to successfully implement MCS?

Industry and Company Overview

In 1991, there were nearly 37,000 supermarkets and grocery stores in the United States, with total sales of $309 billion. There were 28 companies in the United States that operated more than 200 stores each; their combined annual sales were over $125 billion. Of the 2,146 companies that operated grocery stores and supermarkets, 1,594 of them carried private label products.[1] Exhibit 2A compares the top three chains in terms of sales and number of retail outlets, manufacturing plants, and employees.

In 1990, American Stores Company of Salt Lake City was the largest chain, with approximately 940 outlets and sales of $22 billion. American Stores was a holding company which conducted business through its subsidiaries: Acme Markets, Jewel Food Stores, Lucky Stores, Star Market, Osco Drug, and Savon Drug.

With sales of $19 billion, the Kroger Company, based in Cincinnati, Ohio, had the second-largest sales volume in 1990 and 2,231 stores. Kroger manufactured a broad array of private-label dairy, bakery, delicatessen, and grocery products in its 37 manufacturing and processing facilities. Kroger-brand products accounted for 20 percent of Kroger stores 1990 grocery sales.

Safeway, headquartered in Oakland, California, ranked third in the grocery industry, with sales in 1990 of $14.8 billion (see Exhibit 2B). At the

---

[1] *1993 Directory of Supermarket, Grocery, & Convenience Store Chains* (Tampa, Florida: Business Guides, Inc.), p. IX.

EXHIBIT 2B   Financial Highlights (in Millions)

	1990	1989
Statement of income		
For the year:		
Sales	$14,873.6	$14,324.6
Gross profit	3,976.6	3,689.5
Operating profit	535.5	462.4
Net income	87.1	2.5
Capital expenditures	489.6	375.5
Balance sheet		
Assets		
Cash	150.6	123.2
Receivables	141.1	141.3
Merchandise inventory	1,208.1	1,167.7
Other current assets	82.8	56.2
Total current assets	$ 1,582.6	$ 1,488.4
Property, net	2,295.3	2,153.6
Other assets	861.2	896.0
Total assets	$ 4,739.1	$ 4,538.0
Liabilities		
Current liabilities	1,379.7	1,703.3
Long-term debt	3,004.5	2,698.9
Other liabilities	538.3	524.7
Total liabilities	$ 4,922.5	$ 4,926.9
Stockholders' deficit	$ (183.4)	$ (388.9)
Total liabilities and stockholders' deficit	$ 4,739.1	$ 4,538.0
Number of stores	1,121	1,117

end of 1990, Safeway operated 1,117 stores in the United States and Canada and had approximately 110,000 full- and part-time employees. Peter A. Magowan was the chairman, president, and chief executive officer. Exhibit 3 highlights the corporate organization structure. Safeway had seven divisions: one for each of the six US regional divisions, plus the manufacturing division (SMD), also known as supply, headed by Senior Vice President Walter Schoendorf, Sr. (Canada Safeway Limited was a separate corporate entity.)

SMD management considered Kroger's manufacturing organization to be its closest private-label competitor. Kroger was the only other grocery chain in the country that had a large manufacturing base. SMD's other main competitors were large US-based food manufacturers, including Pillsbury, Beatrice, Kraft-General Foods, and R.J.R. Nabisco.

In 1986, a corporation formed by the private investment firm of Kohlberg Kravis Roberts & Co. acquired Safeway Inc.'s predecessor, Safeway Stores, Incorporated, a publicly held corporation,

EXHIBIT 3   Safeway Inc. Corporate Structure—June 1991

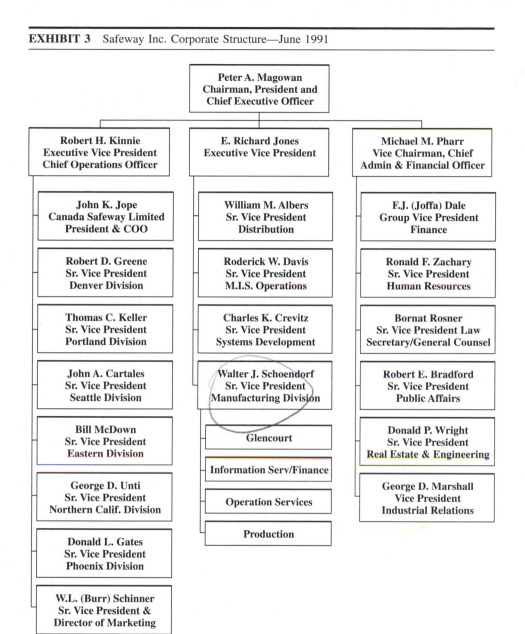

EXHIBIT 4 Safeway Store and Plant Locations—1991

Plant & Retail Locations

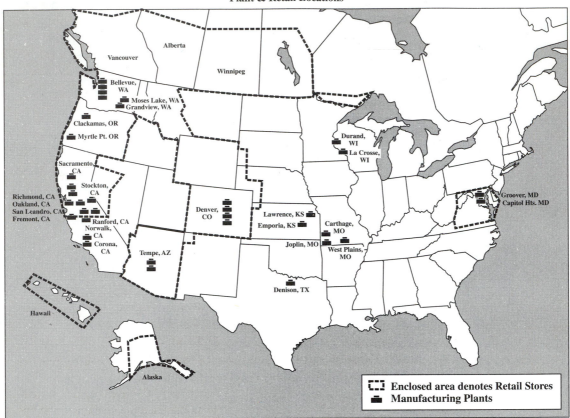

in a $4.2 billion leveraged buyout. After the acquisition, the company had total debt of $5.8 billion.[2] Between 1986 and 1988, Safeway extensively restructured its operations and substantially improved its operating results. It sold 11 major

operations, including approximately 1,000 stores along with 45 associated manufacturing and food processing facilities, and certain other assets and facilities. Proceeds from these sales, $2.4 billion, was applied toward the debt incurred by the acquisition. Strong operating results since the acquisition allowed Safeway to restructure its capitalization through the issuance of common stock and the early redemption of much of the high interest rate debt from the acquisition.

Exhibit 4 summarizes Safeway's store and plant locations in 1991. Safeway management believed that Safeway had the leading market share in at least four of its markets and ranked second in the

[2]For further general, financial, and other information on Safeway before, during, and after the leveraged buyout transaction, see HBS cases No. 192-095, *Leveraged Buyouts and Restructuring: The Case of Safeway, Inc.* by Professor Karen H. Wruck and Research Associate Steve-Anna Stephens, and No. 192-094, *Leveraged Buyouts and Restructuring: The Case of Safeway, Inc.—Media Response* by Research Associate Steve-Anna Stephens and Professor Karen H. Wruck.

EXHIBIT 5   SMD Organization—June 1991

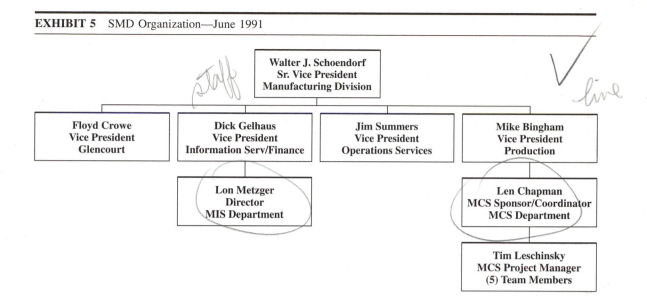

other two. In the past several years, Safeway had expanded the number of "superstores," which had such specialty departments as bakery, pharmacy, fresh fish, floral, and salad bar. Whereas in 1986 superstores made up only 32 percent of the total, by 1991 they made up almost 50 percent.

Safeway Manufacturing Division (SMD)

Manufacturing operations were an important part of Safeway's business. The principal activities of these operations were to manufacture, process, and purchase private-label merchandise to be sold in Safeway stores. Yet, Safeway stores were not the manufacturing division's only customers. Since the LBO, an increasingly important part of the manufacturing division's sales were to customers outside of the Safeway chain (referred to as *public sales*). By 1991, outside sales were projected to be $300 million of the division's forecasted $1.5 billion, although Walt Schoendorf expressed that his goal was public sales of 30 to 50 percent of the division's total.

Exhibit 5 shows the organization of SMD in June 1991. SMD employed almost 3,500 employees. Plant employees were 95 percent unionized, with contracts consistent with industry practice.

There were several groups within the manufacturing division. The *production group,* headed by Mike Bingham, included the manufacturing operations and plants. The *operations group,* headed by Jim Summers, included purchasing, quality assurance, and human resource management. *Public sales* or *Glencourt,* headed by Floyd Crowe, did the sales and marketing of SMD products to outside, or "public" retail operations. The *information services/finance group* was headed by Dick Gelhaus. Lon Metzger, the SMD MIS director, reported to Gelhaus and provided MIS support to the other areas within SMD.

Within the *production group* were the bakery (including breads, cookies, stuffing mix, and popcorn), grocery (including household cleansers, teas, juice, jam and jelly, beverages, spices), ice cream, meat and cheese, and milk groups. These groups had been known as "divisions" before the LBO;

TABLE A

Milk plants	9
Bakery	8
Ice cream plants	5
Meat and cheese packaging plants	5
Grocery	11
Soft drink bottling plants (4)	
Fruit and vegetable processing plants (2)	
Other food processing plants (2)	
Nonfood plants (3)	
Total	38

---

after the LBO, their independent administrative staffs had been consolidated. The MCS department also resided within the production group.

Table A summarizes the number of SMD plants by type in 1991. Among the "other food" category were plants that produced preserves and spices. Nonfood plants produced charcoal, cat litter, and household products such as laundry detergent.

The brand names of some of Safeway's products were Lucerne, Bel-Air, Cragmont, Nature's Cupboard, Mrs. Wright's, White Magic, Captain's Choice, Smok-a-Rama, Trophy, Edwards, Crown Colony, and TownHouse. Most Safeway brands were produced by SMD. Many other items, including a full line of health and beauty care products, were, according to the 1991 Annual Report, "prepared to our exacting specifications by outside suppliers selected for their attention to quality." Up to two-thirds of Safeway's nearly 3,000 private-label products were sold in a typical Safeway store at any given time, although no store or division was required to buy products from Safeway manufacturing.

Safeway plants varied considerably because of the differences in the products. For example, some, such as Bakery plant products, were made to order, whereas others, for example ice cream, were made to stock. There were also different philosophies with respect to work-in-process and finished-goods inventory. Bakery had no work-in-process or finished-goods inventory on hand and there was a very short span between time ordered and time shipped. Ice cream plants, on the other hand, typically had several months of work-in-process inventory on hand.

Plants also differed in terms of the geographic scope to which they distributed their product. For example, milk plants sold to stores within their region, whereas the charcoal plant distributed its product countrywide.

SMD plants also varied in terms of the degree to which they sold to stores, chains, and other food manufacturers. The plant in Joplin, Missouri, sold 80 percent of its products outside of Safeway. Kmart and Wal-mart bought products made to their specifications from Safeway. Plants also manufactured and sold products to both other private labels as well as to national brands, such as Gatorade and Frito-Lay. There were about 600 public sales customers in all. Chapman, in discussing Safeway manufacturing's outside customers, pointed out that with Anheuser-Busch and Frito-Lay, "Safeway stores are one of their biggest customers and they're two of our [SMD's] biggest customers."

SMD's Existing Computer-Based Systems

SMD's existing computer-based systems could be characterized as either plant based or centralized. In 1991, essentially all of SMD's applications were "home grown," that is, they were developed and supported by manufacturing's MIS department. As one manager observed,

> For many years, we had a very large MIS staff that did all of its own development. Aside from something like Lotus 1-2-3, I can't think of any case in which we bought a package instead of building from scratch.

The plant-based systems ran on either Datapoints,[3] or IBM-compatible personal computers

---

[3] A Datapoint is a minicomputer. In 1991, some models were less powerful than personal computers.

and the centralized systems ran on IBM mainframe computers that were located in Safeway's Salt Lake City data center. In general, the systems were not user friendly, did not provide timely and accurate information, and were not compatible with one another. Significant time was spent consolidating, often manually, the output of the multiple systems resulting in inaccuracies, time delays, and the use of additional personnel resources.

Plant-based systems. Whereas in 1991, all plants had some PCs, most plants had only a small core group of users. The majority of plant employees had no experience of interacting with systems at all. The 38 plants used three different PC-based plant systems that were similar in most respects: PICS was used in milk plants, LAPICS in the grocery plants, and BCS in the bakery plants.[5] These systems primarily provided inventory management and shop floor control, and had some primitive scheduling and production reporting capabilities. Much of the scheduling, however, was done in Lotus 1-2-3 spreadsheets. In the few plants without rudimentary PC skills, scheduling was still being done on ledger paper. Wayne Steffen, production supervisor at a Moses Lake, Washington, milk plant explained,

> Today, very few plant employees interface with the computer. In most plants there is a special group that enters the data that must be reported to Walnut Creek.
>
> I have also found that computer usage varies widely among the plants. There are some that use it only to report to Walnut Creek. Others have elaborate Lotus spreadsheets that supervisors use to help them manage and schedule plant resources. In fact I would guess there must be hundreds of different Lotus spreadsheets across the 38 plants.

Although there was commonality among PICS, LAPICS, and BCS, each system had unique features and capabilities. For example, PICS and LAPICS were based on MRP, whereas BCS was

more of a just-in-time inventory system. Jim Webb, manager MCS implementation, explained,

> LAPICS is MRP-based, but the costing, analysis, and simulation pieces are missing. However, this application is more similar to MCS than, say, the bakery system, which has more of a just-in-time philosophy because of the shorter shelf life and time between order receipt and shipping of the product.

Centralized systems. In addition to the plant systems, the manufacturing division had a foundation of centralized systems. While the plant employees did not interact with these systems in any way, the plant systems did interface with some of the mainframe systems. SMD's mainframe systems included MASS, the companywide general ledger and accounts payable, SOE, SMD's order entry system, and CFS, the cost formula system that performed costing and analysis and had strong interfaces to LAPICS and the other plant systems.

Limitations of existing systems. SMD's management realized that there were significant costs associated with continuing to rely on the existing systems. Plants' limited access to timely operational data caused them to miss out on significant business opportunities. The difficulty of getting daily or shift productivity results and daily loss or yield reports hindered plant managers' ability to monitor and immediately react to problems. Plant managers wanted to know what was produced on the current day or the previous day on any particular line or shift and what were the yields or losses. In general, they wanted answers to the question "How is my manufacturing operation running?" Under the existing systems, significant time lags of many days or weeks were required to gather and analyze information and "slice or dice it in such a way that it would be useful," and even then, capabilities were limited. As one employee explained,

> Under our current system, it takes two to three weeks to close out a period [month]. So we're more than halfway through the next period before we know what was accomplished during the prior

---

[5] PICS, LAPICS, and BCS were the plant-based production inventory control systems in use in 1991.

period. This typifies the fact that information right now is not readily available when you need it from any of our systems.

Another example of the deficiency of the current system was the inability to automatically compile requirements for raw materials to make it possible for SMD to leverage its size with suppliers. For example, sweeteners were used in all beverage, bakery, and ice cream plants as well as some milk and other plants. Yet, sweetener purchases were not always combined into one large order to leverage price.

Not only did Safeway's existing systems constrain plant effectiveness, Safeway's capabilities lagged behind those of its competitors. During and after the LBO, management had been focused on the transaction itself as well as on meeting shareholder expectations. Thus, attention to the corporate infrastructure, including systems, had lapsed. When the dust had settled from the LBO, and attention was turned inward, it became apparent that the business systems used in manufacturing operations no longer provided the Safeway manufacturing division with the "appropriate information and controls to stay in step or maintain a competitive edge in the food and consumer products manufacturing industry," according to an internal document.

MCS

In 1988, Schoendorf formed a seven-person team to develop the MCS proposal. Tim Leschinsky, a long-time Safeway employee with plant and corporate experience, was the MCS project manager. The team conducted a one-month study to assess the current state of SMD systems as compared to other food manufacturers. The study found that MRPII was being used or implemented by many other food manufacturers to operate and manage their plants. The team concluded that SMD's systems were out of date and recommended the implementation of an MRPII system to manage inventory and tie inventory to purchasing, accounts payable, order management, and other functions. Further, the team recommended purchasing an MRPII package, in spite of SMD's tradition of in-house development, since designing an MRPII system from scratch would have been very difficult. The package approach would allow SMD to customize the "core modules," that is, purchasing, costing, order management, and accounts payable, that the vendor system would offer.

Leschinsky then led an eight-person software selection task force with representatives of all the SMD production groups (bakery, cheese, dairy, beverages, etc.) to choose a vendor system. The selection task force documented SMD's requirements and developed a request for proposal which was distributed to 10 vendors. By December 1990, PRMS had been selected as the foundation for MCS. PRMS was an on-line, integrated, business information system which ran on IBM's successful, proprietary AS/400 minicomputers and conformed to MRPII standards.

MCS would replace the three current plant systems (PICS, LAPICS, and BCS) and replace or revise several of the centralized systems such as the order entry system (SOE) and the cost formula system (CFS). It would automate the centralized purchasing function and support Safeway brands purchasing and inventory functions. Finally, it would interface with Safeway's corporate payroll system, general ledger system (MASS), and a Safeway retail order entry system, COM.

Table B summarizes how MCS would impact daily activity in the plants. One significant change that would result from MCS was the delegation of data-entry responsibility to shop floor employees. While previously each employee's actions only directly impacted a few fellow employees, under the MCS system, each employee's activities would impact on many others due to the integrated nature of the system. At the very least, it was felt that the training needed to enable employees to use the system competently to assure data integrity (i.e., that the user entered data in an accurate, complete,

---

TABLE B MCS Impact on Plant Daily Activities

Currently	*Future*
Data must be manually input into multiple systems.	Data will be entered once, for use throughout the system.
Inaccurate data often affects only primary user—stand alone systems.	Inaccurate data affects all users—highly integrated system.
Data is often entered days after an activity.	Data will be entered when activity is performed.
File maintenance is primarily a batch process, controlled by Walnut Creek.	On-line file maintenance, with appropriate security, will provide immediate updates.
Feedback is provided largely via hard copy reports.	On-line inquiries and selection screens will provide alternative to hard copies.

---

and timely fashion). Another challenge would be to get everyone to leverage the information provided by the system to do their jobs more effectively. Leschinsky explained,

> With MCS, people who never had responsibility for information are going to be entering information into a live system. People who work in different areas in the plant will become more interdependent.
>
> Early feedback from the plants suggests that workers are a bit nervous about having to interface with the computer. Similarly, management must communicate how important accuracy will be when employees enter data. The integrity of the system could be jeopardized by one individual's carelessness. We have talked to managers in other companies who have successfully implemented this kind of system and there are validity checks that we can program into our system to reduce the probability of gross errors. Nonetheless, redefining plant floor jobs to include data entry is a big step for us and one that we can only control via education.

Implementation

The team that selected PRMS proposed an implementation plan which delineated four stages: (1) conference room pilot (CRP) planning; (2) the CRP itself, which was considered the most impor-

tant phase of the process; (3) development; and (4) rollout. The implementation was estimated to take five and a half years to complete. Chapman described the implementation approach that the team had defined.

> The team specified four stages. During the *planning* stage the proposal called for having a team that would perform detailed plant interviews to document and analyze the plant's current processes. During the *conference room pilot* [stage] prototypes will be developed to demonstrate the system's ability to carry out those processes. During the *development* stage, we will scale up from prototype systems to full-blown systems and databases. The *rollout* stage will involve implementing the system in the various plants.

Although the software selection team had specified an implementation plan, a number of issues were still being considered. For example, who should do the CRP planning? Should CRP planning be done in the plant by personnel who worked in the plant? Or should a group from headquarters go out to the plant and document current processes? Also, would the implementation team visit all 38 plants or just selected plants?

Another issue related to the conference room pilot and development stages. How would the

---

EXHIBIT 6   PRMS Modules

Inventory control
Purchasing and receiving
Accounts payable
Master production scheduling
Material requirements planning
Capacity requirements planning
Shop floor control
Product costing
Product structure
Replenishment orders
System utilities
Forecasting
Order entry and billing
General ledger

---

implementation team assimilate the information regarding business processes? Should the goal of MCS be to allow plants to perform tasks the way that they do today? Should the implementation team seek to optimize or reengineer processes based on "best practices"? Or alternatively, should the team merely ensure that PRMS could provide the functionality, however it is accomplished, that the plants felt they needed?

Due to the size of the project, decisions also needed to be made about which components of PRMS to implement first. (see Exhibit 6). Should the first applications involve those that impact common processes such as purchasing and accounts payable or those that are more plant specific?

Training and culture. Effective training was viewed by everyone involved with the MCS team as a critical challenge. Consultants and managers experienced with MRPII emphasized that education and training were important enablers of successful MRPII implementations. Chapman acknowledged that it would be a big challenge to train essentially all of the SMD employees in a relatively short time without impacting plant productivity. Not only would the day-to-day activities of people's jobs change, but at the same time, major cultural change would be required on sev-

eral levels. The new system would require virtually every employee at every level, many of whom had never used a computer before, to interact with a complicated, sophisticated computer system. Yet, the approved budget for MCS included only $500,000 for education and training.

As Chapman geared up for the MCS implementation there were a number of issues related to training and education that he needed to address. Who would be responsible for education and training? Should he hire a consultant to develop a program and make the plant managers responsible for the execution of that program in their plants? Did he need to hire a training staff that would reside at SMD headquarters? Should the implementation team be responsible for training and education?

Technical issues. It was clear that Chapman's organization would have to work closely with Metzger's MIS organization to implement MCS. Whereas Chapman's group would define requirements, Metzger's organization would be responsible for making the changes to the software and interfacing with the hardware vendor to ensure that needed capabilities were available.

It was expected that the combination of hardware and modified software in and of themselves would not present any major difficulties, although no previous implementation of PRMS (the MRPII software) had involved as many sites. Diane Lamendola, SMD's IBM marketing representative, confirmed that the previous biggest implementation of PRMS was only 10 plants, but that "it is a concern, but it isn't insurmountable. And 38 locations in the AS/400 world is minuscule."

One major question that loomed, in 1991, was whether to centralize all of the AS/400s at headquarters or to put them at the sites they served. Chapman preferred decentralizing because it would diversify risk, particularly in earthquake-ridden northern California: the link to headquarters would not be critical to operating. Metzger, however, felt that it would be more difficult and more expensive to support 38 or 39 sites (including headquarters) and that a decentralized view would be possible even with centralized processing. Metzger noted:

> If our priority is to give managers the tools that they need to run their businesses autonomously, we can download to plant workstations the required data. If availability and disaster recovery are the issues, we can build redundancy into our systems and networks and develop a disaster recovery plan.

As Schoendorf considered the advice he would give Chapman regarding the MCS implementation challenges, one fact remained clear. The potential of this project to deliver savings to SMD was huge. These savings would result from reduced plant losses, reduced per-unit purchasing costs, inventory value reduction, potential increases in public sales, and overall improvements in productivity. Other benefits were expected due to organized information versus data, improved customer service, improved performance visibility, availability of instant standard-based productivity variances, improved costing/pricing, and full integration of production and business functions. Finally, benefits would accrue to SMD because information and decision making would be pushed down to the level of the process owners, namely the employee performing the work.

Schoendorf concluded that as Chapman moved forward, he would have to manage the risks of MCS while keeping his eye on the ultimate prize.

CASE 8–2: CAPITAL HOLDING CORPORATION—REENGINEERING THE DIRECT RESPONSE GROUP

This case describes a business unit in the midst of a reengineering initiative. The processes that management use to initiate changes in the organization culture, structure, information, and control systems are described, providing an opportunity to examine issues in business process redesign and organizational tranformation.

Preparation Questions

1. What obstacles should managers expect to face as they undertake an organization-wide business transformation initiative?
2. Describe the process that DRG management have taken to reengineering.
3. What recommendations would you make to DRG management as they try to institutionalize some of the initiatives started under the reengineering umbrella?

Case 8–2 Capital Holding Corporation—Reengineering the Direct Response Group*

Caring, listening, satisfying . . . one by one.

—DRG Vision

At the end of 1991, Capital Holding Corporation's direct response group (DRG) was in the midst of a strategic change initiative that management referred to as "reengineering." Norm Phelps, (DRG)'s president, and Pam Godwin, DRG's senior vice president—customer management division (CMD), described why the reengineering initiative had been undertaken. Phelps noted,

> In 1988, we took a close look at the performance of our markets, annuities, and direct response insurance (life, health, property, and casualty), and concluded that direct response insurance business, as it was being conducted, was a slow-growth business. We had had an illusion of high growth because our annuity products were mixed in with our insurance results. As a result, what was happening to the core business was not easily discernable. We were growing and exceeding profit goals but when we looked underneath the covers and took out the annuities we found that the basic insurance business hadn't been growing for years. Further, the profitability of the insurance business was suffering due to excess mortality, terrible persistency, and increasing expenses.
>
> We concluded that the days of mass marketing were over. We recognized that to improve our value to the customer, to increase response rates, and to turn persistency around we would have to move toward strengthening our relationships with existing customers and targeting those customers whose profiles matched our strategies.

To that end, we created a new vision for DRG [Exhibit 1]. Basically, our vision is to be exactly what most people don't expect us to be—an insurance company that cares about its customers and wants to give them the best possible value for their premium dollar. We initiated a comprehensive vision communication program and a strategic planning process which would enable the implementation of our new vision.

Godwin continued:

> In 1990, we took stock of our progress toward the implementation of our vision. And while we were making headway, we realized that we hadn't really attacked the fundamental business model and processes that make it all work. It wasn't a matter of bending and shaping our current systems into new models. We had to build new models from the ground up. We had to change our business, not on our terms, but on the customers' terms. And we had to make those changes fast, while maintaining profitability and generating a return to our shareholders. We had to create a step-by-step strategy for change—a strategy we call *reengineering.*

DRG's reengineering initiative started in the fall of 1990. By the end of 1991, over 150 employees organizationwide were engaged in the process of reengineering and DRG estimated it had spent $5 to 10 million on systems and personnel. Eight teams of employees were prototyping new ways of working in the future, designing and developing ideas, and conducting tests to refine the organization's understanding of how these new ways of operating would enable it to realize its business goals. Joan Chandler was the director of reengineering implementation and reported to Godwin.

---

*Professor Donna B. Stoddard prepared this case with the assistance of Research Associate C. J. Meadows. Copyright © 1992 by the President and Fellows of Harvard College. Harvard Business School case 192-001 (Revised May 12, 1992).

EXHIBIT 1   DRG Vision

Our Vision
Caring, Listening, Satisfying . . . One by One

Each of us is devoted to satisfying the financial concerns of every member of our customer family by:

- Deeply caring about and understanding each member's unique financial concerns.
- Providing value through products and services that meet each member's financial concerns.
- Responding with the clear information, personal attention, and respect to which each member is entitled.
- Nurturing an enduring relationship that earns each member's loyalty and recommendation.

To carry out our vision we must:

- Find and serve people who have a strong sense of affiliation, reaching them through new or existing membership groups.
- Provide our members with a broad range of insurance and savings products.
- Communicate personally with each member through direct response, emphasizing telephone and technology to build close relationships.

Our unmatchable spirit of dedication to member satisfaction sets us apart. It is the promise on which current members rely, to which new members are attracted, and by which each of us lives.

"We've committed tremendous resources to the reengineering initiative," noted Chandler.

> Often when people in other organizations talk about reengineering, they mean business process redesign. At DRG we are changing our strategy, culture, processes, *and* products, while staying within our core competencies. Further, as we learn from the various reengineering prototypes we refine our business model.
>
> We're learning by doing . . . our prototypes are living rough drafts.

As DRG senior management moved forward into 1992, there were concerns. "Can we make the dramatic changes that will be necessary to fund our growth into the 21st century? Do we have the right vision? What else do we need to do to ensure the success of our business?"

Company and DRG Overview

Capital Holding Corporation (CHC) is a diversified financial services company. In 1991, its revenues were in excess of $2.7 billion and it had over $19 billion in assets (Exhibit 2). CHC was organized into four business units: agency group, direct response group (DRG), accumulation and investment group (AIG), and banking group. Descriptions of and financial data for each business unit are summarized in Exhibit 2.

DRG offered a full line of life and health insurance and property and casualty insurance to individuals via mail, telephone, and other direct-response methods. Exhibit 3 highlights the structure of DRG at the end of 1991. Headquartered in Valley Forge, Pennsylvania, DRG included two organizations, and their affiliates: National Liberty Corporation, which underwrote and sold life and health insurance, and Worldwide Underwriters Insurance Company, a property/casualty underwriter and sales organization. National Liberty Corporation was best known in the early 1980s for its television advertisements featuring celebrity endorsers such as Lorne Green, Michael Landon, Art Linkletter, Ed Asner, and Tennessee Ernie Ford. In

---

EXHIBIT 2 Capital Holding Corporation—Financial Summary and Description of Business Units

---

Financial Summary (in Millions)

	1991	*1990*
Total revenues	$ 2,670.7	$ 2,577.3
Net income	250.2	166.2
Shareholders' equity	1,930.9	1,552.5
Assets	18,873.0	16,668.5

Description of Business Units

Agency group
  Premium income: $374 million
  Revenues: $663 million
  Pretax earnings: $169.5 million
  Margin on policy holder reserves—life: 9.2%
  Margin on premiums—health: 2.0%

A major "home service" provider of life and health insurance to middle-income households in the Southeast and Mid-Atlantic states. 3,000 representatives serve this market, with traditional whole life and interest-sensitive insurance products and services designed to meet customers' ongoing needs, based on income levels.

Direct-response group
  Premium income: $568 million
  Revenues: $654 million
  Pretax earnings: $74 million
  Margin on premium—life: 17.3%
  Margin on premium—health: 18.2%
  P&C pretax earnings: $1.2 million

DRG offers a wide range of whole life plans; term life plans; various accident and health plans including hospital indemnity, automobile, homeowners; and personal umbrella liability insurance.

Accumulation and investment group
  Customer deposits: $10.2 billion
  Revenues: $887 million
  Pretax earnings: $80 million
  Margin on mean deposits: 1.15%

AIG seeks to develop differentiated products for targeted market niches in which it can price appropriately for the risks assumed, and maintain low operating costs. Institutional products include guaranteed investment contracts (GICs) that are indexed to published market rates. Retail products include single- and flexible-premium deferred annuities, variable annuities, structured settlements, and pension buyouts.

Banking group
  Revenues: $451 million
  Pretax earnings: $73 million
  Margin on mean assets: 2.2%

First Deposit operates a direct-response consumer lending and deposit business. It uses a credit card as a vehicle to make cash loans. State-of-the-art analytical tools are used to develop and execute stringent underwriting criteria to make loans to the reliable, consistent borrower.

EXHIBIT 3   DRG Structure and Staffing

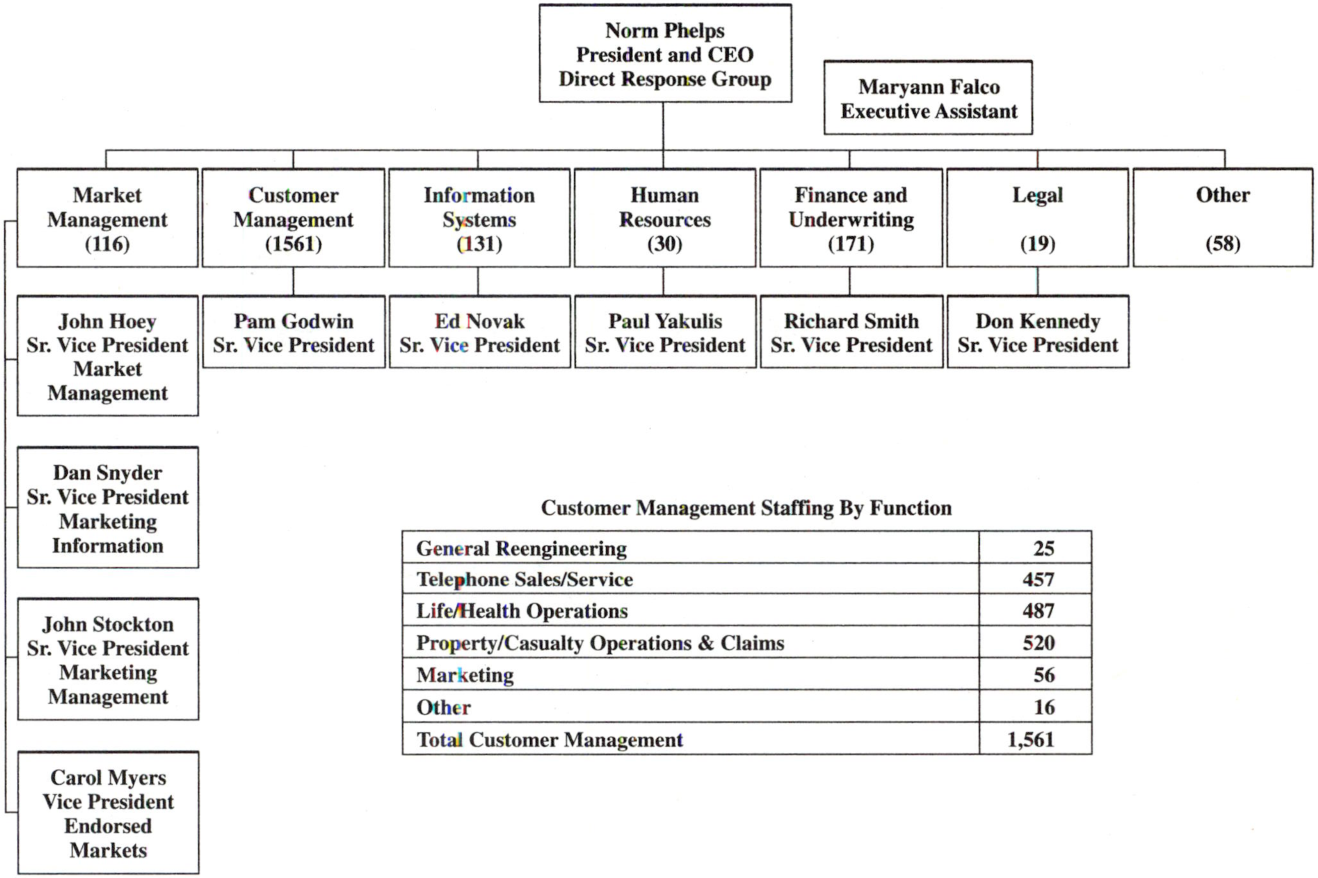

Organization chart:

Norm Phelps — President and CEO, Direct Response Group

Maryann Falco — Executive Assistant

Reporting units:

- Market Management (116)
- Customer Management (1561)
- Information Systems (131)
- Human Resources (30)
- Finance and Underwriting (171)
- Legal (19)
- Other (58)

- Pam Godwin, Sr. Vice President — Customer Management
- Ed Novak, Sr. Vice President — Information Systems
- Paul Yakulis, Sr. Vice President — Human Resources
- Richard Smith, Sr. Vice President — Finance and Underwriting
- Don Kennedy, Sr. Vice President — Legal

Under Market Management:
- John Hoey, Sr. Vice President, Market Management
- Dan Snyder, Sr. Vice President, Marketing Information
- John Stockton, Sr. Vice President, Marketing Management
- Carol Myers, Vice President, Endorsed Markets

Customer Management Staffing By Function

General Reengineering	25
Telephone Sales/Service	457
Life/Health Operations	487
Property/Casualty Operations & Claims	520
Marketing	56
Other	16
Total Customer Management	1,561

addition to television commercials, newspaper inserts and direct-mail advertising were used to make contact with prospects. Exhibit 4 highlights the market segments upon which DRG focused in 1991.

DRG competed with insurance and financial services companies. Other major direct response insurance companies included Prudential, Physicians Mutual, JC Penney Life, and Allstate, to name a few.

In agent-sold insurance companies, variable acquisition costs consist primarily of agent compensation which is paid throughout the life of the policy. At DRG, the variable costs associated with a TV commercial or mail campaign are front-end loaded. Phelps estimated that between 85 percent and 150 percent of a product's first-year premium was spent in marketing costs before a single policy was sold. Further, Geoff Banta, vice president, noted, "Our experience suggests that for every 1 million prospective customers that we contact in a mass marketing campaign, we can expect to convert 50,000 of those prospects into customers."

When CHC began direct response distribution, the group's financial performance was excellent. In 1986, National Liberty was touted as having one of the fastest-growing distribution channels in the insurance industry—it was the quintessential insurance mass marketer. By 1989, however, the picture looked different.

DRG's Traditional Approach to Business

Godwin described DRG's business strategy in the 1980s:

> We were a direct-response insurance company engineered for the mass market. We built a highly efficient factory for marketing on the averages. A one-size-fits-all approach to selling insurance. Out of that factory came products and advertising targeted by rudimentary demographics—like age, state, and zip code. The processes yielded a huge volume of names to feed the assembly line, as many as one million prospects in a single year. This volume added about $100 million of new business

each year until the late 1980s and generated double-digit earnings growth.

As shown in Exhibit 3, DRG had traditionally been organized along functional lines. As a result, while many were experts in their respective area, few understood where they fit in the "big picture." At the end of 1991, DRG employed over 2,000 employees, 70 percent of whom worked in Godwin's organization (CMD), which included the operations, the customer marketing, and the customer management teams.

Customer Management

Exhibit 5A shows a typical customer interaction with DRG's customer service department in the late 1980s. Traditionally, a customer might call to make two requests: "Increase my accident and health coverage and give me information about my life insurance policy beneficiaries." The customer service representative (CSR) would submit action requests via the accident and health on-line system (Challis 3) and via the life insurance system (Life 70). Exhibit 5A illustrates the routing of the requests to the various departments involved. Within two weeks of phoning into the customer service center, the customer would receive two separate responses. Godwin described the traditional and planned customer interaction processes:

> In the past, our interaction with the customer suffered from the curse of departmentalization. We handed the business off one stage at a time until somebody got back to the customer. Further, since there was a lack of responsibility for any individual customer, we seldom used an interaction with a customer to find out more about the customer and probe for unmet needs. For example, suppose a life insurance customer called to report an upcoming change of address. Typically, we would make the address change and confirm the change by mail.
>
> With the customer management teams (CMT) [described below] that we are prototyping, rather than just make the change, the representative would probe for unmet needs and perhaps find that the customer was purchasing a new home and didn't have homeowners coverage yet. After discussing his

EXHIBIT 4 DRG Products and Markets

DRG Products

National Liberty, DRG's life and health company, offers a wide range of whole life plans, term life plans, and various accident and health plans, including hospital indemnity. DRG is well-known for its Medicare supplement insurance. Worldwide, DRG's property and casualty company offers automobile, homeowners, and personal umbrella liability insurance.

DRG Markets

	Annualized Premiums As of 6/91
Broad market	$ 86,000
Senior services	105,000
Veterans	143,300
Endorsed markets	68,900
Property and casualty	137,500
Credit union	30,300
	$ 571,300

Broad Market

DRG life and health business that is not targeted to a particular affinity group is a part of the broad market segment. Over half of the policy holders have been customers for 10 years or more and 90% of the life and 95% of the accident and health policy holders are over 40. The major portion of the customer base is clustered at the mid-point as far as wealth is concerned; 71% have incomes in the $20,000 to $50,000 range.

Veterans Market

Mass-marketing techniques, including TV, direct mail, telemarketing, and alternate media (newspaper inserts, take-ones, etc.) have been used to attract customers for the veterans market since the 1970s. The primary products sold have been supplemental insurance, low face-amount life insurance to the 50+ market, and somewhat higher underwritten life products to the under-50 market. 90% of the veterans market customers were >40 years of age. A further breakout shows that 46% of policy holders were 40+ with incomes in the $15,000 to $35,000 range, and 30% were 40+ with income >$35,000.

Endorsed Market

Markets supplemental life and health insurance to credit card and deposit customers of major banks and oil companies. Because these organizations are not permitted to sell insurance on their own, they contract with National Liberty to sell products to their customers under their name. In exchange for this endorsement and the billing and collection process that is part of the program, the client earns compensation, typically in the form of an administrative fee and a marketing/list fee.

(*continued*)

EXHIBIT 4 *(concluded)*   DRG Products and Markets

Credit Union

In 1983, National Liberty formed a joint venture with the CUNA Mutual Organization to service the life and
health insurance needs of the individual credit union member. CMIG had a virtual monopoly in the credit
union market serving nearly 97% of all credit unions with their credit life products.

Property and Casualty

A variety of products, including automobile, homeowners, and personal umbrella liability insurance, marketed
via DRG's Worldwide Insurance Company. DRG sought to exploit the synergy that existed with the life and
health and property and casualty business through targeted product matching and total customer service capabilities.

---

needs, the CSR could propose that the customer
purchase our homeowners coverage.

Further, the new systems that we are developing
will make it possible to confirm policy changes in
writing within days, not weeks [Exhibit 5B]. Also,
whereas in the past, a number of functional areas
were responsible for individual tasks associated with
a customer's request for a change to their policy,
our new systems will give control of the interaction
with the customer to the CMT.

Sales and Marketing

As a direct-response company, DRG used television commercials, newspaper inserts, and direct-
mail advertising to make contact with prospects. A
typical interaction with a life insurance prospect
in the mid-1980s might have started when an
individual called in to request product information
in response to a television advertisement targeting
veterans and featuring Roger Staubach. Alternatively, an individual might have called DRG in
response to a newspaper insert describing a product offering to the broad market. In response to
that phone call, the prospect would receive three
mailings. First, a kit describing the product would
be mailed to the potential customer via Western
Union (to highlight the importance and urgency of
responding). Second, within five days, the customer would receive another sales kit (whether or
not he or she had responded to the first) to remind

the customer of the insurance inquiry and opportunity. If the customer did not respond, he or she
might receive a phone call from a telemarketing
sales representative who would attempt to close
the sale. A third package would follow within five
days of the phone conversation.

Mary Ann Farrow, vice president, commented:

Traditionally we had a product focus. We would
typically develop a new product and then market
that product to a broadly defined market, such as
veterans. Typically, our systems were such that
if at the beginning of a campaign for a new
product we decided that we would send three
kits to a customer, the customer received three
kits, even if he or she responded to us after the
first.

As we move into the future, our goal is to be
more customer focused. Being customer focused
includes developing products that our customers
have told us they want and need, responding
appropriately to those needs, and not sending out
unwanted mail.

DRG had successfully identified and developed
several target markets including veterans, credit
card holders, credit union members, and senior
citizens. At the end of 1991, the marketing department was organized to concentrate on DRG's key
market segment: veterans, nonveterans or the
broad market, and sponsored markets (Exhibit 4).

EXHIBIT 5A   DRG's Service Process Today

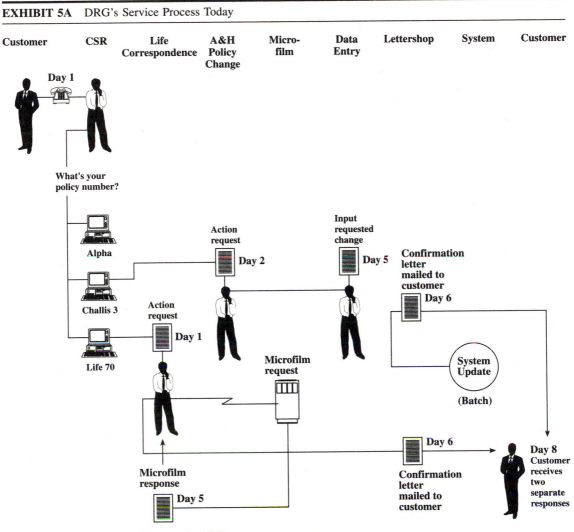

** Increase my A&H coverage
 * Give me information about my Life Policy beneficiaries

DRG's largest and most successful target marketing program was the one geared toward the veterans market. A popular life insurance product in the late 1980s was a "dollar-a-week" term insurance product that was marketed to both the veterans market and to the broad market. DRG had also been successful marketing a Medicare supplement policy to senior citizens. DRG's Medicare supplement policy was an acknowledged industry leader and was labeled a "best buy" by *Consumer Reports* in 1989.

In 1988 DRG implemented the personal service representative (PSR) program to better meet the needs of the senior market. There were eight PSR teams, each of which included three to five teleservice representatives. Each Medicare supplement

EXHIBIT 5B How DRG's Service Process Will Change

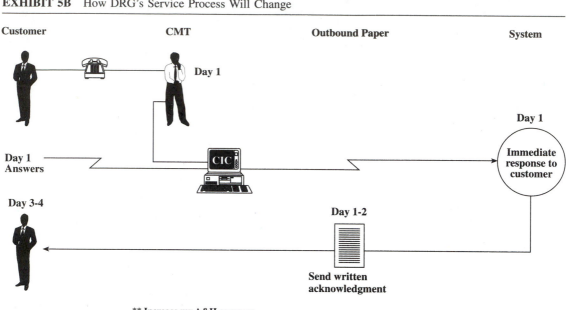

** Increase my A&H coverage
* Give me information about my Life Policy beneficiaries

policy holder was assigned to one of the teams. Roe Lombardi, manager of the PSR, described the relationship of the PSR and customer.

> There is very little that the PSRs won't do for the customer. We have been known to call Social Security and Medicare on behalf of a customer if that was necessary. We will also call family members to discuss the mechanics of our policies.
>
> Our objective is to forge a relationship with each of our customers. The first call from the PSR to the customer occurs approximately three weeks after the policy is issued. A member of the team calls the customer to introduce the team and to make sure the customer understands the product.
>
> Some of our customers rely heavily on the PSR. One of the most poignant examples is a case where a customer was having a heart attack and called someone he knew and trusted, the PSR. The PSR called for an ambulance, contacted a family member, and stayed on the phone with the customer until help arrived.

Many PSR customers wrote letters to DRG senior management to express their enthusiasm for the service provided by the PSRs.

Information Technology (IT)

Information technology was a critical resource exploited by most areas within DRG. It was crucial to those in marketing to enable the development of mailing lists for mail campaigns. It was important for the telemarketing area, since IT made it possible to quickly capture customer information so that product information could be mailed to a customer. Similarly, it was imperative that customer service representatives be able to access customer policy information while the customer was on the phone.

Traditionally, DRG's applications were product focused and aligned with the DRG's functional organization. As such, there were few links between systems and it was not possible to create a view of DRG relationships with any one customer.

DRG operated in an IBM mainframe environment with a CPU that could process 65 million instructions per second (MIPS). In 1989, DRG made a decision to install an IBM DB2 relational database. At the end of 1991, its database consumed more than 100 gigabytes of disk storage and included information on more than 15 million customers and prospects.

At the end of 1991, DRG had completed the consolidation of the Worldwide and National Liberty data centers. The DRG data center was scheduled to be consolidated into the CHC corporate data center in early 1992.

Human Resources

DRG's traditional human resources policies were similar to what would have been found in any organization during the 1980s. Employees were hired into a functional area to perform a task. Employees were compensated as individual contributors based on a merit review system. Training was minimal. Most employees learned by doing and were not encouraged to gain knowledge of multiple functions or related processes. Functional experts were rewarded with promotions into management positions within their respective areas.

The Need for Change

In 1987–1988, DRG's management noted some alarming trends with respect to its financial measures. Margins had declined due to underwriting risks, problems with persistency, and higher costs to acquire new customers. Further, sales were no longer enough to offset lapsed policies, let alone grow the business.

Changes in the marketplace and issues raised by regulators in the late 1980s further underscored a need for change. Godwin noted:

> Regulators were clamping down hard on the use of celebrity endorsers, which just about every direct response company, including National Liberty, relied on to move policies. This controversy made front-page news, and frankly, made the use of celebrities in our advertising more trouble than it was worth. Also, consumer mail boxes were

overflowing and our creative, well-designed pitches were more and more likely to hit the trash unopened. Further, markets were beginning to fragment as customers demanded more individual attention.

> And so there we were . . . the quintessential mass marketer . . . with no mass market.

By 1990, five key areas of performance, referred to as *imperatives,* had been identified. Those imperatives were: profitable sales, customer retention, claims management, expense control, and reengineering. DRG senior management concluded that accomplishment of the imperatives would enable the best chance of realizing the DRG vision.

Accomplishment of the reengineering imperative was viewed as critical to achieving the others. Phelps explained:

> We felt that to really accomplish our vision, we would have to redefine how we approach our customers from both a sales and service perspective. Very basically, reengineering is an umbrella for a series of projects, pilots, prototypes, and tests through which we will build the new business model to support our customer-driven, profit-driven goals.

Reengineering DRG

DRG began the process of reengineering during the autumn of 1990. Reengineering was not viewed as one project, but as an umbrella for a series of projects, pilots, prototypes, and tests where successes could be quickly built upon and failures could be learned from and quickly discarded.

According to Godwin,

> Our first major initiative under the reengineering umbrella was a cultural audit that has given us a critical base point for understanding employee attitudes. We recognized that it would be impossible to reengineer our systems and processes without an understanding of the cultural barriers—the people issues—that might stand in our way.

Exhibit 6 summarizes the "cultural rules of DRG" highlighted by employees during the cultural

EXHIBIT 6   DRG Cultural Audit Findings

Underlying Assumptions or Cultural "Rules" of DRG	Implications
1. You can only trust your friends.	Lack of trust may indicate a lack of confidence in the organization and may impede the organization's ability to implement change. If ideas aren't shared, there is likely to be less innovation. Withholding "bad news" gives an incomplete picture, which can result in poor decisions.
2. Employees are overhead, not assets.	If people don't feel valued, they are likely to underperform. There is little motivation for taking risk. As a result, risk takers are less likely to stay. Little motivation exists for thinking and learning within the organization.
3. Conflict is bad.	Lack of conflict inhibits risk taking and innovation since people are reluctant to challenge ideas. Decisions are made slowly or prematurely because diverse opinions are not voiced. The quality of decisions and product/services often suffers because issues and expectations aren't raised and resolved.
4. Information/knowledge is power.	Sometimes information is withheld to influence decision making. People don't feel valued, or that they are key players or part of a team—this leads to a caste system based on who's in the know. People may resist shared databases.
5. Internal competition is healthy.	Lose sight that the real competition is external—develop products that compete against each other. Loss of business that requires cooperation between units— they don't pass on "winners" to other areas and ultimately don't satisfy the customers. Competition inhibits teamwork and collaboration.
6. Excellent performance is not a core value.	Results orientation and quality work are not recognized and rewarded. Employees are not clear about what *excellence* is beyond "doing your job." People lose motivation.
7. The customer is incidental.	DRG doesn't train, develop, or reward people for being customer focused. No one really owns the customer—no one feels responsible for service or bottom-line financial results.

EXHIBIT 7   The New Business Model

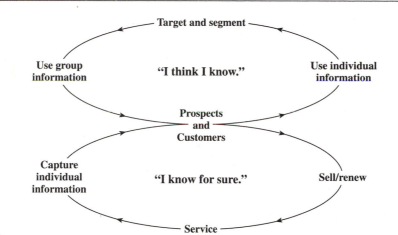

audit. "Issues highlighted by the cultural audit contributed to some major changes that are underway in human resource management," noted Chandler.

> We're redesigning our promotion and reward systems. In the future, compensation will be based on job skills, willingness to continue to learn and develop, and the ability to function in a team environment. Our new job evaluation system will motivate people to develop a wider array of skills. Goal sharing will tie individual rewards to the performance of the team and the corporation as a whole. Further, our training and development programs have been revamped to feature a wide array of courses designed to support life in a team-based environment and to support the redeployment of people.

The next stage of the reengineering initiative was the development of a new business model that described how DRG would approach customers from both a sales and service perspective. The third stage involved changes to the systems and processes underlying the business.

The New Business Model
A cross-functional, multilevel team of six DRG employees worked with representatives from a management consulting firm to develop a *new business model* (Exhibit 7), which was to guide the transformation of the organization. This model was completed in April 1991.

The new business model highlighted a dual focus: customer management and market management. As shown in Exhibit 7, the two halves of the model formed a "figure eight," with information flowing between the customer and market management areas.

The bottom loop, the customer management area, was where DRG would deliver the new level of responsive, personalized service they felt their customers wanted. The customer management organization was responsible for building the capability to provide personalized service and sales to individual customers. It would have responsibility to close all sales to new customers and current customers. Customer management was described as the "I know for sure" part of the model because that was where DRG employees talked directly to customers to learn about their needs and how DRG could address those needs.

Market management, the top half of the "figure eight," was responsible for taking the information DRG collected from customers, as well as data gathered from outside sources, and using it to identify leads for profitable new business. Those working in the market management area would also develop new markets and new products for both the life/health and property/casualty businesses. Because this segment was based on hypotheses about the aggregate marketplace, it was referred to as the "I think I know" part of the model.

A DRG internal document that described the new business model highlighted the importance of prototyping to the reengineering process.

> The process of prototyping serves as a catalyst to cultural change and enables us to test ideas as we develop them prior to making substantial investments in technology and our organization. Prototype ideas are derived from the critical elements of the new business model. They are being examined rigorously to determine their viability in our business from two perspectives: "Will it work?" and "Will it pay?" We will continue to refine, adapt, and add to these ideas continuously during the next several years.

Prototypes planned and under way to enable the implementation of the new business model are summarized in Exhibit 8. Following is a discussion of the customer management team (CMT) and market management team (MMT) pilots.

The Customer Management Team

DRG began to pilot its customer management team (CMT) concept in September 1991. The CMT was viewed as the centerpiece of the customer-driven strategy; a critical component that would enable DRG to move from its product-driven, mass-marketing strategy to a customer-driven strategy of "caring, listening, satisfying . . . one by one."

The first CMT provided sales and service to a group of 40,000 customers from the veterans business in 16 states where DRG marketed life, health, property, and casualty products. The CMT sold those customers new products, provided some services directly (such as policy changes), and acted as an interface and advocate when other departments provided services, such as claims or underwriting. A CMT member recounted an opportunity to serve as an advocate for a customer:

> A customer called whose policy had lapsed five months ago and wanted the policy reinstated. I was told that it would take one month to pull the customer's file so that we could determine the premiums due! Well that wasn't good enough! I spoke to a number of people and was able to get back to the customer in three days!!

CMT members were selected and trained specifically for this program. The team consisted of 10 insurance agents who had worked in the DRG telemarketing area and were, therefore, licensed to sell the insurance products. In addition to the 10 agents, the team included one member from the marketing, operations, and systems areas. All were trained intensively in the new customer service philosophy and procedures that the pilot was testing.

The team's first calls were generated by a letter telling customers they were being assigned to a specific customer team that would handle all their insurance needs. "We were surprised by the number of calls we received during the first few weeks of the CMT," noted Banta, who was responsible for the CMT.

> Our customers were overwhelmingly positive . . . they're very interested in this approach.

> The CMT members are focused on (1) meeting the customers' needs and (2) producing financial results. As such, when a customer calls in, the CMT member should service the customer, get additional information about the customer (e.g., income, upcoming events that would trigger an insurance need, referrals, etc.), discuss insurance needs, and make a proposal/sale, if appropriate.

The online IT system that supported the CMT was one of DRG's first attempts to support teleservice representatives with a client/server architecture. The system that was developed allowed the CMT member to initiate multiple windows and therefore access a number of systems simultaneously. For example, in the hypothetical example described earlier where a customer called to re-

EXHIBIT 8 The New Business Model and Reengineering Prototypes

New Business Model Implementation

Projects	Scope
CMT prototype/pilot	Prove that individualized service and needs analysis will pay Roll out the model to the organization
C-I-C development	Design and develop C-I-C to support model by rapid and frequent rollout of capabilities Strengthen I/S-business partnership
Human resources	Provide training and support for the organization throughout the change process Implement new management models to foster the development of our thinking culture (e.g., rewards, incentives, performance measures, etc.)
Financial	Implement new financial reporting system Develop a sales decision support system (e.g., risk scoring, sales potential) Design and build CMT management reporting systems
Marketing	Identify and create customer packages Integrate lead acquisition, aggregate analysis
Product development	Define product portfolio Simplify policy forms to facilitate bundling
Customer logistics	Integrate processes transformed by reengineering internal operations

Redesigning Business Processes

Claims processing	Reduce costs of claims processing by diminishing unnecessary handoffs Focus efforts on essential activities
Application processing	Increase customer satisfaction and paid-for rate by reducing time in process and increasing data capture
Mail and correspondence handling	Transform "handling" of all paper both inbound and outbound to improve service and reduce costs
ISD/ISS renewal	Transform the I/S process and organization to enable successful contribution to business goals by improving and gaining new skills, strengthening business partnership, developing coordinated plans and architecture, and adopting tools and methodologies to ensure flexibility
Product development	Integrate product development into a single process Streamline application and product development process
Marketing operations assessment	Streamline information systems to increase coordination and decrease costs
Aggregate marketing pilot	Implement targeted strategies and programs to realize maximum potential with respect to sales

quest an address change for his/her life insurance policy, the CMT member could access the Life 70 system and retrieve the name and address information associated with the customer's policy. The CMT member could then open a second window to submit an action request to change the customer's address. Similarly, a third window could be opened to take an application for the homeowners policy that was proposed by the CMT member.

Banta described the new IT system:

> At this point, we have tried to make our old transaction systems more accessible by making them available in a windows environment where one can simultaneously log onto multiple systems. The old transaction-based systems are still unfriendly and often cumbersome to use, but the additional access to information has made it possible for the CMT members to be responsive to customer requests.
>
> We occasionally suffer from windows clutter . . . it is easy to get to the point where you have too many windows open and lose your way. That's an area that needs work.

CMTs were expected to be entrepreneurial. The plan was that where feasible, teams would be self-managing and report to a CMT manager who would be responsible for several CMTs. As such, DRG was exploring the feasibility of having the teams, under the direction of a CMT manager, set and manage individual goals, team revenue and profitability goals, and team incentives. It was anticipated that CMTs would take the opportunity to explore and introduce unique CMT behaviors, tools, and techniques, to further their contribution to DRG.

The Market Management Team

Market management focused on information about individuals that had been aggregated to understand the market and guide the CMTs to the most desirable customers. The five critical activities of market management were: (1) aggregation of individual information from internal and external sources; (2) dynamic segmentation and analysis of market trends and opportunities; (3) identifying the basis for competitive advantage for each chosen market segment and developing the marketing

strategies and plans for those segments; (4) matching segment needs with specific product benefits; (5) delivering to the CMTs high-value leads with needs and product benefits identified.

A market management team pilot was also started in the fall of 1991. Farrow described the objective of the MMT:

> There are two objectives of the market management team pilot. First, we want to determine how market management will behave in the future, particularly how it will interact with CMTs. To that end, members of the MMT are working with the information collected from customers via the CMT, as well as data that we get from outside sources, and are using these data to generate leads for profitable new business. The second objective of the MMT is to identify new market opportunities—new products, new market segments that fit with our strategy, or new opportunities for partnerships with other organizations.

The data from outside sources to which the MMT had access were provided by the organization headed by Dan Snyder, senior vice president of marketing information and underwriting systems. Snyder's group had responsibility for the marketing database, which included more than 15 million customer records and external data from Equifax Microvision, MRI, SRI, and Donnelly Marketing, to name a few. The database allowed for the identification of market segments displaying promising characteristics of long-term growth and facilitated market research, predictive modeling, etc. Snyder noted,

> My organization's mission is to provide the tools that will allow us to understand who our current and potential customers are based on a variety of demographic and psychographic data that go beyond those used by traditional mass marketers. Armed with that data we will be positioned to tailor products to our target market segments.
>
> What I am describing is not traditional mass marketing. Rather, we are trying to focus on the individual—individual service and individually designed products. We are trying to merge the customer approach with the efficiency of mass marketing.

Redesigning Business Processes

Exhibit 8 summarizes the projects planned and under way at the end of 1991 to redesign critical DRG business processes. DRG management expected to begin to realize quantifiable benefits from these initiatives in 1992 through expense reductions, sales increases, and improvements in customer retention and claims management.

The claims processing, life/health applications processing, and mail- and correspondence-handling projects were related to customer logistics. "Expert service teams" (i.e., teams of experts) related to applications processing and claims management were planned to support CMTs and MMTs in the new business model environment. Prototype teams for applications processing and claims management were under way at the end of 1991.

Life/Health Applications Processing Prototype

Applications processing was an important area for DRG and all life insurers. A life insurance application and supplemental information that could be pulled on an applicant from the medical information board (MIB) suggested the degree of underwriting risks associated with each policy applicant.

In 1991, DRG processed over 600,000 life and more than 400,000 accident and health applications. According to Suzanne Munley, applications processing manager, in routine cases DRG sought to respond to a customer's insurance application within 10 days. Munley described the objective of reengineering:

> We are redesigning our work flow for both underwritten and nonunderwritten products. Today the applications processing area is very specialized with one group focused on contacting the customer via phone, another area responsible for interfacing with outside sources—for example doctors or the MIB—and another that makes a decision on the application. In the future we plan to have individual case workers who "own" customers until the issue decision is made. The intent is to not only eliminate hand-offs and duplicate work, but also to provide an underwriter with much more information on the applicant so that better risk analysis can be performed.

Some of the information entry and inquiry screens currently being designed for the CMTs prompt agents to collect data relevant to underwriting decisions directly from the customer, as a normal part of a conversation.

Claims Management Prototype

Marty Renninger, senior vice president, life/health operations, described the claims management system that was under development:

> The new claims system will allow us to significantly restructure the work in this area. In the future, a nonclaims expert (perhaps a CMT member) will be able to take claims information over the phone from the customer. The computer will be able to approve those straightforward cases where documentation to support the claim exists in our files. The system's "intelligence" will also make it possible for us to more easily identify speculators (those who submit repeated or fraudulent claims). We will only need to involve the claims examiners in the more difficult cases.

The claims management prototype was a personal computer– and client/server–based system that would add an "automated adjudication module" to the existing claims system. This module would allow the system to make decisions on simple claims and refer complicated claims to an examiner for research. The new system was also expected to enable communication with other DRG areas such as underwriting or with the CMT.

The Role of Information Systems

DRG executives believed that availability and access to information would be *the* critical enabler of the new business model. Therefore, information technology was viewed as a key facilitator to becoming a high-service, cost-effective provider of insurance and other financial products and services.

A reorganization of the information services division (ISD) in the fall of 1991 by Ed Novak, senior vice president of information systems, sought to realign ISD to maximize support of DRG's

EXHIBIT 9   ISD Organization

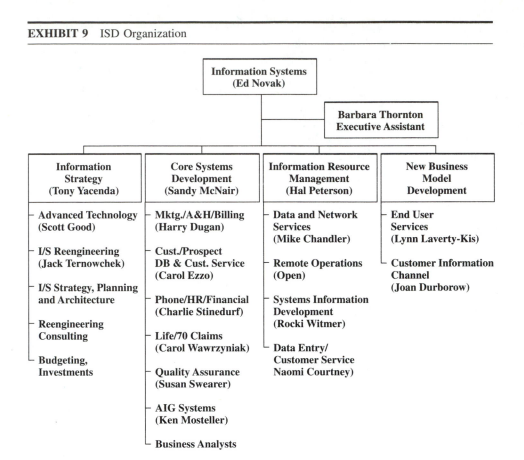

customer driven business model (Exhibit 9). The objectives for ISD at the end of 1991 are summarized in Exhibit 10.

ISD was committed to supporting all of the aforementioned reengineering projects. Another major ISD reengineering initiative at the end of 1991 was the definition and support of the customer information channel (CIC). The objective of the CIC was to provide the users an easy-to-use workstation that allowed access to information in formats that were appropriate to their needs.

The CIC supported distributed customer databases and application systems. Upon rollout, each CMT would have its own "copy" of the "core" applications and own and manage all the information about its customers. The architecture provided

to the CMT was to provide: (1) fail-safe business operation at the CMT level, (2) standard core systems available for all functions, (3) modularity to support constant and transformational business improvements, (4) broad abilities to customize at the end-user's location and (5) modular simplicity of technology.

Novak described the strategy of ISD:

We must be able to quickly develop systems that provide the functionality required by the business. To that end we have tried to divide initiatives into manageable chunks and have begun to use a number of tools that are available in a PC LAN environment that make it possible for us to rapidly develop systems.

EXHIBIT 10   ISD Objectives and Strategies

Objectives

1. Establish an integrated technology architecture and systems blueprint for the future.
2. Provide all the systems support and technology necessary to service the CMT/MMT business model development.
3. Establish business partnerships between IS and make certain all investments are directly tied to the achievement of business objectives.
4. Dramatically reduce the time required to effect system changes through the use of advanced development tools.
5. Leverage the use of IS to obtain order of magnitude improvement in basic business processes through reengineering.
6. IS will work effectively in teams, while providing opportunities for individuals to grow and develop.

Strategies

1. Develop a three-year strategic plan to include the future operational business model and the supporting IS requirements.
2. IS will develop a partnership with the CMT/MMT processes to clearly understand the requirements of the new business model.
3. Continue to provide support for nonreengineering projects that are in need of IS support.

Clearly we do not have the time to rewrite all of our old systems. Instead, we are trying to develop new client-server architecture based systems that work around the weaknesses in our core systems.

Human Resources

A significant implication of the reengineering initiative was a move from a focus on individual contributors toward more team-based work. Further, it was expected that, where appropriate, teams would be self-managing and therefore control many aspects of team life including the setting and monitoring of goals, work assignments, and work schedules.

In 1992, DRG introduced a "total rewards" program that would radically change the way DRG compensated its employees. The two major objectives of the total rewards program were to empower employees to transform DRG into the company described in its vision, and to reward (at a rate higher than the industry average, assuming results that were higher than industry average) the people who make the transformation happen.

There were five parts to the DRG total rewards program. (1) *Base pay*—an individual's base pay would be set by comparing the value of the job with similar jobs at other companies. Base pay would increase as the individual of team increased his/her value to the company by adding new job skills and improving performance. (2) *Goal sharing*—the goal sharing component of total rewards sought to compensate an individual for helping DRG reach its goals. (3) *Performance management and development*—performance management and development would reward individuals for setting and reaching their own objectives as well as team objectives. (4) *Benefits*—the flexible benefits program would provide cost effective protection for DRG employees and their families in light of their unique needs. (5) *Recognition*—finally, monetary rewards and other gifts would provide recognition when an individual's or team's work, suggestions, or actions exceeded expectations.

Phelps commented on the move to the total reward program:

> We believe that total rewards will help to shape us into the customer-driven DRG that we hope to become. We understand that the move to this new compensation structure, which encourages employees to expand their skills and knowledge of our business and to innovate, will be intimidating to some . . . but as we move forward we need for all our employees to be committed to changing, growing, and learning.

Managing Change

"We're taking a modular approach to allow for constant change and improvements," noted Godwin.

We're handling each of our reengineering efforts in manageable pieces to learn quickly and cheaply if we're on the right track. When we're correct, we will integrate our learnings right away into as many parts of the organization as they apply.

This theory of developing and testing is only possible because of the partnership we have forged with our information systems people. Plus, when we test in small manageable chunks, we're able to run our prototypes on personal computers—and by avoiding the mainframe environment, we shorten development time and reduce significantly the costs of a test.

Reengineering is nothing less than massive redesign of DRG's entire infrastructure. And it all has to be done while supporting the current business. It is a process that could be overwhelming but we have been learning by doing in manageable chunks. It's amazing how much you can get done if you break a huge challenge down into manageable pieces.

Chapter 9

Information Technology and Tomorrow's Manager

INTRODUCTION

This chapter looks to the future. As described in Chapter 6, information technologies have evolved at a rapid pace and are likely to continue to do so for the foreseeable future. This means that effective managers will continue to face the problems and seize the opportunities posed by technological discontinuities. Effective assimilation of emerging technologies will continue to be a function of careful, continuous assessment of their potential contribution to and corresponding changes in organizational structure, management control systems, and human resources. Some of these technologies will play key roles in enabling significant business transformation. Organizations that neither exploit these technologies nor develop effective alternative strategic choices are at great risk. Some managers will have the skills and insights to use new technologies to transform entire industries.

The first half of this chapter briefly examines emerging information technologies, and discusses steps that managers can take to keep abreast of changing IT capabilities. Two promising emerging technologies—neural networks and virtual reality—are described. The KPMG Peat Marwick case illustrates how one company, faced with a promising technological capability, considered whether to adopt it and how it could be used to transform the organization.

The chapter closes with an article that appeared in the *Harvard Business Review* in 1988, "Information Technology and Tomorrow's Manager." In it, Harvard Business School professors Lynda Applegate, Jim Cash, and Quinn Mills examined predictions made by Harold Leavitt and Thomas Whisler in 1958. Leavitt and Whisler predicted many—but not all—significant IT trends and organizational changes that were realized in the 1980s. Applegate, Cash, and Mills attempted the same task, looking toward the next millennium.

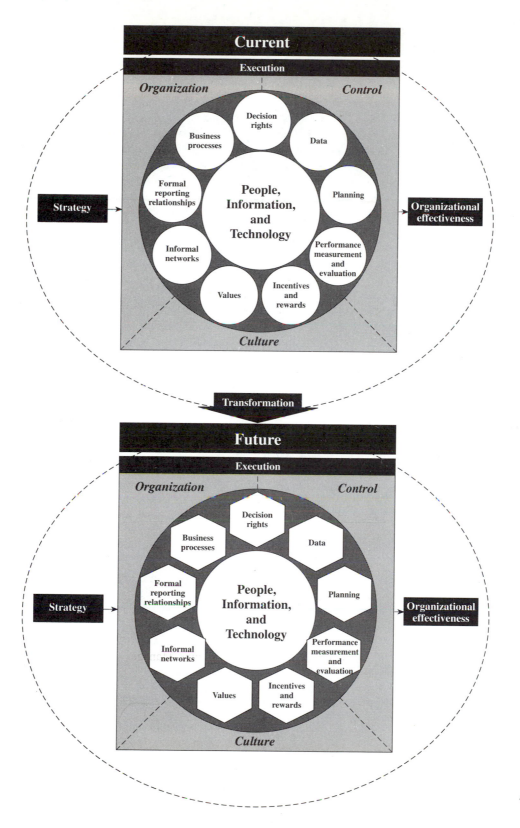

EMERGING TECHNOLOGIES AND THE CHALLENGE OF CHANGE

A cartoon depicts a forlorn, ragged man slumped on a park bench. Two well-dressed fellows are walking by; one says to the other, "Poor guy—an IT manager—he took a two-week vacation and fell behind in the technology." Perhaps we can go ahead and take our vacations (and for better or worse, bring along our notebook PCs and cellular phones), but we ignore at our peril the rapid pace of technology change.

Figure 9–1 outlines some of "yesterday's" and "today's" emerging technologies. Figure 9–2 summarizes the results of surveys conducted by CSC/Index in 1991, 1992, and 1993. Respondents—IS managers at large ($250 million or greater) North American corporations—were asked to indicate which of a list of 35 technologies were of greatest interest to their companies. The survey results suggest a sharp increase in interest in client-server computing and a declining interest in database tools, local area networks, and expert systems—possibly because these are no longer viewed as "emerging" technologies.

The two technologies described in the accompanying boxes—neural networks and virtual reality—were not mentioned in the CSC-Index survey as of 1993, even though a small number of organizations were already exploring their potential. These are but two of many promising emerging technologies. By the time this book goes to press, other technologies will also have come on the scene. An understanding of current IT capabilities, combined with insights about the potential of new technologies, can help managers identify promising new products, new ways of doing business, and new career opportunities.

Chapter 6 briefly discussed the pace of technology change, and recommended that organizations establish a technology scanning and assessment function. As that discussion suggested, an emerging technologies group identifies promising new technologies, assesses whether a particular technology is a radical or incremental

FIGURE 9–1   Yesterday's Emerging Technology Is Today's Established Technology

1980s	1990s
Personal computers	Personal digital assistants
MS-DOS	Windows, OS/2, pen-based OS
Facsimile machines	Voice-to-text, handwriting recognition
Local area networks	Client-server computing
Electronic mail	Network navigators
Cellular phones	Wireless communications, VSATs
CD-ROM	Multimedia/interactive video
Relational databases	Hypertext
CASE	RISC, object-oriented programming (OOPs)
Expert systems	Neural networks, fuzzy logic, virtual reality

FIGURE 9–2   CSC/Index Emerging Technologies Survey: Senior IS Executives, Large North American Corporations

What are the three emerging technologies of greatest interest to your company?

	1993	1992	1991
Client-server technology	47%	26%	7%
Imaging systems	29	49	41
CASE	17	19	76
Open systems	14	10	4
Electronic data interchange (EDI)	14	11	8
Network integration	13	NR	NR
Executive information systems	12	NR	NR
Object-oriented development	10	10	3
Local area networks	9	20	22
Cooperative/distributed processing	8	8	10
Graphical user interface	7	3	3
Wireless technology	7	NR	NR
Software reengineering	6	NR	NR
Database tools and management systems	6	9	17
Groupware	5	NR	NR
Optical storage media	5	4	3
Decision support systems	5	3	4
Scanner/barcoding/POS	5	4	4
Pen-based computers	5	2	NR
Expert systems/artificial intelligence	5	18	35
Joint application development tools	5	NR	NR
Multimedia applications	4	4	1
Video/teleconferencing	4	6	4
RISC	4	NR	NR
Portable and hand-held computers	3	6	2
4GLs, end-user programming languages	3	3	2
Geographic information systems	3	NR	NR
Business process simulation tools	2	NR	NR
Automated operations (lights-out centers)	2	1	3
Advanced workstations/PCs	2	7	9
Private/hybrid networks	2	NR	NR
VSAT	2	NR	NR
Voice recognition/synthesis	1	6	3
Manufacturing software tools	1	1	2
Data security	1	NR	2
Other	7	34	NR

Source: *CSC/Index Survey of I/S Management Issues,* 1991, 1992, 1993.

Emerging Technology: Neural Networks

Yesterday's emerging technology is today's production system. In the 1980s, expert systems, which tackled problems previously considered too unstructured for algorithmic computer programs, were considered an emerging technology. Today, expert systems are in widespread use across many domains, including credit checking, urban planning, chemical analysis, medical diagnosis. A newer outgrowth of artificial intelligence research, the neural network, is another technique for examining poorly structured problems. Neural networks use large numbers of linked microprocessors and software that tackles a problem in a unified, rather than sequential, manner:

> The neurocomputer learns; that is, it's a self-programming system that creates a model, based on its input and output. A conventional computer processes a datum once; the neurocomputer processes it many times. As it does, it learns to recognize patterns and relationships in the data. Neurocomputing is particularly suited to evaluating application forms, such as loan or credit applications. Both accepted and rejected loan applications are input into the neurocomputer. The facts about the applications—income, assets, down payment, etc.—are known; this is the input. Resulting decisions about the applications are known also; they were approved or disapproved. This is the output. The neurocomputer processes and reprocesses input and output data, learning the characteristics of all types of loans. The neural system sees the complex patterns and relationships between input data and output data. It finds patterns that corroborate why loans are either approved or rejected and learns them. Eventually, its learning completed, it can make its own decisions on new loan applications.[1]

Neural network software and hardware have been applied to evaluating credit applications (as noted above), characteristics of potential oil fields, spotting faulty paint finishes and diagnosing engine problems at a major automobile manufacturer, and analyzing price and volume patterns in stock trading. This technology appears to be excellent at identifying patterns in "fuzzy" data, including spoken words and fingerprints. However, the software's path to a solution is unpredictable. Unlike expert systems, neural network software is unable to "explain" its solution, although some developers have addressed this problem by successfully integrating expert systems and neural networks (achieving the best of both approaches).

[1]Rochester, Jack B. "New Business Uses for Neurocomputing," *I/S Analyzer* 28(2): 1–12, February, 1990, p. 5. See also: O'Reilly, Brian, "Computers that Think Like People," *Fortune,* February 27, 1989: pp. 99 ff.

innovation, and examines its potential impact on the firm's existing IT architecture and management practices.

To assess the potential impact of a new technology on the firm's existing IT architecture, it is necessary to acquire robust hands-on experience with the new tool, in order to understand its strengths and limitations. The emerging technologies group assesses the technology in terms of its potential impact on IT structures, processes, and tools (for a review, see Figure 4-5). Consider, for example, the impact of client-server technologies on *IT* processes:

Emerging Technology: Virtual Reality

- "... Engineers at Northrop Corporation ... are using a virtual reality system from Simgraphics Engineering Corp. to help redesign the Air Force's F-18 fighter jet. They model air-intake ducts on computers to make sure they fit through bulkheads, rather than building expensive hard models. An operator wearing wraparound goggles moves parts around with a mouse, making sure they fit together in virtual space. The software even simulates resistance, so engineers know when parts 'bump' against each other. ..."[2]

- Architects designing a day-care center have their clients don headgear and "walk" through the building by viewing images in the architect's CAD database through stereoscopic, digital projection glasses. "Let's see how this looks from the child's point of view," suggests the architect. Immediately, clients are viewing the new design as if they were less than two feet tall. "Let's put a nonbreakable window in the lower portion of this door, and also lower that wall mirror," suggests one of the clients.

- "Virtual operating rooms" enable surgeons to explore three-dimensional images to determine the best sequence of surgical procedures, and their likely effects. These facilities combine computer tomography, magnetic resonance imaging, analytical software, and a database of surgical cases. The surgeon can see, for example, how removal of a craniofacial tumor will affect the patient's facial features. The patient spends less time under the knife and risks fewer complications and surprises than under traditional surgical practice.

These are examples of "virtual reality," a capability that combines artificial intelligence, multimedia, and other technologies to give the user the experience of "being there." What is virtual reality? The subject is still quite new, and there is no single, accepted definition as yet. Benn Konsynski and Espen Andersen suggest that three characteristics are present in virtual reality:[3]

Using more than two senses: Traditional human-computer interaction uses the senses of touch (hands on the keyboard or mouse) and sight (viewing the screen). Virtual reality headgear adds realistic, binaural sound and three-dimensional imaging, and "data gloves" give the user a far more sophisticated ability to "feel" computer-generated objects, "move" them around, or change their form.

Using natural movements as input: In the example of designing a day-care center, neither the client nor the architect gave explicit commands to the computer to tell it where they are moving in the virtual building. Instead, they "walk" in that direction on a treadmill or in the line of infra-red sensors that determine their spatial positions. Video games incorporate these features in "power gloves" and "power pads." A system called "The Activator" permits "virtual violence." Two players each stand on mats that radiate eight infrared beams that surround them. As the players punch or kick the air, each break in the beam translates into movements of cartoon figures on the computer screen. Players get safe exercise, without bruises, and with the sensation of directly controlling the video game.[4]

---

[2] "Virtual Reality: How a Computer-Generated World Could Change the Real World," *Business Week* (January 23, 1993).
[3] Benn Konsynski and Espen Andersen, "Virtual Reality and the General Manager: Toys Becoming Tools," Harvard Business School Note N9-192-090 (February 11, 1992).
[4] Michael Antonoff, "Virtual Violence: Boxing without Bruises," *Popular Science* (April 1993): 60.   (*continued*)

Emerging Technology: Virtual Reality—(*continued*)

Locking out external stimuli: As the architect and client "walk" around in the building they see only the building image that the computer has generated, and hear only what the designer intends for them to hear. Wide-angle stereoscopic projection and binaural sound reinforce the feeling of "being there."

The potential contribution of virtual reality is just beginning to become apparent. Applications in designing products of all kinds are easy to envision. Complex processes, such as designing automobiles and aircraft, can greatly benefit from this approach. Even the design of simple objects can greatly improve, since virtual reality can explore how users interact with each design.

Virtual reality also holds great promise for exploring complex processes, especially dangerous ones (surgery, nuclear power, war). For example, applications in medicine should lead to significant improvements in surgical procedures, and far less use of invasive exploratory surgery. Pilots in training use virtual reality before taking up a jet aircraft, and platoons of soldiers or their officers practice dangerous maneuvers before putting their lives on the line.

As a commercial product, virtual reality is already a winner in the entertainment industry and at the video arcade (experience race-car driving without the inconvenience of blowing up a real Corvette; "battle without bruises" in the virtual boxing ring). Over the coming decade, however, we are likely to see many useful applications that prove its worth as a tool, not just a toy.

Data storage: Will we continue to maintain a central, mainframe-based database? If so, which data will remain on it, and which will migrate to distributed servers?

Data transport: What network equipment and standards are required for client-server technologies? What can we salvage from our existing network infrastructure?

Data transformation: Which applications software, development tools, and maintenances tools will we migrate to client-server technologies? Which, if any, will remain in the mainframe environment?

Similarly, the emerging technologies group might be charged with assessing the impact of client-server technologies on existing IT structures. Some of the questions they will address include:

Who pays? What services will be covered by our existing chargeout policy? How will our chargeout systems have to change?

Who manages? What new processes or policies are needed to establish responsibility for data accuracy and security? Who will be in charge of updating software?

How much? What are the hardware, software, and support costs for client-server computing compared with our existing systems?

FIGURE 9–3   Benefit/Beneficiary Matrix*

	Efficiency	Effectiveness	Transformation
Individual			
Functional unit			
Organization			

Source: Cyrus F. Gibson and Barbara Bund Jackson. *The Information Imperative: Managing the Impact of Information Technology on Businesses and People* (Lexington, Mass.: Lexington Books, 1988).

Effective emerging technologies groups also assess the potential *business impacts* of new technologies. The Benefits/Beneficiaries Matrix (Figure 9–3) introduced in Chapter 8, can serve as a useful framework for assessing the potential contribution of a new technology, and also for monitoring the changing use of the technology over time. Consider what happened with personal computers. When they were first introduced to organizations in the early 1980s, word processing and spreadsheets on PCs primarily served users' individual efficiency (producing work faster) and effectiveness (producing more thorough/higher-quality work) needs. In many organizations, standard personal computer applications were subsequently developed for individuals doing the same work. For example, most public accounting firms developed software for auditors' "working papers." This is an example of a functional unit/efficiency benefit. Many of these applications are now mounted on client-server systems, enabling a new set of benefits and beneficiaries. Chapter 8 discussed an accounting firm that developed specialized PC software for conducting audits of particular financial instruments. This can be considered a "transformation" benefit, since the software enabled this firm to capture an entirely new market niche. Hence, the emerging technologies group can use the Benefits/Beneficiaries Matrix to predict the impact of a new technology, and also to subsequently assess actual uses of it over time.

A key task of the emerging technologies group is to help users adopt those new technologies that are considered promising. Recall that the IT stages discussion in Chapter 6 emphasized the importance of balancing "control" and "slack." Early in the assimilation of a new technology (initiation, contagion stages) a high-slack/low-control climate fosters exploration of the tool's potential. During these stages, purchase and use justifications may be based on loose criteria. Generally, costs are absorbed into overhead or charged to an R&D budget, rather than charged directly to users. Hardware and software standards, set for mature, established technologies, are relaxed to permit experimentation with new technologies. This is required to assess the potential of the new technology, since optimal protocols, data representation schemes, or other features may not yet be evident. Eventually, however, the accumulated experience with a technology reveals features that should be standardized. For example, early in the assimilation of CD-ROM technology there were multiple forms of data representation and retrieval; now the industry is converging on a couple of CD-ROM standards.

With accumulated experience also comes user awareness of the benefits of a technology, which in some instances can lead organizations to remove the item from overhead or R&D and charge directly for its use. Standards and chargeback are examples of measures that institute increased control over a specific technology.

At this point of transition from "slack" to "control," which generally coincides with users' perceptions of the technology as "established" rather than "new" or "emerging," the emerging technology group passes responsibility to established operational units. Either its adoption and use is delegated directly to a business unit or other user group, or it becomes the responsibility of an IT support organization.

CASE 9–1: KPMG PEAT MARWICK: THE SHADOW PARTNER

This case describes several emerging technologies for the support of knowledge work, and discusses their potential role in transforming a professional consulting firm.

Preparation Questions

1. What are the challenges that KPMG Peat Marwick faces over the next 5 to 10 years? What are the organizational implications of these challenges?
2. What contributions can the Shadow Partner project make toward meeting these challenges? Attempt to map the potential impacts using the Benefits/Beneficiaries Matrix.
3. What other technologies could make a contribution? Have KPMG Peat Marwick managers converged too quickly on this set of technologies?
4. Why is the Shadow Partner project facing resistance? If you were its champion, what would you do?

Case 9–1 KPMG Peat Marwick: The Shadow Partner*

Imagine: one morning you arrive at your office at the accounting company where you are a tax

*Research Associate Julie A. Gladstone prepared this case under the supervision of Professor Robert G. Eccles. Copyright © 1991 by the President and Fellows of Harvard College. Harvard Business School case 492-002.

partner, and your "shadow partner" informs you that one of your clients has been targeted with a hostile takeover bid. You do not panic because you know that your shadow partner has all the information you need to address the crisis.

This particular morning, when you logged on to your shadow partner, three icons appeared on the screen of your microcomputer: a voice-mail message from the chief financial officer of Amalgamated Pulp & Paper (AP&P); a news report on AP&P; and a draft opinion on a tax matter submitted by one of your managers. Before responding to the voice-mail message, you decide to read the news report. You click on the news report with your mouse.

A report that AP&P has been targeted with a hostile takeover bid by Worldwide Industries appears on the screen. Before calling AP&P's CFO, you tap the resources of your shadow partner. You quickly call to the screen the relevant tax laws and regulations on mergers and acquisitions, and refresh your memory on the key concepts. You review the news stories and analysts' reports on Worldwide Industries for the last month. In addition, you retrieve and review Worldwide Industries' financial statements and most recent annual report.

You then point to the voice mail icon (noting its receipt at 6:55 AM), click on the message, and hear: "This is Jen Green. Something's come up, and I need to speak with you as soon as possible." You point to the voice-mail icon's "return call" button and the shadow partner retrieves Green's direct-dial phone number and dials it. In seconds Green is on the line to talk about, as anticipated, the hostile bid. The discussion with Green is very substantial, as you are informed about the bid and the bidder and the relevant laws and regulations. Green wants immediate advice on defense strategies and tax implications of the takeover, and you arrange to meet the following morning.

Before tomorrow morning's meeting, you need to develop defense strategies. You start by logging into your shadow partner's proposals database to find all the recent engagements in which the firm assisted companies under attack, especially pulp and paper companies. You discover the firm recently assisted a number of clients, including Dominion Pulp and Paper, a company similar to AP&P, in comparable circumstances. You review the advice the firm gave in that situation. You also request information on the KPMG partner in-

volved in that case (John Mac) and the fees that were charged.

You click on Mac's name, and get him on the telephone to discuss the AP&P case. You realize that you can have your staff adapt Mac's materials for the AP&P case, so you click on the staff scheduling icon to review staff availability. You note that a senior accountant is available for a few days and you forward the relevant Dominion material to the accountant's shadow partner with brief instructions. You also instruct the accountant to retrieve financial and operating data for all KPMG's paper and pulp clients worldwide and prepare comparative analyses in graphic display of efficiency, market value, and tax status so Green can get a broad view of AP&P's worth in the marketplace, whether AP&P can expect additional bidders, and what strategic moves might drive up AP&P's market value.

You also note that the Dominion Pulp & Paper case resulted in several services being rendered in connection with the tender offer that had not been requested by Green. These included development of pro forma financial statements of the potential consolidated company, searches for the outplacement of redundant executives, and various required regulatory filings. You call Green and suggest that AP&P will need to prepare for these same eventualities. She agrees and asks you to prepare a proposal immediately. You review the firm's recent proposals, including the Dominion engagement, and find several other relevant recent examples. The examples include graphics and fee information, which you forward to your administrative assistant for formatting for the meeting.

You proceed to write a brief description of the AP&P situation and a request for help, and electronically mail it to KPMG's entire mergers-and-acquisitions specialists' mailing list. Within seconds, an icon of your request appears on the screens of all the M&A specialists currently logged on to their shadow partners. Three of them have relevant experience and click their "return call" buttons to speak to you. One specialist is available to come to your office in the morning.

While the M&A specialist is on the phone, you touch your "conference call button" and add Green to the phone call. The M&A specialist suggests several lines of defense and agrees to arrive at Green's office in the morning to start assisting AP&P with its defense.

With AP&P matters under momentary control, you turn to the draft tax opinion in your mailbox. You call it to the screen, review it, make minor changes, and return it to the manager with instructions to deliver the opinion and submit the bill. Next you review the status of your current engagements. You request a graphic display that compares time and expense charges to date, and estimated costs to complete each engagement. It highlights all engagements which are likely to exceed their anticipated costs. You click on the names of each of the project managers in turn to telephone them and discuss the problems.

A quick review of your "lock up" (unbilled time and expenses plus uncollected receivables) sorted in descending order of size shows that two engagements with tardy billings yesterday had been billed out and three large delinquent receivables had been collected since yesterday, reducing your lock up to 21 days. You check your personal investment portfolio to see if there are any stocks you want to buy.

It is now 12:30 and a reminder appears on the screen that you have to leave in 15 minutes if you are to be on time to your lunch with Lester Bigg, CEO of Bigg, Inc., and a member of your list of top client prospects. Before leaving for lunch, you call to the screen all recent publicity on Bigg, Inc., and Bigg himself. You review Bigg's *Who's Who* entry and note that he's president of the board of trustees of the local museum, and a founding member of Help International. In hurrying to the lunch appointment you forget to log-off your shadow partner. Your shadow partner, sensing no activity in the last 10 minutes, issues an on-screen alert that if you do not identify yourself, it will log you off. Receiving no reply, it logs you off. (This protects the system from unauthorized access through your microcomputer during your absence,

which is especially important because, as a partner, you have top security clearance.)

After lunch, you log on to your shadow partner and realize that the concept of shareholder value, which you only vaguely understand, is relevant to advising Green. You click on the "training" button and review the available training materials on shareholder value. One of these is a half-hour executive-summary-level course. You click the course icon. An interactive course module quickly assesses your current knowledge and knowledge objectives and presents you with a course tailored to your specific needs.

It occurs to you that one possible approach to the AP&P tender offer would be to reduce the hostility level through mediation. You recall the Worldwide Industries annual report to the screen and select (by pointing to) the names of all the officers and directors. You cross check this list with KPMG's contacts database. You see that Worldwide's CEO is a friend of Pam Spring, the senior partner of your office. You file away the information for possible later use with Green.

Your administrative assistant's graphics are ready and are sent to you via your shadow partner. You print them out and other information you collected on AP&P and Worldwide Industries during the day, tuck the material away into your brief case for study that night, and log off your shadow partner.

The Shadow Partner

As of March 1991, the shadow partner was a vision—a technologically possible vision with a prototype to attest to its feasibility. The shadow partner had not yet been implemented at KPMG Peat Marwick, and whether or not it would be implemented and then to what extent had not yet been decided.

The shadow partner in its fully developed form was intended to be a worldwide information network that would link all KPMG professionals to each other and to a wealth of databases and information services. The databases would include information, updated daily, about the experiences and contacts of the partners; public information, such as directories, online news services, and the Dow Jones report; and training courses on business topics. The shadow partner would also include more standard functions, such as word processing, voice mail, and resource-scheduling functions.

Partners, by sharing and gathering information through the network, would be able to use the entire company's knowledge and experience to serve clients. As Floyd Kuehnis, managing partner of the Minneapolis office and area partner for the surrounding region, stated, "We need to use the information we have as a company to provide clients with more value-added service. Clients will hire us, not out of tradition or loyalty, but because we deliver services of value to them in the environment of the 1990s. We should use our information to become business advisors to our clients."

The results of a survey KPMG sent to 80 percent of its clients in 1989 indicated that clients wanted their accounting firms to bring the full range of the firm's experience and knowledge to individual clients' needs. Also, firms needed to respond to the expanded needs of clients for ongoing advice.

Bob Elliott, strategic planner and the individual known as one of the firm's "visionaries," described the clients' desire for wider, more integrated services: "Clients demand solutions, not simply products. The solutions need to be integrative, combining the knowledge of all the functional areas—tax, auditing, and consulting. To provide integrated solutions, each partner needs to access the knowledge of all the functions." Elliott said that the internal accounting system impeded cross-functionality: "The functional areas are separate because our profit and cost accounting system supports the separation of functions. We need to change to an integrated, information orientation, not a product and functional orientation."

Overall, the shadow partner would allow partners to access the full range of knowledge in the firm, to grow professionally through learning about a wider range of partners' experiences, and to provide superior service to meet clients' expanded needs.

Design of the Shadow Partner

Elliott envisioned the shadow partner as "a complete, concise, quality-controlled representation of the company's expertise." Another executive described the shadow partner as a "reservoir of practice and knowledge." Elliott believed that the information in the databases should be "unstructured," because any structure imposed on the information would be based on past experience. The data inputted into the system would come from public information sources, published company reports, and partners' reports, proposals, letters, and other business-related material. The database would also include all employees' resumes and time reports (recording how they spent their time). Information in the database could be retrieved, looked at, and presented in whatever way imagined. To Elliott, an unstructured database connoted creative responsiveness to novel client issues.

Competitors and the Shadow Partner

Similar to KPMG, some competitors were looking for innovative ways to bring more value-added services to clients. Among KPMG's professionals, there were different perceptions about the competition's progress. According to Tony Sapienza, chief information officer and, from 1990, chairman of the technology committee, KPMG was far ahead of the competition: "Our competitors are starting to think of something like the shadow partner, but they have no long-term strategy like KPMG does. It will take the competition two years to figure out what we did, two years to decide if they want it, and two years to figure out how to do it."

Other partners, such as Bob Barry, managing partner of the Pittsburgh office, believed that the competition had made significant headway: "Some of our competitors are farther along than we may think. Some of them have networks and the ability to share data across offices. We do not have automated information sharing across offices yet." Barry continued that implementation of the shadow partner was mandatory:

> I don't think we have much choice but to go ahead with the shadow partner. One of the givens down the road is that to provide quality products we'll need certain technology. Those firms that use their information best will thrive. Adopting the shadow partner requires an open-mindedness and a belief that dinosaurs become extinct because they don't adapt.

Origin of the Shadow Partner

The shadow partner was Elliott's vision, which took shape in the early 1980s. Elliott believed that the company had to consider the strategic use of information technology in the business: "As a member of the strategic planning committee, I argued that technology issues are an important part of strategy and that the company had to address that fact. Some offices were using technology, but there was no technology component in the firm's overall strategy." In 1986, Larry Horner, CEO from 1984 to 1990, asked the strategic planning committee to appoint a technology task force to explore the issue. The technology task force recommended that the firm establish a technology committee, which would report to the strategic planning committee (which included the COO, partner-in-charge of auditing, partner-in-charge of tax, partner-in-charge of consulting, partner-in-charge of professional practice, and partner-in-charge of international relations) and the operating committee (which included the CEO, COO, partners-in-charge of auditing, tax, consulting, professional practice, and international, and the six area partners).

The Technology Committee

The technology committee, headed by Bob Elliott, was composed of the following members: one senior representative of each of the three functional departments—auditing (Elliott), tax (Jack McGowan), and consulting (Dick Nolan, who was co-founder of Nolan, Norton, an information technology consulting firm that KPMG acquired in April 1987); the individual in each functional department responsible for technology development for that function; the chief financial officer (Harry Baird); the head of the firm's computer resource center in Montvale, New Jersey; the partner-in-charge of banking; the partner-in-charge of middle market practice; and managing partners of two offices—Minneapolis (Floyd Kuehnis) and Pittsburgh (Bob Barry). Kuehnis and Barry represented the partners who would be the end-users of the system.

Before becoming managing partner of the Minneapolis office, Kuehnis had been managing partner of the San Jose office from 1978 to 1986. The San Jose office was situated in Silicon Valley, a hub of technology development in the United States. Kuehnis was aware of the potential of information technology for strategic purposes, and was seeking ways to use the technology in his office for improved client service. In 1982, Kuehnis was given funding from the operating committee to explore ways to use technology to improve client service. Kuehnis established a program called WAR, which stood for "who and referral" system. WAR contained a database of the officials of a number of KPMG clients and information about the specialties in San Jose and a few other KPMG offices. When Kuehnis joined the Minneapolis office in 1986, he established the WAR system there and expanded it to include 150,000 contacts and to track the business of the office. The client database in WAR foreshadowed the client database that would be in the shadow partner.

Barry was asked to be on the technology committee because his office was using technology in some basic ways for tax and auditing purposes, and he had a good sense of the operational needs of the office environment. Barry explained his role on the committee: "My basic responsibility was to relate the day-to-day, basic operating needs of the office. I was grounded in practicality, while most of the other members thought more conceptually."

The technology committee met quarterly and in between quarters on an ad hoc basis. The committee conducted studies regarding the databases that existed in the company at the time and how the company conducted professional practices. In addition, the committee surveyed 10 percent of the partners to see what features they wanted displayed on the shadow partner. In 1987, Doug Brockway, a consultant from Nolan, Norton, joined the technology committee. Brockway complemented the studies being done on technology by conducting a comprehensive study of the information architecture of the firm. The various studies helped the technology committee devise a technology strategy and create a detailed design for the shadow partner.

There was also an international technology committee, which was responsible for coordinating technology development throughout the global company and was involved in shadow partner development. The North American representatives on the international technology committee were Bob Elliott; Ross Walker, chairman of KPMG Canada and chairman of the international technology committee; and Dick Nolan, cofounder of Nolan, Norton.

The United States technology committee presented the shadow partner formally for the first time in January 1989 at a meeting of the operating committee and a meeting of the strategic planning committee. Some of the members of these committees responded enthusiastically to the shadow partner idea, while others were skeptical.

During 1989, Elliott and the other members of the technology committee made presentations of the shadow partner concept. In September 1989, Elliott demonstrated a prototype of the shadow partner to 200 partners at the KPMG international conference. The prototype was a program on a microcomputer that showed the capabilities of the shadow partner and how the user would interact with the system. In November 1989, Elliott showed the shadow partner prototype to all the United States partners at the annual partners meeting. Following partners meetings, it was customary to survey the partners through a questionnaire about their impressions of the meeting. Elliott's presentation received, what he described as, "pretty good" ratings. Some individuals were very excited about the shadow partner, but overall the response was one of caution.

If the technology was available, the clients were demanding more value-added services, and the technology experts in the firm believed that the shadow partner was a vital competitive tool, why was the firm not wholeheartedly committed to the project? There were both cultural issues and cost issues to consider in understanding the firm's attitude toward shadow partner development.

Cultural Issues

The cultural issues that affected the decision about whether or not to fund the shadow partner ranged from the dynamics of the accounting industry, to the fact that the firm was a partnership, to the mind frame of the members of the firm.

The Accounting Industry

The pioneers of the accounting profession in the United States established practices and norms that shaped the accounting industry and that persisted throughout its development. Peat, Marwick, Mitchell & Co. was one of the pioneers. It was created in 1911 from the merger of Marwick, Mitchell & Co., an American accounting firm founded in 1897 by two recent Scottish immigrants, and William B. Peat & Co., an English firm established in 1870. Peat, Marwick, Mitchell & Co. had strong roots in Anglo-American countries. On April 1, 1987, Peat, Marwick, Mitchell & Co. merged with Klynveld Main Goerdeler (KMG). KMG was a confederation that included prestigious national firms in Western Europe and that sought to become more international in orientation. The merger created a global powerhouse, which had dominant market share in 4 of 22 critical markets, 6,000 partners worldwide (1,850 in the United States), and 75,000 to 80,000 employees worldwide (20,000 in the United States) in

650 cities and 120 countries around the world. KPMG Peat Marwick (hereinafter referred to as KPMG) achieved revenues in excess of $5.1 billion for FY1990.

The accounting industry traditionally was dominated by a few firms, known as the Big Eight. The Big Eight included Coopers and Lybrand; Deloitte, Haskins & Sells; Price Waterhouse; Touche Ross; Arthur Young; Peat, Marwick, Mitchell & Co.; Ernst and Whinney; and Arthur Andersen. Executives at KPMG described the industry as traditionally having a relatively low level of competition. In fact, there was a sense of fellowship among firms in the industry. Senior representatives from the major firms met regularly to discuss professional issues. The accounting services provided and the fees charged were generally consistent across firms. Salaries for partners were also fairly consistent. Client loyalty to firms was strong, and clients discontinued audit relations with one firm in favor of another less than 5 percent of the time.

Until the 1980s, the industry dynamics remained relatively unchanged, with the same eight firms dominating the industry. Then, in the mid-1980s, a few firms began to discuss potential mergers, and some mergers were implemented. Deloitte, Haskins & Sells and Price Waterhouse announced they would merge in 1986. The merger, however, did not occur because the firms could not reach a mutually acceptable agreement. In 1987, when Peat, Marwick, Mitchell & Co. merged with KMG, KMG was the ninth largest firm in the industry. After witnessing KPMG's merger, other firms realized that mergers were possible. Also, through the merger KPMG expanded its global presence, and other firms hoped to accomplish expansion through mergers of their own. In 1989, Ernst and Whinney merged with Arthur Young, and Deloitte, Haskins & Sells merged with Touche Ross. Arthur Andersen and Price Waterhouse discussed the possibility of a merger, but it was never implemented. So, the Big 8 went to the Big 6, almost the Big 5, and then stabilized as the Big 6.

The Business

From the start, KPMG performed a range of services in auditing, tax, and consulting. The percentage of resources devoted to each area, though, shifted over time. Auditing, the examination of an organization's or an individual's financial statements, was the main function upon which KPMG built its identity. Auditing currently generated 60 percent of the firm's revenues. The tax function included preparing tax returns and advising clients on issues such as how to organize and manage their business to minimize long-term tax liability. The types of consulting services provided included management accounting consulting (e.g. helping clients design and implement accounting systems), information technology consulting, and benefits and compensation consulting.

Personal Networks

Most partners began with the firm directly upon college graduation and stayed until retirement. During many years of work with the firm, partners developed strong relationships with each other and developed personal networks of contacts within the firm. The networks usually were composed of partners who shared a similar area of expertise. Annual partners' meetings strengthened these networks. In serving clients, partners gathered information through contacting those in personal networks, but more often through daily conversation with the other partners at their operating office. Each of the 102 operating offices in the United States was intended to be sufficient in size to enable each partner to find all the resources and expertise needed to serve the client within the local office.

After the merger, the limitations of personal networks became more evident. The breadth of information reached through personal networks and the operating offices declined in comparison to the potential amount of information available. As Elliott commented:

Personal networks are well developed and well utilized. But they're relatively slow and do not cover a wide area of information in the company. After the merger, all of a sudden we had 2,500 new partners, and no easy way to learn about each other's experiences and to expand information networks.

Information sharing through networks occurred mostly over the telephone. There was some exchange of information through local area electronic networks, and about 20 percent of the partners engaged in this type of information sharing through local area networks.

There were 5,000 to 6,000 partners worldwide. About 55 percent of the partners were between ages 30 and 40, 35 percent were between 40 and 50 years old, and 10 percent were between 50 and 60 years old. The pension plan encouraged early retirement, so many partners retired between ages 55 and 57. There was mandatory retirement at age 60. Elliott described the profession as a "high burnout" one. "It is hard to remain as energetic and aggressive as you need to be," he said.

Partnership Procedures

Since the firm was a partnership, not a corporation, the partners owned the firm, and the CEO and COO were expected to act on behalf of the partners. Therefore, the CEO's decision about whether to fund a project such as the shadow partner had to reflect the partners' wishes. The CEO and COO were elected by the partners every six years. Partners also voted on the admission of new members, members of the board of directors, and changes to the partnership agreement.

The CEO, COO, and senior management committees could not force partners to adopt a certain policy. As Elliott explained, "The CEO and COO must manage by consensus. They cannot deliver mandates to the partners. The firm is based more on consensual agreement than management from the top."

Similarly, the CEO's commitment to a project, without the partners' support, was not sufficient. Elliott explained: "The CEO can be convinced of the value of funding a particular project or pursu-

ing a particular path, but in a partnership that's not enough. You need the partners' buy-in. Partners must be convinced of the value of a project before they will adopt it."

Since the partners were the owners of the firm, there was a sense among partners that investments in the business were personal investments and expenditures. Many of the partners, especially the older partners, were hesitant to fund a project if the monetary returns were not certain upfront. One senior executive commented: "Partners' mind frame makes them reluctant to accept a project in which the return on investment cannot be proven before implementation. Accountants are often skeptical. They focus on the cost side."

In promoting the shadow partner, the technology committee focused on both facets of corporate management—the partners and the senior executives. If the senior executives were convinced of the benefits of the shadow partner, they would try to get the partners enthusiastic about it. Similarly, if the partners were enthusiastic about the shadow partner, they would encourage the senior management to endorse the project.

Senior Management

Jon Madonna was elected CEO in October 1990, after having been managing partner of the San Francisco office for three years and a partner at the firm for nearly 20 years. Jim Brocksmith, who was elected chief operating officer at the same time, had been managing partner of the Chicago office. Elliott described Madonna's orientation to technology: "Madonna has told me he feels he needs to gain a better understanding of the strategic benefits of technology to the firm." Since becoming CEO, Madonna had not had time to discuss strategic technology issues with Elliott. They had only met to discuss legislative and professional issues. Their first strategic meeting was planned for April 1991.

Elliott described his impression of Brocksmith's orientation to technology: "Brocksmith sees the tactical advantages of information technology in terms of cost reduction and quality improvement, but he remains to be convinced of the strategic use of information technology in our business."

Use of Technology

As of 1991, 20 to 25 percent of the audit partners and 100 percent of the tax partners in the United States used computers for professional applications as well as communications and other basic functions. A few offices had more sophisticated information technology systems, such as the San Jose office, and were seeking ways to use their technology more strategically. Each operating office also had an IBM personal computer that connected it to a central financial database. Each operating office did its own record keeping, payroll, and other financial accounting, and regularly downloaded this information to a central IBM computer in Montvale, New Jersey. The central computer system, which was built in the 1960s, did processing and printed reports that were sent to the operating offices.

Financial Issues

Revenue

Growth in the accounting profession began to slow in the fall of 1989 due to a variety of factors. One factor was that there had been few recent changes to the tax laws, and changes in tax laws generated business. The number of mergers and acquisitions decreased, banks failed, and cash flow decreased in certain businesses, all of which adversely affected growth. Firm revenue grew in the early 1980s at about 20 percent each year, but for 1990 and 1991 real growth was flat.

Another general reason growth stalled was that the accounting firm's product had become a commodity product. As Kuehnis explained:

> Firms have been doing things one way for 40 years. Everyone knows how to deliver the product. Clients are not trying to pay firms less for the traditional service, but they won't pay more either.

Partners' Compensation

Partner compensation averaged $250,000, and ranged from $120,000 for younger partners to $1 million for senior partners. It took, on average, 12 years to become a partner. Compensation figures for partners were published and distributed to all partners annually. The compensation was based on the firm's profits and the performance of the individual partner. Partners, once a year, did self-evaluations and met with their supervisors to discuss their performance during the last year and to set goals. They set one-year goals and three-year goals.

For nonpartners, the performance evaluation system was more complex. Since teams were formed to serve the clients on an individual basis, nonpartners would usually work in many teams and under many supervisors throughout the year. After each engagement, the supervisor of the team evaluated the performance of each nonpartner in the team. All of a nonpartner's evaluations were accumulated once a year and considered in the compensation decision.

The slowed growth in 1989 and 1990 caused the company to decrease the number of partners by 5 percent. The number of nonpartners decreased as well, but that decrease resulted primarily from the need for fewer administrative assistants due to the use of technology.

Cost Issues and the Shadow Partner

The cost of shadow partner development as of 1991 was approximately $5 million. The first $2 million of that cost included the time and resources the partners and Nolan, Norton consultants devoted to the project. The next $3 million was the cost for Nolan, Norton to develop the "engineering drawings" for the system. The drawings detailed the network hardware and software specifications.

The cost to deploy the shadow partner ranged from a low of $30 million, to a median of $70 million, to a high of $100 million. The different estimated costs depended on the degree to which the shadow partner was implemented.

If fully deployed, the system would include workstations on every desktop linked to Connection Machines which would operate on a wide-area network. The workstations were the personal computers at the operating offices, which were both freestanding personal computers and windows into the Connection Machines. Each workstation would have the same software. Many workstations would be linked to one Connection Machine. Connection Machine was a brand name that referred to a massively parallel processor system produced by Thinking Machines based in Cambridge, Massachusetts. Parallel processor machines had the ability to execute multiple, independent operations simultaneously. The parallel processors on the network would have the ability to rapidly process KPMG's 140 gigabits of current information, which roughly equalled the amount of information in 250,000 250-page books. The information in the system would be comprehensive and unstructured. Each Connection Machine cost $5 million for 64K parallel processors. The wide area network would connect all the Connection Machines and hence all of the workstations. In addition to providing shared database access, the network would allow global electronic communication (i.e., e-mail).

The median implementation of the vision would include 80 percent of the capabilities of the full vision. There would be fewer Connection Machines, and the ability to process fewer gigabits of information. The company would have to be more selective about what information was included in the databases. Experts in certain areas would decide the "best of practice" material that would be included in the database. In a sense, there were people who did this already; they received information from partners, reviewed it, and fed it back to partners. Also, the median implementation would mean that workstations did not have to have identical functionality—only similar. There could be IBM or Apple workstations, and their interfaces would be similar but not identical. The low cost version of the shadow partner would include a few Connection Machines and a curtailed amount of data. Once the system was developed, all offices would be responsible for funding the implementation and maintenance of the system at their particular locations.

Future of the Shadow Partner

The concern of the technology committee and other proponents of the shadow partner was whether the firm would provide the necessary funding to develop the shadow partner. Sapienza, who was made head of the technology committee in 1990, and Brockway both commented that the operating committee would be hesitant to endorse the shadow partner because of the difficulty of proving the value of the shadow partner upfront. As Sapienza explained, the system would not reduce the cost of service as much as it would enhance service:

> One of the problems with the shadow partner is that the company has to buy it on faith. I can't show all the benefits of the system or cost justify it until it is implemented. The natural tendency of the operating committee is to ask: Where will it save money? Where will it reduce cost? The payback will be in new clients, better service for current clients, and more business from current clients.

Brockway did not believe the partners would make the initial investment: "I do not think the partners are going to spend $100 million, especially when they cannot be shown upfront that there is going to be a monetary payback." Elliott summed up this viewpoint by stating, "It's easy to quantify costs. It's hard to quantify benefits."

Some executives believed that if some offices installed the shadow partner and a limited network was established, then the other offices would follow suit. Brockway stated: "We need to get a few machines out there to prove the value of the system. Until the partners interact with the technology themselves, it is hard for them to envision its value. Those that use the system will realize its value and will convince others that they cannot live without it."

Elliott commented that in order for the shadow partner to be really effective a critical number of executives had to adopt it: "In order for an unstructured database to work in a network, you need critical mass. Many people need to use it. E-mail, for instance, was never very useful here because too few people adopted it. I think if enough partners use the shadow partner, there will be enough of an information explosion to make it indispensable."

Ross Walker believed that offices would adopt a limited version of the shadow partner: "Each office has autonomy as to what technology they want to use, and I don't see everyone wanting to buy the same exact hardware or software systems. Instead, I see there being a 'band of technology' within which everyone will stay if they want to be a part of the international network. I see some offices buying in enthusiastically and other offices dragging their feet. I think if the offices in the major countries buy in, the others will."

Kuehnis stressed that partners' adopting the shadow partner depended partly on their overcoming any cultural aversion they had toward technology: "I think that the technology models of the future are not technology issues, they're cultural issues. The culture of the company has to support information sharing through technology and more strategic uses of information." Walker remarked that many members of the international executive committee (which included senior partners of the largest offices) did not completely understand the benefits of technology in general: "I would say that the international executive committee supports the shadow partner, but there is a lack of full appreciation of its implications."

Sapienza was scheduled to make a presentation to the operating committee in February 1991, and this committee had the authority to fund development of the shadow partner in the United States. Should the senior executives authorize funding for the full development, or a limited version, of the shadow partner?

Reading 9–1: Information Technology and Tomorrow's Manager

This chapter closes with a *Harvard Business Review* reprint, "Information Technology and Tomorrow's Manager."

Preparation Questions

1. Consider the technology trends that Applegate, Cash, and Mills examined. Did they miss any technologies in 1988 that appear significant today?
2. Evaluate the authors' four predictions about the impact of IT on organizational structure.
3. Evaluate the authors' four predictions about the impact of IT on management processes.
4. Evaluate the authors' five predictions about the impact of IT on human resources.
5. How will you prepare for these changes? What other changes would you predict?

INFORMATION TECHNOLOGY AND TOMORROW'S MANAGER

By Lynda M. Applegate, James I. Cash, Jr., and D. Quinn Mills*

The year is 1958. It's a time of prosperity, productivity, and industrial growth for US corporations, which dominate the world economy. Organizations are growing bigger and more complex by the day. Transatlantic cable service, which has just been initiated, and advances in transportation are allowing companies to expand into international markets. To handle the growth, companies are decentralizing decision making. To keep track of these burgeoning operations, they are hiring middle managers in droves. In fact, for the first time ever, white-collar workers outnumber blue-collar workers. Large companies are installing their first computers to automate routine clerical and production tasks, and "participatory management" is the buzzword.

It's also the year Harold J. Leavitt and Thomas L. Whisler predicted what corporate life would be like 30 years later. Their article "Management in the 1980s" (*HBR* November–December 1958)[1] and its predictions ran counter to the trends that were then underway. Leavitt and Whisler said, for instance, that by the late 1980s, the combination of management science and information technology would cause middle-management ranks to shrink, top management to take on more of the creative functions, and large organizations to centralize again. Through the 1960s, 1970s, and early 1980s, Leavitt and Whisler's predictions met strong criticism. But as the 1980s draw to a close, they don't seem so farfetched. Instead, they seem downright

visionary. (See the insert, "Their Future, Our Present.")

Downsizing and "flattening" have been common in recent years. One estimate has it that organizations have shed more than one million managers and staff professionals since 1979. As companies have reduced the number of middle managers, senior managers have increased their span of control and assumed additional responsibilities. Consider these two examples:

- Within weeks after a comprehensive restructuring thinned management by 40 percent, the president of a large oil company requested an improved management control system for his newly appointed senior management team. In response, a sophisticated, online executive information system was developed. It did the work of scores of analysts and mid-level managers whose responsibilities had been to produce charts and graphs, communicate this information, and coordinate operations with others in the company. The president also mandated the use of electronic mail to streamline communication throughout the business.

- A large manufacturing company recently undertook a massive restructuring to cut the cost and time required to bring a new product to market. The effort included layoffs, divestitures, and early retirements, which thinned middle management by 30 percent. The company adopted a sophisticated telecommunications network, which linked all parts of the multinational company, and a centralized corporate database, which integrated all aspects of the highly decentralized business. Senior managers used the database and networks to summarize and display data from inside and outside the company and to signal to employees the kinds of things they should focus on.

[1]Reprints of "Management in the 1980s," by Harold J. Leavitt and Thomas L. Whisler, HBR November–December 1958, p. 41, are available by calling (617) 495-6192. Reprint number 58605.

Information technology, which had once been a tool for organizational expansion, has become a tool for downsizing and restructuring. Both these companies used technology to improve centralized control and to create new information channels. But this improved centralized control did not come at the expense of decentralized decision making. In fact, the need to be responsive led to even more decentralized decision making. The companies reduced the number of middle managers, and the computer systems assumed many of the communication, coordination, and control functions that middle managers previously performed. The line managers who remained were liberated from some routine tasks and had more responsibility.

These effects are similar to what Leavitt and Whisler predicted. Taking their clues from the management science and technology research of the 1950s, Leavitt and Whisler contemplated how technology would influence the shape and nature of the organization. They understood that technology would enable senior management to monitor and control large organizations more effectively and that fewer middle managers would be needed to analyze and relay information. They did not anticipate, however, that microcomputers would enable simultaneous improvement in decentralized decision making.

In the past, managers had to choose between a centralized and a decentralized structure. Today there is a third option: technology-driven control systems that support the flexibility and responsiveness of a decentralized organization as well as the integration and control of a centralized organization.

What Next?

Now that this wave of information technology has worked its way into practice, it's time to think about where we're headed next. When we turn to research to see what technical breakthroughs are on the horizon, as Leavitt and Whisler did, we find that the horizon itself has changed. It's now much closer. Since the 1950s, development time has been cut in half. What once took 30 years to get

from pure research to commercial application now takes only 10 to 15.

Moreover, when earlier generations of technology were commercialized, managers tended to adopt the technology first and then try to figure out what to do with the new information and how to cope with the organizational implications. But for many companies, that approach is now grossly inadequate. The new technology is more powerful, more diverse, and increasingly entwined with the organization's critical business processes. Continuing to merely react to new technology and the organizational change it triggers could throw a business into a tailspin.

At the same time, the business environment is changing ever faster, and organizations must be more responsive to it. Yet certain facts of life restrain them from doing so. Companies want to be more flexible, yet job descriptions, compensation schemes, and control mechanisms are rigid. They want to use their resources effectively, yet it's not always clear who can contribute most to a project, especially among people in different functional areas. They want to be productive, but every time an employee goes to another company, a little bit of corporate history and experience walks out the door.

With the help of technology, managers will be able to overcome these problems and make their organizations far more responsive than they are today. We can look forward, in fact, to an era in which managers will do the shaping. Large organization or small, centralized or not—business leaders will have options they've never had before. The technology will be there to turn the vision into reality and to change it as circumstances evolve. With that in mind, making a next round of predictions and waiting to see if they come true seems too passive. It makes more sense to begin thinking about the kind of organization we want and taking the steps necessary to prepare for it.

We already see glimpses of the future in some progressive companies that have used technology creatively, but even they do not give us a complete picture of the kind of organization that will be

Information Technology and Tomorrow's Manager   **475**

possible—maybe even prevalent—in the twenty-first century. Some companies will choose to adopt a new organizational form that we call the "cluster organization."[2] By doing so, they will be able to run their large companies like small ones and achieve the benefits of both.

In the cluster organization, groups of people will work together to solve business problems or define a process and will then disband when the job is done. Team members may be geographically dispersed and unacquainted with each other, but information and communication systems will enable those with complementary skills to work together. The systems will help the teams carry out their activities and track the results of their decisions. Reporting relationships, control mechanisms, compensation schemes—all will be different in the cluster organization.

Technology will offer new options even to companies that don't wish to make all of the changes the cluster organization implies. The first step in understanding these options is to look, as Leavitt and Whisler did, at the technologies that will make them possible.

Tomorrow's Machines

Much of the technology that will give managers the freedom to shape their organizations is already being commercialized—expert systems, group and cooperative work systems, and executive information systems. Expert and knowledge-based systems (a subset of artificial intelligence technology) are rapidly appearing in commercial settings. Every large company we've polled expects to have at least one production system using this technology by late 1989. Group and cooperative work systems have sprung up in a number of companies, primarily for use by multidisciplinary teams. Executive information systems, which track both internal and external information, enable senior managers to

monitor and control large, geographically dispersed and complex organizations.

By the turn of the century, these and other technologies will be widely available. Companies will be able to pick and choose applications that fit their requirements. Computers will be faster, smaller, more reliable, and easier to use. They'll store vast amounts of information, and they'll be flexible enough to allow companies to change their information and communication systems as the environment changes.

In the twenty-first century, desktop computers will be as powerful as today's supercomputers, and supercomputers will run at speeds over a thousand times faster than today's. Computer chips now with one million processing elements will have more than one billion, and parallel processing (the ability to share a task among a number of processing units) will boost power tremendously.

It will be possible to communicate voluminous amounts of information in a variety of forms over long distances within seconds. Standard telephone lines and advanced cellular radio technology will provide access to high-speed networks that will whisk data, text, graphics, voice, and video information from one part of the world and send it to another instantly. Improved reliability and security will accompany the significantly higher network speeds and the improved performance.

Plugging all shapes and sizes of computers into tomorrow's network will be as easy as plugging in a telephone today. Telephones, in fact, will be replaced by computer phones that can convert speech into machine-readable text and can simultaneously transmit video images, voice, and data. Storing messages, transferring documents, paying bills, and shopping at home will all be possible through the same connection.

Computers the size of a small book will have the information-processing power and storage capabilities of today's desktop workstations, yet will fit in a briefcase. They'll enable us to create and revise documents, review and answer mail, and even hold video conference meetings from anyplace that has a phone jack. Cellular terminals will

[2]See D. Quinn Mills, *The Cluster Organization: A New Alternative to the Hierarchy* (1989).

Their Future, Our Present

Harold J. Leavitt and Thomas L. Whisler's "Management in the 1980s" appeared in the November–December 1958 issue of the *Harvard Business Review.* In that article, the two authors hypothesized what the organization of the future would look like. They predicted that in the 1980s . . .

. . . *the role and scope of middle managers would change.* Many of the existing middle management jobs would become more structured and would move downward in status and compensation. The number of middle managers would decrease, creating a flatter organization. Those middle-management positions that remained would be more technical and specialized. New mid-level positions with titles like "analyst" would be created.

. . . *top management would take on more of the innovating, planning, and creating.* The rate of obsolescence and change would quicken, and top management would have to continually focus on the horizon.

. . . *large organizations would recentralize.* New information technologies would give top managers more information and would extend top management's control over the decisions of subordinates. Top executives chose to decentralize only because they were unable to keep up with the changing size and complexity of their organizations. Given the chance, however, they would use information technology to take more control and recentralize.

---

allow even more freedom, since they won't require a wired telephone connection. And we will no longer be a slave to the keyboard; voice recognition technology will allow us to dictate messages and create and revise text as easily as using a dictaphone.

As computers become faster at processing and communicating information, we'll need better ways of storing and managing it. Optical storage media, similar to the compact-disk technology that is used today to store music, will hold much more information than is possible today and will retrieve information much more quickly.

And no longer will it be necessary to store data in static databases that must be reprogrammed every time the business changes. Flexible, dynamic information networks called associative networks will do away with these rigid systems. Associative networks will allow us to store and manipulate information in a manner similar to the way we think. They will store data, voice, video, text, and graphics—but beyond that, they will store the relationships between information elements. As needs change and the network is reconfigured, the relationships among the data remain intact. Primitive associative information systems, used primarily to process large-text databases (e.g., hypertext), are currently on the market. We can expect significant enhancements to these associative information systems in the next several years.

Tomorrow's computers will truly be more intelligent. Today's computers are designed to process information sequentially, one command at a time. This capability works well if the problem or task is structured and can be broken down into a series of steps. It doesn't work well for complex, unstructured tasks involving insight, creativity, and judgment. "Neural network" computers will change that.

Rather than processing commands one at a time, a neural network computer uses associative reasoning to store information as patterns of connections among millions of tiny processors, all of which are linked together. These computers attempt to mimic the actions of the human brain. When faced with a new pattern, the computer follows rules of logic to ask questions that help it figure out what to do with the anomaly.

Prototypes of neural network computers already exist. One group of researchers developed a neural network computer that contained the logic to understand English phonetics. The researchers gave the computer typed transcripts, containing 1,024 words, from a child in first grade, and it proceeded to read out loud. A human instructor "told" the computer each time it made a mistake, and within 10 tries, the computer was reading the text in an understandable way. Within 50 tries, the computer was reading at 95 percent accuracy. No software programming was ever done.[2] The computer learned to read in much the same way that humans do.

We can also expect that by the twenty-first century there will be many companies that routinely use expert systems and other artificial intelligence applications. Knowledge bases, in which expertise is stored along with information, will become as commonplace as data bases are today. Technology will increasingly help people perform tasks requiring judgment and expert knowledge. Already, fighter aircraft technology is moving toward having the plane respond to what the pilot is thinking rather than his physical movements.

This type of technology will no longer simply make things more efficient; instead, the computer will become a tool for creativity, discovery, and education. Interactive technology based on optical storage is currently used in flight simulators to help pilots learn to make decisions. Some companies are experimenting with similar systems, described as digital video interactive, to help planners, analysts, researchers, functional specialists, and managers learn to make decisions without the risk and time associated with traditional experiential learning. These should help managers learn to be effective much more quickly.

Technologies will be well developed to meet the needs of senior executives. Sophisticated analytical, graphical, and computer interface capabilities will be able to aggregate, integrate, and present data in flexible and easy-to-use formats. Computers and special software will support executive planning, decision making, communication, and control activities. Some executives already use these applications to manage their businesses.

While in the past computers primarily supported individual work, the computer systems of the future will also be geared toward groups. Research on computer support for cooperative work has gained momentum over the past five years, and many companies are developing promising new technologies. Several companies are installing automated meeting rooms, and a number of vendors are working on software to support group activities. Researchers are now testing electronic brainstorming, group consensus, and negotiation software, and general meeting support systems. To help geographically dispersed group members work together, some companies are developing electronic communication software and applications that make communication and the exchange of documents and ideas faster and easier. These applications will allow skills to be better allocated.

The Structure, the Process, and the People

These and other advanced technologies will give managers a whole new set of options for structuring and operating their businesses. In the twenty-first century, like today, some companies will be small, some will be large; some will be decentralized, others will not. But technology will enable new organizational structures and management processes to spring up around the familiar ones, and the business world will be a very different place as a result. Here we describe the organizational structures, management processes, and human resource management strategies associated with the cluster organization and how the technology will make them possible in years to come.

Organizational Structures

Companies will have the benefits of small scale and large scale simultaneously.

Even large organizations will be able to adopt more flexible and dynamic structures.

The distinctions between centralized and decentralized control will blur.

The focus will be on projects and processes rather than on tasks and standard procedures.

---

[2]Terrence Sejnowski and Charles Rosenberg, "Parallel Networks That Learn to Pronounce English Text, *Complex Systems,* vol. 1, 1987, p. 145.

The hierarchy and the matrix are the most common formal organization designs for large companies today. They structure communication, responsibility, and accountability to help reduce complexity and provide stability. But, as implemented today, they also tend to stifle innovation. With the environment changing as quickly as it does, the challenge has been to make large companies, with their economies of scale and other size advantages, as responsive as small ones.

Small companies, of course, have fewer layers of management and less bureaucracy, so the organization is less rigid. They adapt more easily to change and allow for creativity. Leadership and control are generally easier in small businesses because top management can communicate directly with workers and can readily trace the contribution individuals make. Information is also easier to track. Much of the knowledge is in people's heads, and everyone knows whom to go to for expertise on a particular subject. People often have a chance to get involved with a broad range of responsibilities and therefore have a better understanding of the business as a whole.

These small organizations, especially those that are information-intensive and have a large percentage of professional employees, tend to be structured differently. We have termed the most fluid and flexible forms "cluster." Other authors talk of a network organization or an adhocracy.[3] In the network organization, rigid hierarchies are replaced by formal and informal communication networks that connect all parts of the company. In the adhocracy, a set of project-oriented work groups replaces the hierarchy. Both of these forms are well known for their flexibility and adaptiveness. The Manned Space Flight Center of NASA, an example of an adhocracy, changed its organization structure 17 times in the first 8 years of its existence.[4]

In what will be an even faster changing world than the one we now know, businesses of all sizes will need the ability to adapt to the dynamics of the external environment. Automated information and communication networks will support the sharing of information throughout a large, widely dispersed, complex company. The systems will form the organization's infrastructure and change the role of formal reporting procedures. Even in large corporations, each individual will be able to communicate with any other—just as if he or she worked in a small company.

The technologies that will allow these more fluid organizational forms are already coming into use in the form of electronic mail, voice mail, fax, data networks, and computer and video conferencing. Speed and performance improvements will collapse the time and distance that now separate people who could benefit from working together. The large organizations of the future will seem as tightly connected as small ones.

Computers will also help identify who in the company has the expertise needed to work on a particular problem. Databases of employees' skills and backgrounds will ensure that the mix of talent can be tailor-made for every task that arises. The systems will keep track of who knows what, and how to prepare an individual for the next project.

Managers in large companies will also have technological help in keeping track of where information resides and how to analyze it. Associative information networks and neural network computers will preserve the relationships among data elements and will store and manage information in a manner similar to the way we think. They will provide concise snapshots of the vast activities and resources of a large corporation. This will prevent managers from being overwhelmed by the scale and complexity.

[3]See Robert G. Eccles and Dwight B. Crane, "Managing through Networks in Investment Banking," *California Management Review* (Fall 1987): 176; and Henry Mintzberg, "The Adhocracy," in *The Strategy Process,* ed. James Brian Quinn, Henry Mintzberg, and Robert M. James (Englewood Cliffs, N.J.: Prentice Hall, 1988), p. 607.

[4]As reported in Henry Mintzberg, *Structuring in Fives: Designing Effective Organizations* (Englewood Cliffs, N.J.: Prentice Hall, 1983).

Conversations with Leavitt and Whisler

In January 1988, Lynda Applegate, Mark Cannon (a research associate), and James Cash visited with professors Leavitt and Whisler and asked them to reflect on their 1958 article. Here are excerpts from those conversations.

What prompted you to write the article "Management in the 1980s"?

Leavitt: As a graduate student at MIT in the late 1940s, I was exposed to all kinds of new ideas about machines that might be able to learn and even think. It was an expansive and optimistic time of very rapid technical change. Management theory was also changing to a much more human approach. The emphasis was shifting away from hierarchical formalism toward decentralization and participative management. Tom and I wanted to shake people up and get them to look at not only the human side, but also the technical and social sides. We wanted to stimulate debate—and we did.

Whisler: Hal and I shared an office at the University of Chicago. I was interested in organization structure and technology's influence on it. Hal was a social scientist interested in organization and management theory. We had a number of lively discussions on how computers would change organizations. We believed the trend toward decentralization was a response to increasing complexity. We were convinced that given the right tools to deal with the complexity, managers would recentralize. We saw the computer as one of those tools.

How would you evaluate your predictions today?

Leavitt: One thing we didn't anticipate was the tremendous impact of miniaturization. We thought of computers as massive, centralized machines. We couldn't even imagine modern PCs sitting on our desks. The whole question of centralization versus decentralization becomes almost irrelevant when you consider the potential of decentralizing computer processing.

Whisler: In our 1958 predictions, we focused on the influence of information technology, although we knew that other factors also affected organization structure. A major development to which we did not pay sufficient attention was the rapidly expanding economy of the 1960s and the consequent explosive growth of companies. These companies needed more middle managers to keep them under control, which had a decentralizing effect. For a while, growth upstaged the special kind of "downsizing" of middle management we foresaw. As growth slowed in the late 1970s and 1980s, and competition became intense, the effect of information technology became evident. The timing of events was fortunate for us.

You were among the first, if not the first, to use the term information technology. *What did you mean by it?*

Leavitt: We were influenced by the early research on artificial intelligence, heuristic programming, and quantitative modeling by people like Norbert Wiener and Herbert Simon. So we were looking at the computer from a human and managerial—not a data processing—point of view. We were thinking about computers that might influence human learning and decision making—not computers that would automate routine work.

Whisler: The mid-1950s were a time of intense interest in management science. The computer was seen as a tool to support complex, quantitative modeling. We used the term *information technology* because we wanted to stress the use of the computer to support decision making and organizational information processing. Many people misinterpreted our perspective.

Executives and senior managers will be less insulated from operations because executive information systems will help them get the information they need to monitor, coordinate, and control their businesses. Rather than waiting for the analysts and middle managers to prepare reports at the end of a prolonged reporting period, executives will have immediate access to information. Software will help do the analysis and present it in a usable format. With such immediate feedback, managers will be able to adjust their strategy and tactics as circumstances evolve rather than at fixed time intervals. And if a change in tactics or strategy is warranted, advanced communication technology will send the message to employees promptly.

Top management's ability to know what is going on throughout the organization won't automatically lead to centralization. With feedback on operations readily available at the top, the rigid policies and procedures that now aim to keep line managers on track can be relaxed. The systems will also liberate business managers by giving them the information and analytic support they need to make decisions and control their operations. Individuals and project teams will be able to operate fairly autonomously while senior management monitors the overall effects of their actions by the hour or day.

Most of the day-to-day activity will be project oriented. Because circumstances will change even faster than they do now, no two situations will be exactly alike or call for the same set of experts or procedures. The employees' skills and the approach will vary with the task at hand, so teams of people will form around particular projects and subsequently dissolve. Most responsibilities, then, will be handed over to project managers. Associative information networks will help those managers deploy resources, and software specially designed to support group work will aid communication, decision making, and consensus reaching. People who work together only infrequently will have the tools they need to be at least as effective as the permanent management team in a small company.

Decision making is not well understood in most organizations. Managers often make choices based

---

Management Processes

Decision making will be better understood.

Control will be separate from reporting relationships.

Computers will support creativity at all organizational levels.

Information and communication systems will retain corporate history, experience, and expertise.

---

on thought processes they themselves cannot explain. They gather the information they think is relevant and reach what seems like the best conclusion. In the future, sophisticated expert systems and knowledge bases will help to capture those decision-making processes. Companies can then analyze and improve them.

As the decision processes become more explicit and well defined and as companies learn what information is required, the level of the person making the decision becomes less important. It will still be important to monitor the outcome and to make sure the circumstances surrounding the decision haven't completely changed.

Management control is now exerted through the formal organizational chart. A manager at a given level in the organization is responsible for everything that happens below that level. That same person channels information up through the organization to the person he or she reports to.

But when technology allows top management to monitor data at the lowest organizational level without the help of intermediaries and when employees at all levels and in all functions can communicate directly, formal control systems do not have to be embedded in organizational reporting relationships. The ability to separate control from reporting relationships means that both systems can be handled most effectively. For instance, top management can exercise control directly by monitoring results at all levels, while a different set of relationships exists for reporting purposes. These reporting relationships would focus on employee motivation, creativity, and socialization.

By doing a lot of the analytical work, expert systems and artificial intelligence tools will free up workers at all levels to be more creative. Up to now, only top management jobs have been structured to allow as much time as possible for creative thinking. As technology helps managers with coordination, control, decision making, and communication, they too will have the time and encouragement to make discoveries and use the new resources innovatively.

The transience of even specialized workers won't be nearly the problem in the twenty-first century that it is today. Information systems will maintain the corporate history, experience, and expertise that long-time employees now hold. The information systems themselves—not the people—can become the stable structure of the organization. People will be free to come and go, but the value of their experience will be incorporated in the systems that will help them and their successors run the business.

In this environment, companies will need fewer managers. Those managers that do assume executive positions, however, will lack the experiential learning acquired through years as a middle manager. Their career paths will not take them through positions of increasing responsibility where they oversee the work of others. Executive information systems will enable them to "get up to speed" quickly on all parts of the business. Sophisticated business analysis and simulation models will help them analyze business situations and recognize the consequences, thereby decreasing and managing risk.

Human Resources

Workers will be better trained, more autonomous, and more transient.

The work environment will be exciting and engaging.

Management will be for some people a part-time activity that is shared and rotated.

Job descriptions tied to narrowly defined tasks will become obsolete.

Compensation will be tied more directly to contribution.

In the 1950s and 1960s, computers took on many operational and routine tasks. In the 1970s and 1980s, they assumed some middle-management decision making, coordinating, and controlling tasks. As the technology affects even more aspects of the business, work itself will change and require a different set of skills. People will need to be technically sophisticated and better educated in order to cope with the demands on them. Employees must be capable of leading—rather than being led by—the technology, capable of using technology as a lever against the increased complexity and pace of change in their business environments.

As top management seizes on its ability to monitor without restricting freedom, employees will have more control over their own work. There will be fewer rigid policies from a less visible headquarters. Also, as the nature of the work changes from implementing a particular company's standard operating procedures to participating in a series of projects that call on one's expertise, workers will be less tied to any one organization, and building loyalty to a company will be harder than it is today. In some companies, loyalty may be less critical than having access to the skills a given employee has to offer. As companies pull together the resources they need on a project-by-project basis and as information and communication networks extend beyond the organization, company boundaries will be harder to define. Organizations may draw on expertise that lies in a supplier or an independent consultant if appropriate.

Because workers will be highly skilled and the organization will offer fewer opportunities for advancement, employees will expect the work environment to be rewarding. If they are not stimulated or if their independence is threatened, they will go elsewhere.

In these ways, companies of the future will closely resemble professional service firms today. The most successful firms attract and retain employees by providing an environment that is intellectually engaging. The work is challenging, the projects diverse, and the relationships with clients fairly independent. Some professionals work with more than one firm—like doctors who admit patients to several hospitals.

Management will be a part-time job as group members share responsibility and rotate leadership. Except at the top of the organization, there will be few jobs that consist solely of overseeing the work of others—and then primarily for measurement and control purposes. Each work group may have a different leader. In addition, the leadership of a single group may rotate among members, depending on what the business problem requires. Employees will take on a management role for short periods, and as a result, will have a better understanding of the entire business.

Detailed, task-oriented job descriptions will be less important because the job will be changing all the time. In a sense, everyone will be doing the same job—lending their special skills and expertise to one project after another. In another sense, every job will be unique—people with different kinds of expertise will work on different sets of projects. Information systems will be able to account for the work each person does and the skills and experience he or she possesses.

The ability to track each individual's skill and participation in the company outside the traditional organizational forms creates a whole new freedom: the ability to pay each person for his or her actual contribution to the organization without upsetting an entire pay scale or hierarchical structure. Currently, if the company wants to create an incentive for a particular person, it is often constrained by the compensation system itself. To raise one person's salary requires boosting everyone else above that point in the hierarchy.

Flexible, dynamic compensation packages will allow companies to treat individuals as unique contributors and to reward them based on their particular skills. In some companies, an employee's compensation may follow the pattern of a normal distribution curve, matching the employee's desired work pattern and contribution to the company. Salaries would increase and peak between ages 40 and 50, and then decline.

Be Creative but Be Careful

The new technologies hold great promise that our large, rigid hierarchies will become more adaptive, responsive, and better suited to the fast-paced world of the twenty-first century. But these technologies do not come without risk. Processing information faster may seem like a good idea, but it is possible to process information too fast. As speed increases, efficiency of a process improves only to a point. That point is reached when it is no longer possible to monitor and control the results of the process. Beyond that point, the process of collecting information, making decisions, monitoring feedback, and evaluating performance breaks down. The experience of some companies during the stock market crash of October 19, 1987, shows what can happen when information is processed faster than we can monitor and control it.

There are also risks associated with integrating data from diverse sources. For one thing, we run the risk of data overload, in which case people unable to understand or use the information and the tools that convert data into information may fail. Also, the creation of integrated databases may lead to unintended liabilities. For example, when an elevator manufacturer created a centralized service and repair center, it also created a legal liability. A large, centralized database containing the maintenance and repair records of all of their elevators in North America provided an attractive target for subpoena by any suitor.

Computerization of critical business processes may also create security risks. Sabotage, fraud, record falsification, and theft become more threatening than ever. And with more information stored electronically, privacy issues become more acute.

Leavitt and Whisler were wise to believe that information technology would influence the structure of organizations, their management processes, and the nature of managerial work. Our 30-year history of information technology use in organizations suggests that in the future managers must be much more actively involved in directing technology and managing its influence on organizations.

Technology will not be an easy solution to serious problems and it won't guarantee competitiveness. As always, it will require thoughtful planning and responsible management. But as never before, it will tax the creative powers of the business leaders who must decide when to use it—and to what end.

SUGGESTIONS FOR THE MANAGER'S BOOKSHELF

Organizations

futurist Magazine.

Bartlett, Christopher A., and Sumantra Ghoshal. *Managing across Borders: The Transnational Solution.* Boston: Harvard Business School Press, 1989.

Chandler, Alfred D., Jr. *Scale and Scope: The Dynamics of Industrial Capitalism.* Cambridge, Mass.: The Belknap Press of Harvard University Press, 1990.

Eccles, Robert G., and Dwight B. Crane. *Doing Deals: Investment Banks at Work.* Boston: Harvard Business School Press, 1988.

Eccles, Robert G., and Nitin Nohria. *Beyond the Hype: Rediscovering the Essence of Management.* Boston: Harvard Business School Press, 1992.

Fombrun, Charles J. *Turning Points: Creating Strategic Change in Organizations.* New York: McGraw-Hill, Inc., 1992.

Hackman, J. Richard (ed.) *Groups that Work (and Those that Don't).* San Francisco: Jossey-Bass, 1990.

Kanter, Rosabeth Moss. *When Giants Learn to Dance: Mastering the Challenges of Strategy, Management and Careers in the 1990s.* New York: Simon & Schuster, 1989.

Mills, D. Quinn. *The IBM Lesson.* New York: Time Books, 1988.

Nohria, Nitin, and Robert G. Eccles (Eds.). *Networks and Organizations: Structure, Form, and Action.* Boston: Harvard Business School Press, 1992.

Scott, W. Richard. *Organizations: Rational, Natural and Open Systems.* Englewood Cliffs, N.J.: Prentice Hall, 1981.

Senge, Peter M. *The Fifth Discipline: The Art and Practice of the Learning Organization.* New York: Doubleday/Currency, 1990.

Walton, Richard E. *Innovating to Compete: Lessons for Diffusing and Managing Change in the Workplace.* San Francisco: Jossey-Bass, 1987.

Williamson, Oliver E. *The Economic Institutions of Capitalism.* New York: The Free Press, 1985.

Control

Anthony, Robert N. *The Management Control Function.* Boston: Harvard Business School Press, 1988.

Eccles, Robert G. *The Transfer Pricing Problem: A Theory for Practice.* Lexington, Mass.: Lexington Books, 1985.

Etzioni, Amitaie A. *The Moral Dimension: Toward a New Economics.* New York: Free Press, 1988.

Johnson, Thomas H., and Robert S. Kaplan. *Relevance Lost: The Rise and Fall of Managerial Accounting.* Boston: Harvard Business School Press, 1987.

Merchant, Kenneth A. *Control in Business Organizations.* Cambridge, Mass.: Ballinger, 1985.

Merchant, Kenneth A. *Rewarding Results: Motivating Profit Center Managers.* Boston: Harvard Business School Press, 1989.

Information and Information Technologies

Cash, James I.; F. Warren McFarlan; and James L. McKenney. *Corporate Information Systems Management: The Issues Facing Senior Executives.* Third Edition Homewood, Ill.: Irwin, 1992.

Keen, Peter G. W. *Computing in Time: Using Telecommunications for Competitive Advantage.* Cambridge, Mass.: Ballinger, 1988.

McKinnon, Sharon M., and William J. Bruns, Jr. *The Information Mosaic.* Boston: Harvard Business School Press, 1992.

Walton, Richard E. *Up and Running: Integrating Information Technology and the Organization.* Boston: Harvard Business School Press, 1989.

Zuboff, Shoshana. *In the Age of the Smart Machine.* New York: Basic Books, 1988.

Business Transformation

Beer, Michael; Russel A. Eisenstat; and Burt Spector. *The Critical Path to Corporate Renewal.* Boston: Harvard Business School Press, 1990.

Davenport, Thomas H. *Process Innovation: Reengineering Work through Information Technology.* Boston: Harvard Business School Press, 1993.

Davis, Stan, and Bill Davidson. *2020 Vision: Transform Your Business Today to Succeed in Tomorrow's Economy.* New York: Fireside/Simon & Schuster, 1991.

Hammer, Michael, and James Champy. *Reengineering the Corporation: A Manifesto for Business Revolution.* New York: Harper Collins Publishers, 1993.

Scott Morton, Michael S. (Ed.). *The Corporation of the 1990s: Information Technology and Organizational Transformation.* New York: Oxford University Press, 1991.

Index of Cases

Air Products and Chemicals, Inc.: Project ICON (A), 176

Allen-Bradley's ICCG: Repositioning for the 1990s, 286

APPEX Corporation, 36

Capital Holding Corporation: Reengineering the Direct Response Group, 433

Compaq Computer Corporation, 142

Connor Formed Metal Products, 319

Controls at the Sands Hotel and Casino, 105

Crompton Greaves Ltd., 129

Hill, Holliday, Connors, Cosmopulos, Inc., Advertising (A), 53

Hong Kong TradeLink: News from the Second City, 365

Incident at Waco Manufacturing, 225

Internal Revenue Service: Automated Collection System, 211

Jacobs Suchard: Reorganizing for 1992, 68

KPMG Peat Marwick: The Shadow Partner, 462

Lithonia Lighting, 351

Mrs. Fields' Cookies, 9

Otis Elevator: Managing the Service Force, 233

Phillips 66 Company: Executive Information System, 303

Safeway Manufacturing Division: The Manufacturing Control System (MCS) (A), 420

Singapore Leadership: A Tale of One City, 372

Singapore TradeNet (A): A Tale of One City, 375

Singapore TradeNet (B): The Tale Continues, 388

Symantec, 191

Index

A

Accounting industry, 467–68
Actual performance, 97
Adaptiveness, 400
Advertising industry, 54–57
Airline reservation systems, 255, 341
Air Products and Chemicals, Inc.; Project ICON (A), 176–91
  alternatives to ICON, 186–87
  benefits, 187–90
  business segments, 179
  company background, 178–80
  costs, 187–90
  initial project team, 180–82183
  markets, 179
  MIS organization, 180–82
  network configuration, 186, 187
  organizational challenges, 191
  post-ICON network, proposed, 185–86
  products, 179
  project team findings, 187–91
  quality of service, 183–84
  telecommunications environment, 184–85
Algorithms, 170
Allen, Denise, 40
Allen, Neil, 324
Allen-Bradley's Industrial Computer and Communication
    Group (ICCG), 286–303
  company background, 287
  computer integration, 288–93
  consolidation and reorganization, 295–99
  engineering and manufacturing, integrating, 290–92
  groupwide prioritization, 299–300
  metrics program, instituting, 295–96
  organizational structure, 288, 289
  Pyramid Integrator, 287, 292–93
  quality and customer satisfaction, 294–95
  teaming, 293–94, 298, 300, 301
  Twinsburg, OH facility, 288–90
American Airlines, 160, 341
American Gem Market System, 345
American Hospital Supply (AHS), 342
Analog media, 162
Anderson, Wayne, 317–18
Ansari, Assad, 294
Appex Corporation, 36–52
  circular structure, 42

Appex Corporation—*Cont.*
  company background, 37, 39–40
  divisional structure, 50–52
  employees, forecasted and actual growth in, 40, 41
  hierarchical functional structure, 42–50
  innovative structures, 40–42
  products and services, 38–39
  product team/business team structure, 49
  sales and marketing team's organizational structure, 45–46
  structural changes, 52
Apple Computer, 165
Applegate, Lynda M., 473
Apple Macintosh, 167
Apollo, 343, 346–48
Applications software, 165
Architecture, 161
  information technologies (IT); *see* IT architecture
Arithmetic logic unit (ALU), 163
Armstrong, Steve, 421
Artificial intelligence, 170
ASK software, 149
ASAP, 342, 345, 414
AT&T, 184
Automation, 262

B

Babington, Pat, 292, 293
Bagnell, Bill, 114
Baker, Ted, 52
Bandwidth, 164
Banking funds-transfer systems, 255
Barber, Monk, 225, 226
Barry, Bob, 465
Baseline IT architecture, 172–173
Batchelder, Gene, 303, 310–11, 312, 313, 315–17, 318, 320
Baxter Healthcare, 345
Benefit/beneficiary matrix, 461
  business transformation, 418
Beressi, Howard, 241
Bernard, Ed, 65
Bessler, Phil, 297
Bigg, Lester, 464
Binary digits, 163
Bingham, Mike, 427
Bird, Norman, 246

Blueprints for IT architecture, 174–76
Boesky, Ivan, 305
Bolte, Gunter, 73
Bonuses
    Compaq Computer Corporation, 156
    Connor Formed Metal Products, 328
    Sands Hotel and Casino, 127
    Symantec, 199
Borash, Chuck, 12
Boundaries, organizational, 27, 33
Bowerman, Charlie, 317
Bowman, Bob, 363
Boyle, Brian E., 37, 39, 40
Brandstetter, Carl, 336
Braniff Airlines, 346
Bright, Keith, 312–13
British Telecom (BT), 186
Brockway, Doug, 467, 471
Brown, Tim, 212, 213, 218, 224
Bryant, Charlie, 363–64
Budget
    Compaq Computer Corporation, 153
    Crompton Greaves Ltd., 138–40
    Hill, Holiday, Connors, Cosmopulos, Inc. Advertising, 64
    Symantec, 198
Bunker, Ramo, 347
Burr, Donald, 346
Business processes, 4–6
    definition, 3
    reengineering, 405–14
Business transformation, 399–452
    anticipatory change, 402
    benefit/beneficiary matrix, 418
    business process reengineering, 405–14
    Capital Holding Corporation; reengineering direct response
        group, 433–52
    champion's role, 412
    change partners' role, 411
    design teams' role, 411–12
    discrete to continuous processes, shift from, 405
    existing processes, understanding, 408–14
    horizontal information flows, emphasis on, 405–6
    idea generation, 415
    idea refinement and development, 415
    implementation teams' role, 412–14
    managing uncertainty, shift from predicting events to, 404
    organizational effectiveness, 400
    poor execution, 419–20
    process thinking, 407–8
    required change, determining degree of, 401–3
    roadblocks, 415–20
    Safeway Manufacturing Division; manufacturing control
        system (MCS), 421–33
    scope of change, 403
    sponsor's role, 409
    steering committee's role, 409–10
    stimulus for change, 401–2
    sustaining IT innovation, 414–20
    value analysis, 415, 417, 419
Business Week, 37, 318–20

C

CAD/CAM, 256, 259, 261, 341
Canion, Rod, 144, 148, 149, 154, 155–56, 157
Capital Holding Corporation; reengineering direct response
    group, 433–52
    business processes, redesigning, 449
    claims management prototype, 449
    company background, 435–38
    cultural audit findings, 444
    customer management team, 446
    financial summary and description of business units, 436
    human resources, 451–52
    information systems role, 449–50
    life/health applications processing prototype, 449
    managing change, 452
    market management team, 448
    need for change, 443
    new business model, 445–47
    products and markets, 439–40
    structure and staffing, 437
    traditional approach to business, 438–43
Carrier Corporation, 342–3, 347
Carrot, Robert, 77, 84
Case, John, 331
Cash, James I., Jr., 473
Caterpillar Tractor, 345
CC Mail, 202
Cellular communications, competing standards for, 169–70
Cellular telephone industry, 38
Central processors, 163, 167
Cevoli, Vic, 65
Champion, 412
Chan, Pearleen, 384, 387, 388, 390, 396
Chandler, Joan, 434–35, 445
Change, 411
Channel, defined, 190
Chapman, Len, 421, 423, 431–32, 433
Chilberg, Mary, 199, 201
Chong, Lau Chee, 391
CICS (customer information control system), 190
Clark, Carolyn, 63, 67
Client-server
    applications, 163, 460
    computing, 257
COBOL, 166
Cockfield, Lord, 75
Cohen, Ronnie, 66, 67
"Coming of the New Organization, The" (Drucker), 85–92
Common carriers, 164
Compaq Computer Corporation, 142–57
    annual planning, 153
    budgeting versus forecasting, 153
    company background, 143–44
    compensation, 156
    cost-center management and finance, 150, 152
    culture, 147–49
    demand forecasting, 151–52
    finance function, 149–50
    financial control and measurement, 154–55

Compaq Computer Corporation—*Cont.*
  financial forecasting, 150–55
  international financial controls, 155
  management, 144–47
  manufacturing priorities, 155
  open communications, 148–49
  organization, 144–47
  performance measurement, 155–56
  process, 148
  product history, 145
  product planning, 147
  product pricing and product cost, forecasting, 152
  sales growth, 143
  team performance, emphasis on, 148
Computer-aided software engineering (CASE), 170–71
Computer integrated manufacturing (CIM), 288–93
Conduit host, 340, 349
Connor Formed Metal Products, 320–37
  company and industry background, 321–28
  culture, 327–28
  decision rights, 324
  financial summary, 323
  incentives and rewards, 328
  information technology, 328
  Los Angeles experiment, 328–36
  management control, 325–27
  organization, 321, 323–25
  product service delivery information flow, 335
  shop order, sample, 333
  team meeting report, sample, 326
Connors, Jack, 54, 57, 58–61, 62, 63, 66, 68
Content host, 340, 349
Control systems; *see* Management control systems
Conway, Marc, 364
Cooper Lighting, 356
Coordination mechanisms, 26–27
Cosentiono, John, 246
Cost centers, 100, 101
Compaq Computer Corporation, 150, 152
Cox, Glenn, 320
Crandall, Ted, 295, 296
Creditview, 458
Crompton Greaves Ltd., 129–42
  budgeting and monitoring, 138–40
  company background, 131
  improvement management, 135–38
  measures, 136–38
  operations management, 133–35
  organization structure, 131–32, 133–34
  performance assessment and incentives, 140–41
  performance record, 130
  productivity, 136
  profit improvement plan (PIP), 137
  quality assessment, 136
  statement of values, 135
  strategic management, 138
  strategy of change, 132–38
Crowe, Floyd, 427
CSC-Index, 456
Culpepper, B. J., 312–13, 315, 318

Customer satisfaction, 400
Cypress Semiconductor Corporation, 268–85

D

Darnell, Charles, 352, 356–58, 360, 363
Dartmouth College, 160
DASD (direct-access storage device), 190
Dasgupta, Ranjan, 135
Data, 159, 162
  access, 169; 248–49
  accuracy standard, 167
  object-oriented databases, 168
  security issues, 169
  storage, 167–69, 175, 176, 470
  timeliness, 167–68
  transformation, 170–71, 174, 176, 460
  transport, 169–70, 460
  viability, 168
Database management systems, 166, 170, 254
  hierarchical, 168
  IDMS, 190
Data processing (DP), 254, 261
  personal computing versus traditional, 255, 256
DP era, 254
Davenport, Thomas, 344
Davis, Don, 292, 293
Davis, Larry, 359, 364
Day planner, 23
DB2, 168
Decentralized structure of Jacobs Suchard, 71–73
Decision rights, division of, 26
Decision support systems (DSS), 254
Departmentalization, 26
Design, and management control systems, 100–102
Deskilling, 211
Discontinuity, technological, 254–55
Disney World, 91, 411
Diversification, and Mrs. Fields' Cookies, 21–22
Divisional structure of organization, 30–31, 33, 35
  Appex Corporation, 50–52
Douce, William, 306
Drucker, Peter, 33–34, 85, 209
Dusad, C.P., 137
Dykes, Bob, 197, 199, 200–202, 203

E

Easdon, Don, 57, 61, 62
Eastern Airlines, 346
Economist, The, 54–56
EDIFACT, 345
Effectiveness, defined, 418
Efficiency, defined, 418
Electronic Communications Privacy Act of 1986 (ECPA), 249
Electronic Data Interchange (EDI), 339
  in Hong Kong, 366–72
  protocols, 169

Electronic Data Systems (EDS), 52
Electronic market access forums, 345
Electronic monitoring of employees, 210–11
Elevator industry, 234–35
Elliott, Bob, 465, 466, 467, 468–69, 470
E-mail, 263
Embedding, 262
Emerging technologies, 258, 456–62
   benefit/beneficiary matrix, 461
   creditview, 458
   KPMG Peat Marwick; the shadow partner, 462–72
   neural networks, 458
   virtual reality, 459–60
Employee privacy and information technologies, 209–11,
   248–51
Employee satisfaction and effectiveness, 400
ENIAC, 166
EPIC, 345
Eras, IT, 254–58
Estimated performance, 97
Ethernet, 190
Ethical concerns, and information technologies (IT), 247–51
Eubanks, Gordon E., 192, 197, 198, 199, 200, 202, 203–4
European Economic Community, 75–76
Exceptional coordination, 26

F

Farrow, Mary Ann, 440, 448
Fast Cycle Competition, 264–265
Fields, Debbi Sivyer, 10, 11–16, 19, 21
Fields, Randy, 10, 11–17, 19, 21–23
Financial performance, 400
Finucane, Ann, 62
Fischer, Rudy, 73, 84
Fleming, Pam, 198
Form mail, 23
FORTRAN, 166
Fost, Glenda, 313–14
Frank, Telly, 226
Freeman, Sam, 352
Front-end processor, defined, 190
Frontier, 160
Fuller, Buckminster, 11
Functional structure of organization, 28–30, 33, 35
   Appex Corporation, hierarchical structure of, 42–50

G

Gallucci, Roy, 331
Gambling in New Jersey, 106
Gebhard, Charles, 69
Gelhaus, Dick, 427
General Motors, 340–41, 344–45
Ghosh, Shikhar, 36–37, 39–52
Global Bank, 228–29
Globalized markets, 3
Globalized operations, 4
   Jacobs Suchard, 76–81

Goals, setting, 272–76, 277
Godwing, Pam, 434, 438–40, 443, 452
Gogan, Janis, 256
Gogan, Wanda, 226
Great Bay Casino Corporation (GBCC), 106
Gribi, John, 148, 149
Gudonis, Paul, 42, 47

H

Halkides, George, 322, 325
Hamilton, Keith, 302
Hardware, 162–64
   Mrs. Field's Cookies, 22
Harris, Jim, 144, 149, 154
Hartel, Roger, 295
Harvard Business Review, 349, 455
Hendrix, Gary, 192, 194, 197, 198, 202, 203
Herbert, Brian, 183
Hewlett-Packard system, 200–201
Hill, Holiday, Connors, Cosmopulos, Inc. Advertising, 53–68
   accounting system, 64
   budgeting and allocation systems, 64
   company background, 57–58
   control systems, 64
   corporate culture, 57–58
   creative department, 61–62
   growth, 55, 58–62
   management structure, 62–63
   organization chart, 63
   product expansion, 58–61
   reorganization issues, 64–68
   structure, 62–63
Hill, Jay, 61, 64, 65
Hiring practices, 270–72
Hong Kong Tradelink
   background on Hong Kong, 365–66
   excerpts from articles, 367–72
   Hotline system, 366
   trade-related electronic data interchange in Hong Kong,
      366–72
Hopper, Max, 350
Horizontal dimensions of organization, 26
Horner, Larry, 466
HOTS (Haggar), 345
Howe, Jack, 317
Huber, Joe, 383
Human resources, 5
   Capital Holding Corporation; reengineering direct response
      group, 451–52
   information technologies and, 209
Hyde, Stephen F., 105–6, 127–29
Hypertext systems, 168

I

IBM, 143, 144, 165
   mainframes, 180, 185–186

IBM—*Cont.*
personal computers, 167
Icahn, Carl, 305
IDMS, 190
Implementation Team, 412
Incremental technical innovations, 5
Industry platform, 345
"Informate the Enterprise: An Agenda for the Twenty-first
Century" (Zuboff), 226–33
Information resources, 8, 159
Information technologies (IT), 5, 8–9, 22–23, 159–60
architecture; *see* IT architecture
automation, 262, 263
business transformation and; *see* Business transformation
communicating, 263
Connor Formed Metal Products, 328
data access, 248–49
definition, 159
deskilling, 211
embedding of microprocessors, 262, 263
emerging technologies and challenge of change, 258,
456–62
and employee privacy, 209–11, 248–51
employees, impact on, 208–9
ethical concerns, 247–51
evolution of, 166–67
flexibility, 159
future of, 455–83
human resources issues, new, 209
and the individual, 207–51
informating capacity of, 231, 262
Internal Revenue Service (IRS); automated collection
system, 211–225
interorganizational systems (IOS); *see* Interorganizational
systems (IOS)
Mrs. Fields' Cookies, 19–23
new work, 208
in organizations; *see* IT in organizations
Otis Elevator's North American Operations (NAO),
234–47
stewardship responsibility, 250–51
Symantec, 200–202
Waco Manufacturing, 225–26
working arrangements, new, 208–9
work standards, 211
Informating, 262
"Information Technology and Tomorrow's Manager"
(Applegate, et al.), 472–83
INGRES, 168
Innovation, technological, 4–5
Innovative structures, and Appex Corporation, 40–42
Input devices, 163–64
Integrated circuits, 166
Integration, vertical, 343
Intercarrier services (ICS), 38–39
Internal Revenue Service (IRS); automated collection system
(ACS), 211–225
collection, 213–14
collection office function (COF), 214–19
computer monitoring, 221–22

Internal Revenue Service (IRS)—*Cont.*
contact function, 219–20
employees' reaction to change, 223–24
investigation function, 220
management control systems, 221–22
organization, 212–14
primary function, 212–13
research function, 220
revenue representatives, 216
structure of ACS, 219–21
supervisors' reaction to change, 222–23
tax account representatives, 217
teach reviews, 222
technology, 219
telephone monitoring, 222
transition to ACS, 218–19
Interorganizational systems (IOS), 339–96
channel control, 341–42
competitive risks, 346
conduit host, 340, 349
content host, 340, 349
customer relationships, improvement in, 342–43
definitions, 339–40
electronic market access forums, 345
future of, 349–51
Hong Kong Tradelink, 365–72
industry platform, 345
integration and synergy without risk, 343–44
inventories, improvement of control of, 341
legal and regulatory risks, 347–48
Lithonia Lighting, 351–65
marketing and logistics, 345
motivations for, 340–44, 345
nonprofit organizations, 343
organizational risks, 348–49
paperwork, reduction of, 340–41
participant, 340
partnerships based on, 344
regulatory risks, 347–48
risks, 344–49
share resources/risks, 343
Singapore, 372–96
structure, classification by, 345
supplies, improvement of control of, 341
synergy, integration and, 343–44
technical risks, 346
transaction efficiency, improvement in, 341
virtual systems, 345
Interviewing techniques, 23, 273
Investment centers, 100, 101
IOS; *see* Interorganizational systems (IOS)
IRS; *see* Internal Revenue Service (IRS); automated
collection system
ISDN (Integrated Services Data Network), 190
protocol, 169
Issenmann, Nico, 77, 83
IT; *see* Information technologies (IT)
IT architecture, 159–205
Air Products and Chemicals, Inc.; Project ICON (A),
176–91

IT architecture—*Cont.*
  baseline, 172–73, 174
  basic operations, 165–71
  blueprint, 174–76
  "bottom-up" process, 172
  Dartmouth College, 160
  data, 162
  data storage, 167–69, 175, 176
  data transformation, 170–71, 174, 176
  data transport, 169–70
  definition, 159
  developing, 171–76
  foundations of, 161–71
  hardware, 162–64
  Mrs. Fields' Cookies, 172
  software, 164–65, 174
  structures, 175–76
  Symantec, 192–204
  "top-down" process, 172, 173–74
  vision statements, 173–74, 176
IT in organizations, 253–337
  Allen-Bradley's Industrial Computer and Communication
      Group (ICCG), 286–303
  Connor Formed Metal Products, 320–37
  data processing era, 254, 255, 261
  micro era, 254–56, 261
  network era, 256–59, 261
  "No Excuses Management" (Rodgers), 268–85
  organizational learning and stages theory of IT adoption,
      259–62
  organizational structure, IT-driven changes in, 262–64
  Phillips 66 Company, 303–20
  stages theory of IT adoption and organizational learning,
      259–62
  time-based competition, 264–65
IVANS, 343

J

Jacobs, Irwin, 305
Jacobs, Klaus J., 69, 71, 73, 76–77, 81, 83, 84
Jacobs Suchard, 68–92
  CEO's role, 71
  company background, 70–75
  consolidated financial statements, 70
  corporate principles, 71
  decentralization, 71–73
  global brand sponsors, 77, 79, 81–83
  globalization, 76–81
  international manufacturing centers, 83–84
  job rotation, 73
  organization chart, 72
  Vision 2000 recommendations, 76–77
Jacquesson, Pierre, 75, 82, 83
Jaunich, Robert, 73
Johnson, Kathy, 204
Johnston, Russell, 344, 348
Jones, Ben, 316, 318
Jones, Glenn, 312–13, 315, 318

K

Kang, James, 395
Kaufman, Felix, 34950
Kemeny, John, 160
Kent, Jeff, 291, 301
Khuen, Chan Kah, 383, 391
Kin, Lee Seiu, 392
Kincannon, Felice, 57, 63, 64–68
Kirschner, Sidney, 351
Kisling, Ron, 196
Kobayashi Maru, container ship, 374
Konsynski, Benn, 345
KPMG Peat Marwick; the shadow partner, 462–72
  competitors, 465–66
  cost issues, 470–71
  cultural issues, 467–70
  design of, 465
  financial issues, 470–72
  future of, 471–72
  origin of, 466
  partners' compensation, 470
  partnership procedures, 469
  personal networks, 468–69
  senior management, 469–70
  technology committee, 466–67
  use of technology, 470
Kroll, Rick, 184
Kuehnis, Floyd, 465, 466, 472
Kunkel, Mary, 328

L

Labor, division of, 25–26
Labor scheduler, 23
LANs; *see* Local area networks (LANs)
La Petite Boulangerie (LPB), 21
Lawrence, Paul, 344, 348
Leavitt, Harold J., 473–76, 479, 482
Lee, Albert, 182–83, 186, 191
Lee, Rod, 355, 359
Leschinsky, Tim, 430, 431
LEVILINK, 345
Lithonia Lighting, 351–65
  agencies and distribution chain, 353–56
  company and industry background, 352–53
  competitors and, 355–56
  decentering, 356–57
  distribution chain, 353–56
  future of, 360–63
  Light*Link, 356–60, 361, 363–64
  organization chart, 354
Little, Bill, 293
Local area networks (LANs), 164, 257
  definition, 190
  Ethernet, 190
  protocols, 169
Lombardi, Roe, 442
Low, Joseph, 386

M

Mac, John, 463
Macintosh, 144, 165
Magowan, Peter A., 424
Main control unit, 163
Mainframe computers, 162
Management-by-objectives (MBO), and Sands Hotel and Casino, 127
Management control systems, 5, 95–157
　Compaq Computer Corporation, 142–57
　Connor Formed Metal Products, 325–27
　criteria for comparing measures, 97, 98–99
　Crompton Greaves Ltd., 129–42
　definition, 8, 97
　design, 100–102
　elements of, 97–100
　ethical issues, 250
　exerting control, 96
　Internal Revenue Service (IRS); automated collection system (ACS), 221–22
　loose control, 96, 104
　measures, 97–104
　performance measurement, 97–100, 103–4
　Phillips 66 Company, 309–11
　Sands Hotel and Casino, 105–29
　Symantec, 198–99
　tight control, 96
Management information systems (MIS), 254
　Air Products and Chemicals, Inc., 180–82
　Mrs. Fields' Cookies, 16–18
　Phillips 66 Company, 309–12
　Symantec, 202–3
Managers, role of, 5, 9
Marketing and logistics IOS, 345
Mariott Hotels, 411
Mather, Peter, 177–78, 180, 182, 183, 189, 191
Matrix structure, 31–32, 33, 35
McClung, Jim, 351, 352, 353, 356, 360–61, 362–65
McCoy, Sherman, 226
McDonald's, and management control systems, 96
McFarlan, F. Warren, 344
McKesson Corporation, 348, 404
Measures, 100–104
　behavior, effect on, 100
　criteria for comparing, 97, 98–99
　Crompton Greaves Ltd., 136–38
　definition, 97
　financial results, 103
　in management control systems, 97–104
　perceptual measures, 103
　processes for obtaining and evaluating, 99–100
MEMA/Transnet, 343
Mercury Communications, 186
Merrill Lynch, 404
Mesko, Greg, 290–91
Metzger, Lon, 427, 432–33
Microcomputers, 163, 167
Micro era, 254–56, 261
Microsoft Windows, 165

Midway Airlines, 347
Mills, D. Quinn, 473
Mills, John, 65
Minicomputers, 162–63, 166
MIS; *see* Management information systems (MIS)
Mobile telephone switch office (MTSO), 38
Mrs. Fields' Cookies, 9–23
　company background, 11–13
　competition, 13
　cookie store operations, 18–21
　diversification, 21–22
　financial strategy, 14
　floorplan, 19
　future growth, 22
　information systems applications, 23
　information systems diagram, 20
　information systems hardware, 22
　international expansion, 12–13
　IT architecture, 172
　management control systems, 96–97
　management philosophy, 13–18
　organization, 14–18
　products, 13
MS-DOS, 165
Multiplexer, defined, 190
Murto, Bill, 144

N

Naramore, Tom, 364
Network, 256–59, 261
　devices, 164
　long-distance networking, 257
　neural, 458
　protocols, 169
　structure, 34–35
　Symantec, 201–2
Neural networks, 458
New Jersey, gambling in, 106
New Jersey Casino Control Commission (NJCCC), 106
"No Excuses Management" (Rodgers), 268–85
Nohria, Kewal Krishan, 129–34, 136–42
North, Oliver, 209
Novak, Ed, 449–50

O

Object-oriented databases, 168
Object-oriented programming (OOP), 171
OCR (optical character readers), 163–64
OMAR, 201
Open system interconnect (OSI), 169
Operations, and Mrs. Fields' Cookies, 18–21
ORACLE, 168
Organizational effectiveness, 400
Organizational learning and stages theory of IT adoption, 259–62
　contagion, 259–60

Organizational learning and stages theory of IT
  adoption—*Cont.*
  control, 260
  growth processes, 260–61
  initiation, 259
  integration, 260–61
  Safeway Manufacturing Division; manufacturing control
    system (MCS), 425, 427
Organization structure, 5, 25–92
  accountability, 27
  Allen-Bradley's Industrial Computer and Communication
    Group (ICCG), 288, 289
  Appex Corporation, 36–52
  boundaries, 27, 33
  Compaq Computer Corporation, 144–47
  Connor Formed Metal Products, 323–25
  coordination mechanisms, 26–27
  Crompton Greaves Ltd., 131–32, 133–34
  decision rights, division of, 26
  divisional form, 30–31, 33, 35
  efficiency, 27
  forms of, 28–36
  functional form, 28–30, 33, 35
  functions, 7, 25
  Hill, Holiday, Connors, Cosmopulos, Inc. Advertising,
    58–62
  informal structure, 27–28
  information technologies and, 9, 262–64
  Internal Revenue Service (IRS), 212–14
  Jacobs Suchard, 68–92
  labor, division of, 25–26
  Lithonia Lighting, 354
  matrix form, 31–32, 33, 35
  Mrs. Fields' Cookies, 14–18
  network structure, 34–35
  Otis Elevator's North American Operations (NAO), 235
  reorganization, 33
  responsiveness, 27
  Sands Hotel and Casino, 109–12
  Symantec, 193–96
  timeliness, 27
O'Rourke, J. Tracy, 287, 288
OS/2, 165
Otis Elevator's North American Operations (NAO), 234–47
  Boston, MA, 240–41
  callback operations process, 239
  Dallas, TX, 242–46
  field communications and information tools, 239–40
  field operations, 235–26
  future activities, 246–47
  Glendale, CA, 241–42
  key data terminal (KDT), 241–43, 246, 247
  local solutions and configurations, 240–46
  maintenance mechanics, 236–37
  organization chart, 235
  Otis maintenance management system (OMMS), 245–46
  Otis schedule maintenance (OSM), 246
  POD structure, 242
  repair mechanics, 237
  scheduling and work methods, 237–39

Otis Elevator's North American Operations (NAO)—*Cont.*
  work methods, 237–39
Output devices, 164

P

Pantano, Dick, 61–62, 66
Paper media, 162
Paradox, 168
Partnerships, 105
Pause, Lila, 83
People Express, 160, 346
Performance appraisal, 280–83
Performance measures for management control systems,
    97–100, 103–4
  Compaq Computer Corporation, 148, 155–56
  Crompton Greaves Ltd., 138–41
  Internal Revenue Service (IRS); automated collection
    system (ACS), 221–22
Personal computers, 8–9, 162–63, 167, 170, 255–56
Personal computing, 170
  traditional data processing versus personal computing, 255,
    256
Petroleum industry, 304–5
Pettifer, Gary, 187, 191
Petty, Stan, 324, 328
Pfeiffer, Eckhart, 144, 146, 148, 156
Phelps, Norm, 434, 443, 452
Phillips, Frank, 304
Phillips, L. E., 304
Phillips 66 Company, 303–20
  company background, 303–6
  industry and company background, 303–6
  information management, 311–15
  management information and controls system, 309–11
Pickens, T. Boone, 305
Piney Wood, 227–28
Pohl, Hermann, 69, 73, 81, 83, 84
POPS, 201
PRISM, defined, 190
Privacy of employee and information technologies, 209–11,
    248–51
Processes for obtaining and evaluating measures and criteria,
    99–100
Product development cycles, 3
Productivity
  Crompton Greaves Ltd., 136
  resource allocation for maximum, 276–80
Productivity, Inc., 137
Profit centers, 100, 101
Programmable logic controllers (PLCs), 287–88
Prutzman, Paul, 191
Pyramid Integrator, 287; 287, 292–93

Q

Quality and safety of product, 3
Quarrey, Michael, 321, 330–34, 336–37
Quinn, Paul, 16–17

R

Rajagopal, N., 138
Ramo, Bunker, 347
RAM (random access memory), 163, 165
Rao, P.H., 132, 135, 141
RBase, 168
Read-only memory (ROM), 163
Renninger, Marty, 449
Reorganization, 33
    Hill, Holiday, Connors, Cosmopulos, Inc. Advertising,
        64–68
    Jacobs Suchard, 68–92
Resorts International, 106
Responsibility centers, 100–101
Revenue centers, 100–101
Richman, Tom, 11, 20
RoamAmerica, example of product team structure for, 48
Robertson, Jerry, 237
Robinson, Dick, 317
Rodgers, T. J., 268
Routine coordination, 26

S

SABRE, 343, 346
Safeway Manufacturing Division; manufacturing control
        system (MCS), 421–33
    company and industry background, 423–27
    corporate structure, 425
    costs/benefits, 422
    daily activities, MCS impact on, 431
    existing computer-based systems, 428–30
    financial highlights, 424
    implementation, 431–33
    manufacturing division, 427–30
    organization, 427
    store and plant location, 426
Salas, Rodolfo, 287, 293, 294, 295, 296–301, 302–3
Saltz, Monique, 225, 226
Sands Hotel and Casino, 105–29
    background, 106
    black jack games, operation of, 109–12
    bonuses, 127
    cash control, 109–15
    cash stocks, accountability for, 112
    controls in the casino, 106–29
    counter checks, 114
    drop, interpreting, 122
    flip slip, 114, 115
    future controls, 127–29
    game control, 119
    hold percentage, 122
    industry results report, 128
    licensing, 119
    management-by-objectives (MBO), 127
    master game report, 123–27
    organization, 109–12
    results, monitoring, 122–27

Sands Hotel and Casino—*Cont.*
    security, 115–19
    soft count procedures, 120–21
    standardization of actions at table, 120–21
    supervision, 121–22
    surveillance, 121–22
    table games daily transaction report, 117–18
    transfer of cash procedures, 112–15
    wins, monitoring, 122
Sansolo, Jack, 58, 62, 63, 64
SAS, defined, 190
Schempf, David, 149, 154
Schlein, Ted, 202, 203
Schoendorf, Walter, Sr., 421–23, 430, 433
Schulter, Joe, 182, 184
Secondary storage devices, 164
Shadow partner; *see* KPMG Peat Marwick; the shadow
        partner
Sharpless, Kathy, 57, 65
Shephard, John, 177, 182, 183, 191
Short, James, 344
Siebert, Dana, 196
Silas, C. J., 305–6
Singapore leadership, 372–74
Singapore TradeNet (A), 374–87
Singapore TradeNet (B), 388–96
Skills test, 23
Sloss, Bob, 320, 321, 322–24, 327–28, 330,
        336–37
Sloss, Henry, 322
Sloss, Joe, 322
Smith, Bob, 241
Sneakernet, 169, 275
Snyder, Dan, 448
Software, 164–66, 174
    applications software, 165
    definition, 164
    development methodologies and tools, 170–71
    information technologies (IT); *see* Information
        technologies (IT)
Sornson, Dave, 199, 204
Spanos, Gary, 324
SPEED, 345
Stauback, Roger, 440
Steering Committee, 409
Steffen, Wayne, 429
Steiner, Ray, 317
Stewardship responsibility, 250–51
Stewart, Fran, 197, 201, 202–3, 204
Strategic objectives, 3–4, 5
    definition, 3
Structure (see Organizational Structure)
Summers, Jim, 427
Sutor, Ed, 106, 122, 127
Suttle, Alan, 363
Swavely, Michael, 146, 148, 151, 153, 154, 155
Symantec, 192–204
    budgets, 198
    company background, 192–93
    decision making, 200

Symantec—*Cont.*
Hewlett-Packard system, 200–201
incentives, 199
information flow, 196–98
information technology, 200–202
management control systems, 198–99
MIS department, 202–203
network system, 201–202
organization chart, 194
products, 195
statement of operations, 193
structure, 193–96
System 7, 165

T

TALC, 345
Technological discontinuity, 254–55
Teck, Yeo Seng, 379–80, 386, 389–90
Telecommunications, 170
Air Products and Chemicals, Inc.; Project ICON (A), 184–85
Telecommuting, 208–9
Thompson, James Walter, 56
T1 circuit, defined, 190
Time-based competition, 31, 264–65
Time clock, 23
Time sharing, 166
Tomaso, Shelley, 226
Tooher, Dennis, 241
Total quality management (TQM), 405
TradeGate, 345
TradeLink, 345
TradeNet, 345
Trane, 342–43, 347
Turner, Rod, 193, 196, 198, 202
TVINN, 345

U

United Airlines, 160, 341
Universal product code (UPC), 339

V

Value added networks (VANs), 164
Vanbuskirk, John, 318

Varghese, Susan, 141
Veydt, Jerry, 361, 364
Vieau, Bob, 147, 154, 155
Virtual reality, 459–60
Virtual systems, 345
Vision statements, 173–74, 176
Voice mail, 263
VSAT, 164, 264, 350, 456

W

Waco Manufacturing, 225–26
Wagle, N.M., 132
Wagner, Loretta, 204
Walker, Ross, 467, 472
Wallace, Robert, 303, 306–11, 315, 316, 318, 320
Webb, Jim, 429
Weber, Jim, 295
Wesley, Bob, 240
Wheeler, Dick, 182
Whisler, Thomas L., 473–76, 479, 482
Whitaker, Rick, 234, 247
White, Daryl, 144, 149, 150, 154, 156
Wide area networks (WANs), 164
protocols, 169
Wilt, Bill, 325, 326–27
WINS, 345
Work force diversity, 4
Work standards, 211

Y

Yew, Lee Kuan, 372
Yuen, Georgiana, 385

Z

Zinser, Gerhard, 69, 71–72, 73, 74, 76, 77, 82–83
Zuboff, Shoshana, 207, 209, 226